MICROSOFT
Visual Basic 5
Complete Concepts and Techniques

MICROSOFT
Visual Basic 5

Complete Concepts and Techniques

Gary B. Shelly
Thomas J. Cashman
John F. Repede

SHELLY
CASHMAN
SERIES®

COURSE TECHNOLOGY
ONE MAIN STREET
CAMBRIDGE MA 02142

an International Thomson Publishing company

CAMBRIDGE • ALBANY • BONN • CINCINNATI • LONDON • MADRID • MELBOURNE

MEXICO CITY • NEW YORK • PARIS • SAN FRANCISCO • TOKYO • TORONTO • WASHINGTON

COURSE
TECHNOLOGY

TRADEMARKS

DISCLAIMER

PHOTO CREDITS

Project 1, pages VB 1.2-3, Bride, toy duck, gift box, satellite, and couple, Courtesy of Corel Professional Photos CD-ROM Image usage; Service Merchandise materials courtesy of Service Merchandise; computer paper, images © 1997 PhotoDisc Inc; *Project 2, pages VB 2.2-3*, Mega Studio screen captures, Courtesy of Hollywood Mogel™ Company; Hollywood sign, actor and actress, Courtesy of Corel Professional Photos CD-ROM Image usage; Clapboard, image © 1997 PhotoDisc Inc.; *Project 3, pages VB 3.2-3*, Workers, Courtesy of Corel Professional Photos CD-ROM Image usage; Screen captures, courtesy of National Instruments; *Project 5, pages VB 5.2-3*, X-ray, doctor examining X-ray film, technician reading computer printout, and doctor preparing woman for X-ray procedure images, © 1997 PhotoDisc Inc.; *Project 7, page VB 7.2*, TRAK screen capture and flyer art, Courtesy of Social Tech.

ISBN 0-7895-2777-4

1 2 3 4 5 6 7 8 9 10   BC   02 01 00 99 98

MICROSOFT
Visual Basic 5

Complete Concepts and Techniques

C O N T E N T S

▶ PROJECT SEVEN
CREATING ACTIVEX CONTROLS
AND DISTRIBUTING APPLICATIONS

Preface

The Shelly Cashman Series® offers the finest textbooks in computer education. The Microsoft Visual Basic 5 books continue with the innovation, quality, and reliability consistent with this series. We are proud that both our Visual Basic 3 and Visual Basic 4 books are best-sellers, and we are confident that our Visual Basic 5 books will join their predecessors.

With Visual Basic 5, Microsoft has raised the stakes by adding a number of new features, especially the new integrated development environment (IDE) and control creation capability. The Shelly Cashman Series team has responded with Visual Basic 5 books that present the core programming concepts required in any introductory programming course, as well new features such as ActiveX controls, Visual Basic Wizards, report generators, and compiling and distributing applications.

In our Visual Basic 5 books, you will find an educationally sound and easy-to-follow pedagogy that combines a step-by-step approach with corresponding screens. A new Introduction to Visual Basic Programming section at the beginning of the book gives students the foundation to produce well-written Windows applications. The Other Ways and More About features have been incorporated to offer in-depth knowledge of Visual Basic 5. The all-new project openers provide a fascinating perspective on the subject covered in the project. The Shelly Cashman Series Visual Basic 5 books will make your programming class exciting and dynamic and one that your students will remember as one of their better educational experiences.

 Objectives of This Textbook

Microsoft Visual Basic 5: Complete Concepts and Techniques is intended for a one-quarter or one-semester course covering Visual Basic programming. No experience with a computer is assumed, and no mathematics beyond the high school freshman level is required. The objectives of this book are:

- ▶ To teach the basic concepts and methods of object-oriented programming
- ▶ To teach the fundamentals of the Microsoft Visual Basic 5 programming system
- ▶ To acquaint students with the three-step process of building Windows applications using Visual Basic 5
- ▶ To use practical problems to illustrate application-building techniques
- ▶ To take advantage of the many new capabilities of building applications in a graphical environment
- ▶ To encourage independent study and help those who are working alone in a distance education environment

When students complete the course using this textbook, they will have a firm knowledge and understanding of Visual Basic 5 and will be able to develop a wide variety of Windows applications.

Obtaining a Free Copy of Microsoft Visual Basic 5 Control Creation Edition

You and your students can download the Microsoft Visual Basic 5 Control Creation Edition from the Microsoft Web site at www.microsoft.com/vbasic/controls/download/default.htm. The Control Creation Edition also is available on the Instructor's Resource Kit. The major limitation of the Control Creation Edition is the capability of converting Visual Basic programs to exectuable files that run outside of Visual Basic. The Control Creation Edition, however, does contain most of the basic features and functionality for use with this book.

The Shelly Cashman Approach

Features of the Shelly Cashman Series Visual Basic 5 books include:

Other Ways

1. To open Data Form Designer, press CTRL+U, press F

More About Internet Distribution

If you have a Web site, you can link to your ActiveX documents from any Web page. This is accomplished with a combination of HMTL and VBScript. You even can create a link to your ActiveX document that causes the browser to find and download automatically all components needed to run your ActiveX document.

▶ **Project Orientation:** Each project in the book builds a complete application using the three-step process: creating the interface, setting properties, and writing code.

▶ **Screen-by-Screen, Step-by-Step Instructions:** Each of the tasks required to complete a project is identified throughout the development of the project. Then, steps to accomplish the task are specified. The steps are accompanied by screens.

▶ **Thoroughly Tested Projects:** Every screen in the book is correct because it is produced by the author only after performing a step, resulting in unprecedented quality.

▶ **Other Ways Boxes for Reference:** Visual Basic 5 provides a variety of ways to carry out a given task. The Other Ways boxes displayed at the end of most of the step-by-step sequences specify the other ways to do the task completed in the steps. Thus, the steps and the Other Ways box make a comprehensive reference unit.

▶ **More About Feature:** These marginal annotations provide background information that complement the topics covered, adding interest and depth to learning.

Organization of This Textbook

Microsoft Visual Basic 5: Complete Concepts and Techniques provides detailed instruction on how to use Visual Basic 5. The material is divided into an introductory section and seven projects as follows:

Introduction to Visual Basic Programming   This section provides an overview of application development, user interface design, program development methodology, structured programming, object-oriented programming, and the Visual Basic development system.

Project 1 – Building an Application   Project 1 introduces students to the major elements of Visual Basic. Students develop Converting Dollars to Francs, a currency conversion application. The process of building the application consists of three steps: creating the interface, setting properties, and writing code. Topics include starting Visual Basic; designing a form and adding labels, text boxes, and command buttons; changing the properties of controls; specifying an event procedure; using a function and a method in code; running and saving applications; documenting applications; starting a new project and opening an existing project; and accessing information about Visual Basic using Help.

Project 2 – Working with Intrinsic Controls and ActiveX Controls   Project 2 presents additional properties of the controls used in Project 1, as well as several new intrinsic controls. ActiveX controls also are explained and used in the project to build the Movie Box Office application. Topics include copying controls; copying code between event procedures; using variables and constants in code statements; and using code statements to concatenate string data.

Project 3 – Multiple Forms, Dialogs, Debugging, and EXEs   Project 3 extends the basics of building applications. The Loan Payment Calculator application in this project consists of multiple forms and dialog boxes. Topics include additional properties of the controls presented in Projects 1 and 2; WindowState and modality; adding an icon to a form; using Image, Line, and ScrollBar controls; debugging applications using the features of Visual Basic's Debug window, and creating EXE files.

Project 4 – Menus, Data Controls, Common Dialogs, and General Procedures   Project 4 provides an introductory exposure to accessing a database by building an application that displays information from a World Geography database created with Microsoft Access. The GeoView Database Viewer application built in this project includes a menu bar, menus, submenus and pop-up menus. In addition to presenting the Data control and Font Common Dialog, this project introduces students to control arrays. Students also learn additional properties and methods of some of the controls with which they are already familiar. This project also expands students' abilities to write code by introducing the For...Next loop, the Not operator, the With statement, and writing general procedures.

Project 5 – Drag and Drop Events and More Complex Code Structures   The Traffic Sign Tutorial application built in Project 5 incorporates the activities necessary to add drag-and-drop functionality to applications. Students learn how to accept input from the user through a dialog box created with the InputBox function. Project 4 introduced control arrays. In this project, students write subroutines for common events shared by the controls in an array. In addition, a code method is used that allows one event procedure to initiate another event procedure. Several additional code structures are introduced in this project: nested If...Then blocks, Select Case blocks, and Do...Loop statements. Students also learn more about Visual Basic data types that were introduced briefly in an earlier project.

Project 6 – Database Management and Reporting Applications   After building an application in Project 4 that allowed the user to view records in an existing database, in Project 6, students create a more sophisticated database application, the TrainTrack Inventory System, that allows the user to add, modify, delete, and search for records. Students use data-bound ComboBox controls to allow the user to enter field values by clicking an item in a drop-down list rather than typing. Then, students learn how to use the Visual Data Manager add-in to create or modify a database, and use the Report Designer add-in and Crystal Report custom control to create a report that can be viewed within the application on the desktop or printed.

Project 7 – Creating ActiveX Controls and Distributing Applications   In Project 7, students create a custom ActiveX control. In building the control, students learn about the Timer control and its events and properties. Students also learn how to create custom properties. Students then incorporate the custom control into the Multiplication Quiz application. This application also presents random number generating functions, the Resize event, and several new properties of Command Button controls. Students then compile the Quiz into an .EXE file and use the Visual Basic Setup Wizard to create an installation program for distributing the application on floppy disks. Finally, students use the ActiveX Document Migration Wizard to create a version of the Multiplication Quiz that can be hosted by the Microsoft Internet Explorer application.

End-of-Project Student Activities

A notable strength of the Shelly Cashman Series Visual Basic 5 books is the extensive student activities at the end of each project. Well-structured student activities can make the difference between students merely participating in a class and students retaining the information they learn. The activities in the Shelly Cashman Series Visual Basic 5 books include:

▶ **What You Should Know** A listing of the tasks completed within a project together with the pages where the step-by-step, screen-by-screen explanations appear. This section provides a perfect study review for students.

▶ **Test Your Knowledge** Four pencil-and-paper activities designed to determine the students' understanding of the material in the project. Included are true/false questions, multiple-choice questions, and two short-answer activities.

▶ **Use Help** Any user of Visual Basic 5 must know how to use Help. Therefore, this book contains two Help exercises per project. These exercises alone distinguish the Shelly Cashman Series from any other set of Visual Basic 5 instructional materials.

▶ **Apply Your Knowledge** This exercise requires students to open and manipulate a file on the Data Disk that accompanies the Visual Basic 5 books.

▶ **In the Lab** Three in-depth assignments per project require students to apply the knowledge gained in the project to solve problems on a computer.

▶ **Cases and Places** Seven unique case studies require students to apply their knowledge to real-world situations.

Instructor's Resource Kit

A comprehensive Instructor's Resource Kit (IRK) accompanies this book in the form of a CD-ROM. The CD-ROM includes an electronic Instructor's Manual (called ElecMan) and teaching and testing aids. The CD-ROM (ISBN 0-7895-2778-2) is available through your Course Technology representative or by calling one of the following telephone numbers: Colleges and Universities, 1-800-648-7450; High Schools, 1-800-824-5179; and Career Colleges, 1-800-477-3692. The contents of the CD-ROM follow.

▶ **ElecMan** (*Electronic Instructor's Manual*) ElecMan is made up of Microsoft Word files. The files include lecture notes, solutions to laboratory assignments, and a large test bank. The files allow you to modify the lecture notes or generate quizzes and exams from the test bank using your own word processor. Where appropriate, solutions to laboratory assignments are embedded as icons in the files.

▶ **Figures on CD-ROM** Illustrations for most figures in the textbook are available. Use this ancillary to create a slide show from the illustrations for lecture or to print transparencies for use in lecture with an overhead projector.

▶ **Course Test Manager** Course Test Manager is a powerful testing and assessment package that enables instructors to create and print tests from test banks designed specifically for Course Technology titles. In addition, instructors with access to a networked computer lab (LAN) can administer, grade, and track tests online. Students also can take online practice tests, which generate customized study guides that indicate where in the text students can find more information on each question.

▶ **Lecture Success System** Lecture Success System files are for use with the application software, a personal computer, and projection device to explain and illustrate the step-by-step, screen-by-screen development of a project in the textbook without entering large amounts of data.

▶ **Instructor's Lab Solutions** Solutions and required files for all the In the Lab assignments at the end of each project are available.

▶ **Student Files** All the files that are required by the student to complete the Apply Your Knowledge exercises are included.

▶ **Interactive Labs** Eighteen hands-on interactive labs that take the student from ten to fifteen minutes each to step through help solidify and reinforce mouse and keyboard usage and computer concepts. Student assessment is available in each interactive lab by means of a Print button. The assessment requires students to answer questions.

Shelly Cashman Online

Shelly Cashman Online is a World Wide Web service available to instructors and students of computer education. Visit Shelly Cashman Online at www.scseries.com.

▶ **Series Information** Information on the Shelly Cashman Series products.

▶ **Teaching Resources** This area includes password-protected instructor materials.

▶ **Student Center** Dedicated to students learning about computers with Shelly Cashman Series textbooks and software. This area includes cool links, data from Data Disks that can be downloaded, and much more.

▶ **The Community** Opportunities to discuss your course and your ideas with instructors in your field and with the Shelly Cashman Series team.

Acknowledgments

The Shelly Cashman Series would not be the leading computer education series without the contributions of outstanding publishing professionals. First, and foremost, among them is Becky Herrington, director of production and designer. She is the heart and soul of the Shelly Cashman Series, and it is only through her leadership, dedication, and tireless efforts that superior products are made possible. Becky created and produced the award-winning Windows 95 series of books.

Under Becky's direction, the following individuals made significant contributions to this book: Ginny Harvey, series specialist and developmental editor; Ken Russo, Mike Bodnar, Stephanie Nance, Dave Bonnewitz, and Mark Norton, graphic artists; Jeanne Black, Quark expert; Nancy Lamm, proofreader; Cristina Haley, indexer; Sarah Evertson of Image Quest, photo researcher; and Deborah Fansler and Susan Sebok, contributing writers.

Special thanks go to Jim Quasney, our dedicated series editor; Lisa Strite, senior editor; Lora Wade, associate product manager; Tonia Grafakos, editorial assistant; Jonathan Langdale, online developer; and Kathryn Coyne, marketing manager. Particular thanks go to our reviewers of this book, Leonard Presby and Michael Walton. Special mention must go to Suzanne Biron, Becky Herrington, and Michael Gregson for the outstanding book design; Becky Herrington for the cover design; and Ken Russo for the cover illustrations.

Gary B. Shelly
Thomas J. Cashman
John F. Repede

Shelly Cashman Series – Traditionally Bound Textbooks

The Shelly Cashman Series presents the following computer subjects in a variety of traditionally bound textbooks. For more information, see your Course Technology representative or call one of the following telephone numbers: Colleges and Universities, 1-800-648-7450; High Schools, 1-800-824-5179; and Career Colleges, 1-800-477-3692.

COMPUTERS	
Computers	Discovering Computers 98: A Link to the Future, World Wide Web Enhanced
	Discovering Computers 98: A Link to the Future, World Wide Web Enhanced Brief Edition
	Discovering Computers: A Link to the Future, World Wide Web Enhanced
	Discovering Computers: A Link to the Future, World Wide Web Enhanced Brief Edition
	Using Computers: A Gateway to Information, World Wide Web Edition
	Using Computers: A Gateway to Information, World Wide Web Brief Edition
	Exploring Computers: A Record of Discovery 2e with CD-ROM
	A Record of Discovery for Exploring Computers 2e
	Study Guide for Discovering Computers: A Link to the Future, World Wide Web Enhanced
	Study Guide for Using Computers: A Gateway to Information, World Wide Web Edition
	Brief Introduction to Computers 2e (32-page)
WINDOWS APPLICATIONS	
Integrated Packages	Microsoft Office 97: Introductory Concepts and Techniques, Brief Edition (6 projects)
	Microsoft Office 97: Introductory Concepts and Techniques, Essentials Edition (10 projects)
	Microsoft Office 97: Introductory Concepts and Techniques (15 projects)
	Microsoft Office 97: Introductory Concepts and Techniques Workbook
	Microsoft Office 97: Advanced Concepts and Techniques
	Microsoft Office 95: Introductory Concepts and Techniques (15 projects)
	Microsoft Office 95: Advanced Concepts and Techniques
	Microsoft Office 4.3 running under Windows 95: Introductory Concepts and Techniques
	Microsoft Office for Windows 3.1 Introductory Concepts and Techniques Enhanced Edition
	Microsoft Office: Advanced Concepts and Techniques
	Microsoft Works 4.5* • Microsoft Works 4* • Microsoft Works 3.0*
Windows	Introduction to Microsoft Windows NT Workstation 4
	Microsoft Windows 95: Introductory Concepts and Techniques (96-page)
	Introduction to Microsoft Windows 95 (224-page)
	Microsoft Windows 95: Complete Concepts and Techniques
	Microsoft Windows 3.1 Introductory Concepts and Techniques
	Microsoft Windows 3.1 Complete Concepts and Techniques
Word Processing	Microsoft Word 97* • Microsoft Word 7* • Microsoft Word 6* • Microsoft Word 2.0
	Corel WordPerfect 8 • Corel WordPerfect 7 • WordPerfect 6.1* • WordPerfect 6* • WordPerfect 5.2
Spreadsheets	Microsoft Excel 97* • Microsoft Excel 7* • Microsoft Excel 5* • Microsoft Excel 4
	Lotus 1-2-3 97* • Lotus 1-2-3 Release 5* • Lotus 1-2-3 Release 4* • Quattro Pro 6
Database Management	Microsoft Access 97* • Microsoft Access 7* • Microsoft Access 2
	Paradox 5 • Paradox 4.5 • Paradox 1.0 • Visual dBASE 5/5.5
Presentation Graphics	Microsoft PowerPoint 97* • Microsoft PowerPoint 7* • Microsoft PowerPoint 4*
DOS APPLICATIONS	
Operating Systems	DOS 6 Introductory Concepts and Techniques
	DOS 6 and Microsoft Windows 3.1 Introductory Concepts and Techniques
Word Processing	WordPerfect 6.1 • WordPerfect 6.0 • WordPerfect 5.1
Spreadsheets	Lotus 1-2-3 Release 4 • Lotus 1-2-3 Release 2.4 • Lotus 1-2-3 Release 2.3
Database Management	dBASE 5 • dBASE IV Version 1.1 • dBASE III PLUS • Paradox 4.5
PROGRAMMING AND NETWORKING	
Programming	Microsoft Visual Basic 5*
	Microsoft Visual Basic 4 for Windows 95* (available with Student version software)
	Microsoft Visual Basic 3.0 for Windows*
	QBasic • QBasic: An Introduction to Programming • Microsoft BASIC
	Structured COBOL Programming (Micro Focus COBOL also available)
Networking	Novell NetWare for Users
	Business Data Communications: Introductory Concepts and Techniques, Second Edition
Internet	The Internet: Introductory Concepts and Techniques (UNIX)
	Netscape Navigator 4: An Introduction • Netscape Navigator 3: An Introduction
	Netscape Navigator 2 running under Windows 3.1 • Netscape Navigator: An Introduction (Version 1.1)
	Netscape Composer
	Microsoft Internet Explorer 4: An Introduction • Microsoft Internet Explorer 3: An Introduction
SYSTEMS ANALYSIS	
Systems Analysis	Systems Analysis and Design, Third Edition

*Also available as a Double Diamond Edition, which is a shortened version of the complete book

$\mathcal{S}$helly Cashman Series – **Custom Edition**® Program

If you do not find a Shelly Cashman Series traditionally bound textbook to fit your needs, the Shelly Cashman Series unique **Custom Edition** program allows you to choose from a number of options and create a textbook perfectly suited to your course. Features of the **Custom Edition** program are:

▶ Textbooks that match the content of your course

▶ Windows- and DOS-based materials for the latest versions of personal computer applications software

▶ Shelly Cashman Series quality, with the same full-color materials and Shelly Cashman Series pedagogy found in the traditionally bound books

▶ Affordable pricing so your students receive the **Custom Edition** at a cost similar to that of traditionally bound books

The table on the right summarizes the available materials.

For more information, see your Course Technology representative or call one of the following telephone numbers: Colleges and Universities, 1-800-648-7450; High Schools, 1-800-824-5179; and Career Colleges, 1-800-477-3692.

For Shelly Cashman Series information, visit Shelly Cashman Online at **www.scseries.com**

COMPUTERS	
Computers	Discovering Computers 98: A Link to the Future, World Wide Web Enhanced
	Discovering Computers 98: A Link to the Future, World Wide Web Enhanced Brief Edition
	Discovering Computers: A Link to the Future, World Wide Web Enhanced
	Discovering Computers: A Link to the Future, World Wide Web Enhanced Brief Edition
	Using Computers: A Gateway to Information, World Wide Web Edition
	Using Computers: A Gateway to Information, World Wide Web Brief Edition
	A Record of Discovery for Exploring Computers 2e (available with CD-ROM)
	Study Guide for Discovering Computers: A Link to the Future, World Wide Web Enhanced
	Study Guide for Using Computers: A Gateway to Information, World Wide Web Edition
	Introduction to Computers (32-page)

OPERATING SYSTEMS	
Windows	Microsoft Windows 95: Introductory Concepts and Techniques (96-page)
	Introduction to Microsoft Windows NT Workstation 4
	Introduction to Microsoft Windows 95 (224-page)
	Microsoft Windows 95: Complete Concepts and Techniques
	Microsoft Windows 3.1 Introductory Concepts and Techniques
	Microsoft Windows 3.1 Complete Concepts and Techniques
DOS	Introduction to DOS 6 (using DOS prompt)
	Introduction to DOS 5.0 or earlier (using DOS prompt)

WINDOWS APPLICATIONS	
Integrated Packages	Microsoft Works 4.5* • Microsoft Works 4* Microsoft Works 3.0*
Microsoft Office	Using Microsoft Office 97 (16-page) • Using Microsoft Office 95 (16-page)
	Microsoft Office 97:Introductory Concepts and Techniques, Brief Edition (396-page)
	Microsoft Office 97: Introductory Concepts and Techniques, Essentials Edition (672-page)
	Object Linking and Embedding (OLE) (32-page)
	Microsoft Outlook 97 • Microsoft Schedule+ 7
	Introduction to Integrating Office 97 Applications (48-page)
	Introduction to Integrating Office 95 Applications (80-page)
Word Processing	Microsoft Word 97* • Microsoft Word 7* • Microsoft Word 6*
	Microsoft Word 2.0
	Corel WordPerfect 8 • Corel WordPerfect 7 • WordPerfect 6.1*
	WordPerfect 6* • WordPerfect 5.2
Spreadsheets	Microsoft Excel 97* • Microsoft Excel 7* • Microsoft Excel 5*
	Microsoft Excel 4
	Lotus 1-2-3 97* • Lotus 1-2-3 Release 5* • Lotus 1-2-3 Release 4*
	Quattro Pro 6
Database Management	Microsoft Access 97* • Microsoft Access 7* • Microsoft Access 2*
	Paradox 5 • Paradox 4.5 • Paradox 1.0 • Visual dBASE 5/5.5
Presentation Graphics	Microsoft PowerPoint 97* • Microsoft PowerPoint 7*
	Microsoft PowerPoint 4*

DOS APPLICATIONS	
Word Processing	WordPerfect 6.1 • WordPerfect 6.0 • WordPerfect 5.1
Spreadsheets	Lotus 1-2-3 Release 4 • Lotus 1-2-3 Release 2.4 • Lotus 1-2-3 Release 2.3
	Quattro Pro 3.0 • Quattro with 1-2-3 Menus
Database Management	dBASE 5 • dBASE IV Version 1.1 • dBASE III PLUS
	Paradox 4.5 • Paradox 3.5

PROGRAMMING AND NETWORKING	
Programming	Microsoft Visual Basic 4 for Windows 95* (available with Student version software) • Microsoft Visual Basic 3.0 for Windows*
	Microsoft BASIC • QBasic
Networking	Novell NetWare for Users
Internet	The Internet: Introductory Concepts and Techniques (UNIX)
	Netscape Navigator 4: An Introduction • Netscape Navigator 3: An Introduction • Netscape Navigator 2 running under Windows 3.1
	Netscape Navigator: An Introduction (Version 1.1) • Netscape Composer
	Microsoft Internet Explorer 4: An Introduction
	Microsoft Internet Explorer 3: An Introduction

*Also available as a mini-module

Introduction to Visual Basic Programming

Objectives:

You will have mastered the material in this project when you can:

▶ Describe programs, programming, applications, and application development

▶ List six principles of user interface design

▶ Describe each of the steps in the program development life cycle

▶ Define structured programming

▶ Read and understand a flowchart

▶ Read and understand a HIPO chart

▶ Explain sequence, selection, and repetition control structures

▶ Describe object-oriented programming

▶ Define the terms objects, properties, methods, and events

▶ Read and understand a generalization hierarchy

▶ Read and understand an object structure diagram

▶ Read and understand an event diagram

▶ Define and explain encapsulation, inheritance, and polymorphism

▶ Describe rapid application development (RAD) and prototyping

▶ Describe VBA, VBScript, and the Visual Basic language

Microsoft
Visual Basic 5

Introduction to Visual Basic Programming

Introduction

The **Visual Basic Programming System** encompasses a set of tools and technologies that are being used by more than three million developers worldwide to create computer software components and applications. At the release of version 5 of Visual Basic, Bill Gates, chairman and CEO of Microsoft Corporation, said, "It has been a long time in coming, but the industrial revolution of software is finally upon us." Although not all people would agree with Mr. Gates's characterization of Visual Basic, most would agree that it is an extremely versatile, powerful, and yes — complex development system (the Professional Edition of version 5 contains more than 5,000 pages of user documentation). The popularity and complexity of Visual Basic is evidenced by the several Internet discussion groups dedicated to Visual Basic as well as the many World Wide Web sites and the wealth of books written about Visual Basic.

Schools across the country are teaching Visual Basic in a variety of different settings. These range from using Visual Basic as a general introduction to computer programming to two- and three-semester course sequences with prerequisite courses in subjects such as logic, software design, and structured programming. The two editions of this book (*Microsoft Visual Basic 5: Introductory Concepts and Techniques* and *Introduction to Visual Basic 5*) are designed to provide an introductory to intermediate working knowledge of Visual Basic and the software development concepts and technologies upon which it is built.

You may come to this course already having studied subjects such as systems analysis and design and structured programming, or this may be your first exposure to how a computer is programmed. The purpose of this introductory section is to provide the *big picture* of software design and development. You easily can find entire books and courses on each of the topics covered in this introduction, and your instructor may decide to spend more or less time on these topics depending on your background and the nature of the course you are taking.

Programming a Computer

Before a computer can start to produce a desired result, it must have a step-by-step description of the task to be accomplished. The step-by-step description is a series of precise instructions called a **program**. When these instructions are placed into the computer's memory, they are called a **stored program. Memory** stores the data and instructions that tell the computer what to do with the data.

Once the program is stored, the first instruction is located and sent to the control unit (**fetched**) where it is translated into a form the computer can understand (**decoded**), and then the instruction is carried out (**executed**). The result of the instruction is placed in memory (**stored**). Then, the next instruction is fetched, decoded, and executed. This process, called a **machine cycle**, continues under the direction of the operating system, instruction by instruction, until the program is completed or until the computer is instructed to halt.

In the Windows operating system, you can have multiple windows (programs) open on the desktop at the same time. Unless the computer has more than one CPU (each with its own memory), called **parallel processing**, it still executes only one instruction at a time. It carries these instructions out so fast, however, that it can move back and forth among programs carrying out some instructions from one program, and then some instructions from another program. To the user, it appears as though these programs are running simultaneously. This moving back and forth between programs by the processor is called **multitasking**. Even in a multitasking system, a processor can execute only one instruction at a time.

For the computer to perform another job, a new program is read into memory. By reading stored programs into memory, the computer can be used easily to process a large number of different jobs. The instructions within these jobs can be written, or **coded**, by a computer programmer in a variety of programming languages. Today, more than 2,000 programming languages exist. The process of writing the sets of instructions that make up these jobs is called **computer programming.**

Most computer users do not write their own programs. Programs required for common business and personal applications such as word processing or spreadsheets can be purchased from software vendors or stores that sell computer products. These purchased programs often are referred to as **application software packages,** or simply applications. **Applications** are programs that tell a computer how to accept instructions from the end user and how to produce information in response to those instructions. The process of using a programming language or development environment to build software applications is called **application development.**

User Interface Design

The way that a program accepts instructions from the user and presents results is called the **user interface**. Today, most applications have a graphical user interface (GUI). A **graphical user interface** (**GUI**) provides visual clues such as small pictures, or **icons**, to help the end user give instructions to the computer. Microsoft Windows is the most widely used graphical user interface for personal computers.

After working only a short time with different applications within the Windows operating system, you will begin to notice similarities in the user interfaces — even among applications created by companies other than Microsoft. This is not a coincidence and this similarity greatly reduces the time required to learn a new application.

Examine the packaging for software applications the next time you are in a store that sells software. Many applications have a Windows logo with the words, Designed for Microsoft Windows 95. These applications must follow an extensive set of requirements in order to display the Windows 95 logo on the package. These include requirements ranging from supporting the use of long file names to adherence to very detailed Windows interface guidelines. Whether you want to display the Windows logo on your software or not, some basic principles need to be followed in designing a graphical user interface.

The application always should be under the user's control. The application should present choices that allow the user to initiate and control the application's events. One example would be a user's capability not only to initiate a print function, but if necessary, to cancel the print function before it is completed.

User capabilities and preferences vary greatly and change over time. The user should be able to customize the application to meet his or her preferences. For example, the **ScreenTips** (pop-up help bubbles) that are valuable to a new user of an application may be annoying to a proficient user. A color scheme that one person finds attractive may be distracting to another. The application should allow, but not require, customizing. An initial default interface should be provided for those who do not want to specify customizing options.

Form should follow function. The interface should be designed to provide direct ways to accomplish tasks and not to be glamorous or trendy. Avoid the temptation to try to find some use within the application for your favorite visual elements. For example, a Drop-down ComboBox control should be used when the control you want to give the user is best accomplished with a combo box and not because you feel that combo boxes make your application more professional looking or fun to use. Some of the best interface elements are ones the user does not notice because their use is so intuitive, they do not have to consciously think, Now how do I do this? or What does this thing do?

Use concepts and metaphors that users are familiar with to make the interface parallel real-world experience. A familiar GUI metaphor for lifting and moving a real-world object from one location to another is to use a mouse to complete a drag-and-drop operation. Dragging and dropping an image of a file folder onto an image of a recycle bin is closer to real-world experiences than typing the characters `del filename.doc` next to the `c:\windows>` characters.

Applications should follow basic graphic design principles and should be consistent visually and functionally. For example, each time a dialog box is used to provide a message to the user, it should have a similar shape, location, color, font size, and style. Functional consistency means the user initiates the same set of events in the same way throughout the use of the application. If the same set of print options is offered to the user when printing report A or report B, then report A's options should not be presented as a menu and report B's options presented as a set of check boxes.

The user always should receive immediate feedback after initiating an event. You probably at one time or another have experienced the frustration of clicking a button or icon and then wondering whether anything was happening. When you click an icon and the mouse pointer changes to an hourglass or animated image, you understand that processing has been initiated in response to your click. If you have ever heard the Windows Chimes, Chord, Exclamation, or other sounds, you have experienced **auditory feedback**.

The application should attempt to prevent users from making mistakes as much as possible, rather than allowing mistakes and then pointing them out to the user. Nevertheless, users will make mistakes, and the application should be capable of responding to their mistakes. The user never should be told that he or she made a mistake. Instead, he or she should be told politely why a function cannot be carried out or prompted to reenter data. These messages often are conveyed in dialog boxes, called **error dialogs**, but they should never use language that implies the user is at fault. Many individuals learn how to use an application by trial and error and so the error dialog is a way to provide positive rather than negative feedback to the user.

The Program Development Life Cycle

When programmers build software applications, they just do not sit down and start writing code. Instead, they follow an organized plan, or **methodology**, that breaks the process into a series of tasks. There are many application development methodologies just as there are many programming languages. These different methodologies, however, tend to be variations of what is called the program development life cycle (PDLC).

The **program development life cycle** (**PDLC**) is an outline of each of the steps used to build software applications. Similarly to the way the system development life cycle (SDLC) guides the systems analyst through development of an information system, the program development life cycle is a tool used to guide computer programmers through the development of an application. The program development life cycle consists of six steps, summarized in Table 1 on the next page.

Table 1

STEP	PROCEDURE	DESCRIPTION
1	Analyze the problem	Precisely define the problem to be solved, and write *program specifications* — descriptions of the program's inputs, processing, outputs, and user interface.
2	Design the program	Develop a detailed logic plan using a tool such as *pseudocode, flowcharts, object structure diagrams,* or *event diagrams* to group the program's activities into modules; devise a method of solution or algorithm for each module; and test the solution algorithms.
3	Code the program	Translate the design into an application using a programming language or application development tool by creating the user interface and writing code; include *internal documentation* — comments and remarks within the code that explain the purpose of code statements.
4	Test and debug the program	Test the program, finding and correcting errors (*debugging*) until it is error free and contains enough safeguards to ensure the desired results
5	Formalize the solution	Review and, if necessary, revise internal documentation; formalize and complete end-user (external) documentation.
6	Maintain the program	Provide education and support to end users; correct any unanticipated errors that emerge and identify user-requested modifications (enhancements). Once errors or enhancements are identified, the program development life cycle begins again at Step 1.

Structured Programming

Structured programming, or **structured design,** is a methodology used to facilitate translating the problem analyzed in Step 1 of the PDLC into the specific program instructions in Step 3 (coding). Each module identified in the design step of the PDLC may be broken into a number of smaller and more precise instruction sets. This process can continue for several levels of even smaller, more precise instruction sets. The lowest-level instructions often are called **procedures.** A **hierarchy chart,** also called a **top-down chart** or **hierarchical input process output (HIPO) chart,** is a common way to represent this subdivision of activities visually. A hierarchy chart is shown in Figure 1.

A **flowchart** is a design tool used to represent the logic in a solution algorithm graphically. Table 2 shows a standard set of symbols used to represent various operations in a program's logic.

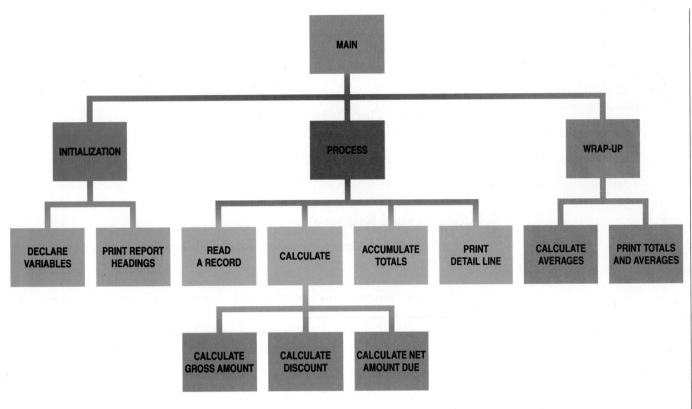

FIGURE 1

Table 2		
SYMBOL	*NAME*	*MEANING*
▭	Process Symbol	Represents the process of executing a defined operation or group of operations which results in a change in value, form, or location of information. Also functions as the default symbol when no other symbol is available.
▱	Input/Output (I/O) Symbol	Represents an I/O function, which makes data available for processing (input) or displaying (output) of processed information.
Left to Right / Right to Left / Top to Bottom / Bottom to Top	Flowline Symbol	Represents the sequence of available information and executable operations. The lines connect other symbols, and the arrowheads are mandatory only for right-to-left and bottom-to-top flow.
⌐---	Annotation Symbol	Represents the addition of descriptive information, comments, or explanatory notes as clarification. The vertical line and the broken line may be placed on the left, as shown, or on the right.
◇	Decision Symbol	Represents a decision that determines which of a number of alternative paths is to be followed.
⬭	Terminal Symbol	Represents the beginning, the end, or a point of interruption or delay in a program.
○	Connector Symbol	Represents any entry from, or exit to, another part of the flowchart. Also serves as an off-page connector.
▯▭▯	Predefined Process Symbol	Represents a named process consisting of one or more operations or program steps that are specified elsewhere.

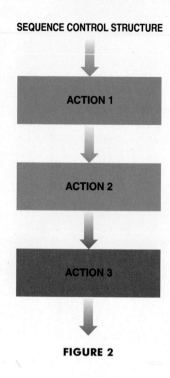

SEQUENCE CONTROL STRUCTURE

FIGURE 2

In structured programming, all program logic is constructed from a combination of three control structures, or constructs. A **control stucture** is a series of instructions that control the logical order in which the program instructions are executed. The three basic control structures are sequence, selection, and repetition.

Sequence Control Structure

The **sequence control structure** is used to show a single action or one action followed in order (sequentially) by another, as shown in Figure 2. Actions can be inputs, processes, or outputs.

Selection Control Structure

The **selection control structure** is used to tell the program which action to take, based on a certain condition. When the condition is evaluated, its result either is true or false. If the result of the condition is true, one action is performed; if the result is false, a different action is performed. This is called an **If...Then...Else** structure (Figure 3).

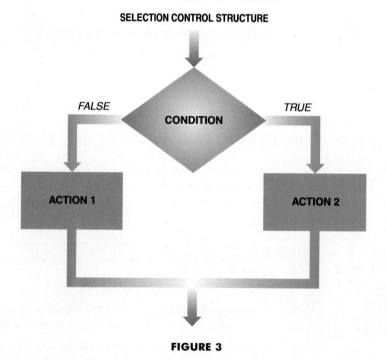

SELECTION CONTROL STRUCTURE

FIGURE 3

The action performed could be a single instruction or the action itself could be another procedure. The **case control structure** is a form of the selection control structure that allows for more than two alternatives when the condition is evaluated (Figure 4).

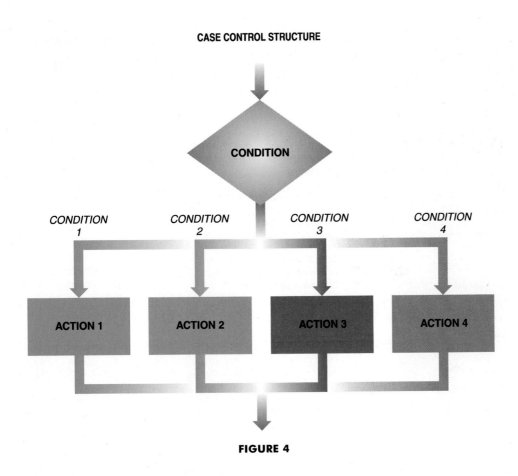

FIGURE 4

Repetition Control Structure

The **repetition control structure**, also called **looping** or **iteration**, is used when a set of actions is to be performed repeatedly. The Do...While and the Do...Until loops are forms of repetition control structures. The **Do...While loop** repeats as long as a condition is true (Figure 5). The **Do...Until loop** is similar, but it evaluates the condition at the end of the loop (Figure 6). This means the action(s) in the Do...Until loop always will execute at least once, where the actions in a Do...While loop may never execute.

Procedures commonly contain more than one control structure. The action specified within a control structure may be a single instruction or may activate other procedures. **Nested control structures** are control structures contained within other control structures. Figure 7 on the next page shows a flowchart that illustrates the processing required to compute the average commission paid to a

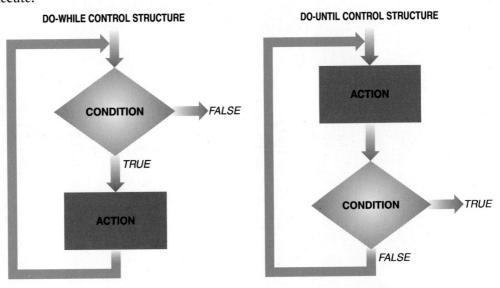

FIGURE 5

FIGURE 6

company's sales personnel and determine the number of male and female salespeople. The flowchart illustrated in Figure 7 contains sequence, selection, and repetition control structures. The selection control structure is nested within the repetition control structure.

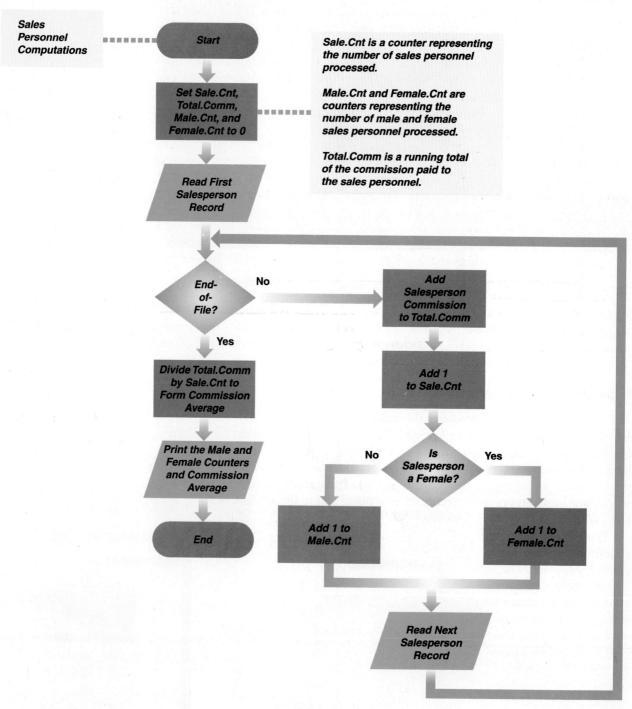

FIGURE 7

Object-Oriented Programming and Design

Object-oriented programming (OOP) and object-oriented design (OOD) represent a more recent methodology of application development than structured programming. This is a methodology that is not as well-defined as structured programming. Today, a number of Internet newsgroups exist in which the definitions, constructs, and implementations of OOP are debated hotly. **Object-oriented programming** has evolved as a way to better isolate logically related portions of an application than is possible in structured design. The benefit is that it is easier to develop, debug, and maintain applications that are becoming tremendously more complex than those created even a few years ago.

Object-oriented design represents the logical plan of a program as a set of interactions among objects and operations. An **object** is anything real or abstract, about which you store both data and operations that manipulate the data. Examples of objects are an invoice, an organization, a computer screen used to interact with a computer program, an airplane, and so on. An object may be composed of other objects, which in turn may contain other objects. A **class** is an implementation that can be used to create multiple objects with the same attributes and behavior. An object is an **instance** of a class. For example, Engine 15 located at 5th Street and Main is an object. It is a member of the class, Fire Truck.

Each class can have one or more lower levels called **subclasses** or one or more higher levels called **superclasses**. For example, Fire Truck is a subclass of Truck. Motor Vehicle is a superclass of Truck. The relationship among the classes, subclasses, and superclasses is called the **hierarchy**. A **generalization hierarchy** (Figure 8) is an object-oriented design tool used to show the relationships among classes of objects.

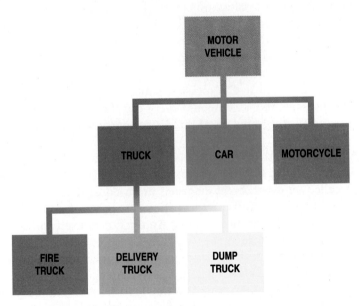

FIGURE 8

In object-oriented terminology, the data stored about an object is called an attribute, or property. **Attributes** are identifying characteristics of individual objects, such as a name, weight, or color. An **operation** is an activity that reads or manipulates the data of an object. In OOD, an operation is called a **service**. In OOP, the code that may be executed to perform a service is called a **method**.

An **object structure diagram** is used to provide a visual representation of an object, its attributes, and its methods (Figure 9 and Figure 10).

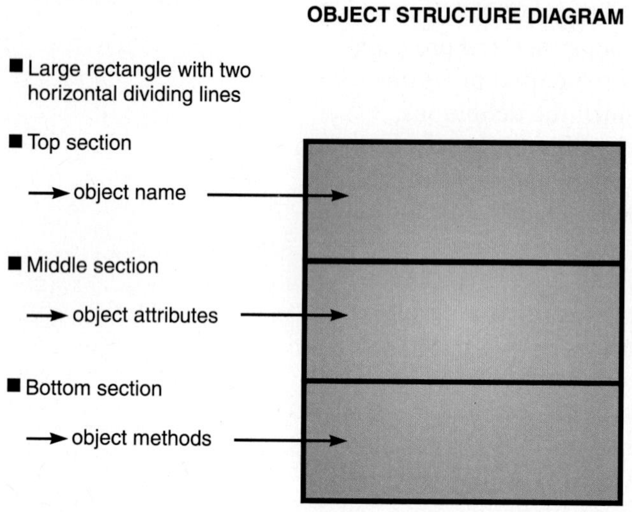

OBJECT STRUCTURE DIAGRAM

- Large rectangle with two horizontal dividing lines

- Top section

  → object name

- Middle section

  → object attributes

- Bottom section

  → object methods

FIGURE 9

SAMPLE OBJECT STRUCTURE DIAGRAM

TRAFFIC LIGHT

Color

Turn Red
Turn Yellow
Turn Green

The operations are described in terms of what they do — not how they do it.

FIGURE 10

For an object to do something, it must be sent a message. The **message** must have two parts — the name of the object to which the message is being sent and the name of the operation that will be performed. An **operation** is an activity that reads or manipulates the data of an object. An operation also can send additional messages. As an example, consider a VCR as a class having a rewind operation, a serial number attribute, and a counter attribute. Your VCR serial number 0023 is an instance of the class, VCR. The tape inside the VCR is not at its beginning and so the value of the counter attribute is something other than 000. To rewind a tape in the VCR, you would send a message similar to, vcr0023_rewind. In response to this message, the VCR would carry out the rewind operation. As a result of the operation, the value of vcr0023's counter attribute would be changed to 0000.

In OOD terminology, the operation is called a **service** and the message is called a **request for service**. In OOP terminology, the service is called a **method** and the message is called an **event**. **Event diagrams** are used to represent the relationships among events and operations. Operations are shown in rounded rectangles and events are shown on lines with arrows. An operation itself can send additional messages (events) (Figure 11).

As shown in Figure 11, nothing happens unless a message is sent (an event occurs). At the conclusion of an operation, the system again will do nothing until another event occurs. This relationship is a key feature of OOP, and programs that are constructed in this way are said to be **event-driven**.

**SAMPLE EVENT DIAGRAM
FOR REWIND OPERATION**

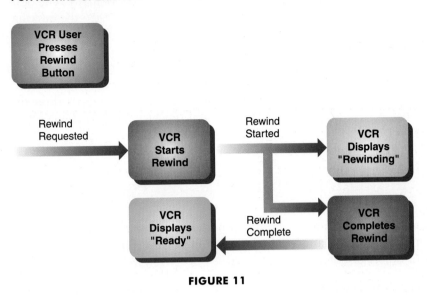

FIGURE 11

The Philosophy of Object-Oriented Programming (OOP)

OOP is not just a different set of tools and methods from structured programming. It represents a different philosophy about the nature of computer programs and how they are assembled. The following case scenario is designed to help illustrate these differences and provide an analogy for discussing the OOP constructs of encapsulation, inheritance, and polymorphism.

Paul Randall is a student of structured programming. He wants to create a work and study area in his room where he can write and draw and be able to cover his work. He wants to sit at the work area, and he wants to store his papers. Paul views the system as a set of functions — sitting, writing, and storing.

After a great deal of effort in drawing up blueprints, Paul has designed a one-piece, integrated study unit consisting of a writing surface with rolltop cover, a bench, and two drawers. By designing an integrated unit, the functions of sitting, writing, and storing will be compatible with each other and he will save on material costs and construction time. Paul travels to several lumber and hardware stores and purchases all the materials.

After considerable construction time, Paul is finished and satisfied with the result. He can work comfortably and does not reach too far to lift up the desktop or pull open the file drawers. Several weeks pass and Paul begins to think about making enhancements to his system. His bench is not as comfortable as he would like, his writing area feels cramped, and his two drawers are full. Paul decides to live with his system's shortcomings, however, because any change would require a substantial effort to dismantle and rebuild the entire system.

Mary Carter is a student of object-oriented programming. She would like to have a study area with the same functionality as Paul's. Mary, however, views the system as a set of objects — a sitting object, a writing surface object, and a storage object. Even though they are separate objects, Mary is confident she can make them interoperate with each other for an effective study area. Mary travels to a furniture factory warehouse and begins evaluating the hundreds of different chairs, desks, and file cabinets for their suitability to her needs and their compatibility with each other.

Mary returns to her room with a chair, a two-drawer file cabinet, and a roll-top desk from the Contemporary Oak line of the Devco Company. The desk has a handle similar to those on the drawers of the file cabinet. When the desk handle is pulled, it activates a hardware mechanism that raises the rolltop. Without too much effort arranging the furniture, Mary's study area is complete.

Although Mary's furniture cost more than Paul's materials, her savings on her labor costs have more than made up for the difference. After several weeks, Mary's file cabinet is full. She returns to the furniture store, buys a three-drawer cabinet from the Contemporary Oak line, and replaces the file cabinet in her study area.

Encapsulation, Inheritance, and Polymorphism

Just as sequence, selection, and repetition are the major constructs of structured programming, encapsulation, inheritance, and polymorphism are the major constructs of object-oriented programming.

Encapsulation

Encapsulation is the capability of an object to have data (properties) and functionality (methods) available to the user without the user having to understand the implementation within the object. Structured programming separates data from procedures. In the object-oriented world, an object contains functions as well as their associated data. Encapsulation is the process of hiding the implementation details of an object from its user. This process also is called **information hiding**. Users know what operations may be requested of an object but do not know the specifics of how the operations are performed. Encapsulation allows objects to be modified without requiring the applications that use them also to be modified.

In the case scenario, both Paul and Mary want drawers that cannot be pulled all the way out accidentally. In constructing his system, Paul had to attend to the details of how drawer stops work, which ones to use, and how to build them into the system. Mary, on the other hand, did not concern herself with *how* the safety stops on her drawers work; only that they *do* work. For Mary, the safety stop functionality and behavior is encapsulated within the file cabinet object.

Inheritance

Inheritance means that a descendent class (subclass) that differs from its superclass in only one way contains just the code or data necessary to explain the difference. Its status as a subclass is enough to give it access to all the superclass's functions and data. This is a very efficient way of reusing code. Also known as **subclassing**, this provides a way for programmers to define a class as an extension of another class, without copying the definition. If you let a class inherit from another class it automatically will have all the data and methods of the inherited class.

Mary's desk, chair, and cabinet all have similar wood grain, color, and style. If you think of the Devco Company's Contemporary Oak line of furniture as a superclass, then Mary's furniture objects are instances of subclasses of that furniture line. Because they are subclasses of the same superclass, they *inherited* the same wood grain, color, and style attributes from the superclass.

Polymorphism

Polymorphism allows an instruction to be given to an object in a generalized rather than specific detailed command. The same command will get different, but predictable, results depending on the object that receives the command. While the specific actions (internal to the object) are different, the results would be the same. In this way, one OOP function can replace several traditional procedures.

Paul must lift up his desktop when he wants to open it. You could say he must perform a *lifting* operation. To open his drawers, he must perform a *pulling* operation. Recall that Mary's rolltop desk has a pull handle with hardware *encapsulated* within the desk that translates the pull of the handle into the raising of the desktop. Mary's desk and file cabinet objects are *polymorphic* with respect to opening. Mary applies the same method, *pulling*, to open either object. She knows that the pull method will result in the object opening. How the object opens, or even that the object does open differently, is not a concern to Mary.

Rapid Application Development (RAD) and the Benefits of Object-Oriented Programming

Rapid application development (RAD) refers to the use of prebuilt objects to make program development much faster. Using prebuilt objects is faster because you use existing objects rather than writing everything yourself. The result is shorter development life cycles, easier maintenance, and the capability to reuse components for other projects. One of the major premises on which industry implementation of OOP is built is greater reusability of code.

The adoption of an object-orientation means that not all members of a development team need to be proficient in an object-oriented programming language such as Visual Basic, Delphi, PowerBuilder, Smalltalk, or C++. A more practical and economical approach is to separate the task of creating objects from the task of assembling objects into applications. Some programmers can focus on creating objects while other developers leverage their knowledge of business processes to assemble applications using OOP methods and tools. The benefits of OOP are summarized in Table 3.

Table 3	
BENEFIT	**EXPLANATION**
Reusability	The classes are designed so they can be reused in many systems or create modified classes using inheritance.
Stability	The classes are designed for repeated reuse and become stable over time.
Easier design	The designer looks at objects as a black box and is not concerned with the detail inside.
Faster design	The applications can be created from existing components.

What Is Microsoft Visual Basic 5?

The **Visual Basic Programming System version 5,** is a tool that allows you to create software applications for the Windows operating system. With **Microsoft Visual Basic 5 (VB5),** you can create Windows desktop applications, reusable software components for building other applications, and applications targeted for the Internet and intranets.

Visual Basic 5 incorporates a set of software technologies called ActiveX. **ActiveX technology** allows the creation, integration, and reuse of software components called controls. **ActiveX controls** are reusable software components that can be integrated into a large number of different software products. More than 2,000 ActiveX controls currently are available. VB5's ActiveX technology also allows you to create ActiveX Documents. **ActiveX documents** are applications that can be delivered dynamically over the Internet or intranets with browsers such as Internet Explorer or Netscape Navigator.

Version 5 of Visual Basic is available in four editions — Control Creation, Learning, Professional, and Enterprise. The Visual Basic 5 **Control Creation Edition (VB5CCE)** allows developers to build ActiveX controls from scratch, customize existing ActiveX controls, or assemble multiple existing controls into new controls. It does not include some of the functionality found in the Learning, Professional, and Enterprise editions and it cannot be used to develop stand-alone applications. The Control Creation Edition is available free to download from the Microsoft Web site. In addition to including control creation capability, the Learning, Professional, and Enterprise editions each offer progressively more application development and project management features.

Visual Basic 5 is based on the **Visual Basic programming language,** which evolved from the Beginner's All-Purpose Symbolic Instruction Code (BASIC). In addition to four editions of Visual Basic 5, two additional editions of the Visual Basic programming language itself are available. The **Applications Edition (VBA)** of the Visual Basic programming language is included within Excel, Access, and many other Windows applications. You can use VBA to customize and extend the capabilities of those applications. The **Scripting Edition (VBScript)** of the Visual Basic programming language is a subset of Visual Basic you can use for Internet programming.

Is Visual Basic Object Oriented?

Visual programming languages are languages where you create the entire program by *visual* means. With Visual Basic, only the interface is created visually. The program still mostly is coded. Visual Basic, therefore, is not a visual programming language in the strict sense.

One of the strengths of Visual Basic is that it is very easy to put the basics of the interface in place, and then go on to develop the functionality of the application a little at a time. Visual Basic is well-suited to prototyping. **Prototyping** is a process where developers iterate between refining the specifications and building working models of the system.

Since its first release in the early 1990s, Visual Basic always has been event-driven and object-based. It does not, however, meet all the requirements to be called an object-oriented programming language. One of the principal distinctions is that Visual Basic implements subclassing through something called *aggregation* and *containment* rather than through inheritance.

In Visual Basic, you create applications by assembling components. Visual Basic has a set of predefined objects and also allows for user-defined objects. Objects have attributes called **properties**. The visual elements common to Windows applications such as check boxes, option buttons, and list boxes, are called **controls** in Visual Basic. The windows that contain an application's controls are called **forms**. Controls and forms are objects that have properties, methods, and events. Messages or requests for service are called **events**. Operations or services are called **procedures**. Procedures include **methods, functions,** and **subroutines**.

Applications are created with Visual Basic in a **three-step process** — creating the interface, setting properties, and writing code. Although Visual Basic has a number of built-in methods and functions that can be applied to objects and controls, you still must write many of the procedures that *glue together* the components. These procedures are written instruction by instruction. The constructs and syntax used to write the procedures are based on the BASIC language. In fact, the approach to coding procedures in Visual Basic uses the constructs and control structures of traditional structured programming.

Visual Basic is well established in the industry as a commercial-grade RAD tool. Thousands of large-scale, complex applications have been built with Visual Basic. Visual Basic also is a powerful tool for learning programming and application development, because it requires an understanding of the concepts and techniques of both structured programming and object-oriented programming.

Summary

This introduction provided an overview of application development, user interface design, program development methodology, structured programming, object-oriented programming, and the Visual Basic software development system. This overview has provided a context within which you can better understand the concepts and technologies involved in the projects that follow. Visual Basic is a powerful and complex event-driven, object-based software development system. Creating applications with Visual Basic is a challenging and exciting undertaking.

A+ Test Your Knowledge

1 True/False

Instructions: Circle T if the statement is true or F is the statement is false.

T F 1. The program development life cycle is an outline of steps used to build software applications.

T F 2. The selection control structure also is called looping.

T F 3. A flowchart is used to show the relationships among classes of objects.

T F 4. In OOP terminology, a message sent to an object is called an event.

T F 5. Inheritance also is called information hiding.

T F 6. Visual Basic is an object-oriented programming language.

T F 7. Event diagrams show the relationship among events and operations.

T F 8. Applications always should direct the user what to do next.

T F 9. In a multitasking system, a processor executes multiple instructions at the same time.

T F 10. The function of an interface should follow from its form.

2 Multiple Choice

Instructions: Circle the correct response.

1. A method is another word for a(n) _____.
   a. service
   b. request for service
   c. event
   d. property

2. Of the following, which is not a structured design tool?
   a. HIPO chart
   b. flowchart
   c. generalization hierarchy
   d. top-down chart

3. The correct order of operations in a machine cycle is _____.
   a. store, decode, fetch, execute
   b. fetch, store, decode, execute
   c. decode, execute, fetch, store
   d. fetch, decode, execute, store

4. An If...Then structure is an example of _____.
   a. sequence
   b. pseudocode
   c. selection
   d. iteration

5. An object is a(n) _____ of a class.
   a. instance
   b. attribute
   c. encapsulation
   d. inheritance

6. _____ allows objects to be modified without requiring the applications that use them to be modified.
   a. Inheritence
   b. Polymorphism
   c. Encapsulation
   d. Instantiation

7. Of the following, which is not a benefit of OOP?
   a. reusability
   b. disposability
   c. stability
   d. faster development

8. In Visual Basic terminology, check boxes, option buttons, and command buttons are called _____.
   a. elements
   b. objects
   c. controls
   d. events

9. _____ refers to the use of prebuilt objects to make application development faster.
   a. SDLC
   b. PDLC
   c. RAID
   d. RAD

10. In the PDLC, internal documentation is written during the _____ procedure.
   a. documenting
   b. maintaining
   c. designing
   d. coding

 Test Your Knowledge

3 Understanding Flowcharts

Instructions: A flowchart representation of part of a cariovascular disease risk assessment is shown in Figure 12. The higher the point total, the greater the risk. In the spaces provided, write the point total for the following persons.

1. A 33-year-old non-smoker with normal blood pressure who eats a high fat diet

   _____

2. A 19-year-old non-smoker with high blood pressure who eats a high fat diet

   _____

3. A 50-year-old non-smoker with high blood pressure who eats a high fat diet

   _____

4. A 27-year-old smoker with high blood pressure who eats a low fat diet

   _____

5. A 43-year-old smoker with high blood pressure who eats a high fat diet

   _____

6. A 17-year-old non-smoker with normal blood pressure who eats a high fat diet

   _____

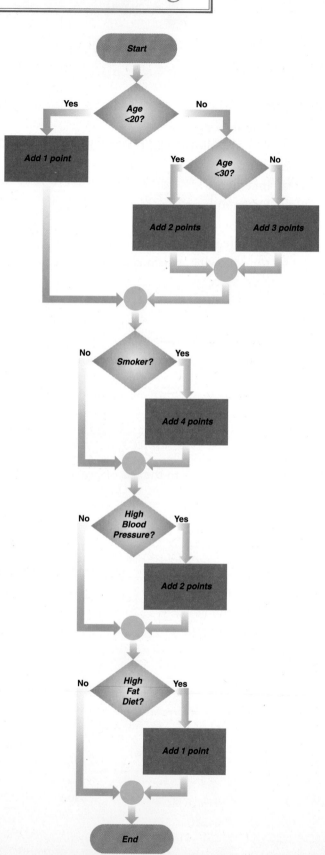

FIGURE 12

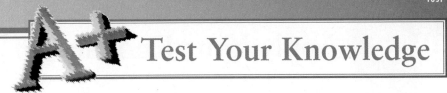

4 Understanding Event Diagrams

Instructions: Refer to Figure 13 to answer the following questions.

1. List each message and operation pair that follows.
2. Which of these operations includes a subsequent message? List any pairs of operations and their message.
3. Which of these operations changes the value of an attribute of an object? List the operation, attribute, and the attribute's value before and after the operation.

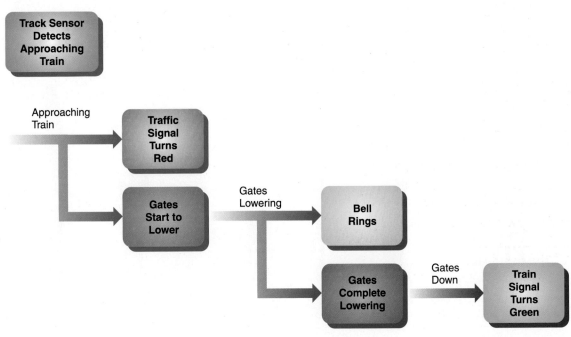

FIGURE 13

Apply Your Knowledge

1 Creating a Generalization Hierarchy

Instructions: Pick any class of objects that interests you (for example, clothes, musical instruments, physical fitness equipment, etc.). Create a generalization hierarchy showing at least four levels of subclasses and superclasses. For each subclass, identify several attributes inherited from each of its superclasses.

2 Creating a Flowchart

Instructions: Draw one flowchart that enables the mechanical man to accomplish the objectives efficiently in both Phase 1 and Phase 2, as illustrated in Figure 14.

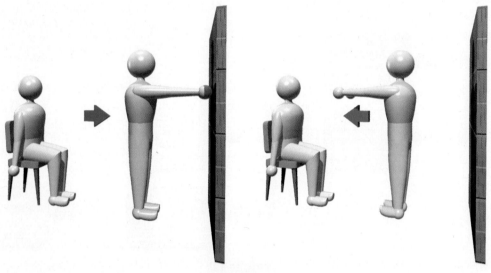

FIGURE 14

The mechanical man possesses the following properties:
1. He is restricted to a limited set of operations.
2. He is event-driven (doing nothing unless given a specific instruction).
3. He must carry out instructions one at a time.
4. He understands the following instructions:
   a. Physical movement:
      (1) Stand
      (2) Sit
      (3) Take one step forward
      (4) Raise arms straight ahead
      (5) Lower arms to sides
      (6) Turn right (90 degrees without taking a step)

Apply Your Knowledge

b. Arithmetic:
   (1) Add one to a running total
   (2) Subtract one from a running total
   (3) Store a total (any number of totals can be stored)
c. Logic — the mechanical man can decide what instruction he will carry out next on the basis of answers to the following questions:
   (1) Arithmetic results
       (a) Is the result positive?
       (b) Is the result negative?
       (c) Is the result zero?
       (d) Is the result equal to a predetermined amount?
   (2) Physical status
       (a) Are the raised arms touching anything?

3 Creating Object Structure Diagrams

Instructions: Identify the relevant objects in the mechanical man problem. Draw an object structure diagram for each one. List all the possible values of each of the attributes you identify.

4 Designing a User Interface

Instructions: Based on your previous experience with Windows applications, draw a picture of a user interface for an application that will convert any amount of dollars into the equivalent amount in an international currency. The currencies should include Yen, Lire, Marks, and Francs. Describe the events and methods (the exact exchange rates and calculations are not necessary). Referring to the user interface you designed, what mistakes could a user make? What will your application do in response to those mistakes?

In the Lab

1 Identifying Events and Methods

Instructions: Start any software application available to you. On your own paper, briefly describe what the application generally allows the user to do. Identify five specific events in the application and their corresponding methods (operations). Write your name on the paper and hand it in to your instructor.

2 Principles of Interface Design

Instructions: Start any software application available to you. On your own paper, briefly describe what the application generally allows the user to do. Identify one example of each of the interface design principles discussed in this introduction. Write your name on the paper and hand it in to your instructor.

3 Interface Consistency

Instructions: Explore three different software applications created by at least two different companies. Briefly describe each one on your own paper. List at least five things that all three applications have in common. Write your name on the paper and hand it in to your instructor.

4 User Mistakes

Instructions: Start any software application available to you. On your own paper, briefly describe what the application generally allows the user to do. Intentionally make at least five user mistakes. Describe what you did and how the application responded. Write your name on the paper and hand it in to your instructor.

Microsoft Visual Basic 5

Building an Application

Objectives:

You will have mastered the material in this project when you can:

▶ Start Visual Basic
▶ Select SDI Development Environment options
▶ Start a new Visual Basic project
▶ Change the size and location of a form
▶ Add controls to a form
▶ Describe the functions of the Label, TextBox, and CommandButton controls
▶ Move and resize controls on a form
▶ Set properties of controls
▶ Set a form's Name property
▶ Write an event procedure
▶ Use the Val function and SetFocus method within code statements
▶ Document code with comment statements
▶ Save a Visual Basic project
▶ Print an application's form and code
▶ Open an existing Visual Basic project
▶ Use Visual Basic Help

Touch-Screen Technology Gives Reason to *Celebrate*

Planning a wedding and expecting a baby are two of the more exciting, yet stressful, events in the lives of many couples. Part of the process involves registering for gifts for the special occasions and having friends and relatives purchase these articles. Whether it is housewares for the bride and groom or a stroller for the newborn, selecting the ideal product can be a daunting task.

Not so, if the bridal pair or the parents-to-be shop at Service Merchandise. According to corporate officials, the experience is a *no-hassle, fun way* to register. This positive process is due, in part, to the PC-based Gift Registry touch-screen and scanning system, which uses a Microsoft Visual Basic application developed by software engineers at NCR, a consulting firm and hardware vendor in Georgia.

NCR built the application using the same three-step process of creating the interface, setting properties, and writing code that you will learn in this project. Its programmers produced the system based on surveys stating that shoppers want to reduce frustration and time as they select gifts for the occasion. Using Visual Basic, they designed a graphical user interface that uses a combination of text and graphics to guide registrants and consumers.

The system works like this: registrants visit one of Service Merchandise's stores nationwide and locate the Gift Registry kiosk. Using the touch-screen keyboard developed with Visual Basic, they first select whether they are registering for a wedding, baby, or other special event, such as a retirement, birthday, or anniversary. They then enter their name, address, and event date. After inputting this pertinent information, their records are assigned specific gift registry numbers in the store's main computer processor, and they proceed to the store's information desk.

There they receive a hand-held, radio-frequency scanning gun. They walk through the store and scan the bar codes found on tags attached to specific products. As they enter their gift choices, their records are updated with the item number, description, price, and quantity desired. Once they have selected their items, they return the scanning gun to the information desk. The sales associate then prints a list of the items and announcement cards. This entire process can be accomplished in less than 20 minutes.

Next, these records are transmitted by a roof-mounted satellite dish to Service Merchandise's mainframe located at the corporation's headquarters in Nashville, Tennessee, and added to the database of all registrants.

At this point, relatives and friends throughout the country can visit one of Service Merchandise's more than 300 stores and use the Gift Registry kiosk. They locate the registrant's record by entering the gift registry number or the registrant's name on the touch-screen. The system prints a complete listing of the registrant's gifts, indicating the item number and description, price, number desired, number purchased, and where the item appears in the corporation's catalog. When this customer selects an item on the list, this information is transmitted to the mainframe, and the database is updated immediately.

More than 100,000 individuals register annually for their special events using this system, which makes it one of the country's most popular gift registries. Certainly this no-hassle application calls for a celebration in the eyes of registrants and friends.

no-hassle, fun way

Project 1

Microsoft
Visual Basic 5

Building an Application

Case Perspective

The Farpoint Airport Authority runs a small currency exchange at the entrance to the international concourse of the airport. The currency exchange has significant personnel turnover and cash balancing problems. The Airport Authority is having a difficult time analyzing the problems because the currency exchange's transaction and MIS systems are manual operations. Its most advanced technology consists of a hand-held calculator used for calculating the exchanges. The Airport Authority has published a request for proposal for a stand-alone, PC-based transaction process-ing and management information system.

The company you work for has decided to respond to the Airport Authority's request for proposal. You have been assigned to a team that is building a prototype system as part of the proposal. Visual Basic has been chosen as the development platform for this project. You are responsible for building a Windows-based exchange calculator module of the application. The prototype must demonstrate an intuitive graphical user interface (GUI) for calculating exchange transactions. The transaction-recording module is being built by another member of the team. The capabilities for the user to change the exchange rate and calculate exchanges for multiple currencies will be added later and are not required for the demonstration prototype.

Introduction

The way in which you give instructions to a computer and receive feedback from the computer is called a **user interface**. Microsoft Windows is called a **graphical user interface (GUI)** because it allows you to use both text and graphical images to communicate with the computer. **Applications software**, or **applications**, are computer programs that perform a specific function such as a calendar, word processing, or spreadsheet.

Numerous application software packages are available from computer stores, and several applications are included when you purchase the Microsoft Windows operating system. Although many of these Windows applications are created by different companies or individuals, they have a similar *look and feel* to the computer user. They *look* similar because they contain many of the same graphical images, or objects. Different Windows applications *feel* similar because they respond to the same kinds of user actions, such as clicking or dragging with a mouse. A typical Windows application containing common Windows objects is WordPad, as shown in Figure 1-1.

Visual Basic is itself a Windows application. Its function, however, is to help you build your own special-purpose applications and application components for the Windows operating system. With Visual Basic, professional-looking applications using the graphical user interface of Windows can be created by individuals who have no previous training or experience in computer programming. Because of the ease with which the user interface can be created, Visual Basic is especially useful for prototyping and rapid application development.

Project One – Converting Dollars to Francs

To learn the major features of application development with Microsoft Visual Basic, you will complete a series of projects using Visual Basic to build Windows applications. In this project, you will use Visual Basic to build the currency conversion application shown in Figure 1-2. In this application, the user enters a number in the DOLLARS text box. When the user clicks the CONVERT button, the amount is converted to French francs and displays in the FRANCS text box. The Convert Dollars To Francs application has some of the common features of Windows applications. It occupies a window that the user can move on the desktop, it can be maximized or minimized, and it has a Close button.

Because you are responsible for building only one module of the prototype information system for the airport currency exchange, you will not need to make the application stand-alone. A **stand-alone application**, also called an **EXE**, is one which runs independently of the Visual Basic system. You will learn how to make EXE applications in later projects. In addition, because the application is a prototype it need not contain all of the features and functionality that might be desired in the final application.

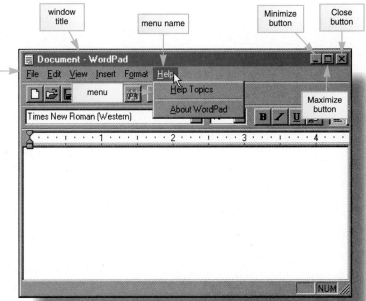

FIGURE 1-1

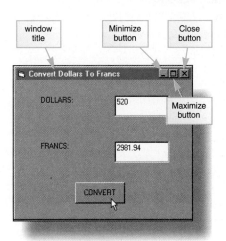

FIGURE 1-2

Project Steps

Applications are built with Visual Basic in a **three-step process:** creating the interface, setting properties, and writing code. You will follow this three-step process to build the currency conversion application. You will complete the following tasks in this project.

1. Start a Standard EXE project in Visual Basic.
2. Set options for the SDI interface.
3. Restart Visual Basic.
4. Set the size and location of a form.
5. Add Label, TextBox, and CommandButton controls to a form.
6. Add controls by drawing and double-clicking.
7. Set Caption, Text, Locked, TabStop, and Name properties.
8. Write an event procedure.
9. Use the Val function and SetFocus method within a procedure.
10. Add comments to a procedure.
11. Save a project.
12. Open and run an existing project.
13. Print a project.
14. Quit Visual Basic.

The following pages contain a detailed explanation of each of these steps.

Starting Visual Basic and Setting Development Environment Options

With Visual Basic 5, not only can you build desktop applications, but also application components and Internet applications. When you start Visual Basic, you can choose to open a recent, existing, or new project. When you select a new project, you must specify which type of project you will be creating.

Visual Basic 5 has an option for either a **multiple document interface (MDI)** or a **single document interface (SDI)**. The SDI presents independent windows on the desktop; the MDI presents windows within windows. The interface you use is one of personal preference; however, the MDI is better suited to larger monitors with higher resolutions.

Visual Basic records the size and location of all of these windows when you close the project so that its **integrated development environment (IDE)** displays the same each time you start Visual Basic. This can be a problem for a student working in a public computer lab, especially a student who is new to Visual Basic, because the IDE may look completely different every time the student comes to the lab and starts Visual Basic. In the following two sets of steps, you will open a new Standard EXE project and make the one IDE arrangement that is used in all of the projects in this book.

Starting Visual Basic and Setting Option Preferences

Whether you use the MDI or SDI, Visual Basic requires a lot of *real estate* on the desktop. Generally, you should minimize or close all other windows on the desktop before starting Visual Basic. This will make it easier for you to work with the Visual Basic windows. The currency conversion is a desktop application, or **Standard EXE**, project type. Perform the following steps to start Visual Basic, open a new Standard EXE project, and set option preferences.

Steps **To Start Visual Basic and Set Option Preferences**

1 **Click the Start button on the taskbar and then point to Programs on the Start menu. Point to Microsoft Visual Basic 5.0 on the Programs submenu, and then point to Visual Basic 5.0.**

The default menu structure for Visual Basic 5.0 is shown in Figure 1-3. Your system may have a different set of menus.

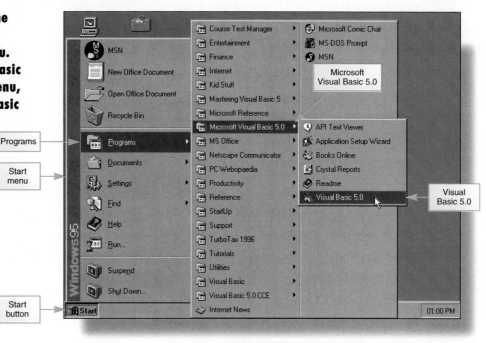

FIGURE 1-3

2 **Click Visual Basic 5.0. Click the New tab and then point to the Standard EXE icon.**

The New Project dialog box displays (Figure 1-4).

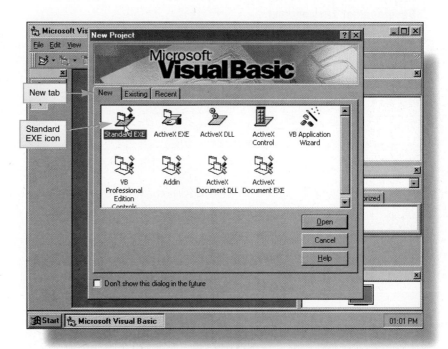

FIGURE 1-4

3 **Double-click the Standard EXE icon, click Tools on the menu bar and then point to the Options command (Figure 1-5).**

The Visual Basic IDE on your desktop may look different from Figure 1-5.

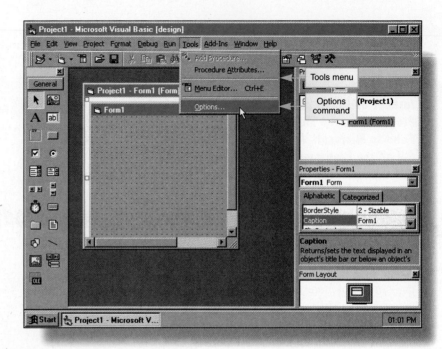

FIGURE 1-5

4 **Click Options, click the Advanced tab, and then point to SDI Development Environment.**

The Options dialog box displays. It contains six tab sheets (Figure 1-6).

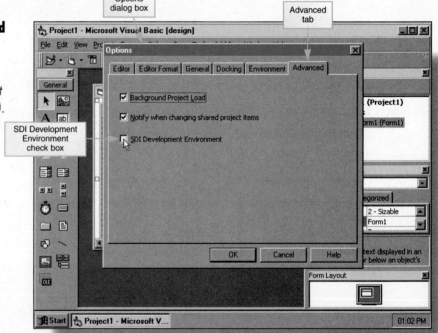

FIGURE 1-6

5 **If necessary, click SDI Development Environment to select it. Click the Editor tab. Point to Default to Full Module View in the Window Settings area.**

If SDI Development Environment was not selected, the MDI to SDI change does not take effect until VB is re-started. The Editor tab of the Options dialog box is shown in Figure 1-7.

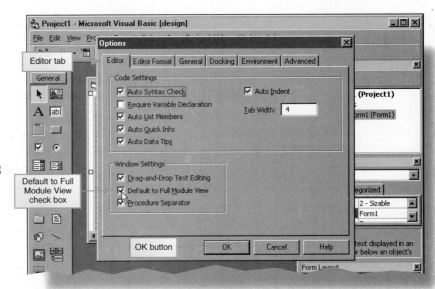

FIGURE 1-7

6 **If necessary, click Default to Full Module View to remove the check mark so that the Full Module View option is not selected. Click the OK button. Point to the Visual Basic Close button.**

The Options dialog box closes (Figure 1-8).

FIGURE 1-8

7 **Click the Close button. Repeat Step 1 through Step 3 to restart VB and open a new Standard EXE project.**

The SDI interface is activated (Figure 1-9)

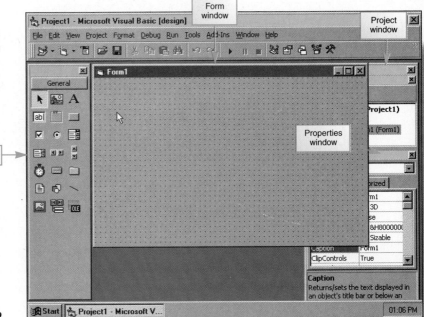

FIGURE 1-9

More *About*
Customizing Toolbars

The Toolbars tab in the Custom dialog box allows you to create, rename, delete, and reset your toolbars. The Options tab allows you to change the appearance of your menu bar and toolbars. The Commands tab allows you to add controls and modify existing controls on the menu bar or any toolbar.

When you start Visual Basic, several windows are added to the desktop. It is possible to work with Visual Basic without clearing the desktop. If other windows already are open, however, the desktop becomes cluttered.

Arranging Visual Basic Toolbars and Windows

The Visual Basic **integrated development environment (IDE)** contains nine different windows, all of which can be **docked**, or *anchored*, to other windows that are dockable and four toolbars that can be docked or float in their own windows. All of the windows can be resized and located anywhere on the desktop. To ensure the windows dock as shown in Figure 1-9 on the previous page, all the Dockable check boxes except Object Browser must be selected in the Docking sheet of the Options dialog box. Perform the following steps to establish a Visual Basic IDE arrangement similar to the one used in this book.

Steps **To Arrange Visual Basic Toolbars and Windows**

1 **With the exception of the Visual Basic menu bar and toolbar window, click the Close button on each Visual Basic window that is open on the desktop.**

Only the menu bar and toolbar remain open (Figure 1-10).

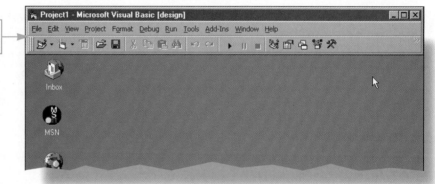

FIGURE 1-10

2 **Click View on the menu bar and then point to Project Explorer.**

The View menu displays (Figure 1-11).

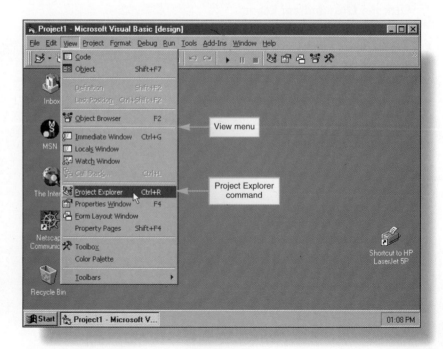

FIGURE 1-11

③ **Click Project Explorer. Click View on the menu bar and then click Properties Window. Click View on the menu bar and then click Toolbox. Right-click the Properties window and then click Description to deselect it. Drag the windows to the locations shown in Figure 1-12 and drag each window's borders to resize the windows to the sizes shown in Figure 1-12.**

Five Visual Basic windows are open on the desktop (Figure 1-12).

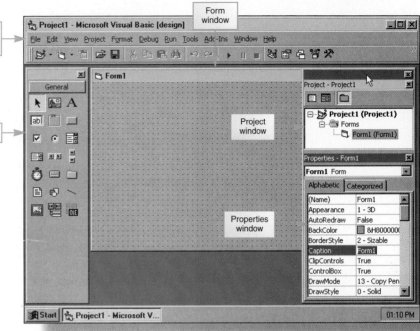

FIGURE 1-12

④ **Right-click the Visual Basic menu bar to the right of the Help menu.**

The shortcut menu displays (Figure 1-13). Your toolbar settings may be different from those shown in Figure 1-13.

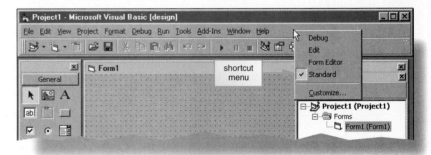

FIGURE 1-13

⑤ **If necessary, click Standard on the shortcut menu to display the Standard toolbar. Right-click the Standard toolbar, and then click any other toolbars that display with a check mark to the left of their names to deselect them.**

Your desktop should display similarly to Figure 1-14, with the Standard toolbar the only toolbar displaying.

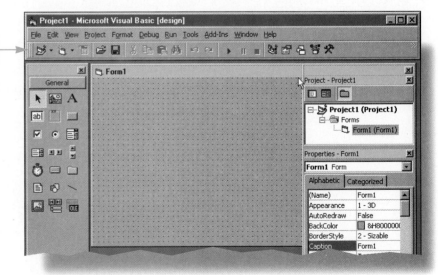

FIGURE 1-14

You can arrange the Visual Basic windows on the desktop in many different ways without affecting Visual Basic's functions. As you become more experienced, you may prefer to work with a different arrangement. Each project in this book uses the sizes and arrangement of the Visual Basic windows shown in Figure 1-14 on the previous page.

Setting the Size and Location of Forms

The time during which you build an application with Visual Basic is called **design time**. In contrast, the time during which you use an application for its intended purpose is called **run time**. In Visual Basic, the applications you build are called projects. A **project** always begins with a form. At run time, a **form** becomes the window the application occupies on the desktop. You will begin building the Convert Dollars To Francs application shown in Figure 1-2 on page VB 1.5 by specifying the size and location where you want the application's window to display on the desktop during run time.

Setting the Size of a Form

The size of an application's window on the desktop during run time is specified by adjusting the size of the form during design time. Adjustments to the form's size can be made at any time during design time.

Perform the following steps to set the size of the Convert Dollars To Francs form.

More *About*
Forms

Forms have properties that determine aspects of their appearance, such as position, size, and color; and aspects of their behavior, such as whether or not they are resizable. A special kind of form, the MDI form, can contain other forms called MDI child forms.

Steps To Set the Size of a Form

1 **Click the Form window's title bar.**

The Form window becomes the active window (Figure 1-15). This can be seen by the color of the title bar and the Form window moving on top of the Project and Properties windows.

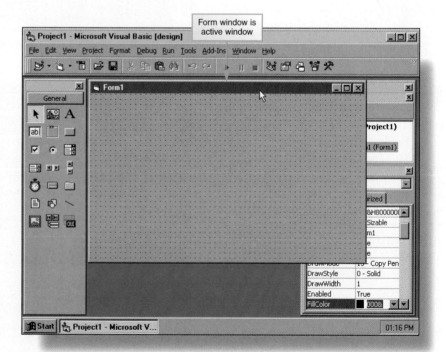

FIGURE 1-15

2 **Point to the form's right border.**

The mouse pointer changes to a double horizontal arrow indicating the form can be sized (Figure 1-16).

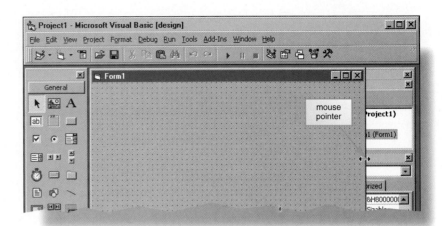

FIGURE 1-16

3 **Without releasing the mouse button, drag the form's right border toward the left side of the screen approximately three inches.**

During the drag operation, the border's new location displays as a shaded gray line (Figure 1-17).

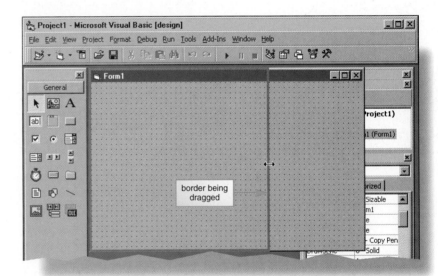

FIGURE 1-17

4 **Release the mouse button.**

The form's right border moves to the new location of the shaded gray line (Figure 1-18). The Project and Properties windows again become visible.

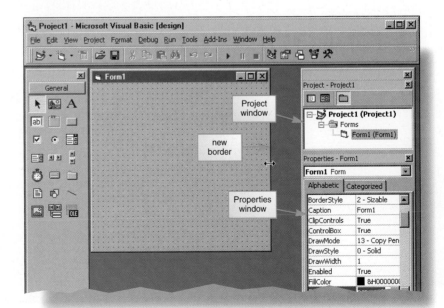

FIGURE 1-18

5 **Without releasing the mouse button, drag the form's bottom border toward the top of the screen approximately one inch.**

The border's new location displays as a shaded gray line (Figure 1-19).

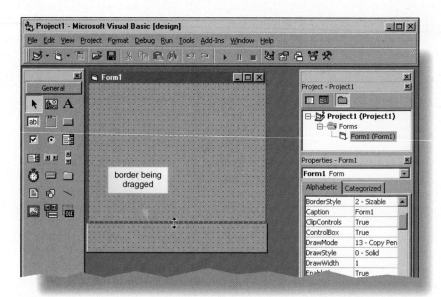

FIGURE 1-19

6 **Release the mouse button.**

The form's bottom border moves to the location of the shaded gray line (Figure 1-20).

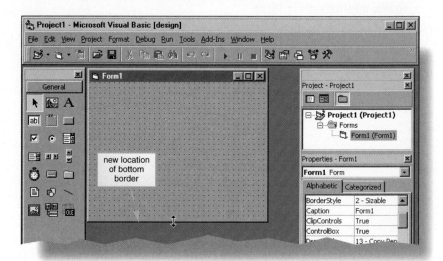

FIGURE 1-20

More *About* Twips

A twip is a unit of screen measurement equal to 1/20 of a printer's point. There are approximately 1440 twips to a logical inch or 567 twips to a logical centimeter (the length of a screen item measuring one inch or one centimeter when printed).

In the preceding steps, you set the form's **Width** and **Height** properties by dragging the form's right and bottom borders. You can drag each of the form's four borders in either an inward or outward direction to change its size. The form's width and height are measured in units called twips. A **twip** is a printer's measurement equal to 1/1440 inch. The width of a twip, however, can vary slightly from one computer monitor to another.

Positioning a Form

The location of an application's window on the desktop during run time is specified by adjusting the location of the form during design time. Adjustments to the form's location can be made at any time during design time. Perform the following steps to set the location on the desktop for the Convert Dollars To Francs window.

Steps To Position a Form

1 **Point to the Form window title bar (Figure 1-21).**

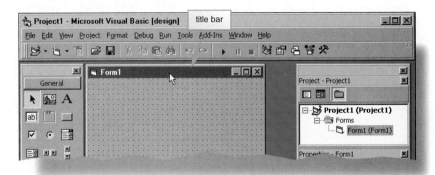

FIGURE 1-21

2 **Without releasing the mouse button, drag the Form window down and to the right.**

During the drag operation, the Form window's new location displays as a shaded gray outline on the desktop (Figure 1-22).

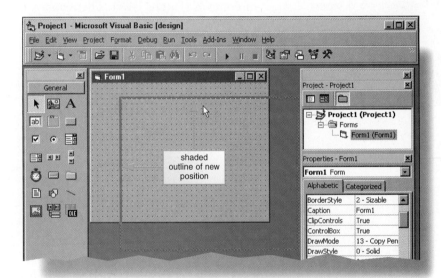

FIGURE 1-22

3 **When the form is approximately centered on the desktop, release the mouse button.**

The form moves to the new location outlined by the shaded gray lines (Figure 1-23).

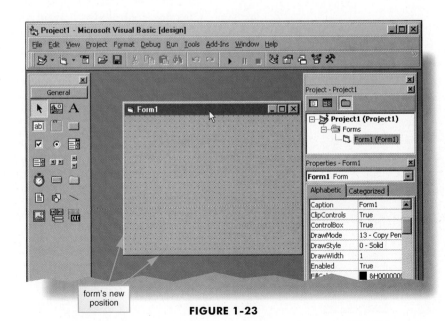

FIGURE 1-23

In the preceding steps, you set the form's location by dragging the form to the desired position. The form's location is given as two numbers. The first number is the value of the Left property. The **Left** property is the distance in twips between the left side of the desktop and the left border of the form. The second number is the value of the Top property. The **Top** property is the distance in twips between the top of the desktop and the top border of the form. The form's location can be changed as often as desired during design time. Sometimes, it is useful to move the form temporarily to work more easily in the other Visual Basic windows.

Adding and Removing Controls

Figure 1-1 on page VB 1.5 shows some of the graphical images, or objects, common to many Windows applications. In Visual Basic, these objects are called **controls**. The Convert Dollars To Francs application contains three different types of controls (Figure 1-24). These controls and their functions are described as follows.

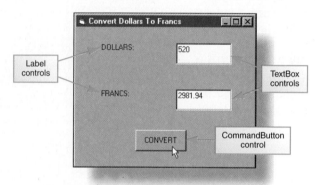

FIGURE 1-24

Label – A **Label control** is used to display text on a form. At run time, the person using the application cannot change the text on a label, such as DOLLARS.

TextBox – A **TextBox control** also is used to display text on a form, but its contents can be changed at run time by the person using the application. It frequently is used as a way for the user to supply information to the application.

CommandButton – A **CommandButton control** is used during run time to initiate actions called **events**.

Adding Controls to a Form

Controls are added to a form using tools in the Visual Basic window called the **Toolbox**. To use a tool, you click its respective button in the Toolbox. Although you can add additional controls to the Toolbox, the Toolbox contains twenty **intrinsic** controls. More than 2,000 additional controls are available from Microsoft and from third-party vendors. Specific controls and their functions will be discussed as they are used throughout the projects in this book. Figure 1-25 identifies the intrinsic tools in the Toolbox.

Complete the following steps to use the Toolbox to add controls to the form.

General

TextBox
Frame
CheckBox
ListBox
HScrollBar
Timer
FileListBox
Shape
Image

Label
PictureBox
CommandButton
ComboBox
OptionButton
VScrollBar
DirListBox
DriveListBox
Line
OLE
Data

FIGURE 1-25

Steps To Draw Label Controls on a Form

1 **Point to the Label button in the Toolbox (Figure 1-26).**

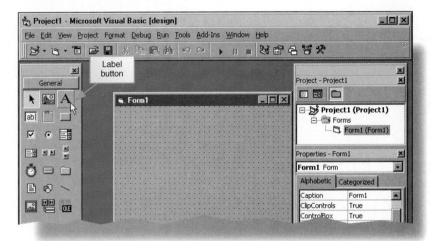

FIGURE 1-26

2 **Click the Label button. Position the cross hair mouse pointer near the upper-left corner of the form by moving the mouse pointer.**

*The Label button in the Toolbox is recessed, and the mouse pointer changes to a **cross hair** when it is over the form (Figure 1-27). The upper-left corner of the Label control will be positioned here.*

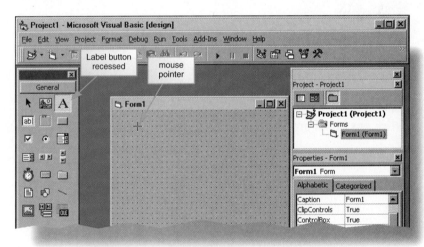

FIGURE 1-27

3 **Drag down and to the right.**

A gray outline of the Label control displays (Figure 1-28).

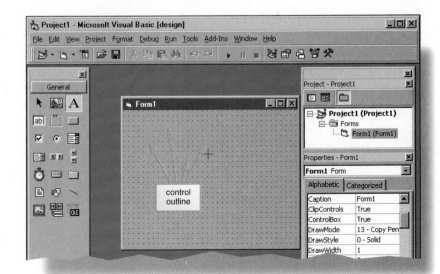

FIGURE 1-28

4 **When the Label control outline is the desired size, release the mouse button.**

The gray outline changes to a solid background. The name of the Label control (Label1) displays on the control. Small sizing handles display at each corner and in the middle of each side of the Label control (Figure 1-29).

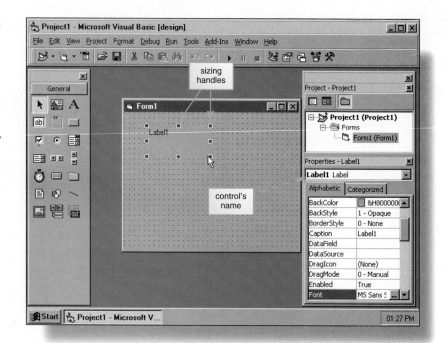

FIGURE 1-29

5 **Repeat Step 1 through Step 4 to draw a second Label control on the form in the size and position shown in Figure 1-30 and then click any blank area on the form.**

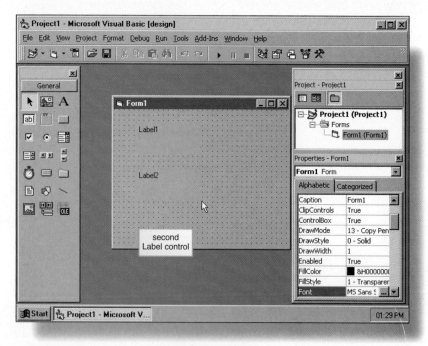

FIGURE 1-30

Two Label controls now have been added to the form by drawing them with the Label tool selected from the Toolbox. Complete the following steps to add two TextBox controls to the form.

Steps **To Draw TextBox Controls on a Form**

1 **Point to the TextBox button in the Toolbox (Figure 1-31).**

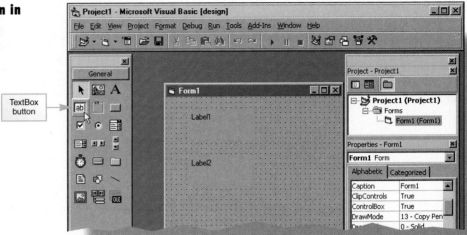

FIGURE 1-31

2 **Click the TextBox button. Position the cross hair mouse pointer toward the middle-right side of the form.**

The TextBox button is recessed in the Toolbox and the mouse pointer changes to a cross hair (Figure 1-32). The upper-left corner of the Label control will be positioned here.

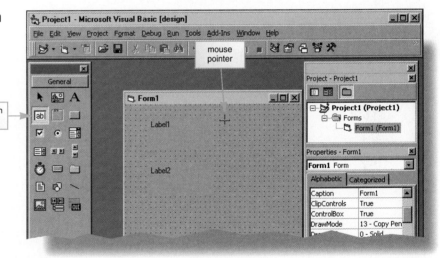

FIGURE 1-32

3 **Drag down and to the right.**

A gray outline of the TextBox control displays (Figure 1-33).

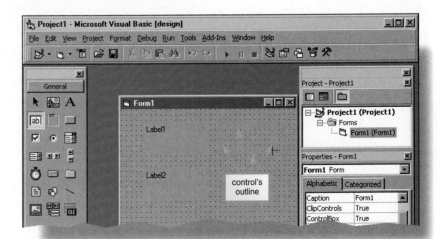

FIGURE 1-33

4 **When the TextBox control outline is the desired size, release the mouse button.**

The gray outline changes to a solid background. The name of the TextBox control (Text1) displays on the control. Sizing handles display at each corner and in the middle of each side of the text box control (Figure 1-34).

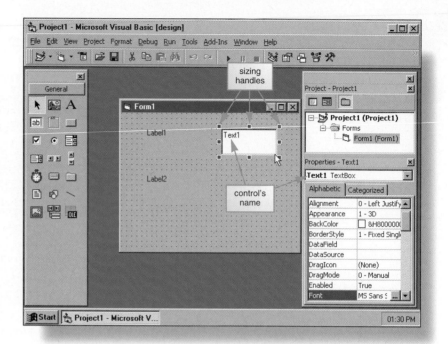

FIGURE 1-34

5 **Repeat Step 1 through Step 4 to place a second TextBox control on the form as shown in Figure 1-35.**

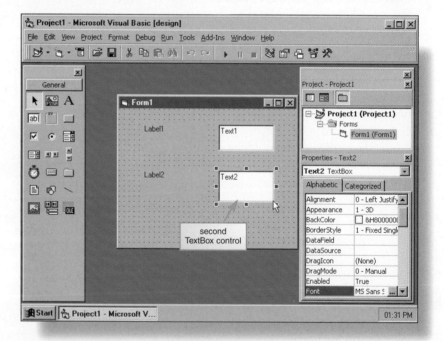

FIGURE 1-35

Two TextBox controls were added to the form in the same way as the two Label controls by clicking the button in the Toolbox and then drawing the control's outline on the form. This method can be used for adding any of the controls in the Toolbox to a form. This method, however, is not the only way to add controls to a form. The following steps use an alternative method to add a CommandButton control to the Convert Dollars To Francs form.

Steps To Add Controls by Double-Clicking

1 **Point to the CommandButton button in the Toolbox (Figure 1-36).**

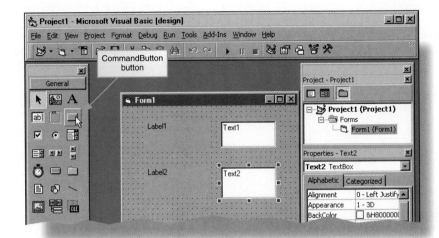

FIGURE 1-36

2 **Double-click the CommandButton button.**

The CommandButton control displays in the center of the form. The control's name, Command1, displays on the control. Sizing handles display around the CommandButton control (Figure 1-37).

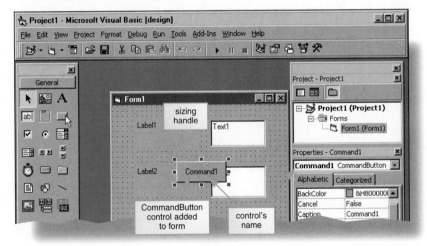

FIGURE 1-37

As you have just seen, double-clicking a button in the Toolbox adds a default-sized control to the center of the form. If another control already is located in the center of the form, this method will add the new control on top of the previous control.

Removing Controls

If you click the wrong button in the Toolbox or want to modify the project, controls can be removed from the form at any time during design time. Use the following steps to remove a control.

TO REMOVE A CONTROL

1 Point to the control you want to remove.

2 Click the control to select it.

3 Press the DELETE key.

Changing the Location and Size of Controls

If you add a control to a form by double-clicking a button in the Toolbox, you will need to move the control from the center of the form, and frequently, you will want to change its size from the default. The location and size of any of the controls on a form can be changed at any time during design time.

Moving a Control on a Form

A control can be moved by dragging it to a new location. Perform the following steps to move the CommandButton control from the center of the Convert Dollars To Francs form.

 Steps **To Move a Control on a Form**

1 **Point to a location in the interior (not on any of the handles) of the Command1 CommandButton control (Figure 1-38).**

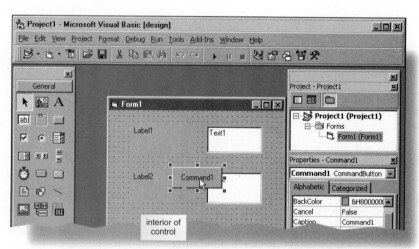

FIGURE 1-38

2 **Drag the Command1 control toward the bottom of the form.**

A gray outline of the CommandButton control displays (Figure 1-39).

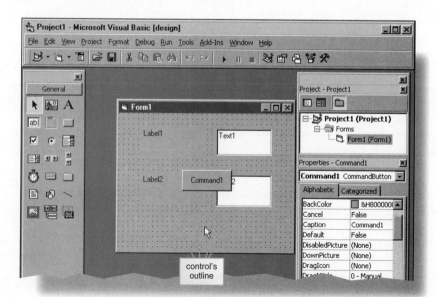

FIGURE 1-39

3 Position the gray outline at the desired location on the form, and then release the mouse button.

The control moves to the location of the outline (Figure 1-40).

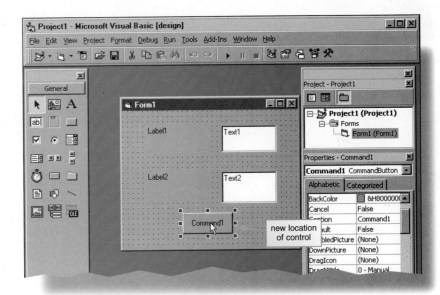

FIGURE 1-40

The location given to a control by dragging during design time is where the control will display at the beginning of run time. Dragging the control changes the values of its Top and Left properties. A control does not have to remain in its original location during run time. Changing a control's location during run time will be covered in a later project.

Changing the Size of a Control

Controls can be made larger or smaller by dragging the sizing handles located around the control. Perform the following steps to make the Text1 control smaller.

More *About* **Control Location**

The Top property is the distance between the internal top edge of a control and the top edge of its container. The Left property is the distance between the internal left edge of a control and its container. A container is any control that can contain other controls, such as a Form control.

 Steps To Change the Size of a Control

1 Click the Text1 TextBox control.

Sizing handles display around the control (Figure 1-41).

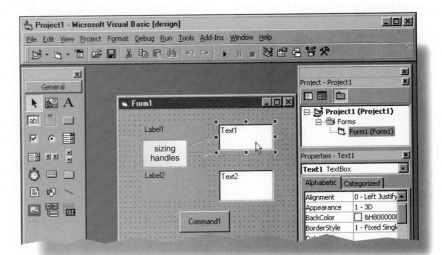

FIGURE 1-41

2 **Point to the handle located at the center of the bottom border of the control.**

The mouse pointer changes to a double vertical arrow (Figure 1-42).

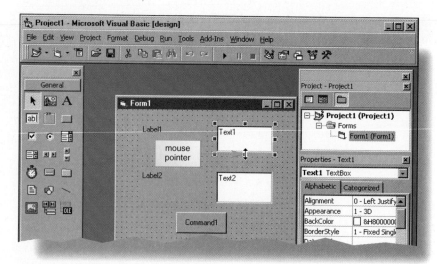

FIGURE 1-42

3 **Drag the border toward the top of the screen approximately one-quarter inch.**

The new position of the bottom border displays as a shaded gray line (Figure 1-43). Dragging a handle located in the center of one of the borders of a control moves that one border. Dragging one of the handles located at the corner of a control simultaneously moves the two borders that form the corner.

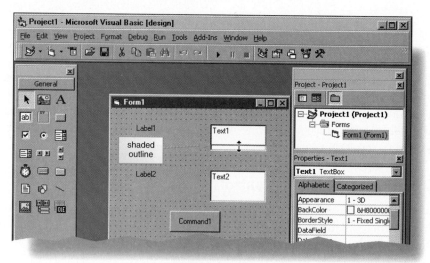

FIGURE 1-43

4 **Release the mouse button.**

The bottom border of the Text1 TextBox control moves to the location of the outline (Figure 1-44).

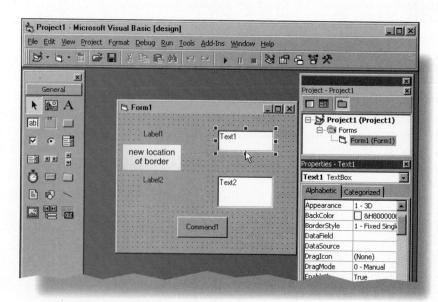

FIGURE 1-44

5 **Repeat Step 1 through Step 4 to resize the Text2 TextBox control to the size shown in Figure 1-45.**

The Form window now resembles the one shown in Figure 1-45.

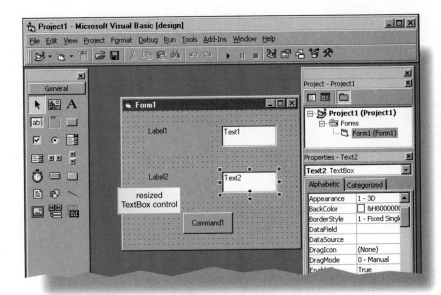

FIGURE 1-45

You may have noticed how similar the procedures are for setting the location and size of the form and for setting the locations and sizes of the Label, TextBox, and CommandButton controls on the form. This similarity should not be surprising, because a Visual Basic form also is a type of control. You will work more with Form controls in Project 3.

Setting Properties

Now that controls have been added to the form, the next step in Visual Basic application development is to set the controls' properties. **Properties** are characteristics, or attributes, of a control, such as its color or the text that displays on top of it. Properties are set at design time by using the **Properties window** (Figure 1-46).

The Properties window consists of the following elements.

Object box – The **Object box** displays the name of the currently selected object, or control, whose properties are being set.

Properties list – The **Properties list** displays the set of properties belonging to the control named in the Object box and the current value of those properties. The Properties list has two tab sheets. The **Alphabetic tab sheet** lists the properties in alphabetical order. The **Categorized tab sheet** groups the properties by category.

Different controls have different sets of properties. Because some controls' Properties lists are very long, the Properties window has a scroll bar to move through the list. It is not necessary to set every property of each control because Visual Basic assigns initial values for each of the properties. You need to change only the properties that you want to differ from their initial values, called **default** values. The major properties of controls will be discussed as they are used throughout the projects in this book.

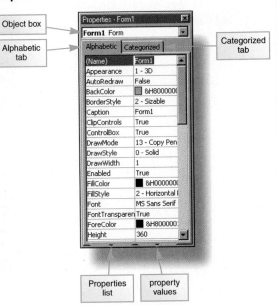

FIGURE 1-46

The Caption Property

The **Caption property** of a control contains the text to be displayed on the control. Complete the following steps to set the Caption property of the Label1 control.

Steps To Set the Caption Property

1 Select the Label1 Label control by clicking the control on the form.

Handles display around the selected control. The control's name (Label1) displays in the Object box of the Properties window. The currently selected property (ForeColor) is highlighted in the Properties list (Figure 1-47). Another property may be highlighted on your screen.

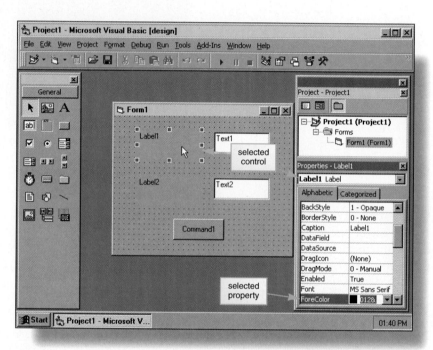

FIGURE 1-47

2 Scroll the Properties list until the Caption property is visible in the list and then double-click the Caption property.

The Caption property is highlighted in the Properties list. The current value of the property, Label1, is highlighted (Figure 1-48).

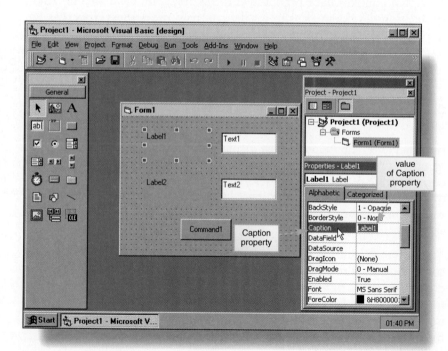

FIGURE 1-48

3 **Type** DOLLARS: **as the new value.**

When you type the first character, the old value of the caption is replaced by that character. As you continue typing characters, they display in the Properties list and on the Label control on the form (Figure 1-49). If you make a mistake while typing, you can correct it by using the BACKSPACE key or the LEFT ARROW and DELETE keys.

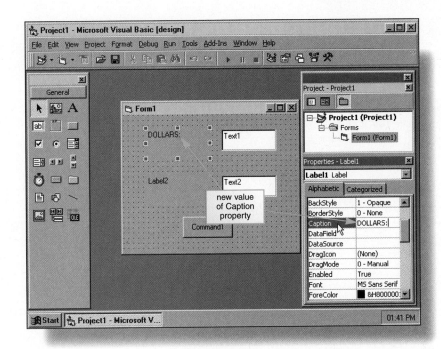

FIGURE 1-49

4 **Repeat Step 1 through Step 3 to change the caption of the second Label control from Label2 to FRANCS:. Repeat Step 1 through Step 3 to change the caption of the CommandButton control to CONVERT.**

5 **Select the Form1 control by clicking an empty area of the form that does not contain any other controls.**

The form should display as shown in Figure 1-50.

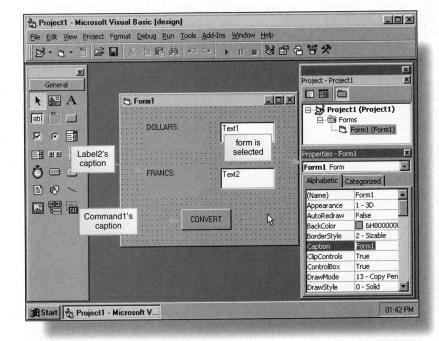

FIGURE 1-50

6 Repeat Step 1 through Step 3 to change the Form control's caption from Form1 to Convert Dollars To Francs.

The form's caption displays in the title bar (Figure 1-51).

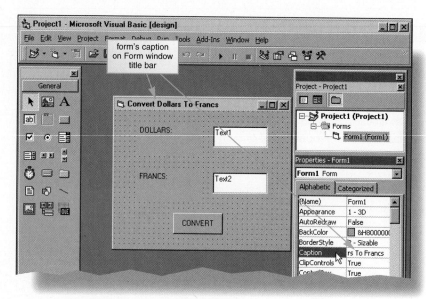

FIGURE 1-51

In the preceding steps, you changed the Caption property of four different types of controls. The caption of a Label control displays as text in the Label control's location. This control frequently is used to place text in different locations on a form. The Caption property of a form displays as text on the title bar of the form.

An alternative method of selecting the control whose properties you want to change is to click the Object box arrow (Figure 1-52), and then click the control's name from the list box that displays. This list expands as you add more controls to a form.

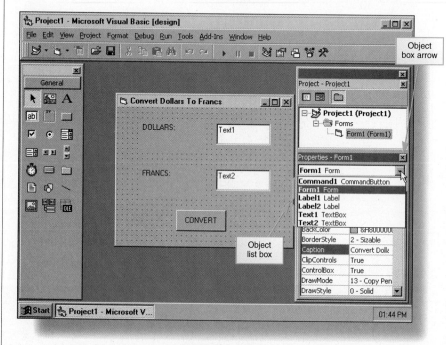

FIGURE 1-52

The Text, Locked, TabStop, and TabIndex Properties

The **Text property** of a text box is similar to the Caption property of a label. That is, whatever value you give to the Text property of a TextBox control displays in the text box at the beginning of run time. Later in this project, you will see how to change the Text property during run time.

The default value of a text box's Text property (the text that displays within its borders) is the name of the control. In the Convert Dollars To Francs application, the two text boxes should be empty when the application begins, so you will set their Text property to be blank. In addition, the user should not be able to edit the contents of the text box that displays the result in dollars. This is accomplished by changing the text box's **Locked property** value from False to True.

It is common in Windows applications for the user to be able to move the focus from one control to another by pressing the TAB key. The order in which the control gets the focus by tabbing is determined by the control's **TabIndex property**. You can cause the focus to skip a control by changing its **TabStop property** value from True to False.

Perform the following steps to set the text boxes' text values to blank, prevent the FRANCS text box's text from being changed by the user, and disable tabbing in the application.

More *About*
Tab Order

By default, Visual Basic assigns a tab order to controls as you draw them on a form. If you change the value of a control's TabIndex property to adjust the tab order, Visual Basic automatically renumbers the TabIndex of the other controls to reflect insertions and deletions.

Steps **To Set Text, Locked, and TabStop Properties**

1 **Click the Text1 TextBox control on the form.**

The selected control's name displays in the Object box of the Properties window (Figure 1-53).

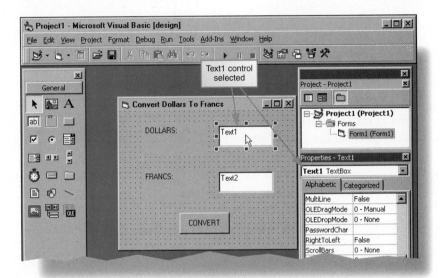

FIGURE 1-53

2 **Scroll the Properties window Properties list to display the Text property and then double-click the Text property.**

The Text property is highlighted in the Properties list, and the current value of the property, Text1, is highlighted (Figure 1-54).

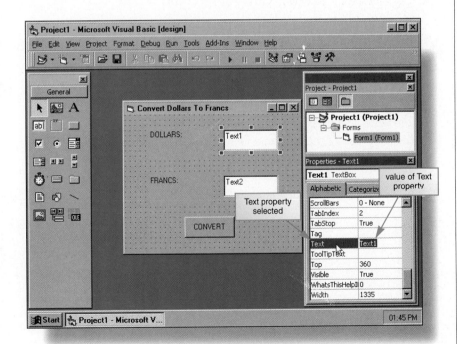

FIGURE 1-54

3 Delete the value of the TextBox control by pressing the DELETE key.

The selected text box is blank (Figure 1-55).

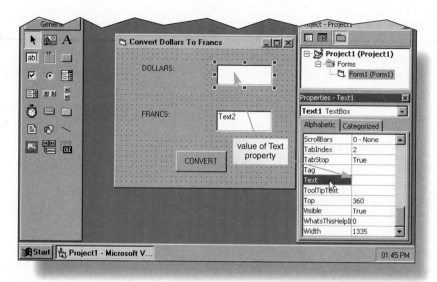

FIGURE 1-55

4 Repeat Step 1 through Step 3 for the Text2 TextBox control and then point to the Locked property in the Properties list.

The form displays as shown in Figure 1-56.

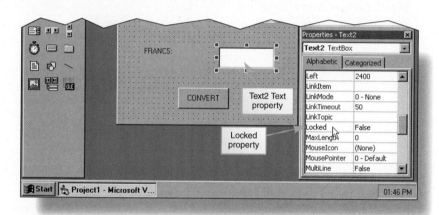

FIGURE 1-56

5 Double-click the Locked property. Scroll the Properties list and then double-click the TabStop property.

The value of the Text2 control's Locked property changes from False to True and the value of the Text2 control's TabStop property changes from True to False (Figure 1-57).

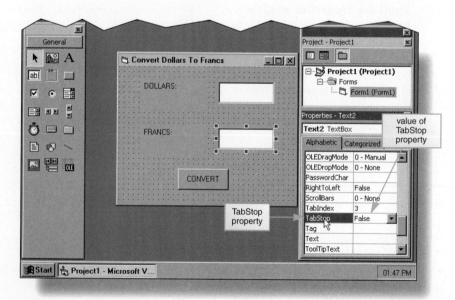

FIGURE 1-57

6 **Select the CommandButton control and then double-click its TabStop property in the Properties list.**

The CommandButton control's TabStop property is now False (Figure 1-58).

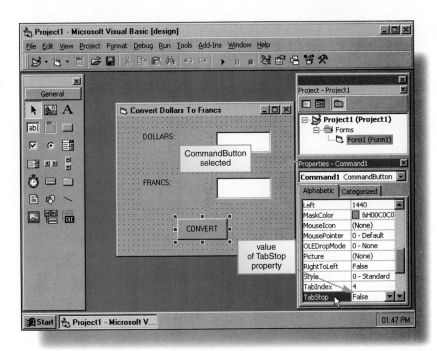

FIGURE 1-58

You used the same procedure for setting the Text property of the text boxes and for setting the Caption property of the labels. This same basic procedure is used for setting most of the properties of any type of control during design time. Label controls never have the capability of receiving the focus on a form and therefore do not have a TabStop property. They do, however, have a TabIndex property used internally by Visual Basic for other purposes.

Naming Controls

Visual Basic assigns unique default names to controls, such as Form1, Label1, Label2, Text1, and Command1. These names are reflected in the control's **Name property**. Although Visual Basic initially sets the caption of some controls to be equal to the name of the control, the name of a control and the caption of a control are two different properties. For example, the caption of the command button in your application is CONVERT; its name is Command1.

Each control has its own unique name to distinguish it from another instance of the same class of objects. For example, the Convert Dollars To Francs application has more than one text box. It is very important in the application to distinguish which text box gets what text printed in it. Many times, it is useful to give a different name to a control. This renaming often is beneficial with forms, which are themselves a type of control.

You will see in Project 3 that a single Visual Basic project can have more than one form and that forms created in one project can be used in other projects. For these reasons, it is advisable to give each form you create a unique name. Forms are named by setting the Name property of the form control. Perform the steps on the next page to change the Name property of the Form1 control.

More *About* **Control Names**

An object's Name property must start with a letter and can be a maximum of 40 characters. It can include numbers and underline (_) characters but cannot include punctuation or spaces.

Steps To Set the Name Property of a Control

1 Select the Form1 control by clicking an area of the form that does not contain any other control.

The form's name displays in the Object box of the Properties window. Clicking an empty area allows you to select the form instead of one of the controls on the form (Figure 1-59).

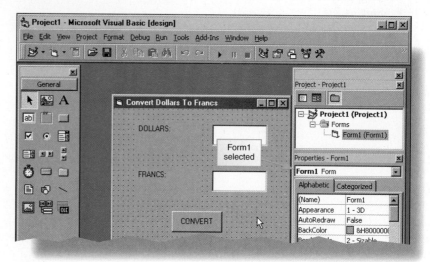

FIGURE 1-59

2 Scroll the Properties list and then double-click the Name property (the first property in the list) in the Properties list.

The Name property and its value, Form1, are highlighted in the Properties list (Figure 1-60).

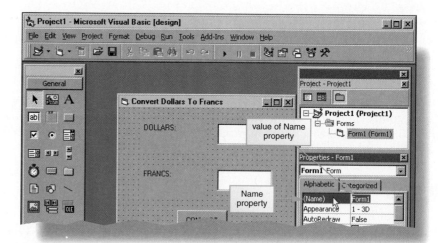

FIGURE 1-60

3 Type DLR2FRNC as the new value and then press the ENTER key.

The value of the form's name in the Object box and the Project window is changed to DLR2FRNC (Figure 1-61). Notice that the form's caption in the title bar is unchanged because the Caption property is different from the Name property.

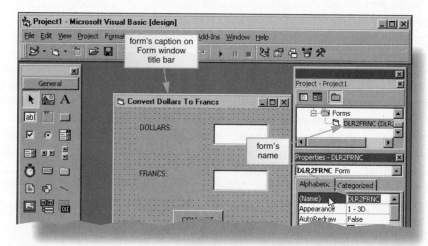

FIGURE 1-61

When you save a Visual Basic project, forms are saved as separate files with a file extension **.frm**. The default file name for the form is the current value of the form's Name property. You can, however, assign a file name different from the form's Name property.

Writing Code

You began the development of the Convert Dollars To Francs application by building the user interface, which consisted of a form and controls. You then set the properties of the controls. The remaining step in developing the application is to write the **code**, or *actions*, that will occur within the application in response to specific events.

Events are messages sent to an object when the application runs. Events can be initiated by the user, such as clicking or dragging a control. Events also can be initiated by the application itself. Events trigger **procedures**, which are groups of code statements, sometimes simply called code. **Code statements** are instructions to the computer written at design time for the computer to execute at run time. Visual Basic has its own language, which are the words and symbols used to write these instructions. This language is very similar to Beginner's All-Purpose Symbolic Instruction Code (BASIC).

In Visual Basic, certain controls are capable of recognizing certain events. For example, the **Click** event, which is clicking the left mouse button, is recognized by most types of Visual Basic controls. CommandButton controls are one type of control that can recognize the Click event. A control's name is used to associate an event with a specific control on a form in order to initiate the procedure or code statements you write. For example, when the mouse is clicked with its pointer positioned on a specific CommandButton control, such as Command1, the **Command1_Click event procedure** is executed.

Many times, the actions you want to occur in response to events can be expressed as changes in the values of the properties of objects on the form. The generalized code statement would be

> *controlname.propertyname = propertyvalue*

Functions and methods are additional types of procedures within Visual Basic. A **function** is code that transforms one or more values into a new value. For example, the **Val** function takes whatever value is given and converts it to a number. If it cannot convert the value to a number, it returns a zero. For example, val(8) = 8 and val("hello") = 0. **Methods** are code statements that can be applied to an object to change its attributes or behavior. For example, the **SetFocus** method causes the focus to be changed to a specific control on a form. The code statement, Text1.SetFocus applies the SetFocus method to the Text1 control. Visual Basic has many predefined functions and methods that you can use in your code. You will learn more about these in later projects.

Programmers often add comments within their code statements as a form of **internal documentation**. A **comment** is text added within a procedure that explains how the code in the procedure works. Each comment line must begin with an apostrophe (') or the letters Rem.

The currency conversion application has an event procedure that is triggered when the user clicks the command button. The procedure should take the number of dollars entered by the user, convert it to francs and display the result. If the user enters text instead of a number, the answer should be zero. The procedure should contain a statement of explanation. Perform the steps on the next page to write the Command1_Click event procedure.

More *About* **Writing Code**

Code in a Visual Basic application is divided into blocks called procedures. You write code for the Visual Basic application in a separate window, called the Code window. Using the Code window, you can view and edit any of the code quickly. You can choose to display all code procedures in the same Code window, or display a single procedure at a time.

Steps To Write an Event Procedure

1 **Point to the Command1 CommandButton control.**

Although you changed the CommandButton control's caption to CONVERT (Figure 1-62), its name is still Command1, which is the name supplied by Visual Basic when you added the control to the form. If you had more than one command button on the form, you might want to change the control's name to cmdConvert or something that more clearly identifies its function.

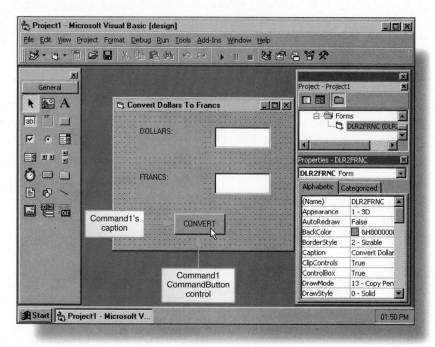

FIGURE 1-62

2 **Double-click the CommandButton control on the form.**

The Code window opens on the desktop (Figure 1-63). The name of the control you selected displays in the Object box of the Code window. Two lines of code for the Click event procedure display in the Code window.

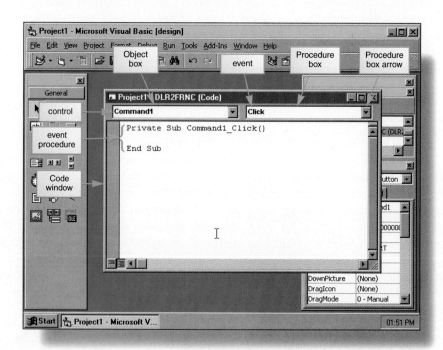

FIGURE 1-63

3 **Click the Procedure box arrow.**

The Procedure list box displays, containing all the event procedures that can be associated with the Command1 control (Figure 1-64).

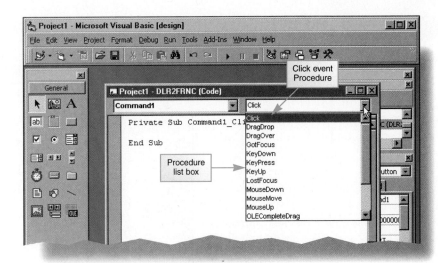

FIGURE 1-64

4 **Click the Click event procedure in the list.**

The insertion point displays at the beginning of a blank line in between the two code statements (Figure 1-65).

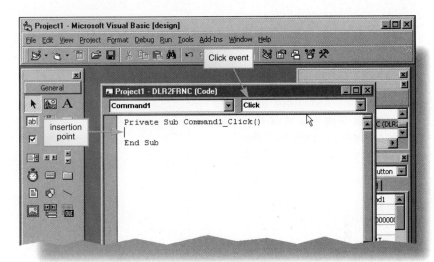

FIGURE 1-65

5 **Type** 'Display AmtFrancs as val of UserInput * ExRate **and then press the ENTER key. If necessary, resize the Code window by dragging its right border so the entire code statement displays as shown in Figure 1-66.**

The insertion point moves to the next line. The statement changes color because Visual Basic recognizes it as a comment and not a code instruction.

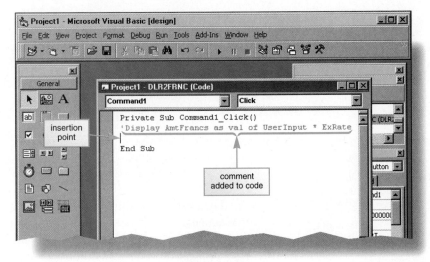

FIGURE 1-66

6 **Type** text2.text = val(text1.text) * 5.7345 **on one line and then press the ENTER key.**

The code displays in the second line of the Code window. As you typed the code statement a **pop-up list box** of properties and methods displayed. When you pressed the ENTER key, the editor changed some characters to uppercase (Figure 1-67). This code statement changes the value of the Text property of the Text2 control to equal the value of the Text property of the Text1 control times 5.7345, the exchange rate between dollars and francs.

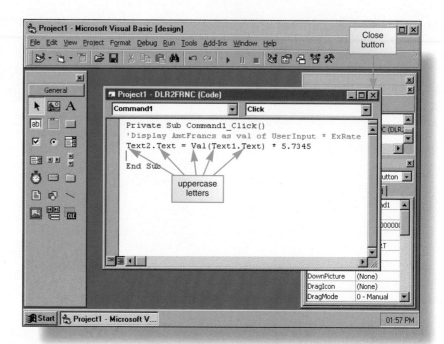

FIGURE 1-67

7 **Type** text1.setfocus **as shown in Figure 1-68 and then close the Code window by clicking the Code window's Close button.**

As you type the period after a control's name, a pop-up list box of that control's properties and methods display depending on your option settings (Figure 1-68).

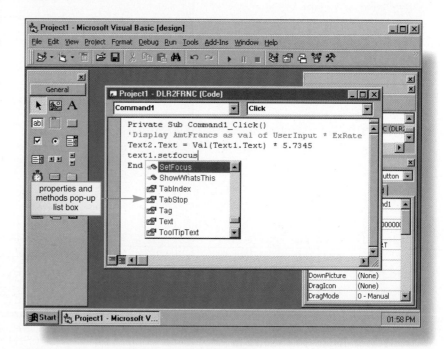

FIGURE 1-68

OtherWays

1. Double-click property or method in pop-up window to insert in code statement

The event procedures in Visual Basic are written in blocks of code called **subroutines.** Each block begins with a statement that includes the subroutine's name and ends with a statement that indicates no further instructions are within that subroutine. These first and last statements are supplied by Visual Basic when you begin a new event procedure subroutine.

The Code window functions as a text editor for writing your code statements. You can add and change text within the window in the same manner as you would with a text editor such as NotePad.

Saving a Project

The Convert Dollars To Francs application now is complete. Before starting a new Visual Basic project or quitting Visual Basic, you should save your work. You also should save your project periodically while you are working on it and before you run it for the first time.

Visual Basic projects are saved as a set of files. Forms are saved as files with a file name and a **.frm** (form) **extension**. If the form contains graphics, an additional file with an **.frx** (form extension) **extension** is saved. In addition to form files, Visual Basic creates an overall project file. This file has a file name and a **.vbp** (visual basic project) **extension**. You specify the path and file name for these files using the Save and Save As dialog boxes, similarly to other Windows applications. Perform the following steps to save the form and project files for this project on a formatted floppy disk in drive A.

Steps To Save a Project

1 **Click the Save Project button on the toolbar.**

The Save File As dialog box opens (Figure 1-69). The default file name in the dialog box is the name you gave to the form previously.

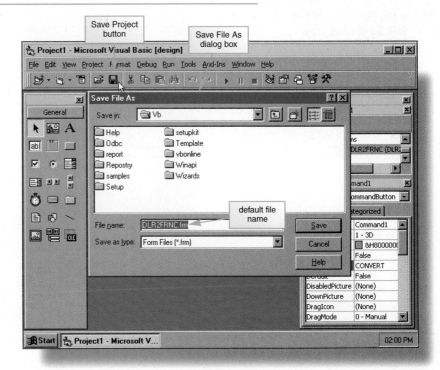

FIGURE 1-69

2 Click 3½ Floppy [A:] in the Save in list box and then point to the Save button.

The Save File As dialog displays as shown in Figure 1-70.

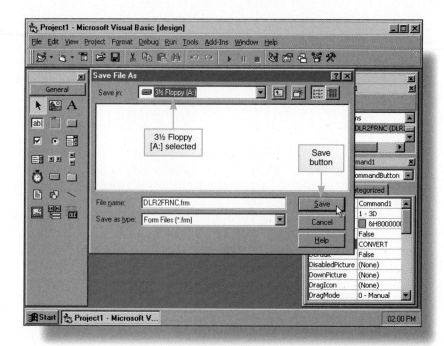

FIGURE 1-70

3 Click the Save button in the Save File As dialog box.

The form is saved as the file DLR2FRNC.frm, and the Save Project As dialog box displays (Figure 1-71). The default project name, Project1.vbp, displays in the File name box.

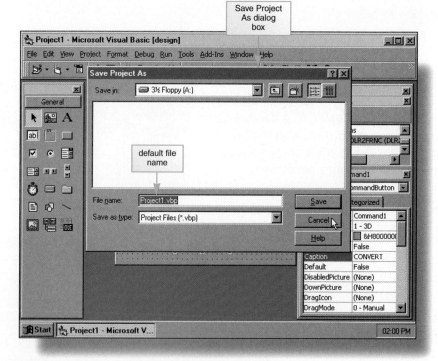

FIGURE 1-71

4 **Type** Currency **in the File name box and then point to the Save button.**

The default name for the project is replaced in the File name box with the characters you typed (Figure 1-72). If you make an error while typing, you can use the BACKSPACE *key or the* LEFT ARROW *and* DELETE *keys to erase the mistake and then continue typing.*

5 **Click the Save button in the Save Project As dialog box.**

The project is saved as Currency.vbp and the dialog box closes.

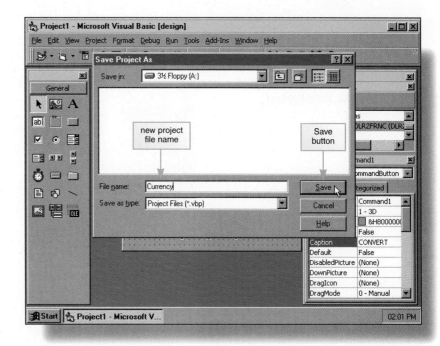

FIGURE 1-72

Other Ways

1. On menu bar click File; click Save Project As

In the Save File As dialog box you specified the drive used to save the form file, but you did not need to change the drive in the Save Project As dialog box. After you change a drive or folder in any of the common dialog boxes, it remains current in all the dialog boxes until you change it again.

You can resave your work without opening the common dialog box by clicking the Save Project button on the Standard toolbar. If you want to save your work with a different file name, folder, or drive, you must click Save File As after clicking File on the menu bar.

Starting, Opening, and Running Projects

In the next sets of steps you will start a new project, open an existing project, and run a project within the Visual Basic environment.

Starting a New Project

When you started Visual Basic, you selected a Standard EXE project from the New tab sheet. The form had no controls or event procedures, and all properties had their default values. It is not necessary to restart Visual Basic each time you want to build a new application. Before beginning a new application, however, you should be certain that you have saved any work you do not want to lose. Because you already have saved the Convert Dollars To Francs application, perform the steps on the next page to begin another project.

Steps To Start a New Project

1 **Click File on the menu bar and then point to New Project.**

The File menu displays (Figure 1-73).

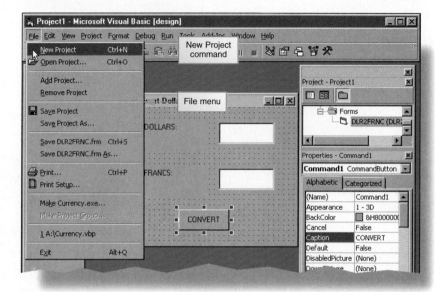

FIGURE 1-73

2 **Click New Project and then point to the Standard EXE icon.**

The New Project dialog box displays (Figure 1-74).

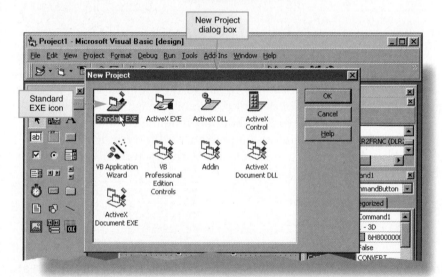

FIGURE 1-74

3 **Double-click the Standard EXE icon.**

A new Standard EXE project is opened on the desktop (Figure 1-75).

FIGURE 1-75

The new form has the default form name, Form1, and the project has the default project name, Project1. If you attempt to open a new project before saving the current project, Visual Basic will display a message box asking if you want to save the previous work.

Opening a Project

Once a project has been saved, you can return to that project and make changes. You instruct Visual Basic which project you want to use in the Open Project dialog box that contains two tab sheets. The first tab sheet, Existing, is similar to the Save File As dialog box. The second tab sheet, Recent, displays a list and location of recently opened projects. Perform the following steps to open the Convert Dollars To Francs application you completed previously.

More *About*
Opening Projects

The names of the four most recently used projects also are displayed on the bottom of the File menu. You can open any of these projects by clicking its name on the File menu. The Recent tab in the Open Project dialog box displays a much longer list of recent projects.

 Steps To Open an Existing Project

1 **Click the Open Project button on the Standard toolbar and then click the Existing tab.**

The Open Project dialog box displays (Figure 1-76). If 3½ Floppy [A:] is not the selected drive, you can change it in the same way you changed the selected drive when you saved the form file.

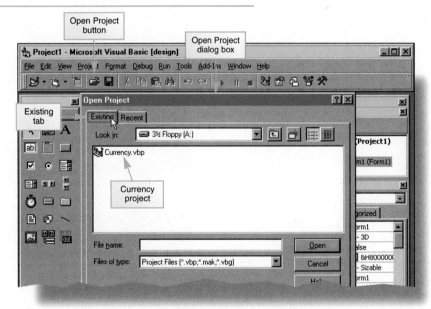

FIGURE 1-76

2 **Double-click the project's name, Currency.vbp, in the File list box. Double-click Forms in the Project window and then double-click DLR2FRNC.**

The Project window shows a tree list view of all of the files that are part of the project (Figure 1-77). The Properties window is empty until a form is selected.

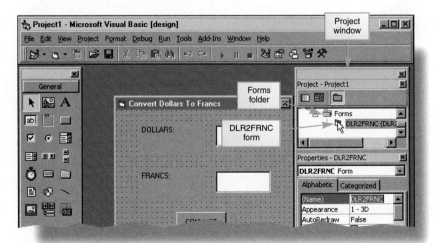

FIGURE 1-77

When you save a project, you can save a form file and project file individually. When you open a project, you only have to open the project file. Any other files associated with that project are opened automatically. All of these files are listed in the Project window.

Running an Application

Perform the following steps to run the Convert Dollars To Francs application from within the Visual Basic environment.

Steps To Run an Application

1 **Click the Start button on the Standard toolbar.**

The word, [design], on the Visual Basic title bar changes to [run]. The application's window displays on the desktop, and the insertion point moves to the first text box (Figure 1-78).

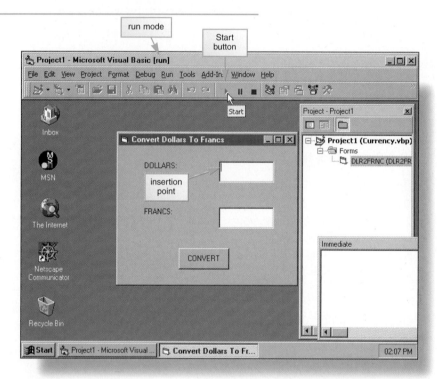

FIGURE 1-78

2 **Type** 520 **in the DOLLARS: text box and then point to the CONVERT button.**

The number displays in the first text box (Figure 1-79). You can change or edit your entry using the BACKSPACE key or the LEFT ARROW and DELETE keys.

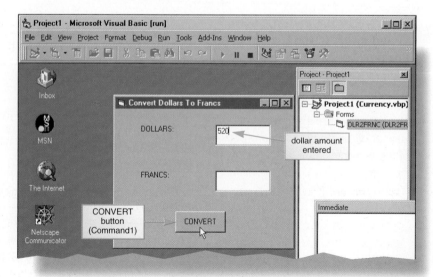

FIGURE 1-79

3 **Click the CONVERT button and then point to the End button on the Standard toolbar.**

The number 2981.94 displays in the second text box (Figure 1-80). Thus, 520 dollars = 2981.94 francs.

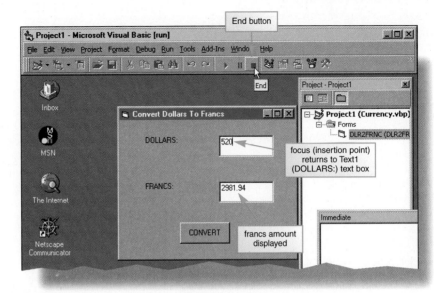

FIGURE 1-80

4 **Click the End button.**

Visual Basic returns to design mode (Figure 1-81).

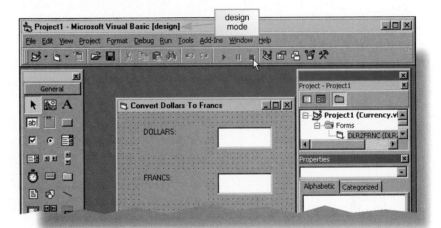

FIGURE 1-81

Run your application again, trying different numbers for the dollars amount. You do not need to restart the application each time you want to perform another conversion. Press the BACKSPACE key several times to erase your entry, and then type a new number. Click the CONVERT button. Enter some characters or a word in the DOLLARS: text box and then click the CONVERT button. Try to change the amount in the FRANCS: text box.

*Other***Ways**

1. On Start menu click Run
2. Press F5

Documenting an Application

Documenting an application refers to producing a printed record of the application. In the Print dialog box, you first must select the current module (form) or the entire project. You then can select any or all of the Print What options. **Form Image** prints the form images; **Code** prints the code for the module or entire project; and **Form As Text** prints a list of all controls and property settings that are different from their default values. Perform the steps on the next page to print a record of the Convert Dollars To Francs application.

Steps To Print a Record of an Application

1 **Click File on the menu bar and then point to Print.**

The File menu displays (Figure 1-82).

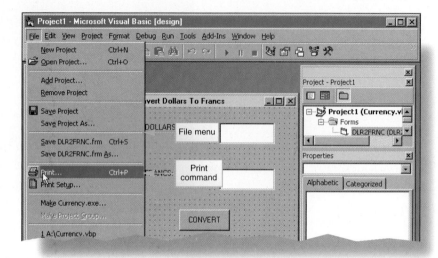

FIGURE 1-82

2 **Click Print. When the Print dialog box opens, click all the check boxes in the Print What area (Figure 1-83). Point to the OK button.**

The Print dialog box displays (Figure 1-83).

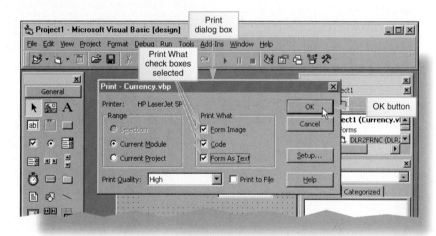

FIGURE 1-83

3 **Click the OK button.**

The form, properties listing, and code are printed. The Print dialog box closes (Figure 1-84).

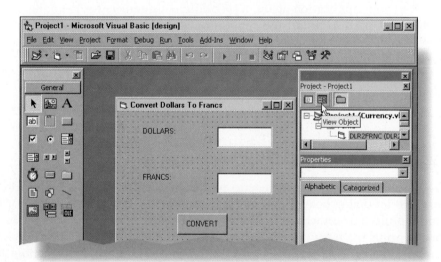

FIGURE 1-84

If the Print to File check box is selected in the Print dialog box, print is sent to the file specified in the Print To File dialog box. This dialog box displays after you click the OK button in the Print dialog box.

Quitting Visual Basic

Similarly to other Windows applications, you can minimize Visual Basic to work with another application temporarily, such as a spreadsheet or word processing document. You then can return by clicking the Visual Basic button on the taskbar.

When you have completed working with Visual Basic, you should quit the Visual Basic system to conserve memory space for other Windows applications. Perform the following step to quit Visual Basic.

 To Quit Visual Basic

1 Click the Visual Basic Close button.

If you made changes to the project since the last time it was saved, Visual Basic displays the Microsoft Visual Basic dialog box (Figure 1-85). If you click the Yes button, you can resave your project and quit. If you click the No button, you will quit without saving the changes. Clicking the Cancel button will close the dialog box.

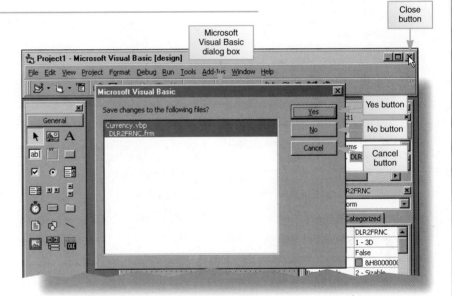

FIGURE 1-85

Visual Basic Help

The Visual Basic programming system includes an extensive online Help system. You can access **Help** any time you are working with Visual Basic by clicking Help on the menu bar and then clicking one of the Help menu commands (Figure 1-86).

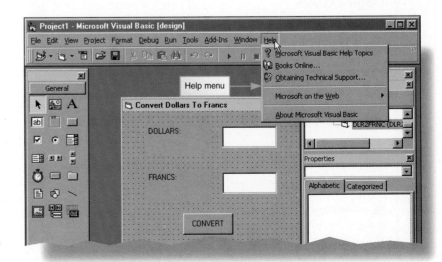

FIGURE 1-86

Help Topics

Clicking **Microsoft Visual Basic Help Topics** on the Help menu opens the Help Topics: Visual Basic 5 Help dialog box from which you can access Help topics from three tabbed sheets. The Contents sheet (Figure 1-87) displays topics organized by category, similarly to the table of contents in a book; the Index sheet displays the Help index, similarly to the index in a book; and the Find sheet (Figure 1-88) provides a text box in which you can type the keyword(s) or phrase you want to find and allows you to navigate the Help system. Once you have accessed VB Help, you can press the F1 key and obtain information about how to use it.

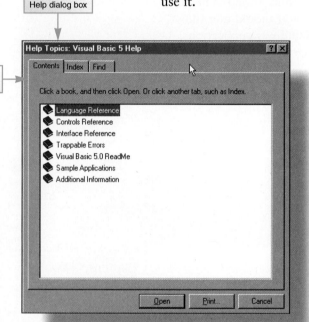

FIGURE 1-87

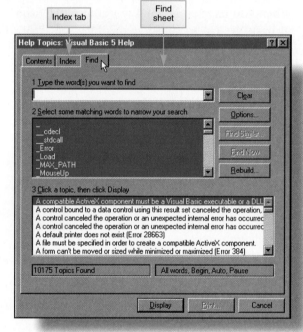

FIGURE 1-88

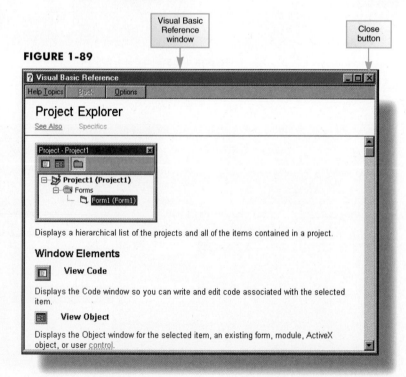

FIGURE 1-89

Context-Sensitive Help

Help on many areas of the Visual Basic screen can be accessed without using the Help menu. This feature, called **context-sensitive Help**, is available by pressing the F1 key. For example, to get Help about Project Explorer, click the Project window title bar and then press the F1 key. The Visual Basic Reference window opens (Figure 1-89), displaying information on Project Explorer (the Project window). To close the Visual Basic Reference window and return to the design environment, click the Close button on the Reference window title bar.

Project Summary

Project 1 introduced the major elements of Visual Basic by developing a Windows application. The process to build the application consists of three steps.

1. Creating the interface — Drawing the form and controls
2. Setting properties – Setting the values of properties for the controls added to the form
3. Writing code — Creating the event procedures that will occur when the application runs

You learned how to start Visual Basic, design a form, and add Label, TextBox, and CommandButton controls to a form. You learned the process for changing the properties of controls by setting Caption, Text, Name, Locked, and TabStop properties. After you built the user interface, you learned how to write an event procedure that included comments, the Val function, and the SetFocus method. You then learned how to run, save, and print your application and how to start a new project or open an existing project. Finally, in Project 1 you learned how to access information about Visual Basic using Help.

What You Should Know

Having completed this project, you now should be able to perform the following tasks:

▸ Add Controls by Double-Clicking *(VB 1.21)*
▸ Arrange Visual Basic Toolbars and Windows *(VB 1.10)*
▸ Change the Size of a Control *(VB 1.23)*
▸ Draw Label Controls on a Form *(VB 1.17)*
▸ Draw TextBox Controls on a Form *(VB 1.19)*
▸ Move a Control on a Form *(VB 1.22)*
▸ Open an Existing Project *(VB 1.41)*
▸ Position a Form *(VB 1.15)*
▸ Print a Record of an Application *(VB 1.44)*
▸ Quit Visual Basic *(VB 1.45)*
▸ Remove a Control *(VB 1.21)*

▸ Run an Application *(VB 1.42)*
▸ Save a Project *(VB 1.37)*
▸ Set the Name Property of a Control *(VB 1.32)*
▸ Set Text, Locked, and TabStop Properties *(VB 1.29)*
▸ Set the Caption Property *(VB 1.26)*
▸ Set the Size of a Form *(VB 1.12)*
▸ Start a New Project *(VB 1.40)*
▸ Start Visual Basic and Set Option Preferences *(VB 1.7)*
▸ Write an Event Procedure *(VB 1.34)*

Test Your Knowledge

1 True/False

Instructions: Circle T if the statement is true or F if the statement is false.

T F 1. A GUI allows you to use both text and graphical images to communicate with the computer.

T F 2. An individual must have previous training or computer programming experience to create Windows applications using Visual Basic.

T F 3. When opened, Visual Basic consists of only one window.

T F 4. A form can be positioned by clicking its title bar, dragging it to a new location, and dropping it.

T F 5. Controls must be added to the form by selecting them in the Toolbox and drawing them individually.

T F 6. The only method of changing the location of a control on a form is by dragging the control to the new location.

T F 7. The Object box of the Properties window is where you enter a value for a specific property.

T F 8. In Visual Basic code, the NUM function is used to return the numbers contained in a string.

T F 9. Comments provide a written record of how your code works.

T F 10. The Form Image of a project cannot be printed.

2 Multiple Choice

Instructions: Circle the correct response.

1. Computer programs that perform specific tasks are _____ software.
   a. system
   b. application
   c. utility
   d. multimedia

2. You must use the _____ to set the size of a form in Visual Basic.
   a. edges
   b. sides
   c. rims
   d. borders

3. A _____ control that is used to display text cannot be changed by the user at run time.
   a. Label
   b. Caption
   c. TextBox
   d. Font

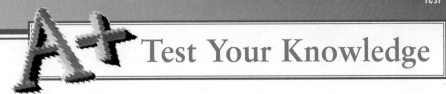

4. The area that displays the name of the control whose properties are being set is called the _____.
   a. Properties list
   b. Object box
   c. Toolbox
   d. Form

5. The _____ property of a TextBox control contains text that will display on the control.
   a. Name
   b. Caption
   c. Text
   d. Label

6. Actions that occur when an application runs are called _____.
   a. codes
   b. commands
   c. responses
   d. events

7. Point to a control and double-click it to open the _____ for that control.
   a. Object box
   b. Properties list
   c. Code window
   d. Save As dialog box

8. A project always should be _____ before it is run.
   a. printed
   b. saved
   c. closed
   d. reviewed

9. Once Help is opened, pressing the _____ key will display information on how to use Help.
   a. F1
   b. HELP
   c. F3
   d. ESC

10. Visual Basic includes online _____ to improve your Visual Basic skills.
   a. tutorials
   b. guides
   c. lessons
   d. books

 Test Your Knowledge

3 Understanding the Visual Basic Environment

Instructions: In Figure 1-90, arrows point to the windows of the Visual Basic environment. Identify the various windows in the spaces provided.

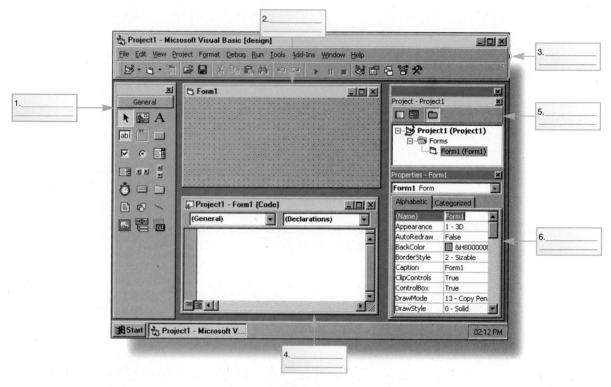

FIGURE 1-90

4 Understanding the Visual Basic Toolbar and Toolbox

Instructions: In Figure 1-91, arrows point to buttons on the Standard toolbar and in the Toolbox. Identify the various buttons in the spaces provided.

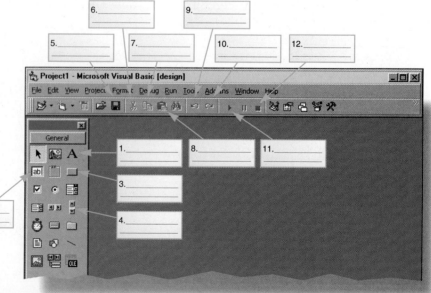

FIGURE 1-91

![Use Help](box icon) **Use Help**

1 Navigating in Help

Instructions: Perform the following tasks using a computer.

1. Start Visual Basic.
2. Click Help on the menu bar and then click Microsoft Visual Basic Help Topics.
3. Click the Contents tab.
4. Double-click the Interface Reference book. Double-click the Menus book. Double-click the File Menu book.
5. Double-click the New Project topic and read the information. Click each of the two green, underlined links to see the ScreenTips. Print the topic by clicking the Options button and then clicking Print Topic on the shortcut menu. Hand in the printout to your instructor.
6. Click the Help Topics button to return to the Contents sheet and then click the Find tab. Type run-time in the top text box labeled 1. Double-click run-time in the middle list box labeled 2. Click ActiveControl Property in the lower list box labeled 3 and then click the Display button. Click the green, underlined links and read the ScreenTips (Figure 1-92). Right-click anywhere in the Visual Basic Reference window and then click Print Topics on the shortcut menu. Click the Example link to display an example of the Help topic currently being viewed. Right-click in the Visual Basic Example window and then print the example. Close the Visual Basic Example window. Click the Help Topics button to return to the Find sheet and then click the Contents tab. Hand in the printout to your instructor.
7. If necessary, double-click the Interface Reference book, double-click the Menus book and double-click the File Menu book.
8. One at a time click the topics Open Project, Remove Project, Save Project/Save Project Group As, and Save. Read the information and then click any green, underlined link. Print the information. Hand in the printout to your instructor.
9. Click the Help Topics button and then click the Print Setup topic. Read the information and then print the information. Click the Help Topics button to return to the Contents sheet. Close the Help window. Hand in the printout to your instructor.

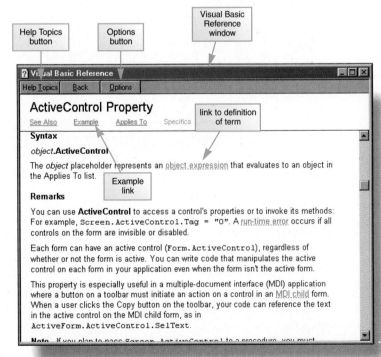

FIGURE 1-92

Use Help

2 Learning More of the Basics

Instructions: Use Visual Basic Help to learn more about Visual Basic concepts and event-driven programming. The Help topics will provide information to answer the questions below. Answers to the questions can be written on your own paper, or the Help information can be printed and handed in to your instructor.

1. Start Visual Basic. Click Help on the menu bar and then click Books Online. Double-click the Programmer's Guide (All Editions) book in the Navigation area. Double-click the Part 1: Visual Basic Basics book in the Navigation area. Read the information in the Topic area. Click the Developing an Application in Visual Basic book in the Navigation area. Read the information that displays in the Topic area (Figure 1-93). Click Visual Basic Concepts under Topics in the Topic area. As you read the text in the Topic area, answer the following questions. Once you have answered the questions, click the Part 1: Visual Basic Basics book in the Navigation area.

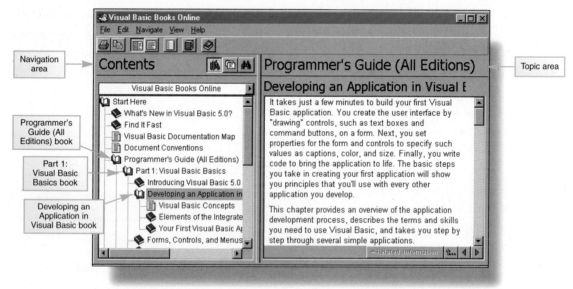

FIGURE 1-93

   a. What are the three essential concepts of the inner workings of Windows?
   b. What is a window?
   c. What is an event?
   d. What is a message?
   e. How do event-driven applications differ from traditional applications?
2. Click the Forms, Controls, and Menus book in the Navigation area. Read the information in the Topic area and then answer the following questions.
   a. What is a form?
   b. How are a form's appearance, behavior, and events defined?
   c. What are controls?
   d. How is the purpose of a control determined?

? Use Help

3. Scroll down and then click the Understanding Properties, Methods and Events topic in the Topic area. Read the information and then answer the following questions. After you answer the questions, close Visual Basic Books Online.
   a. What can an object's properties include?
   b. What kind of methods or actions might an object perform?
   c. What kind of object response can external events cause?
4. Click Help on the menu bar and then click Obtaining Technical Support. Click the Find tab. Type help in the top text box labeled 1. Click Help in the middle list box labeled 2. In the lower list box labeled 3, double-click Choose the Support Option that's Right for You. Answer the following questions.
   a. What are the support options available?
   b. What are the methods of Microsoft Primary Support?
   c. To who is Microsoft Primary Support available?
   d. Does a World Wide Web site exist for Primary Support? If so, what is the Internet address for this site?
   e. Under Primary Support: Other Technical Information Resources, what is MSDL and what is the availability of this service.

Apply Your Knowledge

1 Writing Code in a Visual Basic Application

Instructions: Start Visual Basic and open the project, Moving Shape, from the Data Disk that accompanies this book. This application consists of a form that contains one square Shape control and four CommandButton controls (Figure 1-94).

1. One at a time, change the Caption property of each of the four CommandButton controls. The caption for Command1 is Move Up, for Command2 is Move Down, for Command3 is Move Left, and for Command4 is Move Right.
2. Open the Code window for the CommandButton control captioned Move Up. Add a comment to indicate what the code for this button is accomplishing. Type the code statement shape1.top = shape1.top - 50 and then close the Code window.

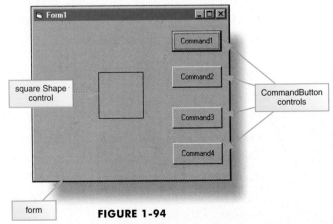

FIGURE 1-94

(continued)

Apply Your Knowledge

Writing Code in a Visual Basic Application *(continued)*

3. Click the Start button on the Standard toolbar to run the application. Click the Move Up command button several times. Click the End button on the Standard toolbar. If necessary, make corrections to the code statement.

4. Open the Code window for the CommandButton control captioned Move Down. Type an appropriate comment and then type the code statement shape1.top = shape1.top + 50 for the command button.

5. Click Command3 in the Object list box. Type an appropriate comment and then type the code statement shape1.left = shape1.left - 50 for the Move Left command button. Click Command4 in the Object list box. Type an appropriate comment and then type the code statement shape1.left = shape1.left + 50 for the Move Right command button.

6. Save the form and the project using the file name, Moving Square.

7. Click the Start button on the Standard toolbar to run the application. Click the command buttons several times. Click the End button on the Standard toolbar, make any necessary corrections to the comments and code statements, and save the project again using the same file name.

8. Print the Form Image, Code, and Form As Text.

In the Lab

1 Creating a Mile to Kilometer Converter

Problem: You want an application to convert the number of miles you enter into the corresponding number of kilometers. Whenever you click the command button, the miles in the first text box should be converted to the appropriate kilometers and displayed in the second text box. Use the conversion of 1 mile equals 1.61 kilometers.

Instructions: Build an application with a user interface that resembles the one shown in Figure 1-95.

1. Open a new project in Visual Basic.

2. One by one, add two Label controls, two TextBox controls, and a CommandButton control by double-clicking their respective buttons in the Toolbox.

3. Drag the Command1 control to the lower-center portion of the form.

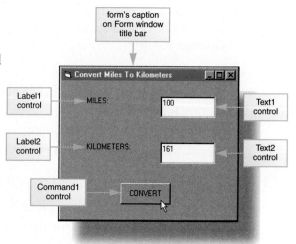

FIGURE 1-95

In the Lab

4. Change the form's Caption property to Convert Miles to Kilometers. Change the Caption property of the Label1 control to MILES and the Label2 control to KILOMETERS.
5. Remove the text from the Text1 and Text2 controls by deleting the existing text.
6. Change the Caption property of the Command1 control to the word, CONVERT.
7. Open the Code window for the Command1 control. Type an appropriate comment to explain the purpose of the code. Type the code statement `text2.text = val(text1.text * 1.61)` for the Command1 control.
8. Save the form and the project using the file name, Convert Miles To Kilometers.
9. Run the application to make certain no errors exist. If any errors are encountered, correct them, and save the form and the project again using the same file name.
10. Print the project Form Image, Code, and Form As Text.

2 Creating an Equivalency Application

Problem: The fabric and notions department of Melman's needs a simple method of converting measurements of inches to centimeters. Create an application that will convert a number of inches beginning at a minimum of zero up to and including a maximum of 100.

Instructions: Perform the following tasks to build an application similar to the one shown in Figure 1-96.

1. Open a new project in Visual Basic.
2. Change the Caption property of the form to Inches To Centimeters.
3. Place Label controls to display the words, INCHES and CENTIMETERS, the minimum values for inches and centimeters, the number of inches selected with the HScrollBar control, the corresponding number of centimeters, and the maximum values for inches and centimeters.
4. Center the form on the desktop. *Hint*: Use the StartUpPosition property.
5. Set the Min property for the HScrollBar control to 0 and set the Max property for the HScrollBar control to 100.
6. Open the Code window for the HScrollBar control. Type `label5.caption = hscroll1.value` to display the inch amounts above the HScrollBar control. On the next line, type `label6.caption = hscroll1.value * 2.54` and the centimeter amounts below the HScrollBar control.
7. Save the form and the project using the file name, Inches To Centimeters.
8. Print the project Form Image, Code, and Form As Text.

FIGURE 1-96

In the Lab

3 Creating and Using a Maturity Calculator

Problem: You are planning to invest money and would like to know what your investment will be worth within a specified period of time. You have decided to develop an application that will allow entry of different amounts, different annual interest rates, and different numbers of years. This will aid you in determining how much you would like to invest. When a command button is clicked, the application displays the maturity value of the investment based on quarterly compounding.

Instructions: Perform the following tasks to create the maturity calculator as shown in Figure 1-97.

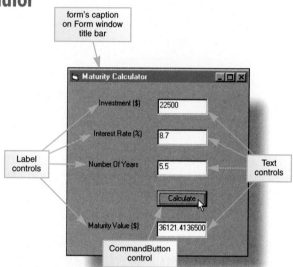

FIGURE 1-97

1. Open a new project in Visual Basic.
2. Size the form appropriately and center it by setting the StartUpPosition property.
3. Add four Label controls, four TextBox controls, and one CommandButton control to the form.
4. Set the form's Caption property to Maturity Calculator.
5. Set the Caption property of each of the four Label controls.
6. Set the Text property of each of the four TextBox controls to be blank.
7. Set the CommandButton control's Caption property.
8. Save the form and the project using the file name, Maturity Calculator.
9. Write the Click event for the Command1 control. *Hint*: Use Text1 for investment, Text2 for rate, Text3 for years, and Text4 for maturity value. Type the code statement `text4.text = val(text1.text * (1 + text2.text/400) ^ (4 * text3.text))` for the CommandButton control.
10. Save the form and the project using the file name, Maturity Calculator.
11. Print the project Form Image, Code, and Form As Text.

Cases and Places

The difficulty of these case studies varies: ❱ are the least difficult; ❱❱ are more difficult; and ❱❱❱ are the most difficult.

1 ❱ Because you are an outstanding student, a local civic organization has awarded you a generous sum of money to pursue your education in England. You also plan to do some sightseeing while you are in Europe. The money currently is in U.S. dollars and you want to know what one U.S. dollar will convert to in English, French, Italian, German, and Spanish currency. Use the concepts and techniques presented in this project to create an application that will accept the U.S. dollar amount, convert the U.S. dollar amount, and display the English, French, Italian, German, and Spanish equivalents.

2 ❱ A Stitch In Time has hired you to assist with taking inventory at its fabric store. Most of the bolts of fabric have been used partially and the amounts remaining are no longer even yards. The clerks will measure the remaining fabric on the bolt in inches and report the number of inches to you. It is up to you to develop an application that allows the entry of amounts in inches. Create the application and then convert the total inches to yards, feet, and total inches of fabric. This application also will have to store a total as the amounts are reported by the clerks and added together. *Hint*: Use Help to find out how to add up the inches and store a total number of inches.

3 ❱❱ To earn some extra spending money, you have taken a part-time position at the Xpress Mart convenience store. Many of the beverages sold by the store are measured in liters. Customers would like to know the equivalent in gallons, quarts, or pints. You have decided to use the knowledge gained in this project to develop an application to perform these conversions.

4 ❱❱ You are an intern at radio station, KNOYZ. The disc jockeys announce the current temperature in both Fahrenheit and Celsius every half-hour. They would like an easy way to display both the Fahrenheit and the Celsius temperatures quickly at the same time. They have requested that you develop such an application for their use and suggest that a scroll bar may be the best solution.

Cases and Places

5 ▶▶ As a consultant for the local telephone company, you determine it requires an application to respond to customer requests. The current customer information system does not permit representatives to supply customers with information regarding competitor's long-distance telephone rates. Your new application will display the telephone companies and rates as shown in the table below.

TELEPHONE COMPANY NAME	TELEPHONE COMPANY ABBREVIATION	RATE FOR FIRST TEN MINUTES BEFORE 7:00 P.M.	RATE FOR FIRST TEN MINUTES AFTER 7:00 P.M.
Canter	Canter	.10	.10
Local Telephone Exchange	LTE	.12	.09
Pacific Telephone & Telegraph	PTT	.15	.13
Regional Communication Interchange	RCI	.11	.08

6 ▶▶▶ As a new employee in the computer information department of The Northwest Indiana Railroad, you have been assigned the task of developing an application to display ticket rates. The railroad makes five different stops along the line with the final destination Chicago, Illinois. Different ticket prices have been established for each stop and different ticket categories. Single-ride ticket prices are South Bend, $8.10, Dunes, $7.30, Gary, $4.60, East Chicago, $4.00, and Hammond, $3.75. The ten-ride ticket costs are the same as ten single ride tickets less two percent of the total cost of ten single ride tickets. The monthly ticket costs are the same as thirty single ride tickets less five percent of the total cost of thirty single ride tickets. The application should display the stops and the rates for each type of ticket for each stop as well as the yearly cost for each category.

7 ▶▶▶ Collecting model cars is among your hobbies. As a collector, it has come to your attention that model cars could be a reasonable investment as well. For your own use, you decide to develop an application that will allow you to enter the current value of a model, a rate of appreciation, and the amount of time you estimate you will keep the model. After these amounts are entered, you want the application to calculate and display the future value of the investment. *Hint*: Refer to Help for assistance in calculating a future value.

Microsoft Visual Basic 5

Working with Intrinsic Controls and ActiveX Controls

Objectives:

You will have mastered the material in this project when you can:

▶ Describe the differences between intrinsic controls and ActiveX controls

▶ Use a ListBox control in an application

▶ Use a Shape control in an application

▶ Use a CheckBox control in an application

▶ Use an OptionButton control in an application

▶ Build an OptionButton group

▶ Use a Frame control in an application

▶ Use the CommonDialog control in an application

▶ Copy controls on a form

▶ Add ActiveX controls to the Toolbox

▶ Set the Locked, MultiLine, FontSize, and ScrollBars properties of TextBox controls

▶ Set the AutoSize and BackStyle properties of Label controls

▶ Name controls

▶ Copy code between procedures in the Code window

▶ Use code to concatenate text

▶ Use the AddItem and ShowColor methods within code

▶ Declare a variable

▶ Use variables and constants within code

▶ Use arithmetic and comparison operators in code

▶ Use the If...Then...Else code structure

▶ Incorporate the ENTER key in applications

▶ Save and run an application

Moviemaking a Reel Delight

Call the Shots in Your Hollywood Studio

Trial Version Tutorial

Movies are made like this:
. You find a screenplay you like
. You give it a budget
. You hire the talent
. You give the movie a "Green Light"
. It goes into pre-production
. It goes into production
. It goes into post-production
. You pick a release date
. You budget the advertising
. You decide how many theaters to show it in
. The movie is released
. You studio receives revenue
. You either make money or lose money

It's really that simple.

Click HERE to continue.

Hollywood film executives spend millions of dollars predicting how their movies will fare with today's audiences. They use their experience, talent, and instincts to attempt to determine how much money the films will make for the studio and whether the actors will win awards.

Now the venue for predicting movie success can move from Hollywood to your personal computer with the advent of Hollywood Mogul™ an interactive business simulation program created with Microsoft Visual Basic.

The object of the game is to make as much money as possible by releasing 100 movies throughout the world. You begin with $1 billion and then decide which books and scripts to buy that ultimately will become the next blockbuster films. Next, you plan a budget, select your producers, directors, and stars, who are called *creatives* in Hollywood lingo, and decide when and where to release the films.

Carey DeVuono used his experience as a screenwriter to develop the initial version of the game in 16 months. It contains 35,000 lines of

Visual Basic code, two forms, and a variety of controls. These controls resemble the ones you will create in this project as you build complex applications with multiple events.

Hollywood Mogul™ game players use a control to select one of five source ideas for the film: original screenplay, novel, stage play, sequel, or the players' own ideas. All the source ideas except the screenplay require the players to hire screenwriters to write the screenplay. Other Visual Basic controls involve obtaining ownership of the idea so it can be made into a film, hiring the creatives, and producing the film, including filming, editing, adding music, and special effects.

The creatives' salaries are above-the-line expenses. In contrast, the physical elements used in film production are termed below-the-line expenses and are added to the total production costs. They include materials to build the movie sets, food, transportation, and lodging. Users add these expenses through more Visual Basic controls. When the film is complete, added expenditures include the print cost to duplicate the movie for theaters worldwide and advertising expenses.

Next, the game players wait for revenues to roll in based on box office receipts worldwide. These results are determined by a probabilities algorithm using 500 variables tracked for each film, such as the major stars, number of special effects, release date, and genre. Additional ancillary revenue is generated by video sales and merchandising, such as clothing and toys.

Awards for Hollywood Mogul™ Version 1.5 include Top 100 Games Of The Year, 1995, *Games* magazine; Special Award, *Computer Game Review* magazine; and *Computer Gaming World* gave Hollywood Mogul™ a 4-Star rating out of 5 possible in its October 1997 issue. You can visit Hollywood Mogul™ online at www.hollywood-mogul.com.

If you decide to use your creative talents and business savvy playing Hollywood Mogul™, you soon will realize the many facets of filmmaking. As an added benefit, you will begin to appreciate the intrinsic capabilities of Visual Basic to produce a variety of applications. And while your applications may not become big moneymakers, your biggest victory may be seeing your name appear in the credits.

Project
2

Microsoft
Visual Basic 5

Working with Intrinsic Controls and ActiveX Controls

*C*ase *P*erspective

The ANC Movie Theater Corporation is upgrading its box office ticket vending technology. Your development team has been assigned the task of developing a prototype of the user interface. The final system will run on a point-of-sale terminal with a touch screen interface. For the prototype, however, you have decided to use a PC running the Windows operating system.

The ANC theaters have two ticket prices — a regular price and a matinee discount price for early show times. Children under 10 years old and seniors receive the matinee price for all show times. The user interface should provide an intuitive way for the salesperson to (1) select the name of the movie, (2) select whether or not a matinee price is available, (3) select the number of tickets and calculate the amount due, and (4) record the transaction.

The final system will include a module that allows the theater manager to change the movie list and ticket prices, and the transactions will be written to a file. These features are not required for the prototype of the salesperson interface. Although the user will not be able to select the color of the interface, you want to include a way to show different color possibilities when you demonstrate the prototype.

Introduction

In Project 1, you built a Windows application that converted an amount of dollars into its corresponding amount of francs. The application consisted of one event and three types of controls: Label, TextBox, and CommandButton. In this project, you will begin building more complex applications with additional controls and multiple events.

In Project 1, you learned how to add basic controls to your application by drawing them on a form using a corresponding button in the Toolbox. This is the way that all controls are added to applications during design time (you also can add controls at run time through code statements). The controls you used in Project 1 belong to a group called intrinsic controls. The **intrinsic controls** are the basic set of twenty controls in the Toolbox. These controls exist within the Visual Basic .exe file. You do not have to add these controls to the Toolbox, nor can you remove them from the Toolbox.

In this project, you will use several more intrinsic controls, as well as an ActiveX control. **ActiveX controls** exist as separate files. In earlier versions of Visual Basic, these were called VBXs (Visual Basic Extensions) and later OCXs (OLE Control Extensions). In VB5, ActiveX controls are separate files with an **.ocx** extension. You can include these controls in your applications by adding them to the Toolbox and then using them the same way you use the intrinsic controls. Microsoft includes a number of ActiveX controls with the Professional and Enterprise editions of VB. Thousands of ActiveX controls are available from software vendors. Version 5 of Visual Basic is the first version to offer the capability of building your own ActiveX controls. This will be covered in a later project.

Application developers often build routines and functions into an application that are not designed for the end user, but exist to help the developer in troubleshooting and revising the application. Sometimes, these functions are available in the end-user version of the product, but they are not documented and they are accessed in a way in which the user is unlikely to notice. In this project, you will include a *hidden* way for you to demonstrate different color choices to the ANC management, even though the end user will not have a color selection option.

Project Two – Movie Box Office

The application in this project is shown in Figure 2-1. This application simulates a ticket vending operation at a movie theater. For each transaction, the name of the movie is selected, whether a matinee discount is available, and the number of tickets to be purchased. When the number of tickets is selected, the total price displays in the Amount Due box. After the money has been accepted, the Enter button is chosen by clicking it, or by pressing the ENTER key on the keyboard. This action adds the name of the movie and number of tickets sold to the transaction list and clears the previous settings.

The Movie Box Office application uses the Label, TextBox, and CommandButton controls presented in Project 1. In addition to learning about some additional properties of these controls, you will learn how to use the ListBox, CheckBox, Shape, and Frame intrinsic controls and the CommonDialog ActiveX control. The intrinsic controls used in this project are identified in Figure 2-2.

To use an ActiveX control in an application, you first must add it to the Toolbox. In this project, you will learn how to add ActiveX controls to the Toolbox. In addition to writing several event procedures, you will learn some new features of the Code window.

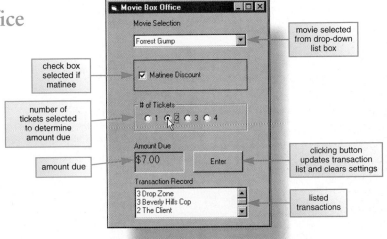

FIGURE 2-1

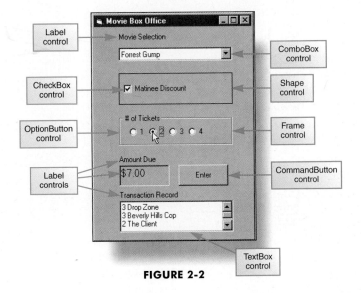

FIGURE 2-2

Project Steps

Applications are built with Visual Basic in the three-step process of creating the interface, setting properties, and writing code. You will follow this three-step process to build the Movie Box Office application. The tasks on the next page will be completed in this project.

1. Start a Standard EXE project in Visual Basic.
2. Set the form's size and position.
3. Add labels and set the AutoSize and BackStyle properties.
4. Copy controls.
5. Add ListBox and ComboBox controls.
6. Add Shape, Frame, and CheckBox controls.
7. Create an OptionButton group.
8. Set the alignment of controls on the form.
9. Name controls and set Caption properties.
10. Set the Style property of the ComboBox control.
11. Set the Locked, MultiLine, and ScrollBars properties of the TextBox control.
12. Set BorderStyle, FontSize, Visible, and Default properties.
13. Declare a variable and use variables and constants in code.
14. Copy and paste code.
15. Use the If...Then...Else code structure.
16. Save and run the project.

The following pages contain a detailed explanation of each of these steps.

Creating the Interface

Creating the interface consists of sizing and locating the form and then adding each of the controls to the form and adjusting their sizes and positions. Before you begin creating the interface, however, you need to start Visual Basic and arrange the Visual Basic windows on the desktop.

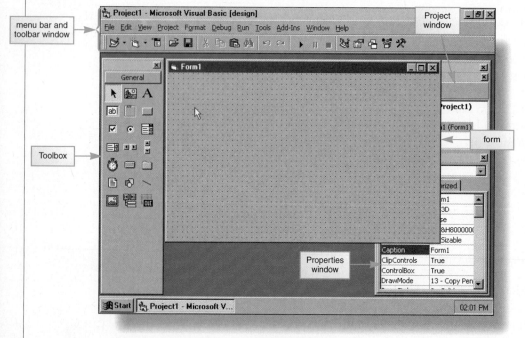

FIGURE 2-3

The Visual Basic Desktop

Begin this project by starting Visual Basic as described on page VB 1.7 in Project 1 or by opening a new Standard EXE project if you already are running Visual Basic. In Project 1, you learned you could change the sizes and positions of the Visual Basic windows on the desktop to whatever arrangement you prefer. All of the projects in this book begin with the Visual Basic windows in the sizes and positions shown in Figure 2-3. If necessary, you should complete the steps on page VB 1.10 in Project 1 to arrange your desktop to resemble Figure 2-3.

Form Size and Position

You can resize a form during design time by changing the values of its **Height** and **Width properties** in the Properties window, and you can change a form's location on the desktop by changing the values of its **Top** and **Left properties**. You also can resize a form by dragging its borders and change its location by dragging and dropping. Perform the following steps to set the size of the form by dragging its borders and set its location by dragging and dropping.

More *About* **Measurement**

The default unit of measurement in Visual Basic is the twip. You can change the unit of measurement to be points, pixels, inches, centimeters, or your own system, by changing the form's ScaleMode property.

 To Set the Size and Location of a Form

1 **Point to the form's lower-right corner. Without releasing the mouse button, drag its corner down and to the left as shown in Figure 2-4.**

Dragging a corner of the form moves the two adjacent borders at the same time (Figure 2-4).

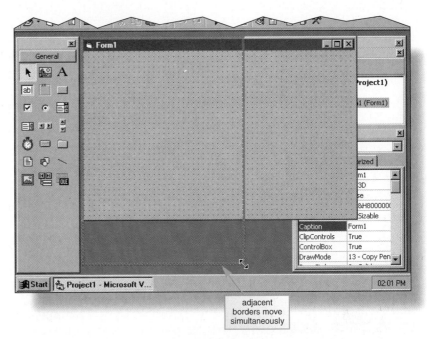

adjacent borders move simultaneously

FIGURE 2-4

2 **Release the mouse button and then drag the form to the location shown in Figure 2-5.**

While you drag the form its new location displays as a shaded gray outline (Figure 2-5).

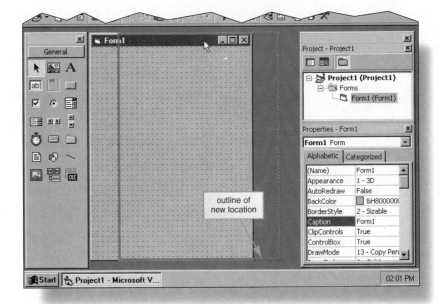

outline of new location

FIGURE 2-5

Release the mouse button.

The form's size and position should display as shown in Figure 2-6.

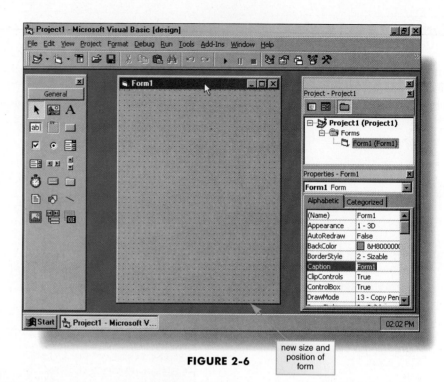

FIGURE 2-6

new size and position of form

Label Controls and the AutoSize and BackStyle Properties

Next, you will add the three Label controls in the Movie Box Office application shown in Figure 2-7. Recall that unlike a text box, the contents of a Label control cannot be directly changed by the user of the application at run time. For example, the words Movie Selection only can be changed with code statements at run time because those words are the caption of one of the Label controls.

When you set the **AutoSize property** of a label to True, the label's size automatically adjusts to the size of the label's caption. Because you will be changing the color of the form later, you will change the value of the label's BackStyle property from opaque to transparent. When a label's **BackStyle property** is **opaque**, the label's **BackColor property** displays within the label's borders. When BackStyle is set to **transparent**, the color of the control below the label (in this case the form) displays within the label's borders.

Although normally you set properties after building the interface, you will set the AutoSize and BackStyle properties of the first label at this time so when you copy the control these property values will be applied to the copies. Perform the following steps to add one Label control to the form and set its AutoSize and BackStyle properties.

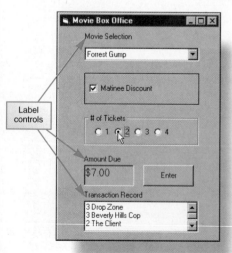

Label controls

FIGURE 2-7

Steps To Add a Label Control and Set its AutoSize and BackStyle Properties

1 Double-click the Label button in the Toolbox, and then point to the AutoSize property in the Properties list.

A default-sized label is added to the center of the form. The Label1 control is the selected control. Its properties display in the Properties window (Figure 2-8).

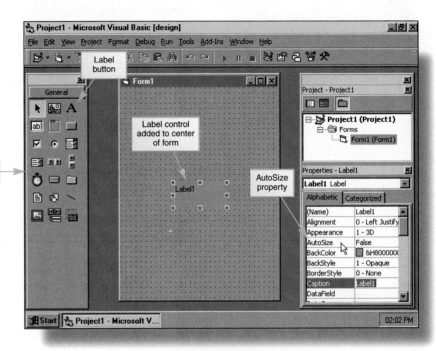

FIGURE 2-8

2 Double-click the AutoSize property in the Properties list.

The value of the label's AutoSize property is changed from False to True in the Properties window, and its size is adjusted on the form (Figure 2-9).

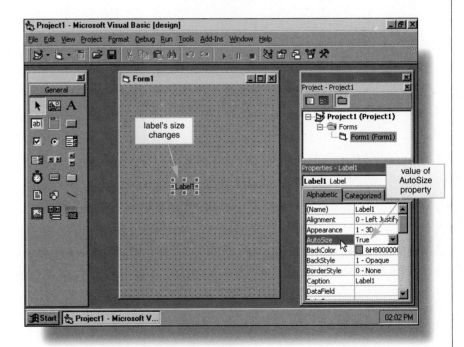

FIGURE 2-9

3 Double-click the BackStyle property in the Properties list and then drag the Label1 control to the position shown in Figure 2-10.

The value of the label's BackStyle property size is changed from opaque to transparent in the Properties window, and its location is changed on the form (Figure 2-10).

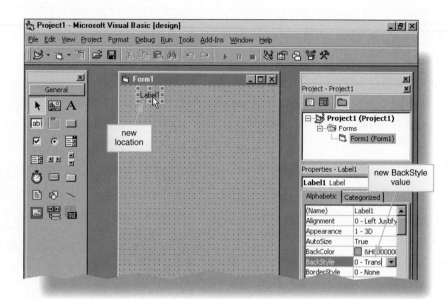

FIGURE 2-10

When a property has fixed values, such as the False/True values of the AutoSize property and the Opaque/Transparent values of the BackStyle property, you can switch between those values by double-clicking the name of the property in the Properties list.

Copying Controls

The two additional Label controls identified in Figure 2-7 on page VB 2.8 are similar to the one that was just added. When you want to add multiple, similar controls to a form, it often is easier to **copy** the control to the Clipboard and then paste copies of it from the Clipboard to the form. Perform the following steps to add two copies of the Label1 control to the form.

 Steps To Copy Controls

1 Click the Label1 control to select it. Click Edit on the menu bar and then point to Copy.

The Edit menu displays (Figure 2-11).

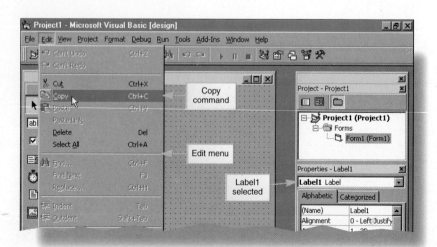

FIGURE 2-11

2 **Click Copy.**

The selected control (Label1) is copied to the Clipboard, and the Edit menu closes (Figure 2-12). The selected control changes to Form1 in the Properties window.

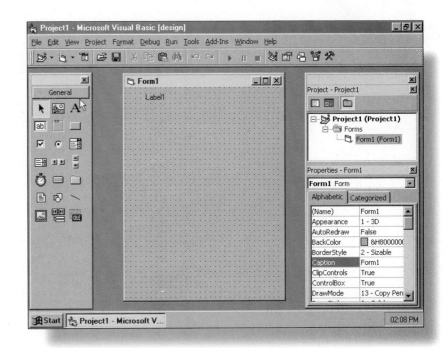

FIGURE 2-12

3 **Click Edit on the menu bar and then click Paste. Point to the No button.**

The Microsoft Visual Basic dialog box displays (Figure 2-13).

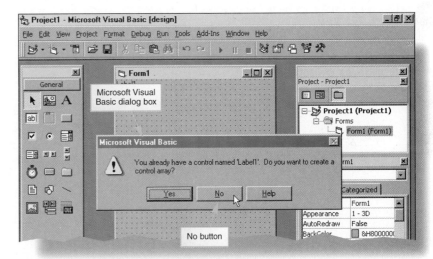

FIGURE 2-13

4 **Click the No button.**

The dialog box closes, and a copy of the control is added to the form (Figure 2-14). The control's Name property automatically is named Label2 and is the selected control. The Caption property (Label1) will be changed later.

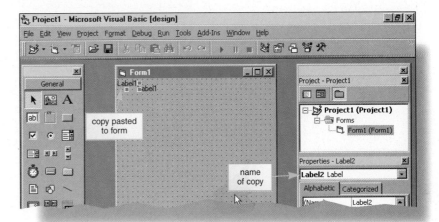

FIGURE 2-14

5 **Drag the new Label control to the position shown in Figure 2-15.**

The label's name shown in the Properties window is Label2, but its caption is Label1 (Figure 2-15).

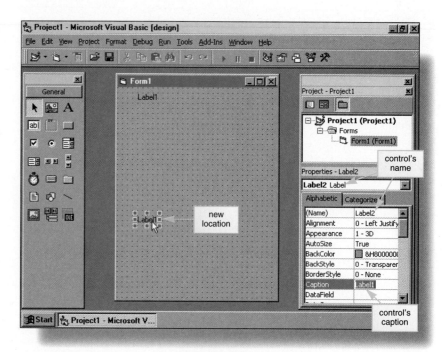

FIGURE 2-15

6 **Repeat the procedures shown in Step 3 and Step 4 to add the third label, and then drag it to the position shown in Figure 2-16.**

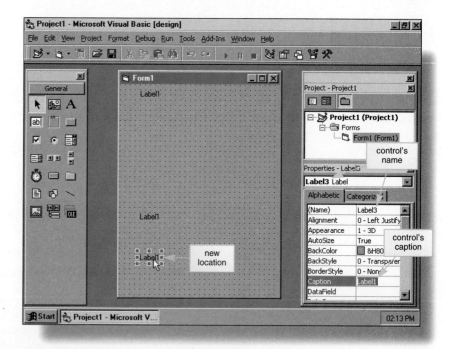

FIGURE 2-16

When you copy a control, the pasted control has a new name but has all of the other properties of the control you copied. Thus, both additional controls are AutoSized, have transparent BackStyles and have the same caption, Label1. The captions will be changed later in this project. Once a control is copied to the Clipboard, multiple copies can be pasted without having to copy the control to the Clipboard each time.

The ListBox and ComboBox Controls

The **ListBox control** and **ComboBox control** are used in applications to present lists of choices. In a list box, part or all of the list of choices displays. When the list of choices is longer than can display in the list box, a scroll bar automatically is added to move the list up or down. When an item is selected from the list by clicking it, the item displays in a highlighted color.

The Movie Box Office application contains a ComboBox control with properties set so the movie names display in a drop-down list of choices (Figure 2-17). With a drop-down list, the list of choices displays only when you click the list box arrow. When you select an item from the list by clicking it, the drop-down list closes, and only the selected item displays in the list box.

At run time, ListBox controls always have one way to select an item from the list. ComboBox controls can have different selection methods and can display differently, depending on the value of its **Style property**. The appearance of ListBox controls and ComboBox controls and the method of selecting an item from these controls at run time are summarized in Table 2-1.

Perform the following steps to add a ComboBox control to the Movie Box Office form. Later, you will set its Style property to 2 (see Table 2-1) to make it a drop-down list.

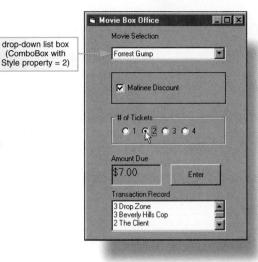

drop-down list box (ComboBox with Style property = 2)

FIGURE 2-17

Table 2-1		
CONTROL	*APPEARANCE OF LIST*	*SELECTION FROM LIST*
ListBox	List always shows, scroll bar added if list is longer than control's size	Click item in list
ComboBox (Style = 0)	Drop-down list	Click item in list or type item directly in ComboBox's text box
ComboBox (Style = 1)	List always shows, scroll bar added if list is longer than control's size	Click item in list or type item directly in ComboBox's text box
ComboBox (Style = 2)	Drop-down list	Click item in list

Steps To Add a ComboBox Control

1 **Double-click the ComboBox button in the Toolbox.**

A default-sized ComboBox control is added to the form (Figure 2-18).

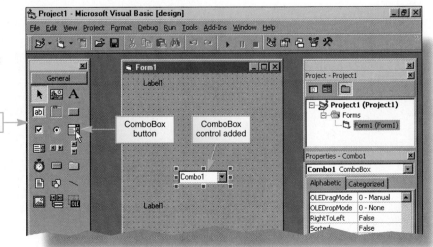

FIGURE 2-18

2 **Drag the combo box to the position shown in Figure 2-19. Point to the right center sizing handle.**

The combo box is moved, and the pointer points to the right center sizing handle.

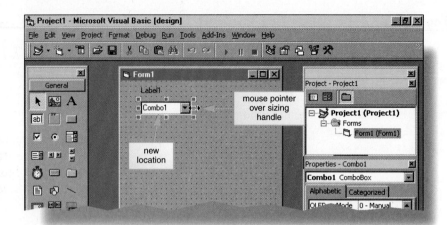

FIGURE 2-19

3 **Drag the sizing handle on the right center side of the combo box to the position shown in Figure 2-20.**

The outline of the control displays on the form.

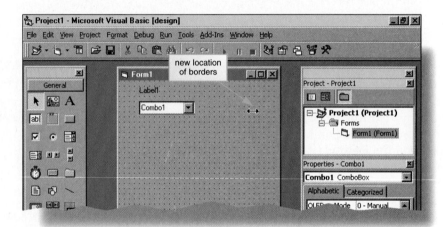

FIGURE 2-20

4 **Release the mouse button.**

The combo box is resized on the form (Figure 2-21).

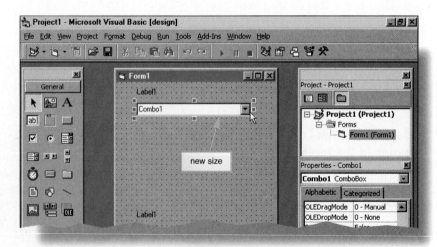

FIGURE 2-21

You will add the names of the movies to the drop-down list box later in this project.

The Shape Control

The **Shape control** is used to add a rectangle, square, oval, or circle to a form. The Movie Box Office application uses a rectangular shape as a border surrounding the Matinee Discount check box (Figure 2-22).

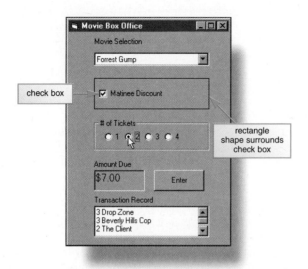

FIGURE 2-22

The only purpose of the Shape control in this application is to enhance the visual balance of the controls on the form. Perform the following steps to add the Shape control to the form.

 Steps To Add a Shape Control

1 **Click the Shape button in the Toolbox, and then move the mouse pointer under the lower-left corner of the ComboBox control, which is where the top-left corner of the shape will display (Figure 2-23).**

The Shape button is recessed in the Toolbox, and the mouse pointer changes to a cross hair.

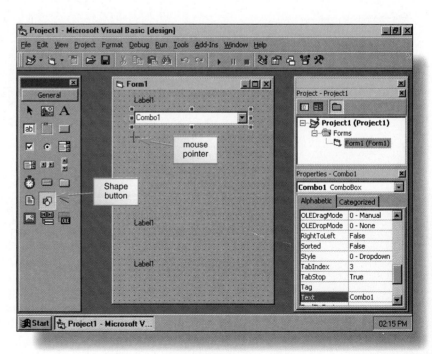

FIGURE 2-23

2 **Drag down and to the right as shown in Figure 2-24.**

A shaded outline of the control displays on the form.

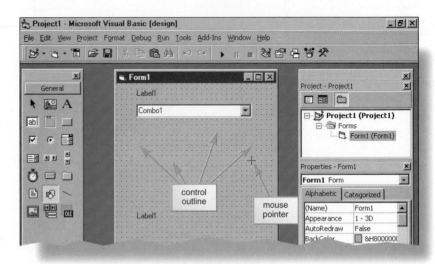

FIGURE 2-24

3 **Release the mouse button.**

The control is sized to fit the area of the shaded outline (Figure 2-25).

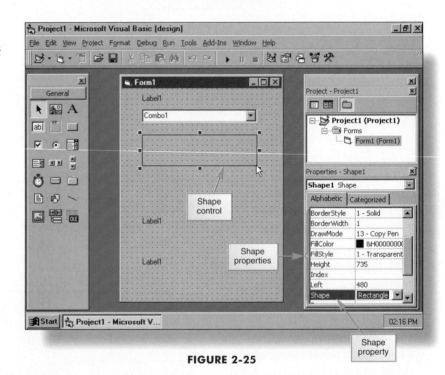

FIGURE 2-25

The different properties of the Shape control, such as the Shape property, display in the Properties list (Figure 2-25). The default value of the **Shape property** of a Shape control is a rectangle.

The CheckBox Control

A **CheckBox control** is used in applications to turn options on or off, such as the Matinee Discount (Figure 2-22 on the previous page). Clicking an empty check box places a check mark in the check box to indicate the option is selected. Clicking a selected check box removes the check mark to indicate the option is not selected. Perform the following steps to add a CheckBox control to the form.

Steps To Add a CheckBox Control

---

1 **Double-click the CheckBox button in the Toolbox.**

A default-sized CheckBox control is added to the form (Figure 2-26).

CheckBox button

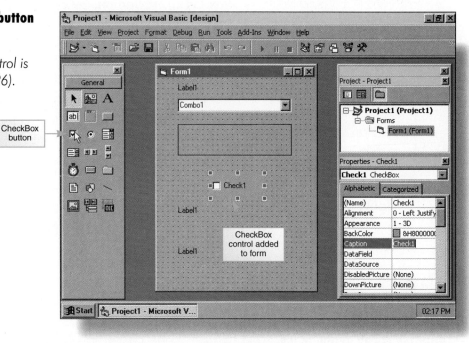

FIGURE 2-26

2 **Drag the CheckBox control to a position inside the Shape control. Drag the sizing handle on the right of the control to extend its width, as shown in Figure 2-27.**

The CheckBox control is positioned inside the Shape control, and its width is extended.

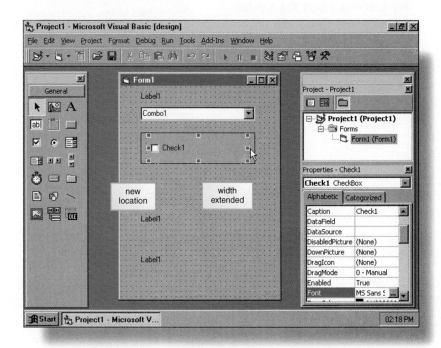

FIGURE 2-27

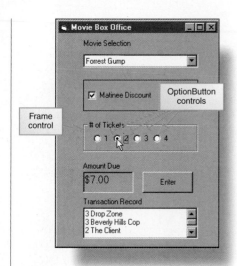

FIGURE 2-28

Check boxes are used to indicate the selection or deselection of individual options. For this reason, any number or combination of check boxes on a form can be selected at the same time. In the Movie Box Office application, the check box is used to switch between the two different prices of the tickets purchased. The two prices will be established later in the code for the application.

The Frame Control

The **Frame control** is used as a container for other controls, as shown in Figure 2-28. It has several properties similar to the Shape control, but it has some important differences:

▶ A frame can have only a rectangular shape.
▶ A frame can have a caption.
▶ When option buttons are added inside a frame, only one can be selected at a time during run time.

Perform the following steps to add the Frame control to the form.

 Steps **To Add a Frame Control**

1 Click the Frame button in the Toolbox, and move the mouse to the position where the top-left corner of the frame will display (Figure 2-29).

The Frame button is recessed in the Toolbox, and the mouse pointer changes to a cross hair.

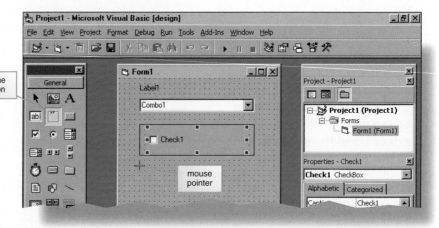

FIGURE 2-29

2 Drag down and to the right as shown in Figure 2-30.

A gray outline of the control displays on the form.

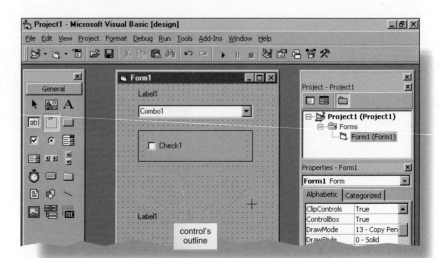

FIGURE 2-30

3 **Release the mouse button.**

The control is sized to fit the area of the shaded outline (Figure 2-31).

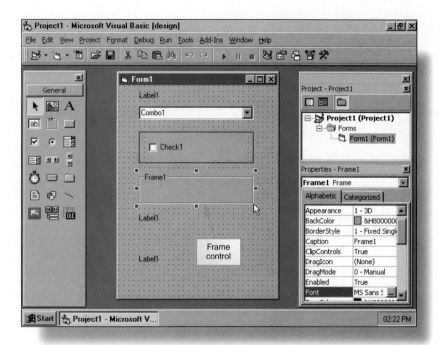

FIGURE 2-31

When controls have been added by drawing them inside a Frame control, dragging the frame to a new position causes the controls inside to be moved as well.

The OptionButton Control

The **OptionButton control** presents a set of choices, such as the number of tickets bought in a single box office transaction (Figure 2-28). Option buttons are placed in **groups** that allow the user to make only one selection from a group, such as the number of tickets sold. All of the option buttons on a form function as one group unless they are placed inside a frame. Multiple groups of option buttons can be created by adding another frame to the form for each option button group. For an option button to be part of a group, it must be added directly inside the frame. You cannot add an option button to the form and then drag it inside a frame if you want it to be part of the group formed by that frame.

The application in this project offers four options for the number of tickets sold (1, 2, 3, or 4). Perform the steps on the next page to create a group of five option buttons within the Frame control already added. The reason for the fifth button will be explained later in this project.

Steps To Build an OptionButton Group

1 **Click the OptionButton button in the Toolbox, and then move the mouse to the position where the top-left corner of the option button will display (Figure 2-32).**

The OptionButton button is recessed in the Toolbox, and the mouse pointer changes to a cross hair.

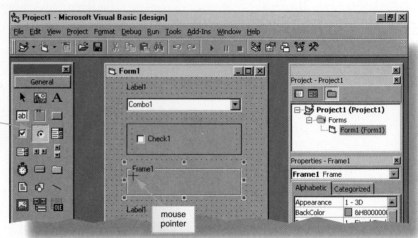

FIGURE 2-32

2 **Drag down and to the right. If necessary, drag the borders to size the control as shown in Figure 2-33.**

A shaded outline of the control displays on the form.

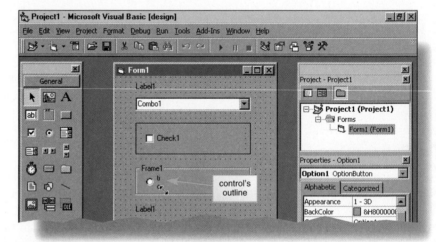

FIGURE 2-33

3 **Release the mouse button.**

The control is sized to fit the area of the shaded outline (Figure 2-34). Only part of the option button's caption, Option1, is visible on the form because of the size of the control.

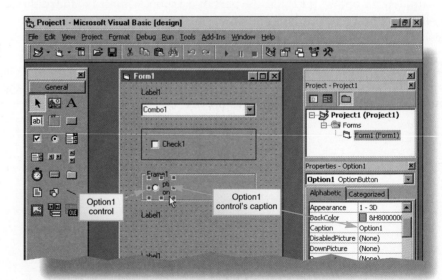

FIGURE 2-34

4 Repeat Step 1 through Step 3 four times to add four more OptionButton controls in the positions shown in Figure 2-35. Click any blank area of the form.

As the OptionButton controls are added, Visual Basic assigns to them the default names Option2 through Option5.

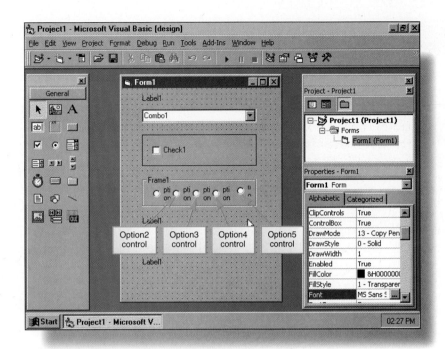

FIGURE 2-35

You may have wondered why Step 4 did not use the cut and paste method or the double-click method to add the last four option buttons. The reason is that both of these methods would have added the option buttons to the form, not to the Frame control. To add the option buttons to a Frame control, the preceding procedure must be used. The option buttons were added to the form inside the Frame control in order to form an OptionButton group.

Label, CommandButton, and TextBox Controls

Three intrinsic controls remain to be added to the form: one additional Label control, a CommandButton control, and a TextBox control as shown in Figure 2-36. You should be familiar with working with these controls from Project 1.

The Movie Box Office application uses a Label control with borders around it to contain the total cost of the transaction (number of tickets times the ticket price). The CommandButton control is used to clear the amount displayed in the label and to add the number of tickets purchased and the name of the movie to a list contained in the Transaction Record TextBox control. Perform the steps on the next page to add these controls to the Movie Box Office form.

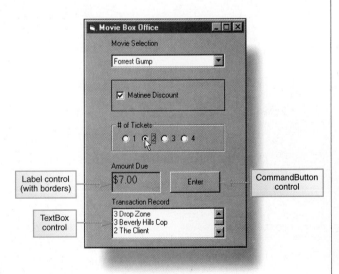

FIGURE 2-36

More *About*
TextBox Controls

At run time, the Microsoft Windows operating system automatically implements a standard keyboard interface to allow navigation in TextBox controls. The user can enter, edit, and delete text with the ARROW keys (UP ARROW, DOWN ARROW, LEFT ARROW, and RIGHT ARROW), and the DELETE, BACKSPACE, HOME and END keys.

TO ADD LABEL, COMMANDBUTTON, AND TEXTBOX CONTROLS

① Click the Label button in the Toolbox, and then draw a Label control on the form in the location and size shown in Figure 2-37.
② Double-click the CommandButton button in the Toolbox and then drag and drop the command button in the location shown in Figure 2-37.
③ Double-click the TextBox button in the Toolbox. Drag and drop the text box under the third Label control and resize it by dragging its borders to the size shown in Figure 2-37.

The locations and sizes of the Label4, Command1, and Text1 controls should display as shown in Figure 2-37.

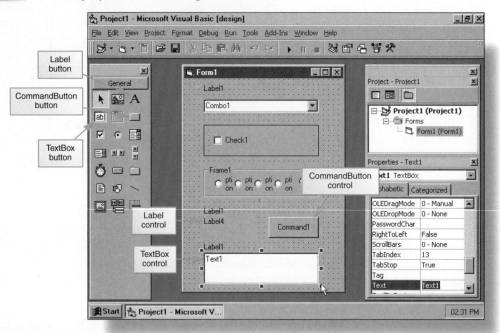

FIGURE 2-37

The CommonDialog Control

You can add the Open, Save As, Color, Print, and Font dialog boxes easily to your applications with the **CommonDialog control**. The CommonDialog control is an ActiveX control and must be added to the Toolbox before you can add it to an application. Although the CommonDialog control displays as a small icon on the form during design time, it never is visible on the form during run time. You cause a dialog box to be opened during run time by applying one of the **Show** methods to the CommonDialog control through code. When a user interacts with the dialog box during run time by selecting a file or clicking a check box, the user is changing values of the properties of the CommonDialog control. You can write code that then uses those new property values.

For example, when the CommonDialog control is used to display the Color dialog box, any color selection the user makes is captured as the value of the CommonDialog control's **Color property**. You then can set (through a code statement) the BackColor property of some other control to be equal to the Color property of the CommonDialog control. The actions from the user's perspective are: (1) the Color dialog box displayed, (2) a color was selected and the OK button was clicked, and (3) the color selected was applied to some other control(s).

More *About*
ActiveX Controls

Over 2,000 ActiveX controls are available today. In addition, version 5 is the first version of Visual Basic that enables you to create your own controls. You can create controls from scratch, customize controls, or combine controls to make new controls.

The movie theater salesperson will not be able to change the Movie Box Office application's color. You will, however, use the Color dialog box to demonstrate different color possibilities to the ANC management when you present the prototype interface. Perform the following steps to add a CommonDialog control to the Toolbox and then add it to the form.

 Steps **To Add a CommonDialog Control**

1 **Right-click the Toolbox and then point to Components on the shortcut menu.**

The shortcut menu displays (Figure 2-38).

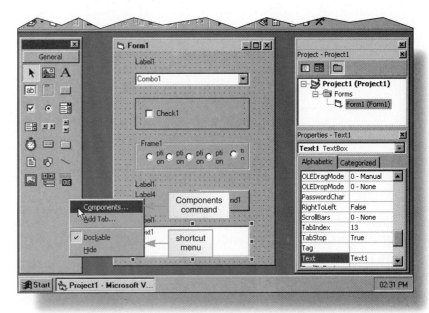

FIGURE 2-38

2 **Click Components on the shortcut menu. If necessary, when the Components dialog box displays, click the Controls tab. Scroll down the list and then click the Microsoft Common Dialog Control 5.0 check box (just clicking the entry does not select the check box). Point to the OK button.**

The Components dialog box displays. The list of ActiveX controls available on your PC may be different from the list shown in Figure 2-39.

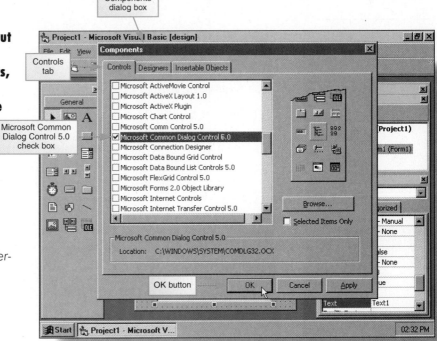

FIGURE 2-39

3 **Click the OK button.**

The Components dialog box closes and the CommonDialog button is added to the Toolbox (Figure 2-40).

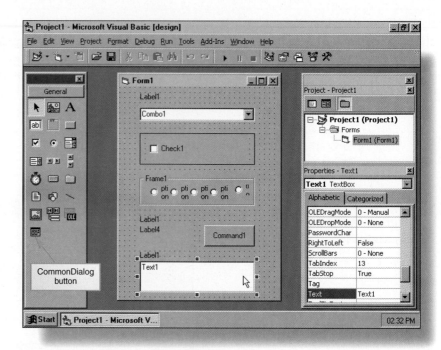

FIGURE 2-40

4 **Double-click the CommonDialog button in the Toolbox. Drag and drop the CommonDialog control to the position shown in Figure 2-41.**

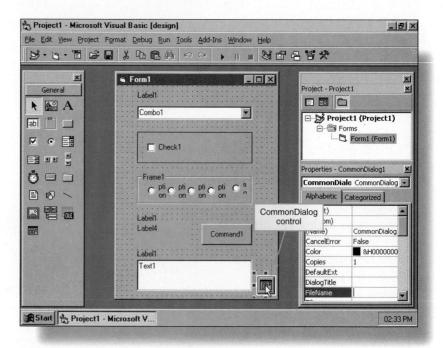

FIGURE 2-41

1. On Project menu click Components
2. Press CTRL+T

You have added the CommonDialog control to the application. Later, you will write the code that activates the control during run time.

Aligning Controls

You can use either VB5's **Format menu** or **Form Editor Toolbar** to access form layout commands that adjust the alignment, spacing, and size of any group of controls on a form. The **Align** command aligns selected objects with each other using the last selected object in a group.

Perform the following steps to select a group of controls on the Form1 control and left-align the selected controls.

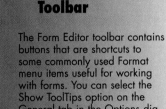

More *About* **the Form Editor Toolbar**

The Form Editor toolbar contains buttons that are shortcuts to some commonly used Format menu items useful for working with forms. You can select the Show ToolTips option on the General tab in the Options dialog box if you want to display ToolTips for the Form Editor toolbar buttons.

 Steps **To Align Controls**

1 **Drag and drop the topmost Label control to the location shown in Figure 2-42.**

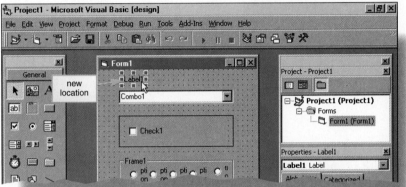

FIGURE 2-42

2 **Click the TextBox control (Text1) at the bottom of the form to select it. Press and hold the CTRL key and then click the Label control above the text box.**

The sizing handles around the text box display as outlines. The text box remains selected while the label also is selected. The label's sizing handles are solid (Figure 2-43).

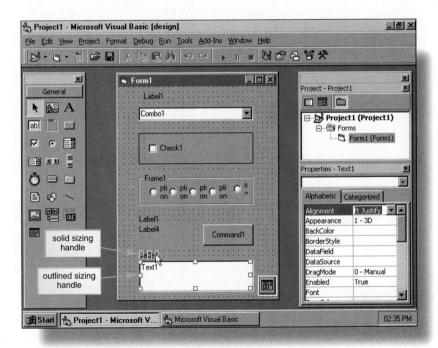

FIGURE 2-43

3 Press and hold the CTRL key and click the remaining controls to be left-aligned as shown in Figure 2-44. Select the topmost label last.

The controls selected as a group display as shown in Figure 2-44.

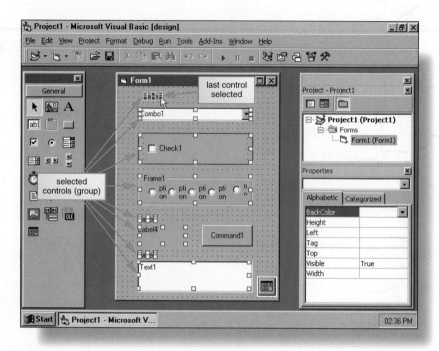

FIGURE 2-44

4 Click Format on the menu bar. Point to Align and then point to Lefts.

The Format menu and Align submenu display (Figure 2-45).

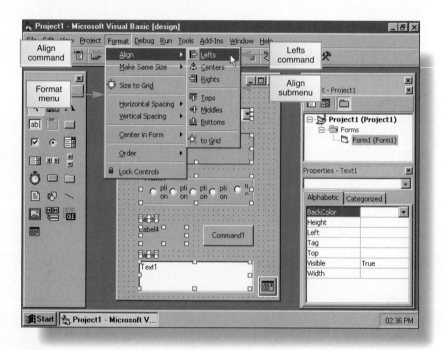

FIGURE 2-45

5 **Click Lefts.**

The left borders of all selected controls are aligned with the left border of the topmost Label1 control (Figure 2-46).

6 **Click any blank area of the form.**

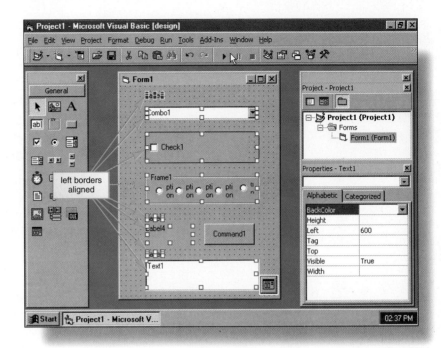

FIGURE 2-46

The interface for the Movie Box Office application now is finished. The form should display as shown in Figure 2-47. Figure 2-48 shows how the form will display at run time after the properties of the controls have been set.

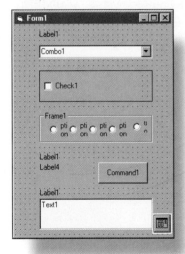

FIGURE 2-47

FIGURE 2-48

Table 2-2

CONTROL	PREFIX	CONTROL	PREFIX
Form	Frm	Image	img
CheckBox	Chk	Label	lbl
ComboBox	Cbo	Line	lin
CommandButton	cmd	ListBox	lst
Data	dat	Menu	mnu
DirListBox	dir	OLE	ole
DriveListBox	drv	OptionButton	opt
FileListBox	fil	PictureBox	pic
Frame	fra	Shape	shp
Grid	grd	TextBox	txt
HScrollBar	hsb	Timer	tmr
		VScrollBar	vsb

Setting Properties

In this section, you will complete the second phase of Visual Basic application development, **setting the properties** of the controls.

Naming Controls

When you add controls to a form, Visual Basic assigns a name to the control, which consists of the type of control and a number, such as Label1. It often is easier to read and edit your code if controls have names that more closely represent the purpose or function of the control within the application. The **Name** of a control is a property of a control and can be changed to whatever seems appropriate. Visual Basic has a suggested standard for naming controls. A control's name should consist of a three-letter prefix that designates the type of control followed by a unique text description. Control types and name prefixes are listed in Table 2-2.

This project follows the Visual Basic conventions for naming controls. Table 2-3 lists the current (default) name of each control (shown in Figure 2-47 on the previous page), its function in the Movie Box Office application, and the new name that will be assigned. Perform the following steps to assign new values of the Name property to several of the controls on the Movie Box Office form.

Table 2-3

CURRENT NAME	CONTROL'S FUNCTION	NEW NAME
Combo1	Selects name of movie	cboMovie
Check1	Selects matinee discount price	chkMatinee
Label4	Displays purchase amount	lblAmtdue
Command1	Enters transaction in list	cmdEnter
Text1	Contains record of purchases	txtRecord
Form1	Movie Box Office form	frmMovies

 Steps To Name Controls

1 Select the control you want to change (Combo1) by clicking it on the form or by selecting its name in the Object list box in the Properties window.

The name of the selected control and its properties display in the Properties window (Figure 2-49).

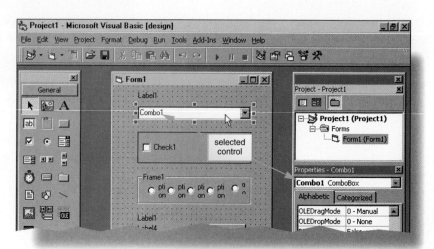

FIGURE 2-49

2 Scroll up to the top of the Properties list. Double-click the Name property in the Properties window.

The current name of the control (Combo1) is highlighted (Figure 2-50).

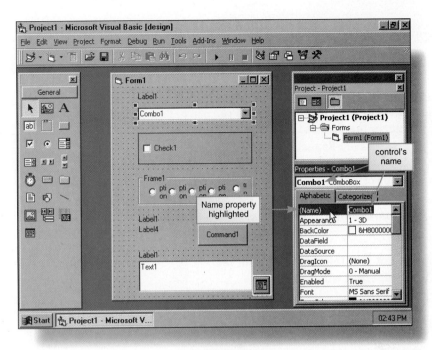

FIGURE 2-50

3 Type cboMovie as the new name and then press the ENTER key.

As you type, Combo1 is replaced with the new value next to the Name property in the Properties list (Figure 2-51).

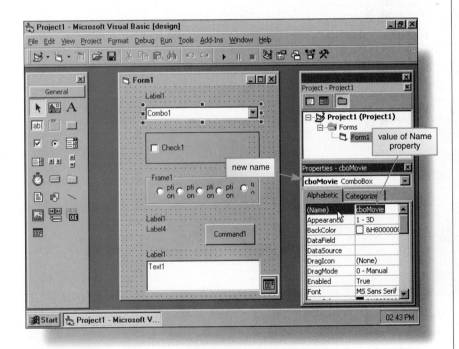

FIGURE 2-51

4 Repeat Step 1 through Step 3 to name the Check1 control `chkMatinee`. Repeat Step 1 through Step 3 to name the Label4 control `lblAmtdue`. Repeat Step 1 through Step 3 to name the Command1 control `cmdEnter`. Repeat Step 1 through Step 3 to name the Text1 control `txtRecord`. Repeat Step 1 through Step 3 to name the Form1 control `frmMovies`.

5 Click the Object box arrow in the Properties window.

The Object list displays showing the new names (Figure 2-52).

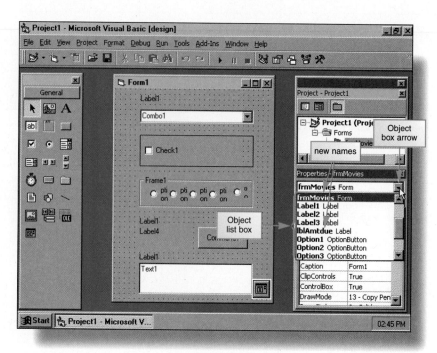

FIGURE 2-52

Changing the control names did not change their appearance on the form because the characters that display on the control are the control's caption, which is separate from the control's name.

Caption and Text Properties

Perform the following steps to add meaningful captions to the controls and clear the initial text in the ComboBox and TextBox controls as shown in Figure 2-53.

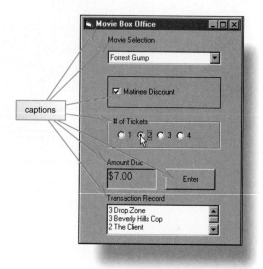

FIGURE 2-53

Steps **To Set Caption and Text Properties**

1 **Select the Label1 control by clicking its name in the Object drop-down list in the Properties window.**

The name of the control and its properties display in the Properties window (Figure 2-54).

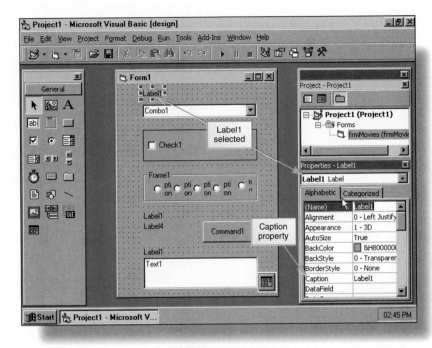

FIGURE 2-54

2 **If necessary, scroll the Properties list until the Caption property is visible. Double-click the Caption property in the Properties list.**

The current value of the control's Caption property displays highlighted (Figure 2-55).

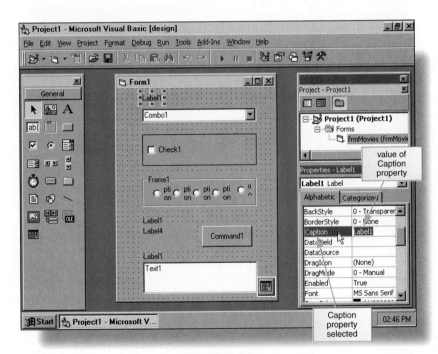

FIGURE 2-55

③ **Type** Movie Selection **as the new caption and then press the ENTER key.**

As you type, the value is replaced with the new caption and displays next to the Caption property in the Properties list (Figure 2-56).

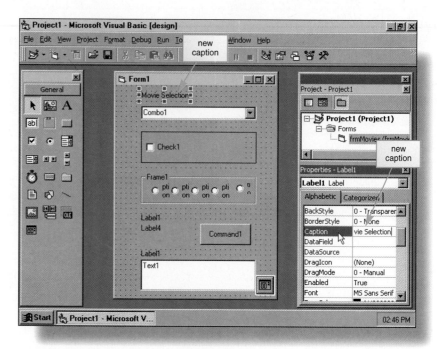

FIGURE 2-56

④ **Repeat Step 1 through Step 3 to change the caption of each control as listed in the New Caption column in Table 2-4.**

⑤ **Follow the procedure in Step 1 through Step 3 to change the txtRecord control's Text property to be blank and the Combo1 (cboMovie) Text property to be blank.**

The Movie Box Office form (frmMovies) displays as shown in Figure 2-57.

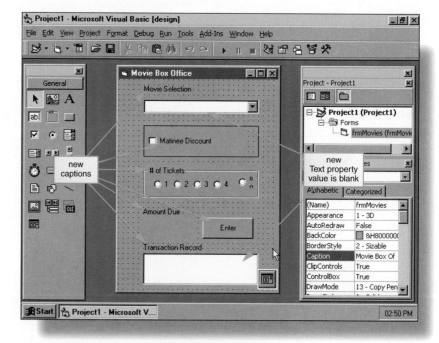

FIGURE 2-57

Style and List Properties

The Movie Box Office application contains a drop-down list for selecting the name of the movie. The ComboBox control selected in Figure 2-58 was added to the form when the other controls were added. Recall from Table 2-1 on page VB 2.13 that a **drop-down list** is one type of a ComboBox control. The type of ComboBox control is set by using the ComboBox control's **Style** property. Perform the following steps to make the ComboBox (cboMovie) control a drop-down list box and add items to its list.

Table 2-4		
CONTROL	*CURRENT CAPTION*	*NEW CAPTION*
chkMatinee	Check1	**Matinee Discount**
Frame1	Frame1	**# of Tickets**
Option1	Option1	**1**
Option2	Option2	**2**
Option3	Option3	**3**
Option4	Option4	**4**
Label2	Label1	**Amount Due**
lblAmtdue	Label4	**[blank]**
cmdEnter	Command1	**Enter**
Label3	Label1	**Transaction Record**
frmMovies	Form1	**Movie Box Office**

 Steps To Set the ComboBox Control's Style and List Properties

1 Select the ComboBox control by clicking it on the form or by selecting its name, cboMovie, in the Object list box in the Properties window.

Sizing handles display around the control and the control's properties display in the Properties window (Figure 2-58).

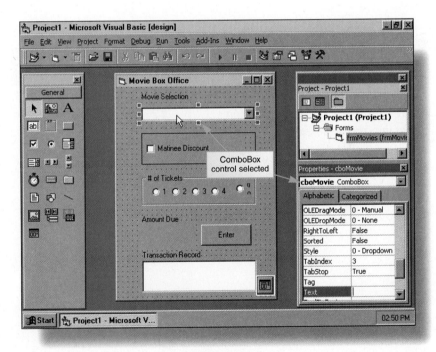

FIGURE 2-58

2 Click the Style property in the Properties list and then click the Style box arrow located on the right of the Style property value.

The default value of the Style property, 0 - Dropdown Combo, displays in the Style property values list (Figure 2-59).

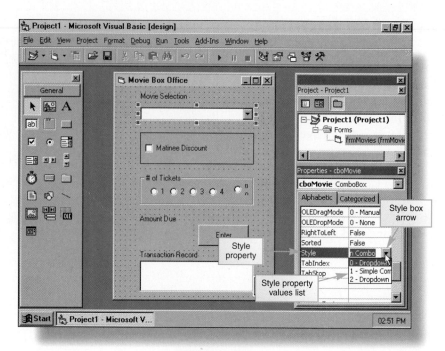

FIGURE 2-59

3 Click 2 - Dropdown List in the Property values list.

The selected value of the Style property displays. The list closes. The Text value changes to the name of the control (Figure 2-60).

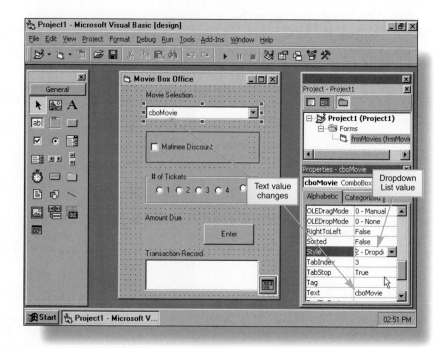

FIGURE 2-60

4 **Scroll the Properties list until the List property is visible and then double-click the List property.**

The List property values list displays (Figure 2-61). The list currently is empty.

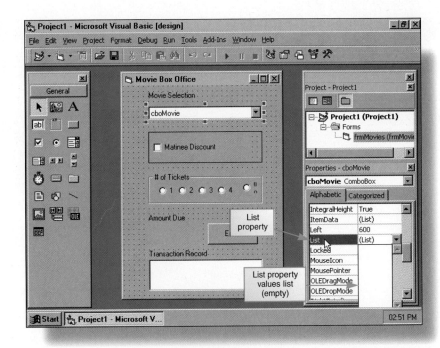

FIGURE 2-61

5 **Type** The Abyss **and then press** **CTRL + ENTER.**

The first item is added to the list (Figure 2-62).

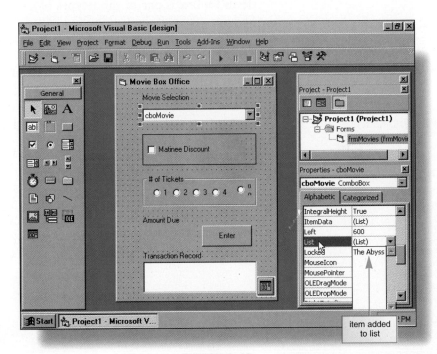

FIGURE 2-62

6 **Repeat Step 5 four times to add**
`Beverly Hills Cop`, `The`
`Client`, `Drop Zone`, **and**
`Forrest Gump` **to the list.**

The list displays as shown in Figure 2-63.

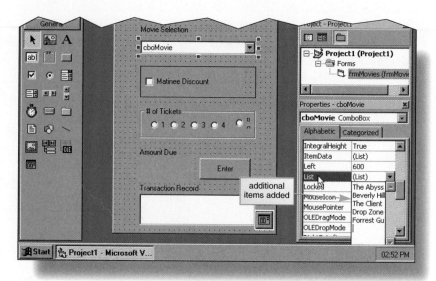

FIGURE 2-63

Although a separate Visual Basic control exists for a simple list box, the **drop-down list box** is one of three types of ComboBox controls specified by setting the Style property of the ComboBox control.

You can add items to a ComboBox or ListBox control during design time by adding to the control's List property as you just did. You can add items to a ComboBox or ListBox control during run time by using the **AddItem method** in code statements.

Locked, MultiLine, and ScrollBars Properties

The Movie Box Office application contains one TextBox control. Its appearance in Figure 2-64 is different from the TextBox controls that were used in Project 1. It contains multiple lines of text (three are visible at a time), it has a vertical scroll bar to move up and down through the text that extends beyond the borders of the control, and the user cannot change its contents. Perform the following steps to add these features by setting the **Locked property, MultiLine property,** and **ScrollBars property** of the TextBox control.

More *About* **the ScrollBars Property**

On some Visual Basic controls, a scroll bar automatically displays when the control's contents extend beyond the control's borders. This is not true of text boxes. You must add scroll bars to text boxes with the ScrollBars property. Scroll bars then will always appear on the text box, even when its contents do not extend beyond its borders.

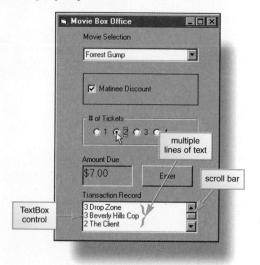

FIGURE 2-64

Steps **To Set the Locked, MultiLine, and ScrollBars Properties**

1 **Select the TextBox control by clicking it on the form or by selecting its name, txtRecord, from the Object list box in the Properties window.**

Sizing handles display around the control, and the control's properties display in the Properties window (Figure 2-65).

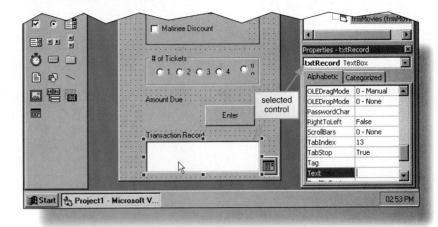

FIGURE 2-65

2 **Double-click the Locked property and then double-click the MultiLine property in the Properties list.**

The value of the Locked and Multi-Line properties change from the default value of False to the new value, True (Figure 2-66).

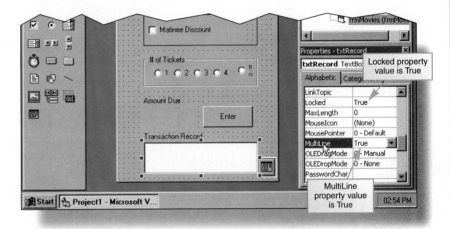

FIGURE 2-66

3 **Click the ScrollBars property in the Properties list. Click the ScrollBars property value box arrow.**

The ScrollBars property values list displays (Figure 2-67).

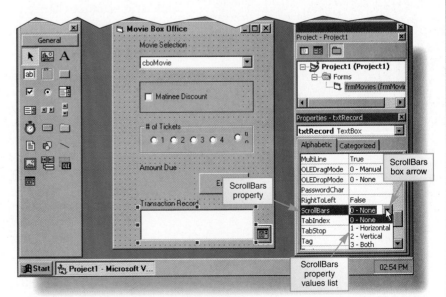

FIGURE 2-67

4 **Click 2 - Vertical in the Property values list.**

A vertical scroll bar is added to the control. The selected value of the property displays and the list closes (Figure 2-68).

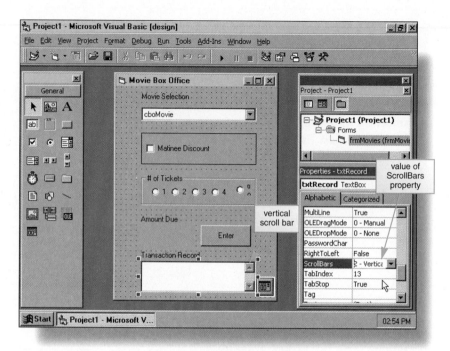

FIGURE 2-68

The ScrollBars property values list also contains values for a horizontal scroll bar or both horizontal and vertical scroll bars to be added to a text box. If the ScrollBars property is not set and the size of the TextBox control is smaller than the text you want to display, you are unable to view the text that extends beyond the borders of the text box.

BorderStyle and FontSize Properties

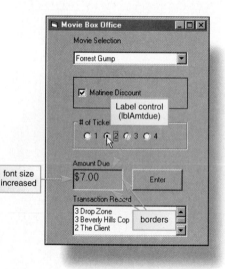

FIGURE 2-69

In the Movie Box Office application, a Label control (lblAmtdue) is used to display the total purchase price (Figure 2-69). A Label control is used instead of a TextBox control so the user of the application cannot change the value displayed during run time. Two features of the Label control (lblAmtdue) shown in Figure 2-69 make it different from the other Label controls in the Movie Box Office application.

First, you may have thought it was a TextBox control because it has a border around it. **Borders** are added to a Label control by setting the **BorderStyle property**. Second, the size of the characters inside the lblAmtdue control is larger than the size of the characters in the other labels on the Movie Box Office form (Figure 2-69). The size of the characters is set by using the **FontSize property** of the control. Perform the following steps to set the BorderStyle property and FontSize property of the labels.

Steps To Set BorderStyle and FontSize Properties

1 **Select the Label control (it displays only as a solid gray rectangle on the form) by clicking it or by selecting its name, lblAmtdue, in the Object list box in the Properties window.**

Sizing handles display around the control, and the control's properties display in the Properties window (Figure 2-70).

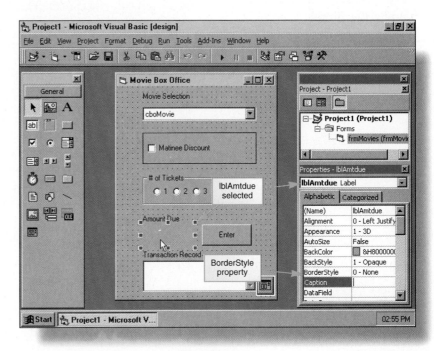

FIGURE 2-70

2 **Double-click the BorderStyle property in the Properties list.**

The value of the BorderStyle property changes from the default value of 0 - None to the new value, 1 - Fixed Single and a border displays around the control (Figure 2-71).

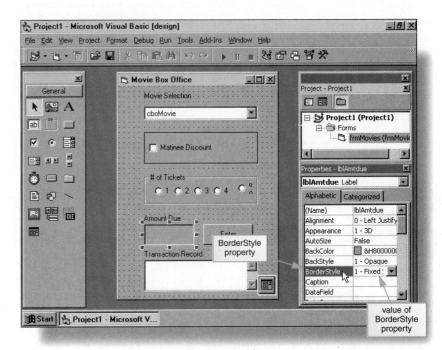

FIGURE 2-71

③ **Scroll the Properties list until the Font property is visible. Click the Font property. Click the Font properties button.**

The Font dialog box displays (Figure 2-72).

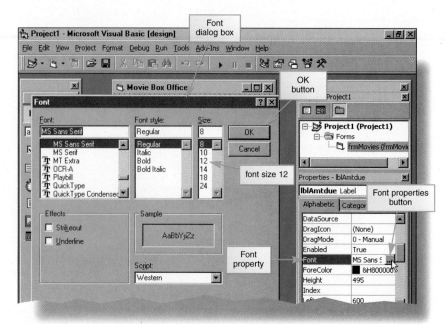

FIGURE 2-72

④ **Click 12 in the Size list. Click the OK button.**

The Font dialog box closes (Figure 2-73).

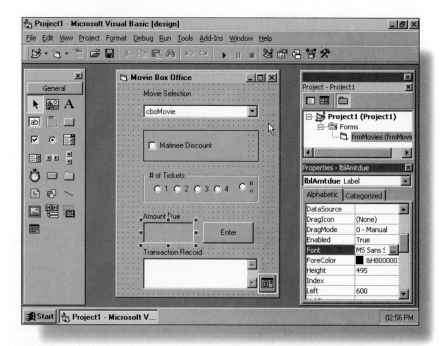

FIGURE 2-73

All controls that contain text or have Caption properties have the FontSize property. Additional Font properties also are available in the Font dialog box. You will work with these other Font properties in later projects.

Visible Property

The five option buttons that form the option group within the Frame control are shown in Figure 2-74. In the earlier discussion of option buttons, you learned that only one option button in a group can be selected at one time. Selecting a second option button automatically deselects the first option button.

When the Movie Box Office application starts, none of the four option buttons representing the number of tickets purchased are to be selected. In addition, when you click the Enter button on the form, all four of these option buttons are to be deselected. These actions are accomplished using the fifth option button added earlier.

Later, you will write code that selects the fifth option button when the Enter button is clicked. Clicking the fifth option button automatically deselects any one of the other four option buttons previously selected. You are making it *seem* that no button is selected, however, by making the fifth button invisible. The **Visible property** of a control determines whether the control can be seen at run time. Perform the following steps to make the Option5 control invisible.

More *About* **the Visible Property**

To hide an object at startup, set the Visible property to False at design time. Setting this property in code enables you to hide and later redisplay a control at run time in response to a particular event.

Steps **To Set the Visible Property**

1 **Select the option button named Option5 by clicking it or by selecting its name from the Object list box in the Properties window.**

Sizing handles display around the control, and the control's properties display in the Properties window (Figure 2-74).

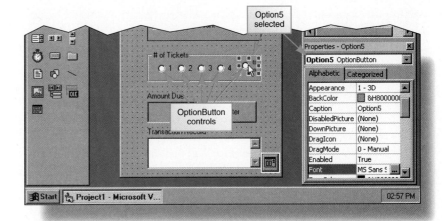

FIGURE 2-74

2 **Scroll the Properties list and then double-click the Visible property.**

The value of the Visible property changes from the default value of True to the new value, False (Figure 2-75).

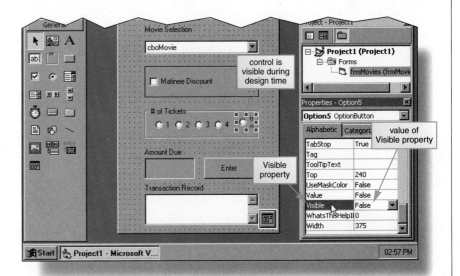

FIGURE 2-75

The Option5 control still is visible on the form during design time. At run time, however, the control will not display on the form.

Writing Code

You have created the interface and set the properties of the controls in the Movie Box Office application. The remaining step is to write the code for the application. Project 1 introduced you to writing Visual Basic code using statements that change the properties of controls during run time. These statements take the following general form:

```
controlname.property = value
```

The name of the control and the name of the property to be changed are separated with a period, and the value of the property to be set follows an equal sign.

Table 2-5		
CONTROL	EVENT	ACTIONS
General	Declarations	Creates a variable that will be used in multiple procedures
Option1	Click	Calculates the cost of one ticket and displays the amount due
Option2	Click	Calculates the cost of two tickets and displays the amount due
Option3	Click	Calculates the cost of three tickets and displays the amount due
Option4	Click	Calculates the cost of four tickets and displays the amount due
cmdEnter	Click	Adds the number of tickets and the name of the movie to the transaction list; clears option buttons, selection box, and amount due box
frmMovies	Double-click	Displays the Color dialog box for developer to allow demonstration of different colors

The Movie Box Office application requires you to write more complex code statements that incorporate variables and the **If...Then...Else statement**. You also will cut and paste (copy) code from one subroutine to another.

Six events in the Movie Box Office application require Event procedures (subroutines). These events and their actions are listed in Table 2-5.

The code for the Movie Box Office application will be written one event at a time using the Code window. Before proceeding with the code writing, you should save the project. In the following steps, the form and project files are saved to a formatted floppy disk in the 3½ Floppy [A:] drive.

TO SAVE THE FORM

1. Click the Save Project button on the Standard toolbar.
2. Type Movies in the File name box in the Save File As dialog box.
3. Click 3½ Floppy [A:] in the Save in list box.
4. Click the Save button in the Save File As dialog box.
5. Type Movies in the File name box in the Save Project As dialog box.
6. Click the Save button in the Save Project As dialog box.

The form and project files are saved. The file names are shown in the Project window (Figure 2-76).

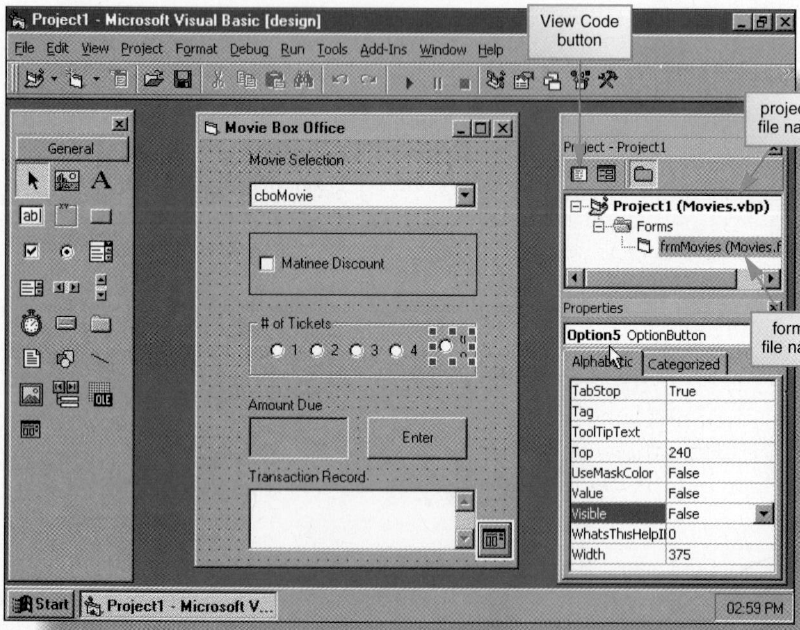

FIGURE 2-76

Variables

Variables are used in code statements to store the temporary values used by other code statements. Visual Basic **variables** have a name you create and a data type. The **data type** determines what kind of data the variable can store (numeric or character). You must follow a few rules when choosing names for variables.

1. The name must begin with a character.
2. The name cannot be more than 255 characters.
3. The name cannot contain punctuation or blank spaces.

The easiest way to create a variable is to assign a value to the variable's name in a code statement, such as `rate = 3.5` or `name = "John"`. Variables created in this way can hold either numbers (numeric data) or characters (string data). Character data, called a **string**, is placed within quotation marks. In addition, variables can be assigned the value of another variable or the value of a mathematical expression. Table 2-6 lists several examples of code statements that create a variable and assign a value to it.

Table 2-6	
EXAMPLE TYPE	*STATEMENT*
Numeric data	Price = 5
Numeric data	Discount = 1.15
String data	movie = "Sneakers"
Value of another variable	Cost = price
Value of an expression	Cost = price * discount
Value of an expression	Amtdue = price * 1.05

When variables are created simply by using them, they are said to be **implicitly declared**. Variables also can be **explicitly declared** in a separate code statement. The declaration statement has the following form:

`Dim variablename As datatype`

Data types of the variable may be Byte, Boolean, Integer, Long, Currency, Single, Double, Date, String, Object, Variant, a user-defined type, or an object type. Data types are discussed in greater detail in a later project. The **scope** of a variable refers to whether or not a variable is available for use by different subroutines. Variables declared within a subroutine can be used only within the subroutine in which they were created and lose their value between calls unless they are declared **static**. For code statements in different subroutines to use the value stored in a variable, the variable must be declared in the form's **General declarations** section.

The Movie Box Office application uses a variable named num that stores the number of tickets to be purchased. The variable is used in more than one event subroutine, and therefore it must be declared in the General declarations section. Perform the steps on the next page to write a declaration for this variable.

More *About* **Variables**

When variables are initialized, a numeric variable is initialized to zero, a variable-length string is initialized to a zero-length string ("") also called a null string, and a fixed-length string is filled with zeros. Variant variables are initialized to Empty.

More *About* **Option Explicit**

When the Require Variable Declaration check box is checked on the Editor tab sheet in the Visual Basic Options dialog box, Visual Basic will display an error dialog box any time you attempt to use a variable that has not been explicitly declared. You also can activate this feature in code by typing Option Explicit in the General declarations section.

Steps To Explicitly Declare Variables

1 **Click the View Code button in the Project window. If necessary, click (General) in the Object list box.**

The Code window opens (Figure 2-77). The insertion point is located at the top-left of the Code window.

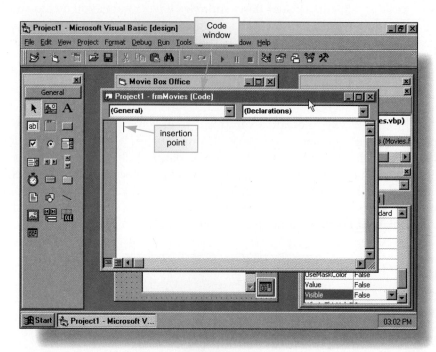

FIGURE 2-77

2 **Type** Dim num As Integer **in the Code window and then press the ENTER key.**

When you press the ENTER key, the insertion point moves to the beginning of the next line (Figure 2-78).

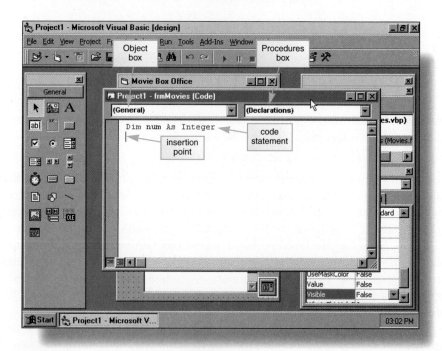

FIGURE 2-78

OtherWays

1. On View menu click Code
2. Press F7

When you press the ENTER key at the end of a code statement, Visual Basic inspects the code for many common errors. If it finds an error, the Microsoft Visual Basic dialog box opens. Some of the characters' case and color are changed automatically for ease in reading the code.

In Project 1, you learned how to open the Code window and select a control from the Object list box by double-clicking the control in the Form window. If you are going to write procedures for several controls, it can be awkward, however, to move between the Form window and the Code window just to select different controls in the Code window. A more general way to enter, edit, or view a subroutine in the Code window involves these steps (refer to Figure 2-78).

1. Select the control to which you will assign code from the Object list box.
2. Select the desired event from the Procedures list box.
3. Enter the code statements.

Arithmetic Expressions and the If...Then...Else Structure

The last two rows in Table 2-6 on page VB 2.43 contain code statements that perform mathematical operations on variables. These **arithmetic expressions** can involve certain Control properties as well as variables. For example, in Project 1, you wrote a code statement that made the Caption property of a label equal to the product of the value of a text box's Text property times a number. Table 2-7 lists the arithmetic operators available in Visual Basic. As is the case in Algebra, a set of parentheses can be used to change the normal **order of precedence,** which is exponentiation, multiplication and division, integer division, modulus arithmetic, addition, and subtraction.

The next step is to write the code for the four visible option buttons (Option1 through Option4) located inside the Frame control labeled # of Tickets (Figure 2-76 on page VB 2.42). The code for each option button is nearly identical. The following paragraphs describe the code for the Click event of the first option button (Option1_Click subroutine). Later, the code will be copied for the Click events of the other three option buttons.

The Click subroutine for each option button must do the following:

1. Assign the number of tickets purchased to the num variable.
2. Determine the ticket price.
3. Calculate the amount due as num * price and display it as dollars and cents in the Amount Due box.

Table 2-7	
ARITHMETIC OPERATOR	MEANING
^	Used to raise a number to the power of an exponent
*	Used to multiply two numbers
/	Used to divide two numbers and return a floating-point result
\	Used to divide two numbers and return an integer result
MOD	Used to divide two numbers and return only the remainder
+	Used to sum two numbers
-	Used to find the difference between two numbers or to indicate the negative value of a numeric expression

The first code statement must set the variable (num) equal to the number of tickets corresponding to that option button (selecting Option1 represents 1 ticket). The values assigned to num for the other three option buttons are 2, 3, and 4, respectively. Thus, for the first option button, the following statement sets the variable num equal to 1:

```
num = 1
```

More *About*
Editor Options

Visual Basic has several optional code writing and editing features such as automatically verifying correct syntax after you enter a line of code. You can enable or disable these features on the Editor tab sheet in the Options dialog box, accessed on the Visual Basic Tools menu.

The second code statement will use a single-line If...Then...Else statement to determine the price of the tickets purchased (based on whether the matinee discount is being given). In the Movie Box Office application, the regular price for all movies is $5, and the matinee price for all movies is $3.50.

Single-line If...Then...Else statements are used to execute one statement or another conditionally. A partial flowchart and the form of the single-line If...Then...Else statement is shown in Figure 2-79. The condition follows the keyword **If**. A condition is made up of two expressions and a **comparison operator**. Table 2-8 lists the comparison operators and their meanings.

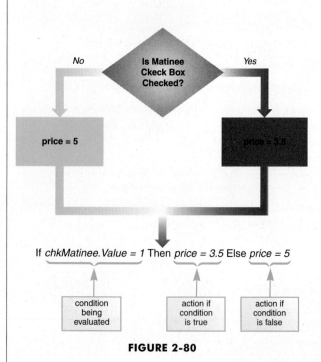

FIGURE 2-79

Table 2-8	
COMPARISON OPERATOR	MEANING
=	is equal to
<	is less than
>	Is greater than
<=	Is less than or equal to
>=	Is greater than or equal to
<>	Is not equal to

The statement to be executed when the condition is true follows the keyword **Then**. The statement to be executed when the condition is false follows the keyword **Else**. Figure 2-80 shows the logic and single-line If...Then...Else statement to determine the price of the ticket(s) purchased.

Recall that the Value property of a CheckBox control is 1 when the box is checked and 0 when it is not checked. The chkMatinee.Value is equal to 1 or 0 depending on whether the user of the application has selected the Matinee Discount option. If the Matinee Discount option is selected, then the price of a ticket is $3.50, or else the price of a ticket is $5.

In the Box Office application, the amount due is equal to the number of tickets purchased times the price. Thus, the formula num * price determines the amount due. The application displays amount due as the caption of the lblAmtdue control, using dollars and cents. The following statement determines the amount due and formats the amount due as dollars and cents:

FIGURE 2-80

```
lblAmtdue.Caption = Format$(num * price, "currency")
```

lblAmtdue is the name of the Amount Due box. **Format$** is a function that takes the first item in parentheses, num * price, and formats it to the second item in the parentheses, "currency". Currency is a predefined format name, which means Visual Basic will display the value num * price in a more readable fashion in the Amount Due box. The **$ character** appended to Format instructs Visual Basic to change the numeric result of num * price to a string before it is assigned as the caption of the Label control lblAmtdue. Table 2-9 summarizes the more frequently used predefined formats in Visual Basic.

Table 2-9

FORMAT	DESCRIPTION
General Number	Displays the number as is
Currency	Displays the number with a dollar sign, thousands separator with two digits to the right of the decimal; negative numbers display in parentheses
Fixed	Displays at least one digit to the left and two digits to the right of the decimal separator
Standard	Displays the number with thousands separator; if appropriate, displays two digits to the right of the decimal
Percent	Displays the number multiplied by 100 with a % sign
Yes/No	Displays No if the number is 0; otherwise displays Yes

Perform the following steps to write the If...Then...Else statement, mathematical expression, and other code for the Option1_Click subroutine.

Steps To Write an If...Then...Else Statement and Mathematical Expression

1 **Click the Object box arrow in the Code window.**

The Object list box displays (Figure 2-81).

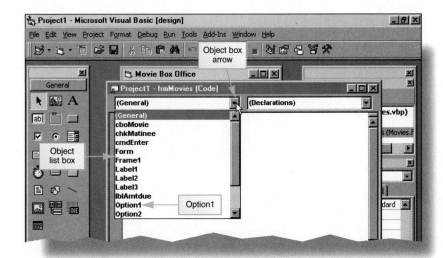

FIGURE 2-81

2 **Click Option1 in the Object list box.**

The Option1_Click subroutine displays in the Code window (Figure 2-82).

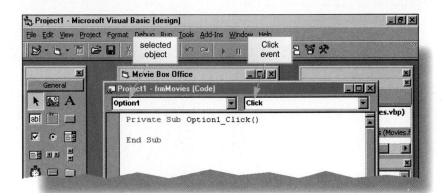

FIGURE 2-82

3 Drag the Code window's right border to extend the Code window's width. Enter the following four statements in the Code window as shown in Figure 2-83.

`'calculate and display amount due`

`num = 1`

`If chkMatinee.Value = 1 Then price = 3.5 Else price = 5`

`lblAmtdue.Caption = Format$(num * price, "currency")`

The Code window displays as shown in Figure 2-83.

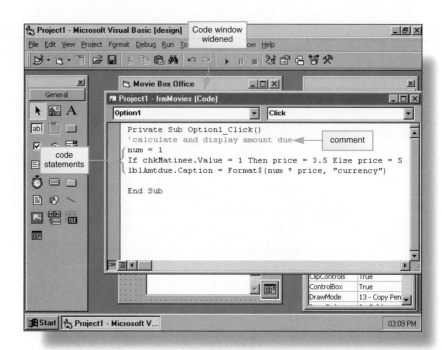

FIGURE 2-83

Copying Code Between Procedures

As previously mentioned, the subroutines for the other three option button Click events are very similar to this first one. Instead of typing all of the code statements in all of the subroutines, you can copy the code from the first subroutine to the other three and then make the necessary minor changes within the copied subroutines. Perform the following steps to copy code between the Option1 and other OptionButton Click event procedures.

 Steps **To Copy Code Between Procedures**

1 Point to the left of the first character (apostrophe) in the second line of code.

The mouse pointer is an I-beam (Figure 2-84).

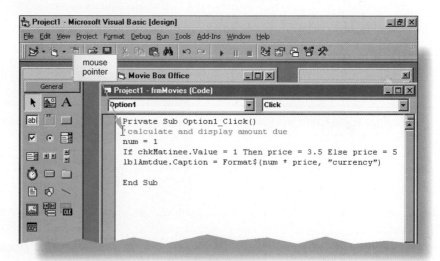

FIGURE 2-84

2 **Drag downward through the next to the last line of code. Click Edit on the menu bar and then point to Copy.**

The code statements are highlighted and the Edit menu displays (Figure 2-85).

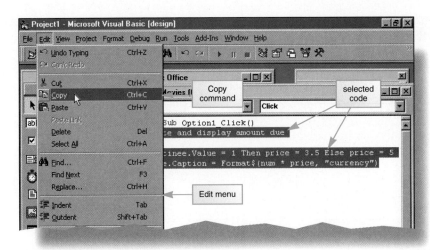

FIGURE 2-85

3 **Click Copy and then click the Object box arrow in the Code window.**

The highlighted text is copied to the Clipboard, and the Object list box displays (Figure 2-86).

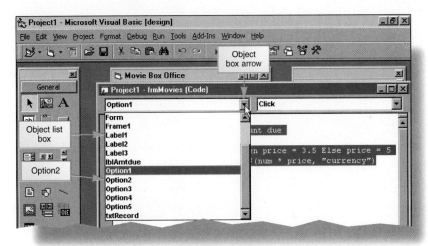

FIGURE 2-86

4 **Click Option2 in the Object list box.**

The Option2_Click subroutine displays with the insertion point at the beginning of the second line (Figure 2-87). If necessary, position the insertion point on the second line.

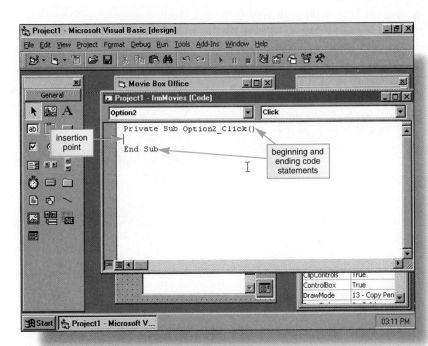

FIGURE 2-87

5 Click Edit on the menu bar and then click Paste.

The code is copied from the Clipboard to the procedure in the Code window (Figure 2-88).

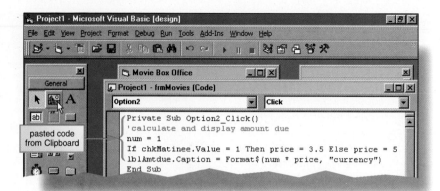

FIGURE 2-88

6 Type num = 2 to edit the code by changing the second line.

This change affects only what is different when 2 tickets are purchased (Figure 2-89).

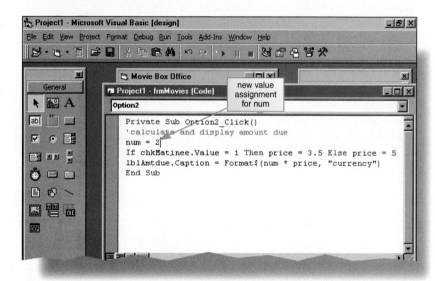

FIGURE 2-89

7 Repeat Step 4 through Step 6 to copy the code and edit it for the Option3_Click event and the Option4_Click event, changing the value of num to 3 and 4, respectively.

The completed Option4_Click event procedure is shown in Figure 2-90.

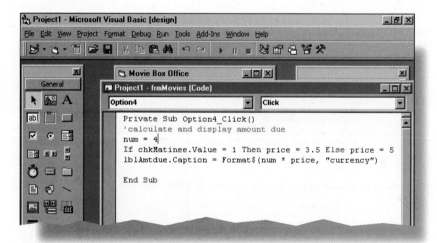

FIGURE 2-90

Once code has been copied to the Clipboard, it is not necessary to copy it each time you want to paste it in a procedure. You can continue to paste it as many times as is needed. Each time you copy code to the Clipboard, the previous contents of the Clipboard are erased.

Using Constants and Concatenating Text

The **cmdEnter_Click event** occurs when you click the Enter button (cmdEnter) on the form. This event adds the number of tickets and the movie's name to the top of a scrollable list in the transaction record (txtRecord) and clears the movie name, number of tickets, and amount due. To accomplish this task, several functions involving the manipulation of string data are used.

The value of a text box's Text property is a single string (group of characters). To have the transaction record behave the way it does, it is necessary to add special **control code characters** to the string that cause a new line to be started each time the cmdEnter event occurs. These characters are chr$(13) and chr$(10). The characters **chr$(13)** instruct Visual Basic to return the insertion point to the beginning of the line. The characters **chr$(10)** instruct Visual Basic to move the insertion point down one line.

A **constant** is similar to a variable in that it is a reserved space in memory. As its name implies, however, it retains a *constant* value throughout the execution of a program. Constants can be defined with the **Const statement** in the General declarations section. Visual Basic has a large set of predefined constants. The **vbNewLine constant** is equivalent to the characters chr$(10) & chr$(13). You can use constants anywhere in your code in place of actual values.

Because the Movie Box Office record must contain all of the previous sales information, it is necessary to add the new data to the old rather than replace it with the new data. This process of adding strings together is called **concatenation** and is performed with the ampersand (&) character. The code statement to accomplish this is as follows:

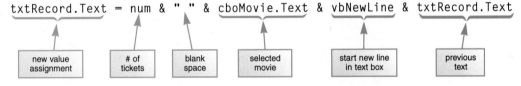

```
txtRecord.Text = num & " " & cboMovie.Text & vbNewLine & txtRecord.Text
```

| new value assignment | # of tickets | blank space | selected movie | start new line in text box | previous text |

More *About*
CommandButton Click Events

You can enable the user to press the ENTER key during run time as a substitute method for clicking a command button by changing that CommandButton control's Default property. Only one command button on a form can be the default command button. When Default is set to True for one command button, it automatically is set to False for all other command buttons on the form.

When you add items to a combo box or list box, Visual Basic assigns each item (in this case movie name) a consecutive number called an **index**. The first item is given an index of 0. When an item is selected by a user during run time, the **ListIndex property** of the control is given the value of that item's index. You can select an item from the list through a code statement by changing the control's ListIndex property. A ListIndex value of –1 means no item is selected. This is how you will clear the Movie Selection. The code statements for the rest of the cmdEnter_Click subroutine are explained as follows:

▶ The list box is returned to an empty state by selecting a blank list item:

```
cboMovie.ListIndex = -1
```

▶ The matinee check box is unchecked by setting its Value property:

```
chkMatinee.Value = 0
```

▶ The selected option button is deselected by selecting the Option5 (invisible) option button:

```
Option5.Value = True
```

▶ The amount due is cleared by setting the value of its Caption property equal to the **null string** (two consecutive quotation marks):

```
lblAmtdue.Caption = ""
```

Perform the following steps to write the cmdEnter_Click subroutine, which includes the use of a constant and text concatenation.

Steps To Use Constants and Concatenate Text

1 **Select the cmdEnter control in the Object list box in the Code window.**

The cmdEnter_Click subroutine displays in the Code window (Figure 2-91).

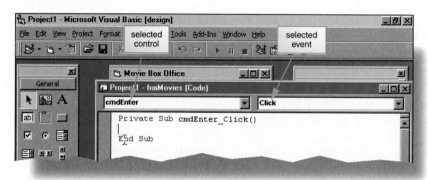

FIGURE 2-91

2 **Enter the following two statements in the Code window:**

```
'update transaction list
    and clear settings
txtRecord.Text = num & ""
    & cboMovie.Text
    & vbNewLine &
    txtRecord.Text
```

As you type the code, the Code window scrolls. Pressing the ENTER key advances the insertion point to the beginning of the next line (Figure 2-92).

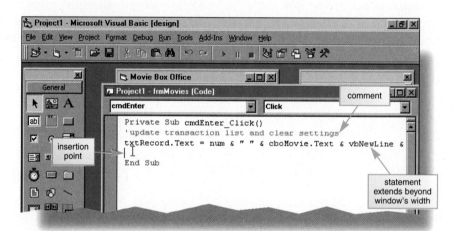

FIGURE 2-92

3 **Enter the following four statements in the Code window:**

```
cboMovie.ListIndex = -1
chkMatinee.Value = 0
Option5.Value = True
lblAmtdue.Caption = ""
```

The Code window displays as shown in Figure 2-93.

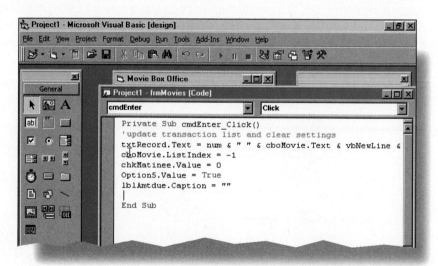

FIGURE 2-93

A code statement that sets a CheckBox control's Value property to 1 checks a check box. Setting the Value property to 0 removes the check mark. An option button is selected and deselected with code by setting its Value property to True or False, respectively. **True** is a Visual Basic constant for the value –1 and **False** is a constant for the value 0. Therefore, the code statement Check1.Value = False is acceptable, but the code statement Check1.Value = True will cause a run time error.

Writing Code for the CommonDialog Control

When you demonstrate the Movie Box Office prototype, you want to show different color possibilities. You do not want to offer this feature to the user, however. For this reason, you have chosen a *hidden* way to access the Color dialog box by double-clicking the form itself.

A common dialog is displayed during run time by applying one of the **Show methods** to the CommonDialog control using code. To display the Color dialog box, you will apply the **ShowColor method**. For each of the dialog boxes available through the CommonDialog control, you can further define the dialog box's properties and behavior with different values of the **Flags property**. In this application you will use the default value of the Flags property.

When the user selects a color and clicks the OK button, the selected color is recorded as the Color property of the CommonDialog control. You must write code that then assigns that color as the **BackColor property** of the form and all controls, which do not have a BackStyle property equal to transparent. Perform the following steps to write code for the CommonDialog control to display the Color dialog box.

> **More** *About*
> **CommonDialog Controls**
>
> The CommonDialog control provides an interface between Visual Basic and the routines in the Microsoft Windows dynamic-link library Commdlg.dll. As such, a common dialog within your application automatically has Windows context-sensitive help. In order for your application to create a dialog box using this control during run time, Commdlg.dll must be in your Microsoft Windows SYSTEM directory.

 Steps To Write CommonDialog Control Code

1. **Select the Form control from the Object list box in the Code window, and then select the DblClick event from the Procedures list box.**

   The frmMovies_DblClick subroutine displays in the Code window (Figure 2- 94).

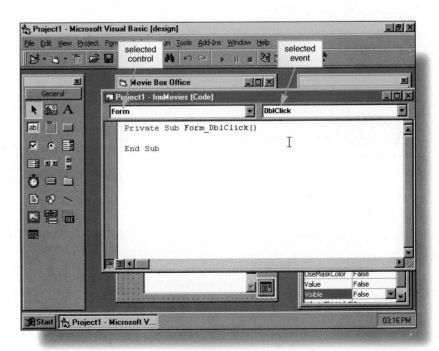

FIGURE 2-94

2 **Enter the following statements in the Code window:**

```
'display color dialog and
    set background color
CommonDialog1.ShowColor
frmMovies.BackColor =
    CommonDialog1.Color
cboMovie.BackColor =
    CommonDialog1.Color
chkMatinee.BackColor =
    CommonDialog1.Color
Frame1.BackColor =
    CommonDialog1.Color
Option1.BackColor =
    CommonDialog1.Color
Option2.BackColor =
    CommonDialog1.Color
Option3.BackColor =
    CommonDialog1.Color
Option4.BackColor =
    CommonDialog1.Color
lblAmtdue.BackColor =
    CommonDialog1.Color
txtRecord.BackColor =
    CommonDialog1.Color
```

The Code window displays as shown in Figure 2-95.

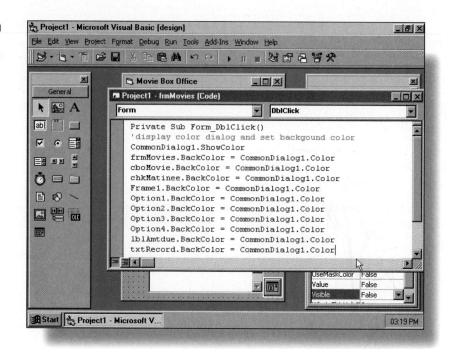

FIGURE 2-95

In the previous steps you wrote code to change the BackColor property of several of the controls on the Movies form. Unlike the Label control, these controls do not have a BackStyle property and, therefore, code must be written.

Saving and Running the Application

The Movie Box Office application now is complete. Before running the application, save the form and the project again.

TO SAVE THE PROJECT

1 Click the Save button on the Standard toolbar.
2 Click the Code window's Close button.

The previous versions of the .frm and .vbp files are replaced. If you wanted to save the form and project with different names, you would have to click Save As on the File menu.

Perform the following steps to run your Movie Box Office application. After Step 14, your application should display as shown in Figure 2-96.

TO RUN THE APPLICATION

1 Click the Start button on the Standard toolbar, or click Start on the Run menu.

2 Select The Client in the MovieSelection list.

3 Click the 2 tickets option button.

4 Click the Enter button.

5 Select Beverly Hills Cop in the movies list.

6 Click the 3 tickets option button.

7 Click the Enter button.

8 Select Drop Zone in the movies list.

9 Click the 3 tickets option button.

10 Click the Enter button.

11 Double-click the form. Click the pale blue color (row 1, column 5) and then click the OK button.

12 Select Forrest Gump in the movies list.

13 Click the Matinee Discount check box.

14 Click the 2 tickets option button.

The application displays as shown in Figure 2-96.

15 To close (end) the application, click the End button on the Standard toolbar, or click the Movie Box Office form's Close button.

16 To close Visual Basic, click File on the menu bar and then click Exit or click the Close button on the Visual Basic menu bar and toolbar window.

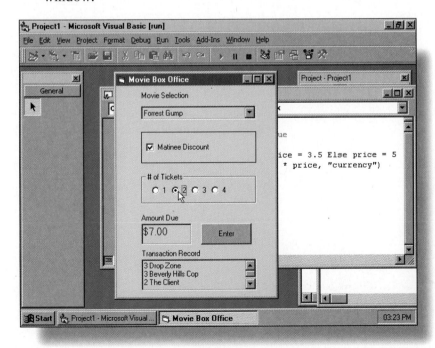

FIGURE 2-96

▶*Other***Ways**

1. Press ALT+R, press S, press F10, press ALT+R, then press E

Project Summary

In this project, you used additional properties of the controls you learned about in Project 1, as well as several additional controls. You added an ActiveX control to the Toolbox and used it in an application. You learned more about writing code by writing six event subroutines and a declaration procedure. You learned how to copy controls and copy code between subroutines. You used variables and constants in code statements and used code statements to concatenate string data. You used an If...Then...Else structure within a procedure.

No single, correct interface exists for a given application, nor is one single method the correct way to write code. In building this application, you may have thought of different ways to design the interface. You may have realized the events and code could have been written in a number of ways. Experiment with other ways to design the interface and to create the events. Building applications in a graphical environment is an exciting, creative enterprise.

What You Should Know

Having completed this project, you now should be able to perform the following tasks:

- Add a CheckBox Control *(VB 2.17)*
- Add a ComboBox Control *(VB 2.13)*
- Add a CommonDialog Control *(VB 2.23)*
- Add a Frame Control *(VB 2.18)*
- Add a Label Control and Set its AutoSize and BackStyle Properties *(VB 2.9)*
- Add Label, CommandButton, and TextBox Controls *(VB 2.22)*
- Add a Shape Control *(VB 2.15)*
- Align Controls *(VB 2.25)*
- Build an OptionButton Group *(VB 2.20)*
- Copy Code Between Procedures *(VB 2.48)*
- Copy Controls *(VB 2.10)*
- Explicitly Declare Variables *(VB 2.44)*
- Name Controls *(VB 2.28)*
- Run the Application *(VB 2.55)*
- Save the Form *(VB 2.42)*
- Save the Project *(VB 2.54)*
- Set BorderStyle and FontSize Properties *(VB 2.39)*
- Set Caption and Text Properties *(VB 2.31)*
- Set the ComboBox Control's Style and List Properties *(VB 2.33)*
- Set the Locked, MultiLine, and ScrollBars Properties *(VB 2.37)*
- Set the Size and Location of a Form *(VB 2.7)*
- Set the Visible Property *(VB 2.41)*
- Use Constants and Concatenate Text *(VB 2.52)*
- Write an If...Then...Else Statement and Mathematical Expression *(VB 2.47)*
- Write CommonDialog Control Code *(VB 2.53)*

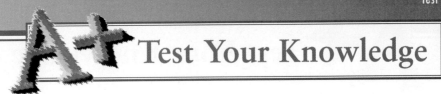

1 True/False

Instructions: Circle T if the statement is true or F is the statement is false.

T F 1. Projects generally are built using a three-step process of creating the interface, setting properties, and writing code.

T F 2. It is not possible to copy an existing control and paste the copy somewhere else on the form.

T F 3. The Shape control can be used only to add ovals or circles to a form.

T F 4. Frame controls are not the same as Shape controls.

T F 5. Within the same grouping, more than one option button can be selected at the same time.

T F 6. Within the same grouping, more than one check box can be checked at the same time.

T F 7. The Name property of a control must have the same value as the Caption property of that control.

T F 8. The type of ComboBox control that displays is determined by its Style property.

T F 9. To make a variable global, it must be declared as Public in the General declarations procedure of a module.

T F 10. When the MultiLine property of the TextBox control is set to True, a ScrollBars control is added automatically to the TextBox control.

2 Multiple Choice

Instructions: Circle the correct response.

1. The _____ property set to True will make a label the size of its caption automatically.
   a. Stretch/Shrink
   b. AutoSize
   c. Min/Max
   d. AutoFit

2. When creating several similar controls, it would not be advantageous to set the _____ property before copying and pasting the controls.
   a. AutoSize
   b. Caption
   c. Appearance
   d. BorderStyle

3. Use a _____ control when the application should have a drop-down list that items must be selected from.
   a. ComboBox (Style = 2)
   b. ListBox
   c. ComboBox (Style = 1)
   d. ComboBox (Style = 0)

(continued)

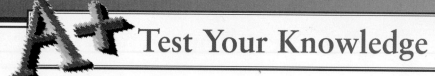

Test Your Knowledge

Multiple Choice *(continued)*

4. The _____ control is used to indicate selection or deselection of one or more individual items at the same time.
   a. CheckBox
   b. ListBox
   c. TextBox
   d. ComboBox

5. A Frame control is used as a _____ for other controls.
   a. container
   b. decoration
   c. shape
   d. border

6. The suggested three-letter prefix for a control name designates the _____ of a control.
   a. order
   b. property
   c. caption
   d. type

7. The _____ property of a TextBox control allows for more than one line of text to be placed in the box.
   a. WordWrap
   b. MoreLines
   c. MultiLine
   d. TextWrap

8. With the Default property of a CommandButton control set to True, the _____ key can be pressed to execute the CommandButton control's code statements.
   a. ENTER
   b. ALT
   c. END
   d. CTRL

9. The syntax of a code statement that changes the properties of a control at run time is in the form of _____ .
   a. property.value = controlname
   b. value.controlname = property
   c. controlname.property = value
   d. value.property = controlname

10. Code statements to be carried out at run time when the form is moved into memory should be placed in the _____ .
    a. Option Click subroutine
    b. General object declarations procedure
    c. Command Click subroutine
    d. Form_Load event

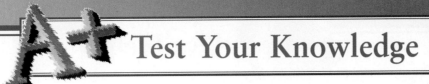 **Test Your Knowledge**

3 Understanding Code Statements

Instructions: Carefully read each of the following descriptions. Write code statements to accomplish specific tasks. Record your answers on a separate sheet of paper. Number your answers to correspond to the code descriptions.

1. Write a code statement that will display the characters Salutations in a Label control with a name of lblGreeting.
2. Write a code statement that will clear a TextBox control with the name of txtBlank.
3. Write a code statement that will create a variable called total to be used in multiple subroutines. The variable should have a data type of Short.
4. Write a code statement that will add Saturday to a drop-down list box with a name of cboDays.
5. Write a code statement that concatenates the contents of two TextBox controls named txtWord1 and txtWord2 to be displayed in a Label control with a name of lblFinal.
6. If a CheckBox control with a name of chkGreeting is checked, write a code statement that displays Salutations in a Label control with a name of lblGreeting otherwise it displays Farewell in the same Label control.

4 Understanding Mathematical Operators in Visual Basic

Instructions: The following variables, controls, and their values are to be used to determine the answers for the following code statements. Each code statement is separate from the others. Write your responses on a separate sheet of paper in the same order as the questions display.

txtRate.Text = 30
time = 40
deduction = 100
chkDeduction.Value = 1
cmdCalculate
lblPay

1. lblPay = txtRate.Text * time
   lblPay.Caption: _____
2. If chkDependent.Value = 0 Then lblPay.Caption = time * txtRate.Text
   lblPay.Caption: _____
3. If time > 40 Then txtRate.Text = txtRate.Text * 1.5
   txtRate.Text: _____
4. deduction = txtRate.Text * time / 24
   deduction: _____
5. cmdCalculate.Default = True
   txtRate.Caption: _____
6. If chkDeduction.Value = 1 Then deduction = txtRate.Text * time / 6 Else deduction = txtRate.Text * time / 20
   deduction: _____

Use Help

1 Reviewing Project Activities

Instructions: Perform the following tasks using a computer.

1. Start Visual Basic.
2. Click Help on the menu bar and then click Microsoft Visual Basic Help Topics.
3. Click the Index tab and then type `default property` in the top text box labeled 1. Double-click Default property in the middle list box labeled 2. Read and print the information.
4. Click the Applies To link and then double-click the topic CommandButton Control. Read and print the information that displays. Hand in the printouts to your instructor.
5. Click the Help Topics button. Type `math operators` in the top text box labeled 1. Click the Display button. Double-click operator precedence in the Topics Found dialog box. Read and print the information. Click each of the green, underlined links and read the ScreenTips. Print each definition that displays by right-clicking the ScreenTip and clicking Print Topic on the shortcut menu. Click the See Also link and then double-click Operator Summary in the Topics Found dialog box. Click Arithmetic Operators and, one by one, click each operator. As you click each operator, read and print the information. Hand in the printouts to your instructor.

2 Expanding on the Basics

Instructions: Use Visual Basic Books Online to understand the topics and answer the questions listed below. Answer the questions on your own paper to hand in to your instructor.

1. Click Help on the menu bar and then click Books Online.
2. In the Navigation area, double-click Programmer's Guide (All Editions) to open the book. Double-click Visual Basic Specification, Limitations, and File Formats. Read the information in the Topic area.
3. Double-click Project Limitations in the Navigation area. Read the information in the Topic area and answer the following questions.
   a. What are at least 3 project identifiers?
   b. How long can a variable name be?
   c. How long can a form, control, module, or class name be?
4. One by one, click Control Limitations, Code Limitations, Data Limitations, and System Resource Limitations in the Navigation area. As you click each one, read the corresponding information that displays in the Topic area and answer all of the following questions.
   a. What can be used to reduce consumption of system resources?
   b. How many control names can be used per form?
   c. What are at least three other controls, their properties, and their limitations?
   d. How long can control property names be?
   e. What is the code line limit?
   f. What is the limit to the number of bytes per line of code?
   g. What is the limit to the number of blank spaces acceptable before text on a line of code?
   h. What is the limit to the number of continuation characters per logical line of code?

Apply Your Knowledge

Complete.

1 Selecting Options Using Multiple OptionButton Control Groups

Instructions: Start Visual Basic. Open the project, Shape Change Properties, from the Data Disk that accompanies this book. This application incorporates multiple OptionButton control groups. One OptionButton control group is used to set the Shape property of the Shape control. The OptionButton group you will add is used to set the BorderStyle property of the Shape control. Perform the following tasks to complete this application as shown in Figure 2-97.

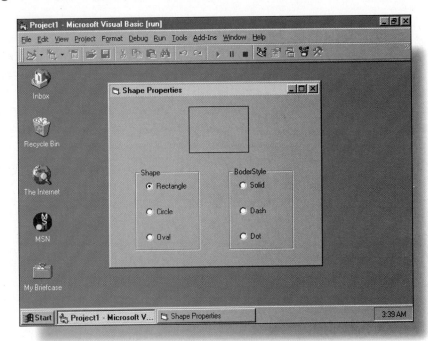

FIGURE 2-97

1. Size and position the form as shown.

2. Add a second Frame control to the right of the existing Frame control. Within the new Frame control, add 3 OptionButton controls. Remember that an OptionButton control is only part of a group if individually placed within a Frame control.

3. Set appropriate Name and Caption properties for each of the new controls. The Frame you have just added contains the option buttons to make the Shape control border style solid, dashed, or dotted.

4. Open the Code window by double-clicking the first new OptionButton control. Type code similar to shpNewShape.BorderStyle = 1 where a border style of 1 is solid. Add a comment to explain what the code is accomplishing.

5. One by one, select the second and third new OptionButton controls from the Object list box in the Code window. Type code similar to shpNewShape.BorderStyle = 1 replacing the 1 with a 2 for a dashed border style for the second new OptionButton control and then a 3 for a dotted border style for the third new OptionButton control. Add comments to explain the code statements.

6. Save the form and the project using the file name, Shape Properties.

7. If necessary, run the application and correct any errors. If changes have been made, save the form and project again using the same file names.

8. Print the Form Image, Code, and Form As Text for the Current Module.

In the Lab

1 Changing Properties at Run Time with CheckBox Controls

Problem: You have decided to build an application to assist the math students whom you tutor. The application should provide the capability of allowing the students to enter two numbers. They also should be able to select whether to add, subtract, multiply, or divide the two numbers or any combination of these operations. The results of each operation should display after they have been calculated. The application should look similar to the one shown in Figure 2-98.

Instructions: Perform the following tasks.

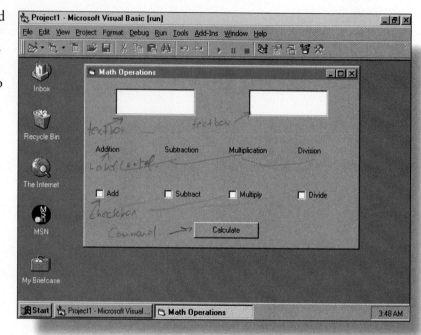

FIGURE 2-98

1. Open a new project in Visual Basic.
2. Add to the form two TextBox controls for typing in numbers, four CheckBox controls to select whether to add, subtract, multiply, or divide, four Label controls to display the results of the math operations, and one CommandButton control to perform the calculations.
3. Name the form and each of the controls appropriately.
4. Set the Caption property of each of the controls that require it.
5. Write the CommandButton control code to execute each of the choices indicated by the four CheckBox controls according to the following sample:

```
If chkCheckBox1.Value = 1 Then
   lblLabel1.Caption = (Val(txtText1.Text) + Val(txtText2.Text))
End If
```

Replace the default control names by the appropriate control names in the actual code. Add comments to explain what the code is accomplishing. Add explanatory comments to code statements.
6. Save the form and project using the file name, Math Operators.
7. Run the application and correct any errors. If any changes have been made, save the form and project again using the same file names.
8. Print the Form Image, Code, and Form As Text for the Current Module.

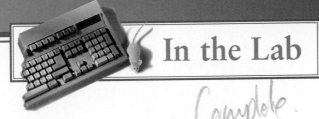

In the Lab

Complete.

2 Changing Properties at Run Time with OptionButton Controls

Problem: As a daycare assistant, you have been asked to develop an application to help children learn both shapes and colors. The finished application is shown in Figure 2-99.

Instructions: Perform the following tasks.

1. Open a new project in Visual Basic.
2. Add one of each circle, square, oval, and rectangle Shape controls to the form.
3. Add one Frame control to correspond to each one of the Shape controls. The Frame controls should be large enough to contain three OptionButton controls each.

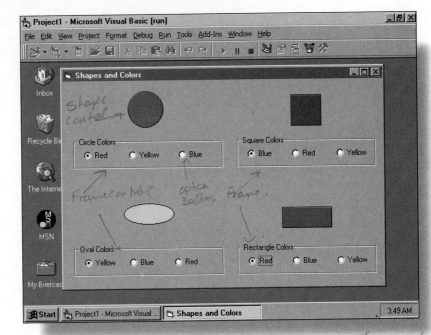

FIGURE 2-99

shpCircle.
shp Square.
shp Oval.
shp Rectangle

4. Add three OptionButton controls to each of the Frame controls.
5. Give the form and all of the controls appropriate names. As you name the controls, keep in mind that each one of the Frame controls contains the OptionButton controls to change the color of one of the Shape controls.
6. Set the Caption property of each of the controls that require it. Set the FillStyle property of each of the Shape controls to 0 - Solid.
7. Write the code for the first OptionButton control in the first Frame control. Sample code is shpShape1.FillColor = VBRed where shpShape1 will be replaced with the actual name given to each of the Shape controls. Constant color values to use for the three OptionButton controls are VBRed, VBYellow, and VBBlue. The code will be similar for each of the three OptionButton controls in each Frame control. Add comments to explain what the code is accomplishing.
8. Save the form and the project using the file name, Shape and Color Changer.
9. Run the application and correct any errors. Remember to resave the form and the project if any changes have been made.
10. Print the Form Image, Code, and Form As Text for the Current Module. *ShapeColorChanger –*

Form –
Project
Save as vb 263.

In the Lab

3 Creating a Drop-Down Application

Problem: You write down people's birthdays on various scraps of paper, on various notepads, and in your pocket calendar. The pieces of paper eventually tend to get lost or misplaced and you do not always carry your pocket calendar, which has incomplete data. Because of this, you miss everyone's birthdays and have decided to organize the data better by building a Visual Basic application. The new application will permit you to view people's names, birthdates, and birth signs by dropping down a list. You further determine that the application should have the capability of adding new data to the existing list.

Instructions: Perform the following tasks to build the application as displayed in Figure 2-100.

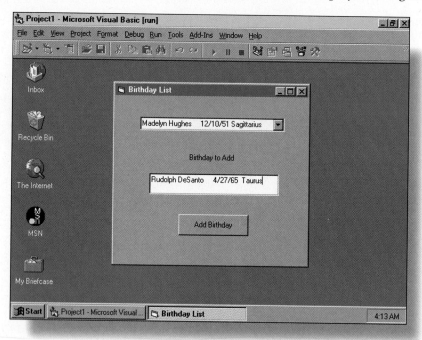

FIGURE 2-100

1. Start a new project in Visual Basic.
2. Add a drop-down ListBox control, a TextBox control, and a CommandButton control to the form.
3. Name the form and each of the controls appropriately.
4. Write the code to add names, birth dates, and birth signs to the drop-down list. Add a comment to explain what the code is accomplishing.
5. Save the form and the project using the file name, Birthday List.
6. Run the application and add the data for several people to the drop-down list.
7. If any errors are encountered, correct them, resave the form and project using the same file names.
8. Print the Form Image, Code, and Form As Text for the Current Module.

Cases and Places

The difficulty of these case studies varies: ❯ are the least difficult; ❯❯ are more difficult; and ❯❯❯ are the most difficult.

1 ❯ Lions, Tigers, and Bears is a progressive pet clinic with personal computers in each examination room. You have been hired to develop an application for the veterinary assistants to record patient temperatures. The assistants want an easy to use application that will display the temperature for the veterinarian. After some discussion, it is determined that they would like to record the patient's temperature by selecting option buttons. The temperature will be represented by a rectangular Shape control that will increase in width and change color. A far below normal temperature will be a short, VBCyan rectangle. A slightly below normal temperature will be the original rectangle width * 2.5 and VBBlue. A normal temperature will be the original rectangle width * 3.5 and VBMagenta. A slightly above normal temperature will be the original rectangle width * 4.5 and VBYellow. A far above normal temperature will be the original rectangle width * 5.5 and VBRed. As a button is selected, the corresponding visual representation of the selection will display. The code for each OptionButton control must set the width of the shape and the color of the shape. The colors used are Visual Basic color constants. Use the concepts and techniques presented in this project to create the application.

2 ❯ Lions, Tigers, and Bears pet clinic is impressed with your previous work for them and have hired you for another small project. The veterinary assistants would like an application that displays basic services. The application should be designed with check boxes to select the various services such as office calls, vaccinations, grooming, hospitalization, heartworm preventive, boarding, dentistry, x-rays, laboratory work, and prescriptions. As each service is selected the charge for the service should display. After all selections have been made, the charges should be added together to arrive at a total amount due and displayed when a CommandButton control is clicked. If the patient's owner thinks the total is too high, a way to clear the CheckBox controls, the corresponding service charges, and the total amount to begin selecting again should be available. Use the concepts and techniques presented in this project to create the application.

3 ❯❯ During tax season, you work for Tax Prep, Inc. Each tax season, several clients pay for their tax preparation with invalid checks. During the past few tax seasons, you have observed that these invalid checks are received from the same clients each tax season. Currently, a handwritten list of these clients is distributed to the tax preparers. These lists frequently are misplaced or accidentally destroyed. You have shared your observation with the manager who has decided you should build a Visual Basic application for the tax preparers. The application should have a drop-down list of these clients including their Social Security numbers as further identification. A text box and an associated command button should be included so additions can be made to the list when new clients pay with invalid checks. Add at least seven clients to the list. Use the concepts and techniques presented in this project to create the application.

Cases and Places

4 ▶▶ The county government computing center where you work has given you a new assignment. The file clerks in the recorder's office frequently encounter problems filing records alphabetically. They would like an application that will allow them to enter two different names and compare them to each other. You have decided command buttons with corresponding code can be used to determine if the two names are equal to each other, one name is less than the other, or one name is greater than the other. Appropriate messages also should display on the form to indicate the result of the comparison and whether it is True or False. *Hint*: This application would be comparing two strings to each other. Visual Basic has a string compare (StrComp) that can be researched using the Contents tab in Help.

5 ▶▶▶ Your city library has hired you on a consulting basis to provide them with an application for overdue charges. The charges apply to overdue books, records, tapes, CDs, and video tapes. The books can be one of two types; either hardbound or paperback. The librarians want an easy way to select the overdue items keeping in mind that a borrower could be returning multiple overdue items of the same type or of different types. Some method of selecting the number of overdue items up to a maximum of five for each item selected should be included. The charges for each category then should be multiplied by the number of overdue items and the amount due should be displayed for each category. The total amount due should be displayed on the form as well. *Hint*: The total amount due is a running total that will require a looping construct. Use Books Online in Help for assistance.

6 ▶▶▶ As an intern for Klassic Kar Insurance, you have received a request to develop an application. The application you will build is to assist the insurance agents in quickly calculating the cost of auto coverage. The application should have a drop-down list to select various coverage types. The coverage types can be obtained from insurance companies along with sample costs. Include a check box to indicate if the insurance client is deserving of a multi-vehicle discount. The costs of coverage also will depend on what category of vehicle is to be covered. It is suggested that the vehicle categories be represented with option buttons. The categories can be obtained from an insurance company. Selections are made from the drop-down list, the check box, and option buttons. After all selections have been made, a total amount due should be calculated and displayed. If the client should change his or her mind, there should be a provision for clearing the selections and amount due to start over.

7 ▶▶▶ You received a generous sum of money in U.S. dollars from the Caribou Club to attend school in Europe. You have decided to develop an application to keep track of what you have spent. This application should be built to accept U.S. dollars, convert them to various currencies, and add each amount spent to a drop-down list. The U.S. dollars spent should be added to a running total and displayed on the form as each foreign currency amount is added to the drop-down list. Current currency conversion rates can be obtained from financial newspapers or via the Internet.

Microsoft Visual Basic 5

Multiple Forms, Dialogs, Debugging, and EXEs

Objectives:

You will have mastered the material in this project when you can:

▶ Add additional forms to a project
▶ Specify a Startup form
▶ Specify a form's Startup location
▶ Set a form's BorderStyle property
▶ Specify an icon for an application
▶ Use an Image control in an application
▶ Use ScrollBar controls in an application
▶ Use Line controls in an application
▶ Build an About... dialog box
▶ Create application dialog boxes with the MsgBox function
▶ Work with multiple form Code windows
▶ Use the IsNumeric function in code
▶ Use the If...Then...Else block code structure
▶ Use the Show, Unload, and SetFocus methods in code
▶ Write code using financial functions
▶ Write procedures for the Change, Scroll, and Load events
▶ Use line continuations in code
▶ Use Visual Basic's Debug features
▶ Make an application executable

Eureka!
I've Created a Virtual Monster!

Desktop Laboratories Enhance Product Development

Albert Einstein and Victor Frankenstein spent hundreds of hours in their laboratories working with test tubes, Bunsen burners, and oscilloscopes to test their theories and develop their creations.

Likewise, scientists and engineers throughout the world today toil in their laboratories to develop potent pharmaceuticals, smaller cellular telephones, and faster computers. Instead of working in rooms stocked with chemicals and test equipment, however, these researchers conduct their experiments and take measurements in their offices using desktop computers.

These computers emulate physical instruments and provide accurate, timely data for analysis. Microsoft Visual Basic plays a role in this experimentation, with researchers using its forms and controls to create a graphical user interface, gather output, and fine-tune the simulations. Similarly, in this project, you will create multiple forms and write code. Emulating researchers' and engineers' efforts, you will debug your code to locate errors and to test your results.

Designers at Asea Brown Boveri (ABB) in Mexico use a Visual Basic application to provide quotes for

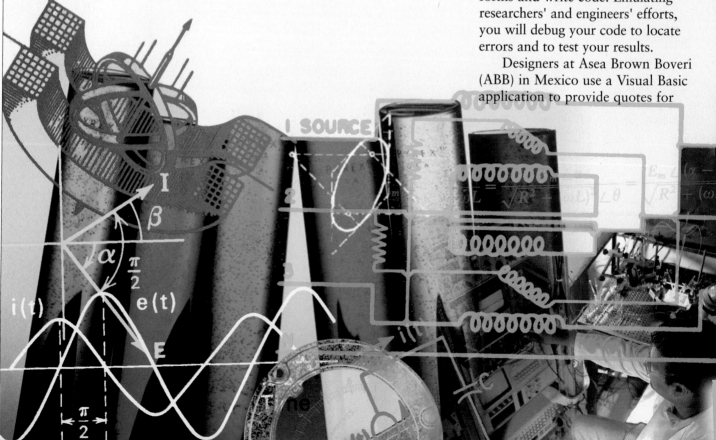

clients in less than 30 minutes, a process that formerly took several days to complete without the program. ABB, a $35 billion engineering corporation with offices throughout the world, specializes in environmental applications related to clean, reliable electric-power generation, transmission, and distribution. Its Mexico City campus develops and manufactures industrial electrical panels.

When potential customers contact ABB, the designers ask a series of questions regarding electrical specifications and budget constraints. Then, they execute the Visual Basic program and work with controls prompting for parameters such as the number of circuit breakers, electrical configurations, and type of electrical panel. This data is used in several algorithms to generate a graphical representation of the proposed panel, a list of materials, and a cash-flow analysis.

Five programmers developed this Visual Basic application in eight weeks, but three of the weeks were spent debugging one piece of code in an algorithm that distributes circuit breakers.

You have used Visual Basic's Toolbox to add a variety of controls to your forms. Researchers using this software, however, often need additional tools to meet their specialized requirements in their desktop laboratories. For example, they may use digital knobs to turn equipment on and off, analog knobs to set a precise value, and thermometers to indicate temperature variations.

National Instruments, a third-party vendor that supplies supplementary controls for scientific and engineering applications, is predominant in computer and instrumentation technology, promoting international technological standards. One of its products, ComponentWorks, adds tools to the Visual Basic Toolbox. With this virtual instrumentation, users can reduce the time needed to manufacture their end products and can improve quality. Augmenting Visual Basic with ComponentWorks, they can create a user interface that mimics the front panel of test equipment and gathers test data. This output can be loaded into spreadsheets or databases and used to generate statistics and monitor production-line tolerances.

Visual Basic applications abound in a variety of locations today — from the business office to the virtual laboratory. But no matter where the venue, the software helps create useful, powerful products in record time.

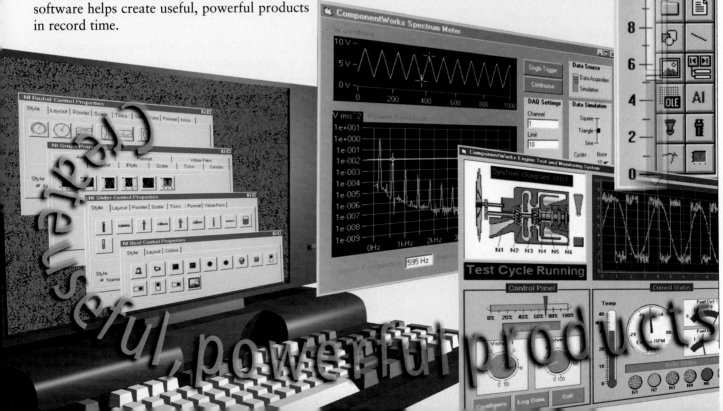

Project

Microsoft
Visual Basic 5

Multiple Forms, Dialogs, Debugging, and EXEs

Case Perspective

The first question people often ask when considering a large purchase is, "How much will the monthly payment be?" This is because many purchases such as a home, car, or appliance are paid for by taking out a loan for the purchase amount. The loan then is repaid by making regular, monthly payments over a certain length of time. Typically, the sum of the payments is more than the purchase price, reflecting the amount of interest paid for the loan. The monthly payment is a function of three things — the loan amount, called the principal; the interest rate, usually expressed as an annual percentage rate (APR); and the number of payments (such as 60 payments for a five-year loan).

The Macrofirm software company sells an operating system that is used on over 90 percent of the personal computers in the country. When you buy its operating system, you also get a number of utility, accessory, and game applications. Many of these applications are created by individual developers who sell their applications and copyrights to the Macrofirm company.

You have an idea for a small application that would fit into Macrofirm's accessories category that you think would be very useful to the average PC user. You have decided to build a prototype of a Loan Payment Calculator for submission to the Macrofirm company for possible inclusion in its bundled software.

Introduction

The applications built in Project 1 and Project 2 consisted of several controls and one form. In this project, you will build an application with additional controls and multiple forms. You also will use Visual Basic's library of built-in financial functions and create dialog boxes within the application. **Dialog boxes** are common in Windows applications and are used during run time to give information about the application to the user or to prompt the user to supply information to the application.

No matter how carefully you build a project, applications often do not work as planned and give erroneous results because of errors in the code. In this project, you will work with the Debug window and some of its features for finding errors in code. The applications you built in Project 1 and Project 2 could not be run outside of the Visual Basic system. In this project, you will make an EXE file that allows your application to run without the Visual Basic development system.

Project Three – Loan Payment Calculator

The completed Loan Payment Calculator application is shown in Figure 3-1. The loan amount is entered into a TextBox control from the keyboard. The number of years and the APR are entered by using ScrollBar controls. As you click the scroll arrows, the value supplied to the loan calculation changes and displays on the form. You can change the value more quickly by dragging the scroll box or by pointing to one of the scroll arrows and then pressing and holding the mouse button.

The Loan Payment Calculator window contains three command buttons labeled Calculate, Clear, and About... . When you click the **Calculate button** or press the ENTER key, the function is computed, and the monthly payment and the total amount to be repaid are displayed on the form (Figure 3-2). If the amount of the loan entered from the keyboard is not a valid numerical amount, the dialog box shown in Figure 3-3 displays to alert you to this input error. Clicking the OK button closes the dialog box and clears the text box so a new loan amount can be entered.

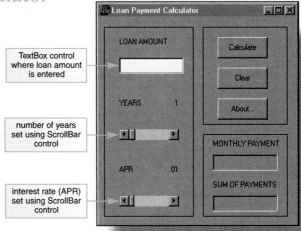

FIGURE 3-1

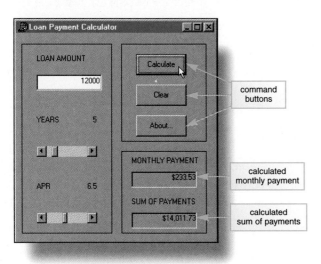

FIGURE 3-2

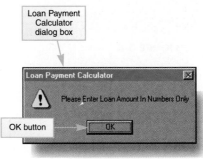

FIGURE 3-3

About Loan
Payment Calculator
dialog box

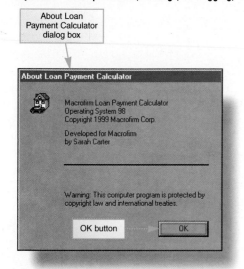

FIGURE 3-4

Minimize
button

Close
button

System
menu

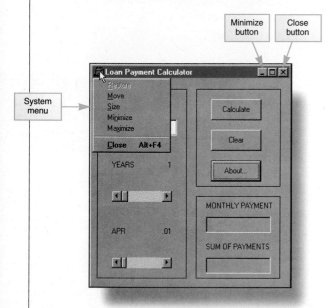

FIGURE 3-5

Clicking the **Clear button** in the Loan Payment Calculator window erases the loan amount, monthly payment, and sum of payments and returns the scroll bars to their lowest values. Clicking the **About... button** in the Loan Payment Calculator window displays the dialog box shown in Figure 3-4. Clicking the OK button in the About... dialog box closes the dialog box.

The Loan Payment Calculator window has a System menu (Figure 3-5) that is opened by clicking the System menu (Control-box) icon. The application can be minimized on the desktop by clicking Minimize on the System menu or by clicking the application's Minimize button. The window is closed by clicking Close on the System menu or by clicking the application's Close button.

Project Steps

Applications are built with Visual Basic in a three-step process: creating the interface, setting properties, and writing code. You will follow this three-step process to build the Loan Payment Calculator application. The following tasks will be completed in this project.

1. Start a Standard EXE project in Visual Basic.
2. Set the About dialog box form's size and position.
3. Add Label, Image, Line, and CommandButton controls.
4. Set the About... dialog box form's border style.
5. Set control Name, Caption, Font, and Picture properties.
6. Save the About dialog box form.
7. Add an additional form to the project.
8. Add Shape, Label, TextBox, ComandButton, and ScrollBar controls.
9. Set Alignment, Caption, Text, and Name properties.
10. Set the properties of a ScrollBar control.
11. Set a form's Icon property.
12. Save the second form.
13. Specify a Startup form.
14. Write the ScrollBar Change and Scroll event procedures.
15. Write the CommandButton Click event procedures.
16. Save, run, and debug the project.
17. Make and run an EXE file for the application.

The following pages contain a detailed explanation of each of these steps.

Creating the Interface

You will create the application's interface (adding controls and setting properties) one form at a time. After the interface is completed, you will write the code for the application. **Creating the interface** consists of sizing and locating the form and then adding each of the controls to the form and adjusting their sizes and positions. Before you begin creating the interface, however, you need to start Visual Basic and arrange the Visual Basic windows on the desktop.

The Visual Basic Desktop

Begin this project by starting Visual Basic as described on page VB 1.7 in Project 1 or by opening a new Standard EXE project if you already are running Visual Basic. If necessary, you should complete the steps on page VB 1.10 in Project 1 to arrange your desktop to resemble Figure 3-6.

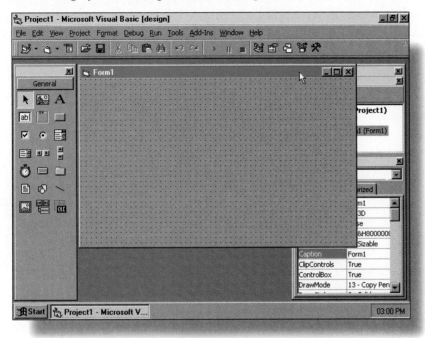

FIGURE 3-6

The About... Dialog Box Form and Its Controls

The About... dialog box shown in Figure 3-4 is created as a form within the project. The **About... dialog box** is common in Windows applications and is used to provide information about the application such as its version number, copyright date, and authors' names. To build the About... dialog box, you will perform the following tasks.

1. Set the size of the form.
2. Add the controls.
3. Set the properties of the form and its controls.
4. Save the form as a file on a floppy disk.

Setting the Size and Position of the Form

In Project 1 and Project 2, the form's size was set by dragging the form's borders. The values of the form's Height property and Width property changed as the borders were dragged to new locations. In the steps on the next page, the size of the About... dialog box form will be changed by directly changing the values of the Height and Width properties in the Properties window. You can change a form's size during run time by writing code statements that, when executed, change the values of the form's Height and Width properties.

The form's Top and Left properties determine the position of the upper-left corner of the form on the desktop. The form's location can be changed at run time by using code statements that change the values of the form's Top and Left properties. The form's **StartUpPosition** property determines where a form first displays on the desktop at run time. In Project 1 and Project 2, the form's first position at run time was the same as its position during design time because its StartUpPosition property was set to manual. This same method will be used for the Loan Payment Calculator application. Perform the following steps to set the size of the About... dialog box form.

Steps To Set the Size of a Form Using the Properties Window

1 **Click the Properties window to make it the active window.**

The Properties window moves on top of the Form window (Figure 3-7).

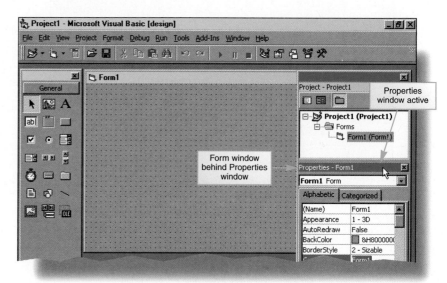

FIGURE 3-7

2 **Scroll through the Properties list, and then double-click the Height property. Type** 4300 **and then press the ENTER key.**

The form's bottom border moves to match the value entered in the properties value box (Figure 3-8).

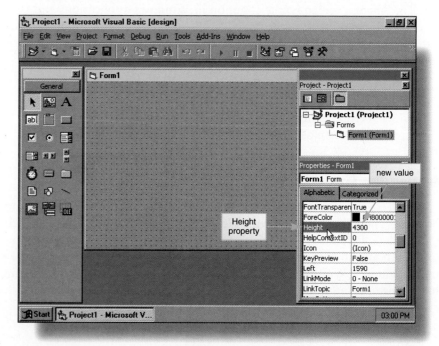

FIGURE 3-8

3 **Scroll through the Properties list, and then double-click the Width property. Type 5000 and then press the ENTER key.**

The form's right border moves to match the value entered in the properties value box (Figure 3-9).

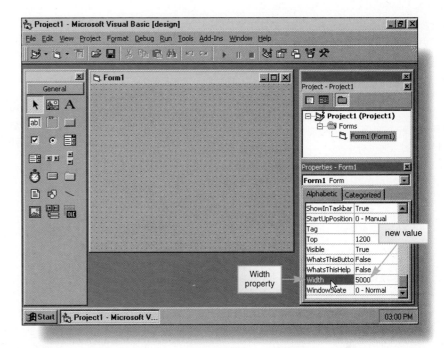

FIGURE 3-9

Because the Top and Left properties were not changed, setting values of the form's Height and Width properties caused only the form's bottom and right borders to move. The form's current location is acceptable for both design time and run time.

Adding the CommandButton and Label Controls

The About... dialog box form contains three Label controls and one CommandButton control, as shown in Figure 3-10. Perform the steps on the next page to add the labels and command button to the About... dialog box form.

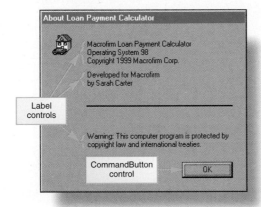

FIGURE 3-10

Steps To Add Label and CommandButton Controls

1 Double-click the Label button in the Toolbox. Drag the Label1 control to the position shown in Figure 3-11.

2 Double-click the Label button in the Toolbox. Drag the Label2 control to the position shown in Figure 3-11.

3 Double-click the Label button in the Toolbox. Drag the Label3 control to the position shown in Figure 3-11.

4 Double-click the CommandButton button in the Toolbox. Drag the Command1 control to the position shown in Figure 3-11.

5 Drag the command button bottom border up one grid mark to reduce its height.

The command button displays on the form with its new height (Figure 3-12).

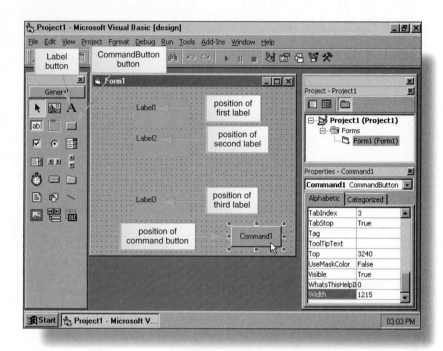

FIGURE 3-11

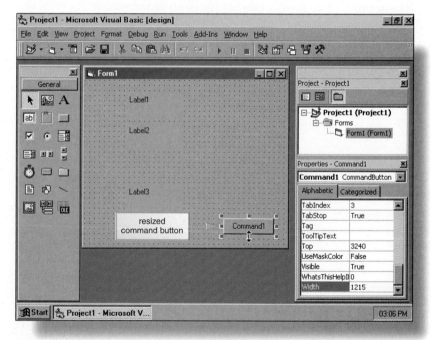

FIGURE 3-12

The Image Control

An **Image control** can be used as a container for graphical images, such as icons or bitmapped graphics files. The Image control acts like a command button, so it often is used to create custom buttons such as those found in Standard toolbars. An Image control is used to add the Loan Payment Calculator application's icon to the About... dialog box form (Figure 3-13). Perform the following steps to add an Image control to the About... dialog box form.

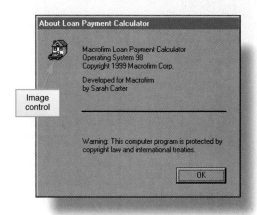

FIGURE 3-13

 Steps To Add an Image Control

1 **Double-click the Image button in the Toolbox.**

An Image control, Image1, is added to the center of the form (Figure 3-14).

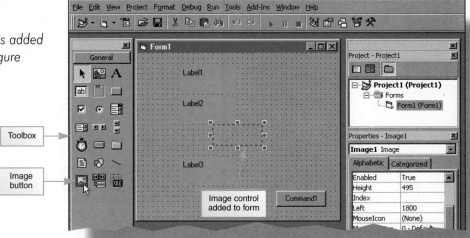

FIGURE 3-14

2 **Drag the Image control to the location shown in Figure 3-15.**

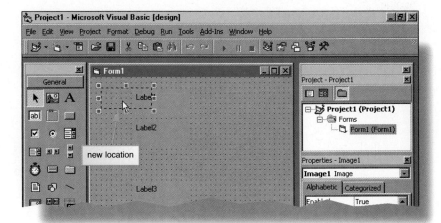

FIGURE 3-15

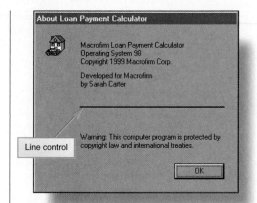

FIGURE 3-16

The Line Control

The **Line control** is used to add straight lines between pairs of points on a form. The About... dialog box form contains a Line control to separate the information on the form visually into two areas (Figure 3-16). Perform the following steps to add a Line control to the About... dialog box form.

 Steps **To Add a Line Control**

---

1 **Click the Line button in the Toolbox. Move the mouse pointer to the location where one end of the line is to display.**

The mouse pointer changes to a cross hair (Figure 3-17).

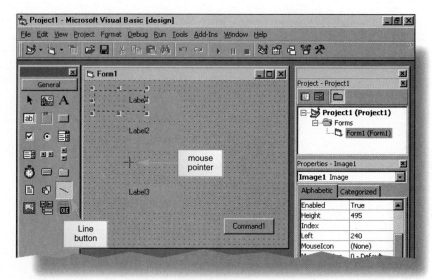

FIGURE 3-17

2 **Drag to the location where you want the other end of the line to display.**

A gray outline of the line displays as you drag the mouse pointer (Figure 3-18).

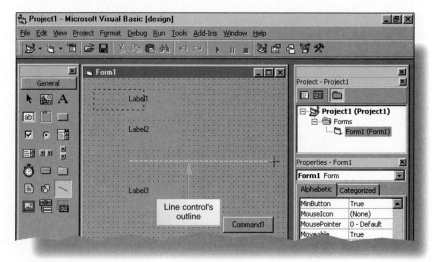

FIGURE 3-18

Release the mouse button.

A solid line replaces the gray outline (Figure 3-19).

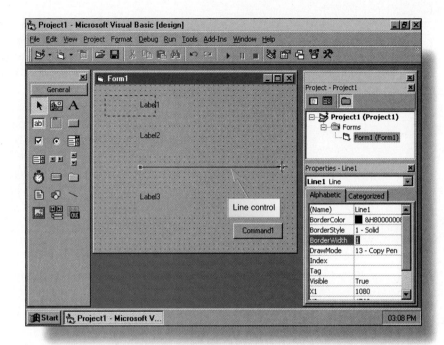

FIGURE 3-19

You can lengthen, shorten, or reposition Line controls by dragging one end at a time to the new position desired.

Setting Properties for the About... Dialog Box Form and Its Controls

The next step is to **set the properties** for the About... dialog box form and its controls. In addition to setting the Name and Caption properties presented in previous projects, the following properties will be set.

▶ WindowState property of forms
▶ BorderStyle property of forms
▶ Font properties of controls
▶ Picture property of Image controls
▶ BorderWidth property of Line controls

The WindowState Property of Forms

The **WindowState property** is a property of a form that corresponds with the window's size on the desktop during run time. The WindowState property takes one of three values, as listed in Table 3-1.

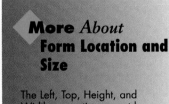

More *About*
Form Location and Size

The Left, Top, Height, and Width properties cannot be changed on a minimized or maximized form.

Table 3-1	
VALUE	*WINDOW'S SIZE*
0 - Normal	Window is open on the desktop
1 - Minimized	Window is reduced to a button on the taskbar
2 - Maximized	Window is enlarged to its maximum size

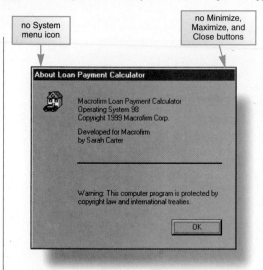

FIGURE 3-20

When the About... dialog box form displays on the desktop at run time, it has a WindowState property value of 0 - Normal (Figure 3-20). If you look closely, you will see that its WindowState property cannot be changed because it does not have a Minimize, Maximize, or Close button in the upper-right corner of the window. Also, the System menu icon is not present.

You can control the capability of making run time changes to the WindowState property by including or removing Minimize and Maximize buttons from the form. You set the values of the **MinButton property** and the **MaxButton property** of the form to True if you want to include the button or to False to exclude the button. Setting the value to False also removes the corresponding command on the System menu. Setting the form's **ControlBox property** to False removes the System menu icon and the Minimize, Maximize, and Close buttons. Perform the following steps to prevent the About... form from having its WindowState property changed during run time.

TO SET THE CONTROLBOX PROPERTY

① Click the Form object name, Form1, in the Object list box in the Properties window.

② Scroll through the Properties list until the ControlBox property is visible. Double-click the ControlBox property in the Properties list.

The new value of False displays in the Properties list (Figure 3-21).

When the ControlBox property is set to False, the form still contains a System menu icon and Minimize, Maximize, and Close buttons at design time (Figure 3-21). At run time, however, the buttons will not display on the form (Figure 3-20).

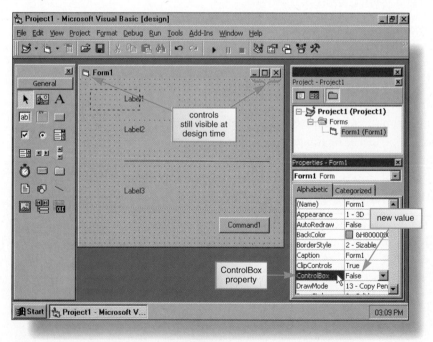

FIGURE 3-21

The BorderStyle Property of Forms

The capability of changing the size of a window at run time by dragging its borders is determined by the value of the form's BorderStyle property. The **BorderStyle property** of a form affects the form's appearance and controls. A sizable form has borders that can be dragged to new positions. A form's BorderStyle property can take one of six values and affects whether certain controls display on the form, as listed in Table 3-2.

Table 3-2						
CONTROL		BORDERSTYLE				
	0 - NONE	1 - FIXED SINGLE	2 - SIZABLE	3 - FIXED DIALOG	4 - FIXED TOOLWINDOW	5 - SIZABLE TOOLWINDOW
Minimize button	No	Optional	Optional	No	No	No
Maximize button	No	Optional	Optional	No	No	No
Control-menu box	No	Optional	Optional	Optional	Optional	Optional
Title bar	No	Optional	Optional	Optional	Optional	Optional
Sizable form	No	No	Yes	No	No	Yes

The **ShowInTaskbar property** determines whether a Form object displays on the Windows 95 taskbar. Changing the setting of the BorderStyle property of a Form object may change the settings of the MinButton, MaxButton, and ShowInTaskbar properties. When the BorderStyle property is set to 1 - Fixed Single or 2 - Sizable, the MinButton, MaxButton, and ShowInTaskbar properties are set automatically to True. When the BorderStyle property is set to 0 - None, 3 - Fixed Dialog, 4 - Fixed ToolWindow, or 5 - Sizable ToolWindow, the MinButton, MaxButton, and ShowInTaskbar properties are set automatically to False.

The About Loan Payment Calculator dialog box is typical of most dialog boxes. Generally, a dialog box's WindowState property cannot be changed, and it is not sizable. Perform the following steps to prevent the About... dialog box form from being resized during run time.

TO SET THE BORDERSTYLE PROPERTY

1. Check to be certain the Form1 form object is selected. If it is not, click its name, Form1, in the Object list box in the Properties window.
2. Scroll through the Properties list until the BorderStyle property is visible. Click the BorderStyle property to select it.
3. Click the BorderStyle property value box arrow.
4. Click 3 - Fixed Dialog in the property values list.

The new value displays in the Properties window (Figure 3-22).

FIGURE 3-22

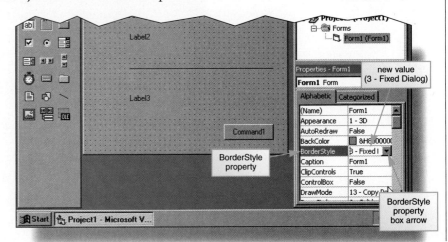

The form remains sizable at design time, no matter what the value of its BorderStyle property. At run time, however, the form displays with the selected value of the BorderStyle property.

Control Names and Captions

In Project 2, you learned that naming controls makes it easier for you to write code and makes your code easier for other people to understand. Not all of the controls in Project 2, however, were given names different from their default names. It is important to name forms, especially in projects that contain more than one form. If only one instance of a type of control is on a form, or if a control is not referred to by an event or procedure, it is not as important to have a name other than the default name Visual Basic assigns.

Perform the following steps to name the form and to assign captions to the controls on the About... dialog box form. To ensure the captions fit inside the controls, you also will set the labels' AutoSize property to True.

✓ TO SET THE NAME, CAPTION, AND AUTOSIZE PROPERTIES

1. Check to be certain the Form1 form object is selected. If not, click its name in the Object list box in the Properties window. Double-click the Name property in the Properties list.
2. Type frmLoanabt and then press the ENTER key.
3. Double-click the Caption property in the Properties list.
4. Type About Loan Payment Calculator and then press the ENTER key.
5. Click the Label1 control in the Object list box in the Properties window. Double-click the AutoSize property in the Properties list.
6. Repeat Step 5 for the Label2 control and then repeat Step 5 for the Lable3 control.
7. Click the Command1 control in the Object list box in the Properties window. Double-click the Caption property in the Properties list.
8. Type OK and then press the ENTER key.

The frmLoanabt form displays as shown in Figure 3-23.

More *About*
Control Names

Forms cannot have the same name as another public object such as Clipboard, Screen, or App. Although the Name property setting can be a keyword, property name, or the name of another object, this should be avoided because it can create conflicts in your code.

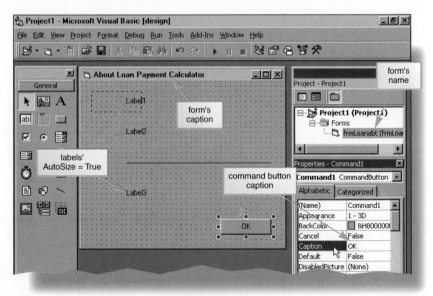

FIGURE 3-23

Font Properties

In Project 2, you changed the size of text characters on a Label control by changing the value of size in the Font dialog box. During design time, you use the **Font dialog box** to change the fonts, the font size, and/or the font style you use for text and data fields. These font characteristics also can be changed at run time through code statements. The property names you use in code statements do not match the Font dialog box directly, as shown in Table 3-3.

You may have questioned why you did not enter the captions for the labels in the previous steps. The reason is that instead of using one label for each line of text that displays in the dialog box, the dialog box uses only three labels, each with multiple lines (Figure 3-24). You will create these multiline captions with code statements later in the project.

The Font, Font Style, and Size settings all have an effect on the size of the text that displays on a control. Although you set a label's AutoSize property value to True, the form does not have a similar property. The selection of a large font size for the Label controls would cause characters to extend beyond the right border of the form where they would not display. Perform the following steps to set the Font properties for the labels in the About... dialog box.

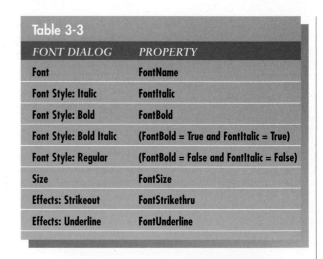

Table 3-3	
FONT DIALOG	*PROPERTY*
Font	**FontName**
Font Style: Italic	**FontItalic**
Font Style: Bold	**FontBold**
Font Style: Bold Italic	**(FontBold = True and FontItalic = True)**
Font Style: Regular	**(FontBold = False and FontItalic = False)**
Size	**FontSize**
Effects: Strikeout	**FontStrikethru**
Effects: Underline	**FontUnderline**

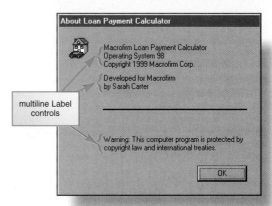

FIGURE 3-24

TO SET THE FONT PROPERTIES

1 Click the Label1 control in the Object list box in the Properties window.

2 Double-click Font in the Properties list to open the Font dialog box (Figure 3-25).

3 Click MS Sans Serif in the Font list box.

4 Click Regular in the Font style list box.

5 Click 8 in the Size list box.

6 Click the OK button in the Font dialog box.

7 Click the Label2 control and repeat Step 2 through Step 6.

8 Click the Label3 control and repeat Step 2 through Step 6.

The Font dialog box for the Label controls displays as shown in Figure 3-25.

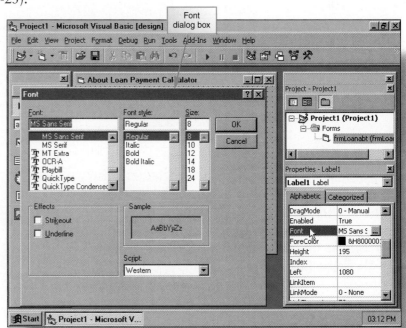

FIGURE 3-25

The list of available fonts (Step 3) depends on which fonts have been installed in your copy of Windows. Style and Effects properties can be used alone or in combination. For example, setting the value of the Font style to Bold and clicking Underline in the Effects area will display the selected font in bold and underlined.

The Picture Property of Image Controls

You can add graphics to forms and certain controls at design time by setting the control's **Picture property** in the Properties window. The graphic image used on the frmLoanabt form comes from the set of icon files with the **.ico extension** supplied as part of the Visual Basic system. It also is available on the Data Disk that accompanies this book. When a form containing graphical data (such as an icon or picture) is saved, Visual Basic automatically creates an additional file with the same file name as the form but with an **.frx extension**.

Perform the following steps to add an icon to the Image1 control.

 Steps To Add a Graphic to an Image Control

1 **Click the Image1 control in the Object list box in the Properties window. Double-click the Picture property in the Properties list.**

The Load Picture dialog box displays (Figure 3-26). The Load Picture dialog box is similar to other common dialog boxes used in Windows applications.

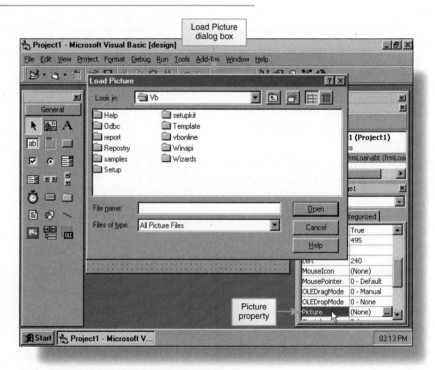

FIGURE 3-26

2 **If necessary, insert the Data Disk that accompanies this book in drive A. Click the Look in box arrow. If necessary, scroll through the list, and then point to 3½ Floppy [A:] (Figure 3-27).**

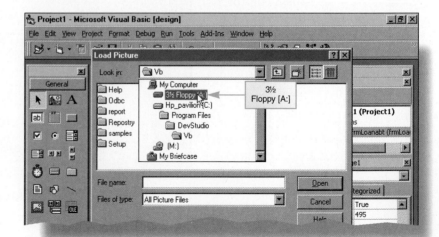

FIGURE 3-27

3 **Click 3½ Floppy [A:] and then point to the House.ico file name.**

All files in the selected folder with any of the eight picture file types that Visual Basic supports display in the list (Figure 3-28).

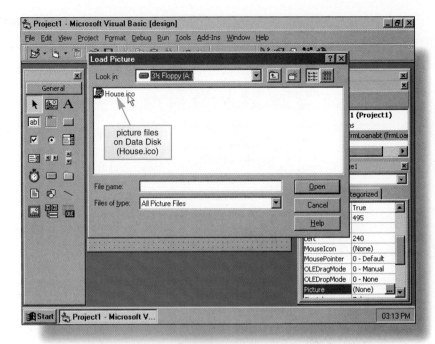

FIGURE 3-28

4 **Double-click House.ico.**

Visual Basic loads the house icon into the Image control located in the upper-left corner of the About... dialog box form (Figure 3-29).

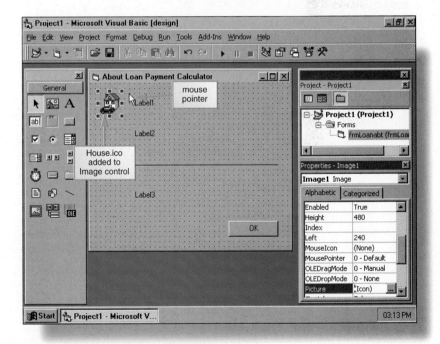

FIGURE 3-29

When Visual Basic loaded the icon, the size of the Image control was adjusted automatically to the size of its contents (the house icon). This automatic sizing occurred because the default value of the Image control's Stretch property is False. If you set the Stretch property of the Image control to True, Visual Basic does not adjust the Image control's size automatically.

Table 3-4

VALUE	DESCRIPTION
0	Transparent
1	(Default) Solid - Border is centered on the edge of the shape
2	Dash
3	Dot
4	Dash-Dot
5	Dash-Dot-Dot
6	Inside Solid - Outer edge of the border is the outer edge of the shape

BorderStyle and BorderWidth Properties of Line Controls

The next step is to change the appearance of the horizontal line that runs across the center of the About... dialog box form. The **BorderStyle property** of the Line control determines the appearance of the line, such as solid or dashed. The seven possible values of the BorderStyle property for the Line control are listed in Table 3-4.

The BorderStyle property of the line on the frmLoanabt form is Solid, which is the default value (Figure 3-30).

The **BorderWidth property** is used to set the width of the line. The values of the BorderWidth property are integers from 1 to 8,192. The line on the frmLoanabt form is wider than the default width of 1 (Figure 3-30). Perform the following steps to change the width of the Line control located on the frmLoanabt form.

TO SET THE BORDERWIDTH PROPERTY OF THE LINE CONTROL

1️⃣ Click the Line1 control in the Object list box in the Properties window.

2️⃣ Double-click the BorderWidth property in the Properties list.

3️⃣ Type 2 and then press the ENTER key.

The Line control displays as shown in Figure 3-31.

FIGURE 3-30

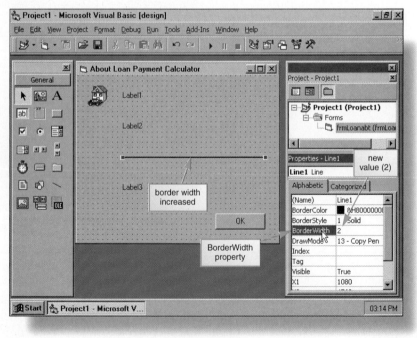

FIGURE 3-31

If the BorderWidth property is set to a value greater than 1, the only effective settings of the BorderStyle property are 1 - Solid and 6 - Inside Solid.

Saving the Form

The frmLoanabt form now is complete. Before proceeding with building the second form in the project, save the form. Perform the following steps to save the form on the Data Disk in drive A.

 Steps To Save a Form File

1 **Click File on the menu bar and then point to Save frmLoanabt As.**

The form's name is listed on the File menu (Figure 3-32).

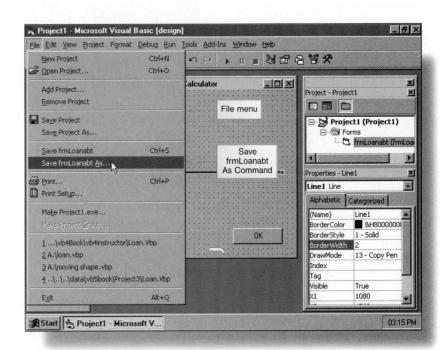

FIGURE 3-32

2 **Click Save frmLoanabt As.**

The Save File As dialog box displays, and the form's name displays in the File name text box (Figure 3-33).

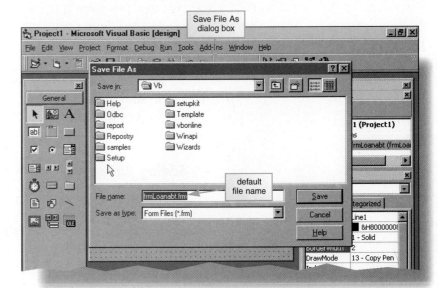

FIGURE 3-33

3 **Type** Loanabt **as the file name. Click the Save in box arrow. If necessary, scroll through the list and then click 3½ Floppy [A:]. Click the Save button in the Save File As dialog box.**

The form is saved as a file on the floppy disk, and the dialog box closes. The form's file name is shown following the form's name in the Project window (Figure 3-34).

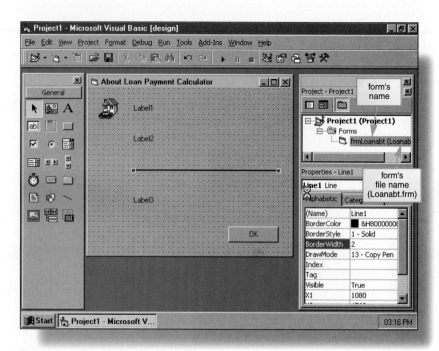

FIGURE 3-34

Because form files automatically have the .frm extension added when you save them, the frm prefix in the form's name was not included in the file name. You can save a file with any name, and the file name can be different from Visual Basic's value of the Name property of the form.

The Loan Payment Calculator Form and Its Controls

The second form in this project is the Loan Payment Calculator form shown in Figure 3-35. Because this form is the second one in the project, you must add a new form. You will build the Loan Payment Calculator form following this sequence of activities.

1. Add a new form to the project.
2. Set the size of the form.
3. Add the controls.
4. Set the properties of the form and its controls.
5. Save the form as a file on a floppy disk.

Adding Additional Forms to the Project

You can have multiple Form windows open on the desktop at the same time. It reduces confusion, however, if you minimize the windows of forms you currently are not using. Perform the following steps to minimize the About... dialog box form (frmLoanabt) and to add a new form to the project.

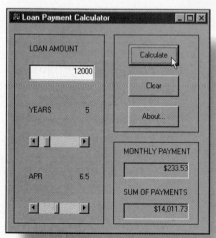

FIGURE 3-35

TO ADD A NEW FORM

① Click the About... dialog box form's (frmLoanabt's) Minimize button.

② Click the Add Form button on the Standard toolbar.

③ Double–click the Form icon on the New tab sheet in the Add Form dialog box.

The About... dialog box form's (frmLoanabt's) window is reduced to a button on the lower-left corner of the desktop. A new form with the default name, Form1, is added to the project, and its window opens on the desktop (Figure 3-36).

Setting the Form Size and Position

The form's current position is acceptable for both design time and run time. Perform the following steps to change the size of the Loan Payment Calculator form by directly changing the values of the Height and Width properties in the Properties window, using the same procedure you used for the About... dialog box form.

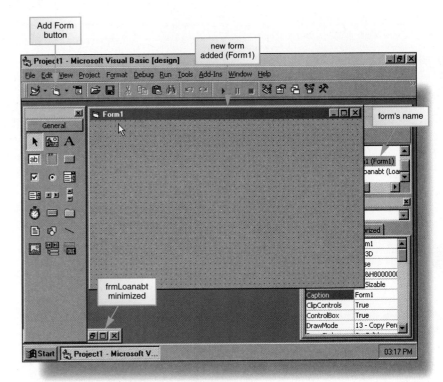

FIGURE 3-36

TO SET THE SIZE OF THE FORM USING THE PROPERTIES WINDOW

① Click the Properties window to make it the active window.

② Scroll through the Properties list, and then double-click the Height property. Type 5265 and then press the ENTER key.

③ Scroll through the Properties list and double-click the Width property. Type 4900 and then press the ENTER key.

The form (Form1) displays as shown in Figure 3-37.

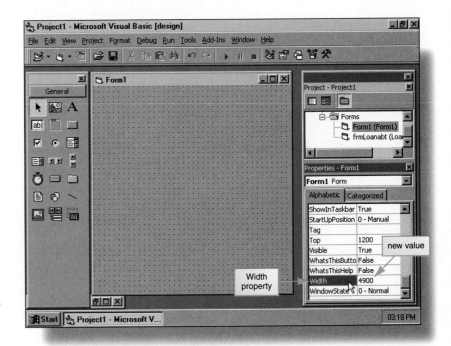

FIGURE 3-37

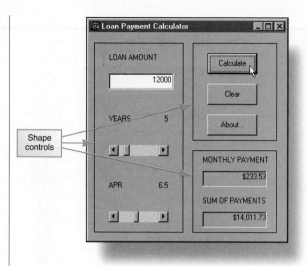

FIGURE 3-38

Adding Shape Controls

The Loan Payment Calculator form has three Shape controls, as shown in Figure 3-38. These controls are not functional within the application because no events or code statements are associated with them. They do serve an important purpose, however.

Shape controls are used in the Loan Payment Calculator application to group related controls on the form visually. All the controls within the shape on the left of the form are related to the **inputs**, or data, needed by the application to carry out its function. The shape on the bottom right of the form groups all of the controls related to the results of the application's function, called **outputs**. The shape located on the top right contains controls used to initiate different actions within the application. Perform the following steps to add three Shape controls to the form.

Steps **To Add Shape Controls**

① **Click the Shape button in the Toolbox, and then move the mouse to the location where the top-left corner of the shape will display.**

The Shape button is recessed in the Toolbox. The mouse pointer changes to a cross hair (Figure 3-39).

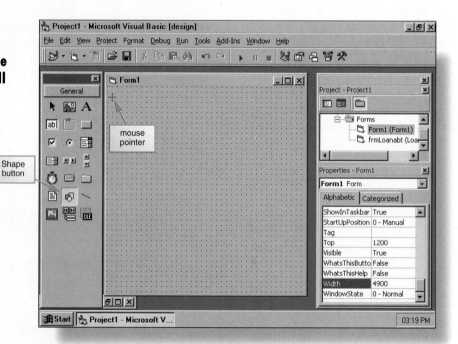

FIGURE 3-39

2 **Drag down and to the right as shown in Figure 3-40. Release the mouse button.**

As you drag the mouse, a gray outline of the control displays on the form. When you release the mouse button, the Shape control is drawn in the position of the outline (Figure 3-40).

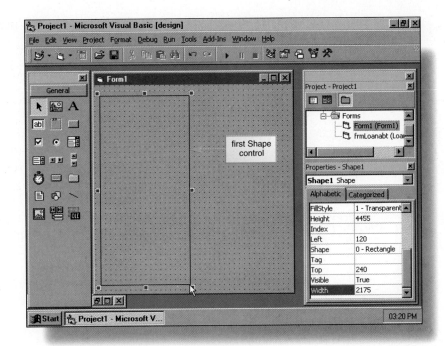

FIGURE 3-40

3 **Repeat Step 1 and Step 2 to draw a second Shape control (Figure 3-41).**

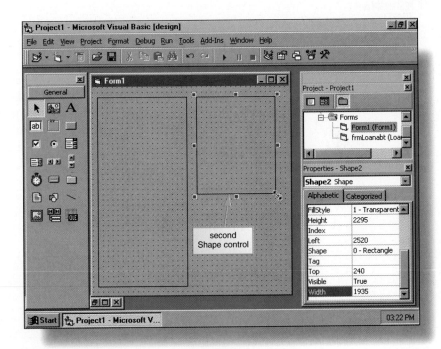

FIGURE 3-41

4 **Repeat Step 1 and Step 2 to draw a third Shape control (Figure 3-42).**

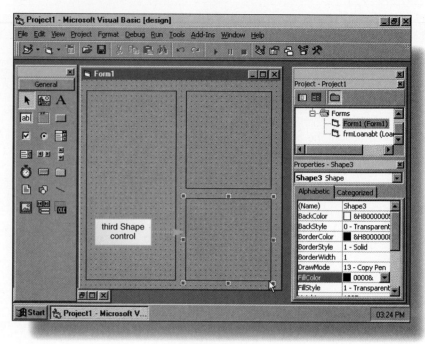

FIGURE 3-42

Adding and Copying Label Controls

The Loan Payment Calculator form contains nine labels, as identified in Figure 3-43. The two labels used to display the outputs of the loan calculation have borders around them. At run time, their contents (captions) are blank until you click the Calculate button. The reason for displaying the outputs in this way is that an empty box visually communicates *something goes here*. The labels above the boxes communicate what that *something* is.

In Project 2, you learned how to copy controls using the mouse and the Edit menu. In the following example, controls are copied using the keyboard. Perform the following steps to add the seven borderless labels and then to add the two labels with borders.

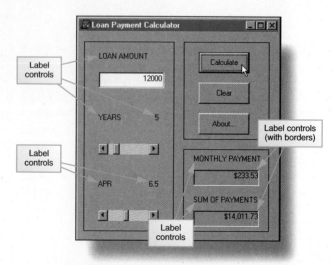

FIGURE 3-43

Steps To Add Borderless Label Controls

1 Add a default-sized Label control to the center of the form by double-clicking the Label button in the Toolbox. Drag the control to the position shown in Figure 3-44.

2 Set the label's AutoSize property value to True by double-clicking the AutoSize property in the Properties window.

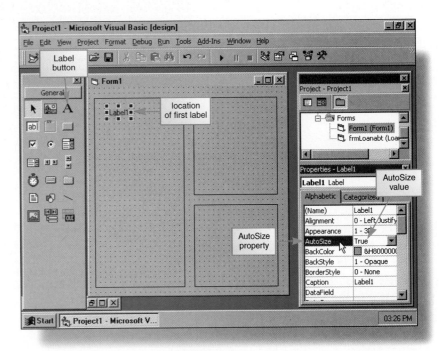

FIGURE 3-44

3 Click the Label control. Press the CTRL+C keys. Press the CTRL+V keys. Click the No button in the Microsoft Visual Basic dialog box.

An additional Label control with its AutoSize property value set to True displays on the form. When you copy a control, all of its property values also are copied. Thus, the second Label control has the caption Label1 (Figure 3-45).

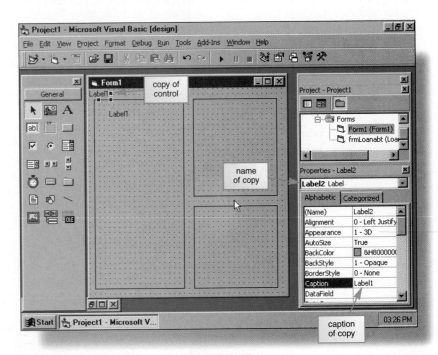

FIGURE 3-45

4 Drag the label to the position shown in Figure 3-46.

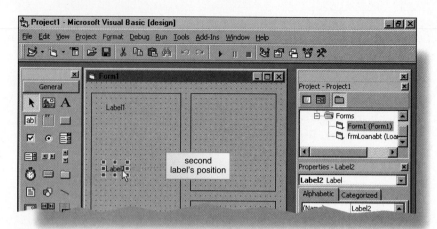

FIGURE 3-46

5 Click a blank area of the form. Press the CTRL+V keys. Click the No button in the Microsoft Visual Basic dialog box. Drag the control to the position shown in Figure 3-47.

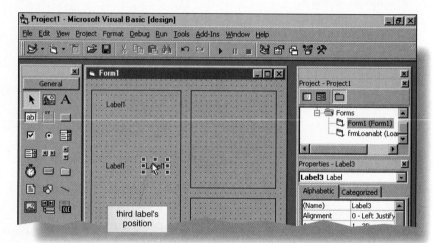

FIGURE 3-47

6 Repeat Step 5 four times to add the remaining labels in the positions shown in Figure 3-48. Be careful to position the labels in the order shown.

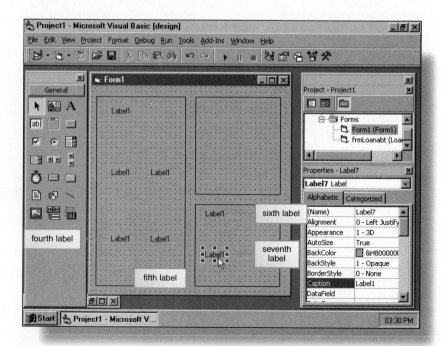

FIGURE 3-48

Pressing the CTRL+C keys copies the selected control to the Clipboard. Pressing the CTRL+V keys pastes the control from the Clipboard to the form. Seven similar labels have been added to the form. Perform the following steps to add the remaining two labels used to contain the application's outputs.

Steps **To Add Additional Label Controls**

1 **Double-click the Label button in the Toolbox and then drag the control to the position shown in Figure 3-49. Double-click the BorderStyle property in the Properties window.**

The label is positioned as shown in Figure 3-49 and the label's BorderStyle property value changes from 0 - No Border to 1 - Fixed Single.

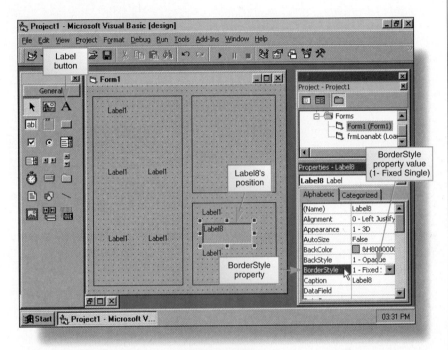

FIGURE 3-49

2 **Drag the Label8 control's lower-right sizing handle up and to the right, as shown in Figure 3-50.**

The new size is shown in a gray shaded line (Figure 3-50).

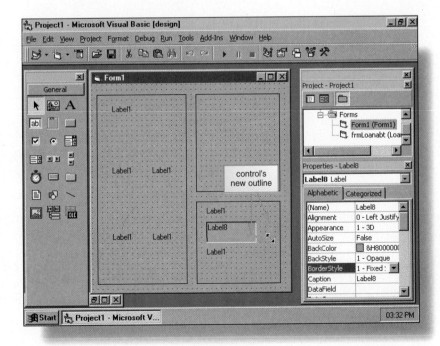

FIGURE 3-50

3 **Release the mouse button. Click the Label8 control. Press the CTRL+C keys. Press the CTRL+V keys. Click the No button in the Microsoft Visual Basic dialog box.**

An identically sized Label control with its BorderStyle property value set to 1 displays on the form (Figure 3-51).

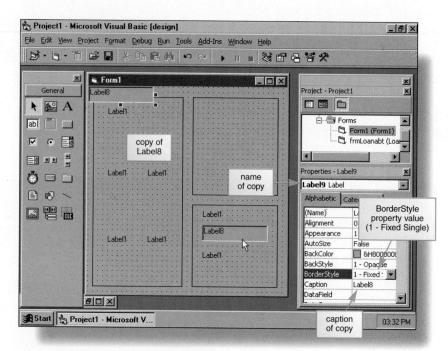

FIGURE 3-51

4 **Drag the label to the position shown in Figure 3-52.**

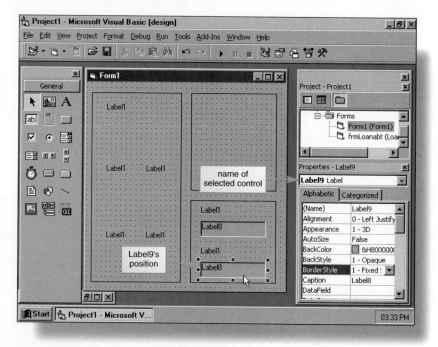

FIGURE 3-52

All of the Label controls now have been added to the form. Compare the positions and appearance of the Label controls in Figure 3-52 to the completed form shown in Figure 3-53. Generally, all of the form's controls are added before setting properties. In the preceding example, you set the AutoSize and BorderStyle properties immediately so you could take advantage of copying property values when copying a control.

Copying the labels with the property values already set will save you time because you will not have to set each label's AutoSize or BorderStyle property when you set the rest of the properties later. By copying the first output label (Label8), you did not have to draw or resize the second output label (Label9) to match the size of the first.

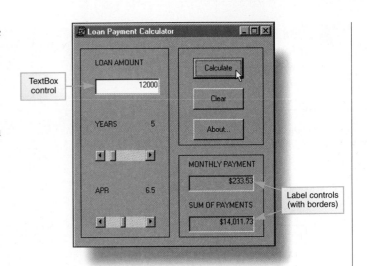

FIGURE 3-53

Adding the TextBox Control

The Loan Payment Calculator form contains one TextBox control, which is used at run time to accept the loan amount (Figure 3-53). You use a **TextBox control** to enter the loan amount instead of a label because a label's contents can be changed during run time only with a code statement.

Perform the following steps to add the TextBox control to the form.

Steps To Add a TextBox Control

① **Double-click the TextBox button in the Toolbox and then drag the control to the position shown in Figure 3-54.**

A default-sized text box is added to the form.

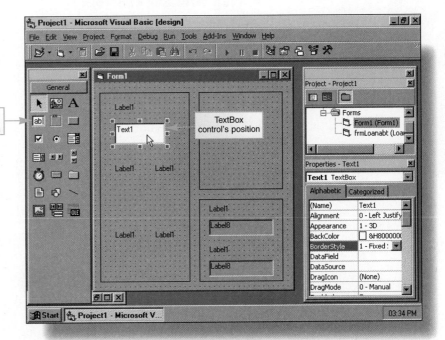

FIGURE 3-54

2 **Drag the control's lower-right sizing handle up and to the right to resize the control as shown in Figure 3-55.**

Dragging the lower-right sizing handle up and to the right decreases the control's height and increases its width (Figure 3-55).

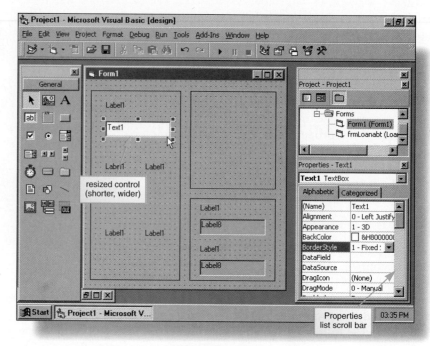

FIGURE 3-55

Adding ScrollBar Controls

More *About*
ScrollBar Controls

When you use a scroll bar as an indicator of quantity or as an input device, you use the Max and Min properties to set the appropriate range for the control. This range can be any integer values between -32,768 and 32,767.

Scroll bars commonly are used to view the contents of a control when the contents cannot fit within the control's borders. An example is the Properties list scroll bar in the Properties window. Visual Basic has two different ScrollBar controls; the horizontal ScrollBar (HScrollBar) control and the vertical ScrollBar (VScrollBar) control. Their names reflect the orientation of the control on the form, not its use. You control its use. For example, you can use a vertical scroll bar to control the horizontal scrolling of a control on a form.

Another use of the ScrollBar control is to give a value to an input. One benefit of using a ScrollBar control for input is that it prevents you from entering an improper value by mistake, such as a letter instead of a number. The two horizontal ScrollBar controls shown in Figure 3-56 are used as input controls for the number of years of the loan and for the annual interest rate.

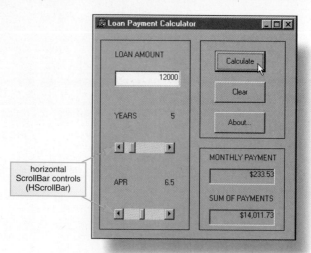

FIGURE 3-56

Perform the following steps to add the two ScrollBar controls.

 Steps To Add ScrollBar Controls

1 **Double-click the HScrollBar button in the Toolbox. Extend the HScrollBar control's width by dragging its sizing handle the distance of two grid marks on the form. Drag the HScrollBar control to the position shown in Figure 3-57.**

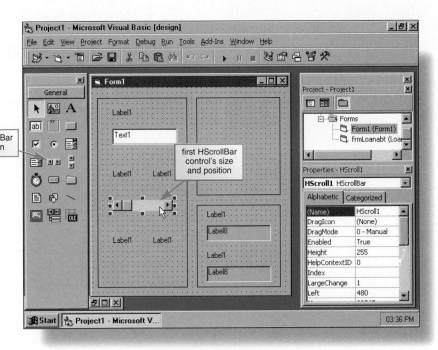

FIGURE 3-57

2 **Double-click the HScrollBar button in the Toolbox. Extend the new HScrollBar control's width by dragging its sizing handle the distance of two grid marks on the form. Drag the HScrollBar control to the position shown in Figure 3-58.**

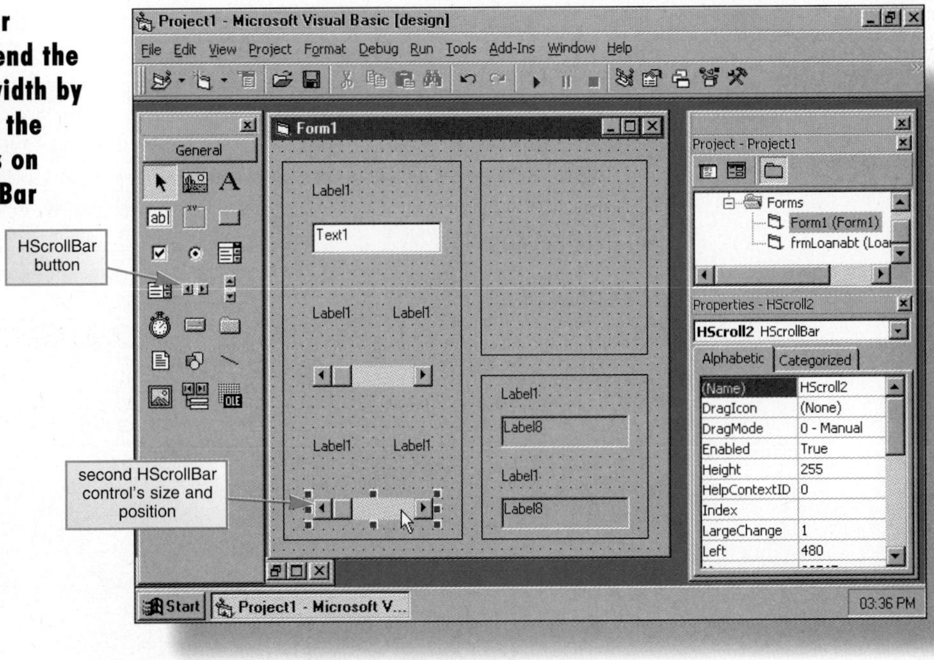

FIGURE 3-58

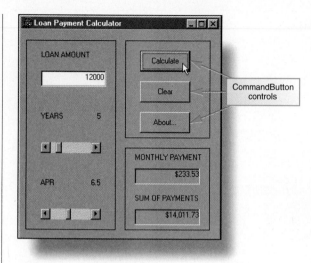

FIGURE 3-59

In the Loan Payment Calculator application, the caption of the label located above the right end of the scroll bar is used to display the current value of the input controlled by that scroll bar. When you click a scroll arrow or drag the scroll box, the scroll bar's **Change event** is triggered. A code statement will be written later in this project that will link the caption of the label to the Change event.

Adding CommandButton Controls

The last three controls to be added to the Loan Payment Calculator form are the three command buttons identified in Figure 3-59.

The command buttons used in this application are the default size, so you can add them to the form by using the double-click method instead of drawing them.

TO ADD COMMANDBUTTON CONTROLS

1. Double-click the CommandButton button in the Toolbox. Drag the Command1 command button inside and to the top of the Shape control in the upper right of the Form window.
2. Double-click the CommandButton button in the Toolbox. Drag the Command2 command button inside and to the center of the Shape control in the upper right of the Form window.
3. Double-click the CommandButton button in the Toolbox. Drag the Command3 command button inside and to the bottom of the Shape control in the upper right of the Form window.

The command buttons display as shown in Figure 3-60.

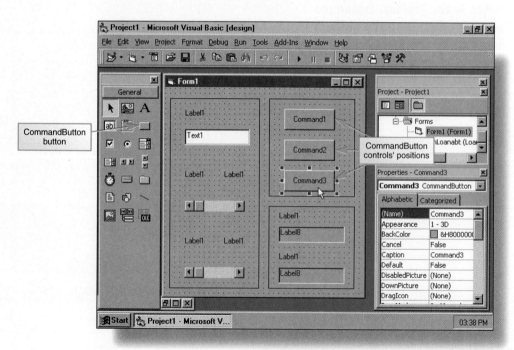

FIGURE 3-60

You now have completed the design of the Loan Payment Calculator form. The next step in the development process is to set the properties for the form and its controls.

Setting Properties of the Loan Payment Calculator Form and Its Controls

In addition to setting the Caption and Name properties of the controls on the Loan Payment Calculator form, you will set the following properties.

▶ Alignment property of text boxes and labels
▶ Min and Max properties of ScrollBar controls
▶ SmallChange and LargeChange properties of ScrollBar controls
▶ Icon property of forms

Setting the Alignment Property of TextBox and Label Controls

The **Alignment property** specifies where the caption will display within the borders of a control, regardless of whether the borders are visible. The values of the Alignment property are listed in Table 3-5.

The default value of the Alignment property is left-justified. Because the values display in the Properties list in the same order as in Table 3-5, you can change from left-justify to right-justify by double-clicking the Alignment property in the Properties list instead of selecting the property values list and then clicking 1 - Right Justify. The five controls with right-justified alignment are identified in Figure 3-61.

The TextBox control is among the five right-justified controls. To change a text box's alignment, the value of its MultiLine property must be equal to True. Perform the following steps to set the Alignment property.

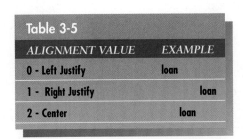

Table 3-5

ALIGNMENT VALUE	EXAMPLE
0 - Left Justify	loan
1 - Right Justify	loan
2 - Center	loan

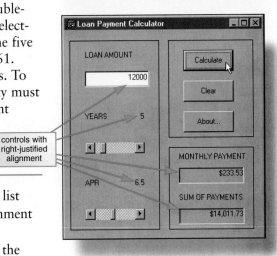

controls with right-justified alignment

FIGURE 3-61

TO SET THE ALIGNMENT PROPERTY

1. Click the Text1 control on the form or in the Object list box in the Properties window. Double-click the Alignment property.
2. Scroll down the Properties list and then double-click the MultiLine property in the Properties list.
3. Click the Label3 control in the Object list box in the Properties window. Double-click the Alignment property.
4. Click the Label5 control in the Object list box in the Properties window. Double-click the Alignment property.
5. Click the Label8 control on the form or in the Object list box in the Properties window. Double-click the Alignment property.
6. Click the Label9 control on the form or in the Object list box in the Properties window. Double-click the Alignment property.

The form displays as shown in Figure 3-62a on the next page.

Setting the Caption and Text Properties

Figure 3-62a shows the Loan Payment Calculator form as it displays in the current stage of development and Figure 3-62b shows how it will display when completed. The differences between these two figures relate to the Caption property of the Form, Label, and CommandButton controls and to the Text property of the one TextBox control. At run time, the text box should start out empty. This text box is made empty by setting the initial value of its Text property to be blank. Perform the following steps to set the Caption property and Text property.

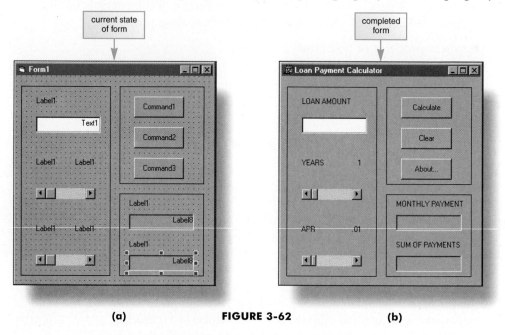

FIGURE 3-62

(a)   (b)

TO SET THE CONTROLS' CAPTION AND TEXT PROPERTIES

1. Click the Form1 form control in the Object list box in the Properties window. Double-click the Caption property in the Properties list. Type Loan Payment Calculator and then press the ENTER key.

2. Click the Label1 control in the Object list box in the Properties window. Double-click the Caption property. Type LOAN AMOUNT and then press the ENTER key.

3. Click the Text1 control in the Object list box in the Properties window. Double-click the Text property. Drag the insertion point over the text to highlight it. Press the DELETE key.

4. Click the Label2 control in the Object list box in the Properties window. Double-click the Caption property. Type YEARS and then press the ENTER key.

5. Click the Label3 control in the Object list box in the Properties window. Double-click the Caption property. Type 1 and then press the ENTER key.

6. Click the Label4 control in the Object list box in the Properties window. Double-click the Caption property. Type APR and then press the ENTER key.

7 Click the Label5 control in the Object list box in the Properties window. Double-click the Caption property. Type .01 and then press the ENTER key.

8 Click the Label6 control in the Object list box in the Properties window. Double-click the Caption property. Type MONTHLY PAYMENT and then press the ENTER key.

9 Click the Label7 control in the Object list box in the Properties window. Double-click the Caption property. Type SUM OF PAYMENTS and then press the ENTER key.

10 Click the Label8 control in the Object list box in the Properties window. Double-click the Caption property. Press the DELETE key.

11 Click the Label9 control in the Object list box in the Properties window. Double-click the Caption property. Press the DELETE key.

12 Click the Command1 control in the Object list box in the Properties window. Double-click the Caption property. Type Calculate and then press the ENTER key.

13 Click the Command2 control in the Object list box in the Properties window. Double-click the Caption property. Type Clear and then press the ENTER key.

14 Click the Command3 control in the Object list box in the Properties window. Double-click the Caption property. Type About... and then press the ENTER key.

The Loan Payment Calculator form displays as shown in Figure 3-63.

> **More** *About* **Command Button Captions**
>
> You can use the Caption property to assign an access key to a CommandButton control. In the caption, include an ampersand (&) immediately preceding the character you want to designate as an access key. The character is underlined. During run time, you can press the ALT key plus the underlined character to execute the command button's Click event.

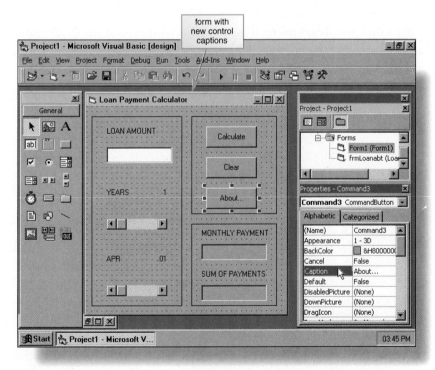

FIGURE 3-63

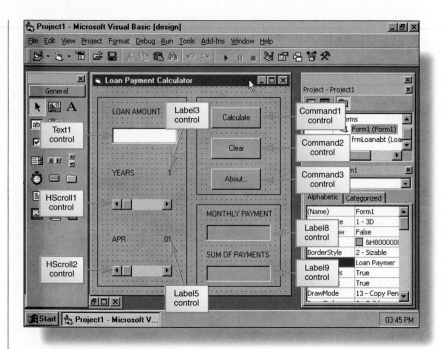

FIGURE 3-64

Naming the Controls

In addition to the form control itself, four labels, two scroll bars, three command buttons, and one text box on the Loan Payment Calculator form will be referred to in the events and code statements that you will write later. These controls, with their current (default) names, are shown in Figure 3-64. It would be confusing to write events and code statements using the default names of these controls. Perform the following steps to rename the controls that will be referred to in code statements.

TO NAME CONTROLS

1. Click the Form1 control in the Object list box in the Properties window. Double-click the Name property. Type the control name frmLoanpmt and then press the ENTER key.

2. Click the Text1 control in the Object list box in the Properties window. Double-click the Name property. Type txtAmount as the control name and then press the ENTER key.

3. Click the Label3 control in the Object list box in the Properties window. Double-click the Name property in the Properties list. Type lblYears as the control name and then press the ENTER key.

4. Click the HScroll1 control in the Object list box in the Properties window. Double-click the Name property in the Properties list. Type hsbYears as the control name and then press the ENTER key.

5. Click the Label5 control in the Object list box in the Properties window. Double-click the Name property in the Properties list. Type lblRate as the control name and then press the ENTER key.

6. Click the HScroll2 control in the Object list box in the Properties window. Double-click the Name property. Type hsbRate and then press the ENTER key.

7. Click the Label8 control in the Object list box in the Properties window. Double-click the Name property. Type lblPayment as the control name and then press the ENTER key.

8. Click the Label9 control in the Object list box in the Properties window. Double-click the Name property. Type lblSumpmts as the control name and then press the ENTER key.

9. Click the Command1 control in the Object list box in the Properties window. Double-click the Name property. Type cmdCalculate as the control name and then press the ENTER key.

10 Click the Command2 control in the Object list box in the Properties window. Double-click the Name property. Type cmdClear as the control name and then press the ENTER key.

11 Click the Command3 control in the Object list box in the Properties window. Double-click the Name property. Type cmdAbout as the control name and then press the ENTER key.

12 Click the Object box arrow to display the Object list of controls with their new names.

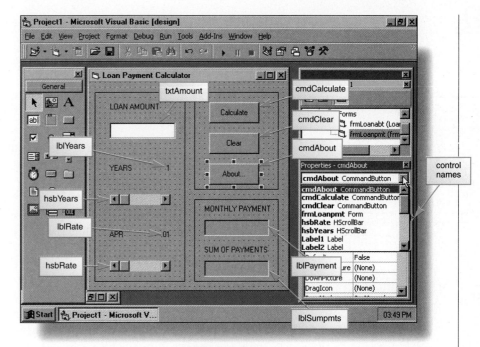

FIGURE 3-65

The controls are identified by their new names as shown in Figure 3-65.

Setting the Scroll Bar Properties

The **Value property** of a scroll bar is an integer number that changes in relation to the position of the scroll box within the scroll bar. The lowest and highest numbers that the Value property can take are set with the **Min property** and **Max property** of the scroll bar. In a horizontal ScrollBar control, these values correspond to the farthest left and farthest right positions of the scroll box.

The amount that the value changes each time you click one of the scroll arrows is set by the **SmallChange property** of the scroll bar. The amount that the value changes by clicking the area between the scroll box and one of the two scroll arrows is set with the **LargeChange property** of the scroll bar. Perform the following steps to set the properties of the ScrollBar controls.

TO SET THE SCROLL BARS PROPERTIES

1 Click the YEARS scroll bar on the form or its name, hsbYears, in the Object list box in the Properties window.

2 Double-click the Max property in the Properties list. Type 30 and then press the ENTER key.

3 Double-click the Min property in the Properties list. Type 1 and then press the ENTER key.

4 Double-click the LargeChange property in the Properties list. Type 5 and then press the ENTER key.

5 Click the APR scroll bar on the form or its name, hsbRate, in the Object list box in the Properties window.

6 Double-click the Max property in the Properties list. Type 1500 and then press the ENTER key.

⑦ Double-click the Min property in the Properties list. Type 1 and then press the ENTER key.

⑧ Double-click the LargeChange property in the Properties list. Type 10 and then press the ENTER key.

The new values of these properties are visible by scrolling through the Properties list.

The preceding steps set properties of the scroll bars so the value of the scroll bar used to set years (hsbYears) will range from 1 to 30 and the value of the scroll bar used to set the APR (hsbRate) will range from 1 to 1500. It was not necessary to set the SmallChange property because its default value is 1. The caption of the label (lblYears), located above the scroll bar at the right end, will be the value of the scroll bar hsbYears, representing the number of years to repay the loan (from 1 to 30).

The annual interest rate displayed as the caption of the label (lblRate), located above the lower scroll bar (hsbRate), will work differently. Percentage rates on loans usually are expressed as a one- or two-digit number followed by a decimal point and a two-digit decimal fraction, such as 12.25 percent or 6.30 percent. Because the value of a scroll bar cannot include a fraction, you will multiply the value of the scroll bar hsbRate by .01 to get the value of the caption of the label (lblRate), located above the scroll bar.

For example, a scroll bar value of 678 will represent an APR of 6.78 percent, and a scroll bar value of 1250 will represent an APR of 12.50 percent. Multiplying a scroll bar value by a decimal is a common way to make scroll bars capable of representing numbers with fractional parts. You set the range of the APR scroll bar (hsbRate) values from 1 to 1500 so it can be used as described above to represent .01 to 15.00 percent.

The Icon Property of Forms

When a window is minimized, it displays on the taskbar as a button with a small graphical image called an **icon**. You can specify the graphical image used to represent the form by setting the form's **Icon property**. Perform the following steps to select an icon for the Loanpmt form.

More *About*
Form Icons

You can see a form's icon in Windows 95 in the upper-left corner of the form when the form's WindowState property either is normal or maximized. If the form is minimized, the BorderStyle property must be set either to 1 - Fixed Single or 2 - Sizable, and the MinButton property must be set to True for the icon to be visible.

Steps **To Set a Form's Icon Property**

① **Click an empty area of the Loanpmt form. Scroll through the Properties list and point to the Icon property (Figure 3-66).**

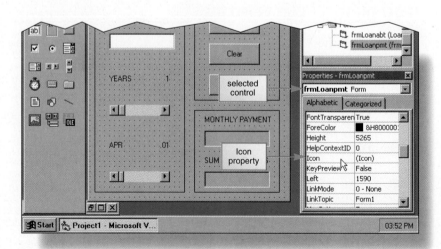

FIGURE 3-66

2 **Double-click the Icon property in the Properties list.**

The Load Icon dialog box displays (Figure 3-67).

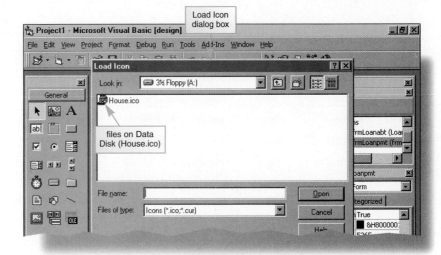

FIGURE 3-67

3 **Double-click House.ico in the File list box.**

The Load Icon dialog box closes, and the icon is added to the form (Figure 3-68).

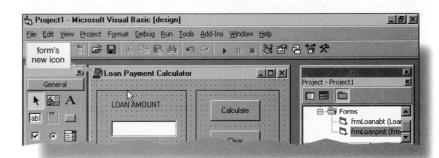

FIGURE 3-68

Saving the Form

The frmLoanpmt form now is complete. Before proceeding, you should save the form. Complete the following steps to save the Loanpmt form on the Data Disk in drive A.

TO SAVE THE FORM

1 Click File on the menu bar and then click Save frmLoanpmt As.

2 Type Loanpmt in the File name text box. If necessary, click 3½ Floppy [A:] in the Save in list box, and then click the Save button in the Save File As dialog box.

3 Minimize the frmLoanpmt window by clicking the Form window's Minimize button.

The frmLoanpmt's name displays in the Project window, followed by its file name (Figure 3-69).

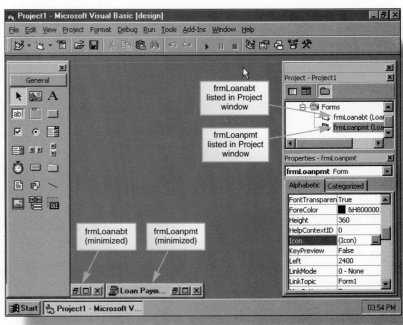

FIGURE 3-69

Table 3-6

FORM	CONTROL	EVENT	ACTIONS
frmLoanpmt	hsbYears	Change	Update caption of lblYears
frmLoanpmt	hsbYears	Scroll	Update caption of lblYears
frmLoanpmt	hsbRate	Change	Update caption of lblRate
frmLoanpmt	hsbRate	Scroll	Update caption of lblRate
frmLoanpmt	cmdCalculate	Click	Perform monthly payment and sum of payment calculations, and display results in lblPayment and lblSumpmts
frmLoanpmt	cmdClear	Click	Clear the contents of txtAmount, lblPayment, and lblSumpmts; reset hsbYears and hsbRate to lowest values
frmLoanpmt	cmdAbout	Click	Add About... dialog box to desktop
frmLoanabt	Form	Load	Set captions of labels
frmLoanabt	Command1	Click	Remove About... dialog box from desktop

 **W**riting Code

Event procedures (subroutines) must be written for nine events in the Loan Payment Calculator application. These events and their actions are listed in Table 3-6.

The code for the Loan Payment Calculator application will be written one event at a time using the Visual Basic Code window in the same manner as in Project 1 and Project 2. In a project that has more than one form, however, each form has its own Code window. Before writing the subroutines, a Startup form for the project will be specified.

The Startup Form

At run time, the **Startup form** is the first form in a project loaded into the computer's memory and added to the desktop. By default, the Startup form is the first form you create in a project. The Loan Payment Calculator application should begin by displaying the frmLoanpmt form on the desktop. Because frmLoanpmt was not the first form created, it must be specified as the Startup form. Perform the following steps to make frmLoanpmt the Startup form.

 Steps To Set a Startup Form

1 **Click Project on the menu bar and then point to Project 1 Properties.**

The Project menu displays (Figure 3-70).

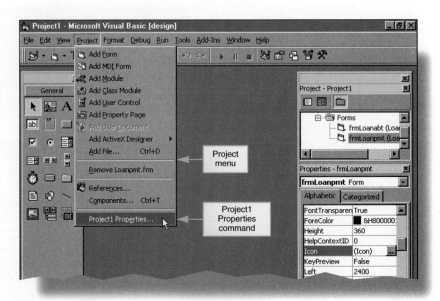

FIGURE 3-70

2 Click Project1 Properties. Click the General tab in the Project1 - Project Properties dialog box.

The Project1 - Project Properties dialog box displays (Figure 3-71).

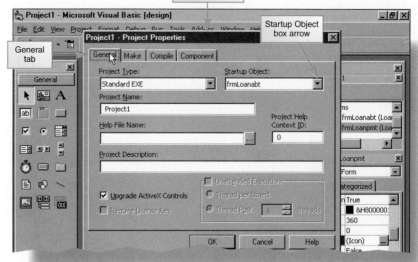

FIGURE 3-71

3 Click the Startup Object box arrow and then point to frmLoanpmt.

The Startup Object list box displays with possible values (Figure 3-72).

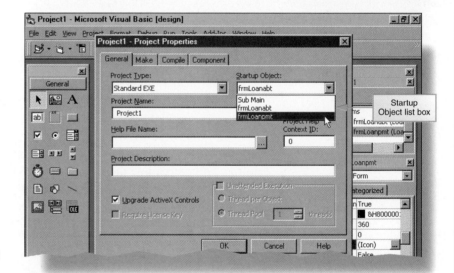

FIGURE 3-72

4 Click frmLoanpmt in the list and then point to the OK button.

frmLoanpmt is now the Startup form (Figure 3-73).

5 Click the OK button.

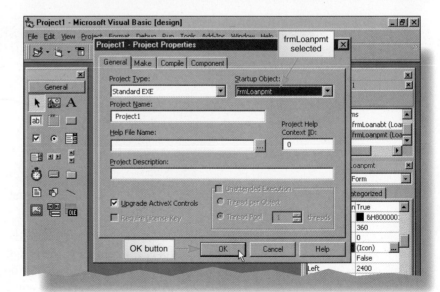

FIGURE 3-73

In Project 1 and Project 2, a Startup form was not specified explicitly because when a project consists of a single form (as those projects did), the form automatically is set as the Startup form.

The frmLoanpmt hsbYears_Change and Scroll Events

A ScrollBar control's **Change event** is triggered any time the control's scroll box is moved by clicking a scroll arrow, releasing the mouse button after dragging the scroll box, or clicking the space between the scroll box and scroll arrow. Each of these three movements also changes the **Value property** of the scroll bar. The **Scroll event** occurs whenever the scroll box is dragged. The scroll event also changes the Value property of the scroll bar.

In the Loan Payment Calculator application, a movement of the scroll box must be linked to a new number displayed in the caption located above the scroll bar. Perform the following steps to establish this link within the Change event procedure by setting the Caption property of the label used to display the years (lblYears) to equal the Value property of the scroll bar located below it on the form (hsbYears).

TO WRITE THE SCROLLBAR CHANGE EVENT PROCEDURE

1 Click the View Code button in the Project window.

2 Click the hsbYears control in the Object list box in the frmLoanpmt (Code) window. If necessary, click the Change procedure in the Procedure list box.

3 Type the following statements in the Code window, pressing the ENTER key at the end of each line.

```
'update lblYears caption when scrollbox is moved
lblYears.Caption = hsbYears.Value
```

The Code window displays as shown in Figure 3-74.

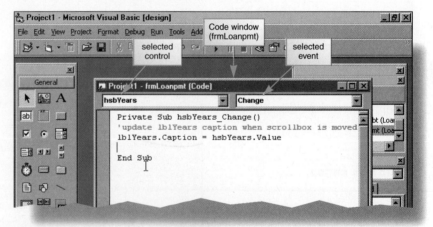

FIGURE 3-74

The lblYears control now will be updated whenever the Change event occurs. To update the lblYears control while dragging the scroll box requires the same code to be written for the Scroll event procedure. Perform the following steps to copy the code to the Scroll event procedure.

TO WRITE THE SCROLLBAR SCROLL EVENT PROCEDURE

1 Highlight the two lines of code you wrote for the hsbYears_Change event.

2 Right-click the selected code and then click Copy on the shortcut menu that displays.

3 Click Scroll in the Procedure list box in the Code window.

4 Right-click the beginning of the second (blank) line in the Code window and then click Paste on the shortcut menu that displays.

The code is copied for the hsbYears_Scroll event (Figure 3-75).

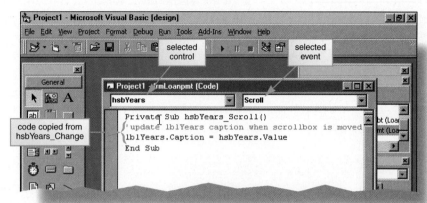

FIGURE 3-75

The frmLoanpmt hsbRate_Change and Scroll Events

This event is similar to the Change event for hsbYears. The only difference is the interest rate displayed as the caption of lblRate must be converted from the value of hsbRate by multiplying it by .01. Perform the following steps to write the hsbRate_Change event and then copy it to the hsbRate_Scroll event.

TO WRITE THE HSBRATE_CHANGE AND SCROLL EVENT PROCEDURES

1 Click the hsbRate control in the Object list box in the frmLoanpmt (Code) window. If necessary, click the Change procedure in the Procedure list box.

2 Enter the following statements in the Code window:
```
'update lblRate caption when scrollbox is moved
lblRate.Caption = hsbRate.Value * 0.01
```

3 Highlight the two lines of code you wrote for the hsbYears_Change event. Right-click the selected code and then click Copy on the shortcut menu that displays.

4 Click Scroll in the Procedure list box in the Code window. Right-click the beginning of the second (blank) line in the Code window and then click Paste on the shortcut menu that displays.

The code is copied for the hsbRate_Scroll event (Figure 3-76).

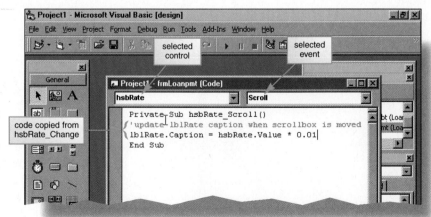

FIGURE 3-76

The frmLoanpmt cmdCalculate_Click Event

The **cmdCalculate_Click event** is used to perform the loan payment calculation and display the results. The actual computation is performed by one of Visual Basic's financial functions, the Pmt function. For a complete list and descriptions of all the Visual Basic financial functions, use online Help to search on the words, financial functions. The **Pmt function** returns the payment for a loan based on periodic, constant payments and a constant interest rate. The function is used in a code statement in the following manner:

Pmt(rate, nper, pv, fv, due)

The entries within parentheses that are supplied to a function are called **arguments**. Arguments within the Pmt function are described in Table 3-7.

Table 3-7	
ARGUMENT	DESCRIPTION
rate	Interest rate per period. For example, if you get a car loan at an annual percentage rate of 9 percent and make monthly payments, the rate per period is 0.09/12 or .0075.
nper	Total number of payment periods in the loan. For example, if you make monthly payments on a five year car loan, your loan has a total of 5 * 12 (or 60) payment periods.
pv	Present value that a series of payments to be made in the future is worth now (to the lender). For example, if you borrow $10,000 to buy a car, its pv is -10,000.
fv	Future value or cash balance you want after you have made the final payment. The future value of a loan is 0.
due	Number indicating when payments are due. Use 0 if payments are due at the end of the period, and use 1 if the payments are due at the beginning of the period.

In the cmdCalculate_Click event, the inputs of the Loan Payment Calculator application are substituted for the arguments of the Pmt function described in Table 3-7. Remember that the value of hsbRate runs from 1 to 1500 and that the decimal interest rate is .0001 times that value. The Pmt function arguments and values assigned in this project are listed in Table 3-8.

When you use the Pmt function, all of the arguments must be numbers (or variables whose value is a number). What if you typed, Hello, as the amount of the loan in the txtAmount text box at run time and then clicked the Calculate button? The function would be unable to calculate a value, and the program would end abruptly. It is possible for you to make an error when typing the loan amount, so you want some way to trap this error and to correct it without the program ending abruptly.

Table 3-8	
ARGUMENT	VALUE
rate	.0001 * hsbRate.Value / 12
nper	hsbYears.Value * 12
pv	−1 * txtAmount.Text
fv	0
due	1

Because the Text property of a text box can be either numbers (numeric) or text (string), you need to write some additional code that checks to see if the contents are numeric. This checking is done with the Visual Basic **IsNumeric function**. The function is used within code statements as follows:

IsNumeric(txtAmount.Text)

The function will return a True value if the contents are a number and a False value if the contents are not a valid number. The logical flow of actions within the cmdCalculate_Click event is shown in Figure 3-77.

In Project 2, this type of logical structure was represented in code by using an If...Then...Else statement. This project uses an extension to the If...Then...Else statement called an If...Then...Else block. The **If...Then...Else block** evaluates a condition similarly to the If...Then...Else statement. The block allows you to have multiple code statements executed, however, as illustrated in Figure 3-78.

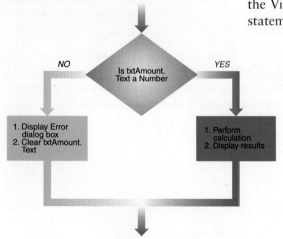

FIGURE 3-77

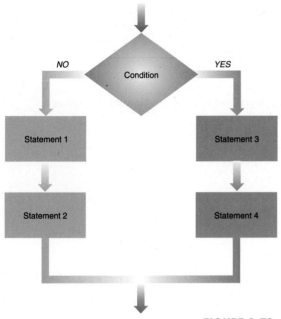

```
IF condition THEN
    statement1
    statement2
ELSE
    statement3
    statement4
END IF
```

FIGURE 3-78

If the value is not a number, you first want to display a dialog box that alerts you to the error, and then erase the contents of txtAmount. Creating customized forms is one way you can add dialog boxes to your applications (as you did with the About... dialog box). Another way is to use the Visual Basic **MsgBox statement** to display message dialog boxes.

The dialog box shown in Figure 3-79 is used to alert the user when an error has been made in entering a value for the loan amount. The dialog box is created with a Msg-Box statement in the application's code. The generalized form of the MsgBox code statement consists of three parts: MsgBox text, type, and title, which are described in Table 3-9.

For a detailed description of how to use different values of type for various combinations of buttons, icons, and modality, use Visual Basic Help to search for help on the MsgBox topic.

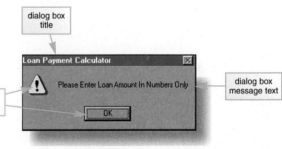

FIGURE 3-79

After the message box displays, you want to place the insertion point back in the txtAmount control for a new loan amount to be entered. You could select the txtAmount control during run time by clicking it, which would place the insertion point in the text box. You can, however, cause this event to occur through code using the **SetFocus method**. The syntax of the statement is:

controlname.SetFocus

The single argument, controlname, is the name of the control that you want to select.

The code statements that make up the cmdCalculate_Click event are shown in Figure 3-80 on the next page.

Table 3-9	
ARGUMENT	**DESCRIPTION**
Text	The text that displays in the body of the dialog box. It is enclosed in quotes in the code statement.
Type	A number that represents the type of button(s) displayed, the icon displayed, and whether or not the dialog box is modal.
Title	The text that displays in the title bar of the dialog box. It is enclosed in quotes in the code statement.

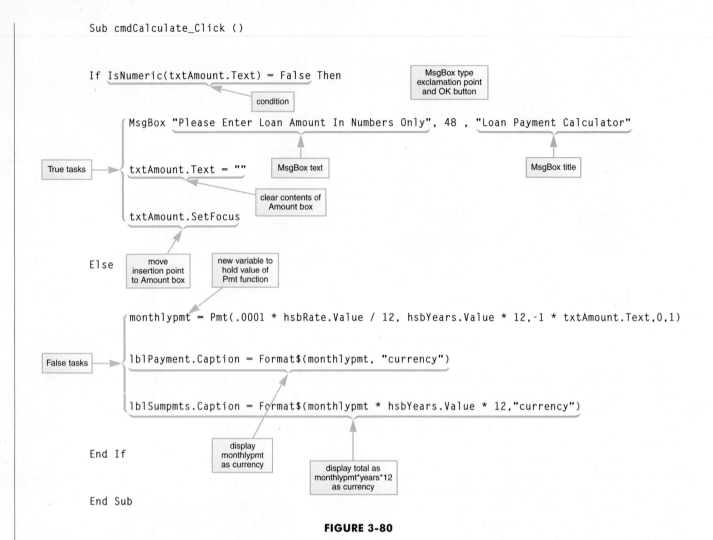

FIGURE 3-80

Perform the following steps to write the cmdCalculate_Click event using IsNumeric, Pmt, and Format$ functions, the If...Then...Else structure, and the MsgBox statement.

TO USE THE ISNUMERIC AND PMT FUNCTIONS AND IF...THEN...ELSE BLOCK IN CODE

❶ Drag the borders of the Code window to extend its width (Figure 3-81).

❷ Click cmdCalculate in the Object list box in the Code window.

❸ Enter the following statements in the Code window. Use the TAB key to indent lines as shown in Figure 3-81.

```
'if amount is not a number then message, else perform
  calculations
If IsNumeric(txtAmount.Text) = False Then
  MsgBox "Please Enter Loan Amount In Numbers Only",
    48,"Loan Payment Calculator"
  txtAmount.Text = ""
 txtAmount.SetFocus
Else
```

```
      monthlypmt = Pmt(0.0001 * hsbRate.Value / 12, hsbYears.Value
      * 12,-1 * txtAmount.Text,0,1)
      lblPayment.Caption = Format$(monthlypmt,"currency")
      lblSumpmts.Caption = Format$(monthlypmt * hsbYears.Value *12,
      "currency")
   End If
```

The Code window should display as shown in Figure 3-81. Indents have no effect on the execution of the code, but make it easier to read.

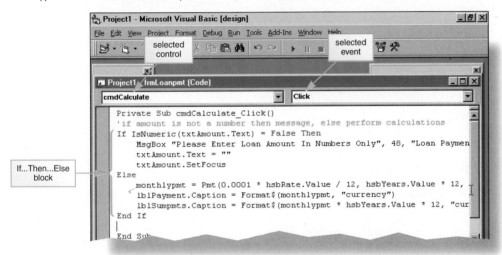

FIGURE 3-81

Line 8 in Figure 3-81 creates a variable named monthlypmt to hold the value returned by the Pmt function. This step makes the statement in Line 9 easier to read, where that value (monthlypmt), formatted as currency, is assigned to the Caption property of the lblPayment control.

In Line 10, the sum of payments is calculated as the monthly payment times the number of years times 12 months in a year, and it also is formatted as currency.

The frmLoanpmt cmdClear_Click Event

During run time, you click the Clear button (cmdClear) to remove any currently displayed inputs or outputs from the form. These include the loan amount (txtAmount.Text), length of loan period (lblYears.Caption), APR (lblRate.Caption), monthly payment (lblPayment.Caption), and sum of payments (lblSumpmts.Caption). You also want the ScrollBars (hsbYears and hsbRate) controls to return to their farthest left positions. Each of these actions will be accomplished by a statement that changes the value of the appropriate property of each control.

You do not need to change the number of years (the caption of lblYears) or the APR (the caption of lblRate directly. A code statement that changes the Value property of the ScrollBar controls activates their Change event, which sets the captions of those labels.

After these actions are completed, you want the insertion point to move back to the Loan Amount box (txtAmount control) for a new amount to be entered. This procedure will be accomplished using the SetFocus method described on page VB 3.47. Perform the steps on the next page to write the code for the Clear event.

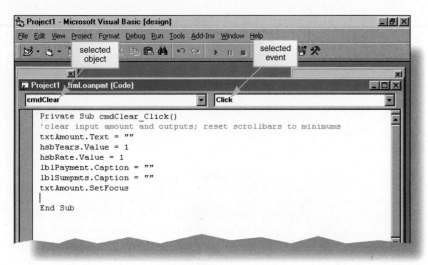

FIGURE 3-82

TO WRITE THE CMDCLEAR_CLICK EVENT

1 Click cmdClear in the Object list box in the Code window.

2 Enter the following statements in the Code window:

```
'clear input amount and outputs;
  reset scrollbars to minimums
txtAmount.Text = ""
hsbYears.Value = 1
hsbRate.Value = 1
lblPayment.Caption = ""
lblSumpmts.Caption = ""
txtAmount.SetFocus
```

The Code window displays as shown in Figure 3-82.

The frmLoanpmt cmdAbout_Click Event

The **cmdAbout_Click event** is triggered at run time when you click the About... command button. This event is used to display the frmLoanabt form. In Windows applications, a dialog box usually displays on top of all other open windows on the desktop, and you cannot work with any other window until you close the dialog box. A form or window with these characteristics is called a **modal** form. Forms without these properties are called **modeless**.

You make forms visible on the desktop and control their modality at run time with the **Show method** in a code statement. The statement has these parts (as described in Table 3-10):

form.Show *style*

Perform the following steps to write the cmdAbout_Click event using the Show method.

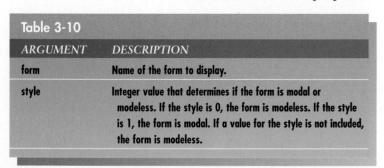

ARGUMENT	DESCRIPTION
form	Name of the form to display.
style	Integer value that determines if the form is modal or modeless. If the style is 0, the form is modeless. If the style is 1, the form is modal. If a value for the style is not included, the form is modeless.

Table 3-10

TO USE THE SHOW METHOD IN CODE

1 Click the cmdAbout control in the Object list box in the frmLoanpmt Code window.

2 Enter the following statements in the Code window:

```
'display modal about dialog form
frmLoanabt.Show 1
```

The Code window displays as shown in Figure 3-83.

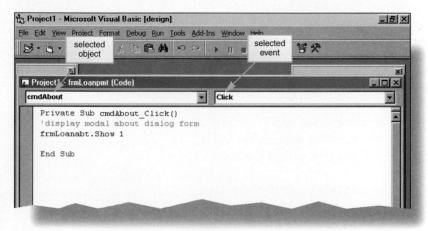

FIGURE 3-83

The frmLoanabt Command1_Click Event

The **Command1_Click event** is triggered when you click the command button labeled OK on the About... form. The action of this event removes the About... dialog box from the desktop. You remove forms from the desktop during run time by using the **Unload method** code statement. Perform the following steps to close the frmLoanpmt Code window, open the frmLoanabt Code window, and write the Command1_Click event using the Unload method.

TO USE THE UNLOAD METHOD IN CODE

1 Click the Close button in the frmLoanpmt Code window.

2 Click the frmLoanabt form in the Project window. Click the View Code button.

3 Click the Command1 control in the Object list box in the Code window. Click the Click event in the Procedure list box.

4 Enter the following statements in the Code window:

```
'remove about dialog form
Unload frmLoanabt
```

The Code window displays as shown in Figure 3-84.

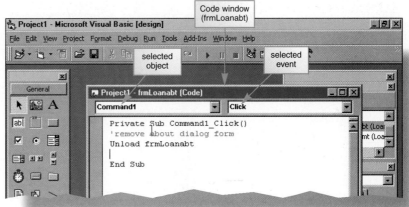

FIGURE 3-84

The Form_Load Event and Line Continuation

A form's **Load event** causes a subroutine of code statements to be carried out when the form is loaded into the computer's memory at run time. You will use the frmLoanabt's Load event to assign the captions of the labels in the About... dialog box.

A **line-continuation character** is the combination of a space followed by an underscore (_) used in the development environment to extend a single logical line of code to two or more physical lines. This has no effect on the execution of code, but can make it much easier to read and understand. You cannot use a line-continuation character to continue a line of code within a string expression and you cannot continue one statement into more than ten lines.

Perform the following steps to write a form Load event that assigns captions to labels and uses line-continuation characters and indents for easier reading.

TO USE LINE CONTINUATIONS IN CODE

1 Be certain the frmLoanabt (Code) window is open. If not, click its name, frmLoanabt, in the Project window and then click the View Code button.

2 Click the Form object in the Object list box in the Code window. If necessary, click the Load event in the Procedure list box.

3 Enter the statements on the next page in the Code window with indents as shown. Be sure that you enter the statements with a space before each underscore (_) character and before and after each ampersand (&).

More *About*
the Form_Load Event

Typically, you use a Load event procedure to include initialization code for a form. For example, this is code that specifies default settings for controls, indicates contents to be loaded into ComboBox or ListBox controls, or initializes form-level variables.

```
'create captions for labels
Label1.Caption = _
    "Macrofirm Loan Payment Calculator" & vbNewLine & _
    "Operating System 98" & vbNewLine & _
    "Copyright 1999 Macrofirm Corp."
Label2.Caption = _
    "Developed for Macrofirm" & vbNewLine & _
    "by Sarah Carter"
Label3.Caption = _
    "Warning: This computer program is protected by" & vbNewLine & _
    "copyright law and international treaties."
```

The Code window displays as shown in Figure 3-85.

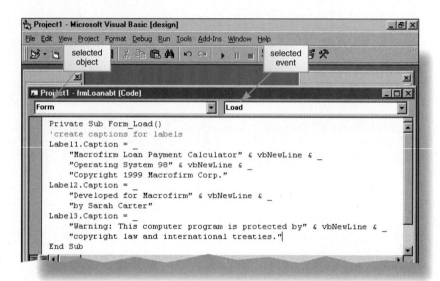

FIGURE 3-85

Saving the Project

The Loan Payment Calculator project is complete. When you save a form, the events you wrote for that form are saved as part of that form's .frm file. The forms were saved earlier, before the code had been written. Before running the project, the form files should be saved again and the project should be saved as a .vbp file.

Perform the following steps to save the forms with their changes and save the project on the Data Disk in drive A.

TO SAVE A PROJECT

1. Close the frmLoanabt Code window.
2. Click the Save Project button on the Standard toolbar.
3. Type LoanCalculator in the File name text box and then click the Save button in the Save Project As dialog box.
4. Click the Start button on the Standard toolbar.
5. Run the application.
6. Click the End button on the Standard toolbar.

When you saved the project, the .frm files were updated and a .vbp file was created. If any errors occurred in the test, you should retrace your steps in creating the project.

Debugging Applications

No matter how carefully you build a project, applications often do not work as planned and give erroneous results because of errors in the code, called **bugs**. The process of isolating and correcting these errors is called **debugging**. When you run an application, Visual Basic opens a special window, called the **Immediate window**, that can be used to help debug your application.

You can temporarily halt the execution of your application by clicking the **Break button** on the Standard toolbar, and then resume execution by clicking the **Continue button**. During the period of time when execution is stopped, the application is said to be in break mode.

Debugging features available through Visual Basic include:

1. Viewing the values of variables and properties (setting and viewing watch expressions).
2. Halting execution at a particular point (setting a breakpoint).
3. Executing your code one line at a time (stepping through the code).
4. Executing code immediately (the Immediate window).

Setting and Viewing Watch Expressions

In **break mode**, you can isolate and view the values of particular variables and properties as a way of checking for errors. You specify which variables and properties you want to monitor by setting **watch expressions**. You can set a watch expression in advance of running the application and then cause the application to break when that expression's value changes. You also can check the value of any variable or property in break mode by setting an **immediate watch**. You can specify a particular point at which you want to break execution by setting a **breakpoint**. Perform the following steps to set a breakpoint and then perform an immediate watch during break mode.

 Steps To Set a Breakpoint and Immediate Watch

1 **Click frmLoanpmt in the Project window. Click the View Code button in the Project window. Click cmdCalculate in the Object list box in the Code window. Click at the beginning of the ninth line of code.**

The insertion point displays at the beginning of the selected code line in the cmdCalculate_Click event procedure in the frmLoanpmt Code window (Figure 3-86).

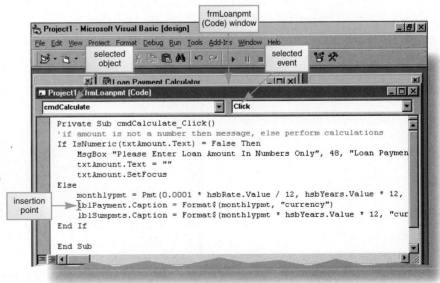

FIGURE 3-86

2 **Click Debug on the menu bar and then click Toggle Breakpoint.**

The code statement is highlighted in red (Figure 3-87).

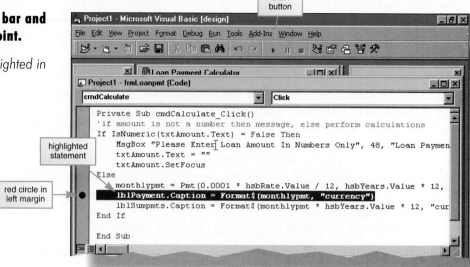

FIGURE 3-87

3 **Click the Start button on the Standard toolbar. Enter** 12000 **for the loan amount,** 5 **for the number of years, and** 6.5 **as the APR. Click the Calculate button.**

The program executes up to the highlighted code statement and then enters break mode. The Code window displays and the next code line to be executed has a yellow highlight (Figure 3-88).

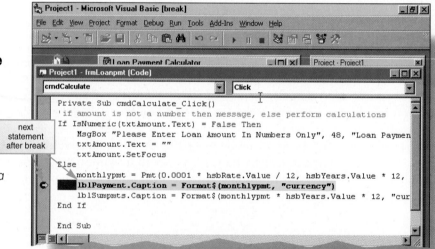

FIGURE 3-88

4 **Highlight monthlypmt as shown in Figure 3-89. Click Debug on the menu bar and then point to Quick Watch.**

The Debug menu displays (Figure 3-89).

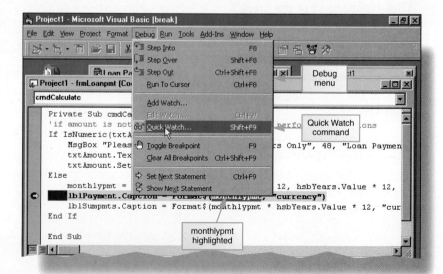

FIGURE 3-89

5 **Click Quick Watch.**

The Quick Watch dialog box displays the context and current value of the monthlypmt variable (Figure 3-90).

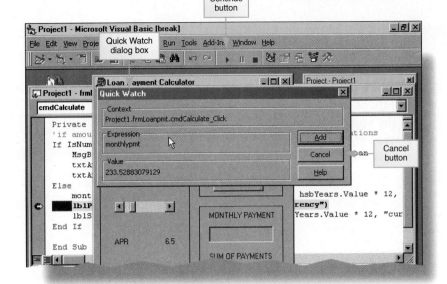

FIGURE 3-90

6 **Click the Cancel button in the Quick Watch dialog box. Click the Continue button on the Standard toolbar.**

The application resumes execution and displays as shown in Figure 3-91.

7 **Click the End button to stop the application.**

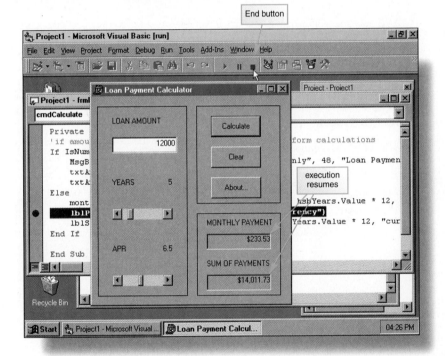

FIGURE 3-91

Other Ways

1. Click beginning of code line, then press F9

In the preceding steps, you used debug commands on the Debug menu. Many of these commands also can be accessed on the Debug toolbar. The Debug toolbar is opened by clicking Debug on the Toolbars submenu of the View menu.

Setting a Watch Expression and Stepping Through Code

You also can set watch expressions in advance of running the application, and also can step through code statements one at a time as additional ways to help isolate errors. Perform the steps on the next page to set a watch expression for the IsNumeric function and then step through the cmdCalculate_Click event procedure.

Steps

1 **Click the red circle in the left margin of the Code window next to the highlighted code statement. Click in the left margin beside the IF statement.**

The breakpoint is changed to the If statement now highlighted in red (Figure 3-92).

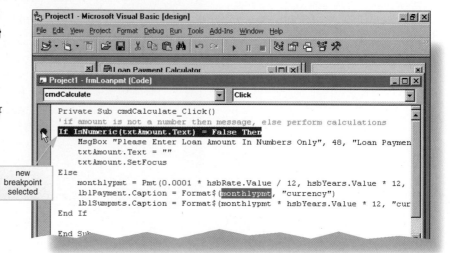

FIGURE 3-92

2 **Highlight IsNumeric(txtAmount.Text). Click Debug on the menu bar and then click Add Watch.**

The Add Watch dialog box displays (Figure 3-93).

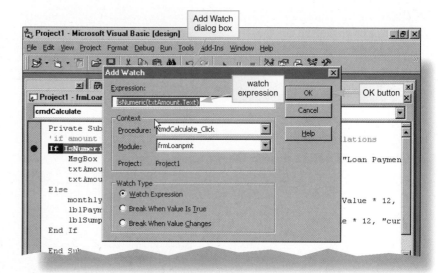

FIGURE 3-93

3 **Click the OK button. Click the Start button on the Standard toolbar. Enter 12000 for the loan amount, 5 for the number of years, and 6.5 as the APR. Click the Calculate button.**

Execution halts at the new breakpoint (Figure 3-94).

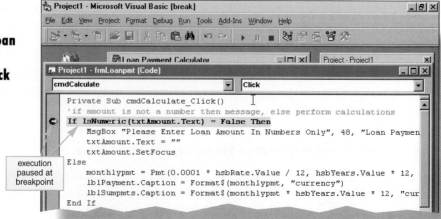

FIGURE 3-94

4 **Click View on the menu bar and then click Watch Window.**

The current value of the IsNumeric function displays (Figure 3-95).

View menu name

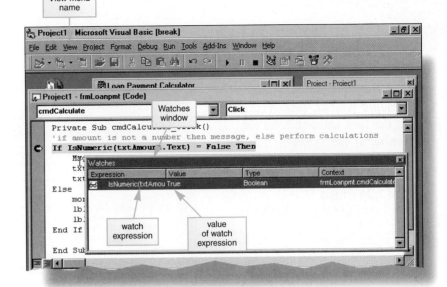

FIGURE 3-95

5 **Click the Code window. Click Debug on the menu bar and then click Step Into.**

The previously highlighted line of code is executed (testing IsNumeric) and the next line of code to be executed is highlighted (Figure 3-96).

6 **Press the F8 key eight times to see line-by-line execution. Click the End button on the Standard toolbar.**

Debug menu name

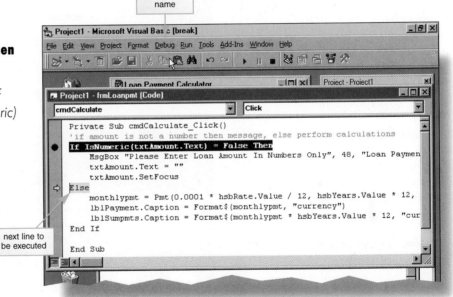

FIGURE 3-96

In the preceding steps, you set a watch expression, a breakpoint, and then stepped through code. In the **line-by-line execution,** the code statements for the input error message box were skipped because the preceding IsNumeric condition was True. A watch expression can be removed by highlighting it in the Watches window and then pressing the DELETE key.

Using the Immediate Window

The **Immediate window** allows you to test out code statements without changing any of your procedures. You can cut and paste code to and from the Immediate window. Perform the steps on the next page to use the Immediate window to check the value of a property.

More *About* **the Immediate Window**

You can open the Immediate window during design time by clicking its name on the View menu or pressing CTRL+G. The Immediate window can be dragged and positioned anywhere on your screen unless you have made it a dockable window on the Docking tab in the Options dialog box. You can close the window by clicking its Close button.

Steps To Use the Immediate Window

1 **Click the Start button on the Standard toolbar. Enter** 12000 **for the loan amount,** 5 **for the number of years, and** 6.5 **as the APR. Click the Calculate button. Click the Immediate window and then type** Print txtAmount.Text **as the entry.**

The Immediate window displays as shown in Figure 3-97.

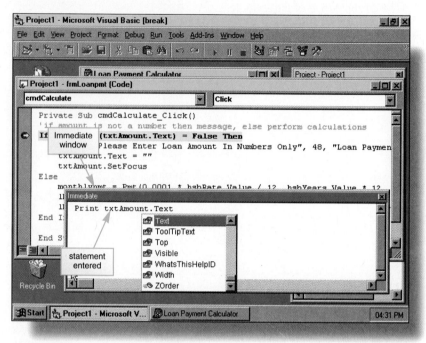

FIGURE 3-97

2 **Press the ENTER key.**

The result of executing the code statement is displayed in the Immediate window (Figure 3-98).

3 **Click the End button on the Standard toolbar.**

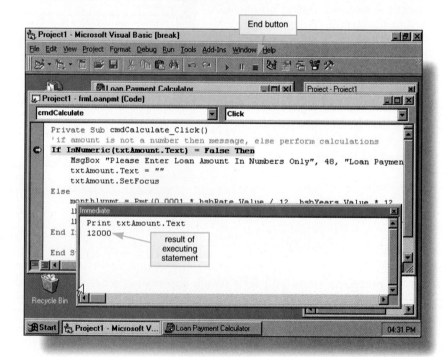

FIGURE 3-98

In the Immediate window, you can type or paste a line of code and then press the ENTER key to run it. You can, however, execute only one line of code at a time.

Making Executable Files

To run an application outside of the Visual Basic programming system, you must **compile**, or convert, the application into an **executable**, or **.exe**, file. Several advanced options are available in the Project Properties window on the Compile tab sheet. Perform the following steps to compile the Loan Payment Calculator using the default compile options and then run the stand-alone application.

Steps To Make and Run an EXE File

More *About*
Code Compilation

More *About*
Code Compilation

You can compile your code either in p-code format or in native code format. P-code is an intermediate step between the high-level instructions in your program and the low-level native code your computer's processor executes. At run time, Visual Basic translates each p-code statement to native code. By compiling directly to native code format, you eliminate the intermediate p-code step.

1 **Click the red circle in the Code window margin. Click File on the menu bar and then point to Make LoanCalculator.exe.**

The File menu displays (Figure 3-99).

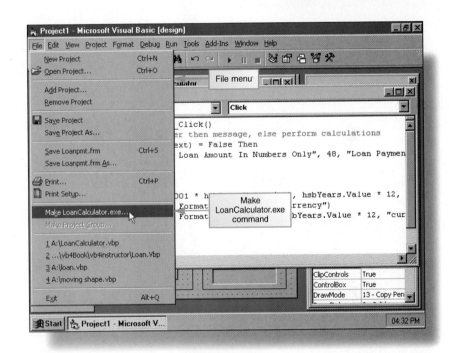

FIGURE 3-99

2 **Click Make LoanCalculator.exe and then point to the Options button in the Make Project dialog box.**

The Make Project dialog box displays (Figure 3-100).

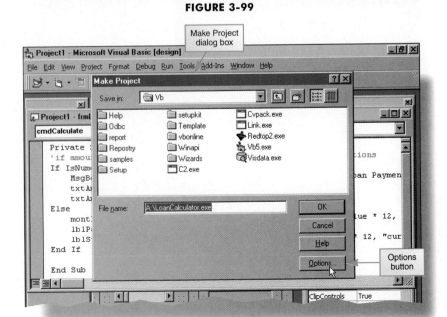

FIGURE 3-100

3 Click the Options button. If necessary, enter the data and make the selections as shown in the Make tab sheet (Figure 3-101). Point to the OK button.

The Make tab sheet displays (Figure 3-101).

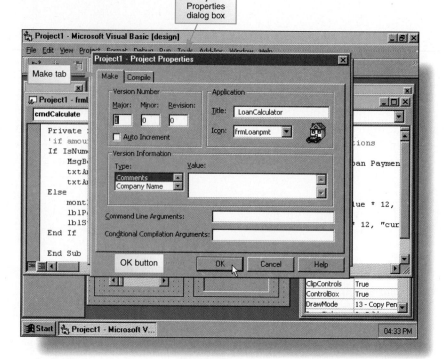

FIGURE 3-101

4 Click the OK button and then type LoanCalculator in the File name text box. Point to the OK button.

The Project Properties dialog box closes and the Make Project dialog box displays (Figure 3-102).

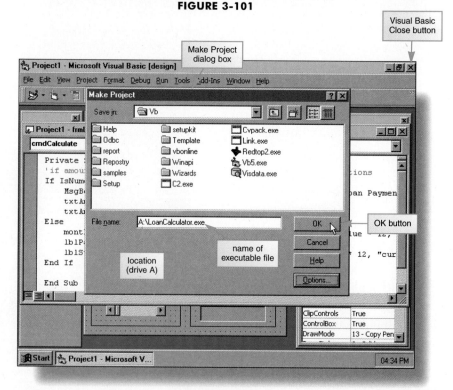

FIGURE 3-102

5 Click the OK button. Close Visual Basic. If prompted to save changes, click the Yes button. Click the Start button on the taskbar and then point to Run on the Start menu.

The Start menu displays (Figure 3-103).

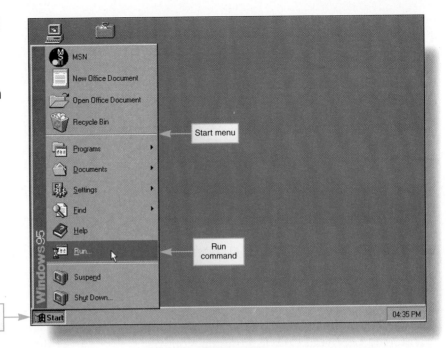

FIGURE 3-103

6 Click Run. Type a:\LoanCalculator.exe **in the Open text box and then click the OK button. Run the application.**

The application is opened on the desktop (Figure 3-104).

7 Close the Loan Payment Calculator application.

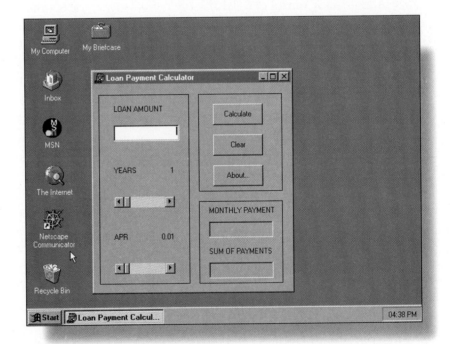

FIGURE 3-104

OtherWays

1. Press ALT+F then press K

Project Summary

Project 3 extended the basics of application building that were presented in Project 1 and Project 2. The application in this project consisted of multiple forms and dialog boxes. You learned about more of the Form control's properties and its WindowState and modality. You also learned how to add an icon to a form.

Several new properties of familiar controls were presented. You also learned how to use Image, Line, and ScrollBar controls. You wrote multiple event procedures for multiple forms that included several new functions and methods. At the end of the project, you learned how to use Visual Basic's Debug menu to isolate and correct errors in code and how to create and run an EXE file.

What You Should Know

Having completed this project, you now should be able to perform the following tasks.

▶ Add a Graphic to an Image Control *(VB 3.18)*

▶ Add Label and CommandButton Controls *(VB 3.10)*

▶ Add a Line Control *(VB 3.12)*

▶ Add a New Form *(VB 3.23)*

▶ Add a TextBox Control *(VB 3.31)*

▶ Add Additional Label Controls *(VB 3.29)*

▶ Add an Image Control *(VB 3.11)*

▶ Add Borderless Label Controls *(VB 3.27)*

▶ Add CommandButton Controls *(VB 3.34)*

▶ Add ScrollBar Controls *(VB 3.33)*

▶ Add Shape Controls *(VB 3.24)*

▶ Make and Run an EXE File *(VB 3.59)*

▶ Name Controls *(VB 3.38)*

▶ Save a Project *(VB 3.52)*

▶ Save a Form File *(VB 3.21)*

▶ Save the Form *(VB 3.41)*

▶ Set a Breakpoint and Immediate Watch *(VB 3.53)*

▶ Set a Form's Icon Property *(VB 3.40)*

▶ Set a Startup Form *(VB 3.42)*

▶ Set a Watch Expression and Step Through Code *(VB 3.56)*

▶ Set the Scroll Bars Properties *(VB 3.39)*

▶ Set the Alignment Property *(VB 3.35)*

▶ Set the BorderStyle Property *(VB 3.15)*

▶ Set the BorderWidth Property of the Line Control *(VB 3.20)*

▶ Set the Control's Caption and Text Properties *(VB 3.36)*

▶ Set the ControlBox Property *(VB 3.14)*

▶ Set the Font Properties *(VB 3.17)*

▶ Set the Name, Caption, and AutoSize Properties *(VB 3.16)*

▶ Set the Size of a Form Using the Properties Window *(VB 3.8, VB 3.23)*

▶ Use Line Continuations in Code *(VB 3.51)*

▶ Use the Immediate Window *(VB 3.58)*

▶ Use the IsNumeric and Pmt Functions and If...Then...Else Block in Code *(VB 3.48)*

▶ Use the Show Method in Code *(VB 3.50)*

▶ Use the Unload Method in Code *(VB 3.51)*

▶ Write the ScrollBar Change Event Procedure *(VB 3.44)*

▶ Write the ScrollBar Scroll Event Procedure *(VB 3.45)*

▶ Write the cmdClear_Click Event *(VB 3.50)*

▶ Write the hsbRate_Change and Scroll Event Procedures *(VB 3.45)*

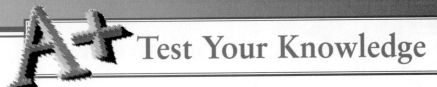

1 True/False

Instructions: Circle T if the statement is true or F if the statement is false.

T F   1. Dialog boxes are used during run time to give information about the application or prompt you to supply information to the application.

T F   2. Image controls can contain graphical images.

T F   3. The WindowState property cannot be changed at run time.

T F   4. When you create multiple forms in a project, it is important to name them.

T F   5. You must close the first form before adding a new form to a project.

T F   6. When a form's Icon property is set and the form is minimized, a button with the icon displays on the taskbar.

T F   7. Entries within the parentheses in a Pmt function are called values.

T F   8. The MsgBox statement can be used to display message dialog boxes.

T F   9. The Unload Form code statement removes a form from the desktop at run time.

T F 10. To help remove errors in code, use the Debug window.

2 Multiple Choice

Instructions: Circle the correct response.

1. The size of a form can be set by changing the _____ and _____ properties values.
   a. Top, Bottom
   b. Left, Right
   c. Height, Width
   d. Bottom, Right

2. The BorderStyle property of a form can have one of _____ different values.
   a. 8
   b. 5
   c. 4
   d. 6

3. Visual Basic creates a file with an extension of _____ when a form with graphical data is saved.
   a. .frx
   b. .ico
   c. .bmp
   d. .exe

(continued)

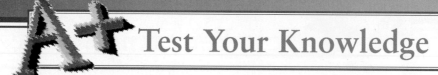

Test Your Knowledge

Multiple Choice *(continued)*

4. To change the appearance of a Line control, set the _____ property and the _____ property.
   a. Text, DrawMode
   b. Name, Visible
   c. BorderStyle, BorderWidth
   d. Caption, DrawMode

5. Use the Shape control to group visually the related _____ and _____.
   a. inputs, outputs
   b. OptionButton controls, CheckBox controls
   c. TextBox controls, Label controls
   d. captions, text

6. The _____ property of a scroll bar sets the amount that the value changes when the scroll arrows are clicked.
   a. Min
   b. SmallChange
   c. LargeChange
   d. Max

7. By default, the _____ form is the first project form moved into memory at run time.
   a. Form1
   b. first
   c. last
   d. Startup

8. The code that checks to see if the contents of a TextBox control are numbers or text is _____.
   a. IsText
   b. IsNumber
   c. IsNumeric
   d. IsAmount

9. Use the _____ method to reposition the insertion point in a TextBox control at run time.
   a. MovePoint
   b. SetFocus
   c. MoveFocus
   d. SetCursor

10. When a dialog box displays preventing work with other windows until it is closed, the dialog box is a(n) _____ type.
    a. modeless
    b. event
    c. eventless
    d. modal

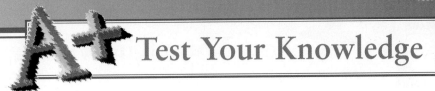

3 Understanding Code Statements

Instructions: Carefully read each of the following descriptions of writing code statements to accomplish specific tasks. Record your answers on a separate sheet of paper. Number your answers to correspond to the code descriptions.

1. Write a code statement to convert the amount displayed as the caption of lblCharge for a ScrollBar control from an integer number to a decimal number.

2. Write a code statement that will display a message dialog box titled, `Important Information`. It should display an exclamation point icon and an OK button. The message text should read, `A Fatal Error Has Occurred`.

3. Write a code statement that will make a TextBox control named txtCursor the active control and place the insertion point in the control.

4. Write a code statement that will cause a form named frmSeeAbout to display on the desktop in a modal state.

5. Write a code statement that will cause a form named, frmGoneAbout, to be removed from the desktop.

6. Write a code statement that will cause a form named, frmSmallAbout, to be minimized on the desktop.

4 Changing Alignment and Font Properties at Run Time

Instructions: Start Visual Basic. Open the project, Text Font Properties, from the Data Disk that accompanies this book. This application has one CheckBox control group and one OptionButton control group. The CheckBox control group is used to set the Font property of the text in the TextBox control. The OptionButton control group is used to set the Alignment property of the caption for the Label control. Perform the following tasks to complete this application as shown in Figure 3-105.

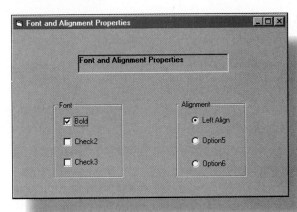

FIGURE 3-105

1. Add two CheckBox controls to the Font CheckBox control group. One should have a caption of Italic and the other should have a caption of Underline. Name the CheckBox controls.

2. Add two OptionButton controls to the OptionButton control group. One should have a caption of Center Align and the other should have a caption of Right Align. Name the OptionButton controls.

3. Open the Code window for the Italic OptionButton control and enter `lblFontAlign.FontItalic = chkItalic.Value` adding a comment to your code to indicate what the command is accomplishing.

(continued)

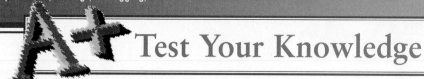

Changing Alignment and Font Properties at Run Time *(continued)*

4. Open the Code window for the Underline OptionButton control and enter
   `lblFontAlign.FontUnderline = chkUnderline.Value` adding a comment to your code to indicate
   what the command is accomplishing.
5. Open the Code window for the Center Align CheckBox control and enter
   `lblFontAlign.Alignment = 2` adding a comment to your code to indicate what the command is
   accomplishing.
6. Open the Code window for the Right Align CheckBox control and enter
   `lblFontAlign.Alignment = 1` adding a comment to your code to indicate what the command is
   accomplishing.
7. Save the form and project using the file name, Font and Alignment.
8. Run the application and make any necessary corrections and resave using the same project file
   name.
9. Print the project Form Image, Code, and Form As Text.

1 Reviewing Project Activities

Instructions: Perform the following tasks using a computer.

1. Start Visual Basic.
2. Click Help on the menu bar and then click Microsoft Visual Basic Help Topics.
3. Click the Contents tab.
4. Double-click the Language Reference book. Double-click the Functions book. Double-click the
   letter F book.
5. Double-click the FV Function topic and read the information. Click each of the green, underlined
   links to see the ScreenTips. Print the topic by right-clicking and then clicking Print Topic on the
   shortcut menu. Click the Example link to display an example of the Help topic currently being
   viewed. Right-click in the Visual Basic Example window and then print the example. Close the
   Visual Basic Example window. Hand in the printouts to your instructor.

Use Help

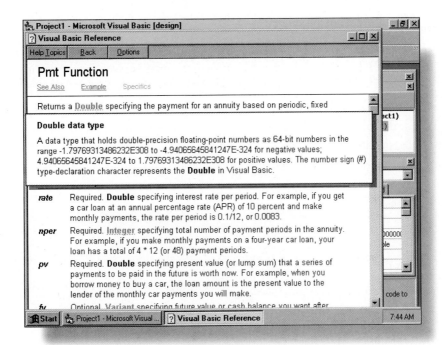

FIGURE 3-106

6. Click the See Also link to display the Topics Found dialog box. Double-click the Pmt Function topic and read the information. Click the green, underlined links and read the ScreenTips (Figure 3-106). Right-click anywhere in the Help window and then click Print Topics on the shortcut menu. Click the Example link to display an example of the Help topic currently being viewed. Right-click in the Visual Basic Example window and then print the example. Close the Visual Basic Example window. Hand in the printouts to your instructor.

7. Click the See Also link to display the Topics Found dialog box. Double-click the PV Function topic and read the information. Click the green, underlined links and read the ScreenTips. Right-click anywhere in the Help window and then click Print Topics on the shortcut menu. Click the Example link to display an example of the Help topic currently being viewed. Right-click anywhere in the Help window and then click Print Topics on the shortcut menu. Close the Visual Basic Example window. Hand in the printouts to your instructor.

8. Click the Help Topics button to return to the Contents sheet and then close Help.

Use Help

2 Learning More of the Basics

Instructions: Use Visual Basic Books Online to learn more about Visual Basic data types, setting focus, and message boxes. The Help topics will provide information to answer the questions below. You can write the answers to the questions on your own paper and hand them in to your instructor.

1. Start Visual Basic. Click Help on the menu bar and then click Books Online. If necessary, in the Navigation area, double-click Programmer's Guide (All Editions) book to open it. Double-click Part 1: Visual Basic Basics in the Navigation area and then double-click Programming Fundamentals. Double-click Introduction to Variables, Constants, and Data Types (Figure 3-107). Read the information that displays in the Topic area. As you read the text in the Topic area, answer the following questions.
   a. What are variables?
   b. What are constants?
   c. What are data types?

2. Click Data Types in the Navigation area and then answer the following questions about data types.
   a. How many data types are included in Visual Basic?
   b. Give at least one example of each data type.

3. Double-click Forms, Controls, and Menus in the Navigation area and then click Understanding Focus. Answer the following questions.
   a. What are the focus events including the one used in this project?
   b. How do each of the focus events work?
   c. Give an example of each one of the focus events.

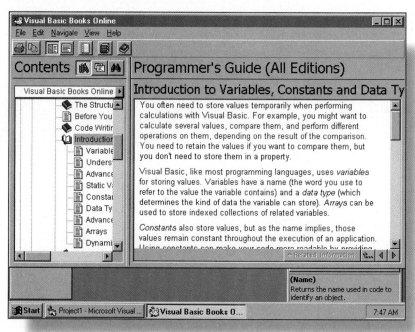

FIGURE 3-107

4. Double-click Part 2: What Can You Do With Visual Basic? in the Navigation area. Double-click Creating a User Interface and then double-click Dialog Boxes. One by one, click the topics below Dialog Boxes in the Navigation area, reading the information in the Topic area. Answer the following questions using the information you read.
   a. What are all of the dialog box types?
   b. What does the owner argument do?
   c. What are the differences between an InputBox and a MsgBox?
   d. How can a custom dialog box be created using a form?
   e. What can be done to customize the form?
   f. How is a custom dialog box displayed?

Apply Your Knowledge

1 Writing Code in a Visual Basic Application

Instructions: Start Visual Basic and open the project, Scroll Bars from the Visual Basic folder on the Data Disk that accompanies this book. This application consists of a form that contains one round Shape control and two ScrollBar controls. (Figure 3-108).

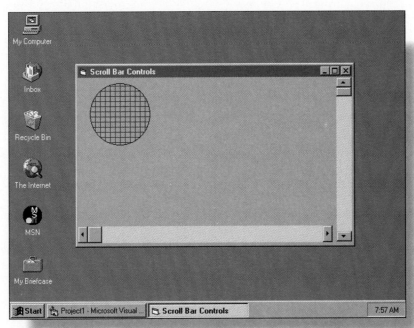

FIGURE 3-108

1. If necessary, click the View Form button in the Project window.
2. One at a time, change the Name property of each of the two scroll bars. For each of the ScrollBar controls, set the Min property to 480, set the Max property to 3600, set the LargeChange property to 200, set the SmallChange property to 50, and set the Value property to 480.
3. Click the View Code button in the Project window.
4. For the horizontal ScrollBar control, add a comment to indicate what the code for this scroll bar is accomplishing. Enter a code statement similar to `Shape1.Width = HScroll1.Value` replacing Shape1 and HScroll1 with the appropriate control names.
5. For the vertical scroll bar (VScrollBar) control, add a comment to indicate what the code for this scroll bar is accomplishing. Enter code statement similar to `Shape1.Height = VScroll1.Value` replacing Shape1 and VScroll1 with the appropriate control names.
6. Save the form and the project using the file name, Moving Scroll Bars.
7. Click the Start button on the Standard toolbar to run the application. Click the scroll arrows on the horizontal and vertical scroll bars several times. Click the End button and make corrections to the code statements, if necessary. Save the form and project again using the same file name.
8. Print the Form Image, Code, and Form As Text.

In the Lab

1 Creating and Modifying a WindowStates Form

Problem: You are a tutor in the computer laboratory at school. The students are having difficulty understanding what the WindowStates of forms is and exactly how it works. You want a simple application to demonstrate the various WindowStates of forms.

Instructions: Build an application with a user interface that resembles the one shown in Figure 3-109. All of the controls should be named properly.

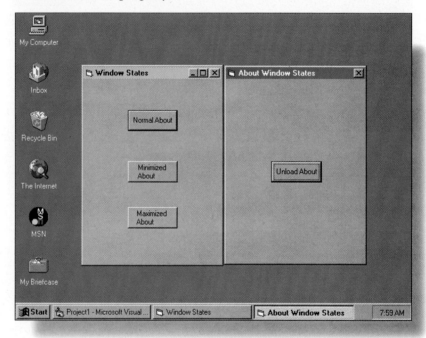

FIGURE 3-109

1. Open a new project in Visual Basic.
2. Add a second form to the project. Size the forms and position them side by side on the desktop.
3. One by one, add three CommandButton controls to the first form and one CommandButton control to the second form by double-clicking the CommandButton button in the Toolbox. Position the CommandButton controls on the forms as they are added.
4. Change the captions on each of the forms. Caption the first form, Window States, and the second form, About Window States.
5. The three command buttons on the Window States form should show the About Window States form in a normal, minimized, and maximized state. Change the Caption property of the CommandButton controls to Normal About, Minimized About, and Maximized About. The CommandButton control on the About Window States form should unload the form from the desktop. Change the Caption property of this CommandButton control to Unload About.
6. Set the BorderStyle property for the Window States form to 2 - Sizable and set the BorderStyle property to 1 - Fixed Single for the About Window States form.

In the Lab

7. Make the Window States form the Startup form. Click Project on the menu bar and then click Properties. Click the General tab. Click the Startup Object box arrow, click the name of the Window States form, and click the OK button.

8. Open the Code window for the Normal About command button. Type an appropriate comment to explain the purpose of the code. Type the code statements `frmAppAbout.Show` and `frmAppAbout.WindowState = 0` for the Normal About CommandButton control. Click the Minimized About command button in the Object list box. Type the code statements `frmAppAbout.Show` and `frmAppAbout.WindowState = 1` and then click the Maximized About command button in the Object list box. Type the code statements `frmAppAbout.Show` and `frmAppAbout.WindowState = 2` and then close the Code window.

9. Open the Code window for the Unload About command button on the About Window States form. Type `Unload frmAppAbout` as the code statement.

10. Save the form and the project using the file name, Window States.

11. Run the application to make certain no errors occur. If any errors are encountered, correct them and save the form and project again using the same file name.

12. Print the project Form Image, Code, and Form As Text.

2 Creating a Comparison Application

Problem: You are working in the library and frequently receive telephone calls requesting population information. You decide that a simple application would be very helpful when answering these questions. It should be generic enough to accept and display city, state, or country names. The application will calculate the difference between the population at the beginning of the year and at the end of the year. It also will display a message dialog box stating an increase or decrease in population.

Instructions: Perform the tasks on the next page to build an application similar to the one shown in Figure 3-110.

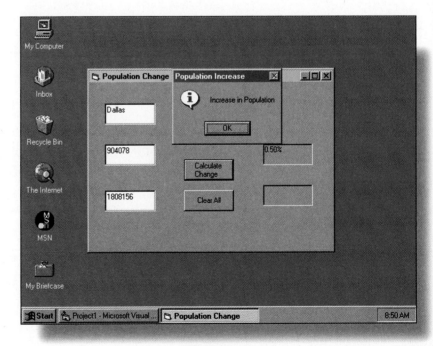

FIGURE 3-110

(continued)

In the Lab

Creating a Comparison Application *(continued)*

1. Open a new project in Visual Basic.
2. Change the Caption property of the form to Compare Population.
3. Place TextBox controls to accept and display the city, state, or country as well as the beginning and ending populations.
4. Place Label controls to display the percentage of increase or decrease in population.
5. Place a CommandButton control to calculate the percentage of increase or decrease in population, and to display the message dialog boxes. Place another CommandButton control on the form to clear all the TextBox controls and the Label controls.
6. Center the form on the desktop. *Hint*: Use the StartUpPosition property.
7. Open the Code window for the CommandButton control for calculations. Write the necessary code statements to calculate the percent of increase or decrease in population and display the percentage of increase or decrease in the appropriate Label control. Write the code to display either a message dialog box to indicate a population increase or a message dialog box to indicate a population decrease.
8. Save the form and the project using the file name, Population Changes.
9. Run the project and make any necessary changes. Remember to save the form and project again if any changes have been made.
10. Print the project Form Image, Code, and Form As Text.

3 Creating and Using a Future Value Calculator

Problem: You have been investing money on a regular basis and want an application that will calculate the value of the investment. You have decided to develop an application that will allow entry of different amounts, the selection of different even annual interest rates from 1 percent to 25 percent without typing in values, and different numbers of years from 1 to 50 without typing in values. Then, when you click a command button, you want the application to display the future value of the investment based on quarterly compounding. This will aid you in determining how much your investment could be worth in the future.

Instructions: Perform the following tasks to create the investment calculator as shown in Figure 3-111.

In the Lab

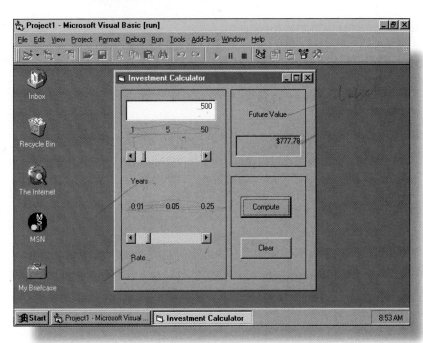

FIGURE 3-111

1. Open a new project in Visual Basic.
2. Size the form appropriately and center it by setting the StartUpPosition property.
3. Add one TextBox control, two ScrollBar controls, seven Label controls, and two CommandButton controls to the form.
4. Set the form's Caption property to Investment Calculator. Set the Icon property to the Calculator icon on the Data Disk that accompanies this book.
5. Set the Text property of the TextBox control to be blank.
6. Set the Caption property of the two CommandButton controls.
7. Write code statements to clear all control values that should be cleared or set them to minimum values when the form is loaded into memory. The code statements for when the form is cleared are the same as when the form is loaded into memory.
8. Each ScrollBar control should have three corresponding Label controls. Write the code statements for the Label control changes that are triggered by use of the ScrollBar controls. For each scroll bar, set the Caption property of the Label controls to reflect values as follows: the minimum value of the scroll bar, the maximum value of the scroll bar, and the change as the scroll bar is used.

(continued)

In the Lab

Creating and Using a Future Value Calculator *(continued)*

9. Write the code statement for the CommandButton control that performs the computations. The code statements should display an error message if the investment amount entered in the TextBox control is not numeric. They should compute the value of the future investment. The amount should be formatted as currency and displayed as the caption of the separate Label control. Remember that the number of years should be multiplied by four and the annual interest rate should be divided by four.
10. Save the form and the project using the file name, Investment Calculator.
11. Run the application and make any necessary corrections. Remember to save the form and project again if any changes have been made.
12. Make the application executable.
13. Print the project Form Image, Code, and Form As Text.

Cases and Places

The difficulty of these case studies varies: ❿ are the least difficult; ❿❿ are more difficult; and ❿❿❿ are the most difficult.

1 ❿   As a student worker employed by various faculty members, you have been given an interesting assignment by a history instructor. Various lands in the United States were purchased from other nations for small sums of money. Your instructor wants to know if the same amount of money were invested in an interest-bearing account, what the investment would be worth today. The application should accept and display the original amount, the interest rate should be selected using a scroll bar, and the period of time should be selected using a scroll bar. An appropriate message should display if the original amount entered is not numeric. The current value of the investment should display on the form. As an example of data that could be entered, use Manhattan Island, which was purchased in 1626 for $24.00.

Cases and Places

Ful Amt = Txt Amount X

2 ▶ You recently were hired at Sparkling Gems to build applications for its accounting department. One of your first assignments is to develop an application to calculate employee yearly raises. You have decided that the yearly salary must be entered with a message displaying if the amount is not numeric. Use OptionButton controls to select the raise percentage rates of 10% for sales, 5% for labor, or 15% for management. The number of years from 1 to 40 can be selected using a ScrollBar control. Use a CheckBox control for people who have worked more than 15 years because they are entitled to an additional 2% raise.

3 ▶▶ As a part-time employee of Mannequin, a clothing store, you have been asked to develop a small application for the salespeople. They require an application that allows them to enter the cost price of a clothing item and select the margin (markup) using a scroll bar. The application then should compute both the selling price of the item and the gross profit of the item. The selling price and gross profit should display for the salesperson. The salesperson should be notified if any errors occur when entering the cost price. You have decided to use the knowledge gained in this project to develop an appropriate application to perform these calculations.

4 ▶▶ Wire-Gram has hired you as a consultant to build an application that will calculate the cost of a telegram. The application should include a way to enter the message and compute the cost based on $4.20 for the first 100 characters and $.02 for each letter over 100. The total number of letters and the total cost should display for the person entering the telegram. You want the company to remember your work and decide to include a form with information about yourself and the application. *Hint*: Search Visual Basic Help for the MultiLine property of a TextBox control as well as the Len function for string data.

5 ▶▶ Your friend, who owns Lullaby Land, knows what a knowledgeable programmer you are and has requested your assistance. She is going to provide around-the-clock child-care. She and her coworkers require a quick, easy way to be able to calculate the total amounts owed by her clients. The application would have to provide a way to enter the beginning and ending times. The rate structure is $3.50 per hour from 8:00 a.m. up to and including 5:00 p.m. and $4.25 per hour after 5:00 p.m. up to and including 8:00 a.m. The number of hours from 8:00 a.m. to 5:00 p.m. should be displayed along with a subtotal amount for this time period. The number of hours from 5:00 p.m. to 8:00 a.m. also should be displayed along with a subtotal amount for this time period. The two subtotals should be added and displayed for a final total amount due. Appropriate error messages should be used with icons and one or more command buttons. An About form also should be developed for the application. *Hint*: See the MsgBox function in the Functions section of the Language Reference in Microsoft Visual Basic Help Topics.

Cases and Places

6 ▶▶▶ As a programmer for Tootsies shoe stores, you have been asked to develop a program to calculate discounts and taxes on items purchased. The form should be neatly arranged. The salespeople should be able to enter the list price of an item as well as the tax rate. Provide a method to select the discount rate. The gross list price should display along with the tax rate and the discount rate. After the calculations have been performed, the net list price also should display. You will want to provide appropriate error messages where necessary. You also want to provide an About form with information about the application and about you. This should be a compiled application.

7 ▶▶▶ You are working as a manager trainee with a well-known national company. One of the benefits of the job is that you can request payroll investment deductions on a quarterly basis. The amount deducted is determined by you at the beginning of each year. The money is invested for a period of years at an annual percentage rate, both of which can vary. You would like to experiment with different values for the investment amount, the period of time, and the annual interest rate to see how much you can earn. You want the form to be well organized. Error messages also should display if amounts entered are not numeric. You also want to remember what the application is for and when you designed it. *Hint*: See the FV function in the Functions section of the Language Reference in Microsoft Visual Basic Help Topics. This should be a compiled application.

Menus, Data Controls, Common Dialogs, and General Procedures

Objectives:

You will have mastered the material in this project when you can:

▶ Describe the general structure of a database

▶ Describe database fields, records, and tables

▶ Build applications that contain menus, submenus, and pop-up menus

▶ Add access keys, shortcuts, separator bars, and check marks to menus

▶ Build applications that use the Data control

▶ Bind data-aware controls to a Data control

▶ Use a Font common dialog in an application

▶ Create control arrays

▶ Write code to select records in a database

▶ Use the For...Next code structure in procedures

▶ Use the With statement in procedures

▶ Write a general procedure

▶ Use the Not operator in code statements

▶ Write code to add and remove menu check marks during run time

▶ Write a procedure for a MouseUp event

Elementary, My Dear Programmer

Database Organizes School Functions

From the registrar to the librarian to the campus police, personnel at your school need to access information about you at various times throughout the academic year. In many cases, the facts about your class schedule, grade point average, overdue library books, and parking tickets are stored in a database, which is a collection of related facts organized in a systematic manner.

Visual Basic provides the tools for creating and maintaining an effective database, as you will learn in this project. While your database will fulfill a class assignment, the application can be used in a very practical way.

Consider the case of IRI/SkyLight Training and Publishing, a Chicago-based company offering classes and books dedicated to enhancing teachers' skills and renewing their vigor for teaching. Company employees were using one computer system for registering students, another for scheduling classes, a third for ordering books, and others for various campus functions. They

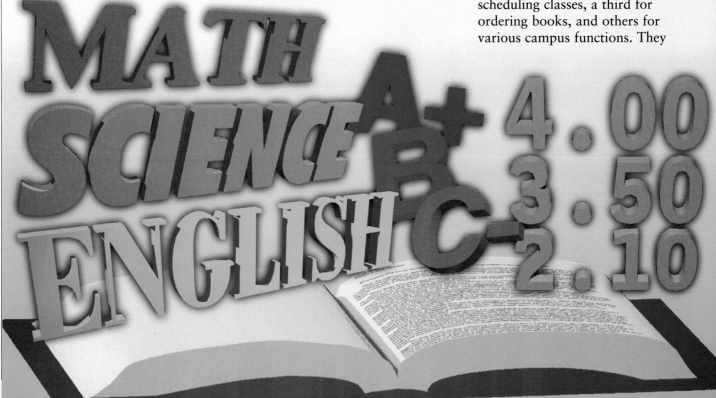

needed one system to organize this data and to streamline their work efforts, so they turned to The Information Management Group (IMG) for help.

IMG provides consulting and technical education services and uses Microsoft developer tools and network technologies. The consulting manager assigned to the IRI/SkyLight project began investigating the school's predicament by analyzing the functioning computer systems and interviewing personnel about their needs and desires. In performing this requirements study, he considered how these employees wanted the new database system to appear and how they would use it.

Next, he used this employee input to design a prototype system. This mock-up specified the components of the database system and described how it would function. He met with the school's employees on a regular basis to obtain their approval on his system and their suggestions for enhancing the proposal. When everyone agreed on the prototype, he then submitted a bid for the project.

Once the contract was approved, he assembled a team of three programmers to write the application using Visual Basic. He selected this software based on its capability of creating applications containing menus, submenus, and Data controls and its user-friendly toolbars and dialog boxes. The programmers developed a classic database containing student records with fields for essential data such as names, addresses, telephone numbers, and classes taken. They tested all the menu options in their system by creating specific scenarios and examining the results. For example, they created a class, assigned a teacher and a textbook, accepted a new student and entered his personal data, registered him for the class, and then dropped him from the class.

The first release of the software took more than 1,000 hours to develop, with the biggest chunk of time devoted to the planning process and design study. IMG's resolution of IRI/SkyLight's problem is based on the elementary principle of taking time at the start to analyze the situation and devise a solution before writing one line of code. If you take the same care in developing your database for this project, you should achieve similar success.

Microsoft
Visual Basic 5

Menus, Data Controls, Common Dialogs, and General Procedures

*C*ase *P*erspective

Your friend, LaTisha is studying elementary education. She is developing a student project to teach grade school children to recognize the flags of different countries and be able to state the name of the country, its capital, and its form of government. LaTisha has some ideas for a PC-based, electronic *flash card* system that she can use in the classroom. The hardware available to LaTisha for the project includes a laptop computer and projector. The laptop has Microsoft Windows and Microsoft Office 97 software.

LaTisha is a competent user of Microsoft Access. She has created a database containing the world geography information she needs, and she is able to use Access to add, modify, and delete data in her database as necessary. LaTisha wants you to develop a *front end* to her database that will present the information one country at a time under her control. She also wants to be able to turn the display of any combination of country name, capital, and government on or off so she can vary the *missing* information during quizzes.

*I*ntroduction

One of the most powerful features of Visual Basic is its capability of creating sophisticated database applications with minimal programming. A **database** is a collection of related facts organized in a systematic manner. A telephone book is an example of a database that contains the names, addresses, and telephone numbers of individuals and businesses in a community. Many database management products, such as Microsoft Access, are available for personal computers and they allow you to store, maintain, and retrieve data quickly and efficiently.

Visual Basic can be used to build applications that display, edit, and update information from databases created by many different database software programs such as Access, dBase, FoxPro, and Paradox. This project provides an introductory exposure to accessing a database by building an application that displays information from a World Geography database created with Microsoft Access. The World Geography database is included on the Data Disk that accompanies this book. This project describes only how to display information in an existing database. Visual Basic can be used to create applications that also query, add, change, or delete information in a database. These features are covered in a later project.

Many of the application-building activities in Projects 1 through 3 involved choosing commands on drop-down menus selected from the Visual Basic menu bar. This structure of menus and commands is common in many types of Windows applications. The application built in this project includes a menu bar, menus, submenus, and pop-up menus. In addition to presenting the Data control and Font CommonDialog, this project introduces you to control arrays. You also will learn additional properties and methods of some of the controls with which you are already familiar. This project also expands your abilities to write code by introducing the For...Next loop, the Not operator, the With statement, and writing your own general procedures.

Project Four — GeoView Database Viewer

The completed GeoView database viewer application is shown in Figure 4-1 as it displays on the desktop during run time. This application accesses an existing database of information about different countries and displays that information one country at a time. The name of the database file is World.mdb.

Each characteristic, or attribute, of a country, such as its name or capital, is represented in the database by a **field**. In addition to text fields, the World database has a field that contains a graphical image of each country's flag. Information about a specific country (the values for that country contained in a group of fields) is represented in a database by a single **record**. A group of records within a database that have the same fields is called a **table**. Although databases can contain more than one table, the World database contains only one table, named Countries.

The information contained in the Countries table of the World database is shown in Table 4-1, where each column represents a field and each row represents a record.

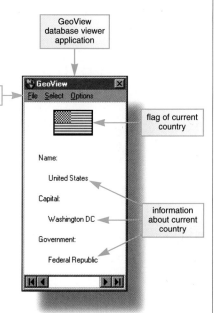

FIGURE 4-1

TABLE 4-1			
NAME	*CAPITAL*	*GOVERNMENT*	*FLAG*
United States	Washington DC	Federal Republic	image
Italy	Rome	Republic	image
France	Paris	Republic	image
Denmark	Copenhagen	Const. Monarchy	image
Turkey	Ankara	Republic	image
Mexico	Mexico City	Federal Republic	image
Brazil	Brasilia	Federal Republic	image
Japan	Tokyo	Const. Monarchy	image
Ireland	Dublin	Republic	image

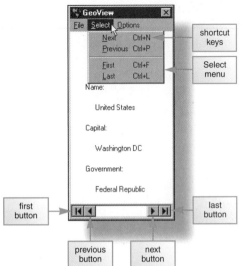

shortcut keys

Select menu

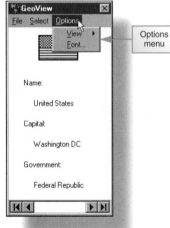

first button

previous button

next button

last button

FIGURE 4-2

Unlike the applications built in previous projects, the GeoView database viewer application does not have any CommandButton, OptionButton, or CheckBox controls for you to initiate events or choose options during run time (Figure 4-1 on the previous page). The reason for this omission is that all run-time interaction with the application occurs by using menus or the Data control.

You can view the information in Table 4-1 during run time by moving forward or backward one record (country) at a time or by moving directly to the first record or to the last record. These actions are initiated by choosing the Next, Previous, First, and Last commands on the Select menu or by clicking the first record, next record, previous record, or last record button on the Data control. The commands on the Select menu also have access keys and shortcut keys (Figure 4-2).

Similar to the Select menu, the Options menu also is available on the menu bar (Figure 4-3). You also can access the Options menu as a **pop-up menu**, also called a **shortcut menu** (Figure 4-4), which displays whenever the user right-clicks anywhere on the form during run time. Pointing to View on the Options menu displays a submenu (Figure 4-4), from which the user can turn on and off the display of any combination of the name, capital, and government fields. The currently displayed fields are indicated by a check mark on the menu.

Clicking Font on the Options menu displays the Font dialog box through which the user can change the Font characteristics of the GeoView application (Figure 4-5).

The application can be moved on the desktop by the user at run time. The user cannot, however, maximize or drag the borders of the application. When the user selects a different font size, the application's window is resized to accommodate the new font size (Figure 4-6). The GeoView application is closed by clicking the Close button or by clicking Exit on the File menu (Figure 4-7).

Options menu

FIGURE 4-3

Options shortcut menu

View submenu

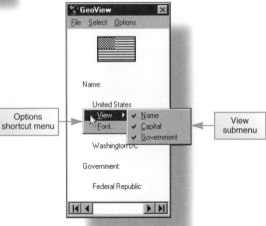

FIGURE 4-4

Font dialog box

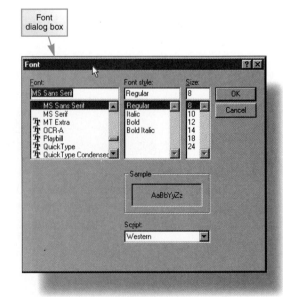

FIGURE 4-5

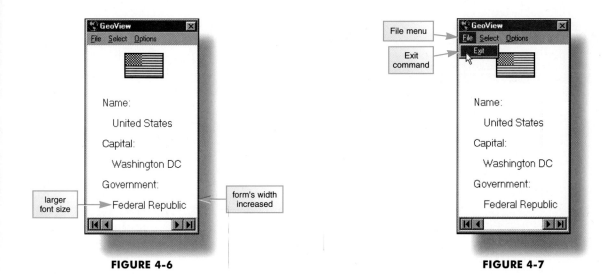

FIGURE 4-6   **FIGURE 4-7**

Project Steps

In this project, you will follow the three-step Visual Basic application development process to build the GeoView application. You will complete the following tasks in this project.

1. Start a Standard EXE project in Visual Basic.
2. Set the form's size and position.
3. Add an Image control and create a Label control array.
4. Add Data and CommonDialog controls.
5. Create the menus.
6. Save the form.
7. Set the form's properties.
8. Set Size and Stretch properties of the Image control.
9. Set control Name and Caption properties.
10. Set properties of the CommonDialog control.
11. Set properties of the Data control.
12. Set properties of the data-aware controls.
13. Save the form again.
14. Write the Exit procedure.
15. Write procedures for the Select menu commands.
16. Write a procedure to display the pop-up menu.
17. Write the Font dialog procedure.
18. Write a general procedure for the View menu commands.
19. Write code to call the general procedure from the View menu commands.
20. Save and test the project.

The following pages contain a detailed explanation of each of these steps.

Getting Started

The database file and the form's icon used in this project are available on the Data Disk that accompanies this book. The database file is named World.mdb and the icon is named Earth.ico. If you will be saving this project on a disk other than the Data Disk, then before starting this project, you should copy these two files to the disk you will use to save the GeoView application.

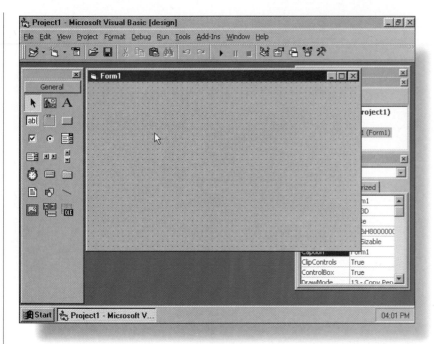

FIGURE 4-8

Begin this project by starting Visual Basic as described on page VB 1.7 in Project 1 or by opening a new Standard EXE project if you are already running Visual Basic. If necessary, you should complete the steps on page VB 1.10 in Project 1 to arrange your desktop to resemble Figure 4-8.

Creating the Interface

In this step, the size and location of the form will be determined, and the controls will be added to the form. The GeoView database viewer form contains one Image control, six Label controls, one CommonDialog control, and one Data control. These controls are shown as they appear on the completed form during design time in Figure 4-9.

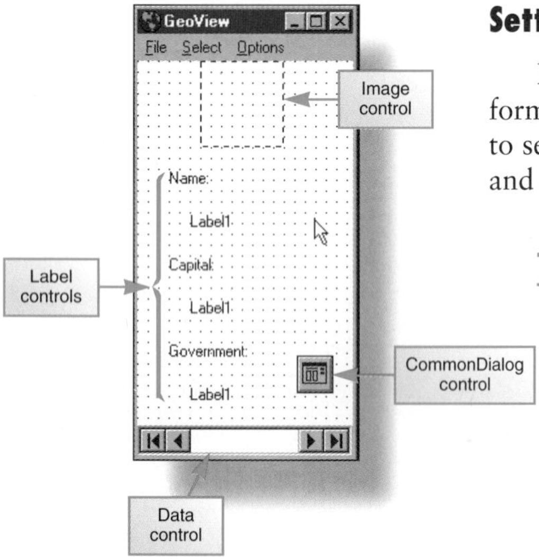

Setting the Size and Location of the Form

In previous projects, you have seen several different ways to set the form's size and location during design time. Perform the following steps to set the form's size by setting the form's Height and Width properties and set the form's position by dragging and dropping.

TO SET THE SIZE AND LOCATION OF A FORM

① Select the Form control by clicking it or by selecting its name, Form1, in the Object list box in the Properties window.

② Double-click the Height property in the Properties list in the Properties window.

③ Type 4800 and then press the ENTER key.

④ Double-click the Width property in the Properties list in the Properties window.

⑤ Type 2600 and then press the ENTER key.

⑥ Drag the form to the center of the desktop.

The form displays as shown in Figure 4-10.

FIGURE 4-9

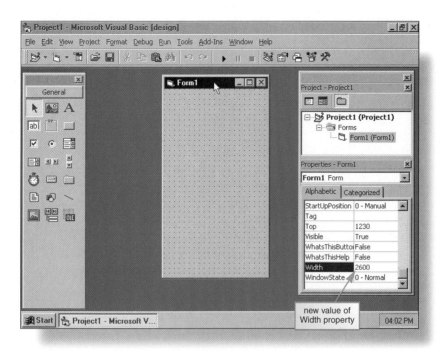

FIGURE 4-10

Adding an Image Control

An **Image control** is used in the GeoView database viewer application to contain the graphical images of the flags of the different countries as shown in Figure 4-11. Perform the following steps to add the Image control.

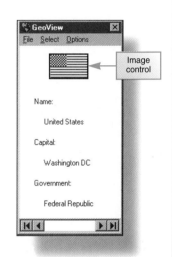

FIGURE 4-11

TO ADD AN IMAGE CONTROL

① Double-click the Image button in the Toolbox.

② Drag the control, Image1, to the location shown in Figure 4-12.

The Image button and Image control's location are shown in Figure 4-12.

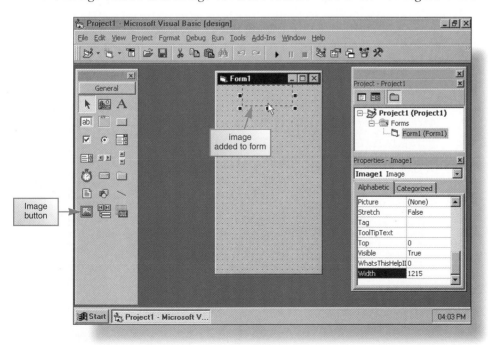

FIGURE 4-12

More *About*
Image Controls

An Image control can display a graphic from a bitmap, icon, or metafile, as well as enhanced metafile, JPEG, or GIF files. The Image control uses fewer system resources and repaints faster than a PictureBox control, but it supports only a subset of the PictureBox properties, events, and methods.

Adding a Label Control Array

Six label controls are used in the GeoView database viewer application (Figure 4-11 on the previous page). Three labels are used to indicate the names of the text fields in the database. The other three labels are used to display the field values for the current record. The six labels are added to the form as a control array.

A **control array** is made up of a group of controls of the same type (for example, all Labels or all TextBoxes). Controls in an array share a common control name and a common set of event procedures. For example, clicking any label in the array triggers the same Click event procedure.

Each control in an array has a unique index number assigned by Visual Basic when the array is created. The value of the index begins at zero for the first control and increases by one for each new control. All items in a control array must have the same Name property setting. All other property settings apply only to the individual control. For example, Label1(0) can have a caption and other property settings different from Label1(1).

Arrays make it easier to change a property of a group of controls to a common value during run time. For example, suppose you wanted to change the FontSize property of all six labels to 12 at run time. As separate controls, this change would require six similar, but separate, code statements. As an array, the FontSize property can be changed much more easily through a simple code structure that will be presented later.

The six labels have their AutoSize property set to True and have the same BackStyle property. Because the controls will be added to the form with the copy method, these two properties will be set for the first control during the interface creation step, instead of during the setting properties step. This will eliminate having to set the two properties for each of the six labels later.

You can use the **Transparent value** of the **BackStyle property** to create transparent controls when you are using a background color on a form. An **Opaque value** of the BackStyle property is used when you want a control to stand out. A control's **BackColor** property is ignored if its BackStyle = 0 (Transparent). Complete the following steps to add one label and set its AutoSize and BackStyle properties. The control then is copied five times to a control array.

Steps **To Create a Control Array**

---

1 Double-click the Label button in the Toolbox.

A default-sized label, Label1, is added to the form (Figure 4-13).

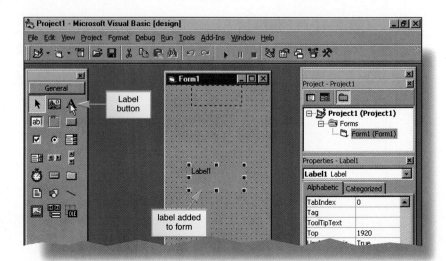

FIGURE 4-13

2 **Double-click the AutoSize property in the Properties list in the Properties window.**

The value of the AutoSize property changes to True (Figure 4-14).

FIGURE 4-14

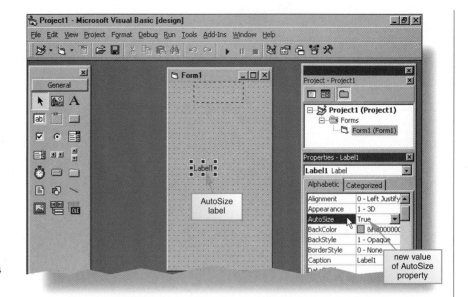

3 **Double-click the BackStyle property in the Properties list in the Properties window.**

The value of the BackStyle property changes to 0 - Transparent (Figure 4-15).

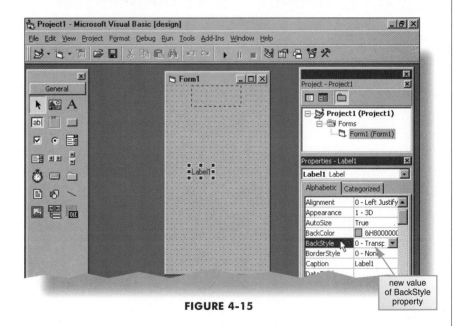

FIGURE 4-15

4 **Drag the label to the position shown in Figure 4-16. Right-click the Label control and then point to Copy on the shortcut menu.**

A shortcut menu displays next to the control (Figure 4-16).

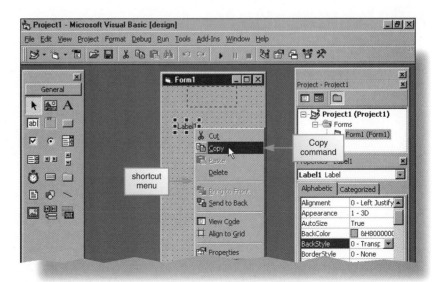

FIGURE 4-16

5 Click Copy.

The control is copied to the Clipboard and the shortcut menu closes (Figure 4-17).

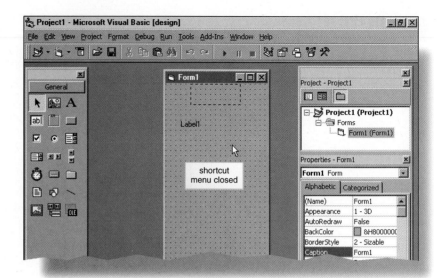

FIGURE 4-17

6 Right-click the form and then point to Paste on the shortcut menu.

A shortcut menu displays (Figure 4-18).

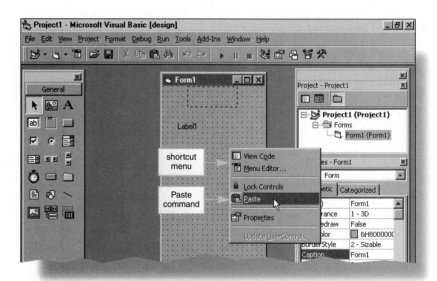

FIGURE 4-18

7 Click Paste and then point to the Yes button in the Microsoft Visual Basic dialog box that displays (Figure 4-19).

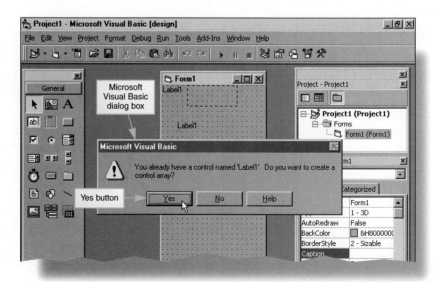

FIGURE 4-19

8 **Click the Yes button.**

The name of the first label changes to Label1(0). A second label control, Label1(1), is added to the upper-left corner of the form (Figure 4-20). The dialog box closes.

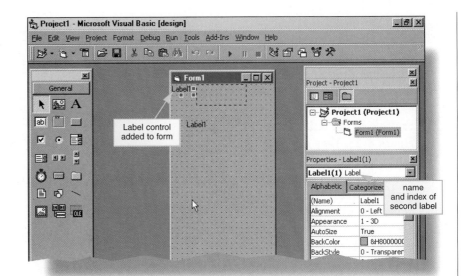

FIGURE 4-20

9 **Drag the second label control, Label1(1), to the location shown in Figure 4-21.**

The property values of the second Label control (including the Caption property) are identical to the property values of the control that was copied, Label1(0).

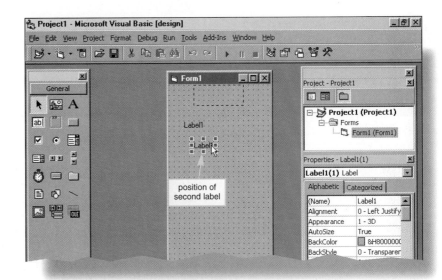

FIGURE 4-21

10 **Press the CTRL+V keys.**

A third Label control is added to the form (Figure 4-22).

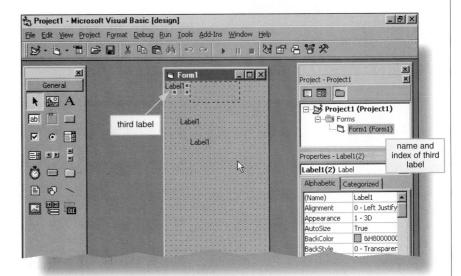

FIGURE 4-22

11 **Drag the third Label control to the location shown in Figure 4-23. Repeat Step 10 three times, each time dragging the control to the location shown in Figure 4-23. Be careful to locate the controls in the order shown in Figure 4-23. They can be confused easily at this point because they have the same caption, Label1. If necessary, adjust the alignment and position of the labels as shown in Figure 4-23. Click the form to deselect Label1(5).**

The six labels in the control array display as shown in Figure 4-23.

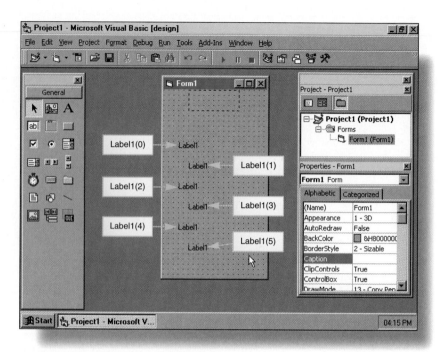

FIGURE 4-23

*Other*Ways

1. Click control to be copied, on File menu click Copy, click form, on File menu click Paste

When controls were copied in previous projects, the Microsoft Visual Basic dialog box displayed each time a copy of a control was placed on the form. This occurred because you clicked the No button in the dialog box each time you were asked if you wanted to start a new control array. Once you clicked the Yes button in the dialog box in the previous steps, it ceased to display because all subsequent copies were added to the array. If you had wanted to add an additional Label control to the form but not as part of the array, you would have had to use a method other than copying, such as double-clicking the Label button in the Toolbox.

Adding a CommonDialog Control and Data Control

You used a Color dialog box in Project 2 to select background colors for the form during run time. The GeoView application uses a Font dialog box that enables the user to change Font properties during run time. Both the Color and Font dialog boxes are among the possible dialog boxes available when you use the CommonDialog control. Recall from Project 2, that although the CommonDialog control is visible on the form during design time, it never is visible during run time. You also should recall from Project 2 that the CommonDialog control is an ActiveX control and must be added to the Toolbox before you can use it in your application.

A **Data control** is used in Visual Basic applications to provide the necessary links to a database file. The Data control is added to a form in the same manner as other controls. A form can contain more than one Data control, and generally one Data control exists for each database table accessed by the application. The Data control has four **record selection buttons** used during run time to move among records in a database, as shown in Figure 4-24. Perform the following steps to add a CommonDialog control and Data control.

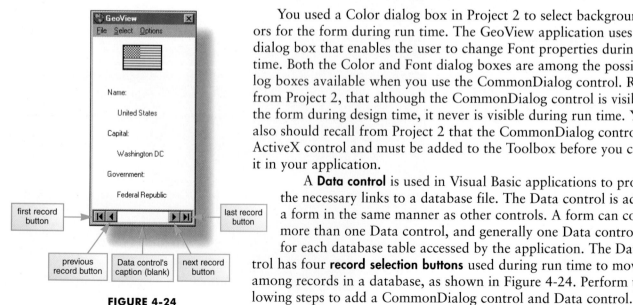

FIGURE 4-24

Steps To Add CommonDialog and Data Controls

1 **Right-click the Toolbox. Click Components. Click the Controls tab in the Components dialog box and then click Microsoft Common Dialog Control 5.0. Click the OK button. Double-click the CommonDialog control button in the Toolbox.**

The CommonDialog button is added to the Toolbox and a default-sized CommonDialog control, CommonDialog1, is added to the form (Figure 4-25).

CommonDialog button added to Toolbox

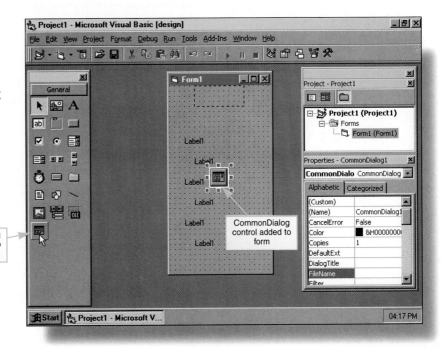

FIGURE 4-25

2 **Drag the CommonDialog control to the location shown in Figure 4-26.**

The location is not critical because the CommonDialog control is not visible during run time.

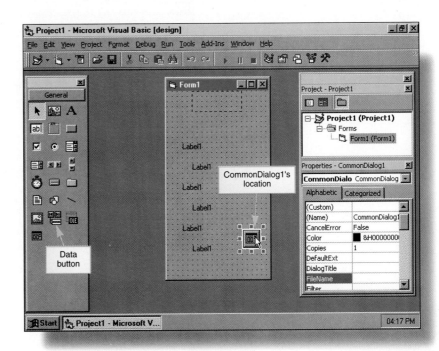

FIGURE 4-26

3 **Double-click the Data button in the Toolbox.**

A default-sized Data control, Data1, is added to the form (Figure 4-27).

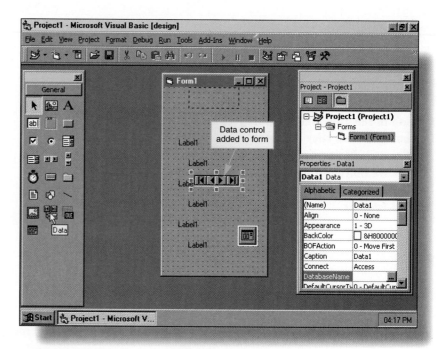

FIGURE 4-27

4 **Drag the Data control to the location shown in Figure 4-28.**

The location is not critical because it will be set later as the property of the Data control.

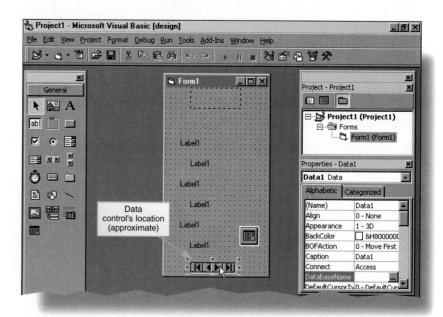

FIGURE 4-28

The GeoView database viewer application contains a Data control to link to the World database. Record selection is controlled through the Data control or the Select menu. Later, code will be written that causes the Select menu commands to trigger the Data control events that make different records in the database the current record. Even though the Select menu commands initiate the record selection actions in this application, a Data control still must be added to make the link between the application and the database. If you wanted to limit record selection to only the Select menu, you could do this by setting the Data control's Visible property to false.

Creating Menus

The GeoView database viewer contains three menus in the menu bar: File, Select, and Options (Figure 4-29). These menus are selected during run time either by clicking their names in the menu bar or by pressing access keys. **Access keys** allow you to open a menu at run time by pressing the ALT key and a letter key. Access key assignments are common in Windows applications and appear as an underlined letter in the Menu control's caption. For example, the letter F is the access key for the File menu (Figure 4-29).

Access keys also can be used for menu commands. When a menu is open, however, you press only the access key of a command (not the ALT key) to choose that command. In the following steps, the three menus in the GeoView database viewer application are created one at a time.

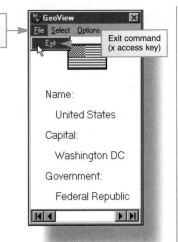

FIGURE 4-29

Creating the File Menu

The **File menu** on the Visual Basic menu bar follows a standard layout for this type of menu in Windows applications. Although the Visual Basic application can be closed by clicking its Close button, File menus always include an Exit (or Close) command as an alternate way to close the application. The File menu in the GeoView database viewer application contains only the Exit command, as shown in Figure 4-29.

Each command you add to a menu is an additional control within the application and it has a name and a Click event. Menus are created during design time with Visual Basic's **Menu Editor**. The Menu Editor dialog box is shown with its major components identified in Figure 4-30.

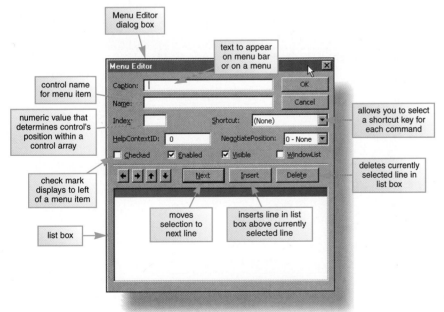

FIGURE 4-30

Perform the steps on the next page to create the File menu for the GeoView database viewer.

Steps To Create a Menu

1 **Click the Menu Editor button on the toolbar. Drag the Menu Editor dialog box to the center of the desktop.**

The Menu Editor dialog box opens on the desktop (Figure 4-31).

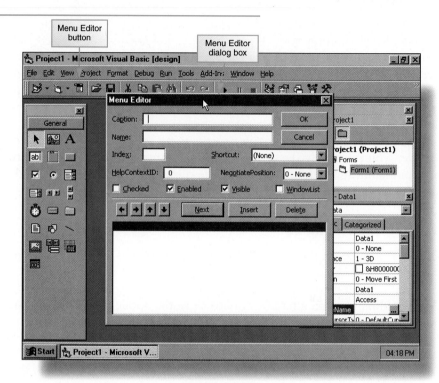

FIGURE 4-31

2 **Type** `&File` **in the Caption text box.**

The caption that will display on the menu bar displays in the Caption text box and in the list box (Figure 4-32). The ampersand (&) is placed before the letter in the caption to be used as the access key. At run time, the ampersand is not visible, and the access key letter is underlined.

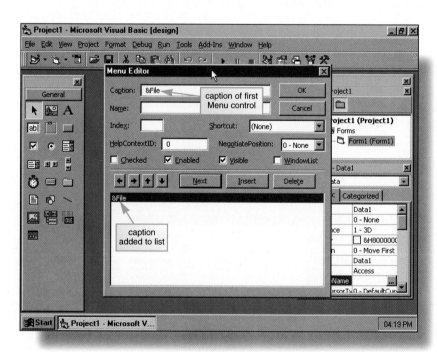

FIGURE 4-32

3 Press the TAB key or click the Name text box to move the insertion point to that box. Type mnuFile and then point to the Next button.

The name of the Menu control, mnuFile, displays in the Name text box (Figure 4-33).

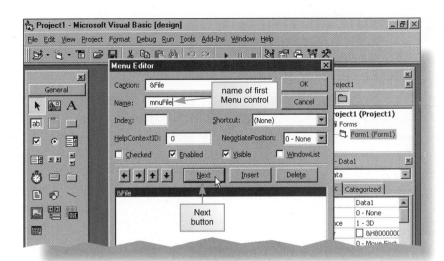

FIGURE 4-33

4 Click the Next button.

The highlighted line in the list box advances to the next line, and the Menu Editor properties boxes are blank (Figure 4-34).

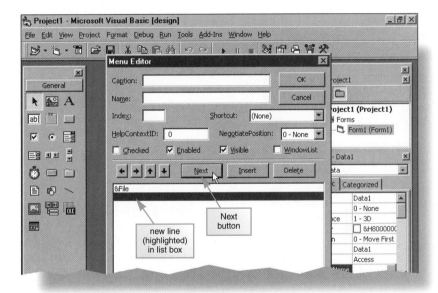

FIGURE 4-34

5 Click the right arrow button. Select the Caption text box by clicking it. Type E&xit as the caption.

A new Menu control with the run time caption, Exit, is added. The caption is preceded by a series of four dots (Figure 4-35). Clicking the right arrow button indents the control's caption and adds dots. This step indicates Exit is a command within the File menu.

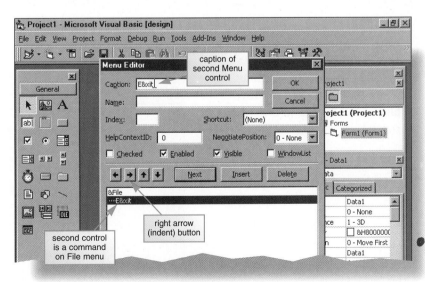

FIGURE 4-35

6 **Press the TAB key and then type**
mnuExit in the Name text box.
Click the Next button. Click the
left arrow button.

Clicking the left arrow button moves
the insertion point flush left in the
list box to indicate the next item will
be a new menu (Figure 4-36).

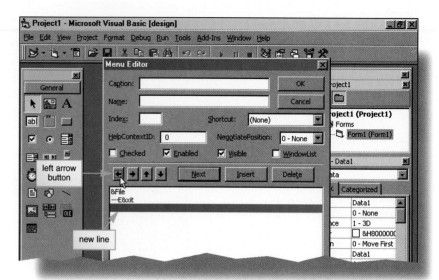

FIGURE 4-36

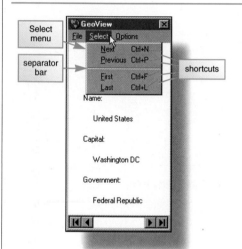

FIGURE 4-37

Adding Shortcuts and Separator Bars to Menus

The **Select menu** is shown in Figure 4-37. The four commands in the menu correspond to the options to move among the records in the database during run time. The four commands each have a keyboard shortcut. A **shortcut** allows you to select a shortcut key or combination of keys that substitute during run time for clicking the command on the menu.

The Select menu also includes a separator bar. A **separator bar** is a horizontal line used to group related commands in a menu visually. Separator bars are added to the menu at design time by typing a hyphen (–) in the Caption text box. Perform the following steps to create the Select menu with keyboard shortcuts and a separator bar.

 Steps To Add Keyboard Shortcuts and Separator Bars to Menus

1 **Type &Select in the Caption**
text box. Type mnuSelect in the
Name text box. Click the Next
button to advance to a new Menu
control.

The Menu Editor dialog box dis-
plays as shown in Figure 4-38.

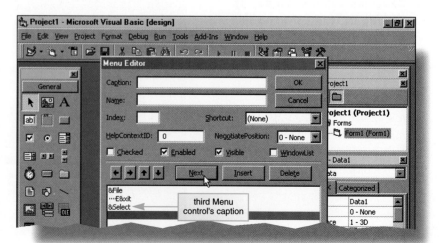

FIGURE 4-38

2 Click the right arrow button to indicate a command within the Select menu. Type &Next in the Caption text box. Type mnuNext in the Name text box. Click the Shortcut box arrow and then click Ctrl+N in the Shortcut list box. Click the Next button. Type &Previous in the Caption text box. Type mnuPrev in the Name text box. Click Ctrl+P in the Shortcut list box.

The Menu Editor dialog box displays as shown in Figure 4-39.

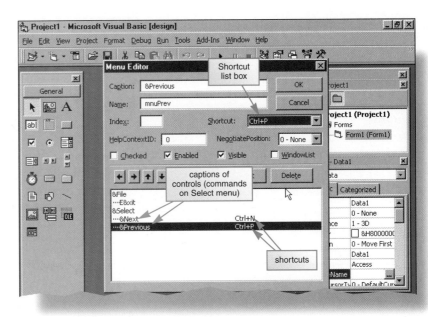

FIGURE 4-39

3 Click the Next button. Add the separator bar to the Select menu by typing - (a hyphen) in the Caption text box. Type Separator in the Name text box. Click the Next button. Type &First in the Caption text box. Type mnuFirst in the Name text box. Click Ctrl+F in the Shortcut list box. Click the Next button. Type &Last in the Caption text box. Type mnuLast in the Name text box. Click Ctrl+L in the Shortcut list box.

The Menu Editor dialog box displays as shown in Figure 4-40. Each separator bar in a menu must be given a unique name even though it does not have a function at run time.

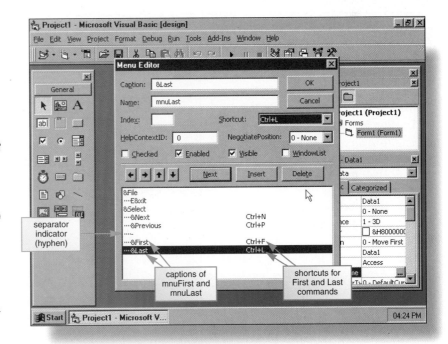

FIGURE 4-40

Submenus and Menu Check Marks

The Options menu is shown in Figure 4-41 on the next page. The **Options menu** displays during run time as either a drop-down menu or a pop-up (shortcut) menu. Both of these types of menus are created in the same way in the Menu Editor dialog box. Later, you will write a code statement that activates the shortcut menu during run time. The Options menu contains a submenu and a command. A **submenu** branches off another menu to present an additional set of commands in a separate grouping.

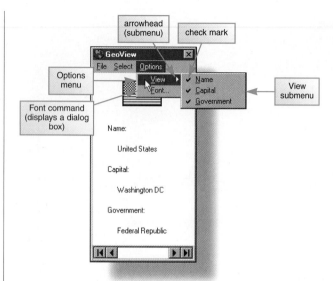

FIGURE 4-41

Each menu created in Visual Basic can have up to four levels of submenus. Menu commands that display submenus have an **arrowhead symbol** at their right edge (Figure 4-41).

The **View submenu** (Figure 4-41) is used in this application to set whether or not the country's name, capital, and government type are shown. During run time, the status of the command is indicated by a check mark if the command is chosen or the absence of a check mark if it is not chosen. The **Font command** is used to open the Font dialog box. Commands that open dialog boxes generally include an ellipsis (...) following the command. Perform the following steps to create the Options menu containing a submenu and menu check marks.

 Steps **To Add Submenus and Menu Check Marks**

1 **Click the Next button. Click the left arrow button to move the insertion point flush left in the list box. Type** &Options **in the Caption text box. Type** mnuOptions **in the Name text box. Click the Next button and then click the right arrow button.**

The Menu control named mnuOptions is added. Its caption, &Options, displays in the Menu control list box. The insertion point is advanced to the next line and is indented once to indicate the next control added will be a command within the Options menu (Figure 4-42).

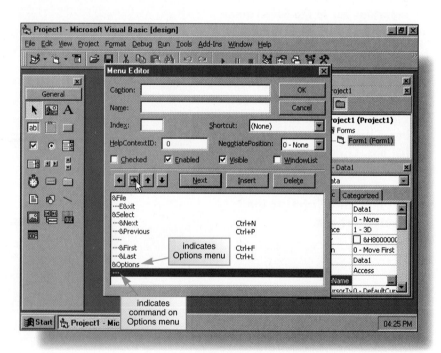

FIGURE 4-42

2 Type &View **in the Caption text box. Type** mnuView **in the Name text box. Click the Next button and then click the right arrow button to indicate that the next control to be added is a submenu. Type** &Name **in the Caption text box. Type** mnuName **in the Name text box. Click Checked.**

The Menu Editor dialog box displays as shown in Figure 4-43. Clicking the Checked check box indicates the mnuName Menu control will have a check mark preceding it at the start of run time.

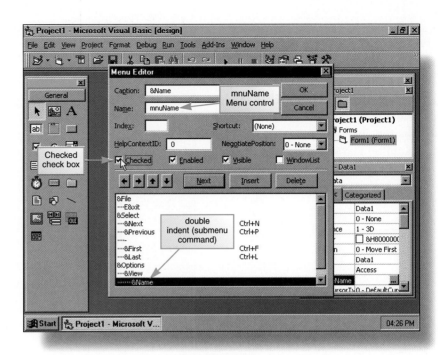

FIGURE 4-43

3 **Click the Next button. Type** &Capital **in the Caption text box. Type** mnuCapital **in the Name text box. Click Checked.**

The Menu Editor dialog box displays as shown in Figure 4-44.

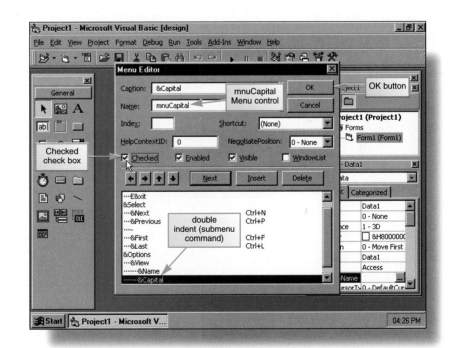

FIGURE 4-44

4 Click the Next button. Type &Government in the Caption text box. Type mnuGovt in the Name text box. Click the Next button. Click Checked. Click the Next button. Click the left arrow button. Type &Font... in the Caption text box. Type mnuFont in the Name text box. Click the OK button.

The Menu Editor dialog box closes and the menus are added to the form (Figure 4-45).

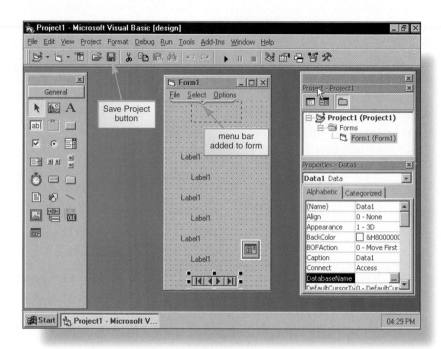

FIGURE 4-45

The menus for the GeoView database viewer application are complete. During design time, menus can be opened in the Form window by clicking the menu name on the menu bar. Click the menu name for each of the menus you just created.

The interface for the GeoView database viewer application now is complete. The second step of application development is to set the properties of the form and other controls.

Saving the Form and the Project

It is a good practice to save your work periodically. Before proceeding with the Property setting, perform the following steps to save the form and project.

TO SAVE A FORM AND PROJECT

1. Insert the floppy disk with the World.mdb and Earth.ico files in the 3½ Floppy [A:] drive.
2. Click the Save Project button on the toolbar.
3. When the Save File As dialog box opens, type GeoView in the File name text box.
4. Click 3½ Floppy [A:] in the Save in list box.
4. Click the Save button in the Save File As dialog box.
5. When the Save Project As dialog box opens, type GeoView in the File name text box.
6. Click the Save button in the Save Project As dialog box.

The form file is saved on the floppy disk in the 3½ Floppy [A:] drive as GeoView.frm. The project file is saved on the diskette in the 3½ Floppy [A:] drive as GeoView.vbp.

Setting Properties

In this section, control properties are set in the following groups of steps:

▶ Properties of the form
▶ Properties of the Image control
▶ Caption property of the Label controls
▶ Properties of the CommonDialog control
▶ Properties of the Data control
▶ Properties of the data-aware controls

Form Properties

In the following steps, you will set several form properties with which you are already familiar. The name of the form will be set to GeoView. No other control names need to be set because all the labels in the array must have the same name, and each of the remaining types of controls appears only once. The form is given a caption to display in its title bar. Additionally, the form's BackColor property is set to white, and an icon is specified to represent the application. The form's BorderStyle is set to fixed single to prevent the user from resizing the form during run time. The MaxButton property is set to false to prevent the user from maximizing the form during run time. Perform the following steps to set these properties for the form.

 To Set Form Properties

① **Select the form by clicking an area that does not contain any other controls. Double-click the Name property in the Properties list. Type** frmGeoView **and press the ENTER key.**

The form's new name displays in both the Project window and the Properties window (Figure 4-46).

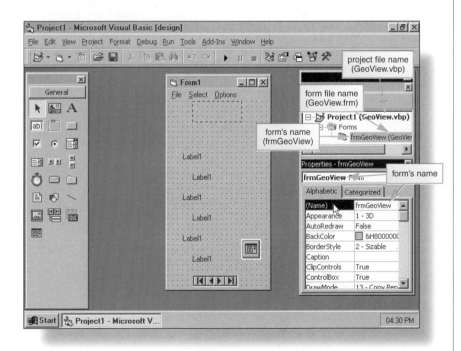

FIGURE 4-46

2 **Double-click the Caption property in the Properties window. Type** GeoView **and then press the ENTER key.**

The form's caption displays in the form's title bar (Figure 4-47).

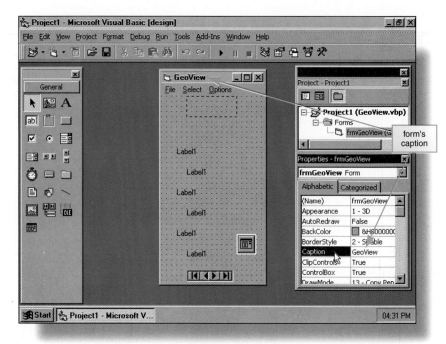

FIGURE 4-47

3 **Double-click the BackColor property in the Properties window. Click the Palette tab. Point to the white color panel identified in Figure 4-48.**

The Color palette opens (Figure 4-48).

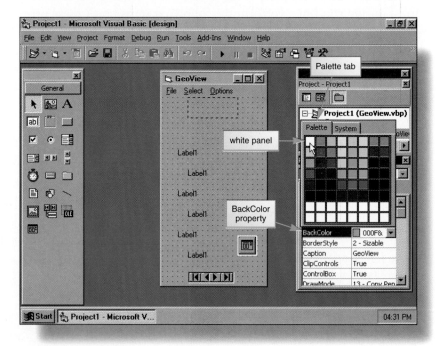

FIGURE 4-48

4 **Click the white color panel.**

The background color of the form control changes to the selected color, and the Color palette closes (Figure 4-49).

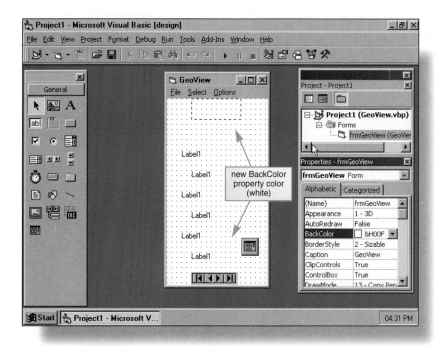

FIGURE 4-49

5 **Double-click the Icon property in the Properties list. Click the Look in box arrow and then click 3½ Floppy [A:]. Point to Earth.ico in the list box.**

The Load Icon dialog box opens (Figure 4-50).

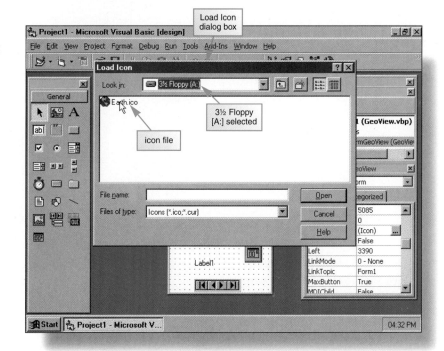

FIGURE 4-50

6 **Double-click Earth.ico.**

Visual Basic loads the icon and closes the Load Icon dialog box (Figure 4-51).

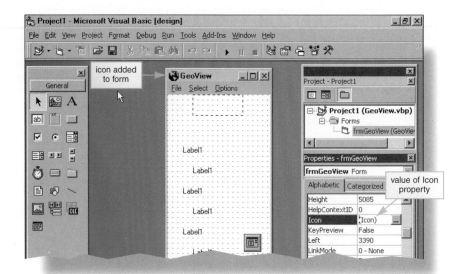

FIGURE 4-51

7 **Double-click the MaxButton property in the Properties list.**

The value changes to False (Figure 4-52).

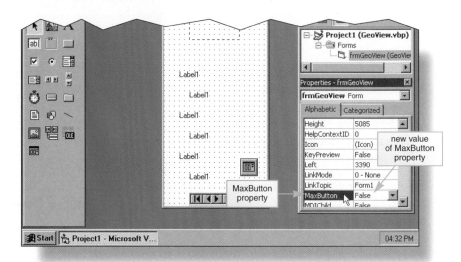

FIGURE 4-52

8 **Click the BorderStyle property. Click the BorderStyle box arrow and then click 1-Fixed Single.**

The value changes to 1-Fixed Single (Figure 4-53).

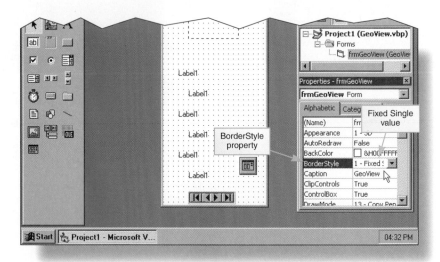

FIGURE 4-53

The MinButton property automatically changes to False. You can change it back to True if you want the user to be able to minimize the window. All of the necessary property settings for the form are complete.

Image Control Properties

The Image control in this application is used to display the flag of the currently selected country. The flags are part of the World database. By default, an Image control will adjust its size to the size of the graphic it contains. The size of the flags is smaller than desired, however, so the Image control's height and width will be increased and its Stretch property will be set to True. When an Image control's **Stretch** property is set to True, the image it contains is stretched to the size of the control. Perform the following steps to set the Image control's properties.

TO SET IMAGE CONTROL HEIGHT, WIDTH, AND STRETCH PROPERTIES

1. Click the Image control to select it.
2. Double-click the Height property in the Properties window. Type 960 and then press the ENTER key.
3. Scroll down the Properties list and then double-click the Width property. Type 960 and then press the ENTER key.
4. Double-click the Stretch property in the Properties list.

The size of the Image control now is enlarged (Figure 4-54) and the flags will be stretched to fit the size of the Image control.

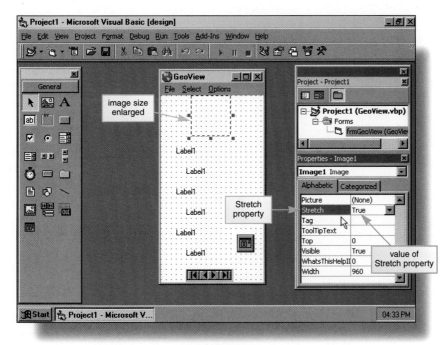

FIGURE 4-54

Label Properties

You already set the labels' BackStyle and AutoSize properties when you created the array. The captions of the three labels aligned to the left on the form are used to show the names of the fields in the database. The captions of the remaining three indented labels are used as containers for the values of the corresponding fields in the current record. Perform the following steps to add the field names to the form as captions of the Label controls.

TO SET LABEL CAPTION PROPERTIES

1 Select Label1(0) by clicking its name in the Object list box in the Properties window. Double-click the Caption property in the Properties list. Type `Name:` and then press the ENTER key.

2 Select Label1(2) by clicking its name in the Object list box in the Properties window. Double-click the Caption property in the Properties list. Type `Capital:` and then press the ENTER key.

3 Select Label1(4) by clicking its name in the Object list box in the Properties window. Double-click the Caption property in the Properties list. Type `Government:` and then press the ENTER key.

The form displays as shown in Figure 4-55.

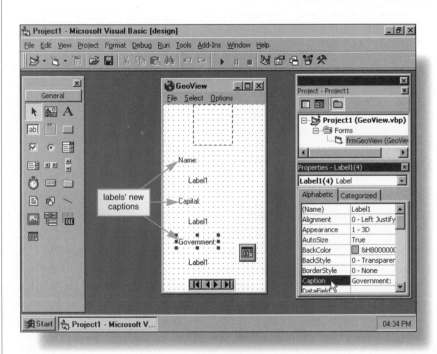

FIGURE 4-55

CommonDialog Control Properties

In Project 2, you used a CommonDialog control to display a Color dialog box. In this project, you will use the CommonDialog control to display a Font dialog box. Although the Font dialog box is displayed by using the **ShowFont** method in code, you still must set some of the CommonDialog control's properties. Recall from Project 2 that the Flags property is used to set dialog box options. When the Flags value is set to 1, the Font dialog box lists only the screen fonts supported by the system. You can search Visual Basic Help on Flags for a complete list of options and their values.

In Visual Basic, the default for the FontName property is determined by the system. Fonts available with Visual Basic vary depending on your system configuration, display devices, and printing devices. For this reason, when the Font dialog box displays on the desktop during run time, a preselected Font does not exist. You must set this font through the CommonDialog's properties either at design time or run time. Perform the following steps to set the CommonDialog's Flags and FontName properties.

TO SET COMMONDIALOG FLAGS AND FONTNAME PROPERTIES

1 Select the CommonDialog control by clicking it on the form or by clicking its name in the Object list box in the Properties window.

2 Double-click the Flags property in the Properties list. Type 1 and then press the ENTER key.

3 Click any one of the Label controls on the form. Scroll through the Properties list and make a note of the default value of its Font property (e.g., MS Sans Serif).

4 Select the CommonDialog control by clicking it on the form or by clicking its name in the Object list box in the Properties window.

5 Double-click the FontName property in the Properties list. Type MS Sans Serif (the default Font) and then press the ENTER key.

The form displays as shown in Figure 4-56.

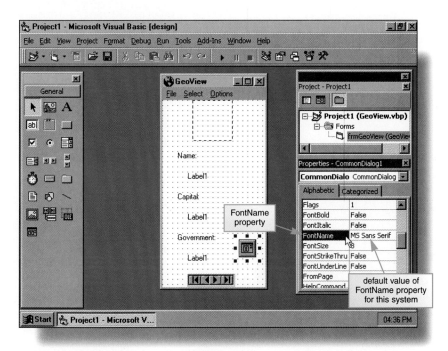

FontName property

default value of FontName property for this system

FIGURE 4-56

FIGURE 4-57

Data Control Properties

The Data control used in the GeoView application is shown as it displays during run time in Figure 4-57. The **Caption** of a Data control is the text that displays between the control's next record and previous record buttons. In the GeoView application, the caption is blank. The Data control's **Align property** determines whether the control can be located anywhere on a form or whether it is sized automatically to fit the form's width and displayed at the top, left, right, or bottom of the form. In the GeoView application the Align property is set to Bottom.

The **DatabaseName property** is used to supply the file name of the database to which the Data control is linked. The **RecordSource property** is used to specify the table name in the database to which the Data control is linked. The **Connect property** is used to specify the type of database (Microsoft Access, FoxPro, dBASE, etc.). When the database to be accessed is a Microsoft Access database (as in this application), it is not necessary to set the Connect property. Perform the steps on the next page to set the properties of the Data control.

Data control (align = bottom)

Data control's caption (blank)

Steps **To Set Data Control Properties**

1 **Select the Data control by clicking it or by clicking its name, Data1, in the Object list box in the Properties window. Double-click the DatabaseName property in the Properties list.**

The DatabaseName dialog box opens (Figure 4-58).

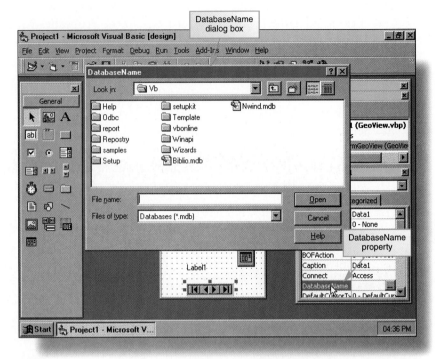

FIGURE 4-58

2 **Make sure the floppy disk to which you copied the World.mdb file earlier is in the 3½ Floppy [A:] drive. Click 3½ Floppy [A:] in the Look in list box box. Point to World.mdb.**

The database file name displays in the list box (Figure 4-59).

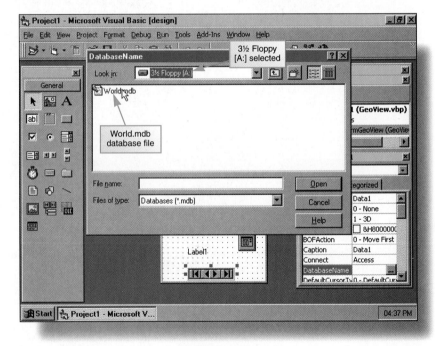

FIGURE 4-59

3 **Double-click World.mdb.**

The file's name displays as the value of the DatabaseName property in the Properties list (Figure 4-60).

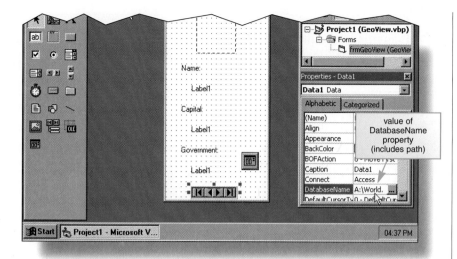

FIGURE 4-60

4 **Click the RecordSource property. Click the RecordSource box arrow.**

The property values list box for the RecordSource property contains all of the tables in the World database (Figure 4-61). Currently, only Countries is listed.

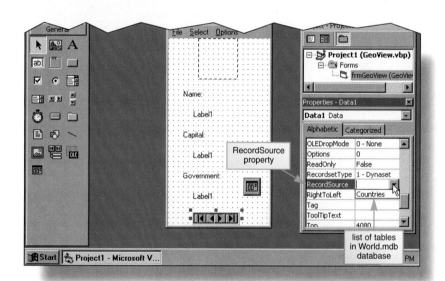

FIGURE 4-61

5 **Click Countries.**

The list closes and the property value (Countries) displays (Figure 4-62).

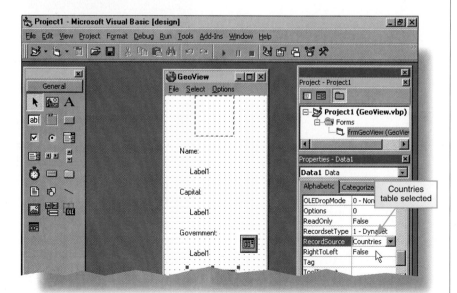

FIGURE 4-62

6 **Click the Align property in the Properties list. Click the Align box arrow and then click 2 - Align Bottom.**

The Data control aligns with the bottom of the form and its width changes (Figure 4-63).

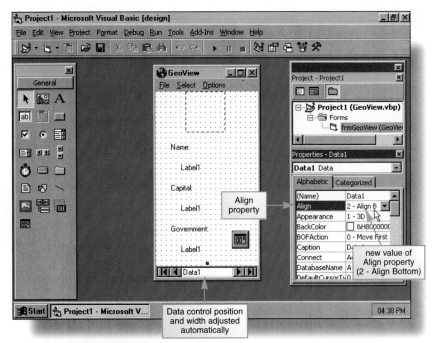

FIGURE 4-63

7 **Double-click the Caption property. Press the DELETE key.**

The caption changes to blank (Figure 4-64).

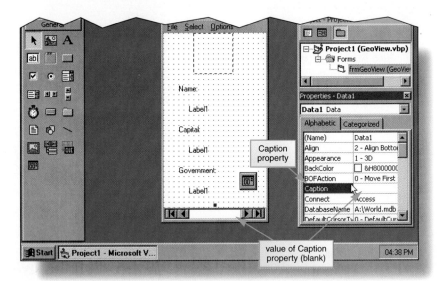

FIGURE 4-64

In Step 4, the property list contained only the name of the Countries table. If the World.mdb database contained more than one table, the values for the RecordSource property would contain all the available tables.

Setting Properties of the Data-Aware Controls

The controls within Visual Basic that can be linked to information in a database are said to be **data-aware**. The data-aware controls include check boxes, images, labels, picture boxes, and text boxes. To use these controls to access a database, the controls must be **bound** to a Data control on the form. In a multi-form application, the bound control and the Data control to which it is bound must be on the same form.

Data-aware controls are bound to a Data control by setting their DataSource and DataField properties. The **DataSource property** of a control specifies the name of the Data control to which it is bound. The **DataField** property of a bound control specifies the name of a field in the database to which the control is linked. Perform the following steps to bind the three Label controls and one Image control in the GeoView database viewer application used to display information from the Countries table of the World.mdb database.

Steps To Bind Data-Aware Controls

① **Select the Label1(1) control by clicking its name in the Object list box in the Properties window. Click the DataSource property in the Properties list. Click the DataSource box arrow.**

The property values list box for the DataSource property contains all the Data controls on the form (Figure 4-65). Currently, only Data1 is listed.

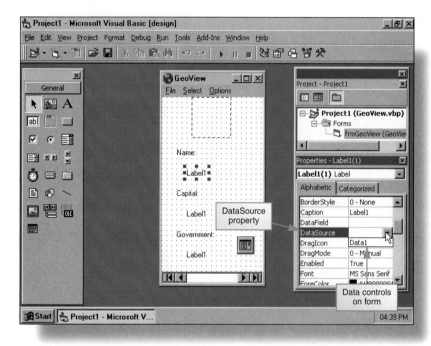

FIGURE 4-65

② **Select the Data1 control by clicking its name in the list box. Click the DataField property in the Properties list. Click the arrow next to the Settings box.**

The property values list box for the DataField property contains all the fields in the Countries table of the World.mdb database (Figure 4-66).

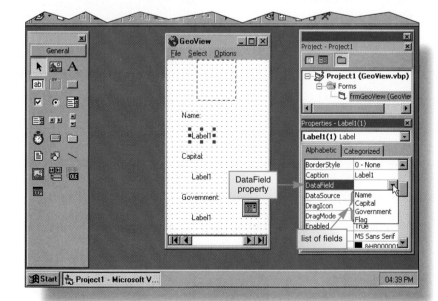

FIGURE 4-66

3 Select the Name field by clicking its name in the list box.

The list closes, and the property value displays (Figure 4-67).

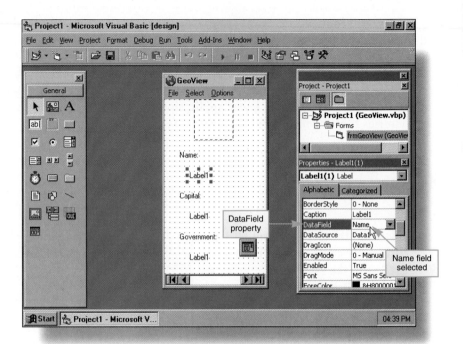

FIGURE 4-67

4 Repeat Steps 1 through 3 three times to accomplish the following: bind the Label1(3) control to the Data1 control, and then set the DataField property equal to Capital. Bind the Label1(5) control to the Data1 control, and then set the DataField property equal to Government. Bind the Image1 control to the Data1 control, and then set the DataField property equal to Flag.

The form displays as shown in Figure 4-68.

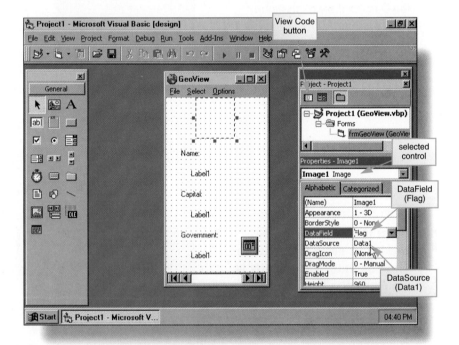

FIGURE 4-68

It is not necessary to change the Caption property of the bound labels to blank because their captions will be given the field values of the first record in the table as soon as the application starts.

The property-setting stage of application development is complete. The third and last stage is to write the code for the application. Click the Save Project button on the toolbar to save the form and project with the updated properties.

Writing Code

Code must be written for ten Event procedures and one general procedure in the GeoView database viewer application. The control, procedure, and a description of the action for the event procedures are listed in Table 4-2. The general procedure is presented later.

The event procedures (subroutines) for the four Menu controls that make up the Select menu are similar. The Click event procedures (subroutines) for the three menu commands that make up the View submenu also are similar. The code-writing activities for the GeoView database viewer application are grouped as follows:

TABLE 4-2

CONTROL	EVENT	ACTIONS
mnuExit	Click	Closes the application
mnuNext	Click	Displays the information from the next record in the table
mnuPrev	Click	Displays the information from the previous record in the table
mnuFirst	Click	Displays the information from the first record in the table
mnuLast	Click	Displays the information from the last record in the table
mnuName	Click	Shows/hides name field and adds/removes menu check mark
mnuCapital	Click	Shows/hides capital field and adds/removes menu check mark
mnuGovt	Click	Shows/hides government field and adds/removes menu check mark
frmGeoView	MouseUp	Displays Options pop-up menu when form is right-clicked
mnuFont	Click	Displays Font dialog box; changes Labels' font properties; resizes form

▶ mnuExit_Click event procedure
▶ Select menu Click event procedures (mnuNext, mnuPrev, mnuFirst, mnuLast)
▶ Pop-up menu display event procedure (MouseUp)
▶ Font menu Click event procedure (Font dialog box)
▶ general procedure
▶ mnuView_Click event procedures (mnuName, mnuCapital, mnuGovt)

Writing an Exit Procedure

When you trigger this event during run time by choosing Exit on the File menu, the GeoView database viewer application closes. For normal termination of a Visual Basic program, you should unload all forms. Before a form is unloaded, the Form_QueryUnload event procedure occurs, followed by the Form_Unload event procedure. Perform the following steps to write the mnuExit_Click event procedure.

TO WRITE AN EXIT PROCEDURE

1. Click the View Code button in the Project window.
2. Select the mnuExit control in the Object list box in the Code window.
3. Enter the following statement in the Code window:
   ```
   Unload frmGeoView
   ```

The Code window displays as shown in Figure 4-69 on the next page.

> **More *About* the QueryUnload Event**
>
> A form's QueryUnload event is triggered automatically when you unload a form. This event typically is used to make sure that before an application closes, no unfinished tasks remain. For example, you can write code in the QueryUnload event procedure to prompt the user to save data.

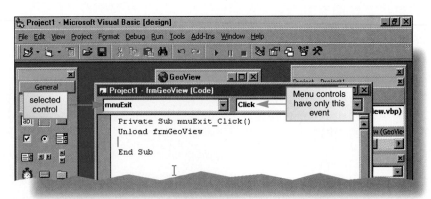

FIGURE 4-69

In the preceding steps, it was not necessary to select the Click event in the Procedure list box in the Code window because Menu controls contain only the Click event.

Data Control Methods

Each of the four commands in the Select menu has one event procedure: mnuNext_Click, mnuPrev_Click, mnuFirst_Click, and mnuLast_Click. When you trigger the mnuNext_Click event during run time by choosing Next on the Select menu, the next record (the one after the current record in the table) becomes the current record, and its information displays in the window. A similar record selection action occurs for each of the other three commands.

These actions are the same as when you click the appropriate record selection button on the Data control for the next, previous, first, or last record to become the current record. These actions are accomplished in code with the **MoveNext**, **MovePrevious**, **MoveFirst**, and **MoveLast** methods. The code statement has the form:

```
DataControlName.Recordset.MoveNext
```

When the Data control's **EOF Action property** is set to 0 - Move Last (its default value), and the current record is the last record in the table and the next record button on a Data control is clicked, the last record remains the current record. When the MoveNext method is used, however, a blank record becomes the current record and the end of file, or **EOF property**, of the recordset changes from False to True. A similar set of events occurs with the MovePrevious method and the beginning of file, or **BOF property**.

The event procedure for the Next command includes an If...Then statement to check if the application has gone past the last record by seeing if the value of EOF is True. If EOF is True, the event procedure makes the first record current. The code to do this procedure is as follows:

```
Data1.Recordset.MoveNext
If Data1.Recordset.EOF = True Then Data1.Recordset.MoveFirst
```

If the MoveNext command causes the current record to move past the last record, then the first record in the table becomes the current record. That is, when the information displayed on the form is from the last country in the table and you choose Next on the Select menu, the information changes to that of the first country in the table. In this way the GeoView database viewer application *loops* through the records. A similar code structure is used in the mnuPrev_Click event procedure. Perform the following steps to write the event procedures for the four commands on the GeoView Select menu.

Steps To Use Data Control Methods in Code

1 **Extend the width of the Code window. Select the mnuNext control in the Object list box. Enter the following two statements in the Code window:**
Data1.Recordset.MoveNext
If Data1.Recordset.
    EOF = True Then
    Data1.Recordset.
    MoveFirst

The Code window displays as shown in Figure 4-70.

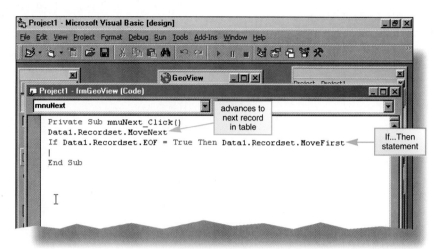

FIGURE 4-70

2 **Select the mnuPrev control in the Object list box. Enter the following two statements in the Code window:**
Data1.Recordset.
    MovePrevious
If Data1.Recordset.BOF
    = True Then Data1.
    Recordset.MoveLast

The Code window displays as shown in Figure 4-71.

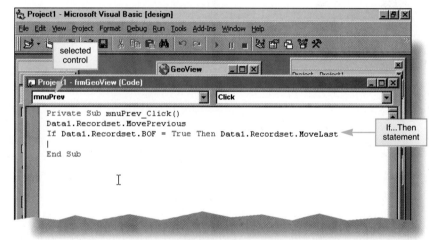

FIGURE 4-71

3 **Select the mnuFirst control in the Object list box. Enter the following statement in the Code window:**
Data1.Recordset.MoveFirst

The Code window displays as shown in Figure 4-72.

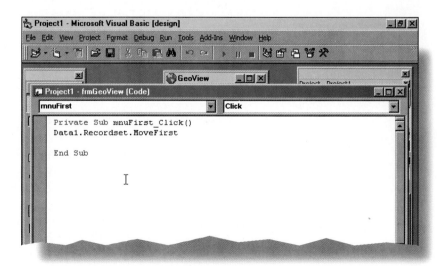

FIGURE 4-72

4 Select the mnuLast control in the Object list box. Enter the following statement in the Code window:

`Data1.Recordset.MoveLast`

The Code window displays as shown in Figure 4-73.

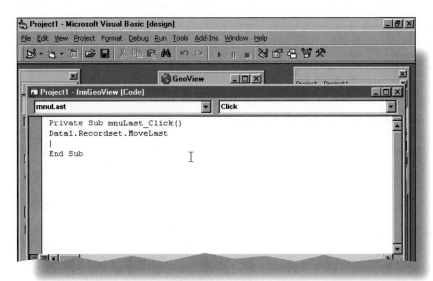

FIGURE 4-73

MouseUp Event

A **MouseDown** or **MouseUp** event procedure is used to specify actions that will occur when a given mouse button is pressed or released. Unlike the Click and DblClick events, MouseDown and MouseUp events enable you to distinguish among the left, right, and middle mouse buttons. In the GeoView database viewer application, this event is used to cause the Options pop-up menu to display when the user right-clicks the form.

Although you can specify where you want the pop-up menu to display, this application uses the default location, which is wherever the mouse pointer currently is located. This is accomplished through a code statement such as

`PopupMenu` *menuname*

where *menuname* is the name of the menu to be displayed. When a MouseUp event occurs, an integer corresponding to which mouse button was released is passed to the event procedure as the value of the variable Button. A value of 2 corresponds to the right mouse button. An If...Then statement within the event is used to check for the release of the right mouse button:

`If Button = 2 Then PopupMenu mnuOptions`

Perform the following steps to write a procedure where the GeoView form's MouseUp event will cause the Options menu to display as a pop-up menu.

TO WRITE A POP-UP MENU EVENT PROCEDURE

1 In the Code window, select the Form control in the Object list box.

2 Select the MouseUp event in the Procedure list box.

3 Type `If Button = 2 Then PopupMenu mnuOptions` and then press the ENTER key.

The Code window displays as shown in Figure 4-74.

More *About* Button Argument

The value of Button is an integer that identifies the button that was pressed (MouseDown) or released (MouseUp) to cause the event. The button argument is a bit field with bits corresponding to the left button (bit 0), right button (bit 1), and middle button (bit 2). These bits correspond to the values 1, 2, and 4, respectively. Only one of the bits is set, indicating the button that caused the event.

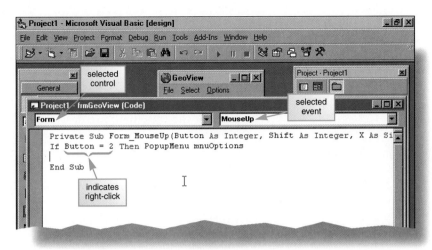

FIGURE 4-74

CommonDialog Code, For...Next Loops, and the With Statement

When the user clicks the Font command on the GeoView Options menu, the Font dialog box displays (Figure 4-75). This action is accomplished by writing a code statement that applies the ShowFont method to the CommonDialog control as follows:

```
CommonDialog1.ShowFont
```

This code statement causes the Font dialog box to display and remain on the desktop until the user clicks the OK button or Cancel button. This is similar to the way you used the CommonDialog control to display the Color dialog box in Project 2. When the user selects a different property value in the Font dialog box and clicks the OK button, the user is changing only the property value of the CommonDialog control. For example, if the current value of the font size is 8 and the user clicks 12 and then clicks the OK button, the following statement now is true:

```
CommonDialog1.FontSize = 12
```

If you then want to apply that property value to another control, you must write an additional code statement such as:

```
Label1.FontSize = CommonDialog1.FontSize
```

A generalized sequence of run-time steps in using the CommonDialog control is as follows:

1. A code statement applies the appropriate Show method to the CommonDialog control.
2. The user changes values of the properties of the CommonDialog control.
3. Code statements use the new property values of the CommonDialog control to change the appearance or behavior of the application.

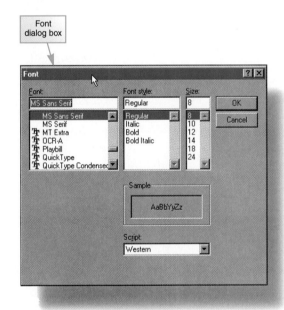

FIGURE 4-75

In the GeoView database viewer application, four font properties selected by the user in the Font dialog box are applied to the six Label controls on the form. You could assign the CommonDialog font properties to the labels by writing twenty-four separate code statements, each changing one property of one label. You can, however, accomplish this more efficiently by using the For...Next loop structure and the With statement.

A **For...Next statement**, also called a **For...Next loop**, repeats a group of code statements a specified number of times. Its syntax is:

```
For counter = start To end
    [statements]
Next
```

The parts of the statement are described in Table 4-3.

A flowchart representation of the For...Next loop is shown in Figure 4-76.

In the GeoView database viewer application, the start and end values of the counter are set to the first and last values of the index of the labels in the Label control array. When the counter increases by one each time it loops, the statements are performed on the next control in the array. For example, the following loop would change the font size of all labels in the array:

```
For Index = 0 to 5
    Label1(Index).FontSize = 12
Next
```

TABLE 4-3

PART	DESCRIPTION
For	Begins a For...Next control structure; must appear before any other part of the structure
Counter	Any variable used as the loop counter
Start	Initial value of the counter
To	Separates start and end values
End	Final value for the counter
[statements]	Code statements executed each time the loop is executed
Next	Ends a For...Next loop

You can use the **With statement** to execute a series of statements on a single object or control. The syntax of the With statement is as follows:

```
With object
[statements]
End With
```

Object is the name of the object or control and [statements] is the group of code statements that operate on *object*. For example, if you want to assign the properties of a Font dialog box to a Label control named Label1, you can use the With statement to shorten the assignment statements as follows:

```
With Label1
    .FontName = CommonDialog1.FontName
    .FontItalic = CommonDialog1.Italic
    .FontBold = CommonDialog1.FontBold
    .FontSize = CommonDialog1.FontSize
End With
```

In the GeoView database viewer application, you will combine the With statement and For...Next statements to assign the CommonDialog font properties to the Labels. A potential problem does exist, however, with allowing the user to change font properties in the GeoView database viewer application in this way.

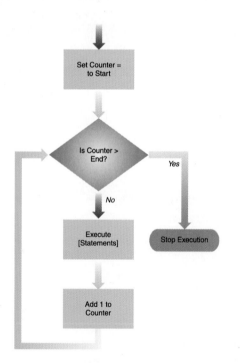

FIGURE 4-76

Even though you set the Labels' AutoSize property to True, it is possible to increase the font size to where the captions extend beyond the form's right border or where they overlap each other top to bottom. The general way to handle this problem is to write code statements that adjust the form's size (Height and Width properties) and controls' locations (Top and Left properties). This can be a significant amount of coding when you take into account the size of the form relative to the desktop and when you have a large number of controls on the form.

In the GeoView database viewer application, you will write code statements to adjust the Width of the form and to center the Image control right to left. Because Label1(5) contains the longest text string (Federal Republic), you can safely base the form's width on the new width of that Label control when United

States is the current record. You will make United States the current record and then adjust the form's width to be equal to the width between the left form border and the beginning of the label (which is the value of Label1(5).Left), plus the width of the label (Label1(5).Width), plus a margin after the label equal to the margin between the left form border and the label above (Label1(4).Left) as shown in Figure 4-77.

In Figure 4-77, you can see that the image is centered right to left on the form when its Left property is equal to a value that is half the distance after the image's width is subtracted from the form's width. The two code statements are as follows:

```
frmGeoView.Width = Label1(5).Left + Label1(5).Width + Label1(4).Left
Image1.Left = (frmGeoView.Width - Image1.Width) / 2
```

Perform the following steps to write the code in the mnuFont_Click event.

TO USE FOR...NEXT AND WITH STATEMENTS

1 In the Code window, select the mnuFont control in the Object list box.

2 Enter the following statements in the Code window:

```
'display font dialog box
CommonDialog1.ShowFont
'assign font properties to labels in array
For X = 0 To 5
  With Label1(X)
      .FontName = CommonDialog1.FontName
      .FontItalic = CommonDialog1.FontItalic
      .FontBold = CommonDialog1.FontBold
      .FontSize = CommonDialog1.FontSize
  End With
Next
'adjust form width to new label width
Data1.Recordset.MoveFirst
frmGeoView.Width = Label1(5).Left + Label1(5).Width + Label1(4).Left
'center image right to left
Image1.Left = (frmGeoView.Width - Image1.Width) / 2
```

The Code window displays as shown in Figure 4-78.

FIGURE 4-77

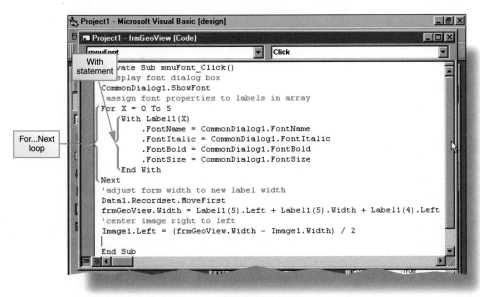

FIGURE 4-78

General Procedures

In addition to writing procedures for Visual Basic events, you can write your own general procedures. **General procedures** include subroutines, also called Sub procedures, and functions. **Function procedures** and **Sub procedures** are separate procedures that can take arguments, perform a series of statements, and change the value of their arguments. Unlike a Function procedure, which returns a value, a Sub procedure cannot be used in an expression.

When multiple events execute similar code statements, it is more efficient to put that code in a general procedure and then activate the general procedure from the appropriate events. You activate, or **call**, a Sub procedure using the procedure name followed by the argument list.

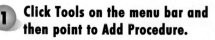

A similar set of actions occurs in the GeoView database viewer application when any one of the three commands on the View submenu (Figure 4-79) is clicked. If the data field currently is visible on the form, it should be made not visible and the check mark on the menu should be removed; if the field currently is not visible, it should be made visible and a check mark should be added to the menu.

If you wrote code for each of these Menu controls' Click events, it would be almost identical. Instead, you will write one general procedure that is called by each of the three Click events. For a single Sub procedure to carry out the actions just described, it needs to know which Menu control was clicked (Name, Capital, or Government) and which Label control contains the corresponding data field (Label1(1), Label1(3), or Label1(5)). This information will be passed to the Sub procedure as two arguments that you will name *ControlName* and *LabelIndex*. You will declare these arguments' types in the declaration of the subroutine.

The **Not operator** is used to perform logical negation on an expression. For example, if a Label, lblMyName, has its Visible property set to True, then the statement:

```
lblMyName.Visible = Not lblMyName.Visible
```

will make its Visible property false. If its Visible property were false, the preceding statement would make its Visible property true.

Perform the following steps to write a general Sub procedure to turn the display of the labels containing the Name, Capital, and Government data on and off.

FIGURE 4-79

 Steps To Write a General Sub Procedure

1 **Click Tools on the menu bar and then point to Add Procedure.**

The Tools menu displays (Figure 4-80).

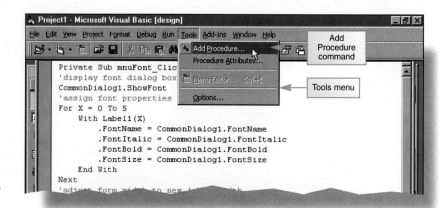

FIGURE 4-80

2 Click Add Procedure. When the Add Procedure dialog box opens, type `ToggleView` in the Name text box and then point to the OK button.

The Add Procedure dialog box displays (Figure 4-81).

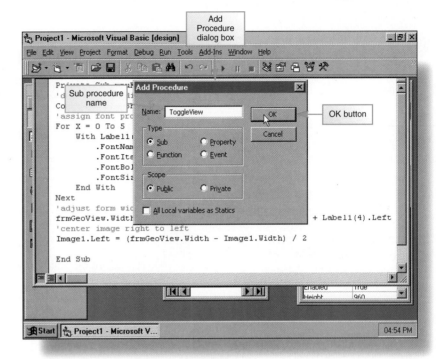

FIGURE 4-81

3 Click the OK button.

A new subroutine is added to the General section of the Code window (Figure 4-82).

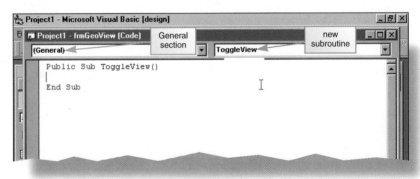

FIGURE 4-82

4 Click inside the parentheses on the first code line. Type `ControlName As Control, LabelIndex As Integer` **and then press the RIGHT ARROW key. Press the ENTER key.**

This code defines the names and then types of the two arguments used by the procedure (Figure 4-83).

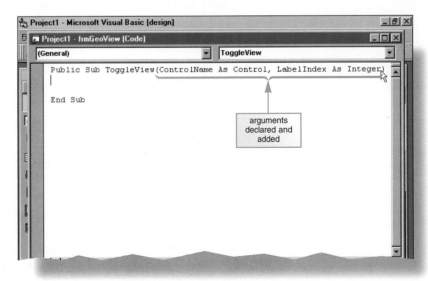

FIGURE 4-83

⑤ Enter the following code statements in the Code window:
```
'toggle display of the
  menu check mark
ControlName.Checked =
  Not ControlName.Checked
'toggle display of the
  label
Label1(LabelIndex).
  Visible = Not Label1
  (LabelIndex).Visible
```

The Code window displays as shown in Figure 4-84.

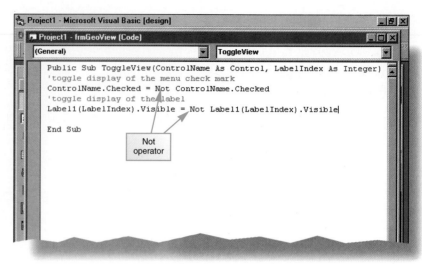

FIGURE 4-84

The code you just wrote will toggle the display of the check mark for whichever Menu control's name is passed to the procedure. Similarly, it will toggle the Visible property of the label whose index is passed to the procedure. You now must write the code that calls the procedure and passes the appropriate arguments.

Calling Subroutines from Other Procedures

Because all of the code to toggle the display of country information is contained in the ToggleView subroutine, the View menu events (mnuName_Click, mnuCapital_Click, and mnuGovt_Click) need to **call** the ToggleView subroutine. You can cause one procedure to initiate a general procedure by inserting a line of code containing the name of the general procedure followed by a list of variables representing arguments that are passed to the Sub procedure. General procedures may have none or one or more arguments. Multiple variables are separated by commas within the calling code statement. After the general procedure is completed, program control returns to the code statement following the one that called the general procedure. Perform the following steps to write the three View menu events.

TO CALL GENERAL PROCEDURES AND PASS ARGUMENTS

① In the Code window, select the mnuName control in the Object list box.

② Enter the following statement in the Code window:
```
ToggleView mnuName, 1
```

③ Select the mnuCapital control in the Object list box.

④ Enter the following statement in the Code window:
```
ToggleView mnuCapital, 3
```

⑤ Select the mnuGovt control in the Object list box.

⑥ Enter the following statement in the Code window:
```
ToggleView mnuGovt, 5
```

The Code window displays as shown in Figure 4-85.

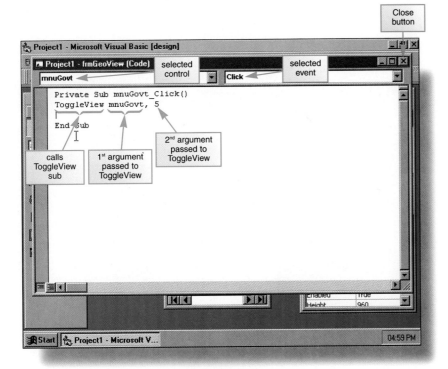

FIGURE 4-85

Saving and Testing the Project

The GeoView database viewer application is complete. Before running an application, always save it. When the GeoView database viewer application starts, it looks for the World database file (World.mdb) on the floppy disk in drive A because A:\World.mdb is the value assigned to the DatabaseName property of the Data control in the application. A floppy disk containing the World.mdb file must be in the 3½ Floppy [A:] drive. This is why you saved the two project files on the disk that already contained the World.mdb file.

An alternative is to copy the World.mdb file to a folder on the hard disk. If you copy World.mdb, then you must change the DatabaseName property to the new drive and folder where the database file is located. Perform the following steps to save and test the GeoView database viewer application.

TO SAVE AND TEST THE PROJECT

1. Click the Code window's Close button.
2. Click the Save Project button on the toolbar.
3. Click the Start button on the toolbar.
4. Close the Immediate window.
5. Close the Project window.
6. Click Options on the GeoView menu bar, click View, and then click Capital on the View submenu.
7. Click Options on the GeoView menu bar and then click Font. Change the font style and size to Bold, 12 and then click the OK button.
8. Click the next record button on the Data control and then press the CTRL+N keys. Click the next record button on the Data control.

The application should display as shown in Figure 4-86 on the next page.

9. Test all remaining menu commands.

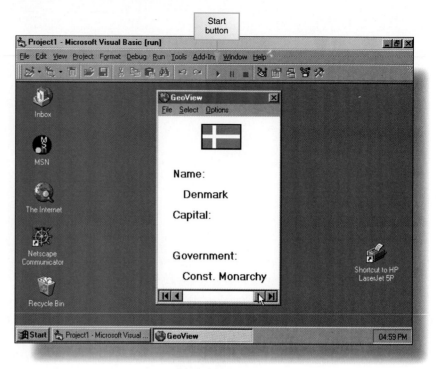

FIGURE 4-86

Project Summary

In this project, you extended the basics of building applications you learned in the first three projects. You built an application by creating the interface, setting properties, and writing code. You used a Data control to link the application to a database and a CommonDialog control to allow the user to change Font properties during run time. You created menus and submenus containing separator bars and check marks using the Menu Editor dialog box. You wrote code that included the use of a control array, the For...Next statement, and the With statement. You wrote a general Sub procedure with two arguments. You wrote code to call the general procedure and pass values to the procedure.

What You Should Know

Having completed this project, you now should be able to perform the following tasks.

▶ Add an Image Control *(VB 4.9)*

▶ Add CommonDialog and Data Controls *(VB 4.15)*

▶ Add Keyboard Shortcuts and Separator Bars to Menus *(VB 4.20)*

▶ Add Submenus and Menu Check Marks *(VB 4.22)*

▶ Bind Data-Aware Controls *(VB 4.35)*

▶ Call General Procedures and Pass Arguments *(VB 4.46)*

▶ Create a Control Array *(VB 4.10)*

▶ Create a Menu *(VB 4.18)*

▶ Save a Form and Project *(VB 4.24)*

▶ Save and Test the Project *(VB 4.47)*

▶ Set CommonDialog Flags and FontName Properties *(VB 4.31)*

▶ Set Data Control Properties *(VB 4.32)*

▶ Set Form Properties *(VB 4.25)*

▶ Set Image Control Height, Width, and Stretch Properties *(VB 4.29)*

▶ Set Label Caption Properties *(VB 4.30)*

▶ Set the Size and Location of a Form *(VB 4.8)*

▶ Use Data Control Methods in Code *(VB 4.39)*

▶ Use For...Next and With Statements *(VB 4.43)*

▶ Write a General Sub Procedure *(VB 4.44)*

▶ Write a Pop-Up Menu Event Procedure *(VB 4.40)*

▶ Write an Exit Procedure *(VB 4.37)*

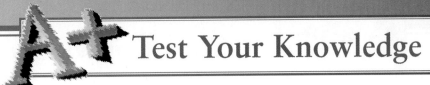

Test Your Knowledge

1 True/False

Instructions: Circle T if the statement is true or F if the statement is false.

T F 1. Databases allow you to store, maintain, and retrieve data quickly and efficiently.

T F 2. A characteristic, or attribute, of an item is the same as a record in a database.

T F 3. A menu in an application can display one or more submenus.

T F 4. Control arrays are made up of a group of controls that are the same type.

T F 5. Opaque values of the BackStyle property are used to make controls stand out.

T F 6. A form can contain only one Data control.

T F 7. Menus are created with Visual Basic's Menu Editor.

T F 8. The RecordSource property is used to specify the type of database to be accessed.

T F 9. The Close statement is used to terminate program execution.

T F 10. A procedure that is not triggered by an event is called a general procedure.

2 Multiple Choice

Instructions: Circle the correct response.

1. Visual Basic applications can be developed to _____, _____, and _____ information in a database.
   a. subtract, access, retrieve
   b. add, multiply, divide
   c. query, divide, report
   d. add, update, delete

2. A _____ menu displays when the user right-clicks anywhere on a form at run time.
   a. pop-up
   b. main
   c. submenu
   d. drop-down

3. The index value of a control array begins at _____.
   a. 2
   b. 1
   c. 0
   d. 5

4. Access keys are used to open a menu at run time by pressing the _____ key and a _____ key.
   a. CTRL, letter
   b. ALT, letter
   c. SHIFT, letter
   d. ALT, number

(continued)

A+ Test Your Knowledge

Multiple Choice *(continued)*

5. Menu choices that display an _____ at the right edge, indicate a submenu is available for that choice.
   a. arrowhead symbol
   b. ellipsis
   c. ampersand
   d. asterisk

6. To increase the height and width of an image in an Image control, set the _____ property to True.
   a. Stretch
   b. Increase
   c. Size
   d. Enabled

7. The _____ property supplies the file name of the database to which a Data control is linked.
   a. DatabaseName
   b. DataField
   c. RecordSource
   d. Connect

8. Data-aware controls must be bound to a _____ control on the same form.
   a. CheckBox
   b. TextBox
   c. Data
   d. Label

9. When MoveNext is used, a blank record becomes the current record and the _____ property of a Recordset changes from False to True.
   a. EOR
   b. EOF
   c. BOR
   d. BOF

10. The _____ and _____ event procedures allow distinguishing among the left, right, and middle mouse buttons.
    a. Click, DblClick
    b. MouseRight, MouseLeft
    c. MouseClick, MouseDblClick
    d. MouseUp, MouseDown

A+ Test Your Knowledge

3 Understanding the Menu Editor Dialog Box

Instructions: In Figure 4-87, arrows point to some of the major components in the Menu Editor dialog box. Identify these numbered items in the spaces provided.

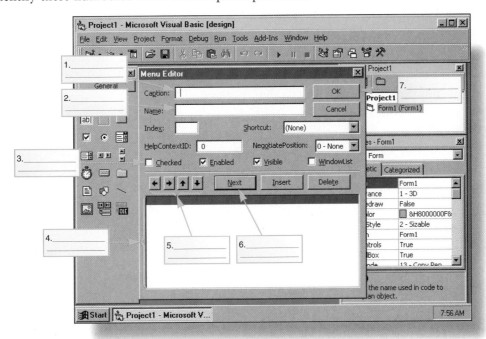

FIGURE 4-87

4 Understanding Menus

Instructions: Figure 4-88 displays the Menu Editor dialog box for an application. On a separate sheet of paper, draw a picture of the menu bar and menus that would be created for the application. Include submenus, access key markings, separator bars, and check marks.

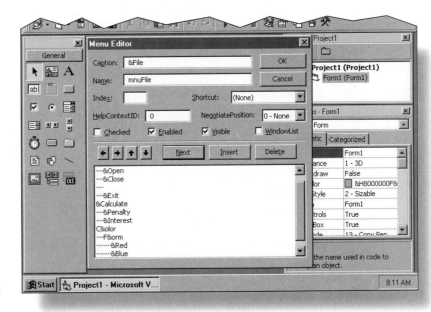

FIGURE 4-88

Use Help

1 Reviewing Project Activities

Instructions: Perform the following tasks using a computer.

1. Start Visual Basic.
2. Click Help on the menu bar and then click Microsoft Visual Basic Help Topics.
3. Click the Contents tab and then double-click the Language Reference book.
4. Double-click the Functions book and then click the A book. Double-click the Array Function topic.
5. Read and print the information. Click any ScreenTip and read each one.
6. Click the Example link and print the example that displays.
7. Hand the printouts in to your instructor.
8. Click the Help Topics button to return to the Contents sheet.
9. Double-click the Controls Reference book. Click the Intrinsic Controls book and then double-click the Menu Control topic.
10. Read and print the information.
11. Hand the printouts in to your instructor.
12. Click the See Also link and then double-click the Menu Editor Dialog Box topic.
13. Read and print the information.
14. Hand the printouts in to your instructor.

2 Learning More of the Basics

Instructions: Use Visual Basic Books Online to learn more about Visual Basic. The Help topics will provide information to answer the questions below. Write the answers to the questions on your own paper and hand them in to your instructor.

1. Start Visual Basic. Click Help on the menu bar and then click Books Online. In the Navigation area, double-click the Programmer's Guide (All Editions) book. Double-click Part 1: Visual Basic Basics and then double-click Programming Fundamentals. Read the information that displays in the Topic area and answer the following questions:
   a. What does a control structure do in a program?
   b. If control structures are not used in a program, what is the normal flow of a program's logic?
2. In the Navigation area, double-click the Introduction to Control Structures book. One by one, double-click Decision Structures, Loop Structures, and Working with Control Structures. Read the information that displays in the Topic area. As you read the text in the Topic area, answer the following questions.
   a. What are the parts of a decision structure?
   b. How do the two types of If statements differ?
   c. Why would the third form of a decision structure be used in a program?
   d. How is it different from the If statements?
   e. What is a loop structure used for?

Apply Your Knowledge

1 Adding a Menu and Writing Code in a Visual Basic Application

Instructions: Start Visual Basic and open the project, Math Tutor, from the Visual Basic folder on the Data Disk that accompanies this book. This application consists of a form that contains two TextBox controls, four CheckBox controls, four Label controls, and one CommandButton control (Figure 4-89).

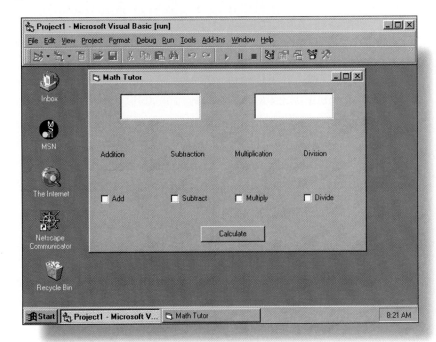

FIGURE 4-89

1. If necessary, click the View Form button in the Project window.
2. Add menus to the application using the Menu Editor dialog box. The menu choices should include selections to exit the application and to perform the addition, subtraction, multiplication, and division calculations.
3. Enter End as the code statement for the Exit menu. Include a comment for this code.
4. Write the following code for the Calculation menu selections in the Code window and include comments for the code statements:

```
If chkAdd.Value = 1 Then
    lblAddition.Caption = (Val(txtNumber1.Text) + Val(txtNumber2.Text))
End If
If chkSubtract.Value = 1 Then
    lblSubtraction.Caption = (Val(txtNumber1.Text) - Val(txtNumber2.Text))
End If
If chkMultiply.Value = 1 Then
    lblMultiplication.Caption = (Val(txtNumber1.Text) * Val(txtNumber2.Text))
End If
If chkDivide.Value = 1 Then
    lblDivision.Caption = (Val(txtNumber1.Text) / Val(txtNumber2.Text))
End If
```

5. For the Calculate CommandButton control, write code statements that are the same as those for the calculation choices on the menus.
6. Save the form and the project using the file name Math Calculations.
7. Click the Start button to test the application. If necessary, make corrections to the code statements. Save the form and project again using the same file name.
8. Print the Form Image, Code, and Form as Text.

1 Creating a Database Viewer Application

Problem: The secretary where you work maintains a database of employees, addresses, and telephone numbers using Microsoft Access. She uses Access to view, add, modify, and delete information in the database. The database file is stored on a networked file server. Other employees want access to the database, but they should not have the ability to modify the database.

Instructions: Build an application to view the employee records with a user interface that resembles the one shown in Figure 4-90. All of the controls should be named appropriately.

1. Open a new Standard EXE project in Visual Basic.
2. Insert the Data Disk with the file Employees.mdb in the 3½ Floppy [A:] drive.
3. Add a Data control to the form.
4. Add fourteen Label controls to the form (seven for the names of the fields and seven for displaying the field values of the current record).
5. Set the appropriate Data control properties to access the Phone table in the Employees database.
6. Set the appropriate properties to bind the seven Label controls to the fields in the Phone table.
7. Set the remaining control properties necessary to make the user interface look like the one shown in Figure 4-90.
8. Save the form as Phone.frm and save the project as Phone.mdb.
9. Print the Form Image, Code, and Form as Text.

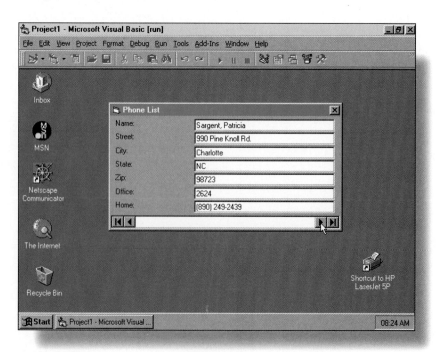

FIGURE 4-90

In the Lab

2 Creating an Application Menu

Problem: You previously designed an application for kindergarten children to display shapes with different borders and in different colors. The original application used check boxes and option buttons to make choices. The teacher using the application now would like to teach the children how to use menus and read the commands listed.

Instructions: Build an application with a user interface that resembles the one shown in Figure 4-91. All of the controls should be properly named and code statements should be properly commented.

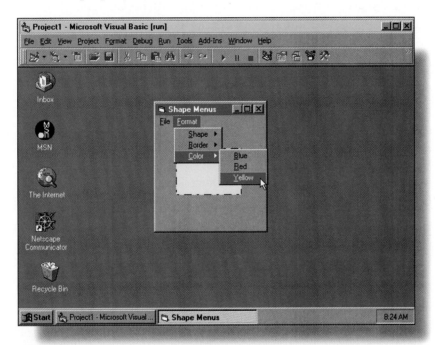

FIGURE 4-91

1. Open a new project in Visual Basic.
2. Size the form, position it on the desktop, and add a rectangle Shape control.
3. Use the Menu Editor to create menus that will allow the user to exit the application and select different shapes, borders, and colors for the shape.
4. Include a submenu for the shape commands of circle, oval, and square; a submenu for the border commands of dash, dot, and solid; and a submenu for the color commands of blue, red, and yellow.
5. Change the Caption property of the form to Shape Menus.
6. Open the Code window for the Exit menu. Enter End in the code window.
7. One by one, select the Shape submenus in the Object list box and then enter code statements similar to shpShape1.Shape = 1 replacing shpShape1 with the appropriate control name and the number 1 with the appropriate number to match the shapes circle, oval, and square.

(continued)

In the Lab

Creating an Application Menu (continued)

8. One by one, select the Border submenus in the Object list box and then enter code statements similar to `shpShape1.Borderstyle = 1` replacing the shpShape1 with the appropriate control name and the number 1 with the appropriate number to match the border styles of dot, dash, and solid.
9. One by one, select the Color submenus in the Object list box. Type the code statements similar to `shpShape1.BackColor = vbBlue` replacing shpShape1 with the appropriate control name and the color vbBlue with vbRed and vbYellow. Close the Code window.
10. Save the form and the project using the file name Shape Menu Choices.
11. Run the application to make certain no errors exist. If you encounter any errors, correct them and resave the form and project using the same file name.
12. Print the Form Image, Code, and Form as Text.

3 Writing a General Procedure

Problem: The application for displaying different shapes with different borders and different back style colors is working as planned. One feature that is missing is a general procedure to clear all of the settings before the application is run or to reset default values before making other selections.

Instructions: Use the application created in In the Lab 2 on the previous page. If this problem was not assigned, quickly create the application following the instructions. Perform the following tasks to enhance the application as shown in Figure 4-92.

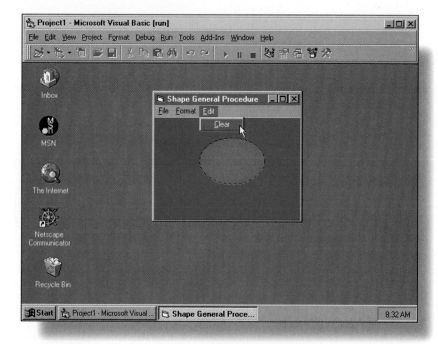

FIGURE 4-92

In the Lab

1. Open the Shape Menus application in Visual Basic.
2. Change the Caption property of the form to Shape General Procedure.
3. Add a menu command for the shape and make it a rectangle. Add a menu command for the border style and make it dash-dot. On the Color submenu, make the Color command for the shape a submenu. On the Color submenu, add another submenu for a Color command for the form back color. On the Shape Color submenu, add the color green as a command. On the Form Color submenu, add the same four Color commands as on the Shape submenu. Add a menu called Edit with a submenu of Clear.
4. Open the general declarations Code window and enter `Public Sub ClearControls` to declare the procedure and make it available to all areas of the program. Write code statements in this procedure to set default beginning values for the Shape, BorderStyle, and BackColor properties of this application. Set the default shape to rectangle, the default border style to dash-dot, the default shape back color to white, and the default form back color to white. End the procedure with the End Sub statement.
5. Enter the code statement `ClearControls` for the Form_Load procedure and for the Clear command on the Edit menu to execute the Public general procedure ClearControls.
6. Save the form and the project using the file name Shape General Procedure.
7. Test the project by running it and make any necessary changes. Remember to save the form and project again if any changes have been made.
8. Print the Form Image, Code, and Form as Text.

4 Using a Control Array and For...Next Loop

Problem: You are tutoring programming students and want an application to demonstrate arrays and looping structures. You want to start with a looping structure that allows control over how many times the loop statements will be executed.

Instructions: Perform the tasks on the next page to create the Checkerboard Array applications as shown in Figure 4-93.

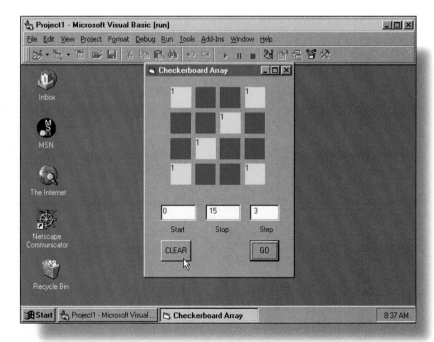

FIGURE 4-93

(continued)

In the Lab

Using a Control Array and For...Next Loop *(continued)*

1. Open a new project in Visual Basic.
2. Size the form appropriately and center it by setting the StartUp Position property.
3. Add one Label control to the form. Size the label to be square in shape. Add 15 more square Label controls to the form using a control array and arrange the squares in a checkerboard pattern of four squares across and four squares down. Add three TextBox controls below the checkerboard, three Label controls below the TextBox controls, and two CommandButton controls near the bottom of the form.
4. Set the form's Caption property to Checkerboard Array. Set the Text property for each of the TextBox controls to be blank. Set the Caption property for the three Label controls to Start, Stop, and Step. Set the Caption property for the two CommandButton controls to Clear and Go.
5. Set the Default property of the Go CommandButton control to True.
6. Open the Code window for the Go CommandButton control and write the For...Next loops to set properties of some of the Label controls in the control array. Enter the following statements in the Code window:

```
For Index = 0 to 15
   Label1(Index).BackColor = vbBlue
Next
For Index = Text1.Text to Text2.Text Step Text3.Text
   Label1(Index).Caption = Label1(Index).Caption + 1
Next
For Index = Text1.Text to Text2.Text Step Text3.Text
   Label1(Index).BackColor = vbYellow
Next
```

Remember to replace Text1, Text2, and Text3 with appropriate control names.

7. Write code statements for the Clear CommandButton control to clear the TextBox controls and to set the BackColor property of the Label controls in the label array to white. Set the focus to the TextBox control for the start value.
8. Write the code statements for the Form Load procedure to clear the TextBox controls and to set the BackColor property of the Label controls in the label array to white.
9. Save the form and the project using the file name Checkerboard.
10. Run the application and make any necessary corrections. Remember to save the form and project again if any changes have been made.
11. Print the Form Image, Code, and Form as Text.

Cases and Places

The difficulty of these case studies varies: ❿ are the least difficult; ❿❿ are more difficult; and ❿❿❿ are the most difficult.

1 ❿ You are serving an internship with the Traffic Court in the city where you live. The clerks in the traffic court office want a simple application that will allow them to enter the actual speed limit, the speed at which the offender was traveling, and the number that represents how many times the person has received a traffic ticket. The application should have a menu system to allow users to exit the application, clear the application, and perform all of the calculations. The application should calculate and display the miles per hour the offender was in excess of the actual speed limit, the cost of the speeding ticket, and court costs. Use ten dollars as the amount to be charged per mile per hour over the speed limit. The court cost should begin at $53.20 and increase by $20.00 for each subsequent offense up to the third offense that will represent the maximum court cost.

2 ❿ As an intern at the planetarium it is your responsibility to develop a small application. The application is to display the planet names, their gravities, and based on the menu command selected, either the distance of the planet to the sun or the distance of the planet to the earth. It should have menus to exit the application, to select the display of distances to either the sun or to the earth, and to display an About form. When the distance to the earth is selected it should display a check mark on the menu and when the distance to the sun is selected it should display a check mark on the menu.

3 ❿❿ You want to improve upon the Math Calculations application you created in the Apply Your Knowledge problem for this project. You have decided to add check marks for the calculation selections to indicate which of the calculations currently is being performed. When a selection is made from the menu, a check mark also should display in the corresponding CheckBox control. You have decided to add an About form and Help form to the application with a menu command to display the About form or display the Help form. The application is a fairly simple one and Help will explain how users can enter numbers and perform the calculations.

4 ❿❿ You work for Northwind Traders on a team assigned to design interface screens for a database that already exists. The database contains many tables. You will begin by building an interface for the customer records. The team has decided to use an invisible Data control to access the records in the database. You also suggest providing menus to select data, to exit the program, to format label captions to bold, to view choices for all information and to hide at least two nonessential fields. It also is decided to provide at least one pop-up menu for the form. If possible, an appropriate icon should be used to represent the minimized form. *Hint*: The Northwind Traders database is a sample database named, Nwind.mdb, that accompanies Visual Basic. It usually is found in the VB folder. See your instructor for directions on where you can locate the database.

Cases and Places

5 ▶▶ At Federal Bank where you work, the tellers need a simple way to calculate charges for checking, savings, and ATM transactions. You decide to build an application with menus as well as Command-Button controls to perform calculations. Include menus for clearing the transactions, exiting the application, and displaying an about form. The tellers must have a way to enter the checking or savings balance or the amount of the ATM transaction. They also must be able to choose the type of transaction, and for savings accounts, they must be able to enter the number of days. In the case of a savings account, charges are based on the remaining account balance. When the balance is less than $100, the charge is $.15 per day for every day the balance is below $100. When the balance is less than $500 the charge is $.10 a day for every day the balance is below $500. When the balance is less than $1,000 the charge is $.05 per day for every day the balance is below $1,000. In the case of a checking account, charges are based on the remaining account balance plus a charge for the number of checks written. The charge for the number of checks written is: $.10 per check for 25 or more checks; $.09 per check for 20 or more but less than 25 checks; $.08 per check for 10 or more but less than 20 checks; and $.07 per check charge for 1 or more but less than 10 checks. In the case of an ATM transaction, the amount charged per transaction is $.50 for savings and $1.00 for checking plus $1.00 for the use of the ATM machine.

6 ▶▶▶ You are developing a prototype for a shareware screen saver that will randomize butterfly images on the screen. You decide to use menus to control exiting, running, and describing the application. You have decided to use the Randomize statement for the application and to use two variables to move the images. The variables should be set using the ScaleWidth and ScaleHeight properties and the Rnd function. Display of the images can be controlled with a For … Next loop. You will set the Top and Left properties of the images with the Rnd function multiplied by an integer. To change the image locations on the screen, set their Move properties using the variables. Keep in mind that this will occupy the entire screen, it should not be sizable, and the ScaleMode may need to be changed. *Hint*: Refer to the section on random numbers in Project 7. The Butterfly1.bmp and Butterfly2.bmp images to create this application are located on the Data Disk that accompanies this book.

7 ▶▶▶ Cover to Cover Book Store has been pleased with your contributions toward organizing the store. The other employees now would like an interface application that can be used to retrieve and view the data from the Booksale.mdb database. The database contains several tables including those for Publishers, Authors, and Titles. The interface should have a visible Data control to access records for at least two of the three tables as well as a menu to select the records. Not all of the employees like the same colors so they should have at least two color choices for the labels and two color choices for the form. Some of the employees think the interface will be cluttered and that some of the data is nonessential. Therefore, a menu should have view choices to see all of the information or to hide at least two fields. They discovered that pop-up menus could be provided for the form and for the labels and have requested these be incorporated as well. Provide an appropriate icon to represent the minimized application. *Hint*: The database and an icon can be found on the Data Disk that accompanies this textbook.

Project

Microsoft *Visual Basic 5*

Drag and Drop Events and More Complex Code Structures

Objectives:

You will have mastered the material in this project when you can:

- ▶ Declare variables using type-declaration characters
- ▶ Write a DragOver event procedure
- ▶ Write a DragDrop event procedure
- ▶ Write code to call event procedures
- ▶ Copy code using keyboard commands
- ▶ Understand Visual Basic data types
- ▶ Write subroutines containing nested code structures
- ▶ Use the Select Case structure in code
- ▶ Use the Do...Loop structure in code
- ▶ Use the InputBox function in applications
- ▶ Use the UCase$ function in applications
- ▶ Change properties of a group of controls

Get the Picture?

*Radiology
Application
Displays
Precise Details*

By the end of this decade, millions of men and women will be diagnosed with a diversity of ailments using services such as X-ray, mammography, ultrasound, and other radiographic technologies.

High-quality diagnostic services are performed at clinics, hospital radiology departments, mobile vans, and private offices. In one such clinic in Charlotte, NC, Dr. Laurene C. Mann and her staff see approximately 30 patients per day. With this volume, they need a system to evaluate the patients and generate reports quickly and accurately.

Previously, Dr. Mann reviewed handwritten notations on a patient's record and dictated her reports. Now, however, she uses a Visual Basic application to expedite this procedure. The

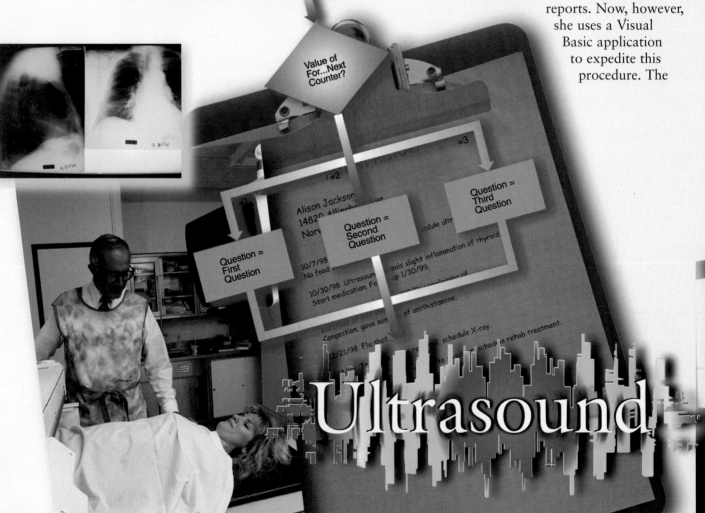

Ultrasound

application uses drag-and-drop functionality, subroutines with nested code structures, and Do...Loops, which are features you will use in the application you create in Project 5.

When a new patient arrives at the clinic, the Visual Basic application assigns the patient a unique ID number. Prompts direct the patients to input their health history into the record by answering questions on a touch screen.

After a patient has completed a test, technicians use another part of the application to enter comments regarding quality assurance, such as whether the X-ray film is good or is too light or too dark.

Next, Dr. Mann reviews this patient's history and the film. The application prompts her to answer questions, and her responses initiate another event procedure. For example, if she responds that the X-ray looks normal, the application transfers control to one subroutine.

In contrast, if the film looks abnormal, the application branches to another subroutine and asks her to input additional information. Specifically, she must identify the irregularity and depict the type of disorder. To help with this identification, the application displays a pectoral area map created with Microsoft Paint, and she uses the Visual Basic drag-and-drop function to place images of various abnormalities at their precise locations on the patient's individual drawing.

Dr. Mann then inputs her impressions, diagnosis, and request for a return visit. When she has completed entering her data, she clicks the OK button on her screen to display the application and then she can print a one- or two-page report.

Timely diagnosis and accurate reports along with state-of-the-art technology and applications like this one created and designed with Visual Basic help doctors get the full picture and are the keys to early detection and ultimately saving lives.

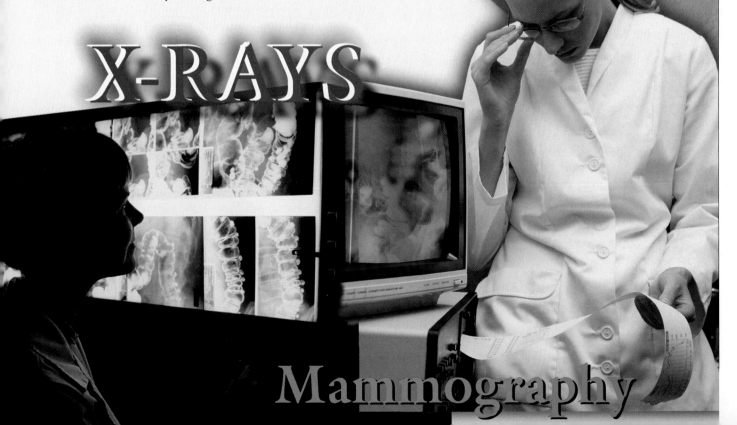

Project 5

Microsoft
Visual Basic 5

Case Perspective

The company you work for is submitting a proposal to develop several CBT (computer-based training) applications for high schools in the local school district. Each of the district's twenty high schools has at least one PC lab, and all labs are running either Windows 95 or Windows NT. Your company feels it can gain a competitive advantage by creating edutainment applications (applications that are both educational and entertaining). You have been assigned to a team that is developing a prototype of one module of a driver's education application.

Your team is responsible for developing a module that teaches driver's education students to identify different road signs correctly. The prototype module need not include all road signs, but it should demonstrate an intuitive and game-like graphical user interface. Users should feel challenged, but not frustrated. The module should provide positive rather than negative reinforcement of user interactions. The user should be made aware of incorrect responses, but never in a judgmental or condescending manner.

Drag and Drop Events and More Complex Code Structures

Introduction

Your interaction with many Windows applications involves dragging and dropping objects and entering information in dialog boxes. The Windows Solitaire game is a good example of dragging and dropping with which most Window's users are familiar. You have used the CommonDialog control in previous projects to create Color and Font dialog boxes. The application built in this project incorporates the activities necessary to add drag-and-drop functionality to your applications. You also will accept information from the user through a special type of dialog box that is created with the InputBox function.

Project 4 introduced control arrays. In this project, subroutines are written for common events shared by the controls in an array. In addition, a code method is used that allows one event procedure to initiate another event procedure. Several additional code structures are introduced in this project: nested If...Then blocks, Select Case blocks, and Do...Loop statements. You also will learn more about Visual Basic data types that were introduced briefly in an earlier project.

Project Five — Traffic Sign Tutorial

The application built in this project is shown in Figure 5-1 as it displays on the desktop during run time. The application is a tutorial that teaches the meanings of several traffic signs. At run time, you are presented with several traffic signs and several containers having labels. You are instructed to drag and drop the signs into the correct containers. If you attempt to drop a sign into an incorrect container, the sign snaps back to its original location.

Three commands are available in the application by using the **Options menu** (Figure 5-2). The menu includes access keys and shortcuts. Clicking the **Clear command** returns all the signs to their original locations. Clicking the **Show command** places all the signs in their correct containers. Clicking the **Quiz command** presents a series of three questions about the shapes of the signs.

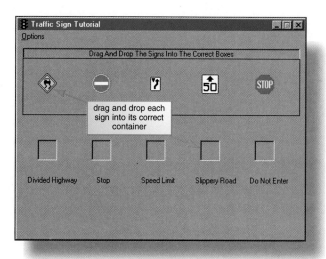

FIGURE 5-1

Project Steps

In this project, you will follow the three-step Visual Basic application development process to build the Traffic Sign Tutorial application. You will complete the following tasks in this project.

1. Start a Standard EXE project in Visual Basic.
2. Set the form's size and position.
3. Add Image, Shape, and Label controls.
4. Create an Image control array for the traffic signs.
5. Create an Image control array for the containers.
6. Create a Label control array.
7. Create a menu.
8. Save the form.
9. Set the form's properties.
10. Set captions of the Label array controls.
11. Set the Picture property of the sign array controls.
12. Set properties for a group of controls (image containers).
13. Set properties of the remaining controls.

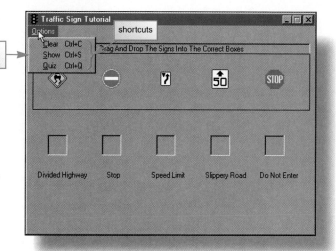

FIGURE 5-2

14. Save the form.
15. Write a general declarations procedure.
16. Write a Form_Load event procedure.
17. Write a DragOver event procedure.
18. Write a DragDrop event procedure.
19. Write Menu Clear and Menu Show command Click event procedures.
20. Write the Traffic Quiz subroutine.
21. Save and test the project.

The following pages contain a detailed explanation of each of these steps.

Getting Started

The traffic sign icons used in this project are available on the Data Disk that accompanies this book. If you will be saving this project on a disk other than the Data Disk, you should copy these files to the disk you will use to save the Traffic Sign Tutorial application before starting this project.

Begin this project by starting Visual Basic as described on page VB 1.7 in Project 1 or by opening a new Standard EXE project if you are already running Visual Basic. If necessary, you should complete the steps on page VB 1.10 in Project 1 to arrange your desktop to resemble Figure 5-3.

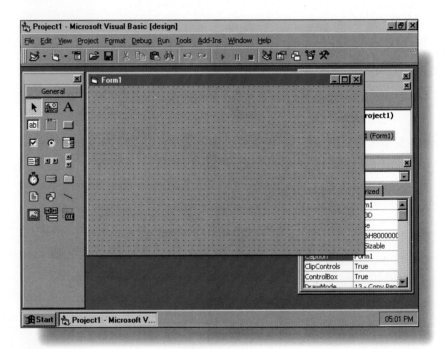

FIGURE 5-3

Creating the Interface

In this step, the size and location of the form is determined, and the controls are added to the form. The Traffic Sign Tutorial form contains one Shape control, one individual Image control, one individual Label control, two arrays of Image controls, and one array of Label controls, as identified in Figure 5-4. After these controls are added to the form, you will create the menu using Visual Basic's Menu Editor.

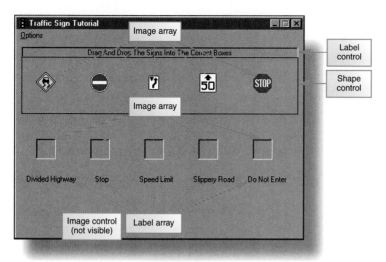

FIGURE 5-4

Setting the Location and Size of the Form

At run time, the form is centered on the desktop. This positioning will be accomplished later in the project through two code statements. Perform the following steps to size the form by setting its Height and Width properties.

TO SET A FORM'S SIZE

1 Select the Form control by clicking it.

2 Click the Properties window. Double-click the Height property in the Properties list.

3 Type 4995 and then press the ENTER key.

4 Double-click the Width property in the Properties list in the Properties window.

5 Type 7080 and then press the ENTER key. Click a blank area of the form.

The form displays as shown in Figure 5-5.

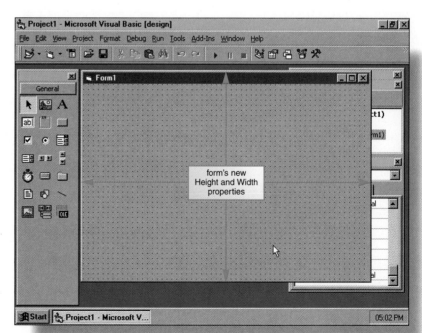

FIGURE 5-5

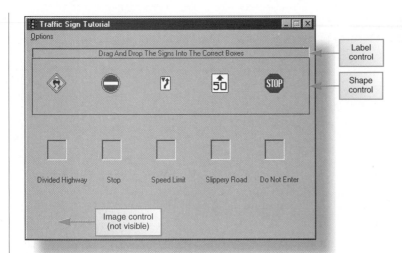

FIGURE 5-6

Adding the Individual Label, Shape, and Image Controls

The individual Label, Shape, and Image controls are identified in Figure 5-6.

The Label control is used to contain the run-time instructions for the application. The Shape control is used to group visually the traffic signs that are to be dragged and dropped. The individual Image control is left blank and is not visible at run time. Its purpose is explained later in this project.

TO ADD LABEL, SHAPE, AND IMAGE CONTROLS

1 Double-click the Label button in the Toolbox. Adjust the Label control's size to that shown in Figure 5-7, and then drag it to the location shown.

2 Double-click the Shape button in the Toolbox. Adjust the Shape control's size to that shown in Figure 5-7, and then drag it to the location shown.

3 Double-click the Image button in the Toolbox. Drag the Image control to the location shown in Figure 5-7.

The form displays as shown in Figure 5-7.

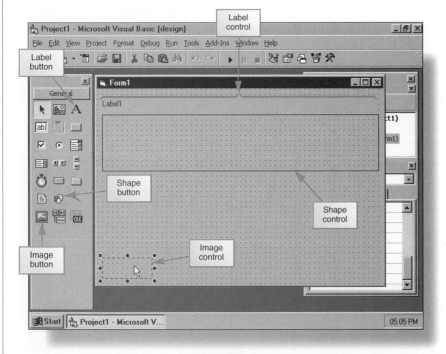

FIGURE 5-7

Adding the Traffic Sign Control Array

Run-time dragging and dropping of a control does not change its location automatically. When the mouse button is released to drop the control, the control retains its original position. Any relocation must be programmed specifically with code statements to occur when the mouse button is released. Many times the control does not actually relocate. The control only appears to relocate by changing the properties of it and other controls, such as the Visible property.

In Visual Basic, the control being dragged is called the **Source control**. The control over which the Source control is located during the dragging operation is called the **target control**.

In the Traffic Sign Tutorial application, a sign appears to move into a container by changing the Picture property of the container from being blank to being equal to the Picture property of the image being dropped. Much of the apparent movement in the Traffic Sign Tutorial application is the result of changing the values of the Picture and Visible properties of Image controls on the form.

The first set of Image controls in this application contains the graphical images of the five signs (Figure 5-8). These controls are grouped in an array to simplify the code writing later. The control array is given the name imgSign.

The ability to drag a control during run time is determined by the value of the control's **DragMode property**. When the DragMode property is set to **Automatic**, the dragging operation is initiated during run time by positioning the mouse pointer on the control and then pressing the mouse button. The DragMode property can be set through code statements or in the Properties window. In this application, you will set the DragMode property to Automatic for the first Image control in the array so that the property will be copied to all Image controls in the array. Perform the following steps to create an Image control array for the traffic signs.

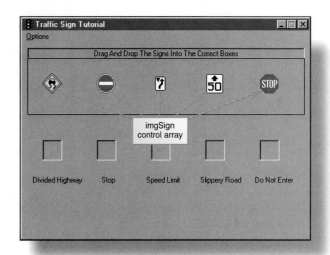

FIGURE 5-8

 Steps To Create an Image Control Array for the Traffic Signs

1 **Double-click the Image button in the Toolbox.**

A default-sized Image control, Image2, is added to the form (Figure 5-9).

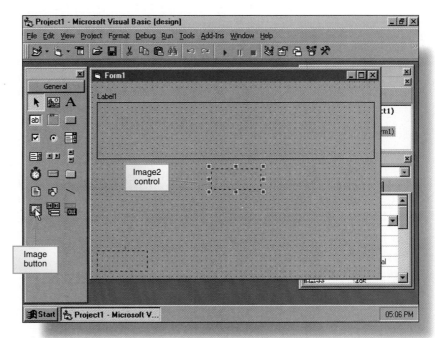

FIGURE 5-9

2 **Drag the Image control to the location shown in Figure 5-10. Its size will be adjusted later.**

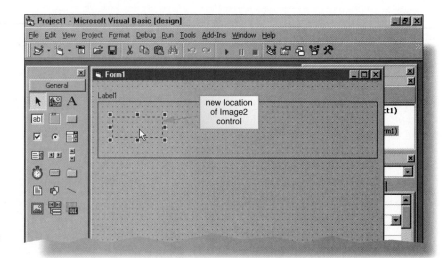

FIGURE 5-10

3 **Click the Properties window. Double-click the Name property in the Properties list. Type** imgSign **and then press the ENTER key. Double-click the DragMode property in the Properties list.**

The control's new name (imgSign) displays in the Object box, and the value of the DragMode property changes to 1 - Automatic (Figure 5-11).

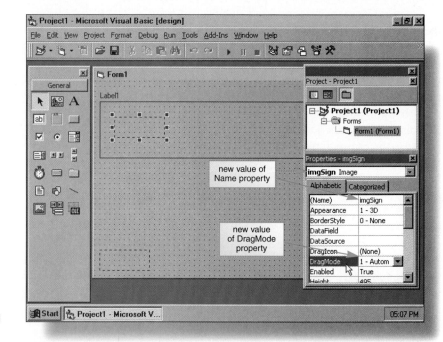

FIGURE 5-11

4 **Click the imgSign control on the form. Press the CTRL+C keys to copy the control to the Clipboard and then press the CTRL+V keys to paste the contents of the Clipboard to the form. Click the Yes button in the Microsoft Visual Basic dialog box to begin a control array.**

The name of the first image changes to imgSign(0). A second Image control, imgSign(1), is added to the upper-left corner of the form (Figure 5-12).

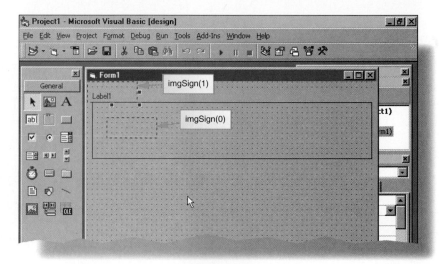

FIGURE 5-12

5 **Drag the second Image control, imgSign(1), from the upper-left corner of the form to the location shown in Figure 5-13. Press CTRL+V to paste the Clipboard contents to the form.**

A third Image control, imgSign(2), is added to the form (Figure 5-13).

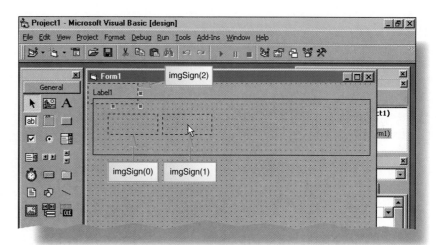

FIGURE 5-13

6 **Drag the third Image control in the array to the location shown in Figure 5-14. Press the CTRL+V keys and then drag the fourth Image control, imgSign(3), to the position shown in Figure 5-14. Press the CTRL+V keys and then drag the fifth Image control, imgSign(4), to the position shown in Figure 5-14.**

Locating the controls in the order shown in Figure 5-14 is important. They easily can be confused because they all have the same appearance on the form.

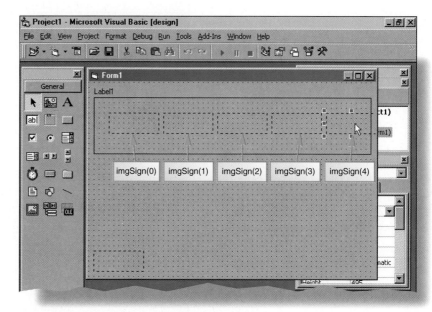

FIGURE 5-14

Creating the Sign Container Control Array

The second set of Image controls is indicated in Figure 5-15. These Image controls act as the containers into which the signs will be dropped. These controls have their BorderStyle property set to Fixed Single to display as empty boxes. Later, you will change the Border-Style property of all of these images as a group. Similar to the imgSign group, the sign container images also are members of a control array. Perform the following steps to create this array, imgContainer, and to locate the controls on the form.

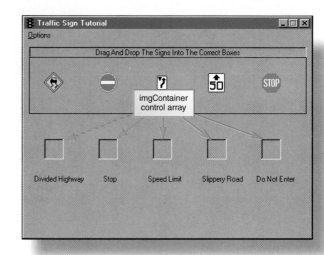

FIGURE 5-15

Steps To Create an Image Control Array for the Traffic Sign Containers

1 **Double-click the Image button in the Toolbox. Double-click the Name property in the Properties list. Type** imgContainer **and then press the ENTER key. Drag the Image control to the location shown in Figure 5-16.**

A new Image control named Image2 is added to the form (Figure 5-16).

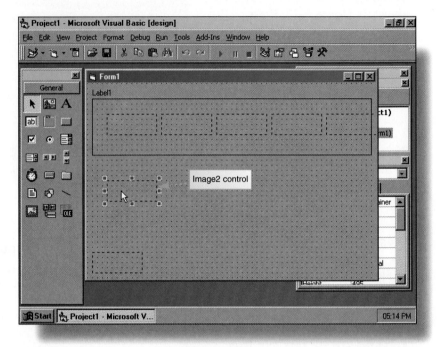

FIGURE 5-16

2 **Press the CTRL+C keys to copy the control to the Clipboard. Press the CTRL+V keys to paste the Clipboard's contents to the form. Click the Yes button in the Microsoft Visual Basic dialog box to start a control array. Drag the second Image control, imgContainer(1), to the location shown in Figure 5-17.**

A second Image control array, named imgContainer(1), is created (Figure 5-17).

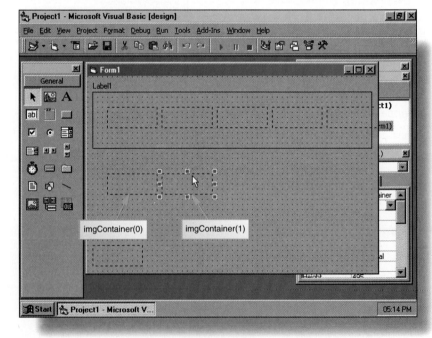

FIGURE 5-17

3 Press the CTRL+V keys to paste the Clipboard's contents to the form and then drag the Image control to the location shown in Figure 5-18. Press the CTRL+V keys two more times, dragging the Image controls to the locations shown in Figure 5-18.

Locating the controls in the order shown in Figure 5-18 is important. They easily can be confused because they all have the same appearance on the form.

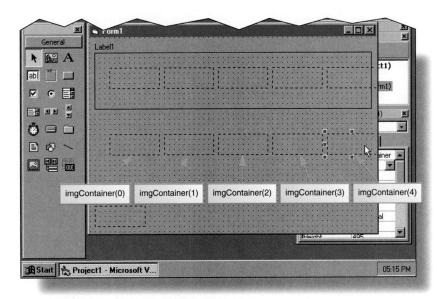

FIGURE 5-18

Adding a Label Control Array

The Label control array is shown in Figure 5-19. These controls are used for the names of the containers. The labels in the array have their AutoSize property set to True. Perform the following steps to create the array of labels used to name the containers.

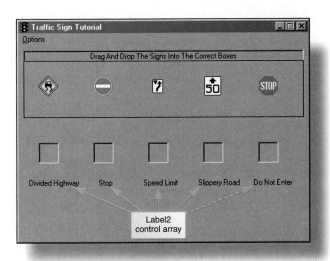

FIGURE 5-19

More *About*
Control Arrays

Adding controls in control arrays uses fewer resources than simply adding multiple controls of the same type to a form at design time. If you want to create a new control at run time, that control must be a member of a control array. With a control array, each new element inherits the common event procedures of the array.

TO ADD A LABEL CONTROL ARRAY

1 Double-click the Label button in the Toolbox.

2 Double-click the AutoSize property in the Properties list. Drag the Label control to the location shown in Figure 5-20.

3 Press the CTRL+C keys and then press the CTRL+V keys. Click the Yes button in the Microsoft Visual Basic dialog box.

4 Drag the second Label control, Label2(1), to the location shown in Figure 5-20.

5 Press the CTRL+V keys to paste the Clipboard's contents to the form. Drag the third Label control to the location shown in Figure 5-20.

6 Press the CTRL+V keys two times, dragging the Label controls to the locations shown in Figure 5-20.

Locating the controls in the order shown in Figure 5-20 is important. They easily can be confused because they all have the same caption, Label2.

Creating the Menu

The Options menu in the Traffic Sign Tutorial application contains three commands, as shown in Figure 5-21. Access keys and shortcuts are designated for the menu selection and command choices. Perform the following steps to create the Traffic Tutorial menu with the Visual Basic Menu Editor.

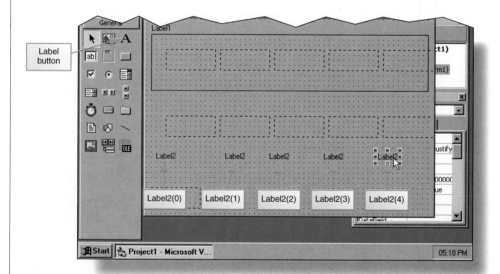

FIGURE 5-20

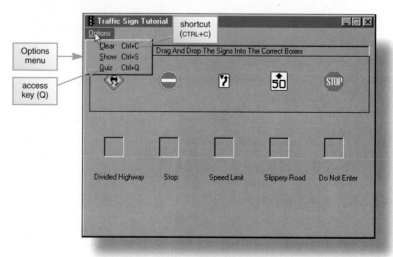

FIGURE 5-21

Steps To Create a Drop-Down Menu

1 **Click the Menu Editor button on the toolbar.**

The Menu Editor dialog box opens on the desktop (Figure 5-22).

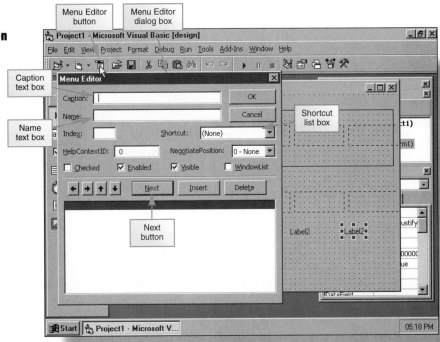

FIGURE 5-22

2 **Type** &Options **in the Caption text box. Press the TAB key. Type** mnuOptions **in the Name text box. Click the Next button.**

The mnuOptions control is added to the menu. Its caption displays in the list box. The highlighted line in the list box advances to the next line and the Menu Editor properties boxes are blank (Figure 5-23).

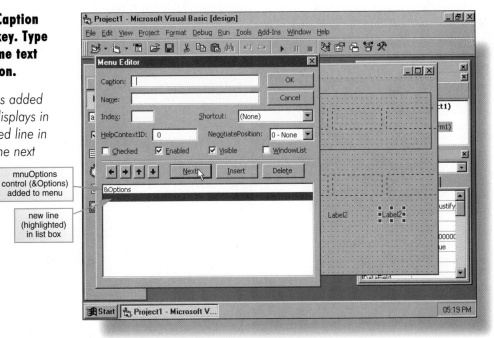

FIGURE 5-23

3 Click the right arrow button in the Menu Editor dialog box. Type &Clear in the Caption text box. Press the TAB key. Type mnuClear in the Name text box. Click Ctrl+C in the Shortcut list box.

The Menu Editor dialog box displays as shown in Figure 5-24.

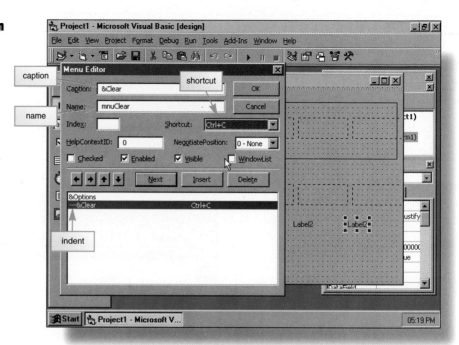

FIGURE 5-24

4 Click the Next button. Type &Show in the Caption text box. Press the TAB key. Type mnuShow in the Name text box. Click Ctrl+S in the Shortcut list box.

The Menu Editor dialog box displays as shown in Figure 5-25.

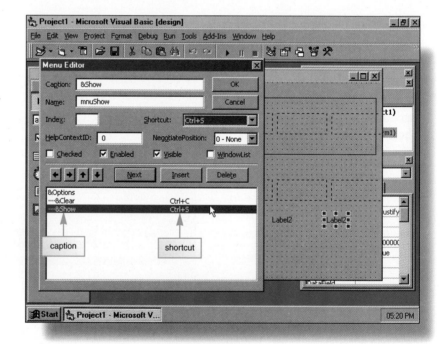

FIGURE 5-25

5 **Click the Next button. Type** `&Quiz` **in the Caption text box. Press the TAB key. Type** `mnuQuiz` **in the Name text box. Click Ctrl+Q in the Shortcut list box. Click the OK button.**

The Menu Editor dialog box closes, and the menu is added to the form (Figure 5-26).

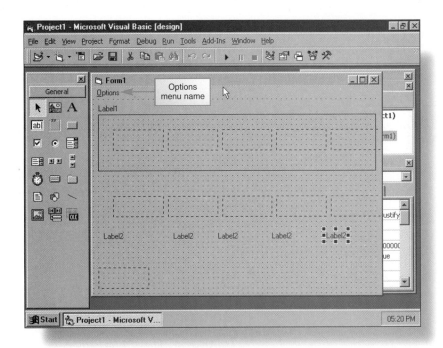

FIGURE 5-26

6 **Click Options on the Form1 menu bar to view the menu structure.**

Menus can be viewed during design time, as shown in Figure 5-27. Click anywhere on the form, or press the ESC key to close the menu.

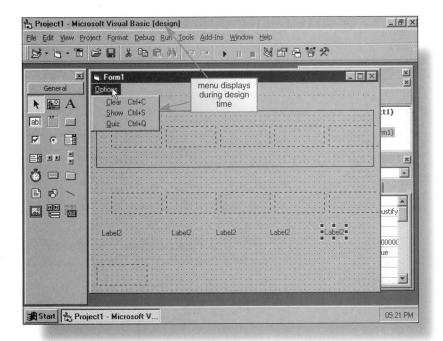

FIGURE 5-27

> **Other Ways**
>
> 1. On Tools menu click Menu Editor
> 2. Press CTRL+E

The interface for the Traffic Sign Tutorial application now is complete. The second step of application development is to set the properties of the form and other controls.

Saving the Form and Project

Before proceeding with setting property values, perform the following steps to save the form and project.

TO SAVE A FORM AND PROJECT

1 Insert the floppy disk with the trffc.ico files in the 3½ Floppy [A:] drive.

2 Click the Save Project button on the toolbar.

3 When the Save File As dialog box opens, type Traffic in the File name text box.

4 Click 3½ Floppy [A:] in the Save in list box.

5 Click the Save button in the Save File As dialog box.

6 When the Save Project As dialog box opens, type Traffic in the File name text box.

7 Click the Save button in the Save Project As dialog box.

The form file is saved on the floppy disk in the 3½ Floppy [A:] drive as Traffic.frm. The project file is saved on the floppy disk in the 3½ Floppy [A:] drive as Traffic.vbp.

Setting Properties

In this section, you will set properties of the form and controls in the following groups of steps.

▶ Properties of the form
▶ Properties of the five Label controls used to display the names of the containers
▶ Properties of the controls in the imgSign array
▶ Properties of the controls in the imgContainer array
▶ Properties of the individual Image and Label controls

Setting Name, Caption, BorderStyle, MinButton, and Icon Properties of the Form

In the following steps, you will set the name of the form, give it a caption to display in its title bar, and specify an icon for the form. At run time, the user should be able to minimize the application, although no need exists to maximize or resize the window. Recall that setting the form's BorderStyle property to Fixed Single prevents the window's borders from being dragged during run time. This BorderStyle property value automatically sets the form's MinButton and MaxButton properties to False, so you will have to reset the MinButton property to True. Perform the following steps to set these properties for the Traffic Tutorial form.

Steps To Set a Form's Name, Caption, BorderStyle, MinButton, and Icon Properties

1 **Click the Properties window to make it visible. Select Form1 in the Object list box. Double-click the Name property in the Properties list. Type** frmTraffic **and then press the ENTER key. Click the BorderStyle box arrow and then click 1 - Fixed Single.**

The form's new name displays in both the Project window and the Properties window (Figure 5-28).

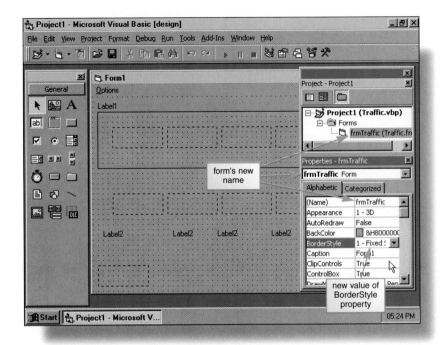

FIGURE 5-28

2 **Double-click the Caption property in the Properties window. Type** Traffic Sign Tutorial **and then press the ENTER key. Double-click the MinButton property. Double-click the Icon property in the Properties list.**

The Load Icon dialog box opens (Figure 5-29).

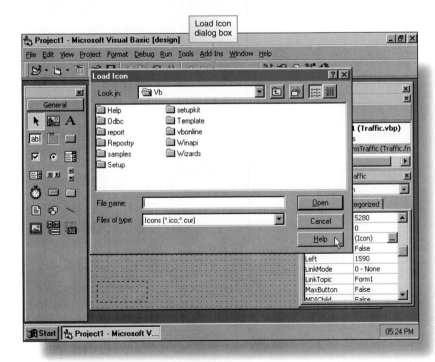

FIGURE 5-29

3 **Click 3½ Floppy [A:] in the Look in list box. Point to Trffc09.ico in the list box (Figure 5-30).**

The floppy disk in the 3½ Floppy [A:] drive either should be the Data Disk or the floppy disk you copied the icon files to at the beginning of this project.

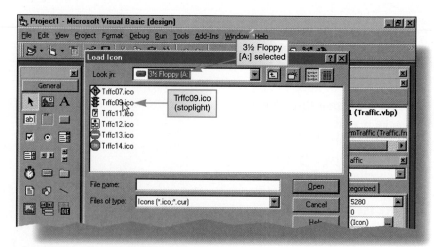

FIGURE 5-30

4 **Double-click Trffc09.ico.**

The Load Icon dialog box closes and the icon is added to the form (Figure 5-31).

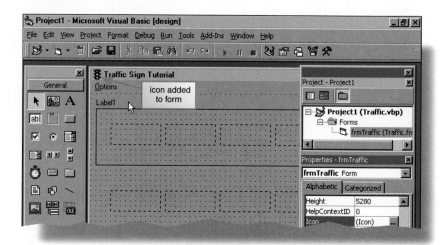

FIGURE 5-31

Setting the Captions of the Label Array Controls

Perform the following steps to set the captions of the Label controls to reflect the names of the sign containers.

TO SET LABEL CONTROL CAPTIONS

1 Select the Label2(0) control by clicking its name in the Object list box in the Properties window. Click the Caption property. Type `Divided Highway` as the name of the label.

2 Select the Label2(1) control by clicking its name in the Object list box in the Properties window. Type `Stop` as the name of the label.

3 Select the Label2(2) control by clicking its name in the Object list box in the Properties window. Type `Speed Limit` as the name of the label.

4 Select the Label2(3) control by clicking its name in the Object list box in the Properties window. Type `Slippery Road` as the name of the label.

5 Select the Label2(4) control by clicking its name in the Object list box in the Properties window. Type Do Not Enter as the name of the label.

6 Click the form to place it on top of the Properties window.

The Label controls' captions display on the form (Figure 5-32).

In previous projects, you set text values of control properties such as the Caption property by double-clicking the property name, typing the new value, and then pressing the ENTER key. In the previous steps, you learned that you also can set text values of properties by clicking the property name and then typing the value. Each time you selected the next Label, the previously selected property (Caption) remained selected, and so you immediately could type the new value. After you become familiar with selecting properties and setting values in the Properties window, you may prefer to use this method as a shortcut.

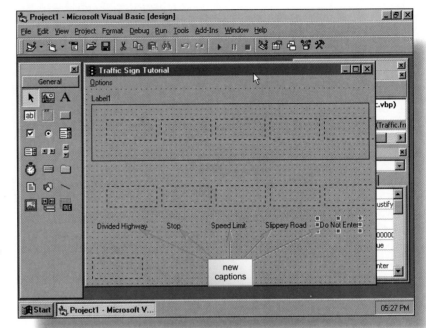

FIGURE 5-32

Setting the Properties of the imgSign Array Controls

Controls in an array must have a common value for their Name property. No other property of controls in an array has this restriction. The following steps load some of Visual Basic's traffic sign icons into the Image controls in the imgSign array by setting the **Picture property** of each of these Image controls.

When dragging is initiated during run time, an outline of the control is moved across the desktop. An image other than the control's outline can display as the control is being dragged by setting the control's **DragIcon property**. Double-clicking the DragIcon property in the Properties list box opens the Load Icon dialog box that was used to set the form's Icon property. In this application, the DragIcon property is set with code statements that will be added later. Perform the following steps to load the traffic icons into the Image controls in the imgSign array and set the Picture properties.

TO LOAD THE ICONS AND SET THE PICTURE PROPERTY OF IMAGE ARRAY CONTROLS

1 Select the imgSign(0) control from the Object list box in the Properties window. Double-click the Picture property in the Properties list.

2 When the Load Picture dialog box opens, double-click trffc11.ico (the Divided Highway icon) in the list box.

3 Select the imgSign(1) control. Double-click the Picture property. Double-click trffc14.ico (the Stop icon) in the list box.

4 Select the imgSign(2) control. Double-click the Picture property. Double-click trffc12.ico (the Speed Limit icon) in the list box.

(5) Select the imgSign(3) control. Double-click the Picture property. Double-click trffc07.ico (the Slippery Road icon) in the list box.

(6) Select the imgSign(4) control. Double-click the Picture property. Double-click trffc13.ico (the Do Not Enter icon) in the list box. Click the form to move it on top of the Properties window.

The traffic icons are loaded into the controls in the imgSign array, as shown in Figure 5-33.

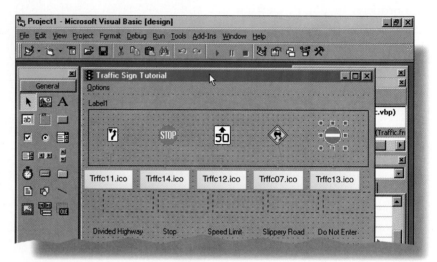

FIGURE 5-33

To load the icons into the Image controls' Picture property in the previous steps, Visual Basic had to access the .ico files on the floppy disk. Once graphic files such as the icons are loaded, the Image controls' Picture property is saved automatically as part of the Traffic.frx (form extension) file, and the graphic files (such as .ico files) are not used again.

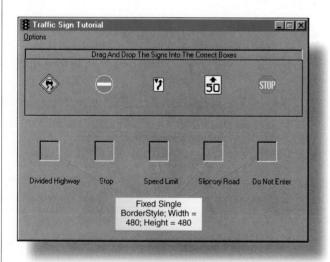

FIGURE 5-34

Setting Properties for a Group of Controls (imgContainer Array)

The values of the BorderStyle, Height, and Width properties of the Image controls in the imgContainer array need to be adjusted. For these controls to appear as containers, the BorderStyle property will be set to 1 - Fixed Single, and the Height and Width properties both will be set to 480 (Figure 5-34).

These properties could be set individually for each control, as you have done many times previously. An easier way exists, however, to set a property for a group of controls when the property value will be the same for all the controls in the group. Complete the following steps to select a group of controls and change its property values.

Steps **To Set Properties for a Group of Controls**

 Click the imgContainer(0) control.

The control is selected (Figure 5-35).

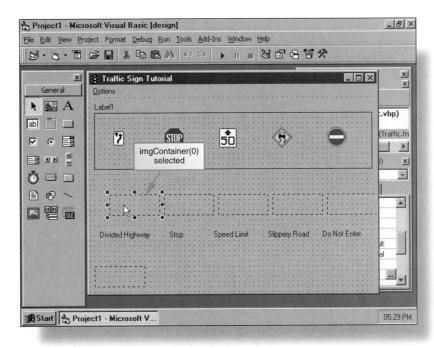

FIGURE 5-35

2 **With the control selected, press and hold down the CTRL key, and then click each additional control in the imgContainer array.**

As additional controls are selected, sizing handles display around the selected control (Figure 5-36).

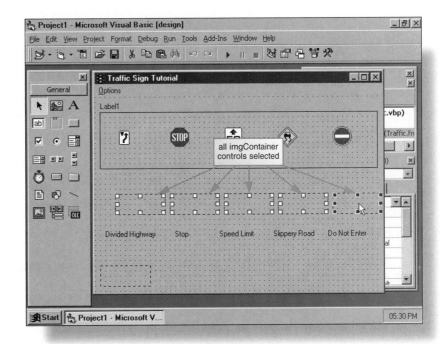

FIGURE 5-36

3 **Double-click the BorderStyle property in the Properties window.**

The BorderStyle property of all selected controls changes to 1 - Fixed Single (Figure 5-37).

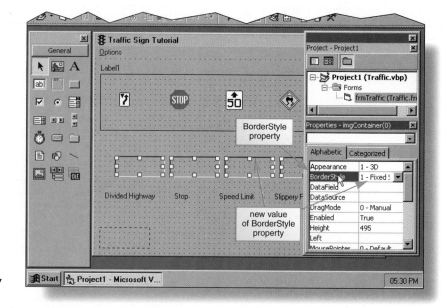

FIGURE 5-37

4 **Double-click the Height property. Type** 480 **and then press the ENTER key.**

The height of all the selected controls changes (Figure 5-38).

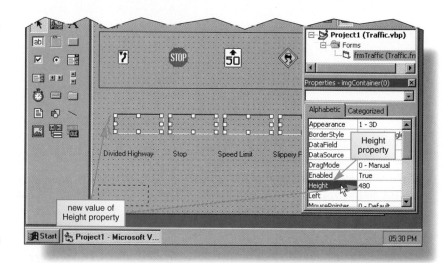

FIGURE 5-38

5 **Double-click the Width property. Type** 480 **and then press the ENTER key. Click an empty area of the form.**

The width of all the selected controls changes, and the group of controls is deselected (Figure 5-39).

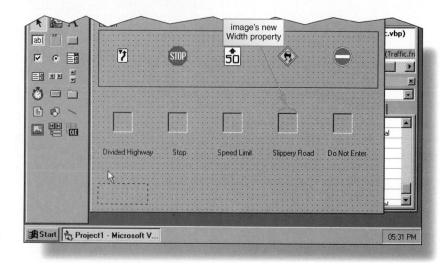

FIGURE 5-39

In the preceding steps, properties for all of the Image controls in the imgContainer array were changed at the same time by first selecting those controls as a group. This same procedure can be applied to a group of dissimilar controls (for example a text box and a label). Only the properties those controls have in common, however, can be changed as a group. You can cancel the selection of a specific control in a group by pressing and holding the CTRL key and clicking the control.

Setting Properties for the Individual Label and Image Controls

The one Label control that is not part of the label array is used to contain the run-time instructions for the Traffic Sign Tutorial application. The instructions are centered in the control by setting the **Alignment property**.

The individual Image control (lower-left corner of the form in Figure 5-39) is not visible at run time. It contains a blank picture that is assigned to other Image controls through code statements to make them appear to move. The control is named imgBlank to aid in understanding the functions of the code statements in which its name is used. Perform the following steps to set the properties for these two controls.

TO SET LABEL AND IMAGE CONTROL PROPERTIES

1. Select the Label control by clicking its name, Label1, in the Object list box in the Properties window.

2. Double-click the Caption property. Type Drag And Drop The Signs Into The Correct Boxes and then press the ENTER key.

3. Double-click the Alignment property in the Properties window. Double-click the Alignment property in the Properties window a second time to center the text.

4. Double-click the BorderStyle property in the Properties list to change the value to 1 - Fixed Single.

5. Select the Image1 Image control (located in the bottom left of the Form window) by clicking its current name, Image1, in the Object list box in the Properties window.

6. Double-click the Name property in the Properties list. Type imgBlank and then press the ENTER key.

7. Double-click the Visible property in the Properties list to change the value to False.

The new property values are visible in the Properties window (Figure 5-40).

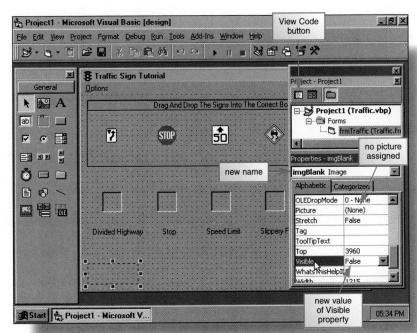

FIGURE 5-40

The design-time property setting is complete. The third and last stage is to write the code for the application. Click the Save button on the toolbar to re-save the form and project with the updated properties.

Writing Code

The code-writing activities for the Traffic Sign Tutorial application include two new events: the DragOver event and the DragDrop event. The **DragOver event** occurs when a drag-and-drop operation is in progress. The mouse pointer position determines which target object receives this event. For example, when imgSign(0) is dragged over a form such as frmTraffic, the Form_DragOver event is initiated. The **source** is imgSign(0). The **target** is frmTraffic.

You can write a code statement that applies to any control being dragged over the target by using the word *source* in the code statement. For example, the statement

```
Source.Visible = False
```

in a DragOver event procedure sets the Visible property to False for any control being dragged over the target control. Note that changing the Source control's Visible property to False does not affect the Source control's DragIcon property. That is, the drag icon still is visible. Changing the Source control's Visible property to False gives the effect that the Source control is being picked up and moved.

Visual Basic automatically adds the following first line to a DragOver event procedure.

```
Private Sub ctrlName_DragOver (Source As Control, X As Single,
Y As Single, State As Integer)
```

The different parts of the DragOver event procedure, called **arguments**, are listed in Table 5-1.

TABLE 5-1	
ARGUMENT	DESCRIPTION
ctrlName	The control that is being dragged over. It also is called the target.
Source	The control being dragged.
X, Y	The current horizontal (X) and vertical (Y) position of the mouse pointer within the target.
State	The transition state of the control being dragged in relation to the target:
	0 - Enter (Source control is being dragged within the range of a target)
	1 - Leave (Source control is being dragged out of the range of a target)
	2 - Over (Source control has moved from one position within the target to another position within the target)

The **DragDrop event** occurs when a drag-and-drop operation is completed as a result of dragging a control over a form or control and then releasing the mouse button. Visual Basic automatically adds the following first line to a DragDrop event procedure:

```
Private Sub ctrlName_DragDrop (Source As Control, X As Single,
Y As Single)
```

The arguments of the DragDrop event procedure are listed in Table 5-2.

TABLE 5-2	
ARGUMENT	*DESCRIPTION*
ctrlName	The control over which the mouse pointer is located when the mouse button is released. It also is called the target.
Source	The control being dragged. You can refer to properties and methods with this argument (for example, Source.Visible = True).
X, Y	The current horizontal (X) and vertical (Y) position of the mouse pointer within the target form or control.

The DragDrop event procedure is used to control what happens after a drag-and-drop operation has been completed. For example, you can use the DragDrop event procedure to move the Source control to a new location or change the Visible property of the Source control.

You must write code for 11 event procedures in the Traffic Sign Tutorial application. The control name, procedure, and a description of the action for the event procedure are listed in Table 5-3.

TABLE 5-3		
CONTROL	*EVENT*	*ACTIONS*
General	Declarations	Declares variable used across procedures.
frmTraffic	Load	Centers the form on the desktop. Sets the DragIcon property for the Image controls in the imgSign array.
frmTraffic	DragOver	Occurs when dragging one of the signs is initiated. Changes the Source control's Visible property to False.
frmTraffic	DragDrop	Dropping a sign on the form (not in a container) is an incorrect placement of a sign. The Source control's Visible property is set back to True so the control appears to *snap back* to its original position.
imgSign( )	DragDrop	Dropping a sign on another sign also is an incorrect placement. Same action as the form's DragDrop event.
Label1	DragDrop	Dropping a sign on the instructions label also is an incorrect placement. Same action as the form's DragDrop event.
Label2( )	DragDrop	Dropping a sign on a label used as a container's name also is an incorrect placement. Same action as the form's DragDrop event.
imgContainer( )	DragDrop	Evaluates whether placement is correct (indexes match) or not correct. If correct, sets the container's Picture property and increments the number correct counter; if not, sets Source.Visible back to True.
mnuClear	Click	Clears all pictures from containers; sets all imgSign( ) Visible properties to True.
mnuShow	Click	Sets all imgSign( ) Visible properties to False; sets imgContainer( ) Picture properties equal to the correct signs.
mnuQuiz	Click	Hides Traffic form; displays three questions (one at a time); keeps displaying a question until the correct answer is given or the Cancel button is clicked; redisplays the Traffic form.

The event procedures (subroutines) for the frmTraffic_DragDrop, imgSign_DragDrop, Label1_DragDrop, and Label2_DragDrop are identical and are written using the same set of steps. The code-writing activities for the Traffic Sign Tutorial application are grouped as follows:

▶ General_Declarations event procedure
▶ frmTraffic_Load event procedure
▶ frmTraffic_DragOver event procedure
▶ Label1, Label2, frmTraffic, and imgSign DragDrop event procedures
▶ imgContainer_DragDrop event procedure
▶ mnuClear_Click event procedure
▶ mnuShow_Click event procedure
▶ mnuQuiz_Click event procedure

Declaring Variables and Type-Declaration Characters

Visual Basic allows variables to have a **Variant data type**, so a given variable can store numbers, text, dates, or times. The Variant data type handles all types of data and converts them automatically. Declaring a data type other than Variant restricts the use of the variable but conserves some memory and makes the code run slightly faster.

The Traffic Sign Tutorial application keeps a count of the number of correct sign placements by adding the number 1 to a variable named NumCorrect% each time a correct placement is made. Because the value of NumCorrect% must be available to more than one subroutine, it must be declared. The concept of declaring variables was introduced in Project 2.

Variables you declare with the **Dim statement** in the general declarations procedure of a form are available to all procedures within the form. Variables you declare at the procedure level are available only within the procedure. When you use the Dim statement in a procedure, generally you put the Dim statement at the beginning of the procedure. You can use the Dim statement at the module (General declarations) or procedure level to declare the data type of a variable. In Project 2, you declared a variable named *num* with the statement

```
Dim num as Integer
```

where Integer was the type. An alternative way to declare the data type is to use a type-declaration character instead of the *as type* clause. A **type-declaration character** is a special character appended to the variable name that identifies its data type. For example, the % sign is the type-declaration character for the Integer type. The statement

```
Dim num%
```

declares a variable named num% as integer type.

Visual Basic data types are listed in Table 5-4.

TABLE 5-4	
DATA TYPE	*DESCRIPTION*
Byte	A data type used to hold positive integer numbers ranging from 0 to 255. Byte variables are stored as single, unsigned 8-bit (1-byte) numbers.
Boolean	A data type with only two possible values, True (-1) or False (0). Boolean variables are stored as 16-bit (2-byte) numbers.
Integer	A data type that holds integer variables stored as 2-byte whole numbers in the range -32,768 to 32,767. The Integer data type also is used to represent enumerated values. The percent sign (%) type-declaration character represents an Integer in Visual Basic.
Long	A 4-byte integer ranging in value from -2,147,483,648 to 2,147,483,647. The ampersand (&) type-declaration character represents a Long in Visual Basic.
Currency	A data type with a range of -922,337,203,685,477.5808 to 922,337,203,685,477.5807. Use this data type for calculations involving money and for fixed-point calculations where accuracy is particularly important. The at sign (@) type-declaration character represents Currency in Visual Basic.
Single	A data type that stores single-precision floating-point variables as 32-bit (2-byte) floating-point numbers, ranging in value from -3.402823E38 to -1.401298E-45 for negative values, and 1.401298E-45 to 3.402823E38 for positive values. The exclamation point (!) type-declaration character represents a Single in Visual Basic.
Double	A data type that holds double-precision floating-point numbers as 64-bit numbers in the range -1.79769313486232E308 to -4.94065645841247E-324 for negative values; 4.94065645841247E-324 to 1.79769313486232E308 for positive values. The number sign (#) type-declaration character represents the Double in Visual Basic.
Date	A data type used to store dates and times as a real number. Date variables are stored as 64-bit (8-byte) numbers. The value to the left of the decimal point represents a date, and the value to the right of the decimal point represents a time.
String	A data type consisting of a sequence of contiguous characters that represent the characters themselves rather than their numeric values. A String can include letters, numbers, spaces, and punctuation. The String data type can store fixed-length strings ranging in length from 0 to approximately 63K characters and dynamic strings ranging in length from 0 to approximately 2 billion characters. The dollar sign ($) type-declaration character represents a String in Visual Basic.
Object	A data type that represents any Object reference. Object variables are stored as 32-bit (4-byte) addresses that refer to objects.
Variant	A special data type that can contain numeric, string, or date data as well as the special values Empty and Null. The Variant data type has a numeric storage size of 16 bytes and can contain data up to the range of a Decimal, or a character storage size of 22 bytes (plus string length), and can store any character text. The VarType function defines how the data in a Variant is treated. All variables become Variant data types if not declared explicitly as some other data type.
User-defined	Any data type defined using the Type statement. User-defined data types can contain one or more elements of any data type. Arrays of user-defined and other data types are created using the Dim statement. Arrays of any type can be included within user-defined types.

In previous projects, you have used three-letter prefixes within control names that identify the control type such as frmLoanPmt or mnuExit. A similar naming convention exists for variables, where a three-letter prefix identifies the data type, such as int, to identify it as an Integer type variable. You should understand, however, that the three-letter prefix does not substitute for declaring the data type with the *as type* clause the way the type-declaration character does. Both the three-letter prefix and type-declaration characters make your code easier to read and understand. The choice between the two is largely one of personal preference or documentation standards of a specific organization.

Perform the following steps to write a general declarations procedure to declare a variable using a type-declaration character.

TO USE TYPE-DECLARATION CHARACTERS

1 Minimize the Form window.

2 Click the View Code button in the Project window.

3 Click General in the Object list box. Enter the following statement in the Code window:

```
Dim NumCorrect%
```

4 Press the ENTER key.

The minimized Form window and the Code window display as shown in Figure 5-41.

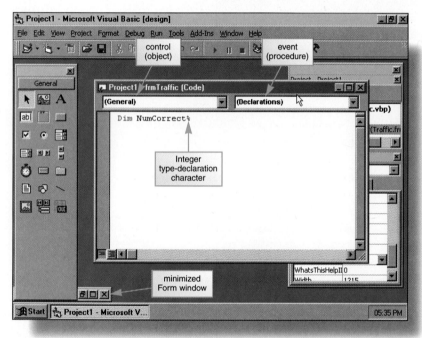

FIGURE 5-41

Writing a Form_Load Event Procedure

The code in this event procedure causes the Traffic form to be centered on the desktop at the beginning of run time. To do this, you will use code statements similarly to the way you centered the flag in the GeoView application. The Form_Load event procedure also assigns a picture to the DragIcon property of each of the controls in the imgSign array. Recall that the default property value for DragIcon is simply an outline of the control. In the following steps, the DragIcon property for each image is set equal to that image's Picture property. For example, the Picture property for imgSign(0) is the Divided Highway sign. The statement

```
imgSign(0).DragIcon = imgSign(0).Picture
```

sets the DragIcon property for that control to be the Divided Highway sign itself rather than just an outline. Because this assignment must be done for all five signs, the For...Next loop presented in Project 4 is used. Perform the following steps to write the frmTraffic_Load event procedure.

TO WRITE A FORM_LOAD EVENT PROCEDURE

1 Maximize the Code window. Select the Form control in the Object list box in the Code window.

2 Enter the following statements in the Code window:

```
'center form on desktop
frmTraffic.Top = (Screen.Height - frmTraffic.Height) / 2
frmTraffic.Left = (Screen.Width - frmTraffic.Width) / 2
'set dragicons for signs
For Index = 0 To 4
    imgSign(Index).DragIcon = imgSign(Index).Picture
Next
```

The Code window displays as shown in Figure 5-42.

In the preceding steps, two remarks were added to help clarify the code statements that follow them. In addition, when the ENTER key is pressed after a remark statement, Visual Basic changes the color of the statement to set it apart further from executable statements.

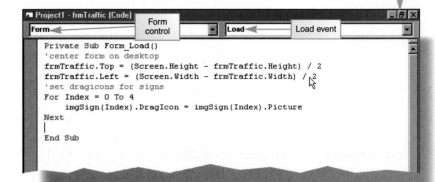

FIGURE 5-42

Writing a DragOver Event Procedure

The frmTraffic_ DragOver event procedure is executed whenever a control is dragged over the form. Because a Shape control does not have a DragOver event, this event occurs in the Traffic Sign Tutorial application when one of the traffic signs is dragged from its original position. To give the appearance that the sign is being moved, this event is used to change the Visible property of the Source control to False. In this way, the Source control's drag icon is visible when dragging occurs, but the Source control is not visible in its original location.

Perform the following steps to write the code statement to set the Visible property to False when the drag-and-drop operation begins.

TO WRITE A DRAGOVER EVENT PROCEDURE

1. Select DragOver in the Procedure list box in the Code window.
2. Enter the following statements in the Code window:

```
'set sign to invisible when dragging begins
Source.Visible = False
```

The Code window displays as shown in Figure 5-43.

It is important to note that the Form_DragOver event is the first event to occur during the drag-and-drop operation in this application because the form is the first control across which a source is dragged when dragging is initiated.

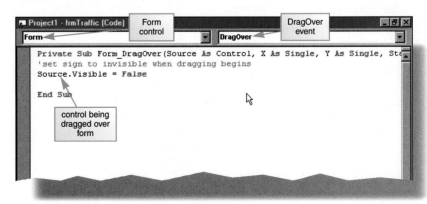

FIGURE 5-43

Writing the frmTraffic, Label1, Label2, and imgSign DragDrop Event Procedures

During the drag-and-drop operation in the Traffic Sign Tutorial application, a control can be dropped on any of the controls on the form including any one of the controls in the imgContainer array. Recall that the Visible property of the Source control (image being dragged) was set to False at the beginning of the drag-and-drop operation in the Form_DragOver event.

The **DragDrop event** occurs at the end of a drag-and-drop operation when the mouse button is released. If the control (traffic sign) being dragged is dropped on any control other than an imgContainer, the placement is incorrect. When this error occurs, setting the Source control's Visible property back to True makes the control appear to *snap back* to its original location. Perform the following steps to write the code statements for the DragDrop events for all controls in the Traffic Sign Tutorial where a drop is not correct.

To Write DragDrop Event Procedures

1 **Click DragDrop in the Procedure list box in the Code window. Enter the following two statements in the Code window:**

```
'unallowable drop; return
  sign to original
  location
Source.Visible  = True
```

The Code window appears as shown in Figure 5-44.

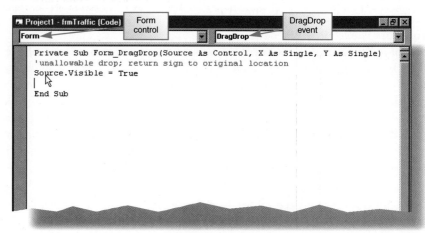

FIGURE 5-44

2 **Move the insertion point to the left of the apostrophe in the second code line. Press and hold the SHIFT key. Press the DOWN ARROW key twice and then release the SHIFT key.**

The two code statements written in Step 2 are highlighted (Figure 5-45).

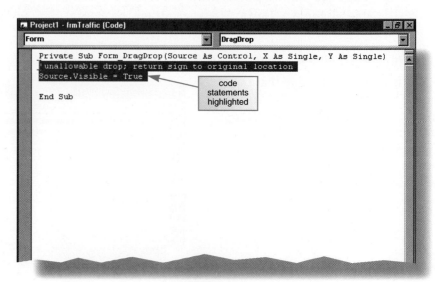

FIGURE 5-45

3 **Press the CTRL+C keys. Click Label1 in the Object list box and click DragDrop in the Procedure list box. Press the CTRL+V keys.**

The highlighted code statements are copied to the Clipboard and then pasted to the Label1_Drag-Drop event procedure (Figure 5-46).

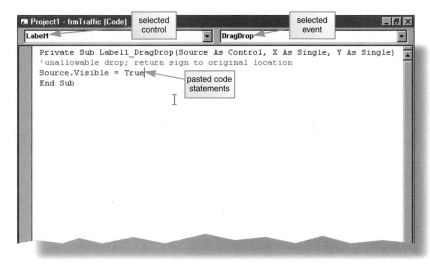

FIGURE 5-46

4 **Click Label2 in the Object list box and then click DragDrop in the Procedure list box. Press the CTRL+V keys.**

The highlighted code statements are pasted to the Label2_DragDrop event procedure (Figure 5-47).

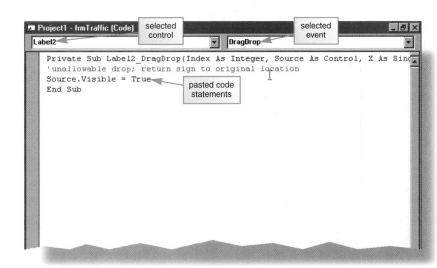

FIGURE 5-47

5 **Click imgSign in the Object list box and then click DragDrop in the Procedure list box. Press the CTRL+V keys.**

The highlighted code statements are pasted to the imgSign_Drag-Drop event procedure (Figure 5-48).

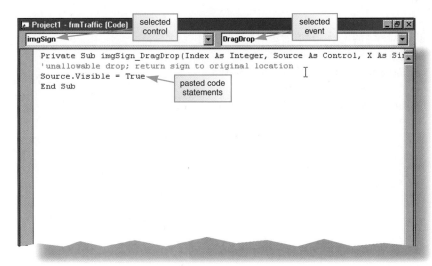

FIGURE 5-48

Project 2 presented a method for copying code between subroutines using the mouse and commands in the Edit menu. The preceding steps presented an alternate method for copying code using keyboard commands only. These same keyboard commands were used to copy and paste controls earlier in this project. The preceding steps also show how one event applies to all controls in an array such as the imgSign and Label2 control arrays.

Writing the imgContainer_DragDrop Event Procedure

Dropping a sign on one of the containers may or may not be a correct placement of the sign, depending upon which container it is dropped on. You added controls in the arrays to the form in a certain order and assigned the pictures of the imgSign array and captions of the Label2 array in the same order.

For example, the Picture property of imgSign(0) is the Divided Highway sign. Label2(0) displays on the form below the imgContainer(0) control, and its caption is Divided Highway (Figure 5-49). By maintaining this consistency in array indexes, the *correctness* of dropping one of the imgSign controls on one of the imgContainer controls is determined by whether their indexes match. Recall that **Index** is a property of the Source control when the Source control is part of an array, and that **Index** also is an argument of the DragDrop event that identifies the specific Target control when the Target control is part of an array. Later, the imgSign controls will be rearranged on the form to make the tutorial more challenging, but this change will not affect their indexes.

In the Traffic Sign Tutorial application, certain actions occur if the placement is correct, and other actions occur if it is not. This type of logical selection is represented in code with the If...Then...Else structure used in previous projects. One of the actions if the placement is correct is to **increment** (add 1 to) the NumCorrect% variable, which is used as a counter. Because the number of signs is five, additional actions are initiated when the counter's value = 5. This logic also is structured as an If...Then block, but the condition NumCorrect% = 5 is evaluated only if the current placement is correct. This If...Then structure within an If...Then...Else structure is called a **nested structure**.

The logical flow of the nested If...Then structure for the Traffic Sign Tutorial application is diagrammed in Figure 5-50. The dialog box that indicates all signs have been placed correctly (Figure 5-51) is created using the **MsgBox function**.

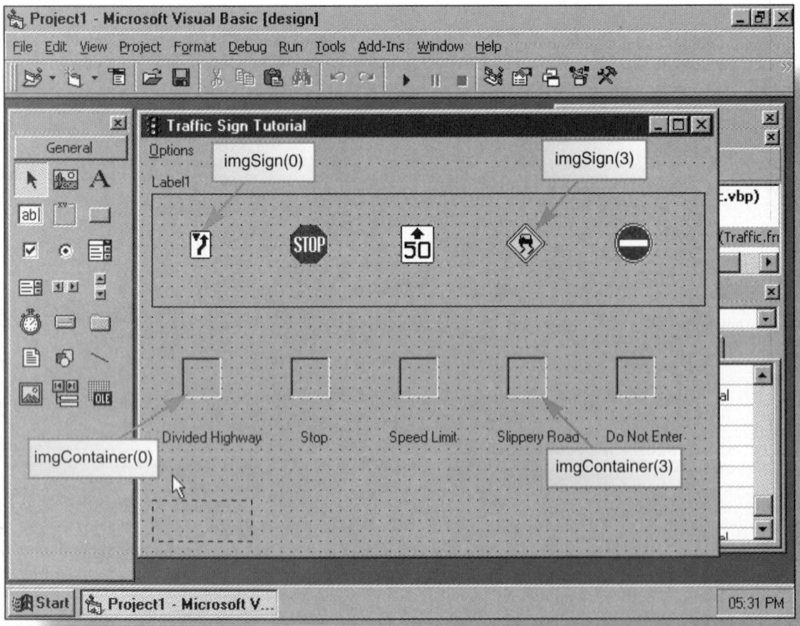

FIGURE 5-49

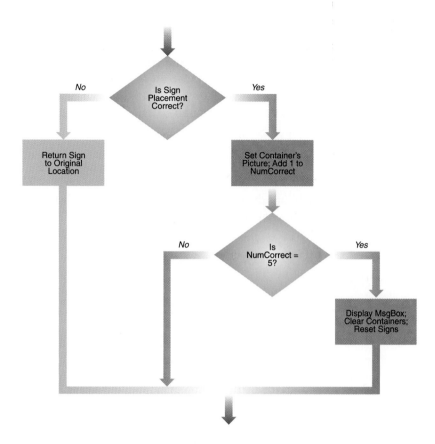

FIGURE 5-50

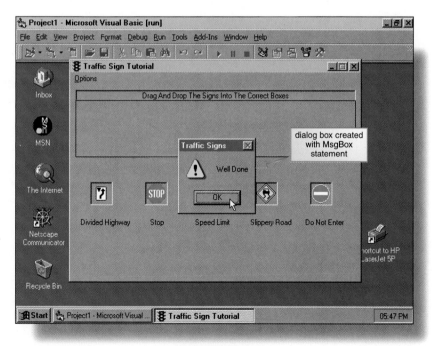

FIGURE 5-51

When the OK button is clicked in the dialog box, the signs are returned to their original positions. This same action occurs when the user clicks the Clear command on the Options menu in the application. Instead of repeating the code statements in both subroutines, you can execute a second subroutine by **calling the event procedure** for the second subroutine from the first. For example, when

Visual Basic encounters the mnuClear_Click event procedure within the imgContainer_DragDrop event procedure, it immediately executes all the code within the mnuClear_Click event procedure and then returns to execute the next code statement in the imgContainer_DragDrop event procedure.

Perform the following steps to write the imgContainer_DragDrop event procedure using the nested If...Then structure and to call the mnuClear_Click event procedure.

TO WRITE NESTED CODE STRUCTURES AND CALL EVENT PROCEDURES

(1) Select the imgContainer control array in the Object list box in the Code window and then select the DragDrop event in the Procedure list box.

(2) Enter the following statements in the Code window:

```
'check for correct drop (indexes match)
If Source.Index = Index Then
        'place sign in container; increment NumCorrect%
        imgContainer(Index).Picture = Source.Picture
        NumCorrect% = NumCorrect% + 1
        'check for last sign
        If NumCorrect% = 5 Then
                'display message; clear signs
                MsgBox "Well Done", 48, "Traffic Signs"
                mnuClear_Click
        End If
Else
        'incorrect drop; return sign to original location
        Source.Visible = True
End If
```

The Code window displays as shown in Figure 5-52.

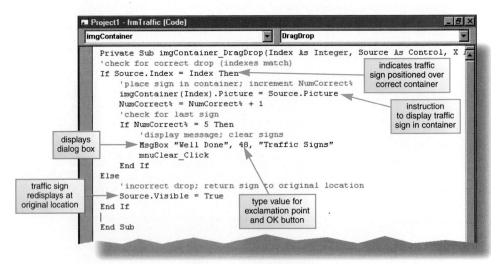

FIGURE 5-52

Clearing Image Controls' Picture Property

When the user of the Traffic Sign Tutorial application clicks the Clear command, all signs currently in containers are returned to their original locations. This command actually involves two actions: clearing any pictures from the container images and setting the Visible property value of the imgSign controls. This subroutine also resets the value of NumCorrect% to 0.

Each container is cleared by setting its Picture property equal to the Picture property of the imgBlank control. Each sign appears to return to its original location by setting the Visible property of the control in the imgSign array to True. Because the property setting must be done for each control in the two arrays, it is more efficient to use a For...Next loop rather than ten individual statements. Perform the following steps to write the code for the mnuClear_Click event procedure.

TO WRITE CODE TO CLEAR IMAGE ARRAY PICTURES

1 Select the mnuClear control in the Object list box in the Code window.

2 Enter the following statements in the Code window:

```
'clear containers and reset signs to original locations
For Index = 0 To 4
        imgContainer(Index).Picture = imgBlank.Picture
        imgSign(Index).Visible = True
Next
'reset counter
NumCorrect% = 0
```

The Code window displays as shown in Figure 5-53.

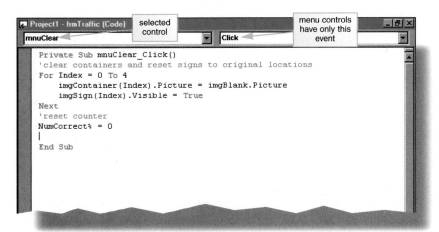

FIGURE 5-53

The mnuShow_Click Event Procedure

When the user clicks the Show command on the Options menu, all the signs appear to move from their original locations to the correct containers. This move is accomplished by setting the imgSign controls' Visible property to False and by setting the Picture property of each imgContainer control equal to the Picture property of its corresponding imgSign control.

You can choose the Show command in the Traffic Sign Tutorial any time during run time. Therefore, movements for all controls must be programmed because you do not know which signs have been placed correctly and which ones have not. Perform the steps on the next page to use a For...Next loop to display all signs in their correct containers.

TO WRITE CODE TO SET IMAGE ARRAY PICTURES

1. Select the mnuShow control in the Object list box in the Code window.
2. Enter the following statements in the Code window:

```
'move all signs to correct containers
For Index = 0 To 4
 imgContainer(Index).Picture = imgSign(Index).Picture
 imgSign(Index).Visible = False
Next
```

The Code window appears as shown in Figure 5-54.

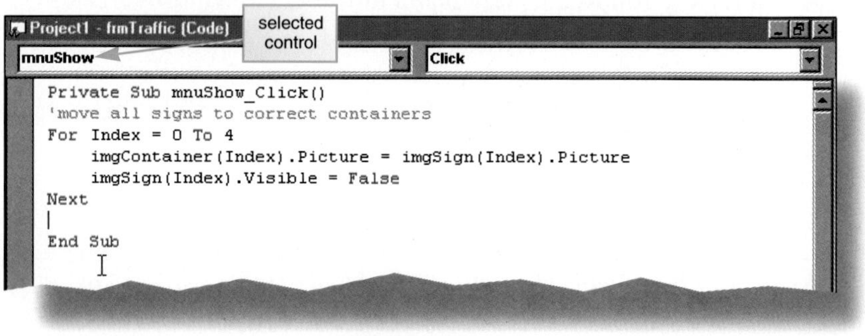

FIGURE 5-54

Writing the mnuQuiz_Click Event Procedure

When the user clicks the Quiz command on the Options menu, a subroutine is initiated that contains several code structures, some of which are nested. The Quiz subroutine presents a series of three questions about the shapes of some signs. A For...Next loop is used to repeat the process of presenting a question and processing an answer.

When the Quiz is displayed, the main form is removed from the desktop. This is accomplished using the Hide method. The **Hide method** removes a form from the desktop and its Visible property is set to False. Unlike the Unload method used in Project 3, however, the form is not removed from the computer's memory and the hidden form's controls are available to the running Visual Basic application. After the Quiz is completed, the form is added back to the desktop using the Show method presented in Project 3.

> **More** *About* **the Hide Method**
>
> If you apply the Hide method to a form that has not yet been loaded, the Hide method will load, but not display, the form.

The questions are displayed using a special dialog box created with the InputBox function (Figure 5-55). An **InputBox function** displays a prompt in a dialog box, waits for the user to input text or click a button, and then returns the contents of the text box to the subroutine.

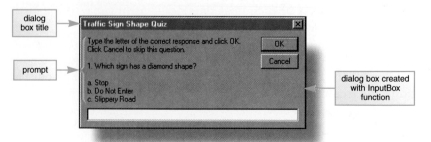

FIGURE 5-55

The syntax of the InputBox function is:

```
InputBox(argumentlist)
```

The most common arguments of the InputBox function are described in Table 5-5.

Additional InputBox arguments are available in Visual Basic. For a complete list, refer to Visual Basic Help.

The prompt shown in Figure 5-55 consists of the question and three answer choices. A new line is started for each answer by using the vbNewLine constant presented previously. If the user clicks the OK button or presses the ENTER key, the InputBox function returns whatever is in the text box. If the user clicks the Cancel button, the function returns a zero-length string ("").

TABLE 5-5	
ARGUMENT	*DESCRIPTION*
Prompt	A string expression displayed as the message in the dialog box. The maximum length of a prompt is approximately 255 characters, depending on the width of the characters used. If prompt consists of more than one line, you can separate the lines using the vbNewLine constant.
Title	Optional. A string expression displayed on the title bar in the dialog box. If you omit Title, the application name is placed on the title bar.
Default	Optional. A string expression displayed in the text box as the default response if no other input is provided. If you omit default, the text box is displayed empty.

Each time the subroutine loops through the For...Next loop, it must select the appropriate question. Project 3 presented the If...Then...Else statement as a method of selection within code. This project uses an additional selection structure, the Select Case structure. The **Select Case structure** executes one of several statement blocks depending on the value of an expression. In its simplest form, its syntax is:

```
Select Case testexpression
    Case expression1
        statementblock-1
    Case expression2
        statementblock-2
    Case Else
        statementblock-n
End Select
```

The parts of the Select Case structure are described in Table 5-6.

TABLE 5-6	
PART	*DESCRIPTION*
Select Case	Begins the Select Case structure. It must appear on a separate line before any other part of the Select Case structure.
testexpression	The name of a variable or any numeric or string expression whose value is compared to the expressions that follow the word Case in each block (e.g., expression1, expression2, and so on). If testexpression matches the expression associated with a Case clause, the statementblock following that Case clause is executed.
Case	Begins a Case clause that groups statements (statementblock) to be executed if the expression following the word Case matches the testexpression.
expression	The value of testexpression that leads to a different statementblock being executed. Similar to the condition in an If...Then statement.
statementblock	A group of Visual Basic code statements.
Case Else	Optional keywords indicating the statement block to be executed if no match is found between testexpression and expression in any of the other Case selections.
End Select	Ends the Select Case structure. It must appear on a separate line after all other statements in the Select Case structure.

In the Traffic Sign Tutorial application, the counter in the For...Next loop is used as the *testexpression*, and the values from 1 to 3 are used in the expressions to select the appropriate question. The logical flow is diagrammed in Figure 5-56.

Although the question displayed in the Traffic Tutorial Quiz InputBox changes, the instructions and the set of possible answers remain the same each time. Code writing is simplified by creating two constants named, Instruction$ and Choice$. The Instruction$ constant holds the text of the instructions and the codes for new lines. The Choice$ constant holds the text of the set of answers. The constants' names then are used in place of all the text.

The code statements and explanatory remarks for the first part of the mnuQuiz_Click event procedure are as follows (notice the use of the line continuation character presented in a previous project):

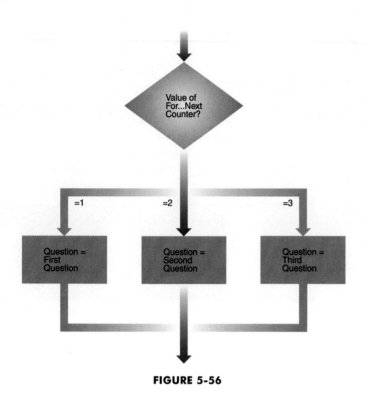

FIGURE 5-56

```
'declare constants and variables
Const Instruction$ = "Type the letter of the correct response and click OK. & vbNewLine & _
                     Click Cancel to skip this question." & vbNewLine & vbNewLine
Const Choice$ = vbNewLine & vbNewLine & "a. Stop" & vbNewLine & _
               "b. Do Not Enter" & vbNewLine & "c. Slippery Road"
Dim QuesNum%, Question$, CorrectAnswer$, Response$
'hide traffic form
frmTraffic.Hide
'loop for three questions
For QuesNum% = 1 To 3
    'assign value to variable Question$ and variable CorrectAnswer$
    Select Case QuesNum%
        Case Is = 1
            Question$ = "1. Which sign has a diamond shape?" & Choice$
            CorrectAnswer$ = "C"
        Case Is = 2
            Question$ = "2. Which sign has an octagonal shape?" & Choice$
            CorrectAnswer$ = "A"
        Case Is = 3
            Question$ = "3. Which sign has a round shape?" & Choice$
            CorrectAnswer$ = "B"
    End Select
```

At this point in the code's execution during run time, the For...Next loop has begun. The first question has been assigned to the variable Question$, and the correct answer to the first question has been assigned to the variable CorrectAnswer$.

Next, the question must be displayed and the user's answer processed. An InputBox function is used to display the question and to get the user's answer. Whatever the user has typed in the text box of the dialog box is assigned as the value of a variable when the OK button is clicked. The variable can be given any valid variable name. This variable is named Response$ in the Traffic Sign Tutorial.

If the user has entered an incorrect answer and has clicked the OK button, the value of the variable Response$ does not match the value of the variable CorrectAnswer$. The Traffic Sign Tutorial application then displays a dialog box created with a MsgBox statement (Figure 5-57).

FIGURE 5-57

The application continues to redisplay the message box and the same question until the correct answer is given or until the user clicks the Cancel button. A For...Next loop is not an appropriate structure of repetition for this activity because the number of repetitions is not known in advance. A **Do...Loop** repeats a block of statements while a condition is True or until a condition is met. In this application, the incorrect answer message box and question are displayed until the answer is correct or until the Cancel button has been clicked. One form of the Do...Loop, called a Do...Until loop, is used. The syntax is as follows:

```
Do Until condition
    statementblock
Loop
```

The parts of the Do Until loop are described in Table 5-7.

TABLE 5-7	
PART	*DESCRIPTION*
Do	Must be the first statement in a Do...Loop code structure.
statementblock	Program statements between the Do and Loop statements that are executed while a condition is true or until a condition is true.
until	Indicates the statementblock is executed repeatedly until the condition is true.
condition	Numeric or string expression that evaluates to True or False.

The logical flow of this Do Until loop is diagrammed in Figure 5-58.

Notice that if the user responds correctly the first time or clicks the Cancel button, the condition is True immediately and the statements inside the loop (statementblock) are not executed. The condition evaluated in the Traffic Sign Shape Quiz is whether the value of the variable Response$ equals the value of the variable CorrectAnswer$ or the value (""). Recall that the zero length string value ("") means the Cancel button was clicked. Notice in the code on page VB 5.40 that the value assigned to the variable CorrectAnswer$ in Case = 1 is the character uppercase C. If the user enters a lowercase c, the condition will evaluate to False and the loop will continue. A way to account for a user responding in either lowercase or uppercase is to use the UCase$ function. The **UCase$ function** returns a string with all letters of the argument uppercase. Its syntax is:

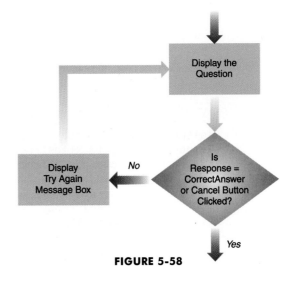

FIGURE 5-58

UCase$(*stringexpr*)

The argument *stringexpr* can be any string expression. Only lowercase letters are converted to uppercase; all uppercase letters and nonletter characters remain unchanged.

An InputBox statement is placed before the Do Until loop to provide the first opportunity for the user to respond. The loop executes until a correct answer is given for each question. That is, the Do...Loop is nested within the For...Next loop, as diagrammed in Figure 5-59.

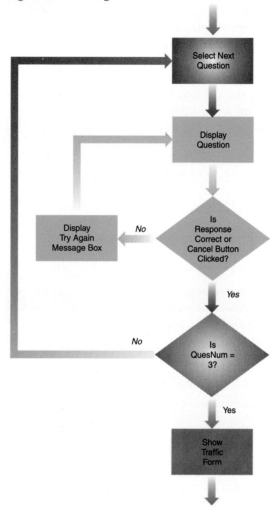

FIGURE 5-59

The additional code for the mnuQuiz_Click event procedure is as follows:

```
'display question; assign returned value to variable Response$
Response$ = InputBox(Instruction$ & Question$,"Traffic Sign Shape Quiz")
    'begin loop for correct answer or cancel button
    Do Until UCase$(Response$) = CorrectAnswer$ Or Response$ = ""
        'display message box for wrong answer
        MsgBox "Your response was not correct. Please try again", , _
            "Traffic Sign Shape Quiz"
        'display question again
        Response$ = InputBox(Instruction$ & Question$, _
                "Traffic Sign Shape Quiz")
    Loop
'add 1 to counter in for...next loop
Next
'display main form after 3rd question
frmTraffic.Show
```

With the second section of code just described, the mnuQuiz_Click event procedure is complete. Perform the following steps to enter the mnuQuiz_Click event procedure in the Code window.

TO WRITE SELECT CASE, INPUTBOX, UCASE$, AND DO...LOOP CODE

1 Select the mnuQuiz control in the Object list box in the Code window.

2 Enter the code as shown in the Code window in Figure 5-60.

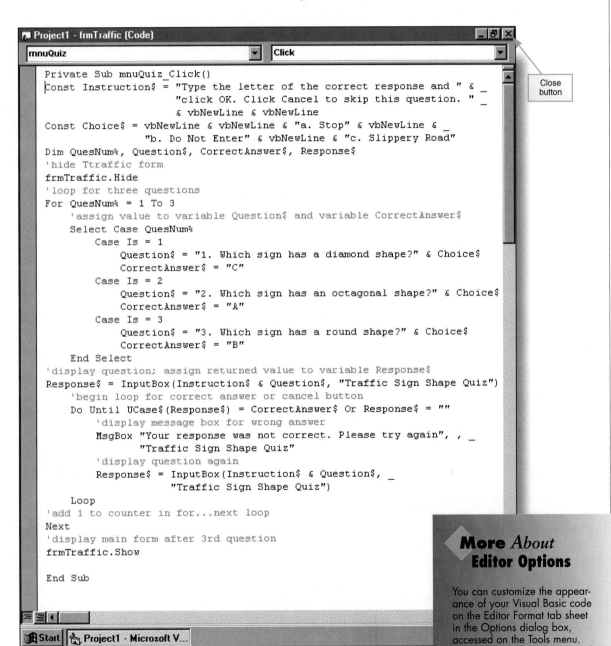

```vb
Private Sub mnuQuiz_Click()
Const Instruction$ = "Type the letter of the correct response and " & _
                     "click OK. Click Cancel to skip this question. " _
                     & vbNewLine & vbNewLine
Const Choice$ = vbNewLine & vbNewLine & "a. Stop" & vbNewLine & _
                "b. Do Not Enter" & vbNewLine & "c. Slippery Road"
Dim QuesNum%, Question$, CorrectAnswer$, Response$
'hide Ttraffic form
frmTraffic.Hide
'loop for three questions
For QuesNum% = 1 To 3
    'assign value to variable Question$ and variable CorrectAnswer$
    Select Case QuesNum%
        Case Is = 1
            Question$ = "1. Which sign has a diamond shape?" & Choice$
            CorrectAnswer$ = "C"
        Case Is = 2
            Question$ = "2. Which sign has an octagonal shape?" & Choice$
            CorrectAnswer$ = "A"
        Case Is = 3
            Question$ = "3. Which sign has a round shape?" & Choice$
            CorrectAnswer$ = "B"
    End Select
'display question; assign returned value to variable Response$
Response$ = InputBox(Instruction$ & Question$, "Traffic Sign Shape Quiz")
    'begin loop for correct answer or cancel button
    Do Until UCase$(Response$) = CorrectAnswer$ Or Response$ = ""
        'display message box for wrong answer
        MsgBox "Your response was not correct. Please try again", , _
            "Traffic Sign Shape Quiz"
        'display question again
        Response$ = InputBox(Instruction$ & Question$, _
                    "Traffic Sign Shape Quiz")
    Loop
'add 1 to counter in for...next loop
Next
'display main form after 3rd question
frmTraffic.Show

End Sub
```

FIGURE 5-60

> ◆ **More** *About*
> **Editor Options**
>
> You can customize the appearance of your Visual Basic code on the Editor Format tab sheet in the Options dialog box, accessed on the Tools menu. You can specify the foreground and background colors used for different types of text, such as Comment text or Keyword text. You also can set the font style and size of the Call code that displays in the Editor.

One last activity must be performed before the Traffic Sign Tutorial is complete. In its current state (Figure 5-61 on the next page), the correct container for each sign is directly below the sign.

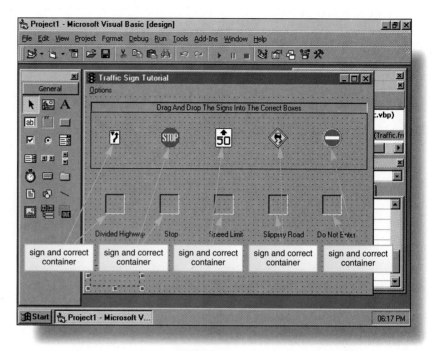

FIGURE 5-61

Perform the following steps to rearrange the imgSign controls to make the tutorial more challenging.

TO REARRANGE THE IMGSIGN CONTROLS

1 Close the Code window by clicking its Close button.

2 Restore the Form window.

3 Rearrange the imgSign controls by dragging them to the positions shown in Figure 5-62.

This rearrangement does not affect the controls' indexes and therefore will have no effect on the function of the tutorial.

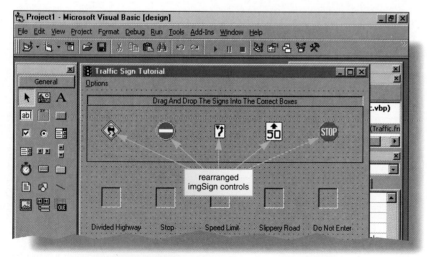

FIGURE 5-62

Saving and Running the Application

The Traffic Sign Tutorial application is complete. Before running the application, the form and project should be resaved. Perform the following steps to resave the project and run it.

Steps To Save and Run the Project

Save Project
button

1 Click the Save Project button on the toolbar.

The form files are resaved on the floppy disk in the 3½ Floppy [A:] drive as Traffic.frm and Traffic.frx. The project file is resaved on the floppy disk in the 3½ Floppy [A:] drive as Traffic.vbp. The desktop displays as shown in Figure 5-63.

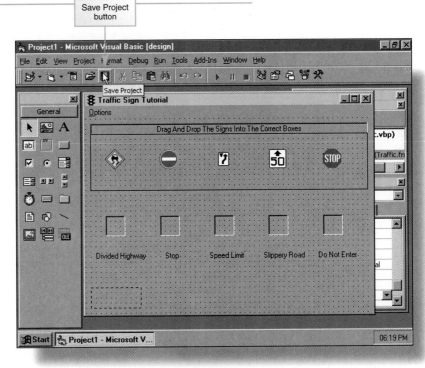

FIGURE 5-63

indicates
run time

Start
button

2 Click the Start button on the toolbar.

The application opens (Figure 5-64).

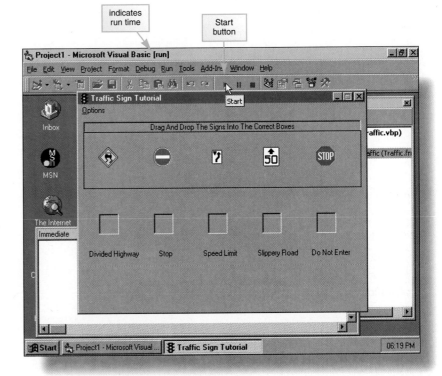

FIGURE 5-64

3 **Click Options on the Traffic Sign Tutorial menu bar and then click Show.**

The signs "move" to the correct containers (Figure 5-65).

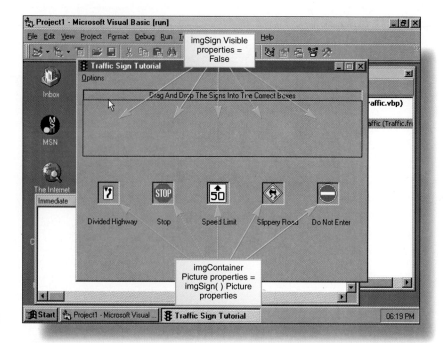

FIGURE 5-65

4 **Press the CTRL+C keys to return the signs to their original locations. Drag and drop one of the signs anywhere on the form other than its correct container.**

During the drag operation the sign appears to move from its original location (Figure 5-66). When dropped incorrectly, it "returns" to its original position.

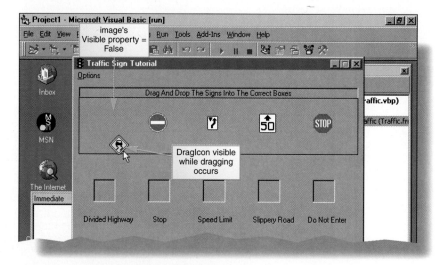

FIGURE 5-66

5 **Click Options on the Traffic Sign Tutorial menu bar and then click Quiz. Enter an incorrect answer and then point to the OK button.**

Because the dialog box is a modal form, you cannot perform any other function (including stopping the application) until the Traffic Sign Shape Quiz (InputBox) dialog box (Figure 5-67) is closed.

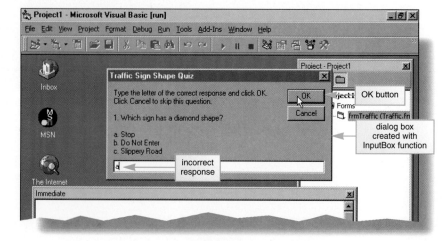

FIGURE 5-67

6 Click the OK button in the Traffic Sign Shape Quiz dialog box and then click the OK button in the next dialog box (MsgBox).

The Do...Loop causes the same question to display again (Figure 5-68).

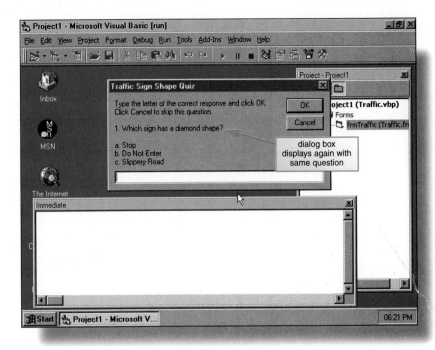

FIGURE 5-68

7 Complete the quiz, and then test the other features of the application. To end the application, click the Traffic Sign Tutorial's Close button or click the End button on the Visual Basic toolbar.

The Visual Basic IDE returns to design mode (Figure 5-69).

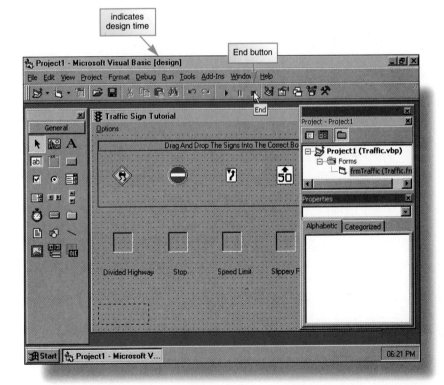

FIGURE 5-69

OtherWays

1. Press F5 to start current application

Project Summary

In Project 5, you used the three-step approach to build a prototype computer-based training application. You used the InputBox and UCase$ functions in code statements. You wrote more complex code using nested structures, the Select Case structure, and the Do...Loop structure.

You learned how to use DragMode and DragIcon properties and DragOver and DragDrop event procedures to add drag and drop functionality to applications. You also learned how to call one event procedure from another event procedure.

What You Should Know

Having completed this project, you now should be able to perform the following tasks.

▶ Add a Label Control Array *(VB 5.13)*

▶ Add Label, Shape, and Image Controls *(VB 5.8)*

▶ Create an Image Control Array for the Traffic Sign Containers *(VB 5.12)*

▶ Create an Image Control Array for the Traffic Signs *(VB 5.9)*

▶ Create a Drop-Down Menu *(VB 5.15)*

▶ Load the Icons and Set the Picture Property of Image Array Controls *(VB 5.21)*

▶ Rearrange the imgSign Controls *(VB 5.44)*

▶ Save a Form and Project *(VB 5.18)*

▶ Save and Run the Project *(VB 5.45)*

▶ Set a Form's Size *(VB 5.7)*

▶ Set a Form's Name, Caption, BorderStyle, Min-Button, and Icon Properties *(VB 5.19)*

▶ Set Label Control Captions *(VB 5.20)*

▶ Set Label and Image Control Properties *(VB 5.25)*

▶ Set Properties for a Group of Controls *(VB 5.23)*

▶ Use Type-Declaration Characters *(VB 5.30)*

▶ Write a DragOver Event Procedure *(VB 5.31)*

▶ Write a Form_Load Event Procedure *(VB 5.30)*

▶ Write Code to Clear Image Array Pictures *(VB 5.37)*

▶ Write Code to Set Image Array Pictures *(VB 5.38)*

▶ Write DragDrop Event Procedures *(VB 5.32)*

▶ Write Nested Code Structures and Call Event Procedures *(VB 5.36)*

▶ Write Select Case, InputBox, UCase$, and Do...Loop Code *(VB 5.43)*

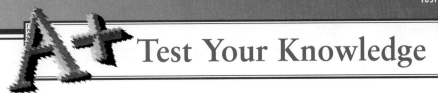

Test Your Knowledge

1 True/False

Instructions: Circle T if the statement is true or F if the statement is false.

T F   1. Run time dragging and dropping of a control always changes the location of the control.

T F   2. The value of the DragMode property determines the ability to drag a control at run time.

T F   3. Each form in Visual Basic can contain only one control array.

T F   4. Parts of the DragOver event procedure are called arguing.

T F   5. When the mouse button is released after dragging a control, the DragDrop event occurs.

T F   6. One event that applies to all controls in an array must be placed in a subroutine.

T F   7. A second subroutine can be executed by calling the event procedure for it from another subroutine.

T F   8. The Hide method works exactly like the Unload method.

T F   9. The Select End statement ends the Select Case structure.

T F 10. The UCase$ function can be used to convert lowercase letters in a string to uppercase.

2 Multiple Choice

Instructions: Circle the correct response.

1. The control being dragged is called the _____ control.
   a. Visible
   b. Source
   c. Target
   d. Image

2. To have an image rather than an outline display as a control is being dragged, set the _____ property for the control.
   a. DragIcon
   b. Image
   c. Visible
   d. DragMode

3. When a drag-and-drop operation is in progress, the _____ event occurs.
   a. DragDrop
   b. DragImage
   c. DragControl
   d. DragOver

4. A data type of _____ allows variables to store text, numbers, dates, or times.
   a. Variant
   b. Double
   c. String
   d. Long

(continued)

A+ Test Your Knowledge

Multiple Choice (continued)

5. In Visual Basic, a(n) _____ can be used to keep track of how many times an event has taken place.
   a. incrementor
   b. adder
   c. counter
   d. tracker

6. When one If...Then structure is placed inside another If...Then...Else structure, it is called a _____ structure.
   a. internal
   b. sub-structure
   c. nested
   d. joined

7. A(n) _____ function prompts for an answer, accepts a response, and returns the response to a subroutine.
   a. QuestionBox
   b. InputBox
   c. AnswerBox
   d. QueryBox

8. A structure used to allow for several choices is called a(n) _____ structure.
   a. Case
   b. For...Next
   c. Do...Loop
   d. If...Then...Else

9. A structure used to repeat a block of statements while a condition is True or until a condition is met is called a(n) _____ structure.
   a. Case
   b. For...Next
   c. Do...Loop
   d. If...Then...Else

10. Adding remarks to code makes it _____.
    a. run faster
    b. remarkable
    c. executable
    d. self-documenting

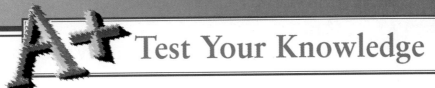

Test Your Knowledge

3 Understanding Case Structures

Instructions: Figure 5-70 shows an interface for a weather application. It displays a common word to describe the temperature based on actual temperature ranges. The temperature ranges and words to describe the ranges are as follows: at least 90^0 and below 130^0 is sweltering; at least 70^0 and below 90^0 is warm; at least 50^0 and below 70^0 is cool; at least 32^0 and below 50^0 is cold; below 32^0 up to and including -70^0 is freezing. When the temperature is above 130^0 or below -70^0, it is out of normal ranges and the user should be notified. When the temperature is entered and it is not numeric, the user should be notified.

Draw a flowchart and write a subroutine using a Select Case structure to select the appropriate description for the temperature entered or to notify users of error conditions.

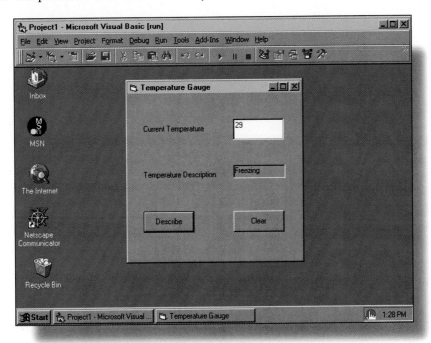

FIGURE 5-70

4 Understanding Do...Loop Structures

Instructions: Figure 5-71 on the next page shows an interface for an application that computes an employee's weekly pay based on a seven-day week. The time for each employee is entered at the end of a work week and the number of entries for each employee cannot exceed seven. When the total number of hours worked exceeds 40 for an individual employee, the employee is paid overtime at 1.5 times the normal rate of pay. When an employee's rate of pay is lower than $5.50 per hour, the employee receives a $10.00 bonus amount for the week in addition to regular and overtime earnings.

(continued)

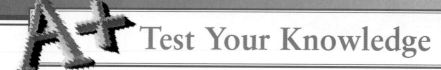

Test Your Knowledge

Understanding Do...Loop Structures (*continued*)

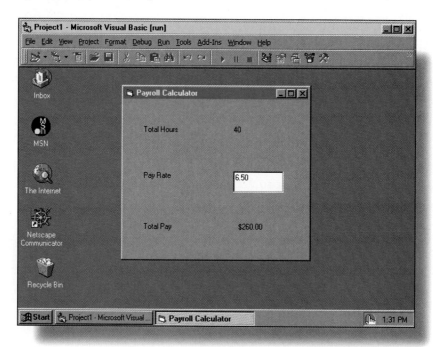

FIGURE 5-71

Draw the flowchart for this application and then build the application based on your flowchart design.

A looping structure in the Form_Load event procedure can be used to accept the hours via an Input-Box function. The other statements in the looping structure's range should accumulate the total number of hours worked and increment the counter for the number of entries. After all of the hours have been entered, the total hours for the week should be labeled and displayed on the form. *Hint*: All variables used in your code statements should be declared and initialized to zero. Also, any variables used in more than one subroutine, may require defining in general declarations.

The remaining code statements should be located in the TextBox object's Change procedure. The code statements located here should accept and display the rate of pay and then calculate and display the total amount of pay.

Use Help

1 Reviewing Project Activities

Instructions: Perform the following tasks using a computer.

1. Start Visual Basic.
2. Click Help on the menu bar and then click Microsoft Visual Basic Help Topics.
3. Click the Index tab and then type `drag and drop` in the top text box labeled 1. Click the Display button. When the Topics Found dialog box displays, click the Display button to display the Drag Method Help topic.
4. Read the information. Right-click anywhere in the Visual Basic Reference window and then click Print Topic. Hand the printouts in to your instructor.
5. Click the See Also link. When the Topics Found dialog box opens, one by one, click the DragDrop Event, DragIcon Property, DragMode Property, and DragOver Event topics. Read the information as it displays. Right-click anywhere in each of the Help windows and then click Print Topic to print the information. Use the Back button to return to the DragMethod Help topic screen. Hand the printouts in to your instructor.
6. Click the Help Topics button to return to the Help Topics: Visual Basic 5 dialog box and then click the Contents tab.
7. Double-click the Language Reference book, the Statements book, and the D book. Double-click the Do...Loop Statement topic.
8. Write the answers to the following questions on your own paper and turn them in to your instructor:
    a. How many types of Do...Loop statements exist?
    b. What statement can be used to leave a Do...Loop early?
    c. What character can be used to include more than one statement on a line?
    d. What character can be used to continue a single logical line onto a second physical line?

2 Learning More of the Basics

Instructions: Use Visual Basic Books Online to learn more about Visual Basic control structures and dragging and dropping. The Help topics will provide information to answer the questions below. Write the answers to the questions on your own paper and turn them in to your instructor.

1. Start Visual Basic. Click Help on the menu bar and then click Books Online. In the Navigation area, double-click Programmer's Guide (All Editions) book. Double-click the following topics in order: Part 1: Visual Basic Basics, Programming Fundamentals, The Structure of a Visual Basic Application, and Introduction to Control Structures. Click the Loop Structures topic. Read the information that displays in the Topic area. As you read the text in the Topic area, answer the following questions:
    a. What is at least one generic example for each type of Do...Loop structure?
    b. Which type of Do...Loop structure will execute at least one time?

(continued)

Use Help

Learning More of the Basics *(continued)*

    c. What are the other types of looping structures supported by Visual Basic 5?

2. In the Navigation area, double-click Part 2: What Can You Do With Visual Basic? and then double-click Responding to Mouse and Keyboard Events. Read the information that displays in the Topic area. As you read the text in the Topic area, answer the following questions:

    a. What are the two types of drag and drop supported by Visual Basic 5?

3. In the Topic area, scroll down to the Topics section. Click the Dragging and Dropping topic. Read the information that displays and answer the following questions:

    a. How is dragging accomplished?

    b. How is dropping accomplished?

    c. Which properties are involved in a drag operation and what do they do?

    d. Which events are involved in a drag operation and what do they do?

    e. Which methods are involved in a drag operation and what do they do?

    f. Which controls cannot be dragged?

4. Click the Back button in the lower-right corner of the Help window. In the Topic area, scroll down to the Topics section. Click the OLE Drag and Drop topic. Read the information that displays and answer the following questions:

    a. What is this feature used for?

    b. Which controls in Visual Basic 5 provide automatic support for OLE drag-and-drop?

    c. What properties must be set for automatic OLE drag-and-drop?

    d. Which controls in Visual Basic 5 provide automatic support for the OLE drag operation?

    e. What property needs to be set for the automatic OLE drag operation?

    f. Which controls in Visual Basic 5 provide support for OLE drag-and-drop events?

    g. Which properties are involved in an OLE drag operation and what do they do?

    h. Which events are involved in an OLE drag operation and what do they do?

    i. Which methods are involved in an OLE drag operation and what do they do?

    j. What is the difference between Automatic dragging and dropping and Manual dragging and dropping?

Apply Your Knowledge

1 Writing Code in a Visual Basic Application

Instructions: Start Visual Basic and open a new project in Visual Basic 5. At completion, this application consists of one blank form, one input box (Figure 5-72a), and two message boxes (Figures 5-72b and 5-72c).

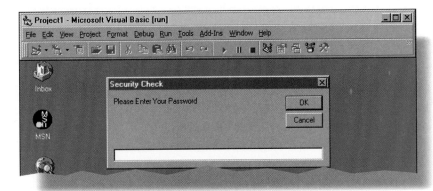

(a)

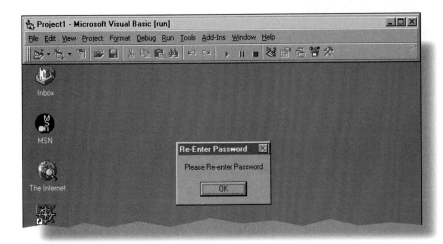

(b)

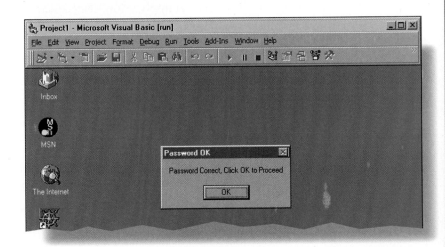

(c)

FIGURE 5-72

(continued)

Apply Your Knowledge

Writing Code in a Visual Basic Application *(continued)*

1. If necessary, click the View Object button in the Project window.
2. Double-click the form to display the Code window. All code for this application will be written in the Form_Load event procedure.
3. The code begins with a Do...Loop structure and will loop until the number of times tried is equal to three.
4. Enter a code statement within the Do...Loop structure to establish a counter and increment it to keep track of the number of times tried.
5. Enter a code statement within the Do...Loop structure similar to the following
   `Password = InputBox$("Please Enter Your Password", "Password Check").`
   This code statement should display an input box for checking the user's password.
6. Enter a Case structure within the Do...Loop structure using the UCase$ function, where the test expression to be used is `Password` for the password being entered. Three Case structures will be used for the three possible actions the user can take.
   a. The first Case is for clicking the Cancel button, where the Case is equal to `""` and the code statement to execute is End.
   b. The second Case is for entering the correct password of "PASS", where the Case is equal to `"PASS"`. This Case should display a MsgBox function to notify the user that the correct password was entered and then to click the OK button to continue, using `vbOKOnly` to display the appropriate OK button, and `"Password OK"` as the title of the message box.
   c. The third Case is a Case Else for entering the incorrect password. In this Case, enter an If-Then-Else structure to test the number of times tried. If the number of times tried is less than or equal to two, then display a MsgBox to prompt the user to re-enter the password, using `vbOKOnly` to display the appropriate OK button, and `"Re-Enter Password"` as the title of the message box.
7. Save the form and the project using the file name Security Check.
8. Click the Start button to test the application. If necessary, make corrections to the code statements. Save the form and project again using the same file name.
9. Print the Form Image, Code, and Form as Text.

In the Lab

1 Creating an Application

Problem: To practice some of the concepts of dragging and dropping in the Visual Basic 5 environment, you have decided to build an application that uses the DragOver event.

Instructions: Perform the following tasks to build an application similar to the one shown in Figure 5-73. Name all of the controls and provide appropriate comments for the code statements.

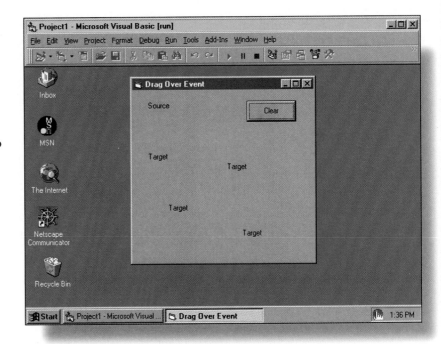

FIGURE 5-73

1. Open a new project in Visual Basic.
2. Change the Caption property of the form to DragOver Event.
3. Place one Label control near the upper-left corner of the form and one CommandButton control near the upper-right corner of the form.
4. Place a Label control array consisting of four labels on the form. Position these controls appropriately.
5. Set the Caption property value of the single Label control to Source and set the DragMode property to Automatic.
6. Set the Caption property value of the CommandButton control to Clear.
7. Center the form on the desktop. *Hint*: Use the StartUp Position property.
8. Open the Code window for the CommandButton control. Write the following code statements, replacing Label2 with the appropriate control name:

```
For Index = 0 to 3
  Label2(Index).Caption = ""
Next
```

9. In the Code window, click Label2 in the Object list box using the appropriate name and click DragOver in the Procedure list box. Write the following code statements for the DragOver event procedure, replacing Label2 with the appropriate control name:

```
If State = 2 Then
  Label2(Index).Caption = "Target"
Else
  Label2(Index).Caption = ""
End If
```

(continued)

In the Lab

Creating an Application *(continued)*

10. Save the form and the project using the file name DragOver Event.

11. Test the project by running it and make any necessary changes. Remember to save the form and project again if you make any changes. To test this project, perform the following steps and write down the answers to the questions on a separate sheet of paper as you are testing the project.

   a. Click the Clear button and then drag the Label control with the caption of the Source control around the form without dropping it. What happens as you drag the Source control around the form?

   b. If necessary, click the Clear button and then drag the Source control around the form again. This time, drop the Source control on the form. What happens when the Source control is dropped on the form?

   c. If necessary, click the Clear button and then drag the Source control around the form. This time, drop the Source control on a target. What happens when the Source control is dropped on a target?

12. Print the Form Image, Code, and Form as Text.

13. Hand the printouts and the separate answer sheet in to your instructor.

2 Creating and Using a DragDrop Event Procedure

Problem: You volunteered to organize the volleyball teams for your company picnic. To keep track of the people signing up to participate in the volleyball competition, you need an application that will accept their names and record their names in some manner. Because they will be assigned to different teams, you decide to type in the names and then drag-and-drop a person's name on a scrollable list.

Instructions: Perform the following tasks to create the Volleyball Assignments application shown in Figure 5-74. Name the controls appropriately and add comments to explain your code statements.

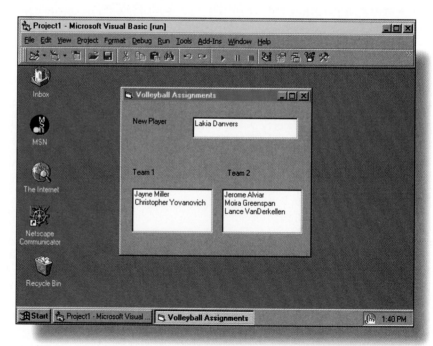

FIGURE 5-74

In the Lab

1. Open a new project in Visual Basic.
2. Size the form appropriately and center it by setting the StartUp Position property.
3. Add three Label controls, one TextBox control, and two simple ListBox controls to the form.
4. Set the Caption property of the form and labels appropriately.
5. Set the TabStop property value of the ListBox controls to False. Set the DragMode property value of the TextBox control to Automatic.
6. Write code statements for the DragDrop event procedures for each ListBox control. Use the AddItem method for adding the text from the TextBox control to the list and then set the Text property of the TextBox control to "".
7. Save the form and the project using the file name Volleyball Assignments.
8. Run the application and make any necessary corrections. Remember to save the form and project again if you make any changes. Add at least two names to each team.
9. Print the Form Image, Code, and Form as Text.

3 Understanding Code Structures

Problem: You are working for the English department, and the instructors require a method of entering student exam scores and calculating the averages of the scores. To practice designing applications, you have decided to draw a flowchart for the application and then build it from your design.

Instructions: Draw an appropriate flowchart and using the flowchart, build an application with an interface that resembles the one shown in Figures 5-75a and 5-75b on the next page.

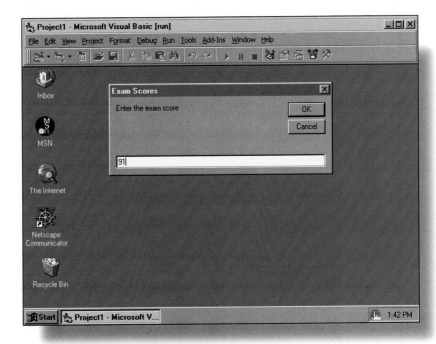

FIGURE 5-75a

(continued)

In the Lab

Understanding Code Structures *(continued)*

1. To represent the application, draw a flowchart with symbols to represent accepting input, processing the scores, and outputting the result of the processing. The flowchart design should include declaring variables, displaying an input box to accept exam scores until all five scores have been entered, accumulating the total of five scores, counting how many scores have been entered, calculating the average of the five exam scores, and displaying the average in a message box.

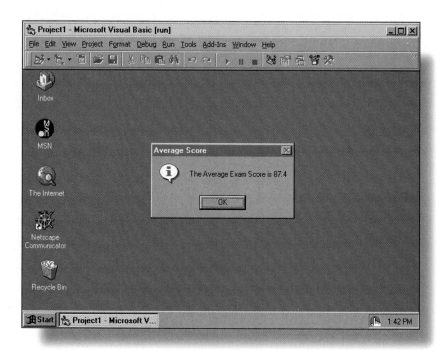

FIGURE 5-75b

2. Open a new project in Visual Basic.
3. Size the form and position it on the desktop.
4. Change the caption on the form.
5. Open the Code window for the form. All code for this application will be written in the Form_Load event procedure.
   a. Enter appropriate comments to explain the purpose of the code.
   b. Declare variables for the number of entries, the total score, and the average score and initialize them to zero.
   c. Enter the code statements in a looping structure that will end when the number of exam score entries is equal to five. The range of code statements inside the looping structure should display an input box for entering the five exam scores, establish an accumulator to keep track of the total of the five exam scores, and establish a counter to keep track of the number of scores entered.
   d. Enter code statements outside of the looping structure to calculate the average exam score and display a message box containing the average exam score.
6. Close the Code window.
7. Save the form and the project using the file name Average Exam Score.
8. Run the application to make certain no errors exist. If you encounter any errors, correct them and resave the form and project using the same file name.
9. Print the Form Image, Code, and Form as Text.

Cases and Places

The difficulty of these case studies varies: ❱ are the least difficult; ❱❱ are more difficult; and ❱❱❱ are the most difficult.

1 ❱ You are an entry-level analyst/programmer working for Clark National Bank. You need to design a new application to compute monthly checking account service charges for the bank's customers. The service charges are based on the number of checks written. The design should take into account the following conditions: A service charge is computed at $.50 plus $.05 on the first ten checks plus $.06 on the next ten checks plus $.07 on the next ten checks plus $.10 on any additional checks.

Draw two different flowcharts to represent the service charges given the number of checks written. The first flowchart should use a Select Case structure. The second flowchart should perform the same calculations using an If...Then...Else structure.

On a separate sheet of paper, explain which of these designs is easier to understand from a programmer's viewpoint and why this is true.

2 ❱ As a teaching assistant for the Visual Basic class, you will perform a demonstration to illustrate the drag-and-drop functionality of Visual Basic. You have determined that you require an application with two Image controls. The first one will contain an image of a file drawer and the second one will contain an image of paper. One group of option buttons will allow the user to select manual or automatic and will set the DragMode property for the first image. Another group of option buttons will allow the user to select none, the first image, or the second image. The second group of option buttons will set the DragIcon property of the first image to be equal to the DragIcon property of the second image, the Picture property of the first image, and the Picture property of the second image.

3 ❱❱ As a tutor for an introductory programming class, it is your responsibility to assist students with learning For...Next and Do...Loop structures. You have determined that this should be fun as well as instructional. You decide that the students should practice by designing a magic number game. This can be accomplished either with a For...Next or a Do...Loop structure, and you decide they should do one of each type to compare how they work. The student should be able to select a number that will be compared to a random number selected by the computer. It should keep track of whether the person or the computer won each round. It also should allow play to continue up to a predetermined number of times. When the predetermined number is reached, the game should end and a message should display to declare the winner. *Hint:* Refer to the section on random numbers in Project 7.

4 ❱❱ While attending school, you have a part-time job at the Leaning Tower of Pizza. To make your job easier and to fulfill a class assignment, you build an application that calculates the purchase price of a pizza. The pizza price will depend on the size of the pizza, the number of pizzas ordered, and the number of pizza toppings ordered. Once selections have been made, the total purchase price should be calculated and displayed. You decide that Case structures would be suitable for building this application. You also decide to provide menus to exit the application, clear the form, calculate the total pizza price, and display an About form.

Cases and Places

5 ▶▶ To entertain yourself and your friends, you design and build a paper, scissors, and rock game. You design it for one human player and the computer as the second player. You decide you should provide at least two methods of choosing paper, scissors, or rock for the human player. Each player should be allowed five turns. The application will have to keep track of whose turn it is; their choice of paper, scissors, or rock; who won the round; and the number of the current round. At the end of five turns, display the players' scores and which player won the game. Recall that in this game, paper covers rock, scissors cut paper, and rock smashes scissors. *Hint:* Refer to the section on random numbers in Project 7.

6 ▶▶▶ As a private math tutor for grade-school children, you design an application to teach multiplication tables. As a prototype for your design, you begin with the number two. One set of controls contains the multiplicand and the multiplier, while the other set of controls contains the product. The game should allow for ten possible matches. The pupils should be allowed three attempts to select the correct product for the corresponding multiplicand and multiplier. When their selection is correct, the background color of the product should change color and a message should display to congratulate the pupil. If a correct selection has not been made after three attempts, a message should display to indicate an error. You also have decided to provide the pupil with a quiz that can be selected from a menu. The quiz should ask at least five questions and have the capability of accepting the answers. When the answer is incorrect, a message should display to notify the pupil. The pupil should be able to continue answering until he or she selects the correct response or be able to escape if he or she does not know the correct response.

7 ▶▶▶ From time to time, you design applications for use by the day-care where you are hired as a consultant. The children have been asking for a new Tic-Tac-Toe computer game. You have analyzed the possibility and determine that it can be accomplished fairly simply. It can be constructed using a looping structure along with a Case structure. It should display an appropriate message to the winner of each round, keep track of the score, and continue for a specific number of times. When a game has ended, a message should display for the winner of the game. The children should have the choice of beginning a new game. The day-care supervisors have asked that the children also have the choice of controls or menus to direct game play.

Database Management and Reporting Applications

Objectives:

You will have mastered the material in this project when you can:

▸ Create and modify database files with the Visual Data Manager Add-In

▸ Create forms with the Data Form Designer

▸ Understand and write code containing Data control methods

▸ Create a form with the Data Form Wizard

▸ Use data-bound ComboBox controls in applications

▸ Write code to create a Recordset search routine

▸ Understand and write code for DataControl Reposition, Validate, and Error events

▸ Understand and write code for Form_Activate events

▸ Create reports with the Report Designer add-in Crystal Reports Pro

▸ Add reports to applications with the CrystalReport ActiveX control

Buttons
and
Bows

Database Tracks
Elaborate Details

As "Painless" Peter Potter in the 1948 comedy *The Paleface*, Bob Hope portrays a cowardly dentist who tames the Wild West and sings of "frills and flowers and buttons and bows." While these items may seem foreign to a Western setting, they are found on costumes worn by his gorgeous co-star, Jane Russell, who plays the gunslinger Calamity Jane.

Performers realize that their elaborately adorned costumes sometimes are the subjects of attention. Apparel companies design, manufacture, and market these products for consumers across the world, and part of their cost of doing business involves acquiring and organizing the fabrics and trimmings used to make these garments.

The Warnaco Group, a leading manufacturer of women's and men's apparel and accessories, has solved the problem of managing the components needed to make their products. Using Visual Basic, the

New York-based company has developed a database application similar to the one you will create in this project, which collects the data describing products stored in its warehouse and then allows the employees to access, retrieve, and use that data. The database consists of records containing details about each item in the warehouse. Each record has fields that describe a specific piece of information, such as the button size and shape or the bow color.

The warehouse receives shipments of thousands of snaps, buttons, bows, and rolls of lace and fabric each year. As each item arrives, employees inspect the product and use a Visual Basic receiving screen to record its details, which are stored in a database record. The program assigns and prints a unique bar code to identify each item and then tells the employees where to store the product and corresponding bar code on shelves.

When a customer places an order, it is entered in Warnaco's host computer system in Connecticut. The system accesses the database to select the specific materials needed to manufacture the products and then transmits the details to the warehouse employees. These workers use portable radio-frequency data terminals, called RF guns, that display the exact shelf location of each required button and bow and fabric. They point their RF guns at the bar code corresponding to the item on the shelf, and a laser scans the bar code and transmits the data to the host computer. The code is verified, and if a match is made, the employee picks the item and brings it to a central area. Using this system, an employee can gather all the required materials for an order in only a few minutes. The items then are sewn and assembled at plants throughout the world.

Warnaco produces approximately eight million garments per year and distributes them to more than 16,000 retailers throughout North America and Europe. Certainly its Visual Basic database application helps maintain its status in the apparel industry by managing the warehouse inventory.

Project 6

Microsoft
Visual Basic 5

Database Management and Reporting Applications

Case Perspective

Geoff Waverman is an avid collector of Lionel® model trains. He spends much of his free time traveling to swap meets buying and selling model trains and accessories. He also maintains a mailing list of other collectors with whom he exchanges price lists. For the past several months, he has been keeping an inventory of his stock with an Excel worksheet, but he has encountered some significant limitations with his current system. Geoff's friend used Microsoft Access to import his worksheet data into a database, but was not able to do anything else with it. In return for creating an inventory application for Geoff, Geoff has agreed to sell your application at train meets (for a small commission).

Geoff wants a Windows–based application that he can take with him on his laptop computer. He needs to keep track of the Lionel stock number, railroad name, description, quantity, and value of each piece in his collection. He needs to be able to search for a specific stock number when he is at a meet. He needs to be able to edit records because values are constantly changing. He also must be able to add and delete records because he buys and sells frequently. Geoff also wants a price list report that can be viewed on his laptop or printed for mailing.

Introduction

Add-ins are extensions to Visual Basic that add special capabilities to the development environment that are not available automatically in Visual Basic. Microsoft and other developers have created several add-ins that you can use in your applications. The Professional Edition of VB5 includes two add-ins that greatly increase your capabilities in creating database applications: the Visual Data Manager and the Report Designer. In addition to these add-ins, Visual Basic has a Data Form Wizard that facilitates form creation for database applications. You will use all of these application development tools in this project.

In Project 4, you built an application that allowed you to view records in an existing database. In this project, you will create a more sophisticated database application that allows you to add, modify, delete, and search for records. In addition, you will use data-bound ComboBox controls to allow the user to enter field values by clicking an item in a list box rather than typing. You will use the Visual Data Manager to add tables to an existing database and you will use the Report Designer to create a report that can be viewed on the desktop and printed.

VB 6.4

Project Six — TrainTrack Inventory System

The main form for the TrainTrack inventory system application is shown in Figure 6-1 as it displays on the desktop during run time. Within this window, Geoff can add, modify, and delete records in his Trains database.

A **data-bound ComboBox control (DBCombo control)** is used for the Railroad Name field. This allows Geoff to edit this field either by typing a value or clicking an item in a list (Figure 6-2). Selecting a field value from a list is a faster way to add new records and also prevents data entry errors.

Geoff also needs to be able to edit the list of values for the Railroad Name field as his collection changes over time. You will add an additional table to Geoff's existing Trains database to hold these values. Geoff can add, modify, and delete items in the Railroads Name list through the form shown in Figure 6-3. This form is opened by clicking the **Edit Railroad List command** on the Options menu of the main form (Figure 6-4).

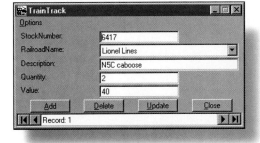

FIGURE 6-1

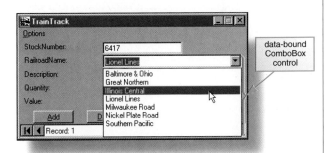

FIGURE 6-2

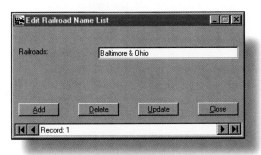

FIGURE 6-3

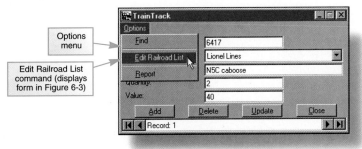

FIGURE 6-4

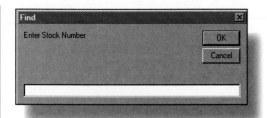

FIGURE 6-5

FIGURE 6-6

Clicking the **Find command** on the Options menu opens the Find dialog box shown in Figure 6-5. This dialog box is used to enter a specific stock number and execute a search. If the stock piece exists within the database, its record becomes the current record; if it does not exist, the message box in Figure 6-6 displays.

A report is available in the application by clicking the **Report command** on the Options menu (Figure 6-7). This report displays on the desktop in its own window (Figure 6-8) and then can be printed if desired (Figure 6-9).

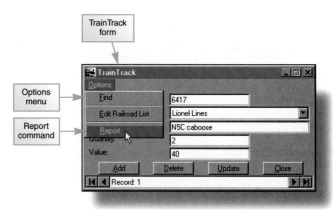

FIGURE 6-7

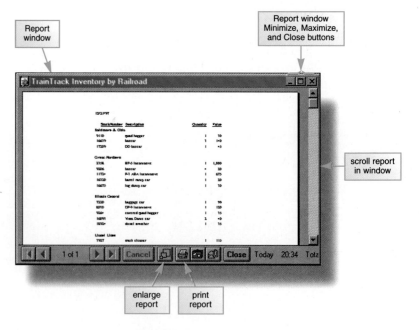

FIGURE 6-8

1/27/99

StockNumber	Description	Quantity	Value
Baltimore & Ohio			
9110	quad hopper	1	30
16639	boxcar	3	140
17209	DD boxcar	1	45
Great Northern			
9206	boxcar	4	20
11724	F-3 ABA locomotive	1	675
16320	barrel ramp car	1	20
16675	log dump car	1	30
Illinois Central			
7220	baggage car	1	99
8030	GP-9 locomotive	1	120
9264	covered quad hopper	1	35
16093	Vista Dome car	2	40
18924	diesel switcher	1	35
Lionel Lines			
6417	N5C caboose	2	40
9378	derrick car	1	30
9408	circus stock car	1	50
16390	flatcar w/ water tank	1	40
16915	gondola	5	10
Milwaukee Road			
9455	boxcar	2	20
16397	I-beam flatcar	1	40
Nickel Plate Road			
16307	flatcar w/ trailers	1	69
19411	flatcar	1	29
Southern Pacific			
9530	baggage car	1	70
9711	boxcar	1	20

FIGURE 6-9

Project Steps

You will complete the following tasks in this project to build the TrainTrack inventory system application.

1. Copy files from the Data Disk that accompanies this book.
2. Start a Standard EXE project and arrange the Visual Basic IDE.
3. Set project properties.
4. Start the Visual Data Manager.
5. Add a table to the Trains database for railroad names.
6. Open the Visual Data Manager Data Form Designer.
7. Create a form for modifying the Railroads table.
8. Modify controls and properties on the Railroads form.
9. Write code for the Railroads form.
10. Save the project and test the Railroads form.
11. Create a main form with the Data Form Wizard.
12. Add data-bound ComboBox and Crystal Reports ActiveX controls to the Toolbox.
13. Add a data-bound ComboBox control to the main form.

14. Modify controls and properties on the main form.
15. Write code for the main form.
16. Save and test the project.
17. Open the Report Designer add-in.
18. Create a report using the Report Designer add-in.
19. Add a Report control to the main form.
20. Set properties and write code for the Report control.
21. Save and test the project again.

The following pages contain a detailed explanation of each of these steps.

Getting Started

The TrainTrack inventory system application will run much faster from a hard drive than from a floppy disk, and the files you create in this project can be saved in a folder on the hard drive. The Trains database (Trains.mdb) and train icon (Train.ico) files used in this project are available on the Data Disk that accompanies this book. You should copy these files to the hard drive folder where the rest of your files will be saved or to a blank formatted disk. As with previous projects, the steps in this book will show the form and project files being saved on a floppy disk.

Begin this project by starting Visual Basic as described on page VB 1.7 in Project 1 or by opening a new Standard EXE project if you are already running Visual Basic. If necessary, you should complete the steps on page VB 1.10 in Project 1 to arrange your desktop to resemble Figure 6-10.

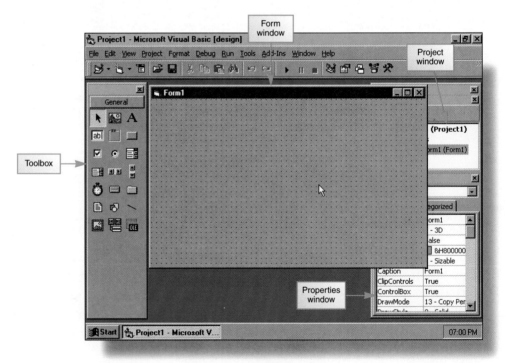

FIGURE 6-10

The Visual Data Manager

The **Visual Data Manager** (**VisData**) is an application that was created using Visual Basic 5. A version of VisData is used as a Visual Basic add-in, accessible from the Add-Ins menu. With VisData, you can create and modify database files; design data forms; and build, view, execute, and save database queries. You can use the **VisData Form Designer** to create data forms and add them to the current Visual Basic project.

Opening a Database in the VisData Add-In

You can use VisData to open an existing database or create a new database of one of several different database types: Microsoft Access (version 7 or 2); dBASE (version 5, IV, or III); FoxPro (version 3, 2.6, 2.5, or 2.0); Paradox (version 5, 4.x, or 3.x); or Text Files. The Trains database you will use in this project is a Microsoft Access type database. Perform the following steps to start the VisData add-in and open the Trains database.

 Steps To Open a Database with the VisData Add-In

① **Click Add-Ins on the Visual Basic menu bar and then point to Visual Data Manager.**

The Add-Ins menu displays (Figure 6-11). The Visual Data Manager command opens the VisData application.

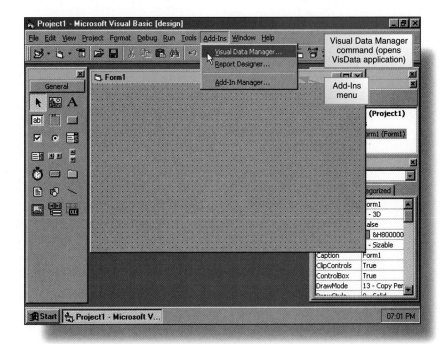

FIGURE 6-11

> **More** *About* **VisData**
>
> The VisData application also is available as a Visual Basic project in the Professional and Enterprise editions of Visual Basic. When you install Visual Basic, Visdata.vbp and all its associated files are copied to the vb/samples/Visdata folder.

2 **Click Visual Data Manager. If the VisData dialog box displays, click the No button. Drag the VisData window to the center of the desktop and then adjust its size as shown in Figure 6-12.**

The VisData window opens on the desktop (Figure 6-12).

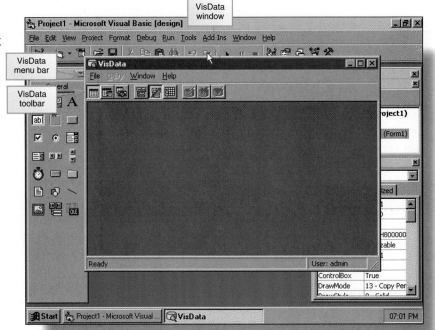

FIGURE 6-12

3 **Click File on the VisData menu bar. Point to Open Database and then point to Microsoft Access.**

The Open Database command contains a submenu of database types VisData can work with (Figure 6-13).

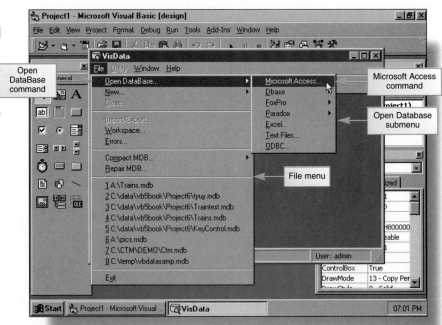

FIGURE 6-13

4 Click Microsoft Access. When the Open Microsoft Access Database dialog box opens, click the Look in box arrow and then click 3½ Floppy [A:]. Point to Trains.mdb.

The Open Microsoft Access Data-base dialog box displays as shown in Figure 6-14. The Open as read-only check box should not be selected.

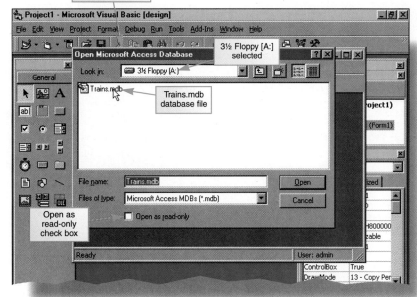

FIGURE 6-14

5 Double-click Trains.mdb.

The VisData:A:\Trains.mdb window displays on the desktop (Figure 6-15).

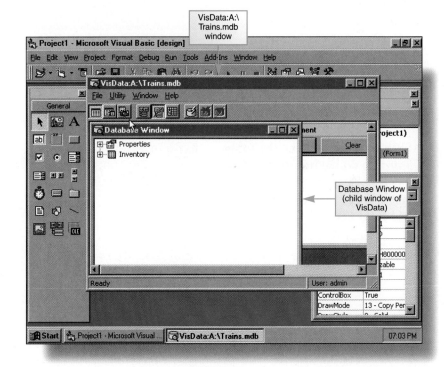

FIGURE 6-15

OtherWays

1. Press ALT+A, press V to open VisData add-in

Adding Tables to a Database

In this project, you will use the VisData add-in to add a table to the Trains database for the values of the Railroads Name field in the Inventory table. You are adding this as a separate table so that Geoff can (1) routinely add and modify inventory records by choosing values in a drop-down list box and (2) periodically add and modify the values contained in the drop-down list box. Perform the steps on the next page to add a Railroads table to the Trains database.

Steps To Add Tables to a Database

1 **Right-click below the list in the Database Window and point to New Table.**

A shortcut menu displays (Figure 6-16).

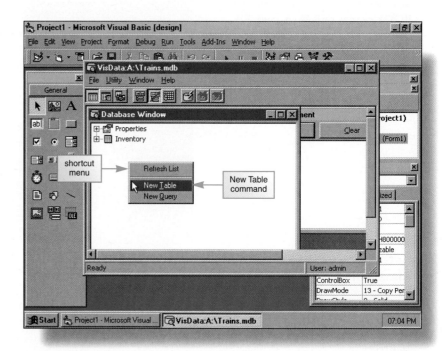

FIGURE 6-16

2 **Click New Table. When the Table Structure dialog box opens, type** `Railroads` **in the Table Name text box and then point to the Add Field button.**

The Table Structure dialog box displays (Figure 6-17). The Field List currently is empty.

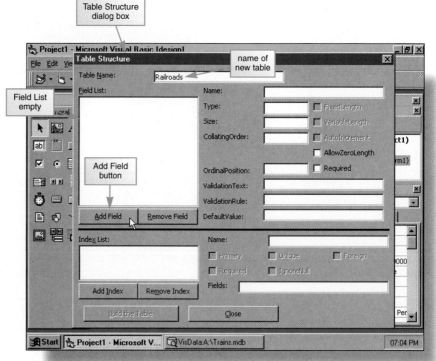

FIGURE 6-17

3 **Click the Add Field button. When the Add Field dialog box opens, type** Railroads **in the Name text box, type** 20 **in the Size text box, and point to the OK button.**

The Add Field dialog box displays as shown in Figure 6-18.

FIGURE 6-18

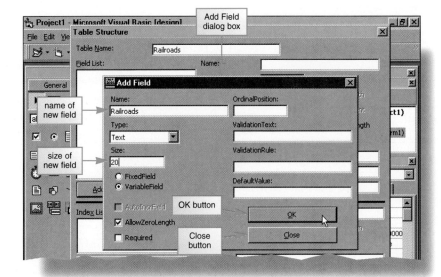

4 **Click the OK button. Click the Close button in the Add Field dialog box, and then point to the Build the Table button in the Table Structure dialog box.**

The Add Field dialog box closes and the new information displays in the Table Structure dialog box (Figure 6-19).

FIGURE 6-19

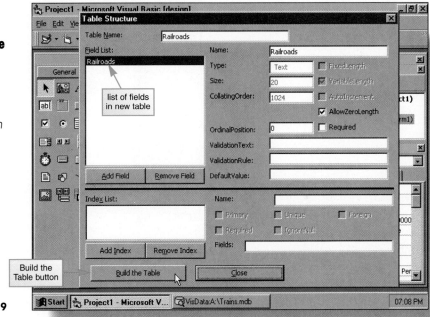

5 **Click the Build the Table button. Click the VisData window.**

The Table Structure dialog box closes and the new table is added to the list in the Database Window (Figure 6-20).

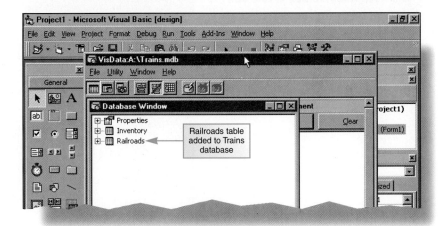

FIGURE 6-20

The Data Form Designer

The **Data Form Designer** is a utility that adds forms to the current Visual Basic project. It is useful for creating forms for browsing and modifying data from a simple table to a complex query. It is available only when VisData has been opened using the Visual Data Manager command on the Visual Basic Add-Ins menu. Perform the following steps to create forms for modifying the values in the Railroads table.

Steps To Create Forms with the Data Form Designer

1 **Click Utility on the VisData menu bar and then point to Data Form Designer.**

The VisData Utility menu displays (Figure 6-21).

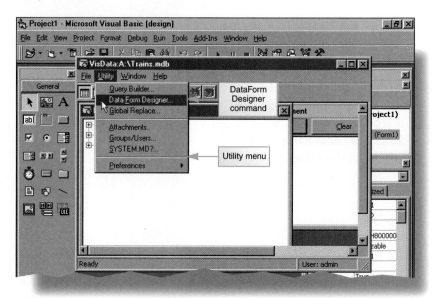

FIGURE 6-21

2 **Click Data Form Designer. When the Data Form Designer dialog box opens, type** Railroads **in the Form Name text box. Click the RecordSource box arrow and then point to Railroads.**

The Data Form Designer dialog box displays (Figure 6-22).

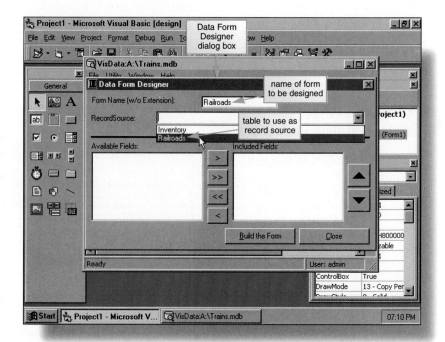

FIGURE 6-22

3 **Click Railroads. Point to the right arrow button between the Available Fields and Included Fields list boxes.**

Railroads is the only field available in the Railroads table (Figure 6-23).

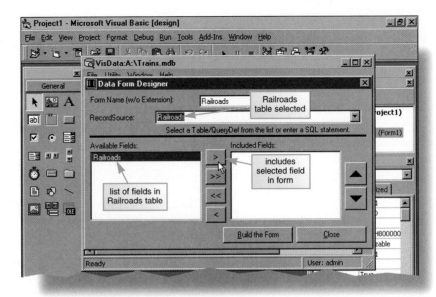

FIGURE 6-23

4 **Click the right arrow button and then point to the Build the Form button.**

The Railroads field is added to the list of fields to be included in the new form (Figure 6-24).

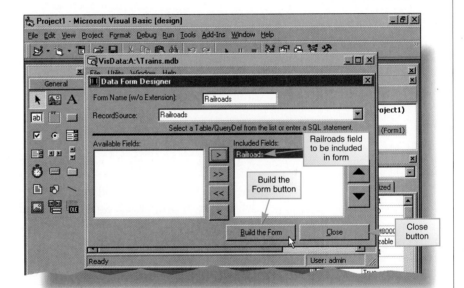

FIGURE 6-24

5 **Click the Build the Form button. Click the Close button in the Data Form Designer dialog box.**

The Railroads form is created and added to the project (Figure 6-25).

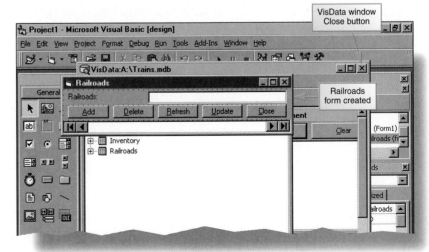

FIGURE 6-25

6 **Click the Close button in the VisData window. Arrange the forms on the desktop as shown in Figure 6-26.**

The new form has been added to the Project window (Figure 6-26).

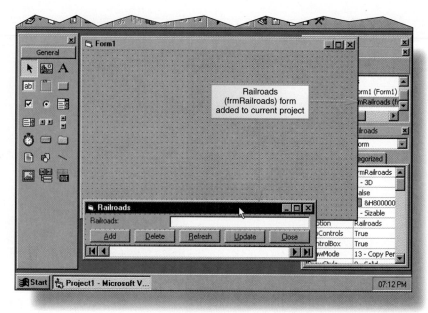

FIGURE 6-26

The Data Form Designer has created a form with a Data control attached to the Railroads table, a text box bound to the RailroadName field in the Railroads table, and five command buttons.

Modifying the Data Form Interface

The Data Form Designer always gives a similar arrangement of controls and default set of properties. Sometimes, you will want to modify the default data form interface the Data Form Designer creates. In the TrainTrack inventory system application, you will modify several of the form's properties. In addition, you will delete the Refresh button (as it is not necessary in single-user applications) and rearrange the layout of the controls on the form. Perform the following steps to modify the Railroads data form.

TO MODIFY A DATA FORM INTERFACE

1 Select the Railroads form.
2 Change the form's BorderStyle property value to 1 - Fixed Single.
3 Change the form's Height property value to 3000.
4 Change the form's Width property value to 5640.
5 Set the form's MinButton property value to True.
6 Set the form's Caption property value to Edit Railroad Name List.
7 Set the form's Icon property value to Train.ico (from the floppy disk).
8 Click the Refresh button on the form and then press the DELETE key.
9 Adjust the locations of the form and its controls to match Figure 6-27.

The Edit Railroad Name List form (frmRailroads) displays as shown (Figure 6-27).

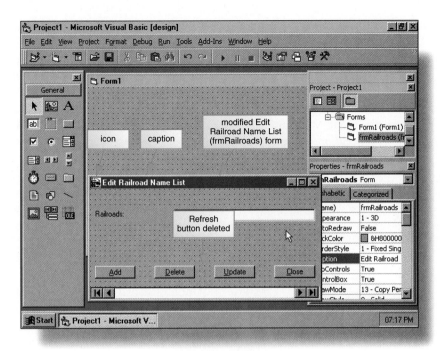

FIGURE 6-27

Modifying Data Form Code

In addition to creating the data form interface, the Data Form Designer wrote several event procedures that are common for most databases. In the groups of steps that follow, you will examine the code written by the Data Form Designer and make some modifications where necessary.

Add, Delete, Update, and Close Click Events

The Data Form Wizard added five command buttons and their corresponding Click events to the Railroads form — Add, Delete, Refresh, Update, and Close. When you modified the interface, you deleted the Refresh button. You did not, however, delete the cmdRefresh_Click event procedure code. When you delete a control from a form, any existing event procedures for that control are moved to the General section of the form's code module (Figure 6-28). As you can see from the remark statement in this procedure, the Refresh method is not needed in this application.

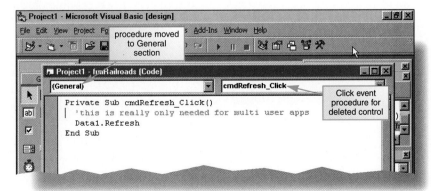

FIGURE 6-28

The **cmdAdd_Click event procedure** (Figure 6-29) applies the AddNew method to the Data1.Recordset object, similarly to the way you applied other methods in Project 4, such as MoveFirst and MoveNext. The **AddNew method** creates and adds a new record in the Recordset object. This method sets the fields to default values, and if no default values are specified, it sets the fields to Null. The record that was current before you used AddNew remains current. If you want to make the new record current, you can set the **Bookmark property** to the bookmark identified by the **LastModified property** value.

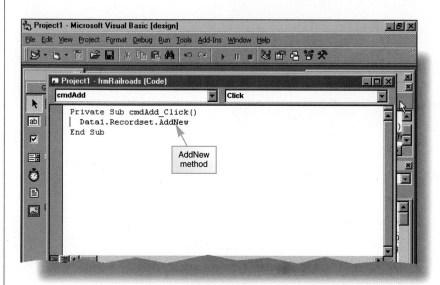

FIGURE 6-29

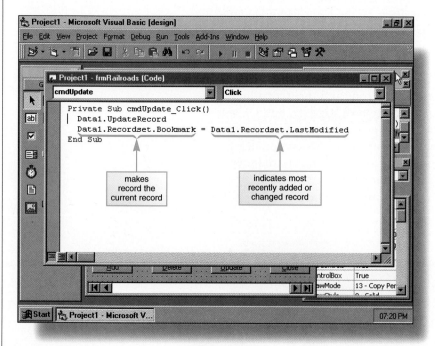

FIGURE 6-30

The **cmdUpdate_Click event procedure** (Figure 6-30) applies the UpdateRecord method to the Recordset object. The **UpdateRecord method** saves the current contents of bound controls to the database during the Validate event without triggering the Validate event again. The UpdateRecord method has the same effect as executing the Edit method, changing a field, and then executing the Update method, except that no events occur.

After applying the UpdateRecord method, the cmdUpdate_Click event procedure sets the bookmark of the Recordset object to be equal to the value of the Recordset object's LastModified property. A bookmark is a property of the Recordset object that contains a binary string identifying the current record. The **LastModified property** of a Recordset object is a bookmark indicating the most recently added or changed record. You can use the LastModified property to move to the most recently added or updated record.

The **cmdDelete_Click event procedure** (Figure 6-31) applies the Delete method and the MoveNext method to the Recordset object. The **Delete method** removes the current record and makes it inaccessible. Although you cannot edit or use the deleted record, it remains current until you move to another record. Once you move to another record, you cannot make the deleted record current again. You should recall the use of the MoveNext method from Project 4.

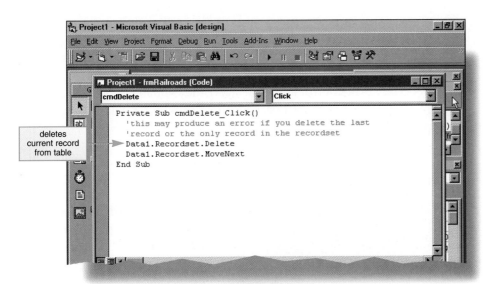

FIGURE 6-31

As noted in the remark statements (Figure 6-31), an error can occur if you delete the last or only record. Because Geoff always will have several records in the Railroads Recordset object, you do not need to address this potential error. You will, however, see how to avoid this error when you create the main form for the TrainTrack inventory system application.

The **cmdClose_Click event procedure** (Figure 6-32) unloads the form from memory, using the Me keyword. The **Me keyword** behaves like an implicitly declared variable. When a class such as a form can have more than one instance, Me provides a way to refer to the specific instance of the class where the code is executing. The statement, Unload Me, applies the Unload method to the current form.

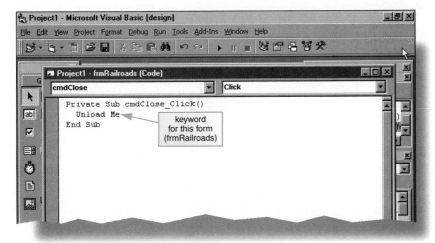

FIGURE 6-32

Before a form is unloaded, the Form_QueryUnload event procedure occurs, followed by the Form_Unload event procedure. When Geoff closes (unloads) the Railroads form, the main form of the application, frmInventory, should display. Geoff can close the Railroads form by clicking the Close command button or by clicking the form's Close button on the title bar. Both of these actions trigger the Form_Unload event procedure. Perform the steps on the next page to modify the Form_Unload event procedure.

TO MODIFY THE FORM_UNLOAD EVENT PROCEDURE

1 Select the frmRailroads form in the Project window.

2 Click the View Code button in the Project window.

3 Select the Form control and then select the Unload event.

4 Enter the code statement `frmInventory.Show` to the Form_Unload event.

The frmRailroads Form_Unload event should display as shown in Figure 6-33.

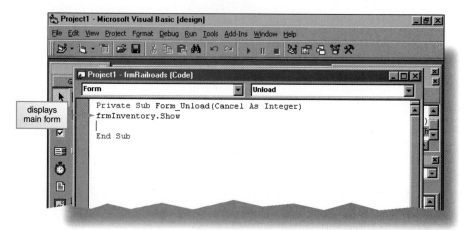

FIGURE 6-33

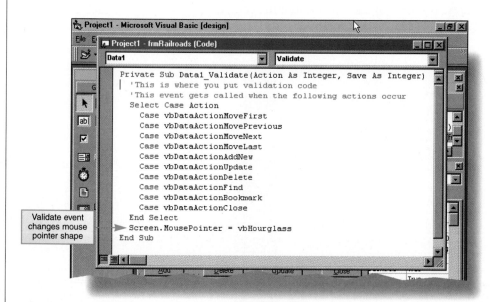

FIGURE 6-34

Data Control Validate, Reposition, and Error Events

The Data Form Designer added code statements to the Data control's Reposition, Validate, and Error events. A Data control's **Validate event** occurs before a different record becomes the current record; before the Update method; and before a Delete, Unload, or Close operation. You can use this event to insure that data entered by the user is valid, and if necessary, change values or notify the user. You also can choose to save data or stop whatever action is causing the event to occur and substitute a different action.

The frmRailroads Data1_Validate event procedure is shown in Figure 6-34. Because Geoff will be the only user of the prototype application, it is not necessary to add code to validate the values he enters. This procedure also changes the mouse pointer shape to the hourglass until the Reposition event returns it to an arrow.

When a Data control is loaded, the first record in the Recordset object becomes the current record, triggering the Reposition event. Whenever a user clicks any button on the Data control to move from record to record, or if you use one of the Move methods, such as MoveNext, the **Reposition event** occurs after each record becomes the current record.

The frmRailroads Data1_Reposition event procedure is shown in Figure 6-35. It is used to display the record number of the current record in the caption of the Data control. This procedure also resets the mouse pointer shape to the arrow (default) to indicate that the Validate event is complete.

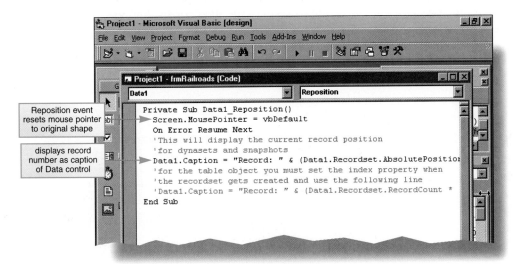

FIGURE 6-35

The Data control automatically opens a database and loads a Recordset object after the Form_Load event, or after a custom control performs an operation such as the MoveNext method, the AddNew method, or the Delete method. If an error results from one of these actions, the Error event occurs. A Data control's **Error event** occurs only as the result of a data access error that takes place when no Visual Basic procedure code is being executed, such as when a user clicks a Data control button.

If you do not write a code procedure for a Data control's Error event, Visual Basic displays a message associated with the error. The frmRailroads Data1_Error event procedure is shown in Figure 6-36. It is used to display a message box describing the error, if one occurs.

Saving and Testing the Data Form

Your work on the Railroads form is complete. Before proceeding with the development of the application's main form and report, you will save the form on a floppy disk and then test the data form by adding records to its corresponding table in the database.

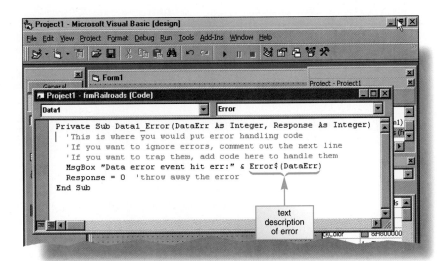

FIGURE 6-36

Saving the Project

At this stage of development, the TrainTrack inventory system application consists of two forms — the default Startup form and the form you created with the VisData Data Form Designer. To be able to test the data form, you first must name the Startup form, add code to display the data forms, and save the project. Perform the following steps to accomplish these tasks.

Steps   To Save a Project for Testing

1 **Close the Code window. Click the Project window. Double-click Form1 in the Project window. In the Properties window, double-click the Name property. Type frmInventory and then press the ENTER key. Point to the View Code button.**

The form's new name displays in the Properties and Project windows (Figure 6-37).

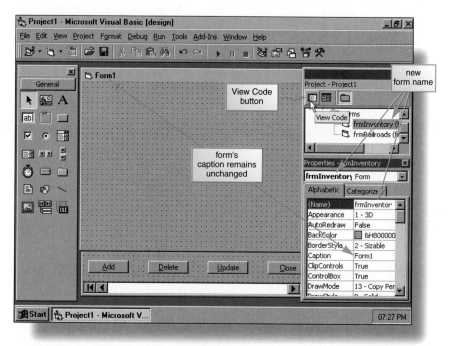

FIGURE 6-37

2 **Click the View Code button. Select the Form control and the Load event in the Code window and then add the two lines of code shown in Figure 6-38.**

This code will load and display the data form when you run the project.

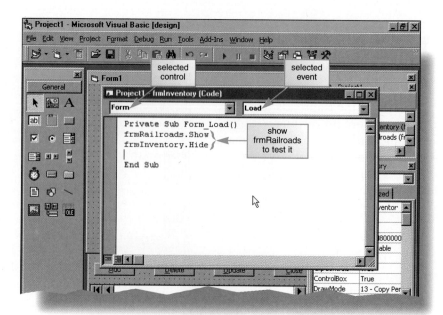

FIGURE 6-38

3 Close the Code window. Click the Save Project button on the toolbar. When the Save File As dialog box opens, click the Save in box arrow, and then click 3½ Floppy [A:]. Type `Railroads` in the File name text box and then point to the Save button.

The Save File As dialog box displays as shown in Figure 6-39.

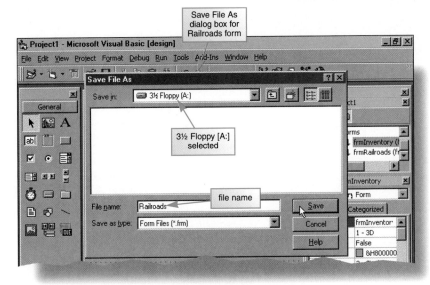

FIGURE 6-39

4 Click the Save button in the Save File As dialog box. Type `Inventory` in the File name text box and then point to the Save button.

The Save File As dialog box displays as shown in Figure 6-40.

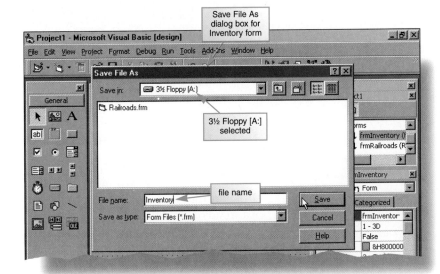

FIGURE 6-40

5 Click the Save button in the Save File As dialog box. When the Save Project As dialog box opens, type `TrainTrack` in the File name text box. Point to the Save button.

The Save Project As dialog box displays as shown in Figure 6-41.

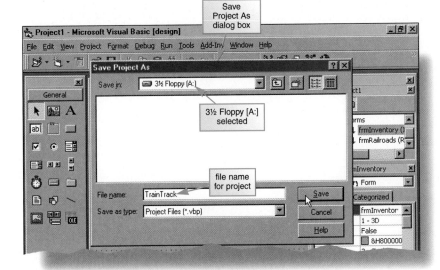

FIGURE 6-41

6 **Click the Save button and then arrange the forms on the desktop as shown in Figure 6-42.**

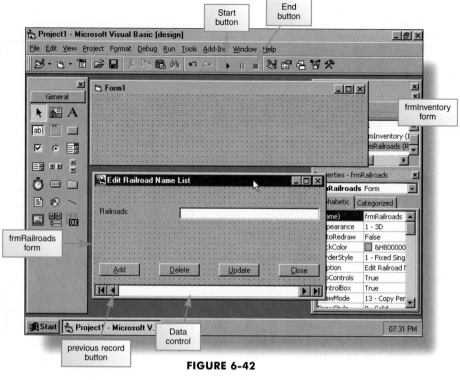

FIGURE 6-42

Testing and Adding Records

TABLE 6-1
NAME
Baltimore & Ohio
Great Northern
Illinois Central
Lionel Lines
Nickel Plate Road

With your work saved, you can now test the Railroads data form and add records to the Railroads table. Table 6–1 lists the initial records for the Railroads table. In the final application, these will display in the drop-down list for the Railroads Name field.

Perform the following steps to test the Railroads form and add records to the RailroadName field in the Railroads table.

TO TEST A DATA FORM AND ADD RECORDS

1 Click the Start button on the toolbar.

2 Click the Edit Railroad Name List form.

3 Click the Add button. Type `Baltimore & Southern` in the Railroads text box.

4 Click the Add button. Type `Great Northern` in the Railroads text box.

5 Click the previous record button on the Data control. Change the value in the Railroads text box to `Baltimore & Ohio` and then click the Update button.

6 Add the remaining records listed in Table 6-1. (Be sure to click Update after you add the last record, Nickel Plate Road).

7 Click the End button on the toolbar.

At this point you have added a new table to the Trains database and you have created the interface and written the code for Geoff so he can add, modify, and delete records in that table. You also have added five records (railroad names) to the Railroads table. The next task is to create the interface and write code for the main form in the application.

The Visual Basic Data Form Wizard

The main form for the TrainTrack inventory system application is shown in Figure 6-43. This form is similar in appearance and function to the Railroads form in several respects — it has a Data control to move among records; Add, Delete, Update, and Close buttons; and text boxes for editing field values. Rather than modify the existing frmInventory form, you will remove the existing frmInventory form from the project and add a new form. You will add the new form by using the Visual Basic Data Form Wizard.

The Visual Basic **Data Form Wizard** automatically generates Visual Basic forms that contain individual bound controls and procedures used to manage information from database tables. You can use the Data Form Wizard to create either single query forms to manage the data from a single table or Master/Detail type forms used to manage more complex one-to-many data relationships. The Data Form Wizard is used in conjunction with either the Data or the RemoteData controls. Perform the following steps to create a frmInventory form with the Data Form Wizard.

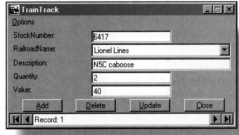

FIGURE 6-43

 To Add a Form with the Data Form Wizard

1 **Right-click frmInventory in the Project window and then point to Remove Inventory.frm.**

A shortcut menu displays (Figure 6-44).

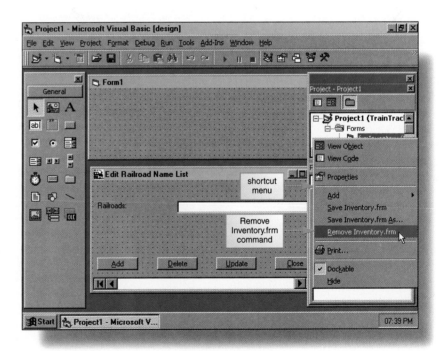

FIGURE 6-44

2 Click Remove Inventory.frm. If a Save dialog box opens, click the No button. Point to the Add Form button on the toolbar.

The frmInventory form is removed from the current project (Figure 6-45).

FIGURE 6-45

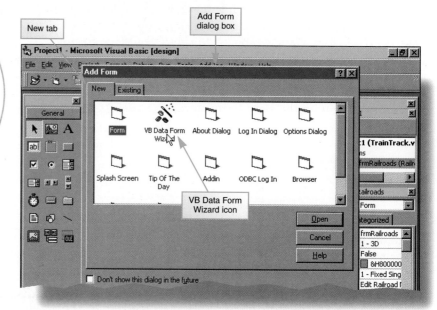

3 Click the Add Form button. When the Add Form dialog box opens, point to the VB Data Form Wizard icon on the New tab sheet.

The Add Form dialog box displays (Figure 6-46).

FIGURE 6-46

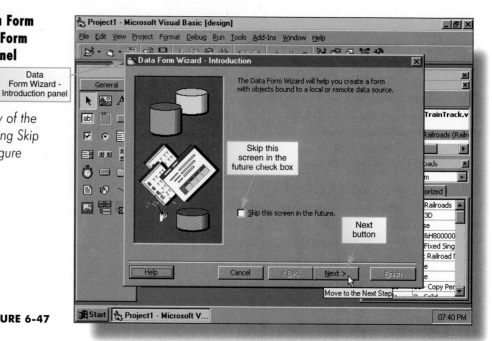

4 Double-click the VB Data Form Wizard icon. If the Data Form Wizard - Introduction panel displays, point to the Next button.

You can disable the display of the Introduction panel by clicking Skip this screen in the future (Figure 6-47).

FIGURE 6-47

5 **If the Data Form Wizard - Introduction panel displays, click the Next button. When the Data Form Wizard - DataBase Type panel opens, click Access and then point to the Next button.**

The Data Form Wizard - Database Type panel displays (Figure 6-48).

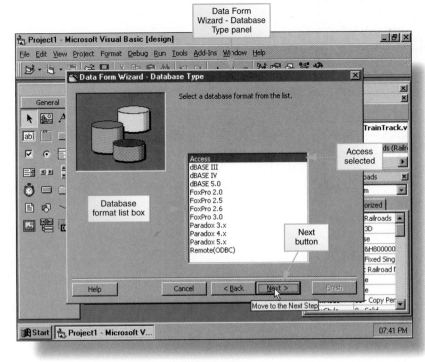

FIGURE 6-48

6 **Click the Next button. In the Data Form Wizard - Database Panel, type** A:\Trains.mdb **in the Database Name text box. In the Record Sources area, Tables should be selected and Queries should not be selected. Point to the Next button.**

The Database panel settings display as shown in Figure 6-49.

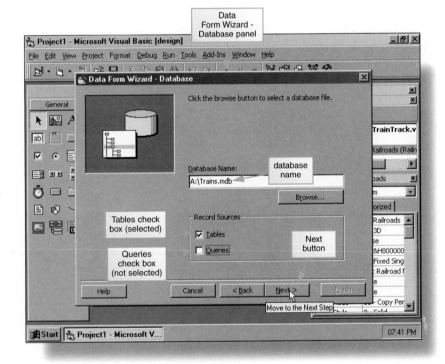

FIGURE 6-49

7 Click the Next button. In the Data Form Wizard – Form panel, click Single record and then point to the Next button.

The Single record layout is selected (Figure 6-50).

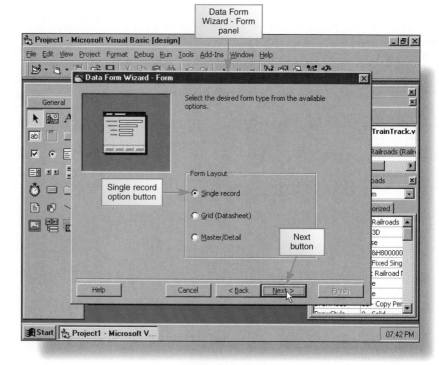

FIGURE 6-50

8 Click the Next button. In the Data Form Wizard – Record Source panel, click the Record Source box arrow and then click Inventory. Point to the right arrow button.

All the fields in the Inventory table are listed in the Available Fields list box (Figure 6-51).

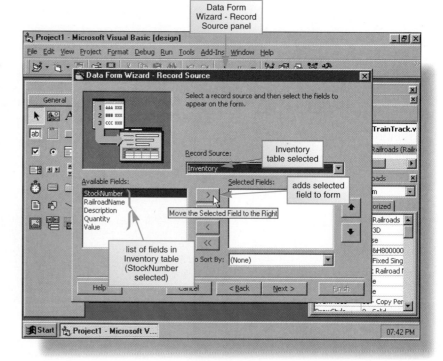

FIGURE 6-51

9 **Click the right arrow button five times. Click the Column to Sort By box arrow and then point to StockNumber.**

All the fields in the Inventory table have been selected (Figure 6-52).

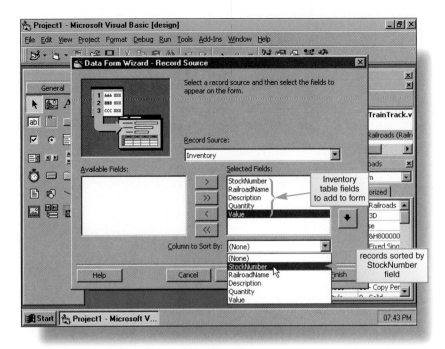

FIGURE 6-52

10 **Click StockNumber. Click the Next button. In the Data Form Wizard - Control Selection panel, click Refresh Button to deselect it and then point to the Next button.**

The Control Selection panel displays as shown in Figure 6-53.

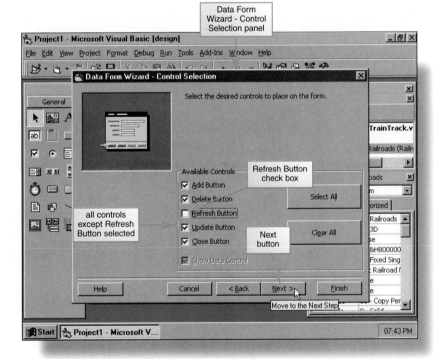

FIGURE 6-53

11 Click the Next button. In the Data Form Wizard – Finished! panel, type `frmInventory` in the What name do you want for the form? text box and then point to the Finish button.

You can click the Back button to move to the previous panel to make changes (Figure 6-54).

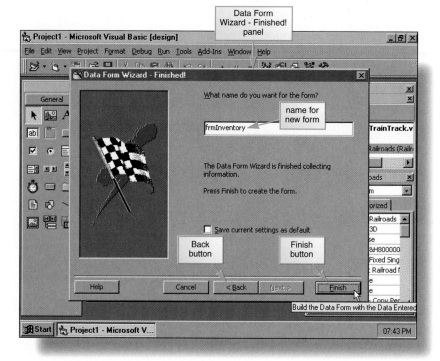

FIGURE 6-54

12 Click the Finish button. Click the OK button in the Data Form Created dialog box that displays.

The form is created (Figure 6-55).

13 Press the CTRL+S keys to open the Save File As dialog box. Type `Inventory` in the File name text box and then click the Save button. Click the Yes button in the Save File As message box.

The new form, frmInventory is saved as Inventory.frm.

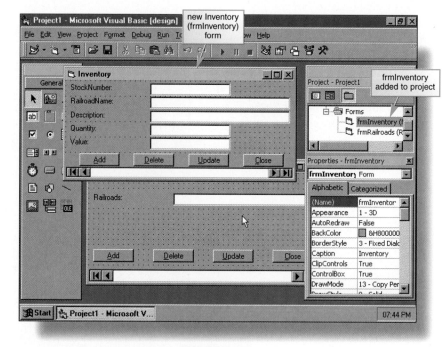

FIGURE 6-55

In the preceding Step 1 and Step 2 on pages 6.25 and 6.26, you removed the original version of frmInventory from the current project. When you remove a form from a project, the form's file (in this case a:\Inventory.frm) is not affected. This is the reason that when you attempted to save the new version of frmInventory as a:\Inventory.frm, you received the message box asking if you wanted to replace the existing file.

Modifying the Inventory Form

By using the Data Form Wizard, you have saved a lot of time and effort in building the Inventory form. You still, however, must make modifications. You will approach changes to the Inventory form using the same three-step process you have used in previous projects; modifying the control interface, modifying properties, and modifying code.

The finished Inventory form contains two ActiveX controls you must add. You should recall from Project 2 that before you can add ActiveX controls to a form, you must first add them to the Toolbox.

Adding ActiveX Controls

The Inventory form in the TrainTrack inventory system application contains two ActiveX controls — the data-bound ComboBox (DBCombo) control and the Crystal Reports control. You will learn more about these controls when you add them to the form. Complete the following steps to add these controls to the Toolbox.

More *About* Adding Controls

The Available Controls list in the Components dialog box displays all the ActiveX controls available on your PC. When the Selected Items Only check box is selected, only those controls in the Available Controls list that you have selected to include in the project display in the dialog box.

Steps To Add ActiveX Controls to the Toolbox

1 Press the CTRL+T keys to display the Components dialog box. If necessary, click the Controls tab to select the Controls tab sheet.

The Components dialog box displays (Figure 6-56).

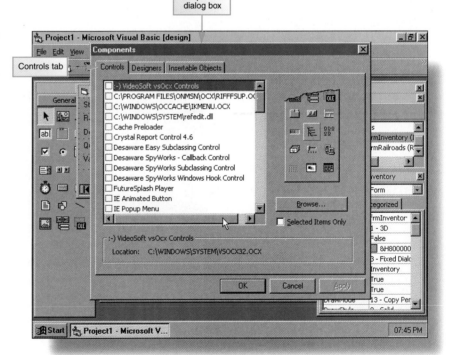

FIGURE 6-56

2 Scroll down the Components list box and click the Crystal Report Control 4.6 check box and then click the Microsoft Data Bound List Controls 5.0 check box. Point to the OK button.

Your list of available controls may be different from the one shown in Figure 6-57.

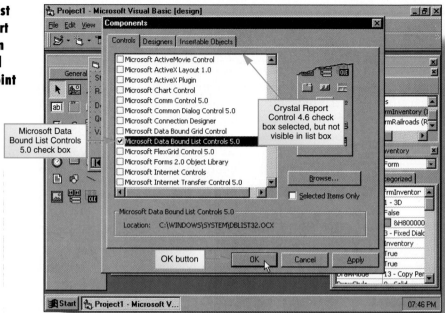

FIGURE 6-57

3 Click the OK button.

Three controls are added to the Toolbox (Figure 6-58).

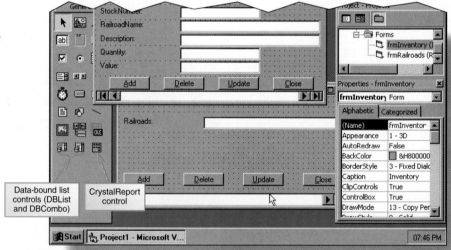

FIGURE 6-58

OtherWays

1. To open Components dialog box, right-click empty area of toolbox, click Components on shortcut menu

Modifying the Interface

You will modify the Inventory form interface by replacing the RailroadName text box with a data-bound ComboBox control, adding a Data control for the data-bound ComboBox control, and creating a menu. The **DBCombo control** is a data-bound combo box with a drop-down list box automatically populated from a field in an attached Data control. The DBCombo control also can be used to update a field in a related table of another Data control. The text box portion of a DBCombo control can be used to edit the selected field. Perform the following steps to add a DBCombo control and Data control to the Inventory form.

Steps **To Add DBCombo Controls and Data Controls**

1 **Select the RailroadName text box. Press the DELETE key. Click the DBCombo button in the Toolbox.**

The textbox is deleted and the DBCombo button is recessed (Figure 6-59).

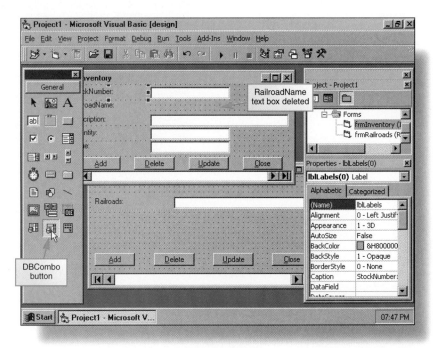

FIGURE 6-59

2 **Draw a DBCombo control on the form in the place of the text box.**

The DBCombo1 control is added (Figure 6-60).

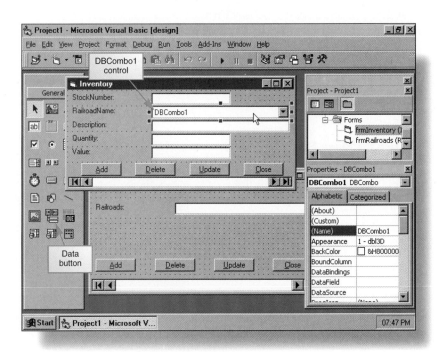

FIGURE 6-60

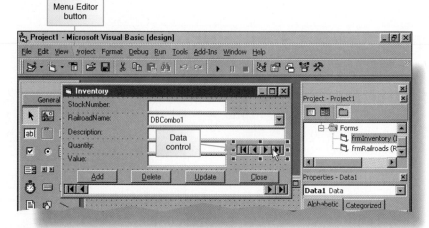

3 Double-click the Data button in the Toolbox and then drag the Data control to the location shown in Figure 6-61.

A Data control (Data1) is added to the form (Figure 6-61).

FIGURE 6-61

TABLE 6-2	
MENU CONTROL CAPTION	*MENU CONTROL NAME*
&Options	mnuOptions
&Find	mnuFind
-	separator1
&Edit Railroad List	mnuRailroads
-	separator2
&Report	mnuReport

The menu for the TrainTrack inventory system application consists of three commands and two separator bars. The Menu control names and their captions are listed in Table 6-2. You will create this menu using the Menu Editor, as you have done in previous projects.

Complete the following steps to build the menu for the TrainTrack inventory system application.

Steps To Build a Menu

1 Click the Menu Editor button on the toolbar and then drag the Menu Editor dialog box to the center of the desktop.

The Menu Editor dialog box displays (Figure 6-62).

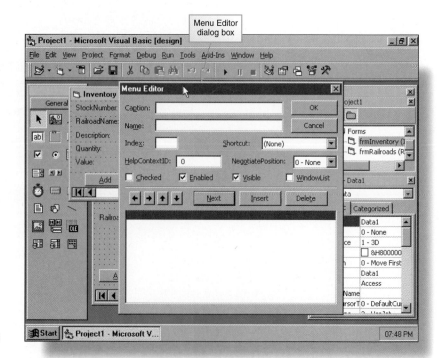

FIGURE 6-62

2 Add the Menu controls and captions listed in Table 6-2 giving them the structure shown in Figure 6-63.

The completed menu structure is shown in Figure 6-63.

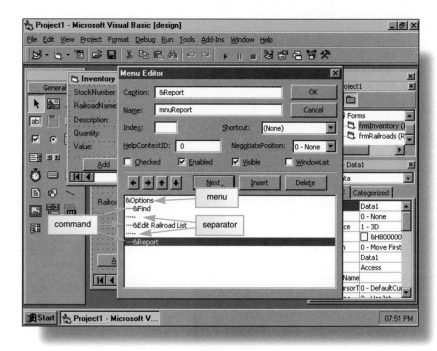

FIGURE 6-63

3 Click the OK button. Click Options on the Inventory form menu bar.

The menu is added to the form and displays as shown in Figure 6-64.

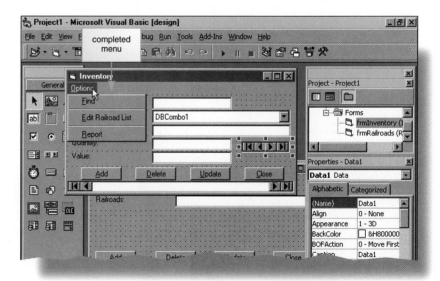

FIGURE 6-64

Other Ways

1. To open Menu Editor, press CTRL+E

Modifying Properties

In the next set of steps, you will set some familiar properties of the form and Data controls. You also will set some properties of the DBCombo and Data controls that you have not set in previous projects.

The DBCombo control's DataSource and DataField properties are the same as those you set for other data-aware controls in previous projects. A DBCombo control's **RowSource property** sets a value that specifies the Data control from which the DBCombo control's list is filled. The **ListField property** sets the name of the field in the Recordset object used to fill the DBCombo's list.

In Project 4, you used the Data control's RecordSource property to set the underlying table for the Data control. In addition to using a table name for the value of the RecordSource property, you can use an **SQL (Structured Query Language) statement** to populate the Recordset object with the records sorted in a certain order. For example, the Data Form Wizard named the Data control datPrimaryRS. When you ran the wizard, you specified that the table was Inventory and that records should be sorted by StockNumber. In the Properties window, the value of datPrimaryRS's RecordSource property is not a table name but is an SQL statement (Figure 6-65).

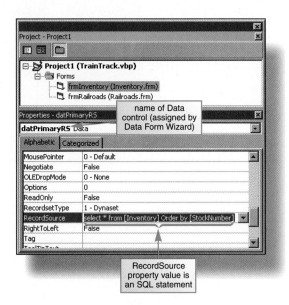

FIGURE 6-65

When you use the AddNew data method, you add a new record to the end of a table. The SQL statement in Figure 6-65 causes the records to be ordered by Stock-Number. You will use a similar SQL statement for the RecordSource property of the Data control to which the RailroadName drop-down list is bound. This will make choices on the drop-down list always display in alphabetical order.

The control name, property name, and value for the properties you will change are listed in Table 6-3.

Complete the following steps to modify the properties of the controls listed in Table 6-3.

TO MODIFY CONTROL PROPERTIES

1. Select the frmInventory control.
2. Double-click the Caption property in the Properties list.
3. Enter TrainTrack as the new value.
4. Repeat Step 1 through Step 3 for each of the controls and properties listed in Table 6-3.

The frmInventory form displays as shown in Figure 6-66.

TABLE 6-3		
CONTROL	PROPERTY	VALUE
frmInventory	Caption	TrainTrack
frmInventory	BorderStyle	1 - Fixed Single
frmInventory	MinButton	True
frmInventory	Icon	Train.ico
Data1	DatabaseName	A:\Train.mdb
Data1	RecordSource	select * from [Railroads] Order by [Railroads]
Data1	Visible	False
DBCombo1	TabIndex	2
DBCombo1	DataSource	datPrimaryRS
DBCombo1	DataField	RailroadName
DBCombo1	RowSource	Data1
DBCombo1	ListField	Railroads

Project
menu name

frmInventory and
controls with new
property values

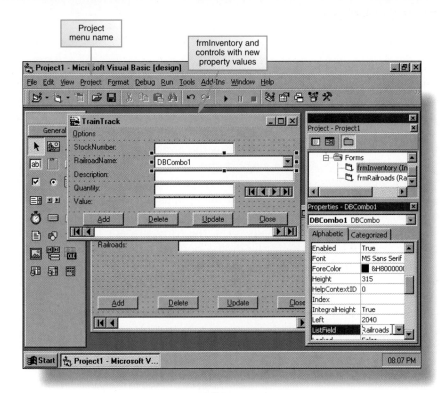

FIGURE 6-66

Setting a Startup Form and Modifying Code

When you open a new project, Form1 is by default the Startup form for the project. When you remove a Startup form from a project, the project's Startup form value is changed automatically to Sub_Main, even if the project contains other forms. Because you removed the original Startup form and then added a new frmInventory, you must specify it as the Startup form for the project.

The Data Form Wizard created several event procedures for the frmInventory form that are similar to the ones created by the VisData Form Designer for the frmRailroads form. In this section, you first will modify the datPrimaryRS_Reposition and cmdUpdate_Click event procedures. You then will write event procedures for the Form_Activate and mnuRailroads_Click events. Later in this project, you will write code for the mnuFind_Click and mnuReport_Click event procedures.

When a DBCombo control displays a field value for the current record, the value displays highlighted in the DBCombo's text box. This allows the user to replace the highlighted text simply by typing. Geoff does not want this functionality, so it is necessary to deselect the text in the DBCombo's text box. The **SelLength property** sets the number of characters selected. The statement DBCombo1.SelLength = 0 will accomplish the deselecting by setting the number of selected characters equal to zero. The best place to do this is in the Reposition event, because this event occurs every time a different record becomes the current record.

When a new record is added to the inventory, it is added at the end of the database table. Because Geoff wants the records to display in order by stock number, it is necessary to sort the records each time a new one is added. This can be accomplished by applying the **Refresh method** to the datPrimaryRS Data control each time Geoff clicks the Update button. You will add the code statement, datPrimaryRS.Refresh, to the cmdUpdate_Click event procedure.

More *About*
Splash Screens

A splash screen is a form that displays on startup and contains information such as the name of the application and copyright information. To learn more about adding splash screens to your applications, search splash screens in Visual Basic Books Online.

Geoff modifies the list of railroads by using the frmRailroads form to modify the Railroads table in the Trains database. After Geoff makes changes in the Railroads table and closes the form, any changes he made to the Railroads table should be reflected in the RailroadName list box on the frmInventory form. For this to occur, the Data1 control on frmInventory must be refreshed with the statement, Data1.Refresh. The Activate event is the appropriate place to refresh the Data1 control. A form's **Activate event** occurs each time a form receives **focus** (becomes the active window) on the desktop. In the TrainTrack inventory system application, this occurs at the Startup of the application and each time Geoff closes the Railroads form.

When Geoff closes the Railroads form, the frmRailroads Data1_Validate event is triggered, which changes the mouse pointer shape to an hourglass. When the frmInventory form is activated, the text in the DBCombo box is highlighted. This means that two additional things must occur in the frmInventory_Activate event procedure: the mouse pointer should change to the default and the DBCombo text should be deselected. You may recall that these two actions occur within the Reposition event, so you need only call the datPrimaryRS_Reposition event procedure from the frmInventory_Activate event procedure.

When Geoff wants to modify the list of railroads, he opens the Edit Railroad Name List (Railroads) form by clicking Options on the menu bar and then clicking Edit Railroad List. In the Click event procedure for mnuRailroad you will add the following code:

```
frmRailroads.Left = frmInventory.Left
frmRailroads.Top = frmInventory.Top
frmRailroads.Show
frmInventory.Hide
```

These statements locate the Railroads form in the same position as the Inventory form and then make it appear that the Railroads form replaces the Inventory form. Perform the following steps to set the Startup form and modify the event procedures just discussed.

Steps **To Set a Startup Form and Modify Code**

① **Click Project on the menu bar and then click Project1 Properties.**

The Project1 - Project Properties dialog box displays (Figure 6-67).

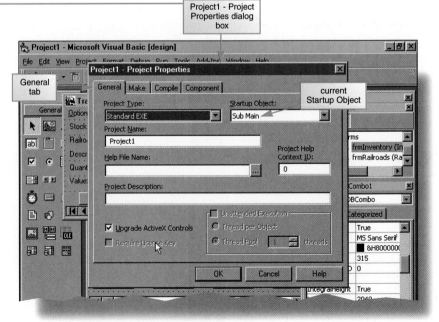

FIGURE 6-67

2 **If necessary, click the General tab. Type** `TrainTrack` **in the Project Name text box and then point to frmInventory in the Startup Object list.**

The Startup Object list box includes all forms in the project (Figure 6-68).

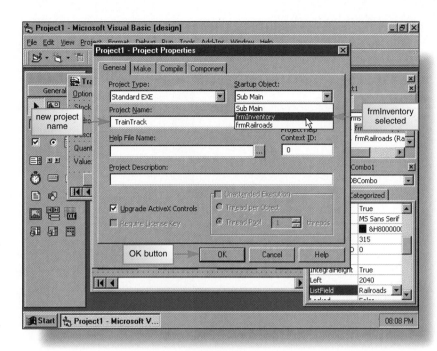

FIGURE 6-68

3 **Click frmInventory and then click the OK button. Click frmInventory in the Project window and then click the View Code button.**

The frmInventory Code window opens on the desktop (Figure 6-69). Your Code window may display differently.

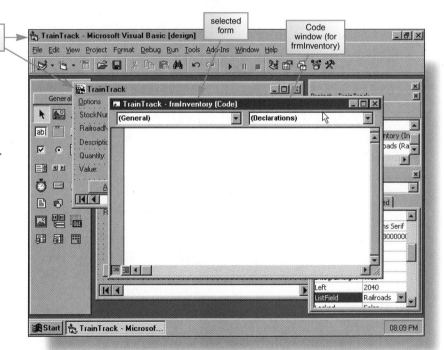

FIGURE 6-69

④ Select the datPrimaryRS_ Reposition event, resize the Code window, and add the code shown in Figure 6-70.

The revised event procedure displays as shown in Figure 6-70.

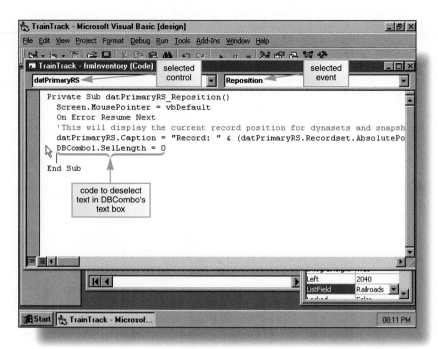

FIGURE 6-70

⑤ Select the cmdUpdate_Click event and then add the code shown in Figure 6-71.

The revised event procedure displays as shown in Figure 6-71.

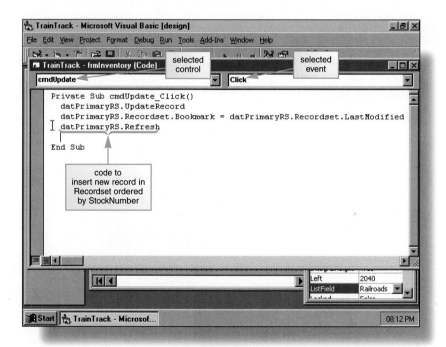

FIGURE 6-71

6 Select the Form_Activate event and then add the code shown in Figure 6-72.

The revised event procedure displays as shown in Figure 6-72.

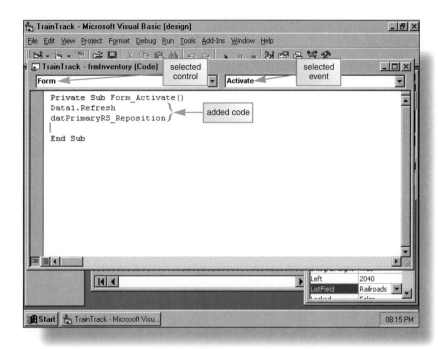

FIGURE 6-72

7 Select the mnuRailroads_Click event and then add the code shown in Figure 6-73.

The revised event procedure displays as shown in Figure 6-73.

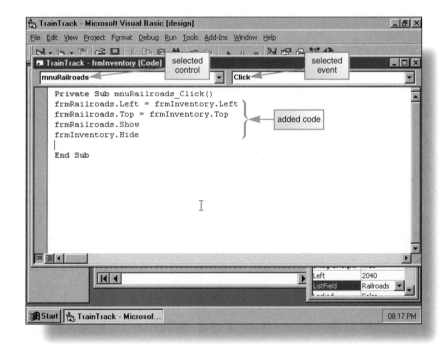

FIGURE 6-73

Writing a Recordset Search Routine

Geoff wants to be able to search his database for a specific stock number and display the corresponding record if it exists in his inventory. When Geoff clicks Find on the Options menu, a dialog box prompts him to enter a stock number (Figure 6-74).

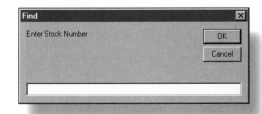

FIGURE 6-74

The dialog box functionality is accomplished with an InputBox function that assigns the user's input to a variable named stocknum. This is similar to the InputBox function you used in Project 5:

```
stocknum = InputBox("Enter Stock Number", "Find")
```

Recall that clicking the Cancel button in an input box returns a zero length string. You can check whether the OK button was clicked through an If...Then statement that looks for a return value not equal to the zero length string:

```
If stocknum <> "" Then
```

Because an "Else" clause is not included in this If...Then block, nothing will happen when the Cancel button is clicked (other than closing the input box).

When Geoff clicks the OK button, a search routine is executed. The routine begins by creating a string variable named SearchString that contains the criteria to be used for the search in the SQL-like syntax. The InputBox function will assign whatever the user types to the value of stocknum — either a number or text. Because the StockNumber field in the Trains database has a number format, a search for a nonnumeric value of the stocknum variable will cause a run-time error. To avoid this, the Val function is used to convert any text characters into the number zero. A search for any numeric value of stocknum that does not exist in the table (including zero) will not cause a run-time error:

```
SearchString = "StockNumber = " & Val(stocknum)
```

The **FindFirst method** locates the first record in a Recordset object that satisfies specified criteria and makes that record the current record. Similar to the Recordset Move methods, related FindLast, FindNext, and FindPrevious methods exist. The statement:

```
datPrimaryRS.Recordset.FindFirst SearchString
```

applies the FindFirst method to the Recordset object of a Data control named datPrimaryRS. The search criteria are contained in a variable named SearchString.

If no match is found to the stock number entered in the input box, a message box informs Geoff (Figure 6-75).

The **NoMatch property** automatically is given a True/False value indicating whether a particular record was found by using one of the Find methods. The value of NoMatch is True if the desired record was not found. The following code displays a message box if no match is found.

```
        If datPrimaryRS.Recordset.NoMatch = True Then
            MsgBox "No Matching Record", 0, "Find"
        End If
End If
```

FIGURE 6-75

The second End If indicates that this If...Then block is nested within the first If...Then block.

Perform the following steps to write the Recordset search routine.

TO WRITE A RECORDSET SEARCH ROUTINE

1 Select the mnuFind control in the Code window.

2 Type the code shown in Figure 6-76.

The completed mnuFind_Click procedure displays as shown in Figure 6-76.

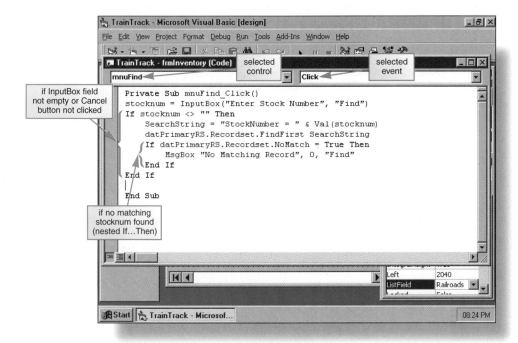

FIGURE 6-76

Before proceeding to the next steps, close the Code window and then click the Save Project button on the toolbar to save the work you have completed since the last save.

Report Designer Add-In

Geoff wants to be able to generate a price list he can send to individuals on his mailing list. Because many of Geoff's customers like to collect pieces for certain railroads, the report must be organized in a way that makes it easy to search Geoff's inventory by railroad name. The finished report is shown in Figure 6-77 on the next page.

1/27/99

StockNumber	Description	Quantity	Value
Baltimore & Ohio			
9110	quad hopper	1	30
16639	boxcar	3	140
17209	DD boxcar	1	45
Great Northern			
2358	EP-5 locomotive	1	1,000
9206	boxcar	4	20
11724	F-3 ABA locomotive	1	675
16320	barrel ramp car	1	20
16675	log dump car	1	30
Illinois Central			
7220	baggage car	1	99
8030	GP-9 locomotive	1	120
9264	covered quad hopper	1	35
16093	Vista Dome car	2	40
18924	diesel switcher	1	35
Lionel Lines			
3927	track cleaner	1	115
6417	N5C caboose	2	40
9378	derrick car	1	30
9408	circus stock car	1	50
16390	flatcar w/ water tank	1	40
Nickel Plate Road			
16307	flatcar w/ trailers	1	69
19411	flatcar	1	29

FIGURE 6-77

More *About* Crystal Reports

The Crystal Report Engine is a dynamic-link library (DLL) that allows your applications to access the same report printing features that are available in the Crystal Reports application. From your application, you access the Report Engine through the Crystal ActiveX control. As a licensed user of Crystal Reports, you receive royalty-free rights to ship the ActiveX control (CRYSTL32.OCX) and the Report Engine DLL (CRPE.DLL) with any application you create.

The Visual Basic **Report Designer Add-In** is a special version of a report-generating software product called Crystal Reports. You can think of the Report Designer Add-In as two separate elements: Crystal Reports, which is the software application used to create reports, and the Crystal Custom Control, which is used to add reports generated with Crystal Reports to your Visual Basic applications. This next section will give you a basic understanding of how to use Crystal Reports to create reports and then add them to your applications.

Crystal Reports is a powerful Windows report writer that you can use to design a nearly endless variety of custom reports. The **Crystal Custom Control** is an ActiveX control that makes it easy for you to build the connection between your application and the reports you create. Using the Crystal Custom Control, you can have your Visual Basic application generate reports and send them to a window on the desktop or to a printer.

The Report Expert

Crystal Reports includes a wizard called the **Report Expert**. You supply information about the report you want to create through a series of tab sheets in a dialog box. When you finish supplying information, the wizard creates the report for you. Similar to other wizards, you can edit and modify the report created by the wizard. Perform the following steps to start Crystal Reports and use the Report Expert to create the basics of the TrainTrack price list report.

Steps **To Use the Report Expert to Create a Report**

1 **Click Add-Ins on the menu bar and then click Report Designer. Maximize the Crystal Reports Pro window.**

The Crystal Reports application opens on the desktop (Figure 6-78).

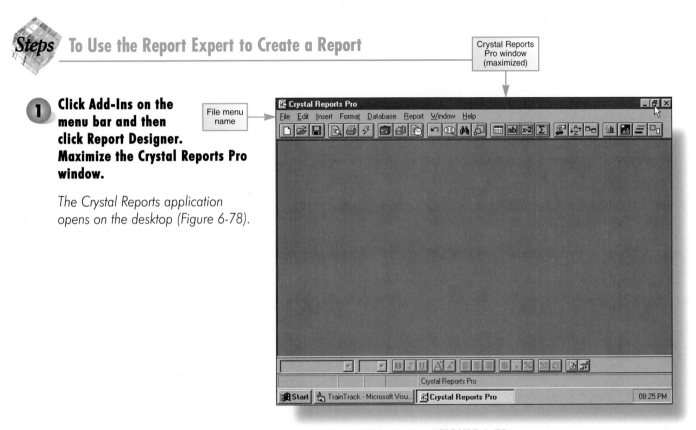

Crystal Reports Pro window (maximized)

File menu name

FIGURE 6-78

2 **Click File on the menu bar and then click New. Point to the Listing button.**

The Create New Report dialog box displays several report template buttons (Figure 6-79).

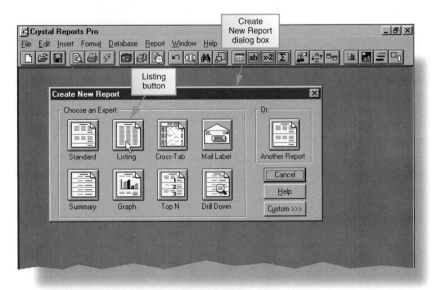

Create New Report dialog box

Listing button

FIGURE 6-79

3 Click the Listing button. If necessary, click the Step 1: Tables tab and then point to the Data File Button.

The Create Report Expert dialog box displays (Figure 6-80).

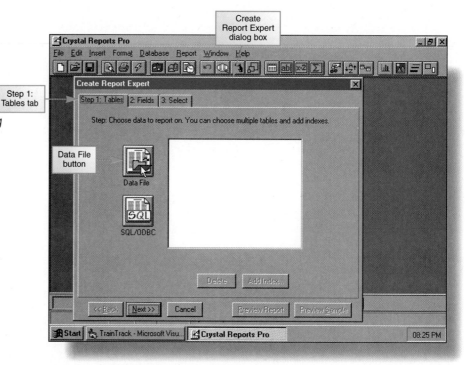

FIGURE 6-80

4 Click the Data File button. When the Choose Database File dialog box opens, click the Drives box arrow and then click a:. Point to Trains.mdb.

The Choose Database File dialog box displays (Figure 6-81).

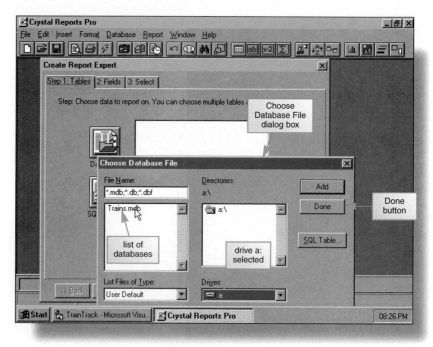

FIGURE 6-81

5 **Double-click Trains.mdb and then click the Done button.**

The dialog box closes and the 2: Links tab sheet displays (Figure 6-82).

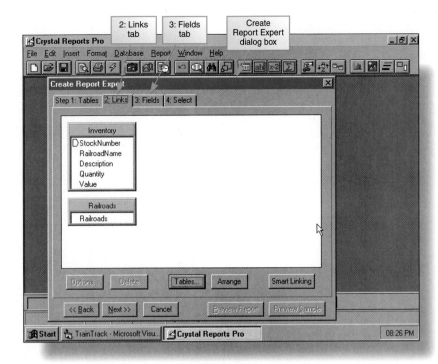

FIGURE 6-82

6 **Click the 3: Fields tab. Click the Add button. Click Description in the Database Fields list box. Click the Add button three more times and then point to the Preview Report button.**

The StockNumber, Description, Quantity, and Value fields are added to the Report Fields list box (Figure 6-83).

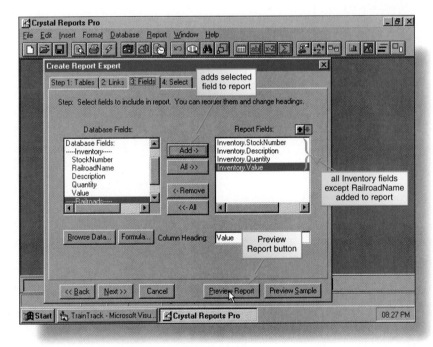

FIGURE 6-83

7 Click the Preview Report button and then click the Zoom button on the toolbar.

A preview of the report displays (Figure 6-84).

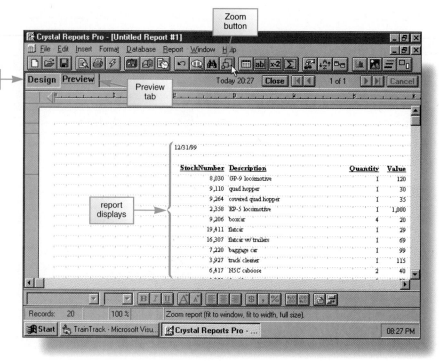

FIGURE 6-84

In Step 6 on the previous page, you did not include the RailroadName field in the report. The reason is that you will add it later as a group heading for the rest of the detail information.

Modifying and Saving a Crystal Report

After you have created a report, you save it as a separate file with an **.rpt extension**. You can open previously created reports and modify them at any time. Perform the following steps to modify the report created by the Report Expert and then save it.

 To Modify and Save a Crystal Report

1 Click the Design tab. Click Insert on the menu bar and then point to Group Section.

The Insert menu displays (Figure 6-85).

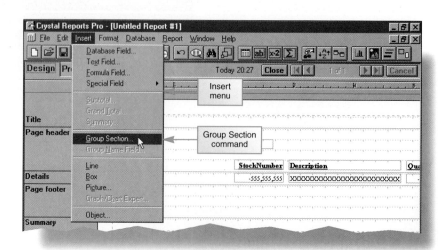

FIGURE 6-85

2 **Click Group Section. When the Insert Group Section dialog box opens, click the top box arrow and then point to RailroadName in the Database Fields section of the list box.**

You can select a field to group by that is not part of the existing report (Figure 6-86).

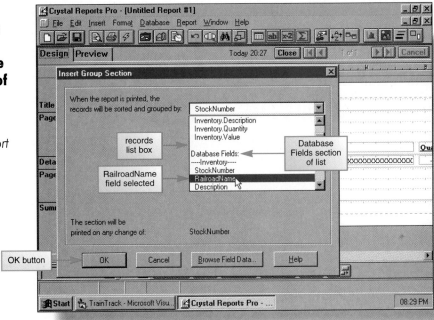

FIGURE 6-86

3 **Click RailroadName. Click the OK button. Click Insert on the menu bar and then point to Group Name Field.**

The report will group records by RailroadName, but the Railroad-Name field is not yet part of the report (Figure 6-87).

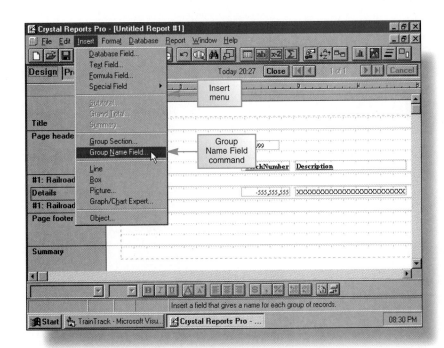

FIGURE 6-87

4 **Click Group Name Field. When the Insert Group Name Field dialog box opens, click Group #1: Inventory.RailroadName – A. Click the OK button. Drag the text box that displays to the position shown in Figure 6-88.**

You can drag the Group Name field to any location on the form (Figure 6-88).

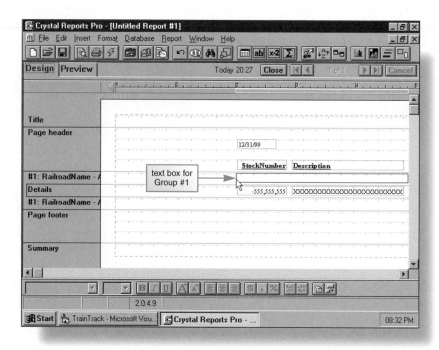

FIGURE 6-88

5 **Without moving the mouse, click the report. Click the Bold button on the Formatting toolbar at the bottom of the Crystal Reports Pro window.**

The Group name field is added to the form and its text will display bold (Figure 6-89).

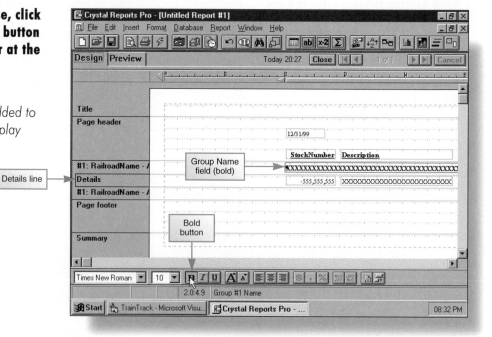

FIGURE 6-89

6 **Right-click the leftmost field on the Details line and then point to Change Format on the shortcut menu.**

The field displaying the stock number is selected and a shortcut menu displays (Figure 6-90).

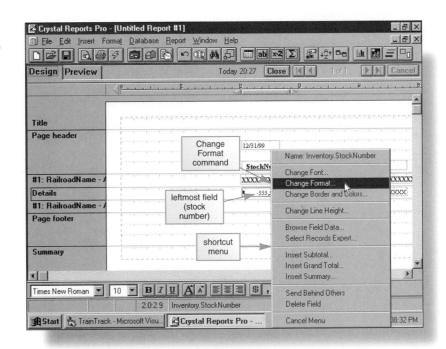

FIGURE 6-90

7 **Click Change Format. When the Format Number dialog box opens, click the Alignment box arrow and then click Thousands Separator to deselect it. Point to the OK button.**

The Format Number dialog box displays as shown in Figure 6-91.

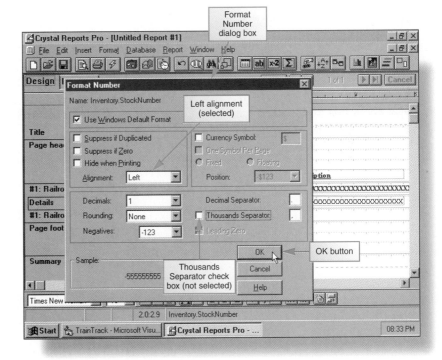

FIGURE 6-91

8 Click the OK button. Click the Sort button on the toolbar. When the Record Sort Order dialog box opens, click the Add button and then point to the OK button.

The report will be sorted by StockNumber within each RailroadName group (Figure 6-92).

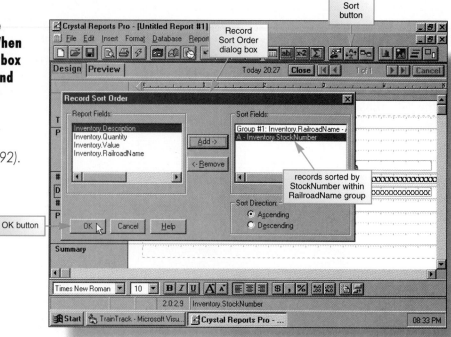

FIGURE 6-92

9 Click the OK button. Click the Save button on the toolbar. When the File Save As dialog box opens, type Inventory in the File name text box, click the Drives box arrow, and click a:. Point to the OK button.

The File Save As dialog box displays (Figure 6-93).

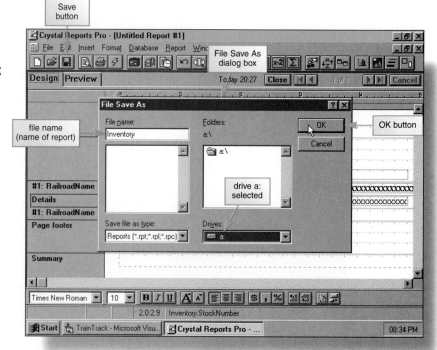

FIGURE 6-93

Click the OK button. Click the Preview tab.

The report is saved as a:\inventory.rpt and displays in the Preview window (Figure 6-94).

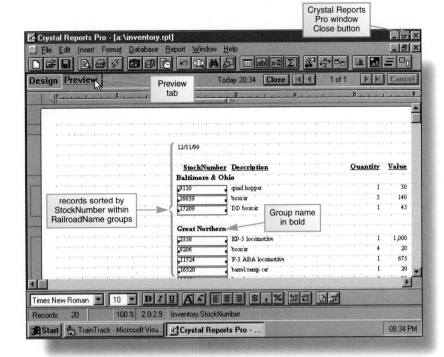

FIGURE 6-94

OtherWays

1. To open Insert Group Section dialog box, press ALT+I, press G

Using the Crystal Custom Control

You added the Crystal Custom Control to the Toolbox earlier in this project. The control is added to a form in the same way as other controls. Once you have the Crystal Custom Control on your form, you build the connection between your application and Crystal Reports by setting the control's properties in the Properties list. The report appearance and actions you can specify using the Properties list include the following:

▶ Name of the report you want to print in response to an event
▶ Destination for the report (window, file, or printer)
▶ Number of copies you want to print from a printer
▶ File information if your report is going to a file
▶ Print window size and location if your report is going to a window
▶ Selection formula information if you want to limit the records in your report

Similar to other controls, the Crystal Custom Control has a default set of property values, and you can set property values either in the Properties window or through code statements. The **WindowTitle property** specifies the caption in the title bar of the report window. The **ReportFileName property** specifies the path and file name of the report to be executed. When the **DiscardSavedData property** is set to True, Crystal Reports ignores any data already in the report file. You will set these properties with the following code statements:

```
CrystalReport1.WindowTitle = "TrainTrack Inventory by Railroad"
CrystalReport1.ReportFileName = "a:\Inventory.rpt"
CrystalReport1.DiscardSavedData = True
```

Setting the **Action property** during run time triggers the printing of the report. You set the Action property to 1 in your procedure code:

```
CrystalReport1.Action = 1
```

to print the report in response to a user event. Perform the following steps to add the Crystal Reports control to the Inventory form and then write the code to activate the report.

Steps To Use the Crystal Report Control

1 **Close the Crystal Reports Pro window. Click the Yes button if prompted to save changes. Double-click frmInventory in the Project window. Double-click the CrystalReport button in the Toolbox and then drag it to the location shown in Figure 6-95.**

The CrystalReport control is visible during design time but not during run time (Figure 6-95).

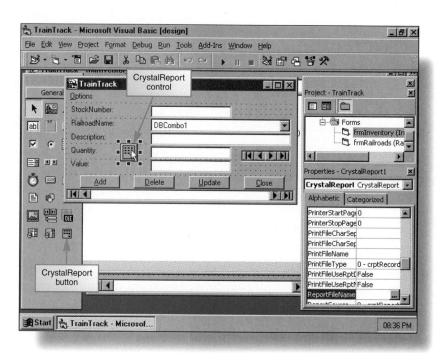

FIGURE 6-95

2 **Select the mnuReport_Click event in the frmInventory Code window. Add the code shown in Figure 6-96.**

The Code window displays as shown in Figure 6-96.

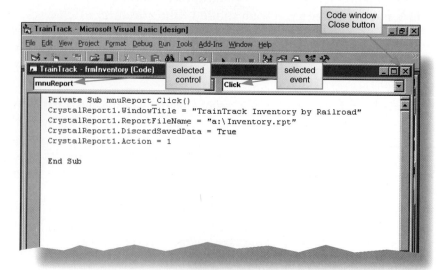

FIGURE 6-96

③ **Click the Code window's Close button. Click the Save Project button on the toolbar.**

The Code window closes and the changes are saved (Figure 6-97).

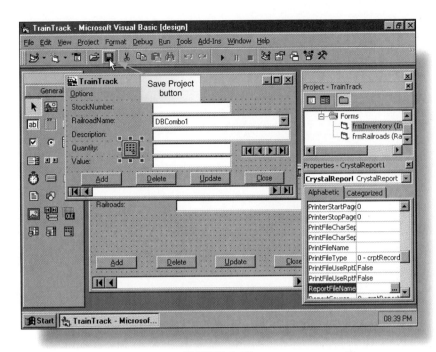

FIGURE 6-97

Testing the Application

The TrainTrack inventory system application is complete. You will test the application by modifying the records in the Railroads table as shown in Table 6-4, adding the records shown in Table 6-5 to the Inventory table, searching for a specific stock item, and generating a report.

TABLE 6-4
NAME
Baltimore & Ohio
Great Northern
Illinois Central
Lionel Lines
Milwaukee Road
Nickel Plate Road
Southern Pacific

TABLE 6-5				
STOCK NUMBER	*RAILROAD NAME*	*DESCRIPTION*	*QUANTITY*	*VALUE*
9455	**Milwaukee Road**	**Boxcar**	2	20
16397	**Milwaukee Road**	**I-beam flatcar**	1	40
9530	**Southern Pacific**	**Baggage car**	1	70
9711	**Southern Pacific**	**Boxcar**	1	20
16915	**Lionel Lines**	**Gondola**	5	10

Perform the following steps to test the TrainTrack inventory system application.

TO TEST AN APPLICATION

1. Click the Start button on the toolbar.
2. Click Edit Railroad List on the Options menu.
3. Add, modify, and delete records so that the table contains the information shown in Table 6-4 on the previous page.
4. Close the Railroads form.
5. Add the records shown in Table 6-5 on the previous page.
6. Use the Find command to make Stock Number 16397 the current record.
7. Click Options on the menu bar and then click Report. Click Print in the Report window.
8. Close the Report window. Close the TrainTrack window.

The printed report should look like the one shown in Figure 6-98.

1/27/99

StockNumber	Description	Quantity	Value
Baltimore & Ohio			
9110	quad hopper	1	30
16639	boxcar	3	140
17209	DD boxcar	1	45
Great Northern			
9206	boxcar	4	20
11724	F-3 ABA locomotive	1	675
16320	barrel ramp car	1	20
16675	log dump car	1	30
Illinois Central			
7220	baggage car	1	99
8030	GP-9 locomotive	1	120
9264	covered quad hopper	1	35
16093	Vista Dome car	2	40
18924	diesel switcher	1	35
Lionel Lines			
6417	N5C caboose	2	40
9378	derrick car	1	30
9408	circus stock car	1	50
16390	flatcar w/ water tank	1	40
16915	gondola	5	10
Milwaukee Road			
9455	boxcar	2	20
16397	I-beam flatcar	1	40
Nickel Plate Road			
16307	flatcar w/ trailers	1	69
19411	flatcar	1	29
Southern Pacific			
9530	baggage car	1	70
9711	boxcar	1	20

FIGURE 6-98

Project Summary

In Project 4, you built an application that allows the user to view records in an existing database. In this project, you created a more sophisticated database application that allows the user to add, modify, delete, and search for records. Using the data-bound ComboBox control, you made it possible for the user to enter field values by clicking an item in a list box rather than typing. You learned how to use the Visual Data Manager add-in to create or modify a database. You used both the Data Form Designer and the Data Form Wizard to create single-record data forms. You used the Report Designer add-in and Crystal Reports Custom Control to create a report that can be viewed within the application or printed.

What You Should Know

Having completed this project, you now should be able to perform the following tasks.

▶ Add a Form with the Data Form Wizard
(VB 6.25)
▶ Add ActiveX Controls to the Toolbox (VB 6.31)
▶ Add DBCombo Controls and Data Controls
(VB 6.32)
▶ Add Tables to a Database (VB 6.12)
▶ Build a Menu (VB 6.34)
▶ Create Forms with the Data Form Designer
(VB 6.14)
▶ Modify a Data Form Interface (VB 6.16)
▶ Modify and Save a Crystal Report (VB 6.48)
▶ Modify Control Properties (VB 6.36)

▶ Modify the Form_Unload Event Procedure
(VB 6.20)
▶ Open a Database with the VisData Add-In
(VB 6.9)
▶ Save a Project for Testing (VB 6.22)
▶ Set a Startup Form and Modify Code (VB 6.38)
▶ Test a Data Form and Add Records (VB 6.24)
▶ Test an Application (VB 6.56)
▶ Use the Crystal Report Control (VB 6.54)
▶ Use the Report Expert to Create a Report
(VB 6.45)
▶ Write a Recordset Search Routine (VB 6.43)

A+ Test Your Knowledge

1 True/False

Instructions: Circle T if the statement is true or F if the statement is false.

T F 1. The Visual Data Manager can be used only to create new Microsoft Access databases.

T F 2. The Data Form Designer is a utility for creating forms.

T F 3. To add a new record using a data entry form, use the AddNew method.

T F 4. To unload the current form, use the Form keyword.

T F 5. The Data Form Wizard can be used to create data entry forms quickly that cannot be changed once created.

T F 6. The RowSource property of a DBCombo control is used to specify the Data control used to fill the DBCombo control's list.

T F 7. In an InputBox control, clicking the Cancel button returns a value not equal to the zero length string.

T F 8. The NoMatch property uses the Match method.

T F 9. Report Designer is not the same as Crystal Reports.

T F 10. Crystal Reports is a stand-alone program that is used to create custom reports.

2 Multiple Choice

Instructions: Circle the correct response.

1. Database tables are defined by adding individual _____ to the table structure.
   a. files
   b. tables
   c. fields
   d. rows

2. On a form created using the Data Form Designer, to attach a Data control to a database table, you must select the _____.
   a. Database Table
   b. RecordSource
   c. Field Name
   d. Data Name

3. To save changes to the current record on a data entry form, use the _____ method.
   a. UpdateRecord
   b. Change
   c. UpdateControl
   d. Refresh

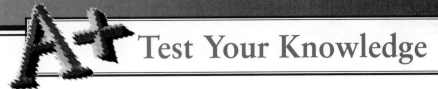
4. The _____ event is caused when a Data control is loaded.
   a. Validate
   b. Error
   c. Query_Unload
   d. Reposition

5. Three selections that must be made in the Data Form Wizard are _____, _____, and

   _____.
   a. Database Type, Database, RecordSource
   b. Database, RecordSource, Fields
   c. Database Type, RecordSource Type, Fields
   d. Database, Column to Sort By, Fields

6. A _____ control is a data-bound control that is populated automatically from a field in an
   attached Data control.
   a. ListBox
   b. TextBox
   c. DBCombo
   d. Label

7. A form's _____ event occurs each time a form receives focus.
   a. Reposition
   b. Activate
   c. Validate
   d. Error

8. When searching records, the _____ property indicates whether a particular record was found.
   a. FindFirst
   b. Match
   c. NoMatch
   d. FindLast

9. For Crystal Reports, the _____ property can be used to trigger printing of a report.
   a. Action
   b. WindowTitle
   c. ReportFileName
   d. Activate

10. A standard report format type in Crystal Reports has rows and columns with _____
    information below the columns.
    a. minimum
    b. average
    c. graph
    d. summary

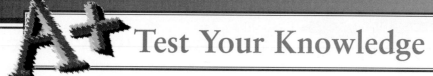

3 Understanding the Data Form Designer

Instructions: In Figure 6-99, arrows point to some of the major components in the Data Form Designer dialog box. Identify these numbered items in the spaces provided.

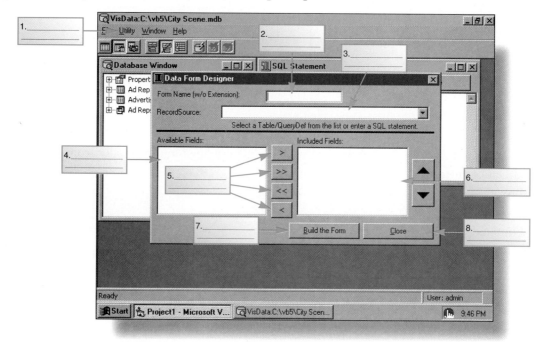

FIGURE 6-99

4 Understanding the Crystal Reports Pro Window

Instructions: In Figure 6-100, arrows point to some of the major components in the Crystal Reports Pro window and the Create New Report dialog box. Identify these numbered items in the spaces provided.

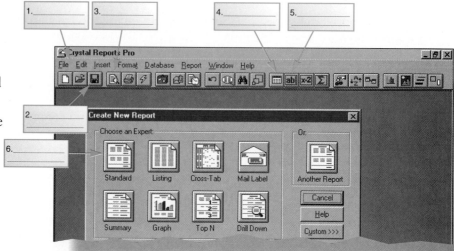

FIGURE 6-100

Use Help

1 Reviewing Project Activities

Instructions: Perform the following tasks using a computer.

1. Start Visual Basic. Click Help on the menu bar and then click Microsoft Visual Basic Help Topics.
2. On the Contents tab, double-click the Controls Reference book. Double-click the Intrinsic Controls book.
3. Double-click the Data Control topic and then read and print the information that displays.
4. Hand the printouts in to your instructor.
5. Click the Help Topics button. When the Contents sheet displays, double-click the ActiveX Controls book.
6. Double-click the DBCombo Control topic and then read and print the information that displays.
7. Hand the printouts in to your instructor and then close Help.

2 Learning More of the Basics

Instructions: Use Visual Basic Books Online to learn more about manipulating database data with code. The Help topics will provide information to answer the questions below. Write the answers to the questions on your own paper and hand them in to your instructor.

1. Start Visual Basic. Click Help on the menu bar and then click Books Online. In the Navigation area, double-click the Programmer's Guide (All Editions) book. Double-click the Part 2: What Can You Do With Visual Basic? book and then double-click the Accessing Data book. Read and then print the text that displays in the Topic area. Hand the printout in to your instructor.
2. In the Navigation area, double-click the Accessing Databases with the Data Control book. Read the text that displays in the Topic area and then answer the following questions:
   a. What activities can you perform using a Data control?
   b. What kinds of databases can be manipulated through Visual Basic?
   c. What other applications can be affected using a Visual Basic Data control?
3. Click the Understanding Database Design and Structure topic in the Navigation area. Read the information that displays in the Topic area and then answer the following questions:
   a. What kind of interface does a Data control provide?
   b. What are the components of a relational database?
   c. Briefly explain each component of a relational database.
   d. Why would an index be used in a database?
   e. How can data be retrieved easily from a database?
4. In the Navigation area, click the Adding, Updating, and Deleting Records topic. Read the information that displays in the Topic area and then answer the following questions:
   a. Name the two methods used in Visual Basic to add, update, and delete records in a database?
   b. What are the BOFAction and EOFAction properties and how do they work?
5. Double-click the Manipulating Records with Code book. Read and print the information that displays in the Topic area. In the Navigation area, one by one, click each topic below the Manipulation Records with Code book, reading and printing the information that displays in the Topic area. Hand the printouts in to your instructor.

Apply Your Knowledge

1 Creating and Modifying Forms with the Visual Data Manager

Instructions: Start Visual Basic and use the Visual Data Manager add-in File menu to open the Microsoft Access database called Museum Mercantile.mdb from the Visual Basic folder on the Data Disk that accompanies this book. This database consists of a table that contains product information and a table that contains vendor information for a museum gift shop.

1. Click Utility on the VisData menu bar and then click Data Form Designer.
2. Type Mproducts in the Form Name text box. Click the RecordSource box arrow and then click Product.
3. Click the double right arrow button between the Available Fields and Included Fields list boxes to add all of the fields to the form.
4. Click the Build the Form button.
5. Repeat Step 2 through Step 4 to create a form named Mvendors, whose record source is the Vendor table, and add all of the fields to the form.
6. Click the Close button in the Data Form Designer dialog box and then click the VisData window's Close button.
7. Arrange the forms on the desktop as shown in Figure 6-101. One at a time, select the forms and perform the following modifications:
   a. Change each form's BorderStyle property value to 1 - Fixed Single.
   b. If necessary, change each form's Height property value to make the forms visually pleasing.
   c. Set each form's MaxButton property value to False.
   d. Set the first form's Caption property value to Museum Products and the second form's Caption property value to Museum Vendors.
   e. Click the Refresh button on each form and then delete it.
   f. Rearrange the controls on each form to group together the Add, Update, and Delete buttons.
8. Open the Code window for the Mproducts form and in the Form control's Load event, type frmMvendors.Show so that both forms display when the project is opened.

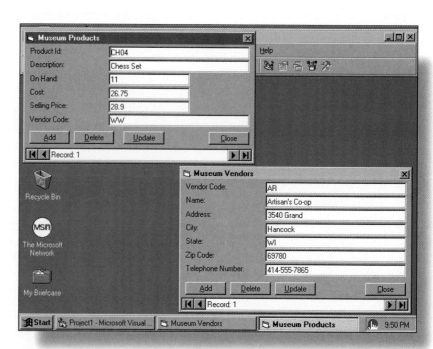

FIGURE 6-101

Apply Your Knowledge

In the (General) control's (Declarations) event, delete the code statements relating to the Refresh button that you removed from the form in an earlier step. Close the Code window. Open the Code window for the Mvendors form and in the (General) control's (Declarations) event, delete the code statements relating to the Refresh button that you removed from the form in an earlier step. Close the Code window.

9. Right-click the project name in the Project window and then click Properties on the shortcut menu. When the Properties dialog box displays, on the General tab, set the frmMproducts form to be the Startup Object and then close the dialog box.

10. In the Project window, delete any unnecessary forms by right-clicking the form name and then clicking Remove (Formname).frm on the shortcut menu.

11. Click the Mproduct form to make certain it is active and save the form as Museum Products. Click the Mvendor form to make it active and save it as Museum Vendors. Close both forms and then save the project using the file name Museum Gifts.

12. Click the Start button to test the application. If necessary, make corrections to the code statement. Save the forms and project again using the same file names.

13. Print the Form Image, Code, and Form as Text.

In the Lab

1 Creating a Database Using the Visual Data Manager

Problem: A store that sells previously listened to CDs currently is using a variety of notebooks, word processing documents, and spreadsheets to keep track of their customers and employees. They want an easier, more efficient way to record and manipulate their data.

Instructions: Build an application with a user interface that resembles the one shown in Figure 6-102.

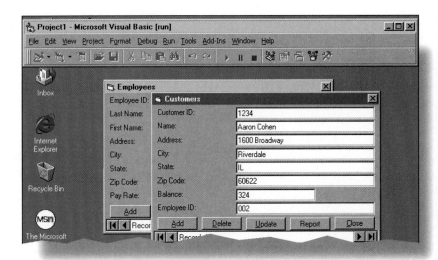

FIGURE 6-102

(continued)

In the Lab

Creating a Database Using the Visual Data Manager *(continued)*

1. Open a new project in Visual Basic and then open the Visual Data Manager add-in.
2. Click File on the menu bar and then click New. Click Microsoft Access. Check with your instructor as to which version of Microsoft Access should be used and then click the suggested version.
3. In the Select Microsoft Access Database to Create dialog box, type the file name Sound Advice, make sure the folder and drive are correct, and then click the Save button.
4. Right-click in the Database Window and click New Table on the shortcut menu.
5. Type Customers in the Name text box and then click the Add Field button in the Table structure dialog box.
6. Type Customer ID in the Name text box, type 4 in the Size text box, click AllowZeroLength to deselect it, click Required to select it, and click the OK button.
7. Type Name in the Name text box, type 15 in the Size text box, and click the OK button. Continue adding the following fields by typing the names and sizes, and clicking the OK button in the Add Field dialog box to add each new field: Address, 15; City, 15; State, 2; Zip Code, 5; Balance, click the Type box arrow and then click Currency; Employee ID, 3.
8. Click the Close button in the Add Field dialog box and click the Build the Table button in the Table Structure dialog box.
9. Repeat step 4 through step 8 to create another table for Employees. The Employees table will have the following fields: Employee ID, 3, click AllowZeroLength to deselect it, click Required to select it; Last Name, 10; First Name, 8; Address, 15; City, 15; State, 2; Zip Code, 5; and Pay Rate, Currency type.
10. Create the data entry forms using the Data Form Designer of VisData. Click Utility on the menu bar and then click Data Form Designer.
11. Type Customers in the Form Name text box. Click the RecordSource box arrow and then click Customers.
12. Click the double right arrow button between the Available Fields and Included Fields list boxes to add all of the available fields to the form. Click the Build the Form button.
13. Repeat step 11 and step 12 to create another form for Employees using the record source of Employees with all of the available fields.
14. Click the Close button in the Form Designer dialog box and then click the Close button in the VisData window.
15. Right-click Form1 in the Project window and then click Remove Form1 on the shortcut menu. Click the No button in the Microsoft Visual Basic dialog box.
16. Arrange the forms on the desktop so the title bars of both forms can be viewed.

In the Lab

17. Click each form one by one and set each form's BorderStyle property value to 1 - Fixed Single. Click the form's Refresh button and then press the DELETE key. Adjust the control locations so the Add, Delete, and Update buttons are next to each other. Double-click each form and delete the Visual Basic code statements that display in the (General) control (Declarations) event for the Refresh button.

18. Double-click the Customers form and enter the following code statement `txtFields(0).SetFocus` under the cmdAdd_Click event procedure below the AddNew statement. Enter the code statement `Screen.MousePointer = vbDefault` under the cmdUpdate_Click event procedure below the LastModified statement. Enter the code statements `Unload Me` and `Screen.MousePointer = vbDefault` under the cmdClose_Click event procedure. Enter the code statement `Data1_Reposition` under the Form_Activate event procedure and `frmEmployees.Show` under the Form_Load event procedure. Close the Code window.

19. Double-click the Employees form and then enter the code statement `txtFields(0).SetFocus` under the cmdAdd_Click event procedure below the AddNew statement. Enter `Screen.MousePointer = vbDefault` under the cmdUpdate_Click event procedure below the LastModified statement. Enter the code statements `Unload Me` and `Screen.MousePointer = vbDefault` under the cmdClose_Click event procedure.

20. Right-click the project name in the Project window and click the Properties on the shortcut menu. When the Properties dialog box opens, on the General tab, set the frmCustomers form to be the Startup Object and then close the dialog box.

21. One by one, click each form and save them using the names Customers and Employees. Save the project using the file name Sound Advice.

22. Run the application to make certain no errors exist. If any errors are encountered, correct them and resave the forms and project using the same file names. Add data to each of the tables using the data entry forms. For the Customers table, add at least four customers. For the Employees table, add at least two employees.

23. Print the Form Image, Code, and Form as Text. See your instructor for directions on handing in this project.

2 Modifying a Database Using the Visual Data Manager

Problem: For In the Lab 1, you created the Sound Advice database consisting of two tables containing the data for the Customers and Employees and two forms for entering the Customers and Employees data. The management of Sound Advice would like to enhance the existing database to record data for the compact discs that are purchased and sold.

Instructions: Perform the tasks on the next page to modify the application created for In the Lab 1. If you did not complete In the Lab 1, see your instructor for directions to obtain a copy of the Sound Advice database and Visual Basic project. The new data entry form you create should be similar to the one shown in Figure 6-103 on the next page.

(continued)

In the Lab

Modifying a Database Using the Visual Data Manager (continued)

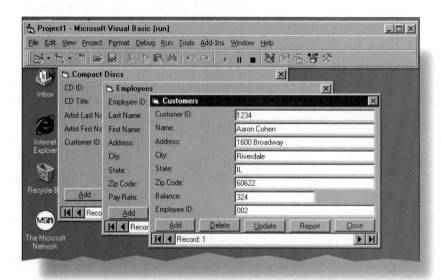

FIGURE 6-103

1. Open the Visual Basic Sound Advice project and then open the Visual Data Manager add-in.
2. Click File on the menu bar and then click Open. Click Microsoft Access.
3. In the Open dialog box, make sure the folder and drive are correct, select the file name Sound Advice, and click the OK button.
4. Right-click in the Database Window and then click New Table on the shortcut menu.
5. In the Table Structure dialog box, type CompactDiscs in the Name text box and then click the Add Field button.
6. Type CD ID in the Name text box, type 4 in the Size text box, click AllowZeroLength to deselect it, click Required to select it, and click the OK button. Continue adding the following fields by typing in the names and sizes, and clicking the OK button to add each new field: CD Title, 30; Artist Last Name, 15; Artist First Name, 8; and Customer ID, 4.
7. Click the Close button in the Add Field dialog box and click the Build the Table button in the Table Structure dialog box.
8. Create the data entry forms using the Data Form Designer of VisData. Click Utility on the menu bar and then click Data Form Designer.
9. Type CompactDiscs in the Form Name text box. Click the RecordSource box arrow and then click CompactDiscs.
10. Click the double right arrow button between the Available Fields and Included Fields list boxes to add all of the available fields to the form and then click the Build the Form button.
11. Click the Close button in the Form Designer dialog box and then click the Close button in the VisData window.

In the Lab

12. Arrange the new form on the desktop so all three forms can be viewed.

13. Click the frmCompactDiscs form and set the form's BorderStyle property value to 1 - Fixed Single. Click the Refresh button on the form and then press the DELETE key. Adjust the control locations so the Add, Delete, and Update buttons are next to each other.

14. Double-click the frmCustomers form and enter the code statement `frmCompactDiscs.Show` above the statement `frmEmployees.Show` under the Form_Load event procedure. Close the Code window.

15. Double-click the frmCompactDiscs form and then delete the Visual Basic code statements that display in the (General) control (Declarations) event for the Refresh button. Enter the code statement `txtFields(0).SetFocus` under the cmdAdd_Click event procedure below the AddNew statement. Enter the code statement `Screen.MousePointer = vbDefault` under the cmdUpdate_Click event procedure below the LastModified statement. Enter the code statements `Unload Me` and `Screen.MousePointer = vbDefault` under the cmdClose_Click event procedure.

16. One by one, click each form. Save them using the names Customers, Employees, and CompactDiscs. Save the project using the file name Sound Advice2.

17. Run the application to make certain no errors exist. If any errors are encountered, correct them and resave the forms and project using the same file names. Close the frmCustomers form to show the frmEmployees form. Close the frmEmployees form to show the frmCompactDiscs form. Add at least 10 compact discs for the CompactDiscs table.

18. Print the project Form Image, Code, and Form as Text. See your instructor for directions on handing in this project.

3 Creating Crystal Reports

Problem: For In the Lab 2, you enhanced the Sound Advice database created consisting of three tables containing the data for the Customers, Employees, and Compact Discs and three forms for entering the Customers, Employees, and Compact Discs data. The management of Sound Advice would like to use the data in the database to report data for the compact discs that are purchased and sold.

Instructions: Perform the following tasks to modify the application created for In the Lab 2. If you did not complete In the Lab 2, see your instructor for directions to obtain a copy of the Sound Advice database and Visual Basic project. The new report forms you create should be similar to the ones shown in Figure 6-104 on the next page.

1. Open the Sound Advice project in Visual Basic.

2. To add the ActiveX control to the Toolbox, press the CTRL+T keys to display the Components dialog box. If necessary, click the Controls tab. Click the Crystal Report 4.6 Control check box and then click the OK button.

3. Add a CrystalReport control to the frmCustomers form, the frmEmployees form, and the frmCompactDiscs form.

(continued)

In the Lab

Creating Crystal Reports *(continued)*

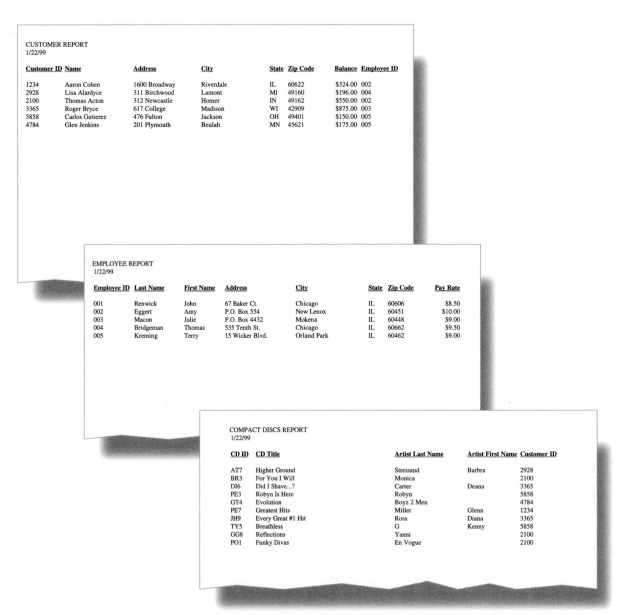

CUSTOMER REPORT
1/22/99

Customer ID	Name	Address	City	State	Zip Code	Balance	Employee ID
1234	Aaron Cohen	1600 Broadway	Riverdale	IL	60622	$324.00	002
2928	Lisa Alardyce	311 Birchwood	Lamont	MI	49160	$196.00	004
2100	Thomas Acton	312 Newcastle	Homer	IN	49162	$550.00	002
3365	Roger Bryce	617 College	Madison	WI	42909	$875.00	003
5858	Carlos Gutierez	476 Fulton	Jackson	OH	49401	$150.00	005
4784	Glen Jenkins	201 Plymouth	Beulah	MN	45621	$175.00	005

EMPLOYEE REPORT
1/22/99

Employee ID	Last Name	First Name	Address	City	State	Zip Code	Pay Rate
001	Renwick	John	67 Baker Ct.	Chicago	IL	60606	$8.50
002	Eggert	Amy	P.O. Box 554	New Lenox	IL	60451	$10.00
003	Macon	Julie	P.O. Box 4432	Mokena	IL	60448	$9.00
004	Bridgeman	Thomas	535 Tenth St.	Chicago	IL	60662	$9.50
005	Kreming	Terry	15 Wicker Blvd.	Orland Park	IL	60462	$9.00

COMPACT DISCS REPORT
1/22/99

CD ID	CD Title	Artist Last Name	Artist First Name	Customer ID
AT7	Higher Ground	Streisand	Barbra	2928
BR3	For You I Will	Monica		2100
DI6	Did I Shave...?	Carter	Deana	3365
PE3	Robyn Is Here	Robyn		5858
GT4	Evolution	Boyz 2 Men		4784
PE7	Greatest Hits	Miller	Glenn	1234
JH9	Every Great #1 Hit	Ross	Diana	3365
TY5	Breathless	G	Kenny	5858
GG8	Reflections	Yanni		2100
PO1	Funky Divas	En Vogue		2100

FIGURE 6-104

4. Adjust the size of the frmCompactDiscs form to match the frmCustomers form and the frmEmployees form.

5. Add one CommandButton control to each of the forms and change the Name property to cmdReport and the Caption property to Report.

6. Click Add-Ins on the menu bar and then click Report Designer. Maximize the Crystal Reports Pro window.

7. Click File on the menu bar and then click New. Click the Listing button in the Create New Report dialog box. If necessary, click the Step 1: Tables tab in the Create Report Expert dialog box. Click the Data File button. Click the Drives box arrow and then click a:. Double-click Sound Advice.mdb and then click the Done button in the Choose Database File dialog box.

8. Click the 3: Fields tab. In the Database Fields list box under Customers, click the first field, press and hold the SHIFT key, scroll down until the last Customers field is in view, and click the last field under Customers. Release the SHIFT key. Click the Add button. Click the Preview Report button and then click the Design tab. Click the Text button, type CUSTOMER REPORT and place the text field on the line for the Page Heading. Click the Save button and save the report using the file name customer.

9. Repeat step 6 through step 8 to create an employee report and a compact discs report. For these reports, add all of the employee fields to the employee report and add all of the compactdisc fields to the compact discs report. Do not sort these two reports. Title the reports, EMPLOYEE REPORT and COMPACT DISCS REPORT, respectively. Save the reports using the file names employee and compact discs. Close the Crystal Report Pro window.

10. In Visual Basic, click the frmCustomers form to make it active and click the CrystalReport control. Double-click the Report CommandButton control. Type the following code statements:

```
CrystalReport1.WindowTitle = "Customer Report"
CrystalReport1.ReportFileName = "a:\customer.rpt"
CrystalReport1.Action = 1
```

11. Repeat step 10 to set the ReportFileName property for the employee report using a:\employee.rpt and for the compact discs report using a:\compact discs.rpt. Write similar code statements for the Report CommandButton controls replacing the WindowTitle with Employee Report and Compact Discs Report and the ReportFileName property with a:\employee.rpt and a:\compact discs.rpt.

12. Save the forms using the names Customers, Employees, and CompactDiscs. Save the project using the file name Sound Advice3.

13. Run the application and make any necessary corrections. Remember to save the form and project again if any changes have been made.

14. Print the Form Image, Code, and Form as Text. Print all three Crystal Reports. See your instructor for directions on turning in this project.

Cases and Places

The difficulty of these case studies varies: ▶ are the least difficult; ▶▶ are more difficult; and ▶▶▶ are the most difficult.

1 ▶ Bill Keller is sales manager for the Midwest Office Furniture Company. Local businesses buy office furniture from Midwest through account representatives who work for Bill. Account representatives are paid a base salary and receive a commission on the sales revenues they generate. Bill has contracted you to build an information system that will keep track of the accounts and account representatives. As a first step, you have decided to create a database with two tables. The Accounts table will contain information on the businesses that buy from Midwest. The Account Reps table will contain information on the representatives. Use the Visual Basic Visual Data Manager to create a database named Sales with an Accounts table structured as shown in Table 6-6. Print the structure of the table.

TABLE 6-6		
FIELD NAME	**DATA TYPE**	**FIELD SIZE**
AccountNumber	Text	4
Name	Text	20
Address	Text	15
City	Text	15
State	Text	2
ZipCode	Text	5
Balance	Currency	
SalesYTD	Currency	
AccRepName	Text	20

2 ▶ The Mercantile Museum Gift shop maintains a database containing a table of information on the products it sells and a table of information on its suppliers. The manager would like you to create a report of product ID and description, grouped by vendor. Use Crystal Reports to create and print this report for the manager. The database is available on the Data Disk as Museum Mercantile.mdb.

3 ▶▶ LaTisha is very pleased with the GeoView database viewer application you built for her in Project 4. She has been using it with great success and plans to add more than 100 records (countries) to the database. She is concerned, however, that when the recordset becomes that large it will be cumbersome for her to find a specific record by moving through all of the records one at a time. Modify the GeoView database viewer application to include the ability for LaTisha to search by country name for a specific record in the database.

4 ▶▶ The Wicker Country Club contracted a small software development company to build a membership database system. The company created an Access database file, entered only a few test records, and then went bankrupt. Wicker Country Club has offered you a free one-year membership if you can salvage the project. Their minimum requirements are that you develop a Windows-based application that they can use to add, modify, and delete membership information. You have decided that the most cost-effective way for you to meet their requirements is to use Visual Basic and its Data Form Wizard to develop the application. The Wicker Country Club.mdb file is available on the Data Disk that accompanies this book.

Cases and Places

5 ▶▶▶ Create a second table for the Midwest Office Furniture database (Cases and Places 1) that contains the account representative name, base salary, and commission rate as listed in Table 6-7. Create an application with a single-record data form that Bill Keller can use to enter information in the Accounts table. He should be able to select the account reps name from a drop-down list of the reps in the Account reps table.

TABLE 6-7		
ACCTREPNAME	*BASESALARY*	*COMMISSION*
Glynn, Nancy	12,000	.07
Halko, Bryan	13,000	.08
Rogers, Helen	12,500	.07
Franks, Peter	11,750	.07
Stubbins, Rachel	13,500	.08

6 ▶▶▶ Your computer consulting firm has been contacted by a new client, Guilford Haberdashers. They need some method of recording stock, vendors, and salespeople information and have hired your firm to analyze the situation and develop a solution. Based on the results of the high-level analysis, you suggest a Microsoft Access database with a Visual Basic interface for entering, modifying, and deleting data as well as for reporting purposes. Design the tables for stock, vendors, and for the salespeople. Develop the database tables. Develop an application to view, add, modify, and delete information in any of the three tables. Design reports that will assist the sales staff in keeping track of inventory in a more efficient manner and incorporate the reports into the Visual Basic database interface.

7 ▶▶▶ From time to time, you do programming work for Night and Day Child Care. They require a method of recording all of the children they care for. What you have decided to provide for them is a Microsoft Access database application that you will create using the Visual Data Manager add-in of Visual Basic. The database will have a Visual Basic interface or forms through which data can be added, updated, and deleted. The data in one table should include information about the parents, such as the parent identification number, parent name(s), home address, home telephone number, and work telephone number(s), and the child identification number(s). The data in another table should include information about each child, such as the child identification number, child name, legal guardian, social security number, doctor name, and any medications the child is to receive. Employees need to be able to search the database by child name or by legal guardian name. To send out advertisements, they would like to print mailing labels for each child cared for at their facility. The mailing labels should be addressed to the parents and should contain the parent name(s), the child name(s), and home address. They also require mailing labels containing each child's name rather than the parent name(s) and the child's address so they can mail out birthday cards to each child.

Creating ActiveX Controls and Distributing Applications

Objectives:

You will have mastered the material in this project when you can:

▶ Create an ActiveX control
▶ Create properties for an ActiveX control
▶ Compile an ActiveX control to an .ocx file
▶ Use a timer control in applications
▶ Write a Resize event procedure
▶ Use the Integer Division and Mod Operators in code
▶ Write a random number generating function
▶ Create a setup program for an application
▶ Use the ActiveX Document Migration Wizard

Get on TRAK

Officers Use Powerful Weapon to Find Missing Children

Of every 42 children in a neighborhood, one will become missing, according to *TIME* magazine. The first two to four hours after an abduction are critical for a safe recovery, so law enforcement officials urge parents to report the incident promptly and supply a high-quality photograph. These officials then can distribute the photo and details of the child, and possibly the abductor, as widely as possible.

The major obstacle faced by legal authorities is technology. The country's 17,600 law enforcement jurisdictions are equipped primarily with a variety of computer and telephone systems. Thus, disseminating the abduction information throughout the country is cumbersome and inefficient when time is of the essence. With a Visual Basic application called the TRAK (Technology to Recover Abducted Kids) Program, however, law enforcement is making headway in coordinating the battle to locate these children.

The moment police determine a child is missing, they launch the user-friendly application and follow the

Main Menu

Create New Flyer

Create New Lineup

Retrieve Existing Flyer

Retrieve Existing Lineup

Load New Remote Flyers
Pending Flyer Count: 0

Transmissions Log

TRAK Administration

Exit

Enter the Person's Te

Case Number:	Height:
Date: 1/3/97	Weight:
Last Name:	Se:
First Name:	Hair:
Alias:	Eyes:
Street:	Complexion:
City:	Race:
State:	Age:
Zip:	Birth Date:
	Social Security #:

This TRAK System sponsored by Funder Name Here

MISSING CHILD

Date:	1/17/97
Case #:	96-650
Name:	Allison Jenkins
Address:	2357 Sycamore Street
	Daly City, CA 94203
Height:	4 Feet 3 Inches
Weight:	65
Age:	9
Eyes:	Hazel
Hair:	Light Brown
Complexion:	Fair
Race:	White
BirthDate:	1/16/86

OTHER INFORMATION BELOW

IDENTIFICATION MARKS:
Allison has a small mole on her upper right shoulder.

CIRCUMSTANCES:
Allison was last seen in Rayburn Park in Daly City at 9 am on Friday January 17.
She was wearing a red sweat shirt and blue jeans.

SUSPECT:
A white male about 30 years old with long dark hair wearing army fatigues and tennis shoes.
The vehicle was a blue Chevy 2-door with Calif plates.

NOTE:
This is a sample flyer created within minutes on the TRAK system. Multiple copies of this flyer can be printed for use by the local agency. The flyer can be electronically transmitted to other TRAK systems and to an unlimited number of fax machines. All are delivered simultaneously in minutes. Other TRAK systems can print the identical color flyer, fax machines will generate a quality black and white flyer. The result is an immediate and effective regional response, one that includes all law enforcement and the community-at-large. Anyone able to help in any way is alert, aware, and looking for the child.

TRAK (SocialTech, Inc.)
1-800-PC4-TRAK   www.trak.org
This flyer produced on a TRAK System. For more information about TRAK see www.trak.org

COMMUNITY ALERT   TEAM MEMBER

TRAK

To Safeguard Our Community

directions on their screen to compose and print a flyer and then distribute it across the country. First, they scan the child's photo. Then, they enter text regarding the child, the suspect, and the crime. This text and digitized photo are added to the flyer automatically. Next, they print color handouts to distribute to local media, schools, and community agencies and businesses. Finally, they transmit the data instantly to participating law enforcement agencies nationwide, where the data is stored in their TRAK systems and a Missing Child flyer is printed on enhanced fax machines. The program also verifies that these agencies received the information correctly.

The program, which uses less than 1 MB of memory, feeds the data into a Microsoft Access database. Developers and programmers at SocialTech, Inc., which is a nonprofit California organization, and InStep Technologies were able to develop the base application in three months and have made enhancements to the system since it was launched in 1996.

When programmers need to develop applications such at TRAK quickly and efficiently, the Visual Basic programming language offers them functionality and creation capabilities, including the Setup Wizard that guides them through the creation of an installation program for distributing the application on floppy disks to the appropriate individuals or agencies. You will work with the Setup Wizard and the ActiveX Document Migration Wizard in this project.

A specific improvement of Visual Basic 5 over previous versions of the program is its number of wizards. Using the Data Form Wizard, SocialTech generated Visual Basic forms that contain procedures and controls to connect the application to a database, which is how TRAK ties into the Access database.

More than 100 law enforcement agencies nationwide have installed the $8,500 TRAK system, including those in five entire counties in California. Most of these departments acquired the funds through fund-raising efforts. This one-time investment helps the community provide one facet of safety for its children. The TRAK instant response system gives officers a powerful weapon in combating child abductions.

application to database

Project 7

Microsoft
Visual Basic 5

Creating ActiveX Controls and Distributing Applications

Case Perspective

The company you work for is applying for a contract from a school district to develop elementary-level, PC-based mathematics practice software. A group of content specialists is developing an outline of subject area and grade level. Your group will develop a prototype for second grade multiplication practice. Specifications for the prototype designate that the software should be easy for an eight-year-old to use; generate new or different exercises; give feedback of correct and incorrect student answers; and display the time taken to complete the exercises.

Displaying elapsed time will be incorporated in all of the grade/subject modules. For this reason, your team also must build an ActiveX StopWatch control that can be used in any future interface that is developed. The Multiplication Quiz application must be capable of running as a Windows desktop application (with an easy-to-use setup program distributed on floppy disks) as well as run as a document within the Internet Explorer browser (for delivery through the school district's future intranet.)

Introduction

In previous projects, you used ActiveX controls such as the CommonDialog control and the DataBound ComboBox control. Hundreds of ActiveX controls are available from Microsoft and other software companies for you to use in building applications. With some applications you create, however, you may be unable to find a control that gives you the functionality you need or you might prefer not to rely on someone else's control. One of the features in Visual Basic version 5 is that you can create your own ActiveX controls and compile them as .ocx files for future use in any application. This control creation capability was not present in earlier versions of Visual Basic.

In this project you will create an ActiveX StopWatch control. In creating the StopWatch control, you also will learn about the Timer control, the Resize event, and how to create your own properties for controls.

You then will incorporate your StopWatch control in the Multiplication Quiz application. This application also will introduce you to random number generating functions and several new properties of CommandButton controls you previously have not used. As in Project 3, you will compile the Multiplication Quiz application into an .EXE file. This time, however, you will use the Visual Basic Setup Wizard to create an installation program for distributing the application on floppy disks. Finally, you will modify the application and then use the ActiveX Document Migration Wizard to create a version of the Multiplication Quiz application that can be hosted by Microsoft Internet Explorer.

Project Seven — Multiplication Quiz

The completed Multiplication Quiz application is shown in Figure 7-1 as it displays on the desktop during run time. The application has been compiled as an executable (.exe) file and is running outside the Visual Basic development environment. When the user clicks the Start button, five multiplication problems are generated randomly and the timer begins. The user then types answers in the corresponding text boxes.

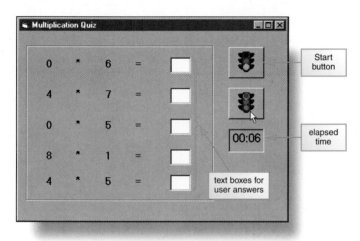

FIGURE 7-1

When the user clicks the Stop button, the timer stops and the background color of the answer boxes changes to indicate correct and incorrect answers — green for correct and red for incorrect. The Start and Stop buttons contain graphic images and display ToolTip text (Figure 7-2).

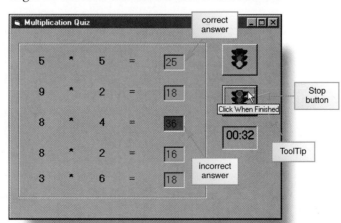

FIGURE 7-2

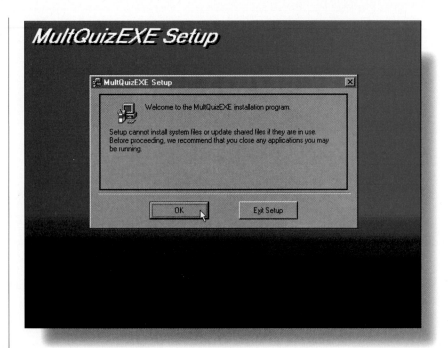

FIGURE 7-3

The Multiplication Quiz application is distributed on two floppy disks and is installed on a target PC by running a Setup program that prompts users for required information and automatically installs the application (Figure 7-3).

The display of elapsed time in the application is accomplished with a StopWatch (StWatch) control shown during design time in Figure 7-4.

The StWatch control is a custom ActiveX control that you will build. The StopWatch control can be activated through code statements or by the user clicking buttons (Figure 7-4). The display of the control buttons is controlled by the value of the Buttons property (Figure 7-5). The Buttons property is a custom property you will create for the StWatch control when you build it.

The Multiplication Quiz application also has an ActiveX document version that allows it to run as a document within Internet Explorer (Figure 7-6).

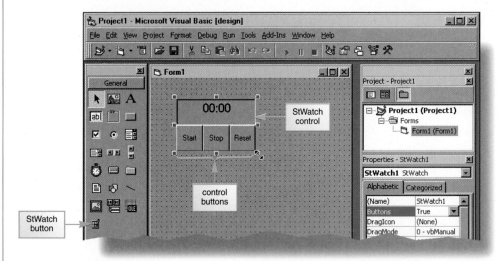

FIGURE 7-4

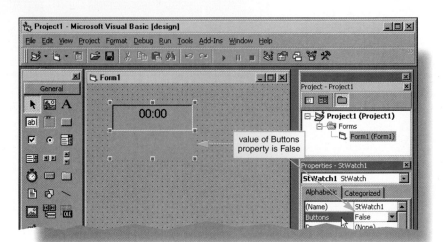

FIGURE 7-5

Internet
Explorer

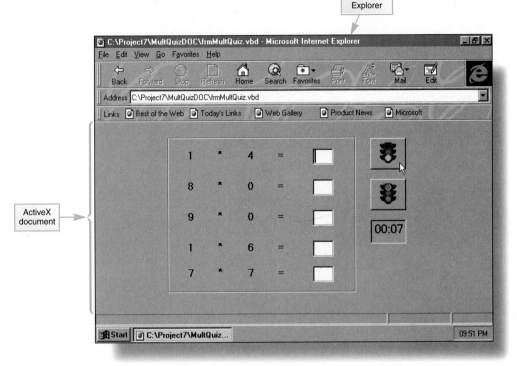

ActiveX
document

FIGURE 7-6

Project Steps

First, you will build, test, and compile the StWatch control. Next, you will build and test the Multiplication Quiz application. You then will create and test a Setup program for the application. Finally, you will create and test an ActiveX document version of the application. The following tasks will be completed in this project.

1. Start an ActiveX Control project.
2. Build a UserControl interface.
3. Set properties of the UserControl and constituent controls.
4. Write code and create properties for the UserControl.
5. Open a Standard EXE project within a project group.
6. Create a Standard EXE project to test the User control.
7. Test the design time and run time behavior of the UserControl.
8. Compile the UserControl into an .ocx file.
9. Open a Standard EXE project and add the ActiveX control to the Toolbox.
10. Create the interface for the Multiplication Quiz application.
11. Set properties for the Multiplication Quiz application.
12. Write code for the Multiplication Quiz application.
13. Test and save the Multiplication Quiz application.
14. Compile the Multiplication Quiz application into an .exe file.
15. Use the Setup Wizard to create a setup program and distribution disks.
16. Test the setup program.
17. Make a copy of the Multiplication Quiz application source code files.
18. Use the Document Migration Wizard to create an ActiveX document version of the application.
19. Test the ActiveX document in Internet Explorer.

The following pages contain a detailed explanation of each of these steps.

Getting Started

You will create many more project files in this project than you have in previous projects, and the Setup Wizard you will be using creates a large temporary directory within the same folder as the project files. For this reason, the steps that follow show the project files being saved in a folder on the PC's hard drive rather than on a floppy disk in the 3½ Floppy [A:] drive. The folder is named Project7 and contains three folders as shown in Figure 7-7. Before you begin this project, you should create these three folders in an appropriate location on your hard drive or file server. Check with your instructor for specific directions. The traffic signal graphics used in this project are available on the Data Disk that accompanies this book. If you are writing the project files to a public access directory, you should copy your files to floppy disk and delete the files from the public access directory after you complete this project.

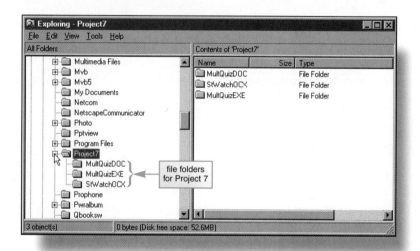

FIGURE 7-7

More *About*
COM and ActiveX

The Component Object Model (COM) is an industry-standard architecture for object-oriented development. ActiveX is Microsoft's brand name for the technologies that enable inter-operability using the Component Object Model.

Creating ActiveX Controls

ActiveX controls are standardized user interface elements you assemble to create an application. With hundreds of ActiveX controls available, you may never need to build your own custom control. ActiveX control creation is, however, a major extension of Visual Basic (and a difficult topic to master). This project will give you an introduction to the basics of control creation.

Visual Basic provides three ways to create controls: (1) create your own control from scratch; (2) modify a single existing control; or (3) assemble a new control from several existing controls. In this project, you will assemble a StopWatch (StWatch) control from existing Label, CommandButton, and Timer controls.

You will begin by starting an ActiveX control project. You then will follow a development process very similar to the one you have been using to create the desktop applications in previous projects. After creating the application, you will add an additional project to the desktop to test the design time and run time behavior of your control. You then will compile the control into an .ocx file for use in other projects.

Starting an ActiveX Control Project

You began previous projects by starting Visual Basic or by opening a new Standard EXE project if you already were running Visual Basic. The process for starting an ActiveX control project is similar. Perform the following steps to start an ActiveX control project.

 Steps To Start an ActiveX Control Project

1 Start Visual Basic or if Visual Basic is already running, click File on the menu bar and then click New Project. Point to the ActiveX Control icon in the New Project dialog box.

If you have another project already open, you will be prompted to save changes. The New Project dialog box displays (Figure 7-8).

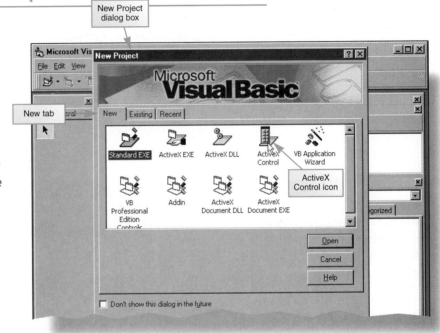

FIGURE 7-8

2 Double-click the ActiveX Control icon. Drag the UserControl's right border approximately ten grid marks to the left. Drag the Designer window's right border to the left and the bottom border up as shown in Figure 7-9.

The ActiveX control Designer window displays (Figure 7-9).

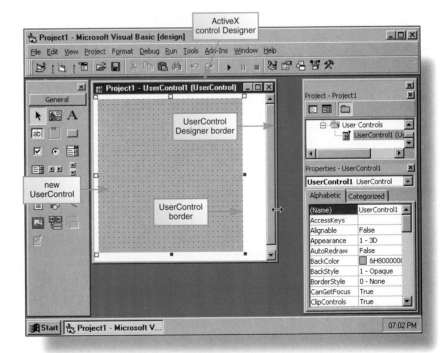

FIGURE 7-9

3 **Click Project on the menu bar and then point to Project1 Properties.**

The Project menu displays (Figure 7-10).

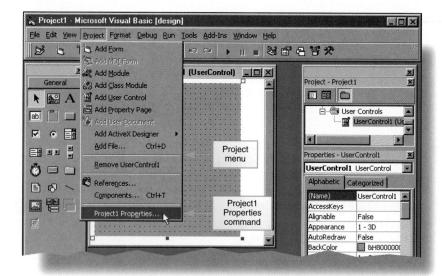

FIGURE 7-10

4 **Click Project1 Properties. If necessary, in the Project1 – Project Properties dialog box, click the General tab. Enter the information shown in Figure 7-11 and then point to the OK button.**

The Project1 – Project Properties dialog box displays as shown in Figure 7-11.

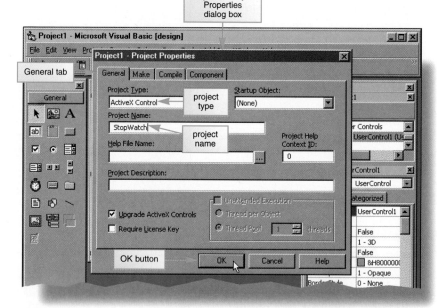

FIGURE 7-11

5 **Click the OK button.**

The new project name, StopWatch, displays in the Project window and Designer window title bars (Figure 7-12).

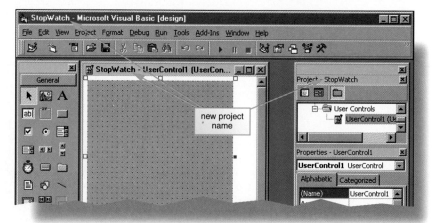

FIGURE 7-12

Creating a User Control Interface

An ActiveX control created with Visual Basic is always composed of a **User-Control** object, plus any controls you place on the UserControl, called **constituent controls**. Like Visual Basic forms, UserControl objects have code modules and visual designers. You add constituent controls to the UserControl object's **Designer window**, in the same way as you add controls to a form.

The StWatch control consists of five constituent controls—three CommandButton controls, one Label control, and one Timer control (Figure 7-13). The Timer control is visible during design time but is not visible to the user during run time.

Perform the following steps to create the control interface.

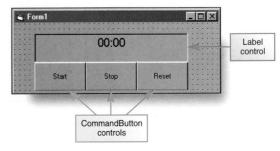

FIGURE 7-13

 To Create an ActiveX Control Interface

1 **Double-click the Label button in the Toolbox and then drag the Label to the upper-left corner of the UserControl.**

A Label control is added to the UserControl (Figure 7-14).

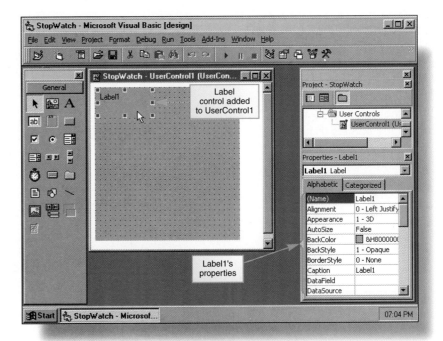

FIGURE 7-14

2 **Add three CommandButton controls to the UserControl and then position them as shown in Figure 7-15.**

Three command buttons are added (Figure 7-15).

FIGURE 7-15

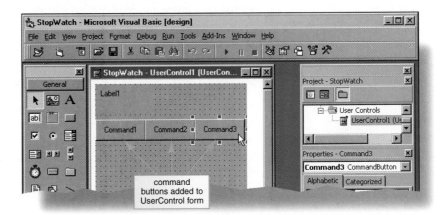

3 **Double-click the Timer button in the Toolbox and then drag the Timer control to the location shown in Figure 7-16.**

A Timer control (Timer1) is added (Figure 7-16).

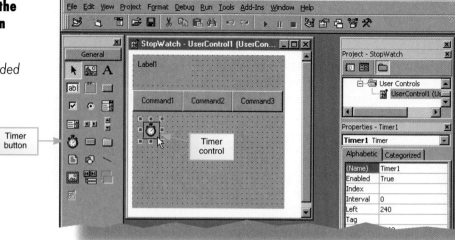

FIGURE 7-16

4 **Drag the lower-right corner of the UserControl upward and to the left to the size shown in Figure 7-17.**

UserControl borders can be dragged in the same way as a form's borders (Figure 7-17).

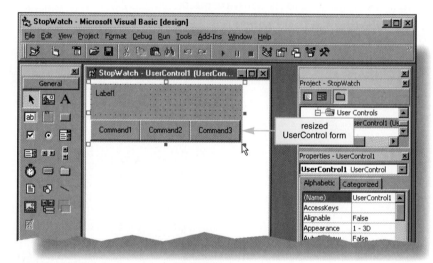

FIGURE 7-17

You can set the size of a UserControl by dragging its borders within the Designer window or by entering values of its Height and Width in the Properties window. The size you set is the default size the UserControl will have when it is added to a form by double-clicking its button in the Toolbox.

Once you have created the control's interface, the next step is to set properties of the UserControl and its constituent controls.

Setting Constituent Control Properties

The StWatch control contains a **Timer control** that is used to update the display of elapsed time. A Timer control has only one event — the Timer event. The **Timer event** occurs when a preset interval for a Timer control has elapsed. The interval's frequency is stored in the control's **Interval property**, which specifies the length of time in milliseconds. You use the Interval property to set the number of milliseconds between calls to a Timer control's Timer event from 1 to 65,535.

The Timer control's **Enabled property** determines whether or not the control responds to the passage of time. You set Enabled to False to turn a Timer control off and to True to turn it on. When a Timer control is enabled, its countdown always starts from the value of its Interval property setting. When it reaches the end of the countdown, it executes whatever code you have added to the Timer event procedure.

In the StWatch control, you will start and stop the Timer control by changing the value of its Enabled property through code statements in the CommandButton Click events. For the Timer event to update the elapsed time every one second, you will set its Interval property equal to 1000.

The additional constituent control properties whose values are different from their default values are listed in Table 7-1.

Similar to controls on a form, constituent control properties can be set in the Properties window during the UserControl's design time or through code statements within the UserControl's procedures. Perform the following steps to set properties of the StWatch UserControl and its constituent controls.

TABLE 7-1		
CONTROL	**PROPERTY**	**VALUE**
UserControl1	**Name**	**StWatch**
Timer1	**Interval**	**1000**
Timer1	**Enabled**	**False**
Command1	**Caption**	**Start**
Command2	**Caption**	**Stop**
Command3	**Caption**	**Reset**
Label1	**Alignment**	**Center**
Label1	**FontSize**	**14**
Label1	**Caption**	**00:00**
Label1	**BorderStyle**	**Fixed Single**

TO SET CONSTITUENT CONTROL PROPERTIES

1 Select UserControl1 by clicking it in the Designer window or by clicking its name in the Properties list box in the Properties window.

2 Double-click the Name property.

3 Type StWatch and then press the ENTER key.

4 Change the remaining properties listed in Table 7-1.

The StWatch control displays as shown in Figure 7-18.

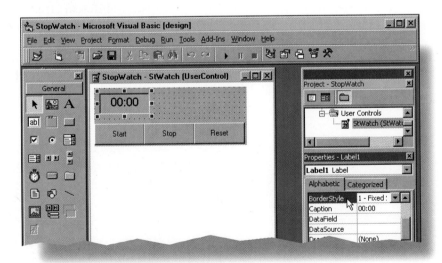

FIGURE 7-18

You have created the UserControl interface and set properties of the UserControl and its constituent controls. Now, you must write code just as you do when developing Standard EXE applications. The code writing for the UserControl is presented in two sections — writing event procedures and writing property procedures.

Writing UserControl Event Procedures

The process for writing event procedures for a UserControl and its constituent controls is the same as if you were creating a desktop application and writing event code for the form and its controls. In fact, you can think of the event code for the StWatch control as though the StWatch was a form with several controls on it.

TABLE 7-2

CONTROL	EVENT	ACTIONS
General	Declarations	Creates a variable to count elapsed time.
UserControl1	Resize	Adjusts the size and locations of constituent controls proportional to the UserControl's size.
Timer1	Timer	Increments elapsed time; displays elapsed time as a caption of the constituent Label control.
Command1	Click	Starts the constituent Timer control.
Command2	Click	Stops the constituent Timer control.
Command3	Click	Sets elapsed time = 0; displays elapsed time as a caption of the constituent Label control.

The control, event, and actions that you must code for the StWatch control are listed in Table 7-2.

Within the StWatch control, a variable is used to keep track of elapsed seconds from Timer start to Timer stop. The variable is named **TotalSeconds**. The Integer data type is appropriate because the number of elapsed seconds is always an integer and the Integer data type has a maximum value equivalent of over nine hours (32,767 from Table 5-4 on page VB 5.29). Because the TotalSeconds variable must be available to both the Timer1_Timer event and the Command3_Click event (Table 7-2) its scope is extended to the module level by declaring it in the general declarations section.

The **Resize event** occurs when a form or a UserControl first is displayed and when the size changes. When the StWatch control is added to a form by double-clicking or when a user draws the StWatch control on a form or drags its borders, its constituent controls should adjust their sizes and positions automatically.

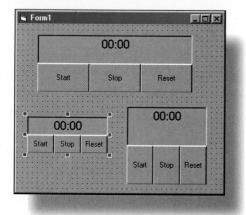

FIGURE 7-19

Figure 7-19 shows three StWatch controls added to a form during design time. Each of the controls is a different size, but the constituent controls always have the same *relative* size and position, as listed in Table 7-3.

When you write the **UserControl1_Resize event procedure**, you will shorten the amount of code needed to accomplish the actions described in Table 7-3 by using the With statement presented in Project 4.

TABLE 7-3

CONTROL	TOP	LEFT	HEIGHT	WIDTH
Label1	0	0	½ UserControl.Height	UserControl.Width
Command1	½ UserControl.Height	0	½ UserControl.Height	1/3 UserControl.Width
Command2	½ UserControl.Height	1/3 UserControl.Width	½ UserControl.Height	1/3 UserControl.Width
Command3	½ UserControl.Height	2/3 UserControl.Width	½ UserControl.Height	1/3 UserControl.Width

The Timer1_Timer event will execute every one second when its Enabled property is True. Elapsed time will be counted as `TotalSeconds = TotalSeconds + 1`. The integer number minutes of elapsed time is calculated using the **integer division operator** (\) as `TotalSeconds \ 60`. The seconds is the remainder of TotalSeconds after the integer division. This is calculated using the Mod operator. The **Mod operator** is used to divide two numbers and return only the remainder, such as `seconds = TotalSeconds Mod 60`.

Perform the following steps to write the StWatch control's event procedures.

 Steps To Write UserControl Event Procedures

1 **Click the View Code button in the Project window. Select General in the Object list box and then select Declarations in the Procedure list box. Type the code shown in Figure 7-20.**

The General_Declarations event procedure displays as shown in Figure 7-20.

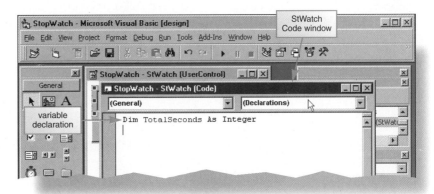

FIGURE 7-20

2 **Select UserControl in the Object list box, select Resize in the Procedure list box, and type the code shown in Figure 7-21.**

The UserControl_Resize event procedure displays as shown in Figure 7-21.

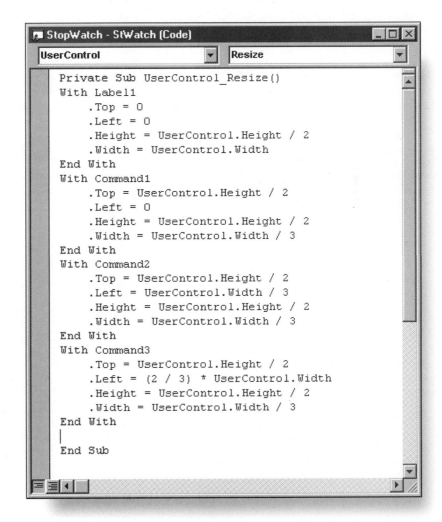

```
StopWatch - StWatch (Code)
UserControl                    Resize
   Private Sub UserControl_Resize()
   With Label1
       .Top = 0
       .Left = 0
       .Height = UserControl.Height / 2
       .Width = UserControl.Width
   End With
   With Command1
       .Top = UserControl.Height / 2
       .Left = 0
       .Height = UserControl.Height / 2
       .Width = UserControl.Width / 3
   End With
   With Command2
       .Top = UserControl.Height / 2
       .Left = UserControl.Width / 3
       .Height = UserControl.Height / 2
       .Width = UserControl.Width / 3
   End With
   With Command3
       .Top = UserControl.Height / 2
       .Left = (2 / 3) * UserControl.Width
       .Height = UserControl.Height / 2
       .Width = UserControl.Width / 3
   End With

   End Sub
```

FIGURE 7-21

3 Select Timer1 in the Object list box, select Timer in the Procedure list box, and type the code shown in Figure 7-22.

The Timer1_Timer event procedure displays as shown in Figure 7-22.

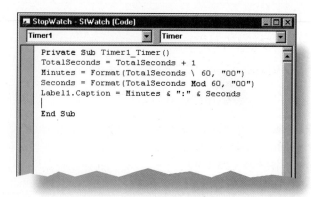

```
StopWatch - StWatch (Code)
Timer1                          Timer
    Private Sub Timer1_Timer()
    TotalSeconds = TotalSeconds + 1
    Minutes = Format(TotalSeconds \ 60, "00")
    Seconds = Format(TotalSeconds Mod 60, "00")
    Label1.Caption = Minutes & ":" & Seconds

    End Sub
```

FIGURE 7-22

4 Select Command1 in the Object list box, select Click in the Procedure list box, and type the code shown in Figure 7-23.

The Command1_Click event procedure displays as shown in Figure 7-23.

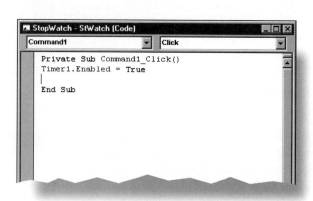

```
StopWatch - StWatch (Code)
Command1                        Click
    Private Sub Command1_Click()
    Timer1.Enabled = True

    End Sub
```

FIGURE 7-23

5 Select Command2 in the Object list box and then type the code shown in Figure 7-24.

The Command2_Click event procedure displays as shown in Figure 7-24.

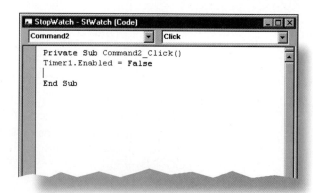

```
StopWatch - StWatch (Code)
Command2                        Click
    Private Sub Command2_Click()
    Timer1.Enabled = False

    End Sub
```

FIGURE 7-24

6 Select Command3 in the Object list box and then type the code shown in Figure 7-25.

The Command3_Click event procedure displays as shown in Figure 7-25.

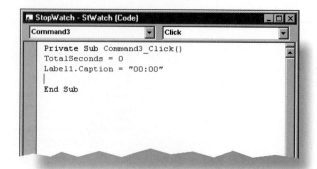

```
StopWatch - StWatch (Code)
Command3                        Click
    Private Sub Command3_Click()
    TotalSeconds = 0
    Label1.Caption = "00:00"

    End Sub
```

FIGURE 7-25

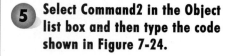
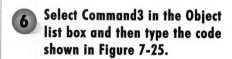
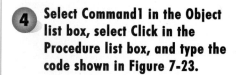

The event procedures for the constituent controls are complete. The next step in the code writing activity is to write property procedures.

Writing UserControl Property Procedures

Every ActiveX control you create automatically has a default set of properties and property values that display in the Properties list. When you are creating an ActiveX control, you also have access to all of the properties of its constituent controls. When the ActiveX control is added to a project, however, you can access only the properties of the UserControl. You no longer can access the properties of the constituent controls directly.

The way that you access the *internal* behavior of the UserControl's constituent controls is to create new properties at the UserControl level and then use changes in those properties to activate changes in the properties of the constituent controls. You write the code to accomplish this in Property procedures. **Property procedures** allow you to execute code when a property value is set or retrieved. You also can use Property procedures to create your own properties.

The typical property will be made up of a pair of Property procedures—a **Property Get procedure** retrieves the value of a property and a **Property Let procedure** assigns a value to a property.

The StWatch control has two additional properties that are used to take values assigned to those UserControl properties and map them to properties of its constituent controls. The Buttons property of the StWatch control gives the user a choice of whether or not the three command buttons in the StWatch are visible. The value of the Buttons property is Boolean (True or False) and these values map directly to the True/False values of the Visible property of the three command buttons. The statement

```
StWatch1.Buttons = False
```

will change the Visible property of the three constituent CommandButtons to False.

If a user of your control decides to make the Buttons property False, then a way is required for the user to start, stop, and reset the StWatch control through code. Recall that when you use a code statement to set the Value property of a CommandButton control equal to True, the CommandButton control's Click event is activated. The second property you will add is the **Action property**. Its values of 1, 2, or 3 will change the Value property of the corresponding CommandButton control to True. The statement

```
StWatch.Action = 2
```

will activate the Click event of the constituent control Command2 (which stops the StopWatch control by setting the Timer control's Enabled property to False). The reason you will not create a True/False Action property that maps to the True/False values of the Timer's Enabled property, is that you need a third (reset) value of the Action property.

At this point you may be thinking that the Action property is more like a method than a property. In Project 2, you opened the Color dialog box by applying the ShowColor method to the CommonDialog control as follows:

```
CommonDialog1.ShowColor
```

You also can display the Color dialog box by setting the CommonDialog control's Action property equal to 3:

```
CommonDialog1.Action = 3
```

◆ **M**ore *About*
Property Pages

A property page presents groups of properties as tabbed pages of a Property sheet. You can open a control's Property Pages dialog box by double-clicking its Custom property in the Properties list. When you create an ActiveX control, properties that you create using Property procedures are shown automatically in the Properties window. You also can connect your control to Property Pages. Refer to Visual Basic Books Online to learn how to create a property page for your controls.

In earlier versions of Visual Basic the Show methods did not exist for the CommonDialog control — you had to use the Action property. In Project 6, you used the statement

```
Report1.Action = 1
```

to print a Crystal Report in response to a user event. This is a property of the CrystalReport control, but it could have been implemented as a method. As the above examples suggest, implementation as a property or a method is sometimes ambiguous and even arbitrary. Although some general guidelines are available for which implementation to use, they are beyond the scope of this discussion.

A UserControl's **WriteProperties event** occurs when an instance of an object is to be saved. This event signals to the object that the state of the object needs to be saved, so the state can be restored later. For example, if you set the BorderStyle property of a label to 1 – Fixed Single, you can close the application, and when you open it later, the Label control's BorderStyle property is still Fixed Single. The **ReadProperties event** occurs when loading an old instance of an object that has a saved state.

The state (property values) of a control are saved within a PropertyBag object. A **PropertyBag object** is passed into an object through the ReadProperties event and the WriteProperties event in order to save and restore the state of the object. Using the methods of the PropertyBag object, the object can read or write properties of itself. The **ReadProperty method** of the PropertyBag object is used to read a value for a property, while the **WriteProperty method** of the PropertyBag object is used to write a value of a property.

The **PropertyChanged method** notifies the object's container (a form in this case) that a property's value has been changed. By notifying the container that a property's value has changed, the container can update the Property window with the new values of the object's properties. Also, this method notifies the container to activate the WriteProperties event to store the new value of the property. Properties that are available only at run time (such as the StWatch's Action property) do not need to call the PropertyChanged method.

The code procedures for implementing the Buttons and Actions properties of the StWatch control are described in Table 7-4.

More *About*
ReadProperty and WriteProperty Methods

The WriteProperty method has three arguments (parts): a string expression that represents the data value to be placed in the property bag, the data value to save in the property bag, and the default value for the data. The ReadProperty method has two arguments: a string expression that represents a data value in the property bag and a value to be returned if no value is present in the property bag.

TABLE 7-4

PROPERTY	PROCEDURE	ACTIONS
Buttons	Property Let	Passes the value of StWatch.Buttons to the Visible property of the constituent CommandButton controls.
Buttons	Property Get	Gets the Visible property of the constituent CommandButton controls as the value of StWatch.Buttons.
Buttons	UserControl_WriteProperties	Saves the application design-time setting of the Buttons property.
Buttons	UserControl_ReadProperties	Gets the saved setting of the Buttons property.
Action	Property Let	Lets the run-time change in the value of StWatch.Action trigger the constituent CommandButton Click events.

Perform the following steps to write the Property procedures for the StWatch control.

1 **Click Tools on the menu bar and point to Add Procedure.**

The Tools menu displays (Figure 7-26).

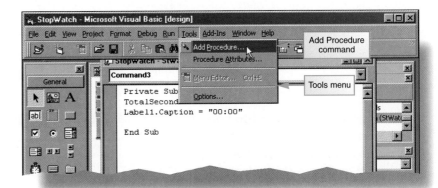

FIGURE 7-26

2 **Click Add Procedure. In the Add Procedure dialog box, type** Buttons **in the Name text box, click Property, and then point to the OK button.**

The Add Procedure dialog box displays as shown in Figure 7-27.

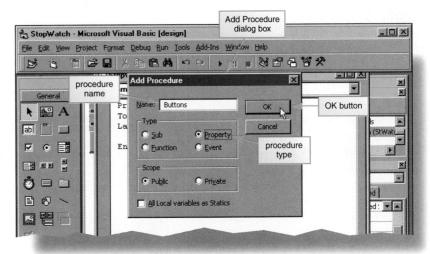

FIGURE 7-27

3 **Click the OK button. Click the Procedure box arrow in the Code window.**

The Code window displays the Buttons [PropertyGet] procedure. A Buttons [PropertyLet] procedure also has been added to the General event (Figure 7-28).

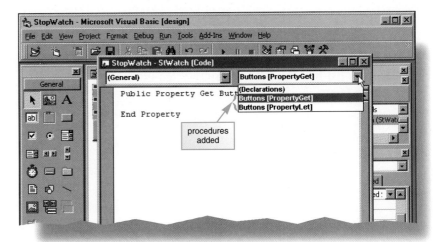

FIGURE 7-28

4 **In the first line of the Buttons [Property Get] procedure, type** Boolean **to change the Variant data type. Type the remaining code shown in Figure 7-29.**

The Buttons [PropertyGet] procedure displays as shown in Figure 7-29.

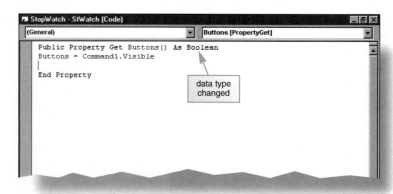

FIGURE 7-29

5 **Click Buttons [Property Let] in the Procedure list box. In the first line of the procedure, type** Boolean **to change the Variant data type. Type the code shown in Figure 7-30.**

The Buttons [PropertyLet] procedure displays as shown in Figure 7-30.

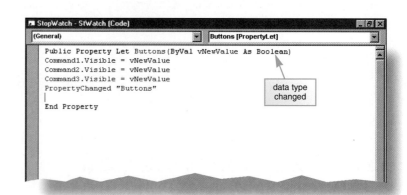

FIGURE 7-30

6 **Select UserControl in the Object list box. Select WriteProperties in the Procedure list box. Type the code shown in Figure 7-31.**

The UserControl_WriteProperties event procedure displays as shown in Figure 7-31.

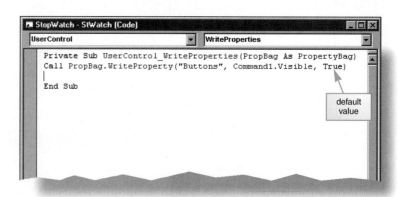

FIGURE 7-31

7 **Select ReadProperties in the Procedure list box. Type the code shown in Figure 7-32.**

The UserControl_ReadProperties event procedure displays as shown in Figure 7-32.

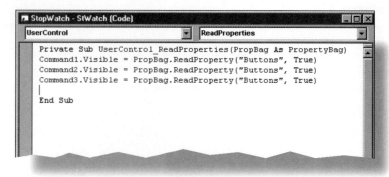

FIGURE 7-32

8 Click Tools on the menu bar and then click Add Procedure. In the Add Procedure dialog box, type `Action` in the Name text box, click Property, and point to the OK button.

The Add Procedure dialog box displays as shown in Figure 7-33.

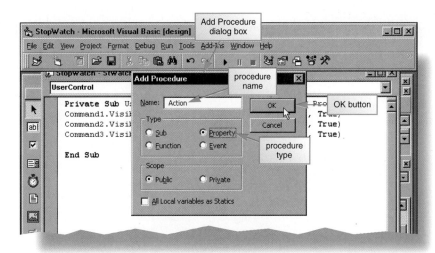

FIGURE 7-33

9 Click the OK button. Click Action [Property Let] in the Procedure list box. Type the code shown in Figure 7-34.

The Action [PropertyLet] procedure displays as shown in Figure 7-34.

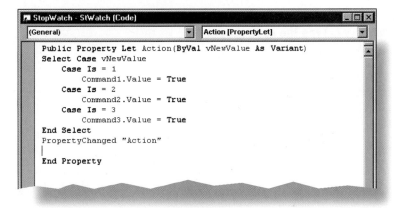

FIGURE 7-34

10 Click Tools on the menu bar and then click Procedure Attributes. In the Procedure Attributes dialog box, click the Advanced button. Click Hide this member attribute to select it and then point to the OK button.

The Procedure Attributes dialog box displays as shown in Figure 7-35.

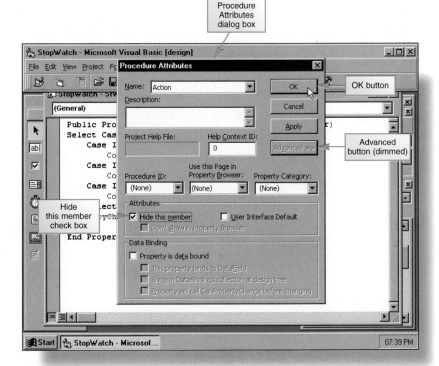

FIGURE 7-35

Click the OK button.

The Procedure Attributes dialog box closes (Figure 7-36).

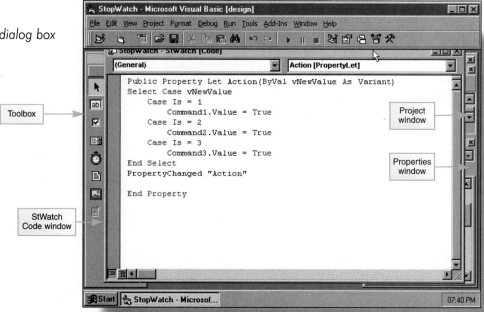

FIGURE 7-36

In Step 10, you selected the Hide this member attribute to keep the Action property from appearing in the Properties list. It was not necessary to write a PropertyGet or ReadProperties procedure and WriteProperties statements for the Action property because the Action property will be used only at run time.

Saving, Testing, and Compiling ActiveX Controls

The StWatch control is complete. Before compiling it as an .ocx file, you will save the ActiveX project and test both design-time and run-time behavior of the StWatch control.

Saving an ActiveX Project

Like forms, UserControls are stored in plain text files that contain the source code and property values of the UserControl and its constituent controls. Visual Basic uses the **.ctl extension** for these source files. If a UserControl or its constituent controls use graphical elements, which cannot be stored as plain text, such as bitmaps, Visual Basic stores those elements in a **.ctx file** with the same name you give to the .ctl file. This is similar to the **.frx files** used to store graphical elements used in forms. The ActiveX project is stored in a project file (.vbp), similarly to Standard EXE project files.

Perform the following steps to save the ActiveX control project.

TO SAVE AN ACTIVEX CONTROL PROJECT

1 Click the Save Project button on the toolbar.

2 In the Save File As dialog box, click the Save in box arrow and then select the StWatchOCX folder in the C:\Project 7 folder.

3 Type StWatch in the File name box.

4 Click the Save button in the Save File As dialog box.

5 In the Save Project As dialog box, type StWatchOCX in the File name box.

6 Click the Save button.

7 Click the Project window.

The UserControl is saved as StWatch.ctl and the project is saved as StWatchOCX.vbp (Figure 7-37).

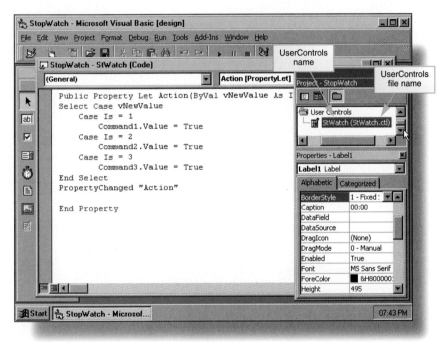

FIGURE 7-37

Adding Multiple Projects to the Visual Basic IDE

Your StWatch control is ready to be tested. You should test the control during both design time and run time. One way to do this is to compile the control as an .ocx file, open a new Standard EXE project, add the control to the Standard EXE project to test it during design time, and then run the Standard EXE project to test the control during run time. A limitation of this method is that if you need to revise the control, you must close the test project, reopen the ActiveX project, make changes, and then compile the control again before testing it again. Visual Basic version 5 provides a more efficient way to test and revise your control.

Version 5 is the first version of Visual Basic that allows you to have multiple projects open in the Visual Basic IDE at the same time. This allows you to open a new Standard EXE project for testing your ActiveX control, while your ActiveX project is still open. In this way, you can test and debug the StWatch control before you compile the StWatch control as an .ocx file.

Perform the following steps to add a second project to the Visual Basic IDE.

Steps To Add a Second Project

1 **Click File on the menu bar and then point to Add Project.**

The File menu displays (Figure 7-38).

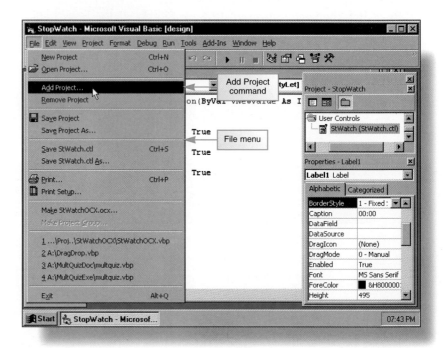

FIGURE 7-38

2 **Click Add Project. In the Add Project dialog box, click the New tab and then point to the Standard EXE icon.**

The New tab sheet in the Add Project dialog box displays (Figure 7-39).

FIGURE 7-39

3 Double-click the Standard EXE icon, drag the bottom border of the Project window down to show both projects, and point to the StWatch button (custom control) in the Toolbox.

All projects currently open display in the Project window and the StWatch control is disabled in the Toolbox (Figure 7-40).

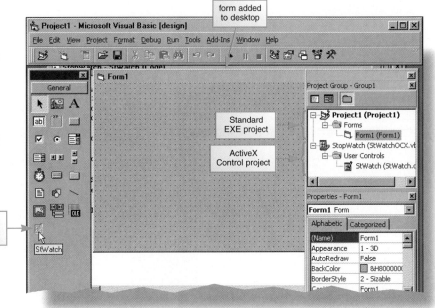

FIGURE 7-40

Other Ways

1. Press ALT+F, press D

In Figure 7-40, you see that the StWatch button is not available for you to use in the new project. This is because the Designer window still is open on the desktop. You will see in the following steps that when you close the ActiveX Designer window, the control becomes available in the Toolbox of your test project.

Testing an ActiveX Control

To test the Action property of the control, you will add three command buttons with click event procedures as listed in Table 7-5.

Perform the following steps to test the StWatch control.

TABLE 7-5

CONTROL	CLICK EVENT PROCEDURE
Command1	StWatch1.Action = 1
Command2	StWatch1.Action = 2
Command3	StWatch1.Action = 3

Steps To Test an ActiveX Control

1 Double-click StWatch (StWatch.ctl) in the Project window and then point to the StopWatch Designer window's Close button.

The Designer window becomes the active window (Figure 7-41).

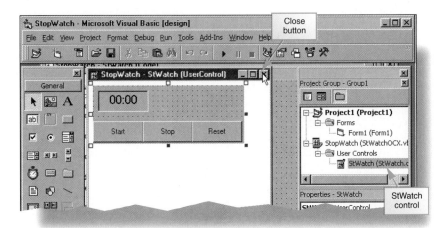

FIGURE 7-41

2 **Click the Designer window's Close button.**

The Designer window closes and the StWatch button now is available in the Toolbox (Figure 7-42).

StWatch button (available)

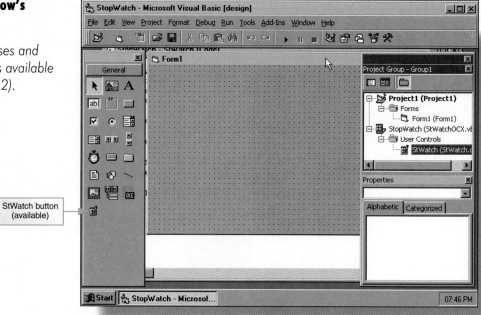

FIGURE 7-42

3 **Resize the form so the Properties window is visible. Extend the top border of the Properties window. Double-click the StWatch button in the Toolbox.**

A default-sized control, StWatch1, is added to the form (Figure 7-43).

StWatch control added to form

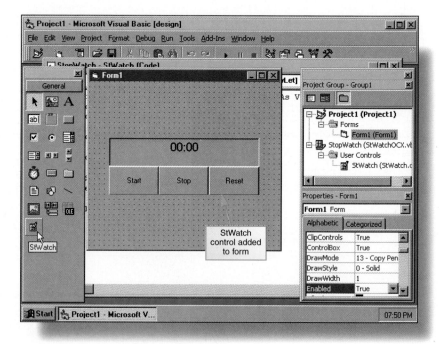

FIGURE 7-43

4 ▸ **Drag the borders of the control to test its resize functionality. Click the Start button on the toolbar. Click each of the command buttons on the control to test its functionality. Click the End button on the toolbar.**

The control is shown during the runtime test in Figure 7-44.

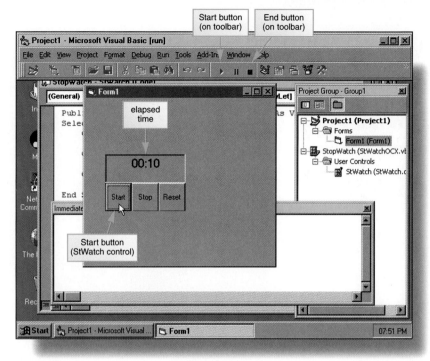

FIGURE 7-44

5 ▸ **Click the form, click StWatch1 in the Properties list box in the Properties window and then double-click the Buttons property.**

The Buttons property changes from True to False and the command buttons in the StWatch control are no longer visible (Figure 7-45).

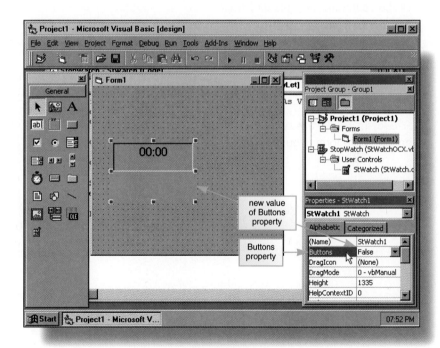

FIGURE 7-45

6 **Add three command buttons to the form, with captions of Start, Stop, and Reset. Write Click event procedures for each as shown in Table 7-5 on page VB 7.25.**

Three command buttons are added to the form (Figure 7-46).

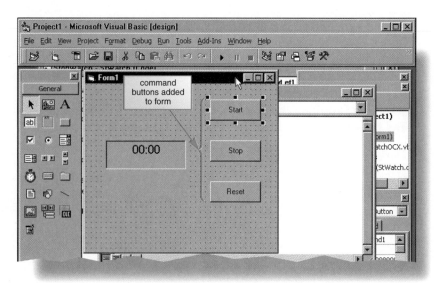

FIGURE 7-46

7 **Start the test project, click each of the command buttons and then end the test project.**

The project is shown after Command1 has been clicked in Figure 7-47.

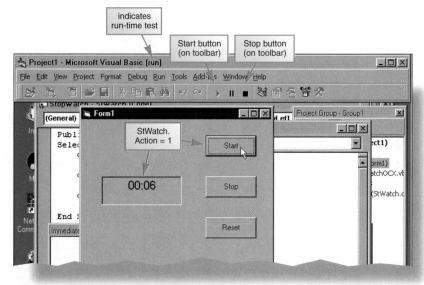

FIGURE 7-47

OtherWays

1. To run a project, press F5

The design-time and run-time tests of the StWatch control were successful. If they were not, you would return to the StWatch project's Designer and Code windows to make any necessary changes.

Compiling an ActiveX Control

The StWatch control exists currently as a .ctl file. You can add a .ctl file to a Standard EXE project and the control will be added to the Toolbox and can be used n the project. When you make the project an .exe file, the control is incorporated into the .exe file and you do not need a separate file for the control.

At least two disadvantages of this method exist, however. First, if you create a newer version of the control later on, you would have to rebuild the project. Second, every project that used the control would have to have the .ctl file incorporated into its .exe file. On the other hand, if the control were available as an .ocx control, it would be available to all applications and would be easy to replace with an updated version.

Perform the following steps to compile the StWatch control, open a new Standard EXE project, and add the StWatch control to the Toolbox.

 To Compile an ActiveX Control

1 **Double-click StWatch (StWatch.ctl) in the Project window.**

The Designer window becomes active (Figure 7-48).

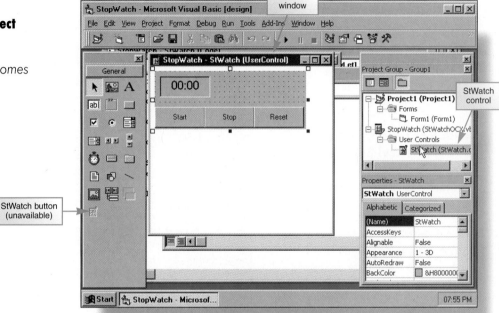

FIGURE 7-48

2 **Click File on the menu bar and then click Make StWatchOCX.ocx.**

The Make Project dialog box opens (Figure 7-49).

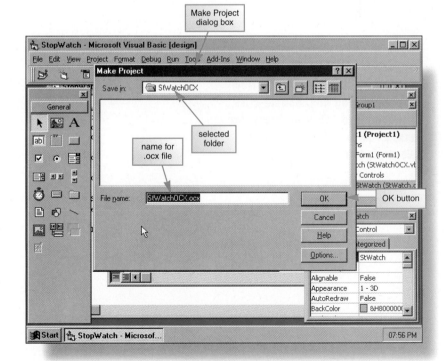

FIGURE 7-49

3 Make sure the C:\Project7\ StWatchOCX folder is selected. Type StWatch in the File name text box. Click the OK button and then click File on the menu bar. Point to New Project.

The StWatch.ocx file is created and the File menu displays (Figure 7-50).

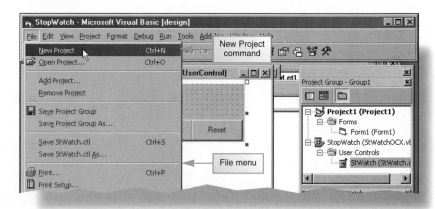

FIGURE 7-50

4 Click New Project. In the Microsoft Visual Basic dialog box, click Group1.vbg, click Project1, click Form1, and point to the Yes button.

Only the StWatchOCX.vbp and StWatch.ctl files are selected for saving changes (Figure 7-51).

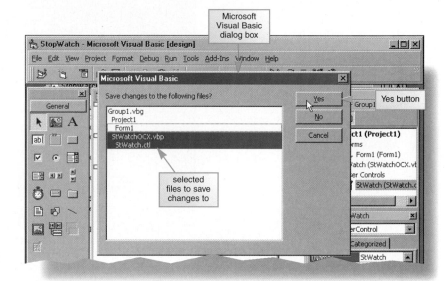

FIGURE 7-51

5 Click the Yes button. In the New Project dialog box, double-click the Standard EXE icon. Press the CTRL+T keys and then click the Controls tab.

The Components dialog opens (Figure 7-52).

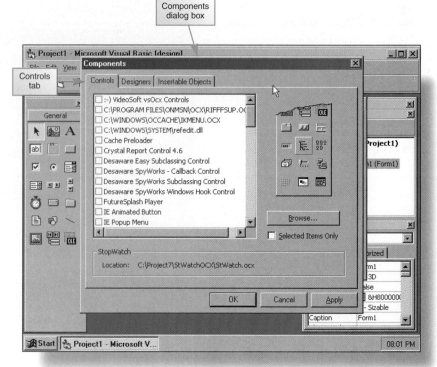

FIGURE 7-52

6 **Scroll down the components list, click the StopWatch check box, and then point to the OK button.**

The StWatch control is added to the components list and selected (Figure 7-53).

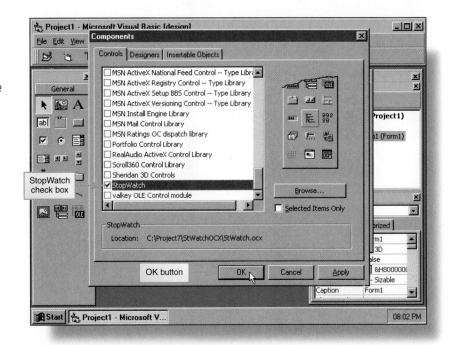

FIGURE 7-53

7 **Click the OK button and then point to the StWatch button in the Toolbox.**

The StWatch control is added to the Toolbox (Figure 7-54).

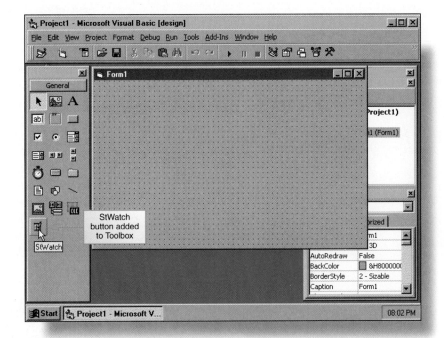

FIGURE 7-54

Other Ways

1. Press ALT+F, press K to open Make Project dialog box

Now that you have created the StWatch control, you can use it in projects like the Multiplication Quiz application.

The Multiplication Quiz Application

The completed Multiplication Quiz application is shown in Figure 7-55 as it displays on the desktop during run time. The command buttons contain graphic images instead of captions. When the mouse pointer is positioned on a command button, ToolTip text displays.

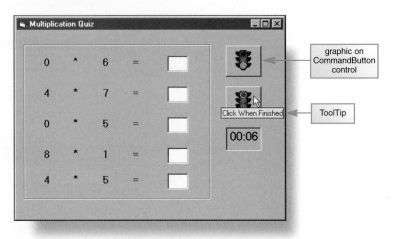

FIGURE 7-55

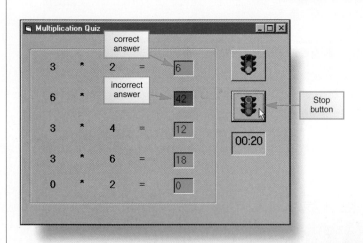

FIGURE 7-56

Each time the Start button is clicked, a new set of multiplication problems displays and the elapsed time begins to count. When the Stop button is clicked, the elapsed time stops counting and the BackColor property of the answer text boxes changes — green to indicate correct and red to indicate incorrect (Figure 7-56).

If the user resizes the Multiplication Quiz window, the controls remain centered within the application's window (Figure 7-57).

You will build the Multiplication Quiz application by creating the interface, setting properties, and writing code.

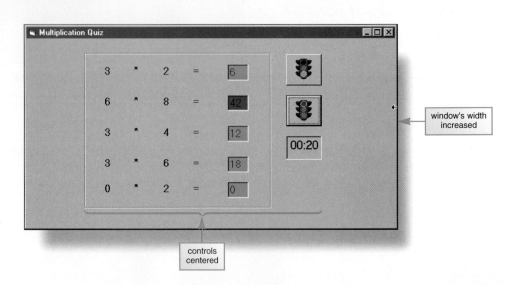

FIGURE 7-57

Creating the Interface

The Multiplication Quiz application consists of one form, one frame, four Label control arrays, one TextBox control array, two CommandButton controls, and one StWatch control as identified in Figure 7-58.

To avoid having to set multiple control properties in later steps, you will set some initial properties of the controls that will be made into arrays. In this way, all controls added to the arrays will have those properties. The properties you will set before creating the arrays are listed in Table 7-6.

The following steps create the interface for the Multiplication Quiz application.

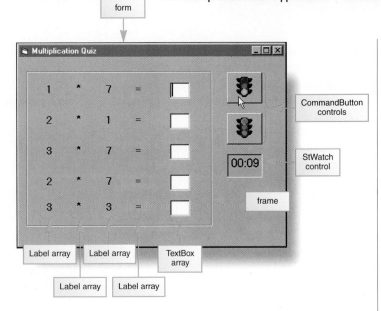

FIGURE 7-58

TABLE 7-6						
CONTROL	*NAME*	*CAPTION*	*TEXT*	*FONT SIZE*	*FONT STYLE*	*AUTOSIZE*
Label1	lblMult1	5	N/A	12	Bold	True
Label2	(default)	*	N/A	12	Bold	True
Label3	lblMult2	5	N/A	12	Bold	True
Label4	(default)	=	N/A	12	Bold	True
Text1	txtProduct	N/A	25	12	Regular	N/A

 Steps To Create the Multiplication Quiz Interface

1 **Double-click the Frame button in the Toolbox. Adjust the size of the form, frame, and Properties window as shown in Figure 7-59.**

A Frame control is added to the form (Figure 7-59).

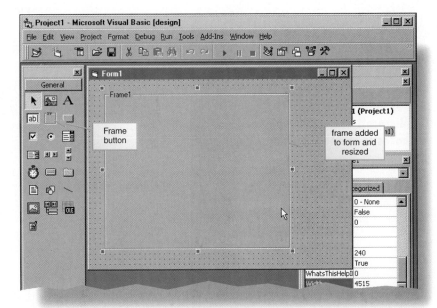

FIGURE 7-59

2 **Draw four Label controls and one TextBox control in the frame as shown in Figure 7-60. (Do not add by double-clicking.)**

By drawing the controls, the Frame becomes their container and not the form (Figure 7-60).

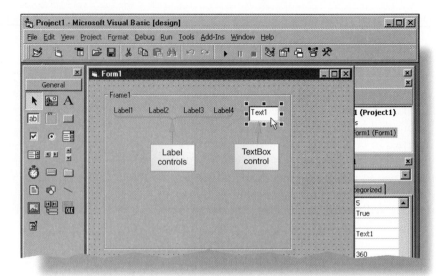

FIGURE 7-60

3 **Change the controls properties as listed in Table 7-6 on the previous page. While holding the CTRL key, click each of the four labels and the text box.**

The five controls are selected as a group (Figure 7-61).

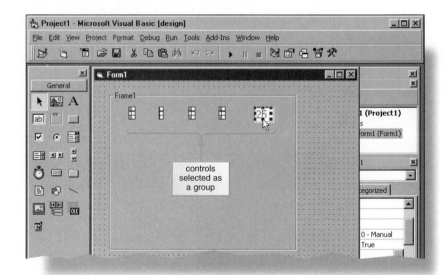

FIGURE 7-61

4 **Press the CTRL+C keys. Click an empty area of the Frame control. Press the CTRL+V keys. Click the Yes button in each of the Microsoft Visual Basic dialog boxes to create the arrays.**

Five control arrays are created and the second control in each array is added to the top of the frame (Figure 7-62).

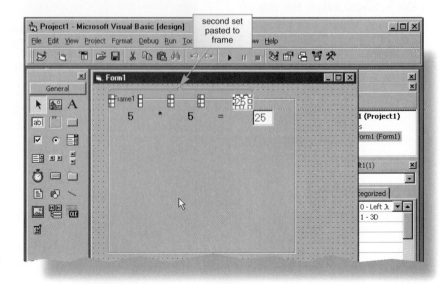

FIGURE 7-62

5 Drag the control group to the position shown in Figure 7-63. Click an empty area of the frame and then press the CTRL+V keys.

A third set of controls is added to the frame (Figure 7-63).

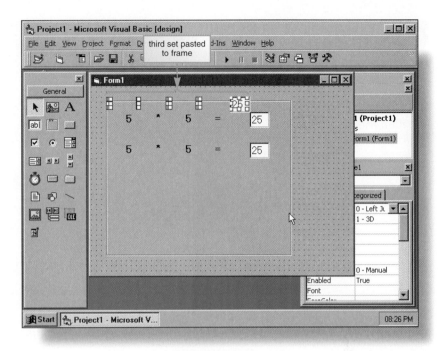

FIGURE 7-63

6 Repeat Step 5 twice to add and position a total of five sets of controls as shown in Figure 7-64.

The four Label and one Textbox arrays are complete (Figure 7-64).

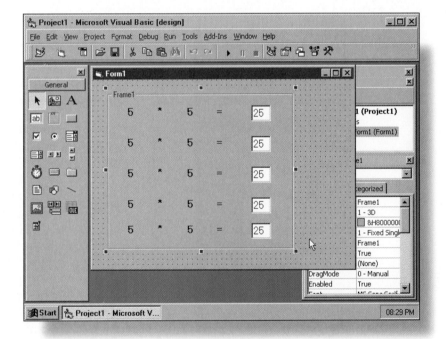

FIGURE 7-64

7 Add two CommandButton controls and one StWatch control to the form in the positions shown in Figure 7-65.

All controls have been added to the form (Figure 7-65).

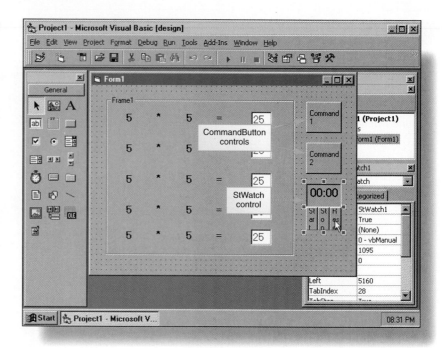

FIGURE 7-65

TABLE 7-7		
CONTROL	PROPERTY	VALUE
Form	Name	frmMultQuiz
Form	Caption	Multiplication Quiz
Frame1	Caption	(no caption)
Command1	Name	cmdStart
Command1	Caption	(no caption)
Command1	Style	1 - Graphical
Command1	Picture	GrnLite.ico
Command1	ToolTipText	Click To Start
Command2	Name	cmdStop
Command2	Caption	(no caption)
Command2	Style	1 - Graphical
Command2	Picture	RedLite.ico
Command2	ToolTipText	Click When Finished
StWatch	Buttons	False

The interface is complete. Next, you will set the properties of the controls.

Setting Properties

In addition to the FontSize, FontBold, and Caption properties of all of the Label and TextBox controls, you must change the properties listed in Table 7-7.

If a CommandButton control's **Style property** is set to 1 - Graphical, then you can use the **Picture property** of a CommandButton control to set a graphic (bitmap, icon, metafile, GIF, JPEG) to be displayed in the command button. You use the **ToolTipText property** of a control to set the text that appears as a ToolTip for that control. A **ToolTip** is a word or short phrase that describes the function of a toolbar button or other button or tool. The ToolTip displays in a small rectangle below an object when you pause the mouse pointer over the object. The two graphics (.ico) files used for the command buttons are available on the Data Disk that accompanies this book.

Perform the following steps to set properties for the controls in the Multiplication Quiz application.

TO SET PROPERTIES OF THE MULTIPLICATION QUIZ CONTROLS

1 Select the form.

2 Click Name in the Properties window and then type frmMultQuiz as the name of the form.

③ Change each of the properties of each of the controls as listed in Table 7-7.

④ Click the form.

The Multiplication Quiz interface displays as show in Figure 7-66.

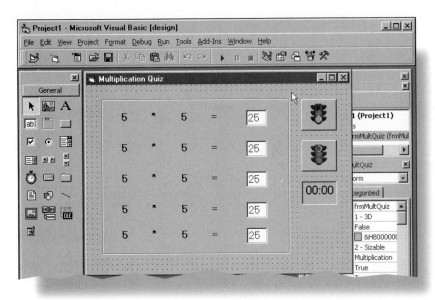

FIGURE 7-66

Writing Code

The Multiplication Quiz application consists of only three event procedures, as described in Table 7-8.

The **Form_Resize event procedure** will be used to keep the controls in the Multiplication Quiz application centered within the application's window when the user resizes it. In some of the earlier projects where the form's BorderStyle property was 2 - Sizable, expanding the size of the window shifted all of the controls up and to the left in the window. This is because the controls' Top and Left properties did not change. Also, the controls retained their original sizes because resizing the form had no effect on the Height and Width properties of the controls on the form.

You can make controls' sizes and locations change in response to changes in the window's size by changing their properties in the Form_Resize event procedure in a manner similar to the way you changed the sizes and relative locations of the StWatch's constituent controls in the UserControl_Resize event procedure. The Multiplication Quiz application is shown as it displays at the start of run time in Figure 7-67.

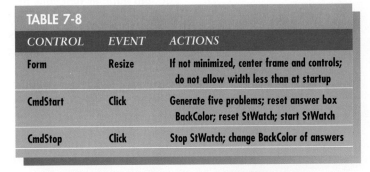

TABLE 7-8		
CONTROL	*EVENT*	*ACTIONS*
Form	**Resize**	If not minimized, center frame and controls; do not allow width less than at startup
CmdStart	**Click**	Generate five problems; reset answer box BackColor; reset StWatch; start StWatch
CmdStop	**Click**	Stop StWatch; change BackColor of answers

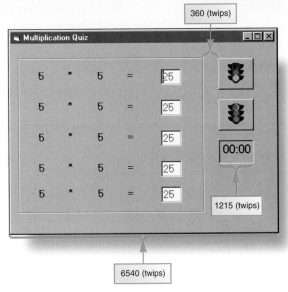

FIGURE 7-67

The Form_Resize event procedure must recognize and respond to three different states:

▶ User minimizes — do nothing
▶ Not minimized and user drags width less than original — return to original width
▶ User makes width greater than original (drags or maximizes) — reposition controls

The code to accomplish these is as follows:

```
If frmMultQuiz.WindowState = 1 Then
        'do nothing
ElseIf frmMultQuiz.Width < 6540 Then
        frmMultQuiz.Width = 6540
Else
        Frame1.Left = (frmMultQuiz.ScaleWidth - Frame1.Width - 360 - 1215) / 2
        cmdStart.Left = Frame1.Left + Frame1.Width + 360
        cmdStop.Left = Frame1.Left + Frame1.Width + 360
        StWatch1.Left = Frame1.Left + Frame1.Width + 360
End If
```

Compare the code above to Figure 7-67 on the previous page to note that 6540 is the startup width of the form, 360 is a fixed margin between the frame and command buttons, and 1215 is the width of the command buttons.

The **cmdStart_Click event procedure** must reset the answer text boxes' BackColor property; generate and display five problems; and reset and start the StWatch control. The problems are generated using a random number function. **Random number functions** are used in applications to model events whose outcome is uncertain. The Multiplication Quiz application generates randomly five sets of multipliers and multiplicands whose values are integers from 0 through 9.

The **Rnd function** returns a value less than one but greater than or equal to zero. If you generated a very large set of numbers with the Rnd function, the numbers would have a **uniform distribution**, meaning they are all equally likely to occur. You can model a system where the outcomes are equally likely and can be represented by integers over a continuous interval ranging from a known lowerbound to a known upperbound with the following function:

```
Int((upperbound - lowerbound + 1) * Rnd + lowerbound)
```

When a computer generates a sequence of random numbers, next number in the sequence is calculated as a function of the preceding number. The first number is calculated as the function of a number called the **Seed**. You can use the **Randomize statement** to set the Seed equal to a function of the system clock to produce a different Seed each time you begin generating random numbers. If you do not change the Seed before you generate the first number in a sequence, the same sequence of numbers will be generated every time.

You can use a For...Next loop to reset the answer text boxes and generate problems because you created the controls in arrays. The following code will generate a pair of multipliers and reset the answer box (five) times and then reset and start the StWatch.

More *About*
Random Numbers

All computers generate a random number in a sequence as a function of the previous number. The function is such that a large set of numbers generated this way will have a uniform distribution (an indication of randomness). Because each number is not independent from the preceding number, however, mathematicians and computer scientists call these numbers pseudo random numbers.

```
Const upperbound = 9
Const lowerbound = 0
Randomize
For Index = 0 To 4
        lblMult1(Index).Caption = Int((upperbound - lowerbound + 1) * Rnd + lowerbound)
        lblMult2(Index).Caption = Int((upperbound - lowerbound + 1) * Rnd + lowerbound)
        txtProduct(Index).Text = ""
        txtProduct(Index).BackColor = vbWhite
Next
txtProduct(0).SetFocus
StWatch1.Action = 3
StWatch1.Action = 1
```

The **cmdStop_Click event procedure** must stop the StWatch and grade the answers. The StWatch control is stopped by setting its Action property equal to 2. Although the pairs of multipliers are generated randomly, the answer can be checked by comparing the value entered in the answer text box to the product of the two numbers. If these two match, the BackColor property is set to green, and red otherwise. The code to accomplish this is placed in a loop and repeated (five) times:

```
StWatch1.Action = 2
For Index = 0 To 4
        If lblMult1(Index.Caption) * lblMult2(Index) = Val(txtProduct(Index).Text) Then
                txtProduct(Index).BackColor = vbGreen
        Else
                txtProduct(Index).BackColor = vbRed
        End If
Next
```

Perform the following steps to write the three event procedures for the Multiplication Quiz application.

 Steps **To Write Event Procedures**

① **Select the Form_Resize event procedure in the Code window. Enter the code as shown in Figure 7-68.**

The Form_Resize event procedure displays as shown in Figure 7-68.

Project1 - frmMultQuiz (Code)

Form — Resize

```
Private Sub Form_Resize()
If frmMultQuiz.WindowState = 1 Then
    'do nothing
ElseIf frmMultQuiz.Width < 6540 Then
    frmMultQuiz.Width = 6540
Else
    Frame1.Left = (frmMultQuiz.ScaleWidth - Frame1.Width - 360 - 1215) / 2
    cmdStart.Left = Frame1.Left + Frame1.Width + 360
    cmdStop.Left = Frame1.Left + Frame1.Width + 360
    StWatch1.Left = Frame1.Left + Frame1.Width + 360
End If

End Sub
```

FIGURE 7-68

2 **Select the cmdStart_Click event procedure in the Code window. Enter the code as shown in Figure 7-69.**

The cmdStart_Click event procedure displays as shown in Figure 7-69.

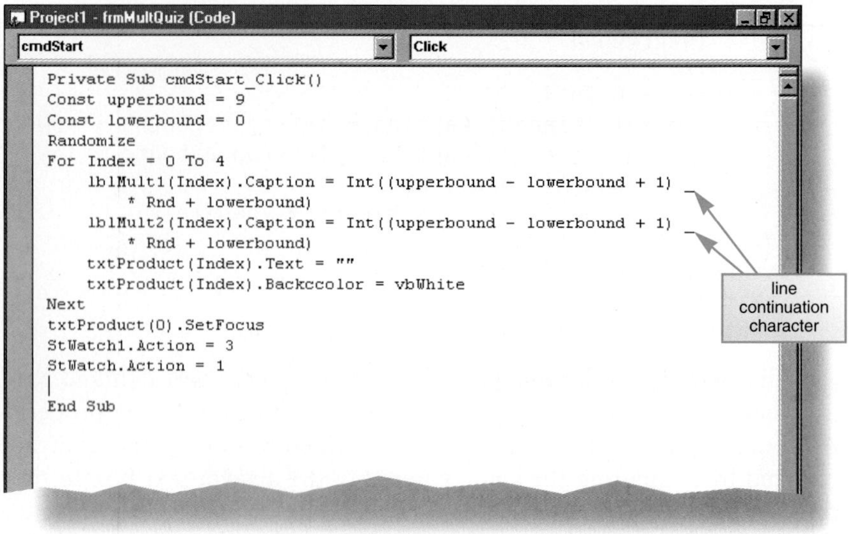

```
Project1 - frmMultQuiz (Code)
cmdStart                              Click

Private Sub cmdStart_Click()
Const upperbound = 9
Const lowerbound = 0
Randomize
For Index = 0 To 4
    lblMult1(Index).Caption = Int((upperbound - lowerbound + 1) _
        * Rnd + lowerbound)
    lblMult2(Index).Caption = Int((upperbound - lowerbound + 1) _
        * Rnd + lowerbound)
    txtProduct(Index).Text = ""
    txtProduct(Index).Backccolor = vbWhite
Next
txtProduct(0).SetFocus
StWatch1.Action = 3
StWatch.Action = 1

End Sub
```

line continuation character

FIGURE 7-69

3 **Select the cmdStop_Click event procedure in the Code window. Enter the code as shown in Figure 7-70.**

The cmdStop_Click event procedure displays as shown in Figure 7-70.

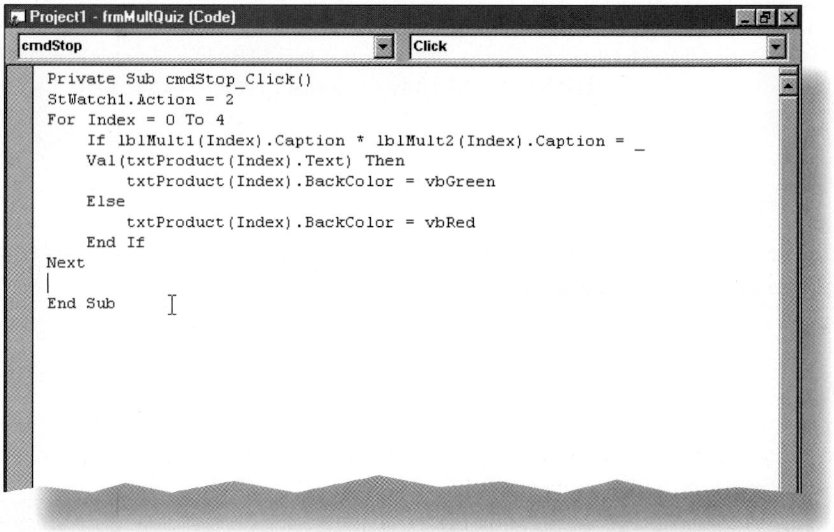

```
Project1 - frmMultQuiz (Code)
cmdStop                               Click

Private Sub cmdStop_Click()
StWatch1.Action = 2
For Index = 0 To 4
    If lblMult1(Index).Caption * lblMult2(Index).Caption = _
    Val(txtProduct(Index).Text) Then
        txtProduct(Index).BackColor = vbGreen
    Else
        txtProduct(Index).BackColor = vbRed
    End If
Next

End Sub
```

FIGURE 7-70

Saving and Testing the Multiplication Quiz Application

The Multiplication Quiz application is complete. Perform the following steps to save and test the Multiplication Quiz application.

TO SAVE AND TEST THE MULTIPLICATION QUIZ APPLICATION

1 Close the Code window and then click the Save Project button on the toolbar.

2 In the Save File As dialog, select the C:\Project7\MultQuizEXE folder, type MultQuiz in the File name box, and then click the Save button.

3 In the Save Project As dialog, select the C:\Project7\MultQuizEXE folder, type MultQuizEXE in the File name box, and then click the Save button.

④ Click the Start button on the toolbar. Click the Start button in the Multiplication Quiz.

⑤ Resize the application window.

⑥ Type answers in the answer boxes, making at least one incorrect answer.

⑦ Click the Multiplication Quiz's Stop button.

⑧ Close the Multiplication Quiz window.

The Multiplication Quiz is shown maximized during run time in Figure 7-71.

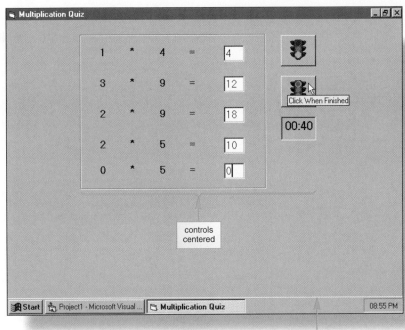

FIGURE 7-71

window maximized

Distributing, Installing, and Removing Applications

In Project 3, you learned how to make an .exe file so your Loan Calculator application could run on the desktop, outside of the Visual Basic IDE. Although the Loancalc.exe file ran successfully on your PC, it may not run on another PC. This is because a Visual Basic application's .exe file requires additional files to be able to run, and these files may or may not be present on another PC. At a minimum, an application requires the MSVBVM50.dll file, Visual Basic's **run time dll**. Other files an application may need include ActiveX controls, data files, and dynamic link libraries (.dll).

Even after you have determined the files required by your application, several reasons exist why you cannot distribute your application by simply copying those files to a floppy disk. The files likely will require more than one floppy disk, preventing the user from running the application from a floppy disk and therefore requiring the files be copied to the hard drive. You then need some way to tell the user what folders to copy the files to. If the user copies a .dll or .ocx file over a newer version of that file used by some other application, your application will run but the other one will not. Even if you get past these problems, the user will still have to create a program group and add the application to the Start menu. Finally, users expect to be able to install software by running a user-friendly setup program that manages all of these issues for them.

You can use the Visual Basic **Application Setup Wizard** to build a setup application and distribution disks for you. The Setup Wizard builds a **dependency file** that determines which files are needed and where they need to be installed on the user's machine. It then creates a setup program for the user, and compresses and writes all of the necessary files to a distribution media you select (floppy disk, network server, or the Internet).

In the next two sets of activities, you first will create a setup program and distribution disks for the Multiplication Quiz application. You then will run the setup program to install the application, test it, and then remove (uninstall) the application.

More *About*
Floppy Disk Distribution

If you plan to distribute your application on floppy disks, you can use the Setup Wizard's Floppy Disk panel to make floppy disks on your computer, or you can use the Disk Directories panel to create floppy disk images in a temporary directory on your computer or a network server. You then can copy the files manually to disks, allow users to copy them from the networked server, or provide them with a floppy disk duplication service.

Creating a Setup Program

The Setup Wizard is a separate application you can run from the Visual Basic group. The Setup Wizard is itself a Visual Basic application and also is available to you as a **.vbp project**. You can use the .vbp project to customize the setup program it creates.

Like other wizards, the Setup Wizard prompts you for information it needs through a series of dialog boxes. In most cases, the dialog boxes contain default values of the information for a *typical* setup. The Setup Wizard offers a number of advanced features and options. You may want to investigate these after you become familiar with the basics.

You will need two additional blank, formatted 1.44 MB floppy disks to use for the distribution media of your application. Perform the following steps to use the Visual Basic Application Setup Wizard to create a setup program and distribution disks for the Multiplication Quiz application.

Steps **To Create a Setup Program and Distribution Disks**

---

1 **Close Visual Basic. Click the Start button on the taskbar, point to Programs, point to Microsoft Visual Basic 5.0, and point to Application Setup Wizard.**

The Programs menu on your PC may be different from the one shown in Figure 7-72.

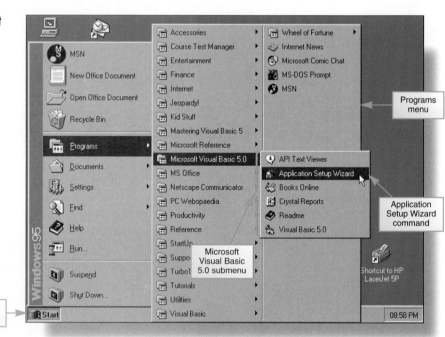

FIGURE 7-72

2 **Click Application Setup Wizard. In the Setup Wizard – Introduction panel, point to the Next button.**

The Introduction panel will not display if the Skip this screen in the future check box has been selected previously (Figure 7-73).

FIGURE 7-73

3 **Click the Next button. In the Setup Wizard – Select Project and Options panel, point to the Browse button.**

The Select Project and Options panel displays (Figure 7-74).

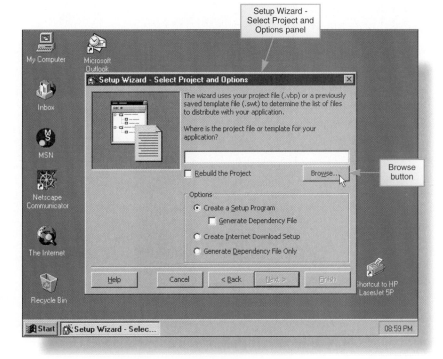

FIGURE 7-74

4 Click the Browse button. In the Locate VB application's .VBP file dialog box, click the Look in box arrow and then select the MultQuizEXE.vbp file in the MultQuizEXE folder in your Project 7 folder on drive C. Point to the Open button.

The MultQuizEXE.vbp file is selected (Figure 7-75).

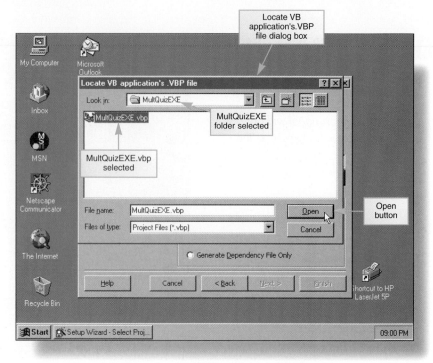

FIGURE 7-75

5 Click the Open button. In the MultQuizEXE – Setup Wizard – Select Project and Options panel, click the Generate Dependency File check box and then point to the Next button.

The Select Project and Options panel displays as shown in Figure 7-76.

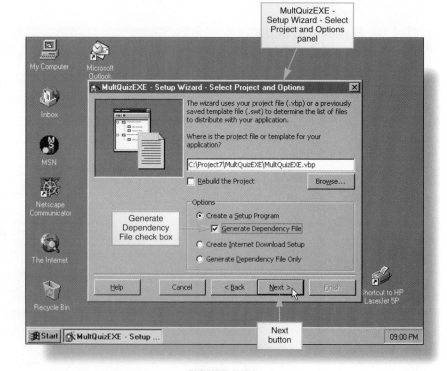

FIGURE 7-76

6 **Click the Next button. If the Missing Dependencies panel displays, click the C:\Project7\ StWatchOCX\StWatch.ocx check box and then click the Next button. In the Distribution Method panel, click Floppy disk and then point to the Next button.**

Three distribution methods are available (Figure 7-77).

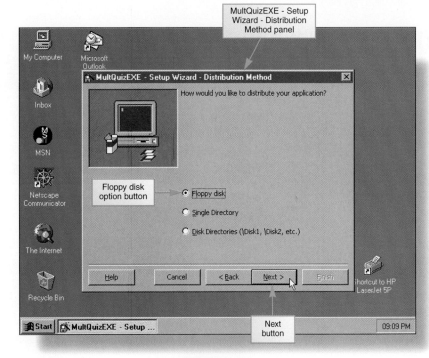

FIGURE 7-77

7 **Click the Next button. In the Floppy Disk panel, select Floppy Drive A: and then select Disk Size 1.44 MB. Point to the Next button.**

The Floppy Disk panel displays as shown in Figure 7-78.

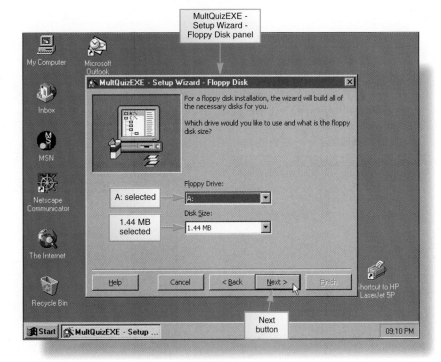

FIGURE 7-78

8 **Click the Next button. In the ActiveX Server Components panel, point to the Next button.**

The application does not use ActiveX server components (Figure 7-79).

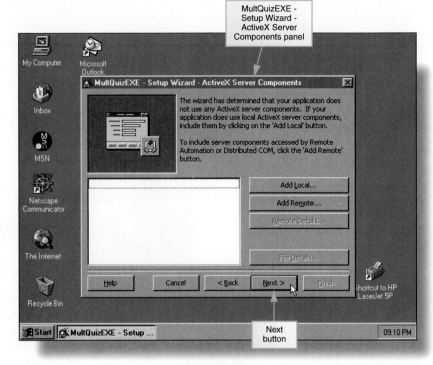

FIGURE 7-79

9 **Click the Next button. In the Confirm Dependencies panel, click the C:\Project7\ StWatchOCX\StWatch.ocx check box and then point to the Next button.**

The application has no other additional dependencies (Figure 7-80).

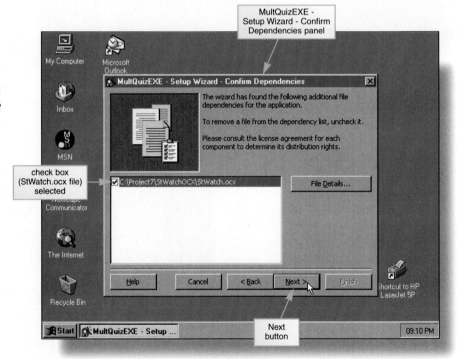

FIGURE 7-80

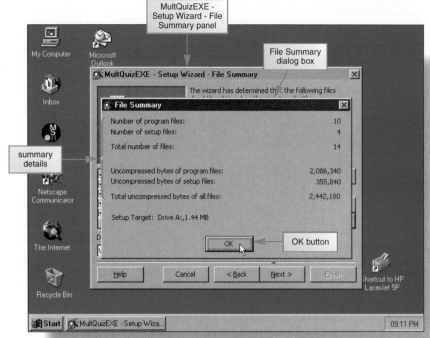

10 **Click the Next button. In the File Summary panel, click the Summary Details button. Point to the OK button.**

Fourteen files will be added to the distribution disks (Figure 7-81).

FIGURE 7-81

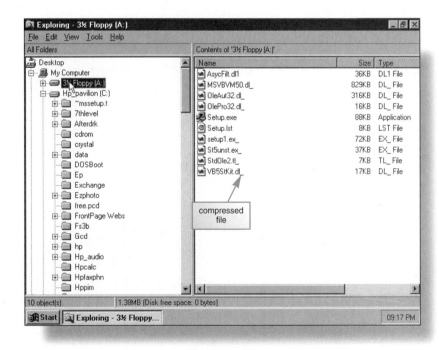

11 **Click the OK button. Click the Next button. In the Finished! panel, click the Finish button. When prompted, insert the first floppy disk and then click the OK button. When prompted, insert the second floppy disk and then click the OK button. When the Setup Wizard closes, locate your files in Windows Explorer.**

The setup is complete and the Setup Wizard closes. The files on the first floppy disk display in Windows Explorer as shown in Figure 7-82.

FIGURE 7-82

Installing, Running, and Uninstalling Applications

When the user runs the setup program, it decompresses the files, copies them to the appropriate folders after checking for newer versions, enters them in the system registry and creates a program group and Start menu links. Similar to wizards, it prompts the user for installation information and suggests default values, such as the folder where the program files will be copied.

Perform the following steps to test the Multiplication Quiz application setup program and then test the Multiplication Quiz application after it has been installed.

TO INSTALL AND RUN AN APPLICATION

1. Close all applications that currently are running.
2. Insert the first distribution disk in the 3½ Floppy [A:] drive.
3. Click the Start button on the taskbar. In the Run dialog box, click Run, type `a:\setup.exe` and then click the OK button.
4. When prompted, insert the second distribution disk and then click the OK button.
5. Click the OK button in the MultQuizEXE Setup dialog box.
6. Click the install button in the next Setup dialog box.
7. Click the OK button in the final Setup dialog box.
8. Click the Start button on the taskbar, point to Programs, click MultQuiz on the Programs submenu.
9. Test the application.
10. Click the Multiplication Quiz window's Close button.

A program group is created as shown in Figure 7-83; however, it does not display on the desktop automatically.

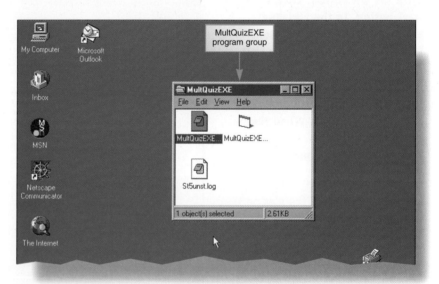

FIGURE 7-83

Removing an Application

When a user runs the setup program, an application removal utility is copied to the user's Windows folder. The setup program also creates a removal log file that contains information about which directories were created, which files were installed and where, what if any changes to the system registry were made, and which program groups, icons, and Start menu were created.

The removal utility and the log file allow the user to uninstall your application through the Add/Remove Programs utility in the Windows Control Panel. Perform the following steps to uninstall the Multiplication Quiz application.

TO UNINSTALL AN APPLICATION

① Click the Start button on the taskbar. Point to Settings and then click Control Panel.

② Double-click the Add/Remove Programs icon in the Control Panel window.

③ Click MultQuizEXE in the program list.

④ Click the Add/Remove button.

⑤ Click Yes in the Application Removal dialog box.

⑥ Click the Remove None button in the Shared Components dialog box.

⑦ Click the OK button in the Application Removal dialog box.

⑧ Close the Add/Remove Programs Properties dialog box.

⑨ Close the Control Panel window.

The Application Removal dialog box shown in Figure 7-84 indicates the application is removed successfully.

You now can copy the two floppy disks and distribute your application to any user of Windows to install it as a Standard EXE application. You may, however, want to target your application to systems that use an Internet browser, such as Internet Explorer, as the user interface. This type of user interface is becoming more popular as companies develop their own intranets and because user interaction with documents rather than applications more closely models the real world. With Visual Basic, you can create applications for this type of interface. They are called ActiveX documents.

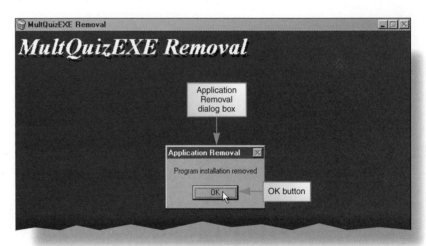

FIGURE 7-84

ActiveX Documents

A Microsoft Word document is not the same as the Microsoft Word application — the Word **document** (with the extension .doc) contains the actual content; the Word **application** (Winword.exe) is used to create the document.

A Word document can be viewed in certain other applications, called **ActiveX containers**. When you open a Word document in a container such as Internet Explorer, the Word application becomes a **server** that supplies the objects that enable the ActiveX container (such as Internet Explorer) to view and activate the document. This same mechanism works for ActiveX documents created with Visual Basic.

When you create an ActiveX document project, you are creating a Visual Basic *document* that can be contained in an ActiveX container (such as Internet Explorer). Compiling the ActiveX document creates both a Visual Basic document file (with the **.vbd extension**) and its corresponding server — which can be an ActiveX .exe file. In other words, the .vbd file is to the .doc file what the ActiveX .exe file is to the Winword.exe file. You can create ActiveX documents from scratch or you can convert existing Standard EXE projects.

More *About* **Internet Distribution**

If you have a Web site, you can link to your ActiveX documents from any Web page. This is accomplished with a combination of HMTL and VBScript. You even can create a link to your ActiveX document that causes the browser to find and download automatically all components needed to run your ActiveX document.

Converting Projects to ActiveX Documents

The process of converting your existing Standard EXE Visual Basic projects into ActiveX documents is called ActiveX Document Migration. The Visual Basic system comes with an add-in that facilitates this conversion — the **ActiveX Document Migration Wizard**. The wizard will convert automatically a form into an ActiveX document object (a file with a .dob extension). When you make the existing project an ActiveX server by making it an ActiveX.EXE file, Visual Basic also converts the document object into an ActiveX Document (file with a .vbd extension).

In order to make an ActiveX.EXE file from an existing Standard EXE project, you first must make some modifications to the project's Startup object. In Project 3, you changed the Loan Calculator's Startup object from frmLoanAbt to frmLoanCalc. In addition to a form, an application's Startup object also can be a special subroutine, Sub Main. There only can be one Sub Main in an application and you must create it within a code module rather than a form.

A code module is similar to the code section of a form. It contains declarations and procedures that you create and it exists as a separate file which can be added and removed from applications like a form. The Startup object of an ActiveX EXE project must be Sub Main, even if the Sub Main procedure does not contain any code.

Perform the following steps to convert the MultQuiz EXE project into an ActiveX EXE project and save the converted project.

More *About*
Commenting Out Code

When the Document Migration Wizard encounters code that is not supported by user documents, such as the Show and Hide methods, the code is **commented out**. This means that the code statement is left intact, but an apostrophe is placed at the beginning of the line, changing it from an instruction to a comment.

Steps **To Convert a Standard EXE Project to an ActiveX Document**

① **Start Visual Basic. Open the MultQuizEXE.vbp project, click Project on the menu bar, and point to Project1 Properties.**

The Project menu displays (Figure 7-85).

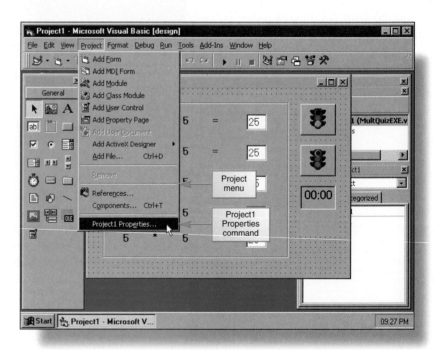

FIGURE 7-85

2 Click Project1 Properties. In the Project1 – Project Properties dialog box, click the General tab, select ActiveX EXE in the Project Type list box, and select Sub Main in the Startup Object list box. Type `MultQuizDOC` in the Project Name text box and then point to the OK button.

The Project1 - Project Properties dialog box displays as shown in Figure 7-86.

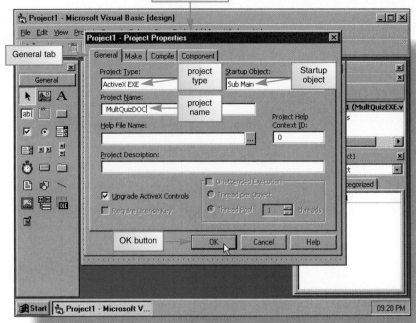

FIGURE 7-86

3 Click the OK button. Click Project on the menu bar and point to Add Module.

The Project menu displays (Figure 7-87).

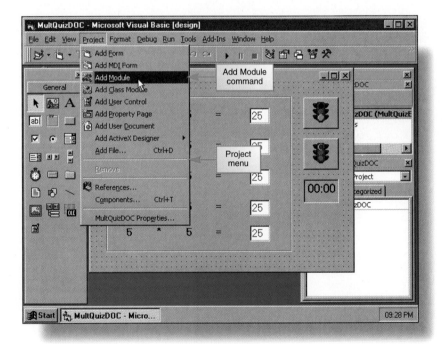

FIGURE 7-87

4 **Click Add Module. In the Add Module dialog box, point to Module on the New tab sheet.**

The Add Module dialog box displays (Figure 7-88).

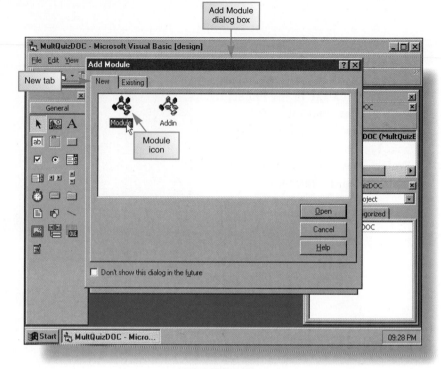

FIGURE 7-88

5 **Double-click Module. Click Tools on the menu bar and point to Add Procedure.**

A Code window for the new module is added to the desktop and the Tools menu displays (Figure 7-89).

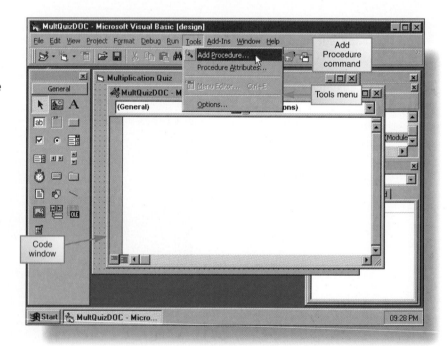

FIGURE 7-89

6 Click Add Procedure. In the Add Procedure dialog box, type Main in the Name text box, click Sub, and point to the OK button.

The Add Procedure dialog box displays (Figure 7-90).

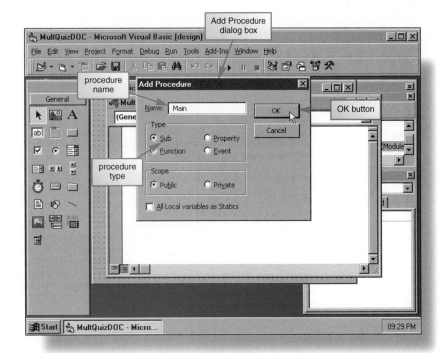

FIGURE 7-90

7 Click the OK button. Click File on the menu bar and then click Save Module1 As. Select the Project7\MultQuizDOC folder, type MultQuiz in the File name text box, and point to the Save button.

The Save File As dialog box displays as shown in Figure 7-91.

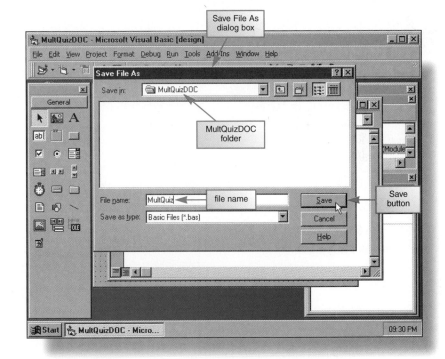

FIGURE 7-91

8 Click Save. Close the Code window and then click the form. Click File on the menu bar and then click Save MultQuiz.frm As. Select the C:\Project7\MultQuizDOC folder, type MultQuiz in the File name text box, and point to the Save button.

The Save File As dialog box displays as shown in Figure 7-92.

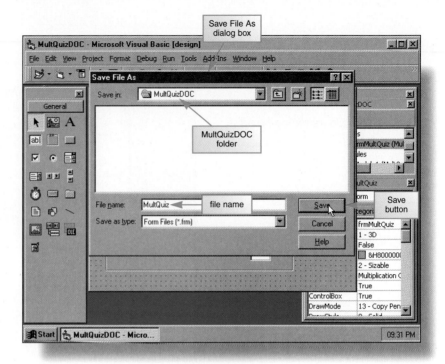

FIGURE 7-92

9 Click the Save button. Click File on the menu bar and then click Save Project As. Select the C:\Project7\MultQuizDOC folder, type MultQuizDOC in the File name text box, and point to the Save button.

The Save Project As dialog box displays as shown in Figure 7-93.

10 Click the Save button in the Save Project As dialog box.

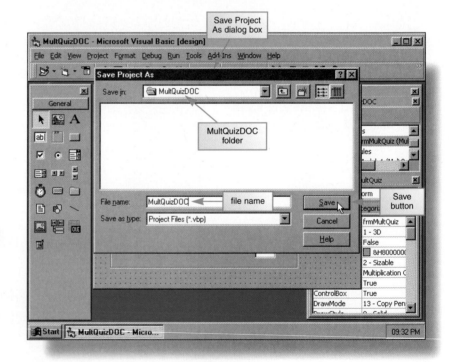

FIGURE 7-93

ActiveX Document Migration Wizard

The **ActiveX Document Migration Wizard** is an add-in that you first must add to the Add-Ins menu with the **Add-In Manager**. Perform the following steps to add the wizard to the Add-Ins menu, and then make and test the Multiplication Quiz application ActiveX Document.

Steps **To Make and Test an ActiveX Document**

1 **Click Add-Ins on the menu bar and then click Add-In Manager. In the Add-In Manager dialog box, click the VB ActiveX Document Migration Wizard check box. Point to the OK button.**

The Add-In Manager dialog box displays as shown (Figure 7-94).

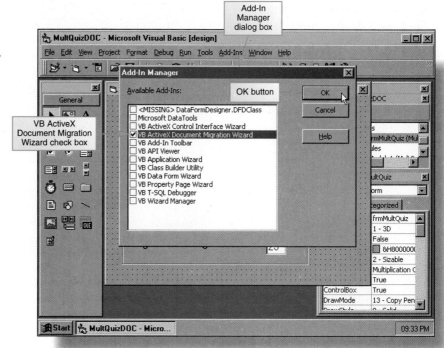

FIGURE 7-94

2 **Click the OK button. Click Add-Ins on the menu bar and then point to ActiveX Document Migration Wizard.**

The Add-Ins menu displays (Figure 7-95).

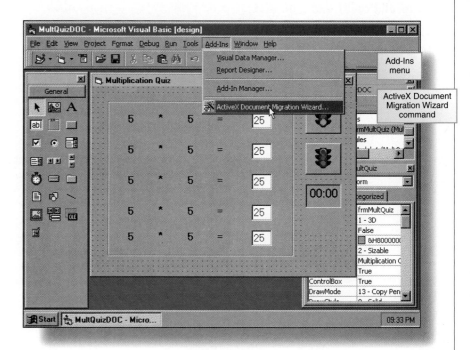

FIGURE 7-95

3 Click ActiveX Document Migration Wizard. If the Introduction panel displays, click the Next button. In the Form Selection panel, click the frmMultQuiz check box and then point to the Next button.

The ActiveX Document Migration Wizard - Form Selection panel displays (Figure 7-96).

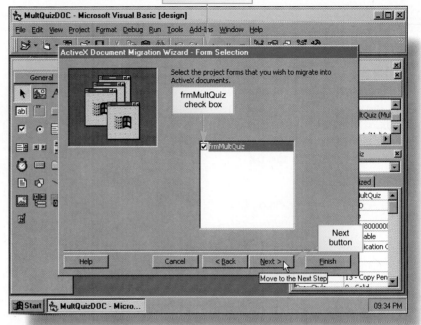

FIGURE 7-96

4 Click the Next button. In the Options panel, click Comment out invalid code? and then click Remove original forms after conversion? Point to the Next button.

The Options panel displays as shown in Figure 7-97.

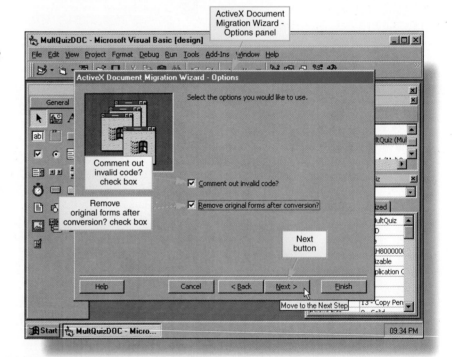

FIGURE 7-97

5 Click the Next button. In the Finished! panel, click No and then point to the Finish button.

The Finished! panel displays as shown in Figure 7-98.

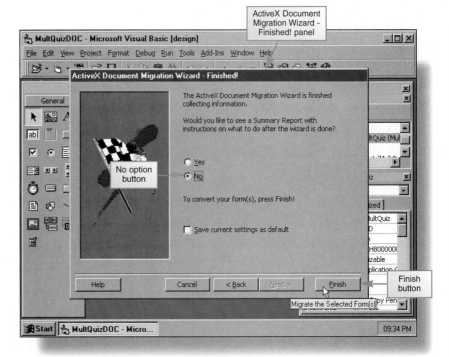

FIGURE 7-98

6 Click the Finish button. If a Confirm dialog box displays, click the Yes button. In the ActiveX Document(s) Created dialog box, point to the OK button.

The form has been converted to an ActiveX document object (Figure 7-99).

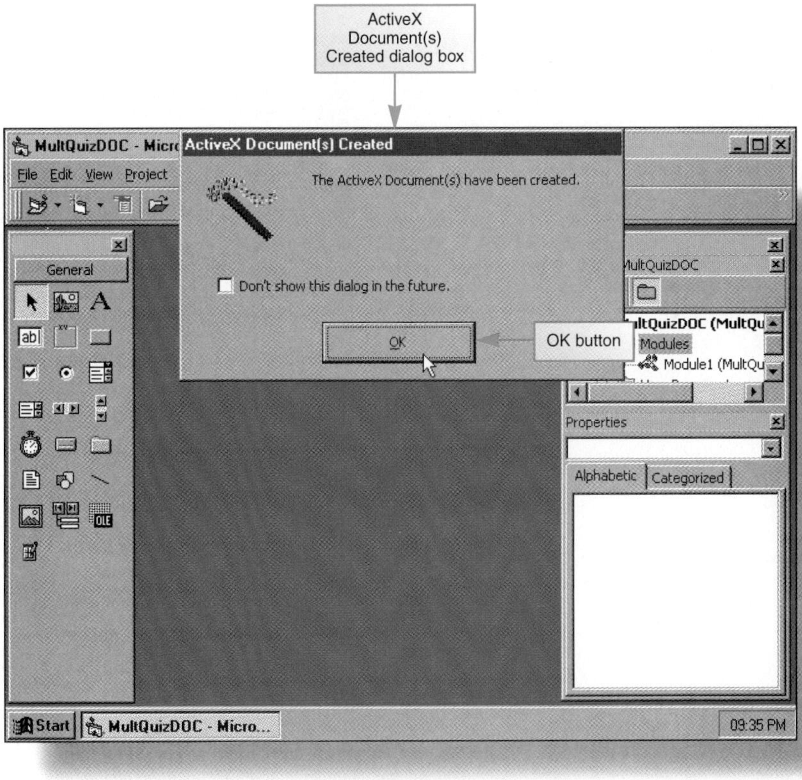

FIGURE 7-99

7 Click the OK button. Click View Code in the Project window and then select the UserDocument_Resize event procedure.

The ActiveX Document Migration Wizard has added comments and modified the code (Figure 7-100).

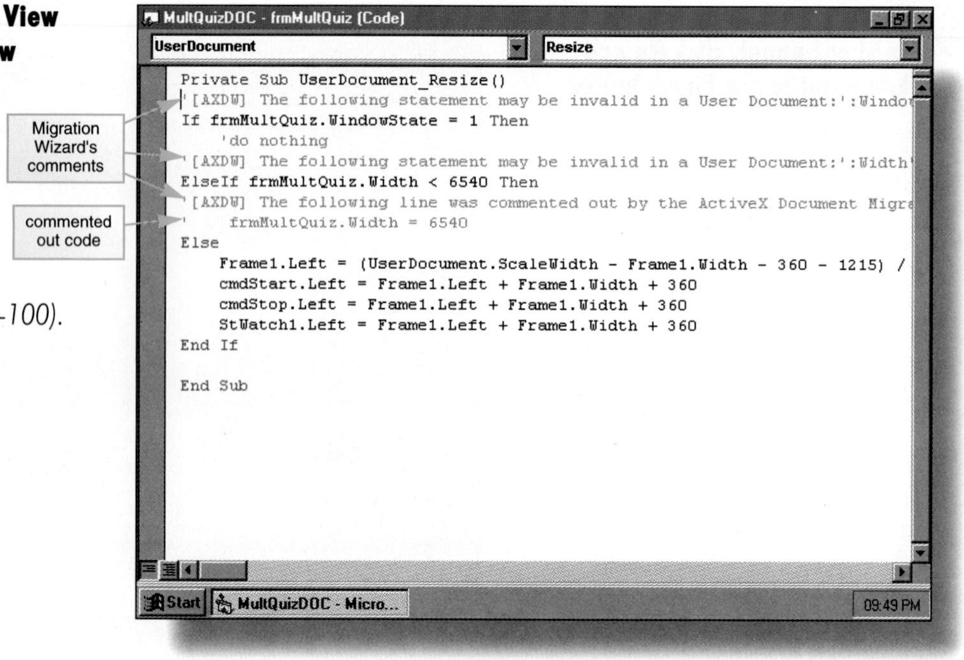

Migration Wizard's comments

commented out code

```
MultQuizDOC - frmMultQuiz (Code)

UserDocument                              Resize

Private Sub UserDocument_Resize()
'[AXDW] The following statement may be invalid in a User Document:':Windo
If frmMultQuiz.WindowState = 1 Then
    'do nothing
'[AXDW] The following statement may be invalid in a User Document:':Width
ElseIf frmMultQuiz.Width < 6540 Then
'[AXDW] The following line was commented out by the ActiveX Document Migra
'    frmMultQuiz.Width = 6540
Else
    Frame1.Left = (UserDocument.ScaleWidth - Frame1.Width - 360 - 1215) /
    cmdStart.Left = Frame1.Left + Frame1.Width + 360
    cmdStop.Left = Frame1.Left + Frame1.Width + 360
    StWatch1.Left = Frame1.Left + Frame1.Width + 360
End If

End Sub
```

```
Start    MultQuizDOC - Micro...                                  09:49 PM
```

FIGURE 7-100

8 Comment out the code as shown in Figure 7-101.

The UserDocument_Resize event procedure displays in the Code window (Figure 7-101).

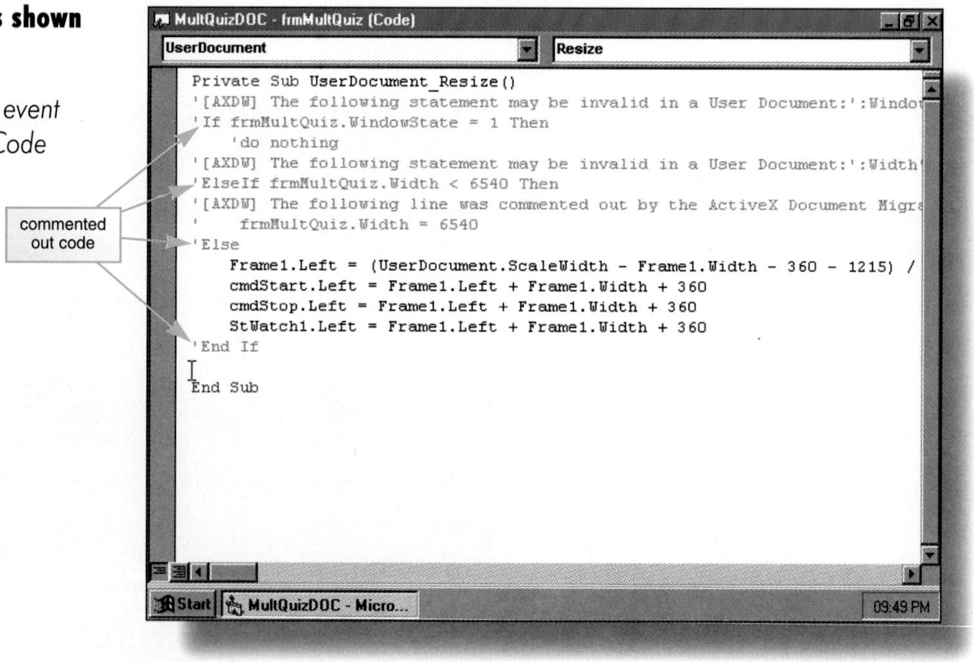

commented out code

```
MultQuizDOC - frmMultQuiz (Code)

UserDocument                              Resize

Private Sub UserDocument_Resize()
'[AXDW] The following statement may be invalid in a User Document:':Windo
'If frmMultQuiz.WindowState = 1 Then
    'do nothing
'[AXDW] The following statement may be invalid in a User Document:':Width
'ElseIf frmMultQuiz.Width < 6540 Then
'[AXDW] The following line was commented out by the ActiveX Document Migra
'    frmMultQuiz.Width = 6540
'Else
    Frame1.Left = (UserDocument.ScaleWidth - Frame1.Width - 360 - 1215) /
    cmdStart.Left = Frame1.Left + Frame1.Width + 360
    cmdStop.Left = Frame1.Left + Frame1.Width + 360
    StWatch1.Left = Frame1.Left + Frame1.Width + 360
'End If

End Sub
```

```
Start    MultQuizDOC - Micro...                                  09:49 PM
```

FIGURE 7-101

9 Close the Code window. Click File on the menu bar and then click **Make MultQuizDoc.exe.** In the Make Project dialog box, select the **C:\Project7\MultQuizDOC** folder, type `MultQuizDoc` in the File name text box, and point to the OK button.

The ActiveX document server will be saved as MultQuizDoc.exe (Figure 7-102).

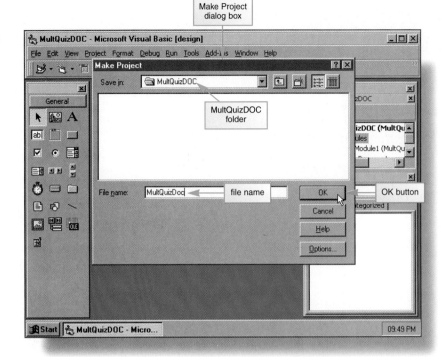

FIGURE 7-102

10 Click the OK button. Close Visual Basic. Click the Yes button if prompted to save changes. Start Internet Explorer. Click File on the menu bar and then point to Browse.

The Open dialog box displays as shown (Figure 7-103).

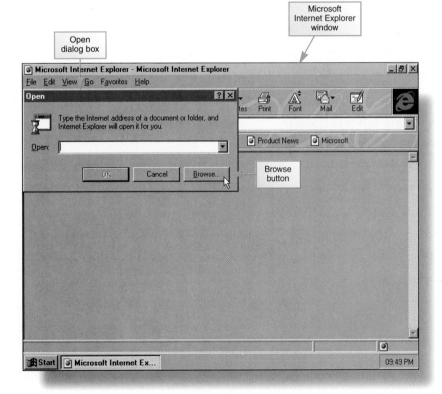

FIGURE 7-103

Open
dialog box

11 Click the Browse button. In the Open dialog box, select the C:\Project7\ MultQuizDOC folder, click the Files of type box arrow, and click All Files. Point to the frmMultQuiz.vbd file.

A second Open dialog box is added to the desktop (Figure 7-104).

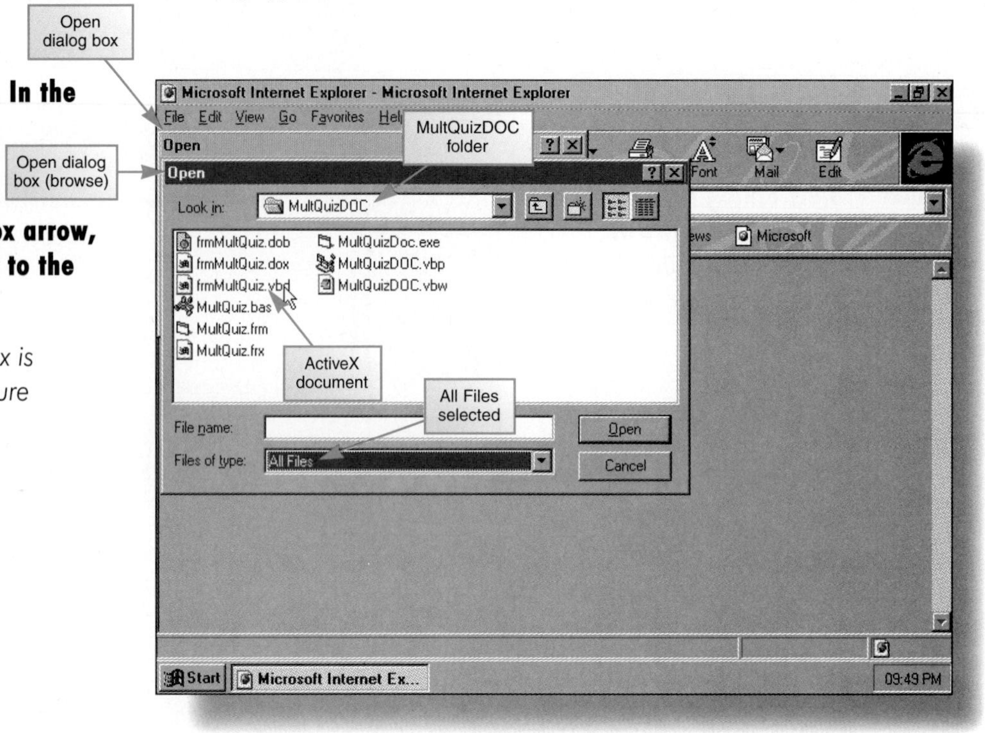

MultQuizDOC folder

Open dialog box (browse)

ActiveX document

All Files selected

FIGURE 7-104

Internet Explorer

12 Double-click frmMultQuiz.vbd and then click the OK button. Test the application and then close Internet Explorer.

The ActiveX document is shown running in Internet Explorer in Figure 7-105.

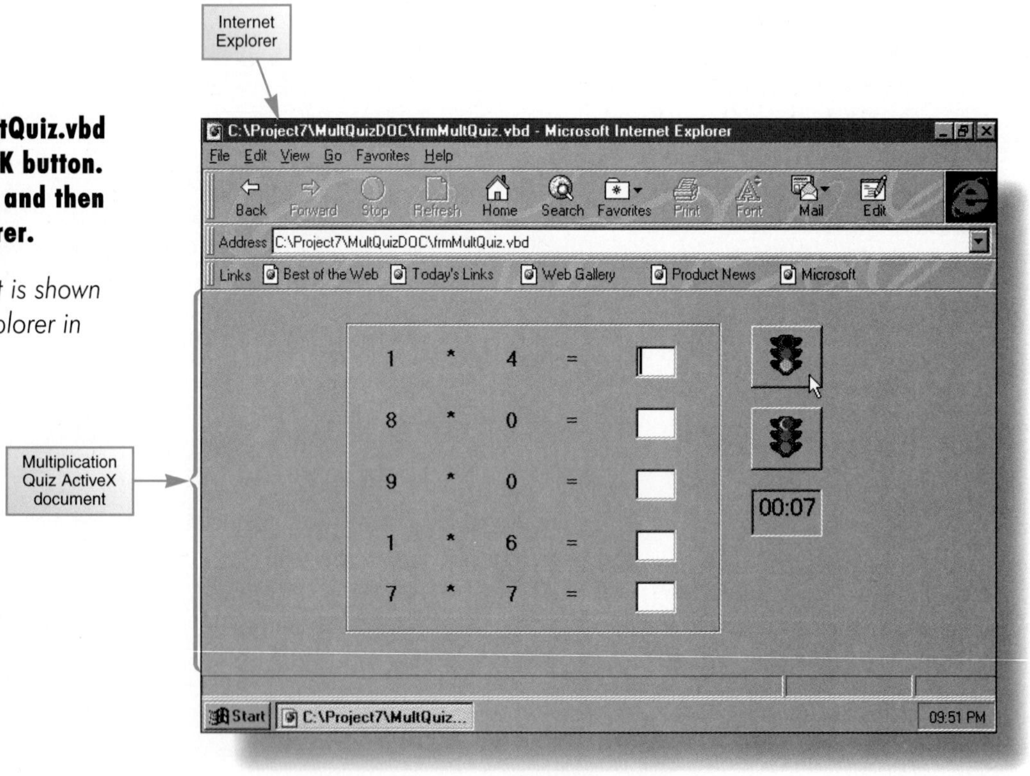

Multiplication Quiz ActiveX document

FIGURE 7-105

Project Summary

In this project, you created a custom ActiveX control. In building the control, you learned about the Timer control and its events and properties. You also learned how to create custom properties. You then incorporated the custom control into the Multiplication Quiz application. In building the application, you learned about random number generating functions, the Resize event, and several new properties of CommandButton controls.

You then compiled the Multiplication Quiz application into an .exe file and used the Visual Basic Setup Wizard to create an installation program for distributing the application on floppy disks. You installed the application, tested it, and uninstalled it. You used the ActiveX Document Migration Wizard to create a document object and then you created an ActiveX document and ActiveX server for the Multiplication Quiz application. You tested the document in Internet Explorer.

What You Should Know

Having completed this project, you now should be able to perform the following tasks.

- Add a Second Project *(VB 7.24)*
- Compile an ActiveX Control *(VB 7.29)*
- Convert a Standard EXE Project to an ActiveX Document *(VB 7.50)*
- Create a Setup Program and Distribution Disks *(VB 7.42)*
- Create an ActiveX Control Interface *(VB 7.11)*
- Create the Multiplication Quiz Application Interface *(VB 7.33)*
- Install and Run an Application *(VB 7.48)*
- Make and Test an ActiveX Document *(VB 7.55)*
- Save an ActiveX Control Project *(VB 7.23)*
- Save and Test the Multiplication Quiz Application *(VB 7.40)*
- Set Constituent Control Properties *(VB 7.13)*
- Set Properties of the Multiplication Quiz Controls *(VB 7.37)*
- Start an ActiveX Control Project *(VB 7.9)*
- Test an ActiveX Control *(VB 7.25)*
- Uninstall an Application *(VB 7.49)*
- Write Event Procedures *(VB 7.39)*
- Write Property Procedures *(VB 7.19)*
- Write UserControl Event Procedures *(VB 7.15)*

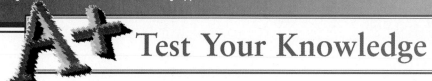

Test Your Knowledge

1 True/False

Instructions: Circle T if the statement is true or F if the statement is false.

T F 1. Controls you add to a UserControl are called constituent controls.

T F 2. A Timer control has only one event.

T F 3. Properties are added to ActiveX controls through event procedures.

T F 4. A percent sign (%) is used as the integer division operator.

T F 5. The Mod operator is used to divide two numbers and return only the remainder.

T F 6. A PropertyBox object is used to save and restore the state of an object.

T F 7. UserControls are stored in plain text files.

T F 8. You can have only one project open in the Visual Basic IDE at a time.

T F 9. ActiveX controls are compiled to .vbx files.

T F 10. A ToolTip is a word or short phrase that describes the function of a toolbar button or other button or tool.

2 Multiple Choice

Instructions: Circle the correct response.

1. The value of a Timer control's Interval property is the number of _____ between Timer events.

   a. seconds

   b. tenths of seconds

   c. hundredths of seconds

   d. thousandths of seconds

2. A CommandButton control can display a graphic if its _____ property is set to 1 - Graphical.

   a. Icon

   b. Picture

   c. Style

   d. Appearance

3. The Startup object of an ActiveX document must be _____.

   a. Form1

   b. Sub Main

   c. UserControl1

   d. Form_Load

4. An ActiveX document file created with Visual Basic has a(n) _____ extension.

   a. .doc

   b. .ocx

   c. .vbp

   d. .vbd

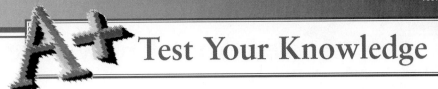

5. With the Setup Wizard, you can distribute applications on _____.
   a. floppy disks
   b. compact disks
   c. a network
   d. all of the above

6. The ActiveX Document Migration Wizard is used to convert Standard EXE projects into _____.
   a. ActiveX documents
   b. ActiveX controls
   c. ActiveX dlls
   d. ActiveX exes

7. A form's Resize event occurs when the form is _____.
   a. first displayed
   b. moved
   c. closed
   d. all of the above

8. The countdown between timer events is started and stopped by setting the Timer control's _____ property.
   a. Timer
   b. Enabled
   c. Action
   d. Interval

9. A _____ procedure retrieves the value of a property.
   a. PropertyRead
   b. PropertyWrite
   c. PropertyLet
   d. PropertyGet

10. The _____ method notifies the object's container that a property's value has been changed.
   a. ValueChanged
   b. PropertyChanged
   c. PropertyLet
   d. PropertyGet

 Test Your Knowledge

3 Understanding the Setup Wizard

Instructions: In Figure 7-106, arrows point to some of the controls in the Select Project and Options panel of the Setup Wizard. Identify the purpose or function of each of these controls in the spaces provided.

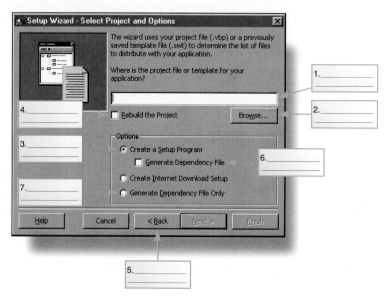

FIGURE 7-106

1. _____

2. _____

3. _____

4. _____

5. _____

6. _____

7. _____

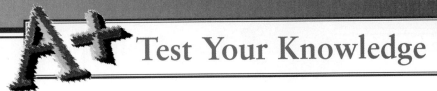

4 Understanding Visual Basic Files

Instructions: In the spaces provided on the right, write a description of each Visual Basic file extension function listed on the left.

FILE EXTENSION	DESCRIPTION
1. .frm	_____
2. .frx	_____
3. .ctl	_____
4. .ctx	_____
5. .dob	_____
6. .dox	_____
7. .vbp	_____
8. .exe	_____
9. .ocx	_____

Use Help

1 More About Creating ActiveX Controls

Instructions: Perform the following tasks using a computer.

1. Start Visual Basic. Click Help on the menu bar and then click Books Online. Locate the section on Creating Property Pages for ActiveX Controls.

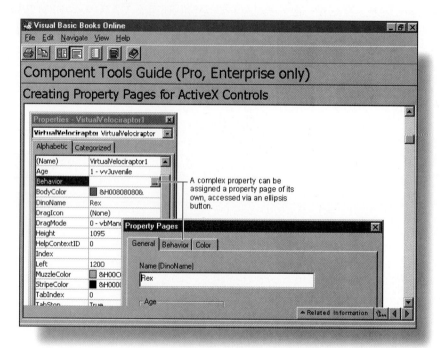

FIGURE 7-107

2. On a separate page, answer the following questions.
   a. What is a Property page?
   b. What is a PropertyPage Designer?
   c. What are standard Property pages?
   d. List at least three design guidelines for Property pages.
   e. What is the Property page Wizard?
3. Hand the answers in to your instructor.

Use Help

2 Visual Basic Professional Controls

Instructions: Use Visual Basic Help to learn more about the ActiveX controls available in the Professional Edition of Visual Basic 5. Write your answers on your own paper and turn them in to your instructor.

1. Start Visual Basic. In the New Project dialog box, double-click VB Professional Edition Controls on the New tab sheet. The Toolbox is shown in Figure 7-108.
2. For each of the controls identified in Figure 7-108, write the name of the control and a brief description of its functions.
3. Hand the answers in to your instructor.

FIGURE 7-108

Apply Your Knowledge

1 Mouse Skill Test

Instructions: Open the DragDrop.vbp project on the Data Disk that accompanies this book. The application displays during run time as shown in Figure 7-109. You can test a person's mouse skills with this application by instructing the person to drag the letter and drop it on the mailbox (a clever Windows user will be able to do it).

1. Set imgLetter's DragMode property to 1 - Automatic.
2. Click the View Code button.
3. Add the following code statement to the Form_DragOver event procedure:

   `Source.Visible=False`

4. Add the following code statement to the Form_DragDrop event procedure:

   `Source.Visible=True`

5. Select the imgMailbox_DragOver event procedure.
6. Complete the last three lines of code in the imgMailbox_DragOver event procedure.
7. Resave the form and project.
8. Test the application.
9. Print the project's code. Write your name on the printout.
10. On the back of the printout, answer the following questions.
    a. Why does the Randomize statement only appear once in the imgMailbox_DragOver event procedure?
    b. Explain the code statement that calculates the upperbound for the new value of the Top property.
    c. What happens if the user drags the form's borders?
    d. Can the imgMailbox_DragDrop event occur in this application — why or why not?

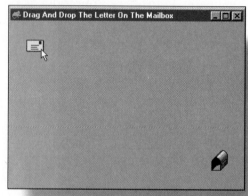

FIGURE 7-109

1 Random Record Selection

Problem: LaTisha wants to select records at random when she uses the GeoView database viewer application (Project 4) to quiz her students. *Hint*: The statement `Data1.Recordset.Move x` (where x is an integer) will make the xth record past the current record become the current record. When the first record is the current record, you can advance any integer number between 0 records and (Data1.Recordset.RecordCount – 1) records.

Instructions: Perform the following tasks to add random record selection to the GeoView database viewer application.

1. Open the GeoView project in Visual Basic.
2. Add a CommandButton control as shown in Figure 7-110.
3. Select the CommandButton control's Click event in the Code window.
4. Enter a code statement to create an integer variable named MoveAmount.
5. Enter a code statement to set a value for the random number Seed.
6. Enter a code statement to set a value for the lowerbound of MoveAmount.
7. Enter a code statement to set a value for the upperbound of MoveAmount.
8. Enter a code statement to assign a random value (of the permissible values) to MoveAmount.
9. Enter a code statement to make the first record the current record.
10. Enter a code statement to advance MoveAmount records.
11. Save the form and the project using the file name GeoView2.
12. Test the project by running it and make any necessary changes. Remember to save the form and project again if you make any changes.
13. Print the Form Image, Code, and Form as Text.
14. Hand the printouts in to your instructor.

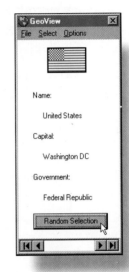

FIGURE 7-110

In the Lab

2 Flashing Label Control

Problem: You want to create an ActiveX control that is a label whose caption flashes off and on. The control is shown during design time in Figure 7-111. In addition to setting the Caption property, you want to be able to set the interval of the flashes. *Hint:* Label1.Visible = Not Label1.Visible will toggle the display of Label1.

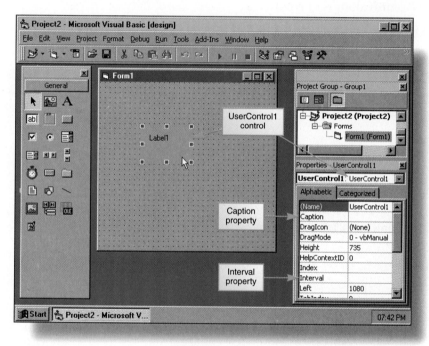

FIGURE 7-111

Instructions: Perform the following tasks to create the Flashing Label control.

1. Open a new ActiveX control project in Visual Basic.
2. Add a Timer and a Label control to the UserControl.
3. Size the UserControl appropriately.
4. Name the control FlashLabel and set any other properties as necessary.
5. Create Property procedures for the Caption property.
6. Create Property procedures for the Interval property.
7. Save the ActiveX control and project.
8. Compile FlashLabel to an .ocx file.
9. Print the Form Image, Code, and Form as Text.
10. Open a new Standard EXE project.
11. Add the FlashLabel control to the Toolbox.
12. Add a FlashLabel control to the project and test it.
13. Hand the printouts in to your instructor.

In the Lab

3 ActiveX Document Migration

Problem: The company that purchased the rights to your Loan Payment Calculator application (Project 3) wants you to create a version that can be hosted by Internet Explorer.

Instructions: Perform the following steps to create an ActiveX Document version of the Loan Payment Calculator application (Figure 7-112).

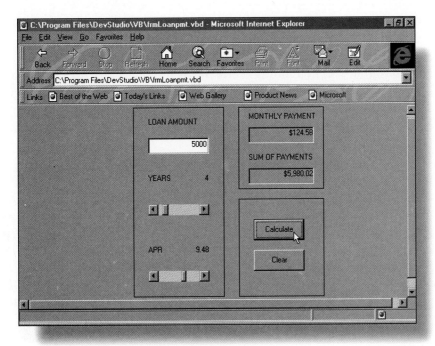

FIGURE 7-112

1. Open the Loan Payment Calculator application in Visual Basic.
2. Remove the AboutDialog form from the project.
3. Delete the cmdAbout button and its Click event procedure.
4. Create a Sub Main procedure.
5. Change the Startup object to Sub Main.
6. Resave the form and project as LoanCalcIE.
7. Run the ActiveX Document Migration Wizard and create a .vbd file.
8. Close Visual Basic and open Internet Explorer.
9. Open LoanCalcIE.vbd in Internet Explorer.
10. Print the document from Internet Explorer.
11. Hand the printout in to your instructor.

Cases and Places

The difficulty of these case studies varies: ❱ are the least difficult; ❱❱ are more difficult; and ❱❱❱ are the most difficult.

1 ❱ When a representative of Macrofirm software company was in town recently, you were able to show him your Loan Payment Calculator application (Project 3). He feels the company might be interested in buying the application from you. To show it to the right people at headquarters, he has asked you to send him the application on a floppy disk with a setup program.

2 ❱ The Farpoint Airport Authority (Project 1) rejected your company's proposal. They have decided that the only user interface that will be running on the PC is Internet Explorer. Your company wants to submit a revised proposal, and you have been directed to create an ActiveX document version of your currency exchange prototype.

3 ❱❱ After end-user testing of the Multiplication Quiz application and several of the other modules, your team has concluded that all of the modules should track elapsed time in minutes, seconds, and tenths of seconds. This means you will have to revise and recompile the StWatch ActiveX control you created in Project 7.

4 ❱❱ The classroom where your Philosophy class meets has a PC at the instructor's desk and a projection system. The instructor frequently uses the system to supplement her presentations with PowerPoint slides. Students have assigned seats for the entire term. The instructor would like to have a seating chart application on the PC. The application should give a visual representation of the seating arrangement in the room, with the corresponding students' names. In question and answer sessions, she would like to be able to call on students at random.

5 ❱❱❱ Your supervisor has reviewed your team's work on the Traffic Sign Tutorial application (Project 5). Although generally she is very pleased, she feels the order of the traffic signs should be different each time the application is run. Revise the Traffic Sign Tutorial to include randomized location of the signs.

6 ❱❱❱ The ANC Movie Theater Corporation has reviewed and tested the prototype Movie Box Office application you built in Project 2. They will commit to full-scale development if you can make the following modifications: the list of currently playing films and their prices should be read by the application from a database; the transaction information should be written to a database; and the application should run within the Internet Explorer interface.

Cases and Places

7 ▶▶▶ Croissant Software sells a large number of different ActiveX controls to developers. They have had many requests from game developers for an ActiveX control that simulates a pair of dice. The control should look like a pair of dice and be sizable. When activated, the control should randomly generate values from 1 to 6 on each die with the same frequencies as real dice. The control should be able to be activated by the user clicking it or through a code statement. The control must have a Value property that is the sum of the die faces currently showing.

Index